# Beginning Databases with PostgreSQL

Richard Stones

Neil Mathew

*Wrox Press Ltd.*

# Beginning Databases with PostgreSQL

Published by Wrox Press Ltd,
Arden House, 1102 Warwick Road, Acocks Green,
Birmingham, B27 6BH, UK
Printed in the United States
ISBN 1-861005-15-6

# Trademark Acknowledgements

Wrox has endeavored to provide trademark information about all the companies and products mentioned in this book by the appropriate use of capitals. However, Wrox cannot guarantee the accuracy of this information.

# Credits

**Authors**
Richard Stones
Neil Mathew

**Contributing Authors**
Jon Parise
Meeraj Kunnumpurath

**Additional Material**
Indu Britto

**Technical Reviewers**
John Cavanaugh
Neil Conway
Peter Eisentraut
Pancrazio' Ezio'de Maura
Devrim Gunduz
David Hudson
Abdul Hussain
Robert Mello
Tobias Ratschiller
Gavin Smyth
Matt Springfield
Branden Williams

**Category Manager**
Dilip Thomas

**Technical Architect**
Dan Maharry
Dilip Thomas

**Author Agents**
Safi Shakir

**Technical Editors**
Manjunath B.V.
Cornellia Boenigk
Indu Britto
Dipali Chittar
Volkar Gobbels
Chris Harshmann
Shiva Nadkarni
Nilesh Parmar
Girish Sharangpani
Will Trillich
Kevin Yank

**Production Manager**
Simon Hardware

**Production Project Coordinator**
Mark Burdett

**ProductionAssistant**
Abbie Forletta

**Index**
Michael Brinkman
Andrew Criddle
Bill Johncocks

**Cover**
Chris Morris

**Proof Reading**
Miriam Robinson

# AUTHORS' ACKNOWLEDGMENTS

We, Richard and Neil, would like to thank our families:

Rick's wife Ann, and children, Jenny and Andrew, for their patience during the many evenings and weekends while the book was written. Rick would also like to thank them for being so understanding about the decision to do more writing.

Neil's wife Christine for her unfailing support and understanding, and his children Alexandra and Adrian, for thinking that it's cool to have a Dad who can write books.

We would also like to thank the many people who made this book possible.

Firstly, all the people who enjoyed our previous books *Beginning Linux Programming* and *Professional Linux Programming*, making them the success they have been, providing useful feedback and spurring us on to write again.

We would like to thank the team at Wrox for their hard work on the book, especially Dan M, who helped us considerably with the initial specification, Grace for her early work on the book, and also the hard working team in Mumbai, particularly Dilip T, Manju, Indu B, Nilesh and Vijay T, as well as the others who worked behind the scenes.

We would also like to thank the people who have contributed additional material to the book; they did some excellent work.

Special thanks are also due to the team of reviewers who worked on our chapters. They provided comments and suggestions of the highest quality, and went to efforts above-and-beyond the call of duty to improve the book. Thank you very much one and all. Any errors that have slipped through are, of course, entirely our own fault.

We would also like to thank our employers, GEHE, for their support while we were writing this book.

We would like to thank the many people who have given their time and effort into making PostgreSQL to superb free database that it is, and wish them every success in the future with this excellent product.

We would also like to pay homage to Linus for the Linux platform, RMS for the excellent set of GNU tools and the GPL, and the ever-expanding throng of unsung heroes who choose to make their software freely available, not forgetting those who continue to promote the cause of Open Source and GPLed software in other ways.

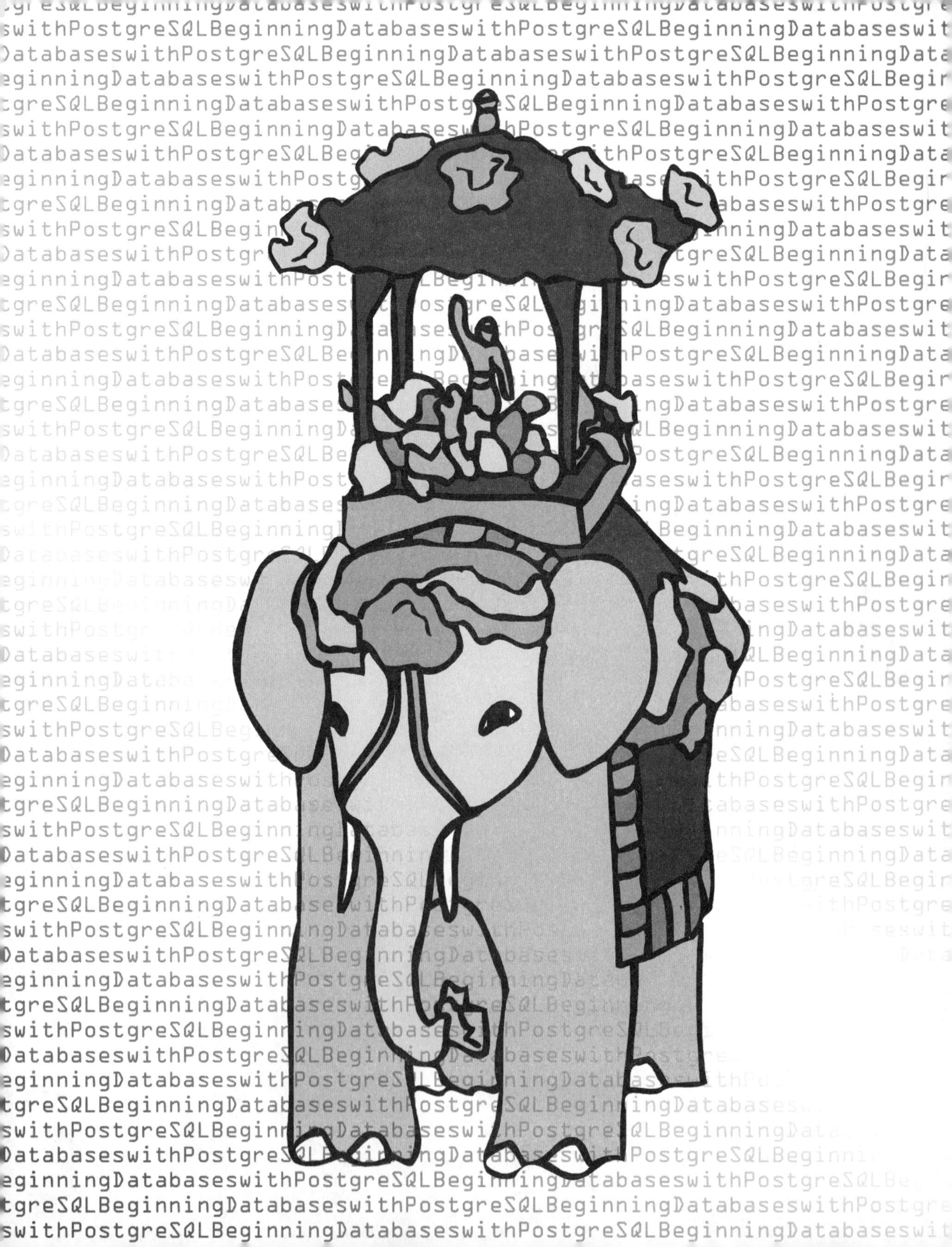
BeginningDatabaseswithPostgreSQL

# Table of Contents

# Table of Contents

# Table of Contents

## Table of Contents

# Table of Contents

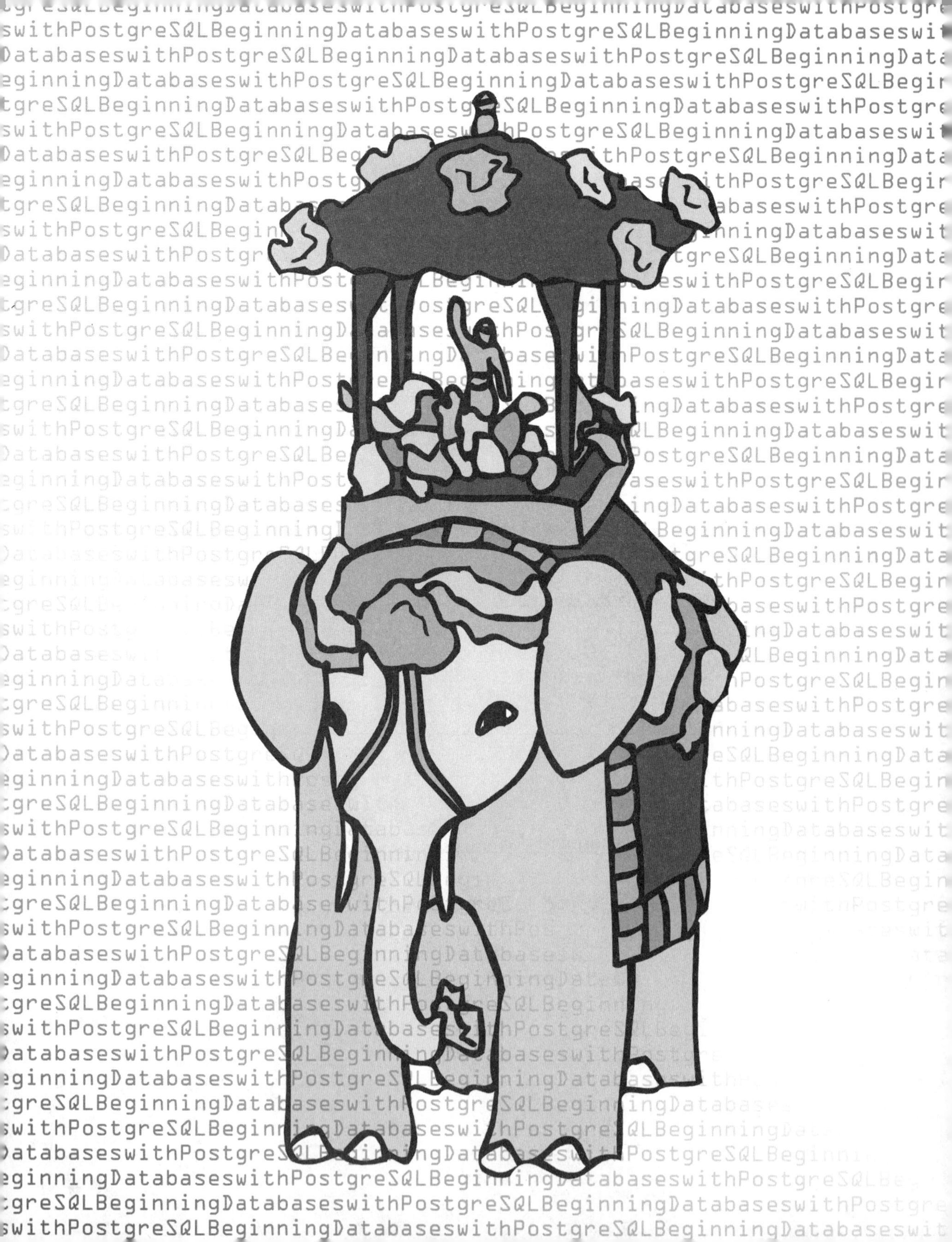
BeginningDatabaseswithPostgreSQL

# Introduction

## How to pronounce PostgreSQL

We think the best way to grapple with any technology, before you can head straight into its rudimentaries, is to learn how to pronounce it. And since it's PostgreSQL, and not the easiest of names to pronounce, we are being that wee-bit extra cautious.

The original database software was called Postgres. When SQL was added to it and its development was taken on to the internet, the name SQL was logically affixed to its fag end.

It is pronounced as Post-gres-cue-el as opposed to postgre-es-cue-el as often wrongly pronounced and referred to.

## What's Covered in this Book

This book is packed with 18 chapters, all combined to give you an introduction to PostgreSQL as a beginner and take you a step further into providing solid fundamentals into Beginning Databases with PostgreSQLs powerful data model, rich data types and high extensibility.

*Chapter 1* introduces you to the whole arena of databases and a little on why they are so useful. Also as to where and how PostgreSQL fits into the picture.

*Chapter 2* goes into more depth on relational database principles with a broad idea about the history and architecture of PostgreSQL that you have assimilated from *Chapter 1*. The chapter then moves on to creating a simple database and explains how to use some of the basic data types in it.

*Chapter 3* walks you through the steps of installing PostgreSQL from binaries or the source code both on UNIX-ish environment and Windows. It also covers the fundamentals of creating tables in the database and populating them.

*Chapter 4* takes a formal look at the heart of the SQL language, the SELECT statement. It covers various options to configure PostgresQL's behaviour in interpreting your data and displaying exactly the information we are looking for.

*Chapter 5* introduces some of the alternatives to psql for accessing and administering PostgreSQL databases like pgAdmin and pgAccess.We also see how to use Microsoft Office products like Microsoft Access and Microsoft Excel to manipulate and report the data.

*Chapter 6* takes a look at the other issues of data manipulation like inserting data with the INSERT command to deleting all rows from a table with the TRUNCATE command.

*Chapter 7* builds on Chapter 4 by covering some of the difficult aspects in SQL. It goes into great depth on the SELECT statement – into aggregate functions, outer joins etc.

*Chapter 8* takes a more formal approach to manipulating data and advanced features like implementing constraints.

*Chapter 9* talks in depth about Transactions, it's ACID rules, the ANSI isolation levels and the implementation of Locks.

*Chapter 10* is quite PostgreSQL specific in that it talks about operators and functions, extending the functionality of PostgreSQL by stored procedures and a loadable procedural language, PL/pgSQL.

*Chapter 11* focuses on database administration. It covers issues such as server control, database maintenance, backup and recovery and more.

*Chapter 12* concerns itself with designing a database. It goes into detail on the various stages of generating a schema, the conventional design patterns etc.

*Chapter 13* is where we turn our attention to creating our own client applications in C.

*Chapter 14* builds on this by looking at a more portable way of interfacing PostgreSQL to C by embedding SQL statements directly in the source code and then using the ecpg translator to generate C code that is then compiled to produce an executable.

*Chapter 15* looks at adding PostgreSQL support to PHP and ways in which the PostgreSQL database can be accessed by the PHP scripting language. It also introduces the PEAR database abstraction interface.

*Chapter 16* examines accessing PostgreSQL databases from Perl. It considers the powerful string manipulation capabilities of Perl, the Perl DBI and DBIx modules to make programming simpler.

*Chapter 17* looks into Java programs using JDBC to access relational data in PostgreSQL databases. It also takes a peek into the new features in the support version 3.0 of the JDBC API.

*Chapter 18* expects that by now you'd have got the confidence to investigate further into the usual and unusual features of PostgreSQL. To help you on your way, it gives you some useful starting points for reference.

# Conventions Used

You are going to encounter various styles of text and layout as you browse through the book. This has been done to keep you from missing different kinds of key information. These styles are:

## Try it Out – A 'Try it Out' Example

'Try it Out' is our way of presenting a practical example.

### How it Works

Then the 'How it Works' explains what is going on.

> **Important information, key points, additional information are displayed like this to make them stand out. Don't ignore them!**

❑   If you see something like `test.sql`, you'll know that it's a filename, object name or function name.

❑   Words that appear on the screen in menus like Control Panel are in a similar font to that which you see on screen.

Code has several fonts. If it's a word that we're talking about in the text, for example, when discussing the `psql` command line tool, it's in a distinctive font. If it's a block of code that you can type in as a program and run, then it's also in a gray box:

```
SELECT * FROM item;
```

Sometimes you'll see code in a mixture of styles, like this:

```
for(n = 0; n < nfields; n++) {
        if(PQgetisnull(result, r, n))
            printf(" %s is NULL,", PQfname(result, n));
        else
          printf(" %s = %s(%d),",
              PQfname(result, n),
              PQgetvalue(result, r, n),
              PQgetlength(result, r, n));
    }
```

This is meant to draw your attention to code that's new, or relevant to the surrounding discussion(in the gray box), whilst showing it in the context of the code you've seen before (on the white background).

Where we show text to be entered at a command prompt, this will be shown as follows:

**# SELECT * FROM item;**

Any output will be in the same font, only lighter:

```
item_id | description  | cost_price | sell_price
--------+--------------+------------+------------
      1 | Wood Puzzle  |      15.23 |      21.95
      2 | Rubic Cube   |       7.45 |      11.49
      3 | Linux CD     |       1.99 |       2.49
      4 | Tissues      |       2.11 |       3.99
      5 | Picture Frame|       7.54 |       9.95
      6 | Fan Small    |       9.23 |      15.75
      7 | Fan Large    |      13.36 |      19.95
      8 | Toothbrush   |       0.75 |       1.45
      9 | Roman Coin   |       2.34 |       2.45
     10 | Carrier Bag  |       0.01 |       0.00
     11 | Speakers     |      19.73 |      25.32
(11 rows)
```

# Downloading the Source Code

As you work through the examples in the book, you might decide that you prefer to type all the code in by hand. Many readers prefer this, because it's a good way of getting familiar with the coding techniques that are used.

Whether you want to type in the code or not, we have made al the source code for this book available at our website, at the following address: http:/www.wrox.com

If you're one of those readers who like to type in the code, you can use or files to check the results you will be getting. They should be your first stop if you think you have typed in an error. If you don't like typing, then downloading the source code from our web site is a must! Either way it'll help you with updates and debugging.

# Errata

We've made every effort to make sure that there are no errors in the text or the code. However to err is human, and as such we recognize the need to keep you informed of any mistakes as they are spotted and corrected. Errata sheets are available for all our books at http://www.wrox.com. If you find an error that hasn't already been reported, please let us know.

Our web site acts as a focus for other information and support, including the code from all our books, sample chapters, previews of forthcoming titles, and articles and opinion on related topics.

# Technical Support

If you wish to directly query a problem in the book with an expert who knows the book in detail then e-mail support@wrox.com , with the title of the book and the last four numbers of the ISBN in the subject field of the e-mail. Your message is delivered to one of the support staff, who are the first people to read it. We have files on the most frequently asked questions and will answer anything general immediately. We also answer general queries about the book and the web site.

Deeper queries are forwarded to the technical editor responsible for that book. They have experience with the general programming language or particular product and are able to answer detailed technical questions on the subject. Once an issue has been resolved, the editor can post the errata the problem brought to light to the web site.

Finally, in the unlikely event that the editor can't answer your problem,  they will forward the request to the author. We try to protect the author from any distractions from their main job. However, we are quite happy to forward specific book-related requests to them. All Wrox authors help with the support on their books. They will either mail the customer directly with their answer, or will send their response to the editor or the support department who will then pass it on to the reader.

# P2P Online Forums

Wrox support doesn't just stop when you finish the book. If you have a question that falls outside the scope of the book, or you have a modified book code for your own ends and need some further support, then the P2P forum is available to you at http://p2p.wrox.com/.

P2P is a community of programmers sharing their problems and expertise. A variety of mailing lists cover all modern programming and internet technologies. Links, resources and archives provide a comprehensive knowledge base. Whether you are an experienced professional or web novice you'll find something of interest here.

The mailing lists are moderated to ensure that messages are relevant and reasonable. This does mean that postings do not appear on the list until they have been read and approved, but prevents the flow of junk mail that unmoderated lists allow. Anonymous access to the lists is allowed for reading, but registration of at least an e-mail address is required to post messages.

# How to Tell Us Exactly What You Think

Our commitment to our readers doesn't stop when you walk out of the bookstore. We understand that errors can destroy the enjoyment of a book and can cause any wasted and frustrated hours, so we seek to minimize the distress they can cause.

Let us know how much you liked or loathed the book, and what you think we can do better next time. You can send your comments, either by returning the reply card in the back of the book, or by e-mail (to feedback@wrox.com). Please be sure to mention the book title in you message.

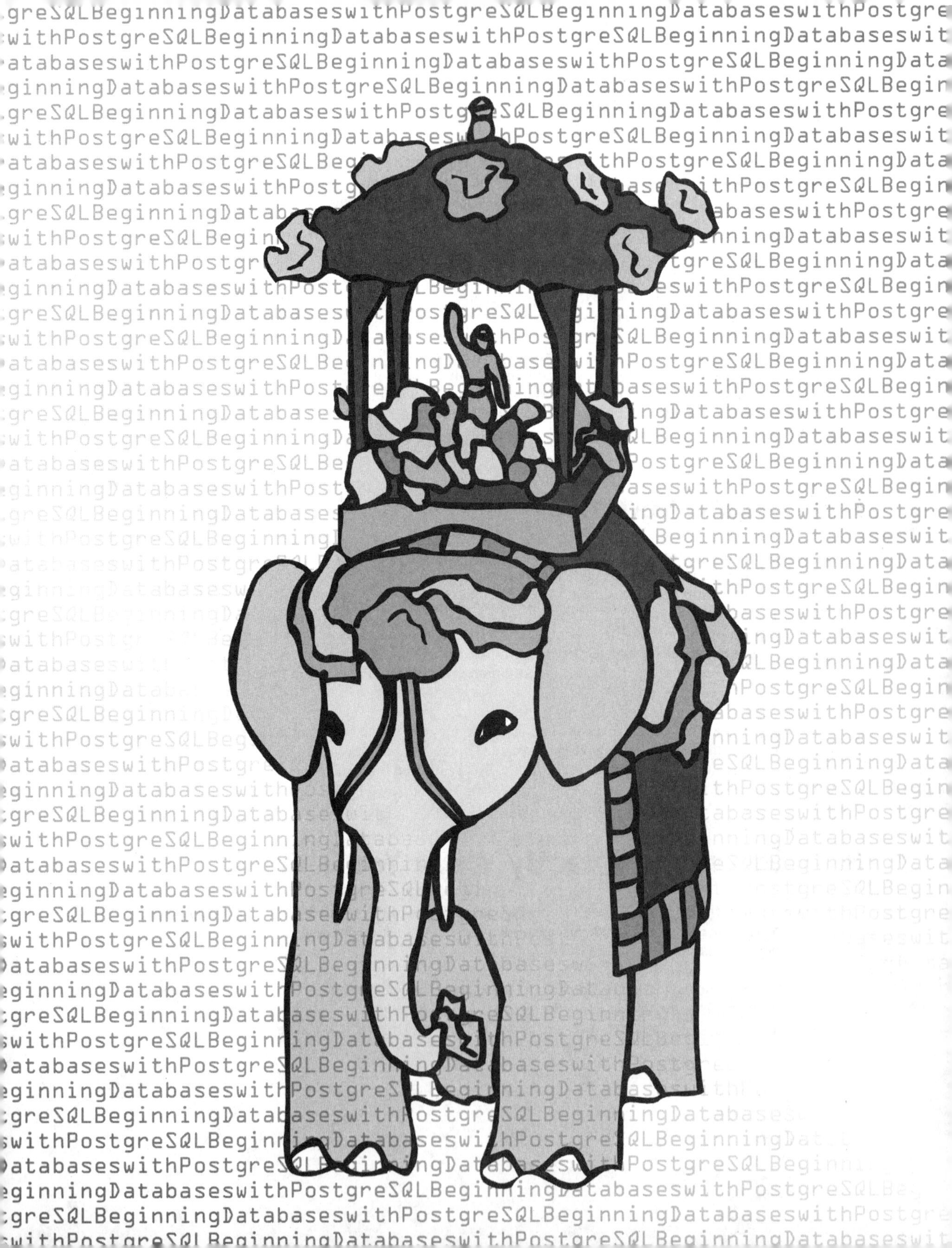
BeginningDatabaseswithPostgreSQL

# 1

# Introduction to PostgreSQL

This book is all about one of the most successful Open Source software products of recent times, a relational database called PostgreSQL. PostgreSQL is finding an eager audience among database aficionados and Open Source developers alike. Anyone who is creating an application with non-trivial amounts of data, can benefit from using a database, and PostgreSQL is an excellent implementation of a relational database, fully featured, Open Source, and free to use.

PostgreSQL can be used from just about any major programming language you care to name, including C, C++, Perl, Python, Java, Tcl, and PHP. It very closely follows the industry standard for query languages, SQL92. It also won the 2000 Linux Journal Editor's Choice Award for Best Database.

We are perhaps getting a little ahead of ourselves here. You may be wondering what exactly PostgreSQL is, and why you might want to use it.

In this chapter, we will try to set the scene for the rest of the book and provide some background information on databases in general, the different types of databases, why they are useful, and where PostgreSQL fits into this picture.

## Programming with Data

Nearly all non-trivial computer applications manipulate large amounts of data, and a lot of applications are written primarily to deal with data, rather than perform calculations.

Some writers estimate that 80% of all application development in the world today is connected in some way to complex data stored in a database, so databases are a very important foundation to many applications. Resources for programming with data abound. Most good programming books will contain chapters on creating, storing and manipulating data. Two of our previous books contain information about programming with data:

- ❑ *"Beginning Linux Programming"* Neil Matthew and Richard Stones, Wrox Press (ISBN 81-7366-156-1), covers the DBM library
- ❑ *"Professional Linux Programming"* Neil Matthew and Richard Stones, Wrox Press (ISBN 1-861003-01-3), contains chapters on the PostgreSQL and MySQL relational database systems

Data comes in all shapes and sizes, and the ways that we deal with it will vary according to the nature of the data. In some cases, the data is simple, perhaps a single number such as the value of   , which might be built into a program that draws circles. The application itself may have this as a "hard-coded" value for the ratio of the circumference of a circle to its diameter. We might call this kind of data "constant" as it will never need to change.

Another example of constant data would be the currency exchange rates used between the currencies of some European countries. In so-called "Euro Land", the countries that are participating in the single European currency (Euro) fixed the exchange rates between their national currencies to six decimal places.

A Euro Land currency converter application could then have a hard-coded table of currency names and base exchange rate, the number of national units to the Euro. These rates will never change.

We are not quite finished, however, as it is possible for this table of currencies to grow. As countries sign up for the Euro, their national currency exchange rate is fixed and they need to be added to the table.

Now, our currency converter needs to be changed, its built-in table changed and the application rebuilt. This will have to be done every time the currency table changes.

A better method would be to have the application read a file containing some simple currency data, maybe the name of the currency, its international symbol and exchange rate. Then we can just alter the file when the table needs to change and leave the application alone.

The data file that we use has no special structure; it's just some lines of text that mean something to the particular application that reads it. It has no inherent structure therefore, we call it a "flat file". Here's what our currency file might look like:

```
France          FRF              6.559570
Germany         DEM              1.955830
Italy           ITL              1936.270020
Belgium         BEF              40.339901
```

# Flat File Databases

Flat files are extremely useful for many application types. As long as the size of the file remains manageable – so that we can easily make changes – a flat file scheme may be sufficient for our needs.

Many systems and applications, particularly on UNIX, use flat files for their data storage or data interchange. An example is the UNIX password file.

The flat file example we've just looked at consists of a number of elements of information, or attributes, together making up what we might term a record. The records are arranged so that each line in the file represents a single record, and the whole file acts to keep the related records together. Sometimes this scheme is not quite good enough and we have to add extra features to support the job the application has to do.

Suppose that we decide to extend the application to record the language spoken in each country, its population, and area. In a flat file, we essentially have one record per line, each record made up of several attributes. Each individual attribute in a record is always in the same place, for example the currency symbol is always the second attribute, so we could think of looking at the data by column, where a column is always the same type of information. Hence, to add the language spoken in a particular country, we might think that we just need to add a new column to each of our lines.

We hit a snag with this as soon as we realize that some countries have more than one official language. So, in our record for Belgium we would have to cater to both Flemish and French. In Switzerland, we have to cater to four languages.

This problem is known as **repeating groups**. We have the situation where a perfectly valid item (language) can be repeated in a record, so not only does the record (row) repeat, but the data in that row repeats as well. Flat files do not cope with this, as it is impossible to determine where the languages stop and the rest of the record starts. The only way round this, is to add some structure to the file, and then it would not be "flat" anymore.

The repeating groups problem is very common and is the issue that really started the drive towards more sophisticated database management systems. We can attempt to resolve this problem by using ordinary text files with a little more structure. These are still often referred to as flat files, but are probably better described as structured text files. Here's another example.

An application that stores the details of DVDs might need to record the year of production, director, genre, and cast list. We could design a file that it looks a little like a Windows `.ini` file, to store this information:

```
[2001: A Space Odyssey]
year=1968
director=Stanley Kubrick
genre=science fiction
starring=Keir Dullea
starring=Leonard Rossiter
...
[Toy Story]
...
```

We have solved the repeating groups problem by introducing some tags to indicate the type of each element in the record.

Now our application has to read and interpret a more complex file, just to get at its data. Updating a record and searching in this kind of structure can be quite difficult. How can we make sure that the descriptions for genre or classification are chosen from a specific subset? How can we easily produce a sorted list of Kubrick films?

As data requirements get more and more complex, we are forced to write more and more application code for reading and storing our data. If we extend our DVD application to include functions that make it useful to a DVD rental store owner with membership details and rentals, returns and reservations, the prospect of maintaining all of that information in flat files becomes very unappealing.

A third, and all too common, problem is simply that of size. Although the above structure could be scanned by 'brute force' to answer complex searching with queries such as "tell me the addresses of all my members that have rented more than one comedy movie in the last three months", not only will it be very difficult to code, but the performance will be dire. This is because the application has no choice but to process the whole file to look for any piece of information, even if the question relates to just a single entry, such as 'How many films were produced in 1968?'

What we need is a general-purpose way of storing and retrieving data, not a solution invented many times to fit slightly different, but very similar, problems as in a generic data handling system.

What we need is a database.

# What is a Database?

The Merriam-Webster online dictionary (http://www.m-w.com) defines a database as a usually large collection of data organized especially for rapid search and retrieval (as by a computer).

A database management system (DBMS) is usually a suite of libraries, applications, and utilities that relieve an application developer from the burden of worrying about the detail of storing and managing data. It will also provide facilities for searching and updating records.

Database management systems come in a number of flavors, developed over the years to solve particular kinds of data storage problems.

# Database Types

During the 1960s and 1970s databases were developed that solved the repeating groups problem in several different ways. These methods result in what are termed **models** for database systems. Research performed at IBM provided much of the basis for these models, which are still in use today.

One of the main drivers in early database system designs was efficiency. It is much easier to deal with database records that are fixed length, or at least have a fixed number of elements per record (columns per row). This essentially avoids the repeating group problem. If you are a programmer in just about any procedural language, you will readily see that in this case you can read each record of a database into a simple C structure. Real life is rarely that accommodating, however, and so we have to deal with inconveniently structured data.

## Network Database Model

The network model introduces the idea of pointers within the database. Records can contain references to other records. So, for example we may keep a record for each customer we deal with. Each customer has placed many orders with us over time (a repeating group). The data is arranged so that the customer record contains a pointer to just one order record. Each order record contains both the order data for that specific order, plus a pointer to another order record. In our currency application then, we might end up with record structures that look a little like this:

```
+-------------+-----------+---------+-----------+
| CountryName |  Symbol   |  Rate   | LangPtr    |
+-------------+-----------+---------+-----------+


+-------------+-----------+
| Language    | LangPtr   |
+-------------+-----------+
```

Once the data is loaded, we end up with a linked (hence, the name *network* model) list used for the languages:

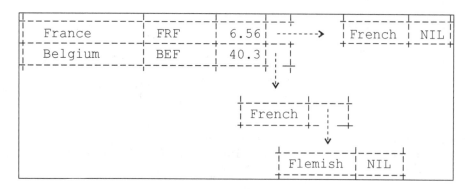

The two different record types we see here would be stored separately, each in their own table.

Of course, to be more efficient in terms of storage, the actual database would not repeat the language names over and over again, but would probably contain a third table of language names together with an identifier (often a small integer) that would be used to refer to the language name table entry in the other record types. This is called a key.

A network model database has some strong advantages. If you need to discover all of the records of one type that are related to a specific record of another type (like here languages spoken in a country), you can find them extremely quickly, by following the pointers from the starting record.

There are however, some disadvantages too. If you want to list the countries that speak French you have to follow the links from all of the country records, which for large databases will be extremely slow. This can be fixed by having other linked lists of pointers specifically for languages, but it rapidly becomes very complex, and is clearly not a general-purpose solution, since you need to decide in advance how the pointers will be designed.

Writing applications that use a network model database can also be very tiresome, as the application typically has to take responsibility for setting up and maintaining the pointers as records are updated and deleted.

# Hierarchical Database Model

The IMS database system from IBM in the late 1960s introduced the hierarchical model for databases. In this model, considering data records to be composed of collections of others solves the repeating groups problem.

The model can be compared to a "bill of materials" used to describe how a complex manufactured product is composed. For example, a car is composed (say) of a chassis, a body, an engine, and four wheels. Each of these major components is broken down further. An engine comprises some cylinders, a cylinder head, and a crankshaft. These components are broken down further until we get to the nuts and bolts that make up every part in an automobile.

Hierarchical model databases are still in use today. A hierarchical database system is able to optimize the data storage to make it more efficient for particular questions, for example to determine which automobile uses a particular part.

# Relational Database Model

The theory of database management systems took a gigantic leap forward in 1970 with the publication of "*A Relational Model of Data for Large Shared Data Banks*", a paper by E. F. Codd (see http://www.acm.org/classics/nov95/toc.html).This revolutionary paper introduced the idea of relations and showed how tables could be used to represent facts that relate to 'real world' objects, and therefore, hold data about them.

By this time, it had also become clear that the initial driving force behind database design, efficiency, was often less important than another concern, data integrity. The relational model emphasizes data integrity much more than either of the earlier models.

There are several important rules that define a relational database management system (RDBMS). Firstly, records in a table are known as tuples, and this is the terminology you will see used in some parts of the PostgreSQL documentation. A tuple is an ordered group of components, or attributes, each of which has a defined type. All tuples follow the same pattern, in that they all have the same number and types of components. Here, is an example of a set of tuples:

```
{"France", "FRF", 6.56}
{"Belgium", "BEF", 40.1}
```

Each of these tuples has three attributes, a country name (string), a currency (string), and an exchange rate (a floating point number). In a relational database, all records that are added to this set, or table, must follow the same form, so the following are disallowed:

```
{"Germany", "DEM"}
    - too few attributes
{"Switzerland", "CHF", "French", "German", "Italian", "Romansch"}
    - too many attributes
{1936.27, "ITL", "Italy"}
    - incorrect attribute types (wrong order)
```

Furthermore, in any table of tuples there can be no duplicates. This means that in any table in a relational database there cannot be any identical rows or records.

This might seem to be a rather draconian restriction, since in a system that records orders placed by customers it would appear to disallow the same customer from ordering the same product from us twice. We will see in the next chapter that in practice there is an easy way to work around this requirement, by adding an additional attribute.

Each attribute in a record must be "atomic", that is, a single piece of data, not another record, or a list of other attributes. Also, the type of corresponding attributes in every record in the table must be the same, as we've seen. Technically, this means that they must be drawn from the same set of values or domain. On practical terms it means they will all be a string, an integer, floating point value, or some other type supported by the database system.

> **The attribute that we use to distinguish otherwise identical records is called a key.**
> **Sometimes a combination of more than one attribute can be used as the key.**

The attribute, or attributes, that we use to distinguish a particular record in a table from all the other records in a table, in other words what makes this record unique, is called a primary key. In a relational database, each relation, or table, must have a primary key, something that makes each record different from all the others in that table.

One last rule that determines the structure of a relational database, is **referential integrity**. This is a desire that all of the records in the database make sense at all times. The database application programmer often has to be careful to make sure that his/her code does not break the integrity of the database. Consider what happens when we delete a customer. If we try to remove the customer from the CUSTOMER relation we need also to delete all of his orders from the ORDERS table too. Otherwise, we will be left with records about orders that have no valid customer.

We will see much more on the theory and practice of relational databases in later chapters. For now, it is enough to know that the relational model for databases is based on some mathematical concepts of sets and relations, and that there are some rules that need to be observed by systems that are built to this model.

# Query Languages

Relational database management systems offer ways to add and update data of course, but their power stems more from their ability to allow users to ask questions about the data stored, in the form of queries. Unlike many earlier database designs, which were often structured around the type of question that the data needed to answer, relational databases are much more flexible at answering questions that were not known at the time the database was designed.

Codd's proposals for the relational model use the fact that relations define sets and sets can be manipulated mathematically. He suggested that queries might use a branch of theoretical logic called the predicate calculus and that query languages would use this as their base. This would bring unprecedented power for searching and selecting data sets.

One of the first implementations of a query language was QUEL, used in the Ingres database developed in the late 1970s. Another query language that takes a different approach is QBE (Query By Example). At around the same time a team at IBM's research center developed SQL (Standard Query Language), usually pronounced "sequel".

SQL is a standardized language, the most commonly used definition is **ISO/IEC 9075:1992, "Information Technology --- Database Languages --- SQL".** This is more simply referred to as SQL92, or sometimes ANSI X3.135-1992, which is an identical US standard, differing only in some cover pages. These standards replaced an earlier standard, SQL89. In fact, there is also a later standard, SQL99, but that is not yet in common usage, and the updates generally don't affect the core SQL language.

There are three levels of conformance to SQL92, Entry SQL, Intermediate SQL, and Full SQL. By far the most common conformance level is 'Entry', and PostgreSQL is very close to this conformance, but there are slight differences. The developers are working to fill in the relatively minor omissions, and PostgreSQL continues to get closer to the standard with each release.

The SQL language comprises three types of commands:

❑ **Data Manipulation Language (DML)**
This is the part of SQL that you will use 90% of the time. It is made up of the commands for inserting, deleting, updating, and most importantly selecting data from the database.

❑ **Data Definition Language (DDL)**
These are the commands for creating tables, and controlling other aspects of the database that are more structural than data related.

❑ **Data Control Language (DCL)**
This is a set of commands that generally control permissions on the data, such as defining access rights. Many database users will never use these commands, because they work in larger company environments where one or more database administrators are employed specifically to manage the database, and usually one of their roles is to control permissions.

As you read through this book, we will be teaching you SQL, so hopefully by the time you get to the end you will be comfortable with a wide range of SQL statements and how to use them.

# SQL

SQL has become very widely adopted as a standard for database query languages, and as we mentioned is defined in a series of international standards. Today, just about every useful database system supports SQL to a greater or less extent. It has become a great unifier, since it means that a database application written to use SQL as the interface to the database can be ported to use another database at little cost in terms of time and effort.

Commercial pressures however, dictate that database manufacturers distinguish their products one from another. This has led to SQL variations, not helped by the fact that the standard for SQL does not define commands for many of the database administration tasks that are an essential part of using a database in the real world. So, there are differences between the SQL used by (for example) Oracle, SQL Server and PostgreSQL.

We will see a lot more of SQL during the rest of the book, but we will take a very brief look at some examples here to show what SQL looks like. We will see that we do not need to worry about the formal basis of SQL to be able to use it.

Here is some SQL for creating a new table in a database. This example creates a table for items that are offered for sale, and will be part of an order:

```
CREATE TABLE item
(
    item_id                 serial,
    description             char(64)        not null,
    cost_price              numeric(7,2),
    sell_price              numeric(7,2)
);
```

We state that the table requires an identifier, which will act as a primary key, and that this is to be generated automatically by the database system. It has type serial, which means that every time an item is added, a new, unique, item_id will be created in sequence. The description is a text attribute of 64 characters. The cost and sell prices are defined to be floating point numbers specified to two decimal places.

Next, we have some SQL that can be used to populate the table we have just created. These are very straightforward:

```
INSERT INTO item(description, cost_price, sell_price)
values('Fan Small', 9.23, 15.75);
INSERT INTO item(description, cost_price, sell_price)
values('Fan Large', 13.36, 19.95);
INSERT INTO item(description, cost_price, sell_price)
values('Toothbrush', 0.75, 1.45);
```

The heart of SQL is the SELECT statement. It is used to create result sets that are groups of records (or attributes from records) that match a particular criterion. The criteria can be quite complex if required. These result sets can then be used as the targets for changes with an UPDATE statement or deleted with DELETE.

Here are some examples of SELECT statements:

```
SELECT * FROM customer, orderinfo
WHERE orderinfo.customer_id = customer.customer_id GROUP BY customer_id

SELECT customer.title, customer.fname, customer.lname,
COUNT(orderinfo.orderinfo_id) AS "Number of orders" FROM customer, orderinfo
WHERE customer.customer_id = orderinfo.customer_id
GROUP BY customer.title, customer.fname, customer.lname
```

These SELECT statements respectively list all customer orders and count the orders each customer has made. We will see the results of these SQL statements in Chapter 2, and learn much more about SELECT in Chapter 4.

With PostgreSQL, we can access our data in several ways. We can:

❑ Use a command line application to execute SQL statements

❑ Embed SQL directly into our application (using embedded SQL)

❑ Use function calls (APIs) to prepare and execute SQL statements, scan result sets, and perform updates from a large variety of different programming languages

❑ Access the data indirectly, using an driver, such as the Open Database Connection (ODBC) or the JDBC standard used by Java programs, or a standard library, such as Perl's DBI , to access our PostgreSQL database

# Database Management Systems

A DBMS, as mentioned above, is a suite of programs that allow the construction of databases and applications that use them. The responsibilities of a DBMS include:

❑ **Creating of the database**
Some systems will manage one large file and create one or more databases inside it, others may use many operating system files, or utilize a raw disk partition directly. Users need not worry about the low-level structure of these files as the DBMS provides all of the access developers and users need.

❑ **Providing query and update facilities**
A DBMS will have a method of asking for data that matches certain criteria, such as all orders made by a particular customer that have not yet been delivered. Before the widespread introduction of the SQL standard, the way that queries like this were expressed varied from system to system.

❑ **Multi-tasking**
If a database is used in several applications, or is accessed concurrently by several users at the same time, the DBMS will make sure that each user's request is processed without impacting the others. This means that users only need to wait in line if someone else is writing to the precise item of data that they wish to read (or write). It is possible to have many simultaneous reads of data going on at the same time. In practice, different database systems support different degrees of multi-tasking, and may even have configurable levels, as we will see in Chapter 9.

❑ **Keeping an audit trail**
A DBMS will keep a log of all the changes to the data for a period of time. This can be used to investigate errors, but perhaps even more importantly, can be used to reconstruct data in the event of a fault in the system, perhaps an unscheduled power down. Typically, a data backup and log of transactions, since the backup can be used to restore the database in case of disk failure.

❑ **Managing the security of the database**
A DBMS will provide access controls so that only authorized users can manipulate the data held in the database and the structure of the database itself (the attributes, tables, and indices). Typically, there will be a hierarchy of users defined for any particular database, from a "superuser" who can change anything, through users with permission to add or delete data, down to users able only to read data. The DBMS will have facilities to add and delete users, and specify which features of the database system they are able to use.

❑ **Maintaining referential integrity**
Many database systems provide features that help to maintain referential integrity, the 'correctness of the data', as mentioned earlier. Typically, they will report an error when a query or update will break the relational model rules.

# What is PostgreSQL?

Now we are in a position to say what PostgreSQL actually is. It is a database management system that incorporates the relational model for its databases and supports the SQL standard query language.

PostgreSQL also happens to be very capable, very reliable, and has good performance characteristics. It runs on just about any UNIX platform, including UNIX-like systems, such as FreeBSD and Linux. It can also be run on Windows NT and 2000 servers, or even Microsoft workstation systems such as ME for development. Oh, and it's free, and Open Source.

PostgreSQL can be compared pretty favorably to other database management systems. It contains just about all the features that you would find in other commercial or Open Source databases, and a few extra that you might not

PostgreSQL features (as listed in the PostgreSQL FAQ):

❑   Transactions

❑   Subselects

❑   Views

❑   Foreign key referential integrity

❑   Sophisticated Locking

❑   User-defined types

❑   Inheritance

❑   Rules

❑   Multi-version concurrency control

We will be looking at many of these as the book progresses.

Since release 6.5, PostgreSQL has been very stable, with a large series or regression tests performed on each release to ensure its stability. With the release of the 7.x series, conformance to SQL92 is closer than ever, and the irksome row size restriction has been removed.

PostgreSQL has proven to be very reliable in use. Each release is very carefully controlled, and beta releases are subject to at least a month's testing. With a large user community, and universal access to the source code, bugs can get fixed very quickly.

The performance of PostgreSQL has been improving with each release, and the latest benchmarks show that in some circumstances it compares well with commercial products. Some less fully featured database systems will outperform it at the cost of lower overall functionality. Then again however, for simple enough applications so will a flat file database.

# A Short History of PostgreSQL

PostgreSQL can trace its family tree back to 1977 at the University of California at Berkeley (UCB). A relational database called Ingres was developed at UCB between 1977 and 1985. Ingres was a popular UCB export, making an appearance on many UNIX computers in the academic and research communities. To serve the commercial marketplace the code for Ingres was taken by Relational Technologies/Ingres Corporation and became one of the first commercially available relational database management systems. Today Ingres has become CA-INGRES II, a product from Computer Associates.

Meanwhile, back at Berkeley, work on a relational database server called Postgres continued from 1986 to 1994. Again, this code was taken up by a commercial company and offered for sale as a product. This time it was Illustra, since swallowed up by Informix. Around 1994 SQL features were added to Postgres and its name was changed to Postgres95.

By 1996, Postgres was becoming very popular and the decision was taken to open up its development to a mailing list, starting what has become a very successful collaboration of volunteers in driving Postgres forward. At this time, Postgres underwent its final name change, ditching the now dated '95' tag for a more appropriate 'SQL' to reflect the support Postgres now has for the query language standard. PostgreSQL was born.

Today a team of Internet developers develops PostgreSQL in much the same manner as other Open Source software such as Perl, Apache, and PHP. Users have access to the source code and contribute fixes, enhancements, and suggestions for new features. The official PostgreSQL releases are made via http://www.postgresql.org.

Commercial support is available from Great Bridge, who also employ some of the PostgreSQL developers. See the *Resources* section at the end of the chapter for more details.

## The PostgreSQL Architecture

One of PostgreSQL's strengths derives from its architecture. In common with commercial database systems, PostgreSQL can be used in a client-server environment. This has many benefits for both users and developers.

The heart of a PostgreSQL installation is the database server process. It runs on a single server (PostgreSQL does not yet have the high availability features of a few enterprise-class commercial database systems that can spread the load across several servers giving additional scalability and resilience).

Applications that need to access the data stored in the database are required to do so via the database process. These client programs cannot access the data directly, even if they are running on the same computer as the server process.

This separation into client and server allows applications to be distributed. We can use a network to separate our clients from our server, and develop client applications in an environment that suits the users. For example, we might implement the database on UNIX and create client programs that run on Microsoft Windows.

The diagram below, shows a typical distributed PostgreSQL application:

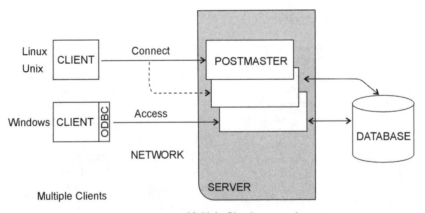

Multiple Simultaneous Access

Here we can see several clients connecting to the server across a network. For PostgreSQL, this needs to be a TCP/IP network – a local area network or possibly even the Internet. Each client connects to the main database server process (shown here as `postmaster`), which creates a new server process specifically for servicing access requests for this client.

Concentrating the data handling in a server, rather than attempting to control many clients accessing the same data stored in a shared directory on a server, allows PostgreSQL to efficiently maintain the data's integrity even with many simultaneous users.

The client programs connect using a message protocol specific to PostgreSQL. It is possible, however, to install software on the client that provides a standard interface for the application to work to, for example, the ODBC standard, or the JDBC standard. The availability of an ODBC driver allows many existing applications to use PostgreSQL as a database, including Microsoft Office products such as Excel and Access. We will see more PostgreSQL connectivity in later chapters.

The client-server architecture for PostgreSQL allows a division of labor. A server machine well suited to the storage and access of large amounts of data can be used as a secure data repository. Sophisticated graphical applications can be developed for the clients. Alternatively, a web-based frontend can be created to access the data and return results as web pages to a standard web browser with no additional client software at all. Again, we will return to these ideas in a later chapter.

# Open Source Licensing

As we start the 21st century, much is being made of Open Source software, of which PostgreSQL is such a good example. But what does this mean exactly?

The term Open Source has a very specific meaning when applied to software. It means that the software is supplied with the source code included. It does not necessarily mean that there are no conditions applied to the software's use. It is still licensed in that you are given permission to use the software in certain ways.

An Open Source license will grant you permission to use the software, modify it and redistribute it without paying license fees. This means that you may use PostgreSQL in your organization as you see fit.

If you have problems with Open Source software, because you have the source code you can either fix them yourself, or give the code to someone else to try to fix. There are now many commercial companies offering support for Open Source products so that you do not have to feel neglected if you choose to use an Open Source product.

There are many different variations on Open Source licenses, some more liberal than others. All of them adhere to the principle of source code availability, and allowing redistribution.

The most liberal license is the Berkeley Software Distribution (BSD) license that says in effect "do what you will with this software, there is no warranty". The license for PostgreSQL echoes the BSD license sentiments and takes the form of a copyright statement that says, "Permission to use, copy, modify, and distribute this software and its documentation for any purpose, without fee, and without a written agreement is hereby granted, provided that the above copyright notice and this paragraph and the following two paragraphs appear in all copies." The paragraphs that follow this statement disclaim liability and warranty.

# Resources

There are many sources of further information about databases in general and PostgreSQL in general – both in print and online.

For more on the theory of databases check out the Tech Talk section of David Frick's site at http://www.frick-cpa.com.

The official PostgreSQL site is http://www.postgreSQL.org where you can find more on the history of PostgreSQL, download copies of PostgreSQL, browse the official documentation, and much more besides, including how to pronounce PostgreSQL.

Commercial support for PostgreSQL is available from Great Bridge, at http://www.greatbridge.com. Great Bridge also support an Open Source project hosting site at http://www.greatbridge.org, which is a great place to look for the latest projects related to PostgreSQL, such as management tools, GUI interfaces and so on.

PostgreSQL is also the foundation of the Red Hat Database. More on the Red Hat database can be found at http://www.redhat.com/products/software/database/.

Some PostgreSQL goodies can be had from the PostgreSQL Inc. site at http://www.pgsql.com.

For more information on Open Source software and the principle of freedom in software, take a few moments to visit these two sites:

❑　　http://www.gnu.org
❑　　http://www.opensource.org

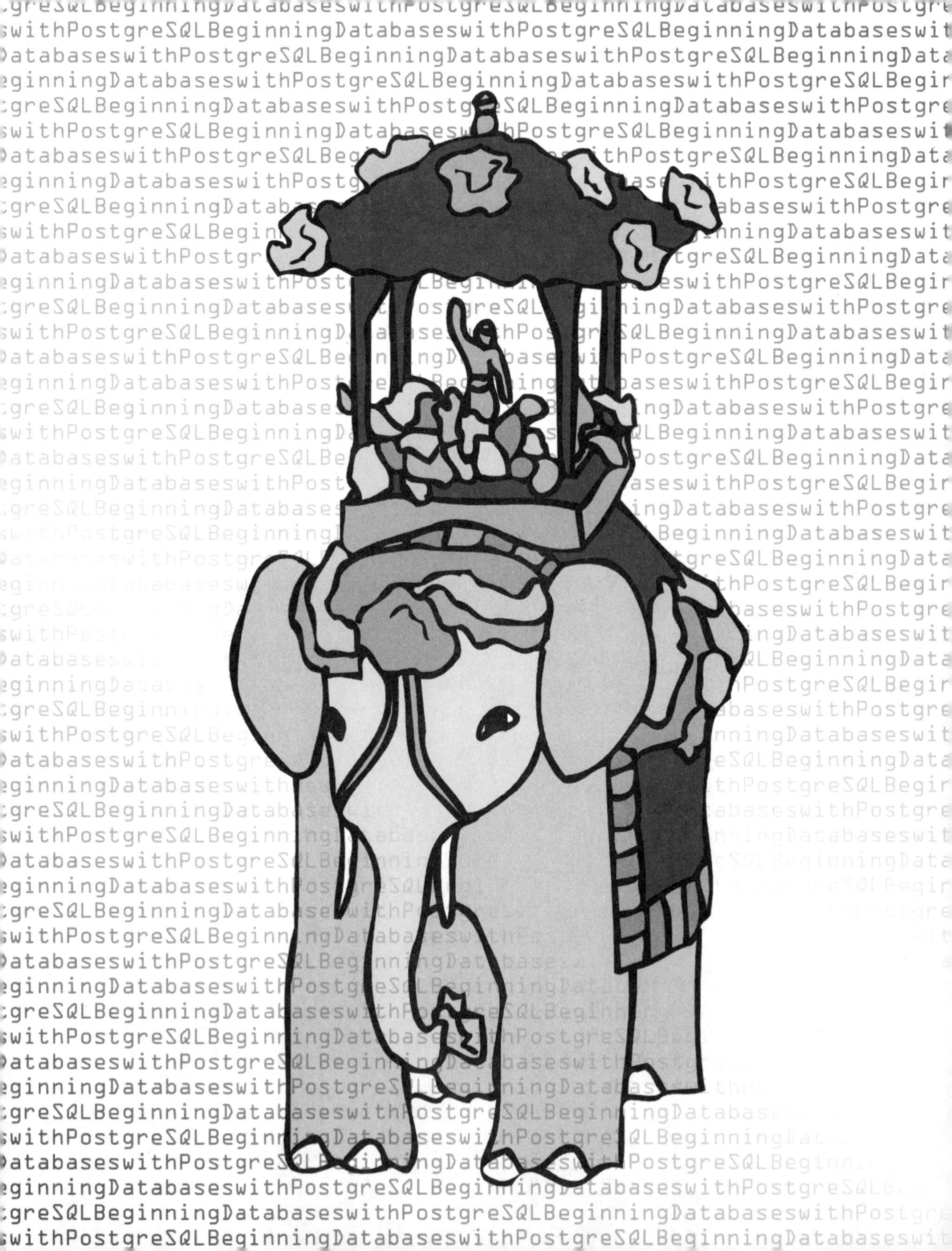
BeginningDatabaseswithPostgreSQL

# Relational Database Principles

In this chapter, we are going to look at what makes a database system, particularly a relational one like PostgreSQL, so useful for real world data. We will start by looking at spreadsheets, which have much in common with relational databases, but also have significant limitations.

We will see how a relational database, such as PostgreSQL, has many advantages over spreadsheets, and how even with a relatively straightforward database, we can take advantage of useful features of PostgreSQL. Along the way we will continue our rather informal look at SQL.

We will be taking a look at the following aspects in this chapter:

- ❑   Spreadsheets – their problems and limitations
- ❑   What's different about a database?
- ❑   Data in a database
- ❑   A basic database design with multiple tables
- ❑   Establishing relations between tables
- ❑   Designing you tables – some basic rules of thumb
- ❑   Demonstrations of a Customer/Order database
- ❑   Some basic data types and NULL

## Spreadsheets

Spreadsheet applications, such as Microsoft Excel, are widely used as a way of storing and inspecting data. Indeed, we often use a spreadsheet as an effective way of taking a set of data and looking at it in many different ways. It's easy to sort the data in different columns and see the features of the data just by looking at it, provided your data is not too large that is.

Unfortunately, people often mistake a tool that is good for inspecting and manipulating data, for a suitable tool for storing and sharing complex data. The two needs are often very different.

Most people will be familiar with one or more spreadsheets, and quite at home with the data being arranged in a set of rows and columns, as we see below in a StarOffice spreadsheet holding a set of customers:

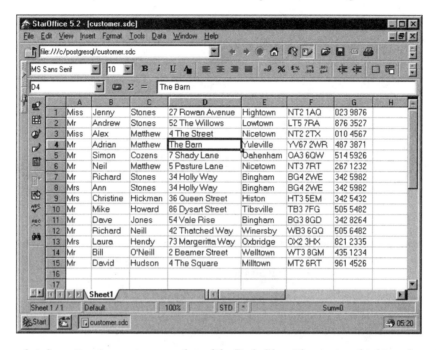

Certainly, such information is easy to see and modify. Probably without even thinking about it, we have designed this spreadsheet to incorporate several features that will be handy to remember when we start designing databases. Each customer has a separate row, and each piece of information about the customer is held in a separate column. For example, their first and last names are held in separate columns, which makes it easy to sort the data by last name, should we want to.

# Some Terminology

Before we move on, let's just ensure we have our terminology straight, by labeling a small section of the data. I'm sure you all know about rows and columns, but here's a refresher:

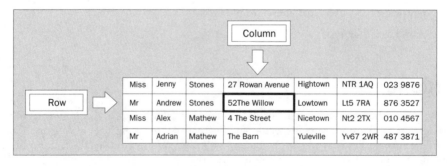

The intersection of a column and a row is a cell. In the StarOffice screen shot above, a single cell is indicated by the arrows, showing the address line '52 The Willows'.

# Limitations with Spreadsheets

So what is wrong with storing our customer information in a spreadsheet? The answer is possibly "absolutely nothing", provided you don't have too many customers and too many details for each customer. Also, provided you don't need to store any other information such as the orders each customer has placed, and there are not too many people who want to update the information at once. That might sound like a long list of possible problems, but it just depends if any of them are applicable for your circumstances.

There are a lot of very good uses for spreadsheets that make them a great tool for many problems. Just like you wouldn't (or at least shouldn't) try to hammer in a nail with a screwdriver, however, sometimes spreadsheets are just not the right tool for the job.

Just imagine what it would be like if a large company, with many thousands of customers, kept the master copy of their customer list in a simple spreadsheet. In a big company it's likely that several people would need to update the list. Although file locking can ensure that only one person updates the list at any one time, as the number of people trying to update the list grows, they will spend longer and longer time waiting for their turn to edit the list. In reality, what we would like, is to allow many people to simultaneously read, update, add, and delete rows. Clearly, simple file locking is going to be totally inadequate to efficiently handle this problem.

Suppose, we also wanted to store details of each order a customer placed? We could start putting order information next to each customer, but as the number of orders per customer grew, the spreadsheet would get more and more complex. Look what happens when we start trying to add some basic order information against each customer:

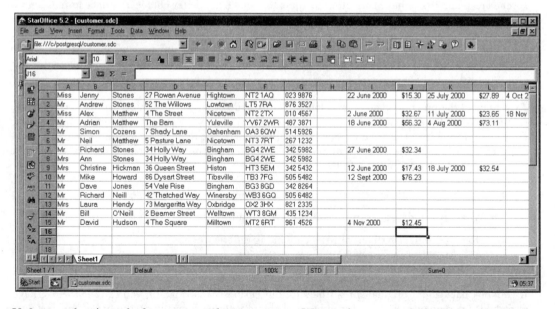

Unfortunately, it's not looking quite so elegant anymore. We now have rows of arbitrary length, which is not an easy way to calculate how much each customer has spent with us. Eventually, we will exceed the number of columns allowed in each row. It's the repeating groups problem we saw in the previous chapter.

Here is an example of how easily you can exceed the capabilities of a spreadsheet. An acquaintance was trying to set up a spreadsheet as a favor for a friend who runs a small business. This small business makes leather items, and the price of the item depended not only on the time to make the item, but also on the unit cost of the leather used in the manufacture. The owner would buy leather in batches, each of which would have a unit price that varied significantly. Then they would use their stock on a 'first in, first used' basis as they made items for sale, normally many per batch. The challenge was to create a spreadsheet to:

- ❑ Track the stock
- ❑ Track as to how many batches of leather was left
- ❑ Track how much had been paid for the batch currently being used
- ❑ Also to make matters more complex, track the number of grades of leather

After days of effort, they discovered that this apparently straightforward stock-keeping requirement is a surprisingly difficult problem to transfer to a spreadsheet. The variable nature of the number of stock records does not fit well with the spreadsheet philosophy.

The point we are making here is that spreadsheets are great in their place, but there are limits to their usefulness.

# What's Different About a Database?

When you look at it superficially, a relational database, such as PostgreSQL, has many similarities to a spreadsheet, but it is much more flexible. It can efficiently store much more complex data than a spreadsheet, and it also has many other features that make it a better choice as a data store, such as managing multiple simultaneous users.

Let's first look at storing our simple single sheet customer list in a database, and see what benefits this might have. Later in the chapter, we will extend this and see how PostgreSQL can help us solve our customer orders problem.

As we saw in the previous chapter, databases are made up of tables, or in more formal terminology, **relations**. We will stick to using the term tables in this book. First, we need to design a table to hold our customer information. The good news is that a spreadsheet of data is often an almost ready-made solution, since it holds the data in a number of rows and columns. To get started with a basic database table, we need to decide on three things:

- ❑ How many columns we need to store the attributes associated with each item?
- ❑ What type of data goes in each attribute (column)?
- ❑ How to distinguish different rows containing different items?

## Choosing Columns

If you look back at our original spreadsheet for our customer information, you can see that we have already decided on what seems a sensible set of columns for each customer, the first name, last name, Zip code, and so on. The first criterion is already met.

## Choosing a Data Type for Each Column

The second criterion is to determine what type of data goes in each column. While spreadsheets allow each cell to have a different type, in a database table each column must have the same type. Just like most programming languages, database columns have types. Most of the time the most basic types are all you need to know; the main choice is between integer numbers, floating point numbers, fixed length text, variable length text, and date. We will come back to PostgreSQL data types in more detail below, and in Chapter 8. Often the easiest way to decide the appropriate type is simply to look at some sample data.

In our customer data, we might decide to use text for all the columns, even though the phone numbers are numbers. Storing the phone number as a literal number could easily result in the loss of leading zeros, preventing us from storing international dial codes (+), using brackets around area codes, and so on. It doesn't take very much thought to determine that a phone number can often be much more than a simple string of numerals.

Using a character string to store the telephone number might not be the best decision, since we could also accidentally store all sorts of strange characters, but it is a better starting point than a number type. We can always refine our initial design later. We can see that the length of the title (Mr, Mrs, Dr) is always very short, and is most unlikely to ever be longer than 4 characters. Similarly, Zip codes also have a fixed maximum length. Therefore, we will make both of these columns fixed length fields, but leave all the other columns as variable length, since we have no easy way of knowing how long a person's last name might be, for example.

The other important difference between spreadsheet rows and database rows, is that the number of columns in a database table must be the same for all the rows. That's not a problem in our original version of the spreadsheet.

## Identifying Rows Uniquely

Our last problem in changing our spreadsheet into a database table is a little more subtle, as it comes from the way databases manage relations between tables. We have to decide on what makes each row of customer data different from any other customer row in the database.

In other words, how do we tell our customers apart? In a spreadsheet, we tend not to worry about the exact details of what distinguishes customers apart, but in a database design this is a key question, since relational database rules require each row to be unique in some way.

The obvious answer to distinguishing customers might seem to be 'by name', but unfortunately, that's not good enough. It is quite possible that we could have two customers with the same name. Another item you might choose is phone number, but that fails when two customers live at the same address. At this point you might try and apply some imagination, and suggest using a combination of name and phone number.

Certainly, it's unlikely that two customers will have both the same name and the same phone number, but quite apart being inelegant, another problem is lurking. What happens if a customer changes phone provider, and changes their phone number? By our definition, a unique customer must then be a new customer, because they are different from the customer we had before. Of course we know that they are just the same customer, with a new phone number.

This sort of problem, identifying uniqueness, turns up frequently in database design. What we have been doing is looking for a 'primary key' – an easy way to distinguish one row of customer data from all the other rows. Unfortunately, we have not yet succeeded, but all is not lost, since the standard solution is to assign a unique number to each customer.

We simply give each customer in turn a unique number, and bingo, we have a unique way to tell customers apart, regardless of them changing their phone number, moving house, or even changing their name. This is such a common problem that there is even a special data type, the serial data type, for helping to solve the problem. We will discover more about this type later in the chapter.

### Order of Rows

There is one other important difference between the data held in a spreadsheet and the same data held in a database table, that we must mention before we continue. In a spreadsheet the order of the rows is normally very important, but in a database table there is no order. That's right, when you ask to look at the data in a database table the database is free to give you the rows of data in any order it chooses, unless you specifically ask for it ordered in a particular way.

# Putting Data Into a Database

Now that we have decided on a database design for our initial table, we can go ahead and store our data in a database. We will come back shortly to the mechanics of defining a database table, storing, and accessing the data, but rest assured it's not difficult. Here is our data sitting in a PostgreSQL database, being viewed using a simple command line tool, psql, on a Linux machine:

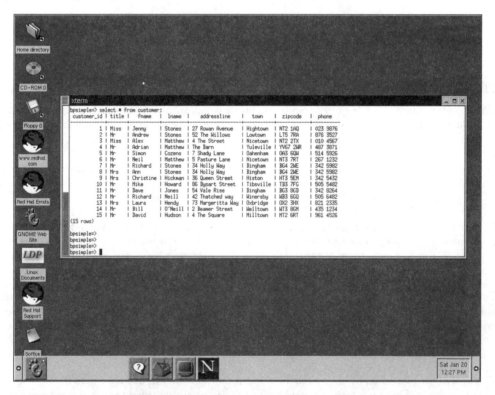

Notice that we have added an extra column, customer_id, as our unique way of referencing a customer. It is our 'primary key' for the table. As you can see, the data looks much like it did in a spreadsheet, laid out in rows and columns.

PostgreSQL is not restricted to command line use. Here is the same table in a graphical tool, pgAccess:

## Access Across a Network

Of course, if we could only access our data on the machine it was held on, we wouldn't have moved forward much from the situation we had with a single file being shared between different people.

PostgreSQL is a server-based database, and as described in the previous chapter, once configured, will accept requests from clients across a network. Of course, the client can also be on the same machine as the database server is running on, but for multi-user access this isn't normally going to be the case. For Microsoft Windows users, an ODBC driver is available. So we can arrange to connect any Windows desktop application that supports ODBC across a network to a server holding our data. We will see the technical details in Chapter 4.

Here is MS Access with a database containing linked external tables via ODBC to access the same data in our PostgreSQL database, which again is running on a Linux machine:

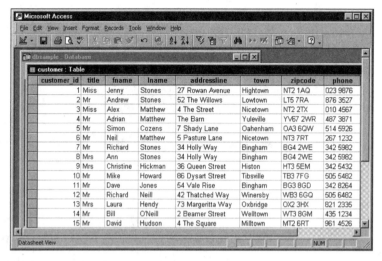

Now we can access the same data from many machines across the network at the same time. So now we have one copy of the data, securely held on a central server, accessible to multiple desktops, running different operating systems, across a network. PostgreSQL, like all relational databases, can automatically ensure that conflicting updates to the database can never occur. It looks to the users as though they all have unrestricted access to all the information at the same time, but behind the scenes PostgreSQL is monitoring updates and preventing conflicting updates.

This ability to apparently allow many people access to the data, but ensuring it is always consistent, is a very important feature of databases. When a user changes a column, you either see it before it changes, or afterwards, you never see partial updates.

A classic example is a bank database transferring money between two accounts. If, while the money was being transferred, someone were to run a report on the amount of money in all the accounts, it's very important that the total is correct. It may not matter in the report which account the money was in at the instant the report was run, but it is important that the report doesn't 'see' the in-between point, where one account has been debited, but the other not credited.

Relational databases like PostgreSQL hide any intermediate states, so they can't be 'seen' by other users. This is termed **isolation**. The report is isolated from the money transfer operation, so it appears to happen either before or after, but never at exactly the same instant. We will come back to this concept of isolation in Chapter 9.

# Slicing and Dicing Data

Now that we have seen how easy it is to access the data once it is in a database table, let's have a first look at how we might actually access that data. There are two very basic operations we frequently need to perform on big sets of data.

Firstly, selecting rows that match a particular set of values, and secondly selecting a subset of the columns of the data. In database terminology, this is called selection and projection respectively, which sounds very clever, but is actually nice and easy.

Let's look at selecting a subset of the rows. Suppose we want to see all our customers who live in the town 'Bingham'. We will go back to PostgreSQLs standard command line tool, psql, to see how we can use the SQL language to ask PostgreSQL to get the data we want.

The SQL command we need is very simple:

```
SELECT * FROM customer WHERE town = 'Bingham'
```

If you are typing this into psql or another graphical client, then you also need to add a semi-colon, which tells psql that this is the end of a command, since longer commands might extend over more than one line. Generally, in this book, we will show the semicolon, since if you are trying the examples as you go along using a GUI, you will need to type it in.

PostgreSQL responds by returning all the rows in the customer table, where the town column is 'Bingham':

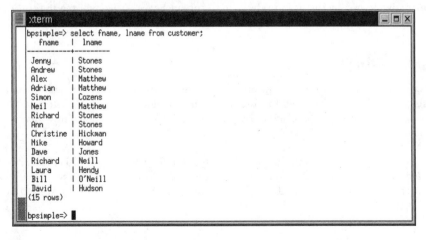

As you can see, that was pretty easy. Don't worry about the details of the SQL statement yet, we will come back to that more formally in Chapter 5. Notice the customer_id column that we added. We will be using it later, when we come to store orders in the database.

So that was selection, where we choose particular rows from a table. Now let's look at projection, or more simply selecting particular columns from a table.

Suppose we wanted to select just the first name and last names from our customer table. You will remember we called those columns fname and lname. The command to retrieve the names is also quite simple:

```
SELECT fname, lname FROM customer;
```

PostgreSQL responds by returning the appropriate columns:

You might reasonably suppose that sometimes we want to do both operations on the data at the same time, that is, select particular column values, but only from particular rows. That's pretty easy in SQL as well. For example, suppose we only wanted to know the first names and last names of all our customers who live in 'Bingham'. We can simply combine our two SQL statements into a single command:

```
SELECT fname, lname FROM customer WHERE town = 'Bingham';
```

PostgreSQL responds:

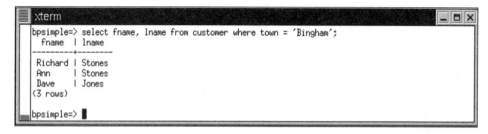

There is one very important thing to notice here. In many traditional programming languages, such as C or Java, we would have written some code to look through all the rows in the tables, stop when we found one with the right town, and print out the names we require. Although it might be possible to squeeze that onto a physical single line of code, it would be a very long and complex line. This is because C, Java, and similar languages are essentially procedural languages. You specify in the language how the computer should behave. In SQL, which is termed a declarative language, you tell the computer what you are trying to achieve, and the internal magic of PostgreSQL works out the 'difficult how' for you.

This might seem a little strange if you have never used a declarative language before, but once you get used to the idea it seems so obvious that it's a much better idea to tell the computer what you want, rather than how to do it. You will wonder how you have managed without such languages till now.

# Adding Additional Information

If what we have seen so far were all that relational databases could do for us, there would not be any great incentive to use databases in preference to spreadsheets. As we will see in this book, however, relational databases such as PostgreSQL are very rich in useful features.

## Multiple Tables

The next feature we will look at is our order problem, where our simple customer spreadsheet suddenly became very untidy once we tried to store order information against each customer. How do we store information about orders from customers, when we don't know in advance how many orders a customer might make?

As you can probably guess from the title of this section, the way to solve this problem with a relational database is to add a second table to store this additional information. Just like we designed our customer table, we start by deciding what information we want to store about each order.

For now we will assume that we want to store the name of the customer who placed the order, the date they placed the order, the date we shipped it and how much we charged for delivery. Just like our customer table, we will also add a unique reference number, so we know we have a unique reference for each order, rather than make any assumptions about what might be unique. To store details of the customer there is obviously no need to store all the customer details again. We already know that given a customer_id, we can find all the details of that customer from the customer table.

You might be wondering about the details of what was ordered, after all that is an important aspect of orders to most customers – they like to get what they ordered! For reasons that will become clear later, we will leave this aside for now. Those on the ball will probably be guessing that it's a similar problem to not knowing in advance how many orders a customer will place. We have no idea how many items will be on each order. The repeating groups problem is never far away. You are quite right, but one thing at a time!

Here is our order information table, with some sample data, again shown in the graphical tool, pgAccess, which as we have seen earlier just allows access to the data in a PostgreSQL database from a graphical interface. We will see more about graphical interfaces in Chapter 4:

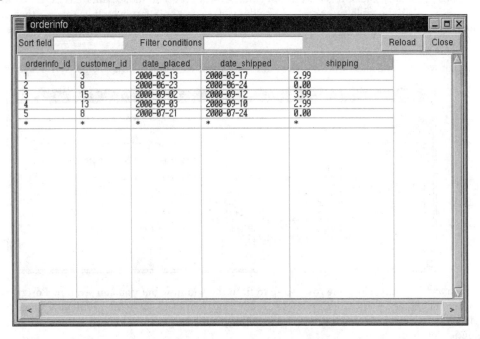

We haven't put too much data in the table, as it is easier to experiment on smaller amounts of data.

# Relations Between Tables

So now we have details of our customers, and at least summary details of their orders, stored in our database. In many ways, this is no different from using a pair of spreadsheets, one for our customer details and one for their order details. It's time to look at what we can do using these tables in combination. We do this by 'selecting' data from both tables at the same time. This is called a join, and after selection and projection from a single table, this is the third most common SQL data retrieval operation.

Suppose we want to list all the orders and the customers who placed them. In a procedural language, such as C, we would have to write code to scan one of the tables, perhaps starting with the `customer` table, then for each customer we look for and print out any orders they have placed. Not difficult, but certainly a bit time consuming and tedious to code. In SQL, I'm sure you will be pleased to know we find the answer much more easily, using a join operation. All we have to do is tell SQL three things:

❑   The columns we want

❑   The tables we want the data retrieved from

❑   How the two tables relate to each other

Don't worry too much about the SQL for now. The command we need is the example we saw in the previous chapter:

```
SELECT * FROM customers, orderinfo WHERE customer.customer_id =
orderinfo.customer_id;
```

As you can probably guess, this asks for all columns from our two tables, and tells SQL that the column `customer_id` in the table `customer` (note the *table.column* notation, which enables us to specify both a table name and a column from within that table) holds the same information as the `customer_id` in the `orderinfo` table.

Now that we have a database with some tables and data, we can see how PostgreSQL responds:

This is a touch untidy, since the rows wrap to fit in the window, but you can see how PostgreSQL has answered our query, without us having to specify exactly how to solve the problem. Of course we could replace the `'*'` with named columns to select only specified columns if we just wanted names and amounts, for example.

Let's leap ahead briefly, and see a much more complex query we could perform using SQL on these two tables. Suppose we wanted to see how frequently different customers had ordered from us. This requires a significantly more advanced bit of SQL, the actual command is:

```
SELECT customer.title, customer.fname, customer.lname,
count(orderinfo.orderinfo_id) AS "Number of orders" FROM customer, orderinfo WHERE
customer.customer_id = orderinfo.customer_id group by customer.title,
customer.fname, customer.lname;
```

That's a complex bit of SQL, but without going into the details, you can see that we have still not told SQL how to answer the question, just specified the question in a very precise way using SQL. We also managed it all in a single statement. For the record, this is how PostgreSQL responds:

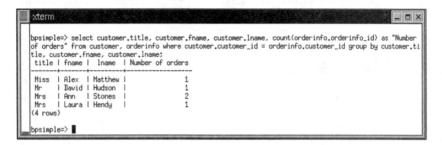

Now while a few database fanatics may quite like typing SQL directly in a window to a command line tool, we have to admit it's not everyone's preference. If users prefer a Windows GUI for example, that's not a problem; they can simply access the database via an ODBC driver, and build their queries graphically. Here is the same query being designed and executed in StarOffice on a Windows NT machine, just to show that StarOffice Base is an alternative to Microsoft Access (a Windows database tool):

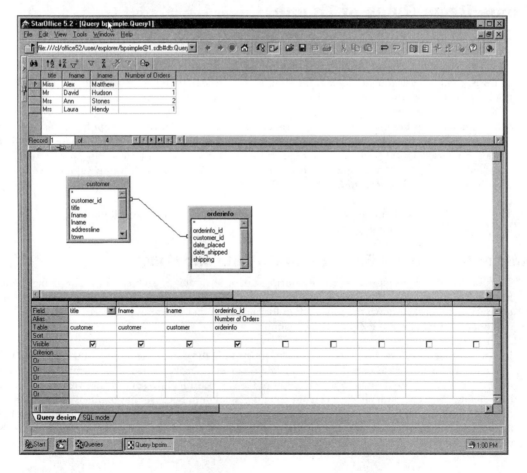

The data is still stored on a Linux machine, but the user hardly needs to be aware of the technical details. Generally, in this book, we will use the command line for teaching SQL, because that way you will learn the basics before moving on to more complex SQL commands, where the GUI tools are not always the most appropriate solution. Of course, you are welcome to use a GUI tool to type in your SQL, rather than a command line terminal; it's your choice.

# Designing Tables

So far we have only two tables in our database, and have not really talked about how we decide what goes in each table, except in the very informal way of doing what looked 'reasonable'. This design, which includes tables, columns, and relationships, is more correctly called a schema. Designing a database schema can be quite difficult to get right. We will cover the principal steps and rules in Chapter 12.

Designing a database with more than a couple of dozen tables is often a serious undertaking. Database designers earn their money by being good at such a difficult task.

# Some Basic Rules of Thumb

Fortunately, for reasonably simple databases, with up to perhaps ten tables, design is usually not that difficult, and with some practice you will usually go a long way towards a sensible design.

In this section, we are going to look at the simple example database we are starting to build, and figure out a way to decide what tables we need.

When a database is designed, it is often 'normalized', that is, a set of rules are applied to ensure that data is broken down in an appropriate fashion. In Chapter 12, we will come back to database design in a more formal way. To get started, all we require are some simple ground rules. We strongly suggest that you don't just read these rules and then dash off to design a database with twenty tables – work your way through the book at least until Chapter 12.

These rules are just to help you understand the initial database, which we will be using to explore SQL and PostgreSQL as the book progresses.

## Rule of Thumb One – Break Down the Data Into Columns

The first rule is only to put one piece of information, or attribute, in each column. This comes naturally to most people provided they consciously think about it. In our original spreadsheet, we had already quite naturally broken down the information for each customer down into different columns, so the name was separate from the Zip code for example.

In a spreadsheet, this rule just makes it simpler to work on the data, for example to sort by the Zip code. In a database however it is essential that the data is correctly broken down into attributes. Why is this so important in databases? From a practical point of view, it is difficult to specify that you want the data between the 29th and 35th characters from an address column, because that happens to be where the Zip code lives. If you have enough data, there is bound to be some data where the rule does not hold, and you get the wrong piece of data. Another reason for the data to be correctly broken down, is that in a database all columns must have the same type.

## *Rule of Thumb Two – Have a Unique Way of Identifying Each Row*

You will remember that when we tried to decide how to identify each row in our spreadsheet, we had a problem of not being sure as to what would be unique. We had no primary key. In general, it doesn't have to be a single column that is unique; it could be a pair of columns taken together, or even the combination of three columns that uniquely identifies a row.

In any case, there has to be a way of saying, with absolute certainty, if I look at X in this row, I know it will have a value, different from all other rows in this table. If you can't find a column, or at most a combination of three columns that uniquely identifies each row, it's probably time to add an extra column, just to fulfill that purpose. In our `customer` table, we added an extra column, `customer_id`, to fulfill the purpose of identifying each row.

## *Rule of Thumb Three – Remove Repeating Information*

Do you remember earlier, when we tried to store order information in the `customer` table, it looked rather untidy because of the repeating groups? For each customer, we repeated order information as many times as was required. This meant that we could never know how many columns were needed for orders. In a database, the number of columns in a table is effectively fixed by the design. So we must decide in advance how many columns we need, what type they are, and name each column before we can store any data. Never try and store repeating groups of data in a single row.

The way round this restriction is to do exactly what we did with our orders and customers data, we split the data into two tables, and used the column `customer_id` to join the two tables together when we needed data from both tables.

More formally, what we had was a many-to-one relationship; that is, there could be many orders received from a single customer.

## *Rule of Thumb Four – Get the Naming Right*

This is occasionally the hardest rule to get right. What do we call a table or column? If you can't decide what to call something, it's often a clue that all is not well in your table and column design.

In addition to the basic question, 'what should this be called?'; most database designers have their own personal 'rules of thumb' that they like to use to ensure the naming of tables and columns in a database is consistent. Don't have some table names singular and some plural, for example 'office' and 'departments'. Instead use 'office' and 'department'. If you decide on a naming rule for an id column, perhaps `tablename_id` then stick to that rule. If you use abbreviations, always use them consistently. If a column in one table is a key to another table (see Chapter 12), then try and give them the same base name.

The goal here is very simple – tables and columns should have short meaningful names, and the naming within the database should be very consistent. Achieving this apparently simple goal is often surprisingly challenging, but the rewards in simplified maintenance are considerable.

# Demonstration of Customer/Order Database

We can draw our database design, or schema, the way it is, using an entity relationship diagram. For our two-table database, such a diagram might look like this:

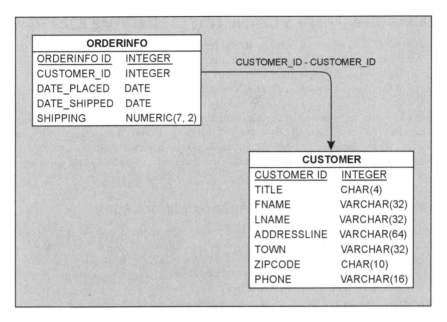

This shows our two tables, the column, data types, and sizes in each column, and also tells us that `customer_id` is the column that joins the two tables together. Notice that the arrow goes from the `orderinfo` table to the `customer` table. This is a hint that for each `orderinfo` entry, there is at most a single entry in the `customer` table, but that for each customer there may be many orders.

It's important that you remember which way round a one-to-many relationship is; getting it confused can cause a lot of problems. You should also notice that we have been very careful to name the column we want to use to join the two tables the same in each table – `customer_id`. This not essential, we could have called the two columns `foo` and `bar` if we had wanted to, but you will find consistent naming a great help.

On a complex database it can get very annoying when names are not quite consistent, for example `customer_id` and `customer_ident`, or `cust_id`, or `cust_no`. It's always worth investing time in getting the naming good and consistent, it will make life much easier in the longer run.

# Extending Beyond Two Tables

Now clearly, the information we have so far is lacking, in that we don't know what items were in each order. You may remember that we deliberately omitted the actual items from each order, promising to come back to that problem? It's time to sort out the actual items in each order.

The problem we have with the items in each order, is that we don't know in advance, how many items there will be in each order. It's almost exactly the same problem as not knowing in advance how many orders a customer might place. Each order might have one, two, three, or a hundred items in it. We have to separate the information that a customer placed an order, from the details of what was in that order. Basically what we might try and do is this:

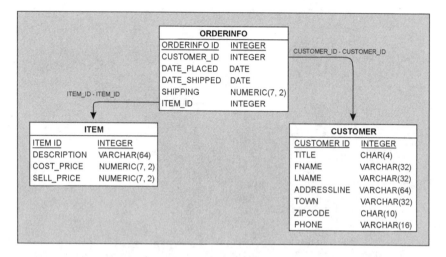

Much like the `customer` and `orderinfo` tables, we separate the information into two tables and then join them together.

We have however created a subtle problem here.

If you think carefully about the relationship between an order and an item that may be ordered, you will realize that not only could each `orderinfo` entry relate to many items, but each item could also appear in many orders, if different customers order the same item. If we try and draw this using an entity diagram, with just these two tables, what we have is:

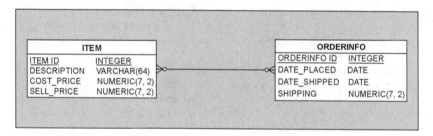

What we have here is actually a many-to-many relationship – each order can refer many items, and each item can appear in many orders. This breaks some of the underlying principals of relational database. We don't wish to go into the detail here, but suffice to say you must never have two tables in a relational database that may have a many-to-many relationship.

We could try and get round this by having a different entry in each row in the `item` table for each order, but then we would have to repeat the description and price information of the item many times. This would break our rule of thumb number three (Remove Repeating Information).

We consider these types of relationship further in Chapter 12, but for now you will be pleased to know that there is a standard solution to this difficulty. You create a third table between the two tables which implements a many-to-many relationship. This is actually easier to do than it is to explain, so let's just go ahead and create a table, 'orderline' to link the orders with the items:

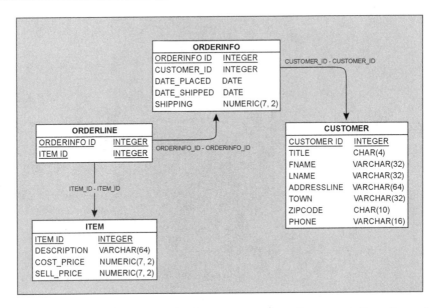

What we have done here is create a table that has rows corresponding to each line of an order. For any single line, we can determine the order it was from using the `orderinfo_id` column, and the item referenced using the `item_id` column.

A single item can appear in many order lines, and a single order can contain many orderliness. Each orderline refers to only a single item, however and can appear in only a single order.

You will also notice that on this occasion we have not had to add a unique id to identify each row. That is because the combination of `orderinfo_id` and `item_id` is always unique. There is one very subtle problem lurking, however. What happens if a customer orders two of an item in a single order?

We can't just enter another row in `orderline`, because we just said that the combination of `orderinfo_id` and `item_id` is always unique. Are we about to have to add yet another special table to cater for orders that contain more than one of any item? Fortunately not. There is a much simpler approach. We just need to add a quantity field to the orderline table, and all will be well.

## Completing the Initial Design

We have just two pieces of information we need to store before we have the main structure of the first cut of our database design in place. We want to store the barcode that goes with each product, and we also want to store the quantity we have in stock for each item.

It's possible that each product will have more than one barcode, because when manufacturers significantly change the packaging of a product, they often also change the barcode. For example, you have probably seen packs that offer '20% extra for free', where the price of (for example) a bottle of drink has not been changed, but there is a promotion pack which contains more liquid than the standard pack. Manufacturers will generally change the barcode, but essentially the product is unchanged. Therefore, we have a many barcodes-to-one item relationship. We add an additional table to hold the barcodes, like this:

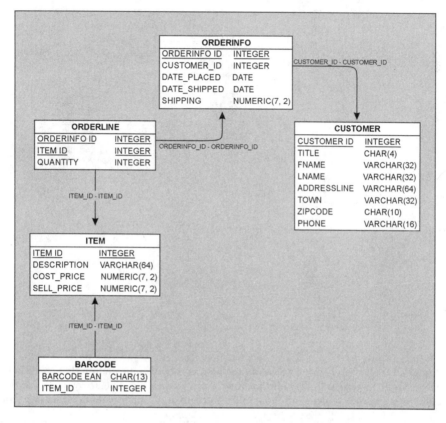

Notice that the arrow points from the BARCODE table to the ITEM table, because there may be many barcodes for each item. Notice that the barcode_ean is the primary key, since there must be a unique row for each barcode, and a single item could have several barcodes, but no barcode can ever belong to more than one item.

The last addition we need to make to our database design, is to hold the stock quantity for each item.

Now there are two ways we could do this. In a situation where most items are in stock, and the stock information is fairly basic, we would simple store a stock quantity directly in the item table.

There are circumstances where we might have a lot of items, however, but only a few are normally in stock, and the amount of information we need to hold for stocked items is quite large. For example, in a warehouse operation we may need to store location information, batch numbers, and expiry dates. If we had an item file with 500,000 items in it, but only held the top 1000 items in stock, this would be very wasteful. There is a standard way of resolving this problem, using what is called a **supplementary table**.

What you do is create a new table to store the 'supplementary' information, such as storage information, and then, create only the rows that are required, of items that are in stock, linking the information back to the main table. Actually, it's much easier than it sounds. Here is our final 'first cut' design of our database that we will be using as the book progresses:

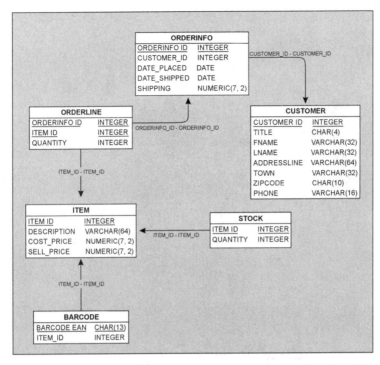

Notice the stock table uses `item_id` as a unique key, and holds information that relates directly to items, using `item_id` to join to the relevant row in the `item` table. The arrow points to the `item` table, because that is the master table, even though it is not a many-to-one relationship in this case.

As it stands, the design is clearly complex, since the additional information we are keeping is so small. We will leave the schema design the way it is to show how it is done, and later in the book we will be showing how to access data where there may be additional information in supplementary tables like this one. For those who like sneaking a look ahead, we will be using what's called an outer join.

You will also notice that some columns are underlined in the drawings – this indicates that the column, or combination of columns (as in the case of the `orderline` table), is guaranteed to be unique. They form the 'primary key' for the table.

# Basic Data Types

When we started talking about data types, we kept the discussion very general. From the schema, it's fairly clear the types we have used, which are not a complete set of PostgreSQL types, rather they are generic types that the design tool knows about, and can be translated into actual PostgreSQL types when you create the real tables.

One minor difficulty we have not tackled so far is generating our unique keys, the fields like `customer_id` and `item_id`. You will remember we said that each row in a table has to be uniquely identifiable, and where there is no clear set of columns that can be used, we add an extra column, a unique id column. Obviously, what we could do is make this an integer, or character field, and each time we add a new row into the database generate a new unique value for the column.

However since the need to add a special unique column is so common in databases, there is a built-in solution, a new type known as SERIAL. This special type is effectively an integer that automatically increments as rows are added to the table, assigning a new unique number as each row is added. When we add a new row to a table that has a serial column, we don't specify a value for the serial column at all, but allow the database to automatically assign the next number.

Most databases, when they assign serial values, don't take account of any rows that are deleted. The number assigned will just go on incrementing for each new row. The design tool we used to draw the above diagrams still shows such fields as INTEGER, because that's the underlying type.

To summarize the types we have used in this schema, we have:

| Data Type | Description |
|---|---|
| INTEGER | A whole number. |
| SERIAL | An integer, but automatically set to a unique number for each row that is added. This is not displayed in the images, but is the type we would use for the '_id' columns. |
| CHAR | A character array of fixed size, with the size shown in parentheses after the type. For these column types, PostgreSQL will always store exactly the specified number of characters. If we use a CHAR(256) to store just 1 character, there will still be (at least) 256 bytes held in the database, and returned when the data is retrieved. |
| VARCHAR | This is also a character array, but as its name suggests it is of variable length, and generally the space used in the database will be much the same as the actual size of the data stored. When you ask for a VARCHAR field to be returned, it returns just the number of characters you stored. The maximum length is given in the parentheses after the type. You might reasonably ask why we bother with CHAR types at all, why not just use the VARCHAR? The answer is efficiency. The database can handle fixed size records much more easily than it can handle variable sized records, so if we know that a title is at most four characters long, we may as well always store four characters, rather than ask the database to track the size each time, since the space we would save is insignificant, but the performance with the fixed length will usually be better. |
| DATE | This allows us to store year, month, and day information. There are of course other related types that allow us to store time information as well as data information. We will meet these later. |
| NUMERIC | This allows us to store numbers with a specified number of digits (the first number in the parentheses) and using a fixed number of decimal places (the second number in the parentheses). Hence, NUMERIC(7,2) would store exactly seven digits, two of them after the decimal place. |

Later in the book we will look at PostgreSQL's other data types, following which we may decide that some of them are more suitable for storing monetary values than NUMERIC, because although NUMERIC is handy, it is not the most efficient way of storing floating point numbers in PostgreSQL.

# NULLs

One topic that often confuses newcomers to databases, is the idea of NULL. In database terminology, NULL generally means a value is unknown, though it also has one or two additional and rather subtle variations on that meaning.

If you look at the orderinfo table you will see that we have both a date ordered and a date shipped column, both of type date. What do we do when an order has been received, but not yet shipped? What should we store in the date shipped column? We could store a special date, a **sentinel value**, that lets us know that we have not yet shipped the order. On UNIX systems we might well use Jan 1, 1970, which is traditionally the date UNIX systems count from. that date is well before the date we designed this system therefore, we will always know that this special date means 'not yet shipped'.

This is however, clearly not ideal. Having special values scattered in our tables shows poor design, and is rather error prone. For example, if a new programmer starts on the project and doesn't realize there is a special date, they might try calculating the average time between order and shipping date, and come up with some very strange answers indeed, if there are a few shipped dates set before the order was placed.

Fortunately, all relational database systems have a very special value called NULL, which usually means 'unknown at this time'. Notice that it doesn't mean zero, or empty string, or anything that can be represented in the type of the field. Unknown is very different from zero or a blank string.

It's very important to take care of NULLs, because they can pop out at odd times and cause you surprises, usually unpleasant ones. So in our orderinfo table we could set date shipped to NULL before an order is shipped, where the meaning 'unknown at this time' is exactly what we require.

There is another subtly different use for NULL (not so common), which is to mean 'not relevant' for this row. Suppose you were doing a survey of people, and one of the questions was about the color of spectacles. For people who don't wear spectacles, this is clearly a nonsensical question. This is a case however, where we might use NULL in the column to record that the information is not relevant for this particular row.

## Testing for NULLs

One feature of the NULL value is that if you compare two NULLs the answer is always that they are different. This sometimes catches people out, but if you think about the meaning of NULL as 'unknown', it's perfectly logical that testing for equality on two unknowns gives the answer 'not equal'.

SQL has a special way of checking for NULL values, by asking 'IS NULL', which allows us to find and test NULL values should we need to.

NULL values do behave in a slightly odd way, therefore it is possible to specify when we design a table that some columns cannot hold NULL values. It is normally a good idea to specify the columns as 'NOT NULL' where you are sure the NULL value should never be accepted, for example primary key columns. Some database designers advocate an almost complete ban on NULL values, but they do have their uses. So we normally advocate allowing NULL values on selected columns, where there is a genuine possibility that 'unknown' values are required.

# The Sample Database

In this chapter, we have been designing, in a rather ad-hoc manner, a simple database to look after customers, orders and items, such as might be used in a small shop. As the book progresses, we will be using this database to demonstrate SQL and other PostgreSQL features. We will also be discovering the limitations of our existing design, and looking at how it can be improved in some areas.

The simplified database we are using has many elements of what a real retail database might look like, however it also has many simplifications. For example, an item might have a full description, a description that appears on the till when it is sold, and yet another description that appears on shelf edge labels.

The address information we are storing for customers is very simplified. We can't cope with long addresses, where there is a village name or a state, nor can we cope with overseas orders. It is often more feasible to start with a reasonably solid base and expand, however, rather than try and cater for every possible requirement in your initial design. This database is adequate for our initial needs.

In the next chapter, we will be looking at installing PostgreSQL, creating the tables for our sample database, and populating them with some sample data.

# Summary

In this chapter, we looked at how a database table is much like a single spreadsheet, with four important differences:

- ❑ All items in a column must have the same type
- ❑ The number of columns must be the same for all rows in a table
- ❑ It must be possible to uniquely identify each row
- ❑ There is no implied row order in a database table, as there would be in a spreadsheet

We have seen how we can extend our database to multiple tables, which lets us manage many-to-one relationships in a simple way. We gave some informal rules of thumb to help you understand how a database design needs to be structured, though we will come back to this in a much more rigorous fashion in later chapters.

We have also seen how to work around many-to-many relationships that turn up in the real world, by breaking them down into a pair of one-to-many relationships by adding an extra table.

Finally, we worked on extending our initial database design so we have a demonstration database design, or schema, to work with as the book progresses.

In the next chapter, we'll see how to get the PostgreSQL up and running on various platforms.

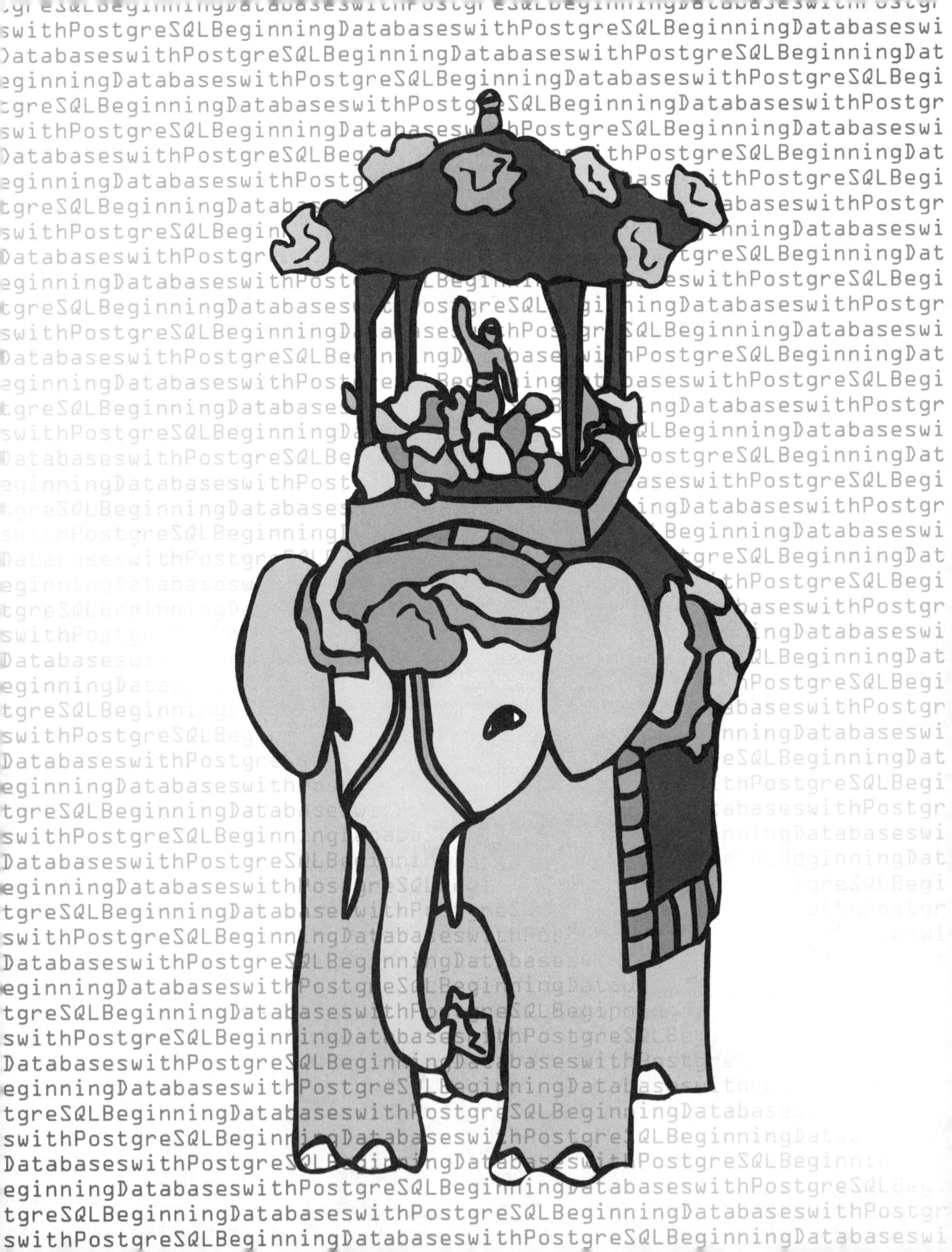
BeginningDatabaseswithPostgreSQL

# Getting Started with PostgreSQL

In this chapter, we will walk the steps of installing PostgreSQL on various operating systems. If you are running a Linux system installed from a recent distribution you may already have PostgreSQL installed or available to you on the installation disks. If you are running a UNIX system, then we'll see how to compile the source code for the UNIX platform.

We'll also see how to install PostgreSQL on Windows platforms, for which we'll have to install some additional software to create a UNIX-like environment, before we can actually install PostgreSQL.

Along the way we'll actually work through the following:

- ❑ Install or upgrade?
- ❑ Installing PostgreSQL from the Linux binaries
- ❑ Anatomy of a PostgreSQL installation
- ❑ Installing PostgreSQL from the source code and starting PostgreSQL
- ❑ Creating databases
- ❑ Creating tables and populating the tables
- ❑ Stopping PostgreSQL
- ❑ Installing PostgreSQL on Windows
- ❑ Cygwin – a UNIX environment on Windows
- ❑ IPC services for Windows
- ❑ Compiling and configuring PostgreSQL on Windows
- ❑ Starting PostgreSQL automatically on Windows

Work on a Solaris release of PostgreSQL is currently in progress. The working release is quite some time away and needs a lot of debugging. As such, the installation of PostgreSQL on Solaris has not been covered in this book. PostgreSQL enthusiasts who wish to work on Solaris can find out more from http://www.greatbridge.org, and can even contribute to the effort.

# Install or Upgrade?

This is the one question that the Linux fans, new to the PostgreSQL, would want answered. As such, there is no single answer to this. The latest release, at the time of writing, is PostgreSQL-7.1.2. To download the latest release visit http://www.postgresql.org, and the ftp mirror sites listed on the site.

If you have a very recent Linux distribution, then in all probability you should have the latest PostgreSQL release bundled along with it. If you already have installed an older Linux distribution that has the 7.1.x release, then you could upgrade to the latest release by downloading the appropriate packages from any of the PostgreSQL ftp sites. We assume here that the reader is new to PostgreSQL and hence suggest a new installation than an upgrade, however, as the process of upgrading is more tedious than a new installation.

The ardent Linux user who has done it before, and who feels better off with an upgrade, could check out the PostgreSQL home site for information on upgrading to the current release.

In the following sections, we describe the installation of PostgreSQL on UNIX-like platforms. That is, we discuss the installation for Linux platforms and on Microsoft Windows. The installation procedure on various Linux distributions or flavors is very similar.

Notably, there are two ways of installing PostgreSQL:

❑   Installing the PostgreSQL using the Linux binaries

❑   Installing the PostgreSQL from the source code

We'll begin the process by learning to install PostgreSQL from the Linux binaries.

# Installing PostgreSQL from the Linux Binaries

Probably the easiest way of installing on Linux, is by using pre-compiled binary packages. The binaries for PostgreSQL are available for download as RPM (RedHat Package Manager) packages for various Linux distributions. As at the time of writing this book, RPM packages had been made available for:

❑   RedHat 6.x and 7.x

❑   SuSe 6.4 and 7.x

❑   TurboLinux 6.x

❑   Caldera OpenLinux eServer 2.3

❑   Mandrake 7.x

❑   LinuxPPC 2000

For a fully functional installation, you need to download and install at least the base and server packages from the packages listed in the table opposite:

| Package | Description |
|---------|-------------|
| postgresql | The base package |
| postgresql-server | Programs to create and run a server |
| postgresql-devel | Header files and libraries for development |
| postgresql-jdbc | Java database connectivity for PostgreSQL |
| postgresql-odbc | Open database connectivity for PostgreSQL |
| postgresql-perl | PostgreSQL interface from Perl |
| postgresql-python | PostgreSQL interface from Python |
| postgresql-tcl | PostgreSQL interface from Tcl |
| postgresql-test | PostgreSQL test suite |
| postgresql-tk | Tk shell and Tk-based GUI for PostgreSQL |

The exact file names will have version numbers appended with the package. It is advisable to install a matching set of packages, all with the same revision level. In a package with the version number 7.1.x, x determines the revision level.

To install the packages, we use the RPM Package Manager application. Make sure that you have logged on as the superuser (root) to perform the installation. You could use the graphical package manager of your choice, such as GnoRPM or Kpackage to install the RPMs. Alternatively, you could place all the RPM files in a single directory and as superuser (root) execute:

```
$ rpm -i *.rpm
```

This will unpack the packages and install all the files they contain into their correct places for your distribution.

You could also install from the PostgreSQL package that is bundled along with your Linux distribution, such as RedHat or SuSE. For example, on SuSe 7.x you can install a version of PostgreSQL by running the YaST installation tool and selecting the packages listed in the table above:

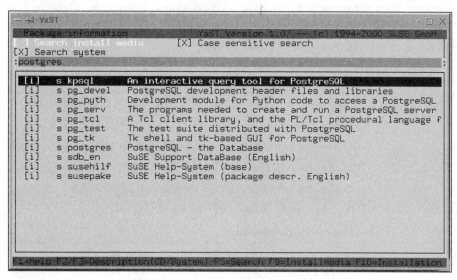

Alternatively, you can download or order on CD, a commercially developed (but the software is still free) version of PostgreSQL that includes an installer and additional documentation as well. One such commercially developed PostgreSQL is available from Great Bridge at http://www.greatbridge.com.

PostgreSQL is under continuous development and, hence, it is likely that new versions will become available from time to time. Installing from RPM packages 'by hand' has the distinct advantage that you can upgrade to the recent version, currently available, by repeating the procedure. To do that, just let the RPM know that you are performing an upgrade rather than a first time install by specifying the −u option instead of the −i option:

```
$ rpm −u *.rpm
```

> **It is strongly advisable to backup your existing data in the database before performing an upgrade. The details of performing an upgrade to the latest release would be available at the PostgreSQL home site.**

The backup and recovery of your existing database is discussed in detail in Chapter 11.

## Anatomy of a PostgreSQL Installation

Unfortunately, at the time of writing this book, there is no established standard for PostgreSQL installations. This could in some ways prove to be a blessing and in some other ways a slight drawback.

A PostgreSQL installation consists of a number of applications, utilities, and data directories. The main PostgreSQL application (postmaster or postgres) contains the server code that services the requests to access data from clients. Utilities, such as pg_ctl, are used to control a master server process that needs to be running all the time the server is active. A data directory is used by PostgreSQL to store all of the files needed for a database. This is used not only for storing the tables and records, but also system parameters.

A typical installation would have all of the components of a PostgreSQL installation, shown in the table below, arranged in sub-directories of one PostgreSQL directory. One common location (and the default when you install from source code) is /usr/local/pgsql.

Sub-directories of the main PostgreSQL directory are:

| Directory | Description |
| --- | --- |
| Bin | Applications and utilities such as pg_ctl and postmaster |
| data | The database itself |
| Doc | Documentation in HTML format |
| include | Header files for use in developing PostgreSQL applications |
| Lib | Libraries for use in developing PostgreSQL applications |
| Man | Manual pages for PostgreSQL tools |
| share | Sample configuration files |

There is a drawback with the one directory approach; both fixed program files and variable data are stored in the same place, which is often not ideal.

The files that PostgreSQL uses fall into different categories. The applications are essentially fixed and they are not modified while PostgreSQL is running. The log file that the database server produces will contain useful information about database accesses and, can be a big help when troubleshooting problems. It effectively just grows as log entries are added. The data files are the heart of the system, storing all of the information of all of our databases.

For reasons of efficiency and administration we might wish to store the different categories of file in a different place. PostgreSQL gives us the flexibility to store the applications, logs, and data in different places, and Linux distributions have made use of this flexibility to good effect.

For example, in SuSE 7.0 the PostgreSQL applications are stored with other applications in `/usr/bin`. The log file is `/var/log/postgresql`. The data is stored in `/var/lib/pgsql/data`. This means that it is easy to arrange backups of the critical data separately from the not-so-critical log files, and so forth.

Other distributions will have their own scheme for file locations. You can use the RPM tool to list the files that have been installed by a particular package. To do this, use the query option, like this:

```
$ rpm -q -l postgres
/usr/bin/createdb
...
/usr/share/man/manl/vacuum.1.gz
$
```

To see where all the files have been installed, you will need to run `rpm` for all of the packages that make up the complete PostgreSQL set:

```
$ rpm -q -l pg_serv
/sbin/conf.d/SuSEconfig.Postgres
...
/var/lib/pgsql/data/pg_options
$
```

Different distributions may also call the packages by slightly different names, here SuSE uses the package name `pg_serv` for the server package. Alternatively, you can use one of the graphical package manager tools, such as `kpackage` that comes with the KDE desktop environment:

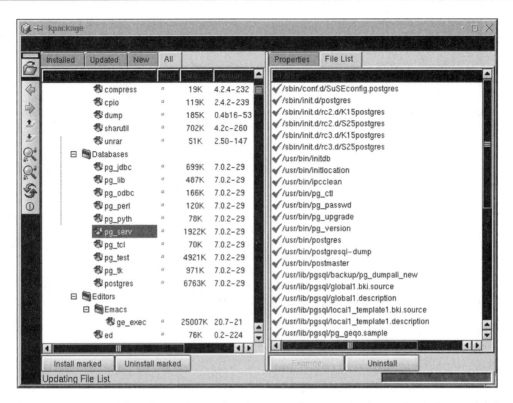

The disadvantage of installing from a Linux distribution is that it is not always clear where everything lives. So if you wish to upgrade to the most recent release, it can be tricky to ensure that you have untangled the original installation.

Sometimes it is better to install PostgreSQL from the source code. If you have no intention of installing from source, you may skip the next section and pick up again with *Starting PostgreSQL* below.

# Installing PostgreSQL From the Source Code

Though RPM packages could be used to install PostgreSQL on all Linux distributions or flavors, you can build and install PostgreSQL from the source on just about any UNIX compatible system.

The source code for PostgreSQL is available at http://www.postgresql.org. Here you will find code for the latest release and often the source code for beta test releases of the next release. Unless you like to live on the edge, it is probably a good idea to stick to the most recent stable release. Some previous releases of PostgreSQL were also available on CD. Check the site for information on current releases and their availability on CDs that could be ordered.

The source code is made available in two forms. The entire PostgreSQL source code can be found in a single 'gzipped-tarball' a file that will have a name similar to:

```
postgresql-7.1.2.tar.gz
```

At the time of writing, the PostgreSQL tarball was around 7.5Mb in size. To ease download, the source is also available in a set of smaller files. These are:

```
postgresql-7.1.2.base.tar.gz
postgresql-7.1.2.docs.tar.gz
postgresql-7.1.2.opt.tar.gz
postgresql-7.1.2.test.tar.gz
```

Again, the exact file names will change with the current version revision number at the time.

Compiling PostgreSQL in fact is a very simple affair. If you are familiar with compiling Open Source products, there will be no surprises for you here. Even if this is your first attempt in compiling and installing an Open Source product, you should have no difficulty. To perform the source code compilation, you will need a Linux or UNIX system with a complete development environment installed. This includes a C compiler, and the GNU version of the make utility that is needed to build the database system.

Linux distributions generally ship with a suitable development environment containing the GNU tools from the Free Software Foundation. These include the excellent GNU C compiler (gcc), which is the standard compiler for Linux. The GNU tools are available for most other UNIX platforms too, and we recommend them for compiling PostgreSQL. You can download the latest tools from http://www.gnu.org. Once you have a development environment installed, the compilation of PostgreSQL is straightforward.

Copy your source code 'tarball' to an appropriate directory for compiling. This does not have to be, and in fact ought not be, the final resting place of your PostgreSQL installation. One possible choice is a subdirectory in your home directory, since we do not need superuser permissions to compile PostgreSQL, only to install it once built. Unpack the 'tarball' to extract the source code:

```
$ tar zxvf postgres-7.1.2.tar.gz
```

We generally prefer to unpack source code into a directory specifically created for maintaining source code products, /usr/src, but you can unpack anywhere you have sufficient disk space for the compilation. You need to allow around 50Mb or so.

The extraction process will have made a new directory, related to the version of PostgreSQL you are building. Move into that directory:

```
$ cd postgres-7.1.2
```

You should find a file, INSTALL, in this directory that contains detailed manual build instructions, in the unlikely event that the automated method outlined here fails for some reason.

The build process makes use of a configuration script, configure, to tailor the build parameters to your specific environment. To accept all defaults you can simply run configure without arguments:

```
$ ./configure
creating cache ./config.cache
checking host system type... i686-pc-linux-gnu
checking which template to use... linux
...
$
```

The `configure` script sets variables that control the way the PostgreSQL software is built, taking into account the type of platform you are compiling on, the features of your C compiler, and so on. The aspect of setting the variables in the `configure` script is beyond the scope of this book. Nevertheless, if you need to set the variables before configuring, run the man pages for `configure`.

The `configure` script will automatically set locations for the installation. The default locations are for PostgreSQL to be compiled to use `/usr/local/pgsql` as the main directory for its operation, with subdirectories for applications and data.

You can use arguments to configure to change the default location settings. The options most often used are:

| Option | Description |
|---|---|
| `--prefix=PREFIX` | Install in directories under `PREFIX`. For PostgreSQL this defaults to `/usr/local/psql` |
| `--bindir=DIR` | Install programs in `DIR`. Defaults to `PREFIX/bin` |
| `--with-tcl` | Compile support for Tcl applications like pgAccess |
| `--with-perl` | Compile support for Perl applications |
| `--with-python` | Compile Python support module |

For a full list of options to configure, you can use the `--help` argument to get a list:

```
$ ./configure --help

Usage: configure [options] [host]
Options: [defaults in brackets after descriptions]
Configuration:
  --cache-file=FILE        cache test results in FILE
...
$
```

We do not have to settle on final locations for the database files and the log file at this stage. We can always specify these locations to the server process, when we start it after installation.

Once the compilation is configured, you can build the software using `make`.

> **The PostgreSQL build process uses a sophisticated set of Makefiles to control the compilation process. Due to this, it is recommended that a version of GNU make is used for the build. This is the default on Linux. On other UNIX platforms, you may need to install GNU make separately. Often this will be given the name gmake to distinguish it from the version of make supplied with the operating system. In the instructions below make refers to GNU make.**

Compile the software:

```
$ make
...
All of PostgreSQL successfully made. Ready to install.
```

If all goes well, you should see a large number of compilations proceeding. You will be finally rewarded with the message that everything has been made successfully.

When `make` has finished you need to copy the programs to their final resting places. We use `make` to do this for us too, but we need to be the `superuser` first:

```
$ su
# make install
...
Thank you for choosing PostgreSQL, the most advanced open source database engine.
# exit
$
```

That's just about all there is to it. We have now got a set of programs that make up the PostgreSQL database server in the right place on our system.

We are in the same situation that we would have been in, had we installed from packages. Now it's time to turn our attention to setting up PostgreSQL to run.

## Starting PostgreSQL

The main database process for PostgreSQL, `postmaster`, is quite a special program. It is responsible for dealing with all data access, from all users, to all databases. It must allow users to access their data, and not allow access to others' data, unless authorized. To do this, it needs to own all of the data files, no normal user can access any of the files directly, and control access by checking permissions granted to the users that request access.

PostgreSQL uses the concept of a pseudo user to manage data access. A user, called `postgres`, is created for the sole purpose of owning the data files. Nobody can log in as the `postgres` user and gain illicit access. This user identity is used by the `postmaster` program to access the database files on behalf of others.

The first step in establishing a working PostgreSQL system is, therefore, to create this `postgres` user.

The precise procedure for making new users differs from system to system. Linux users can (as `root`) simply use `useradd`:

```
# useradd postgres
```

Other UNIX systems may require you to create a home directory, edit the configuration files, or run the appropriate administration tool on your Linux distribution. Refer to your operating system documentation for details about such administration tools.

Now we need to create and initialize database and start the `postmaster` process running.

We will initialize the PostgreSQL database using the `initdb` utility in a moment, specifying where in our file system we want the database files to reside. First, we must create, (as `root`), the directory we are going to use and make it owned by `postgres`:

```
# mkdir /usr/local/pgsql/data
# chown postgres /usr/local/pgsql/data
```

Here we are using the default location for the database. You might choose to store the data separately as we discussed earlier.

To initialize the database we need to assume the identity of the `postgres` user and run the appropriate PostgreSQL program as follows.

Login as `postgres` to change your identity. We need to be `superuser` (`root`), and then become `postgres`:

```
$ su
# su - postgres
pg$
```

Now the programs we run will assume the rights of the `postgres` user and will be able to access the PostgreSQL database files. For clarity, we have shown the shell prompt for commands executed as the `postgres` user as pg$.

> **Do not be tempted to shortcut the process of using the `postgres` user and run these programs as `root`. For security reasons running server processes as `root` can be dangerous. If there was a problem with the process it could result in an outsider gaining access to your system via the network. For this reason `postmaster` will refuse to run as `root`.**

Initialize the database with `initdb`:

```
pg$ /usr/local/pgsql/bin/initdb -D /usr/local/pgsql/data
This database system will be initialized with the user name "Postgres".
This user will own all the data files and must also own the server process.
...
Success.
pg$
```

If all goes well we will have a brand new, completely empty database in the location we specified with the -D option to `initdb`.

Now we start the server process itself. Again we use a -D option to tell `postmaster` where the database files are located. If we want to allow users on a network to access our data we must also specify the -i option to enable remote clients:

```
pg$ /usr/local/pgsql/bin/postmaster -i -D /usr/local/pgsql/data >logfile
2>&1 &
```

By default PostgreSQL will not allow general remote access. To grant permission to connect, you must edit a configuration file, pg_hba.conf. This file lives in the database file area (/usr/local/pgsql/data in our example), and contains entries that grant or reject permission for remote users to connect to the database. Its format is fairly simple, and the default file shipped with PostgreSQL contains many helpful comments for adding entries. You can grant permission for individual users, hosts or groups of computers, and for individual databases if you need to.

Here we will add an entry to allow any computer on the local network to connect to any database without authentication. If you require a different access policy, refer to the comments in the configuration file.

We add a line to the end of pg_hba.conf that looks like this:

```
host all   192.168.0.0 255.255.0.0      trust
```

This means that all computers with an IP address that begins 192.168 can access all databases.

Also, we have redirected the process output to a file (called logfile in the Postgres user's home directory), and merged standard output with standard error by using the shell construction 2>&1. You can of course choose a different location for your log file by redirecting output to another file.

Now we can check that the database is functioning by trying to connect to it. The psql utility is used to interact with the database system and perform simple administration tasks such as creating users, creating databases, and creating tables. We will use it to create and populate the sample database later in the chapter. For now, we can simply try to connect to a database. The response we get will show that we have postmaster successfully running:

```
pg$ /usr/local/pgsql/bin/psql
psql: FATAL 1: Database "postgres" does not exist in the system catalog.
```

Don't be taken aback by the fatal error it displays. By default, psql connects to the database on the local machine and tries to open a database with the same name as the user running the program. We have not created a database called postgres, so the attempt fails. It does indicate however, that postmaster is running and able to respond with details of the failure.

To specify a particular database to connect to we must specify the -d option to psql. A new PostgreSQL system does contain some databases that is used by the system as the base for new databases we might create. One such database is called template1. If we need to, we can connect to this database for administration purposes.

To check network connectivity, we can connect from another PostgreSQL installation on another machine on the network. We specify the host (either name or IP address) with a -h option, and one of the system databases (as we haven't yet created a real database):

```
remote$ psql -h 192.168.0.66 -d template1
Welcome to psql, the PostgreSQL interactive terminal.

Type: \copyright for distribution terms
          \h for help with SQL commands
          \? For help on internal slash commands
          \g or terminate with semicolon to execute query
          \q to quit
```

```
template1=# \q

remote$
```

The final step we need to take is, to arrange for the postmaster server process to be started automatically every time the machine is rebooted.

Essentially, all we have to do is make sure that postmaster is run at startup. Again, there is little standardization between Linux and UNIX variants as to how this should be done. Refer to your installations documentation for specific details.

If you have installed PostgreSQL from a Linux distribution, it is likely that the startup is already configured by the RPM packages you installed. On SuSE Linux, PostgreSQL is automatically started when the system enters multi-user mode, by a script in /etc/rc.d/init.d called postgres.

If you are creating a startup script yourself, the easiest thing to do is make a simple shell script that starts postmaster with the parameters you need, and add a call to your script from one of the scripts that is run automatically at startup, such as those in /etc/rc.d. Be sure that postmaster gets run as the user postgres.

Here is an example script that does the job for a default PostgreSQL installation built from source code:

```
#!/bin/sh

# Script to start and stop PostgreSQL

SERVER=/usr/local/pgsql/bin/postmaster
PGCTL=/usr/local/pgsql/bin/pg_ctl
PGDATA=/usr/local/pgsql/data
OPTIONS=-i
LOGFILE=/usr/local/pgsql/data/postmaster.log

case "$1" in
    start)
            echo -n "Starting PostgreSQL..."
            su -l postgres -c "nohup $SERVER $OPTIONS -D $PGDATA >$LOGFILE 2>&1 &"
            ;;
    stop)
            echo -n "Stopping PostgreSQL..."
            su -l postgres -c "$PGCTL -D $PGDATA stop"
            ;;
    *)
            echo "Usage: $0 {start|stop}"
            exit 1
            ;;
esac
exit 0
```

> **On Debian Linux you may need to use su – in place of su –l.**

Create an executable script file with this script in it, call it say `MyPostgreSQL`. Use the `chmod` command to make it executable:

```
# chmod a+rx MyPostgreSQL
```

Then you need to arrange that it is called to start and stop PostgreSQL when the server boots and shuts down:

```
MyPostgreSQL start
MyPostgreSQL stop
```

For systems (such as many Linux distributions) that use System V type `init` scripting, you can place the script in the appropriate place. For SuSE Linux, for example, we would place the script in `/etc/rc.d/init.d/MyPostgreSQL`, and make symbolic links to it from the following places to automatically start and stop PostgreSQL as the server enters and leaves a multi-user mode:

```
/etc/rc.d/rc2.d/S25MyPostgreSQL
/etc/rc.d/rc2.d/K25MyPostgreSQL
/etc/rc.d/rc3.d/S25MyPostgreSQL
/etc/rc.d/rc3.d/K25MyPostgreSQL
```

Refer to your systems' documentation on startup scripts for more specific details.

Now it's time to create a database.

## Creating the Database

We will be coming back to database administration in more detail later in the book, but for now here is a very brief 'jump start' now that we have PostgreSQL up and running. We are going to create a simple database, which we will call `bpsimple` to support for order database examples. This database is used throughout this book in examples demonstrating PostgreSQL.

Before we start, one simple way to check if PostgreSQL is running on your system is to look for the `postmaster` process:

```
$ ps -el | grep post
```

If there is a process running called `postmaster` (the name might get abbreviated in the display), then you are running a PostgreSQL server.

Each user of a PostgreSQL database system can create databases of their own, and control access to the data it holds. Before we can do this, we have to tell PostgreSQL about the valid users by creating records for them within the system. To do this we use PostgreSQL's `createuser` utility as follows:

Use `su` (from `root`) to become the PostgreSQL user, `postgres`. Then run `createuser` to register the user. The user login name given is recorded as a valid PostgreSQL user. Let's give user rights to the (existing UNIX/Linux) user `neil`:

```
$ su
# su - postgres
pg$ /usr/local/pgsql/bin/createuser neil
Shall the new user be able to create databases? (y/n) y
Shall the new user be able to create new users (y/n) n
CREATE USER
pg$
```

Here we have allowed `neil` to create new databases, but he is not allowed to create new users.

Once you have created yourself as a PostgreSQL user with these rights, you will be able to create a database. Change back to your own (non-`root`) login and run:

```
$ /usr/local/pgsql/bin/createdb bpsimple
CREATE DATABASE
$
```

You should now be able to connect (locally) to the server, using the interactive terminal `psql`:

```
$ /usr/local/pgsql/bin/psql -d bpsimple
Welcome to psql, the PostgreSQL interactive terminal.
...
bpsimple=#
```

You are now logged into PostgreSQL, ready to execute some commands. To exit back to the shell, the command is `\q`.

## Creating the Tables

You can create the tables in your `bpsimple` database by typing in the SQL commands below at the `psql` command prompt, but it's probably much easier to download the code bundle from the Wrox web site, unpack it, and then execute the commands using `\i <filename>`, which executes commands read from a file. The commands are just plain text, so you can always edit them with your preferred text editor if you want:

```
bpsimple=# \i create_tables.sql
CREATE TABLE
...
bpsimple=#
```

It is a very good practice to script all database schema (tables, indexes, procedures) statements. That way, if the database needs to be recreated, then it can be done from the scripts. Scripts should also be used whenever the schema needs to be updated.

Here is the SQL for creating our tables, which you will find in `create_tables.sql` in the code bundle:

```
create table customer
(
    customer_id            serial                          ,
    title                  char(4)                        ,
    fname                  varchar(32)                    ,
```

```
    lname                    varchar(32)             not null,
    addressline              varchar(64)                     ,
    town                     varchar(32)                     ,
    zipcode                  char(10)                not null,
    phone                    varchar(16)                     ,
    CONSTRAINT               customer_pk PRIMARY KEY(customer_id)
);


create table item
(
    item_id                  serial                          ,
    description              varchar(64)             not null,
    cost_price               numeric(7,2)                    ,
    sell_price               numeric(7,2)                    ,
    CONSTRAINT               item_pk PRIMARY KEY(item_id)
);


create table orderinfo
(
    orderinfo_id             serial                          ,
    customer_id              integer                 not null,
    date_placed              date                    not null,
    date_shipped             date                            ,
    shipping                 numeric(7,2)                    ,
    CONSTRAINT               orderinfo_pk PRIMARY KEY(orderinfo_id)
);


create table stock
(
    item_id                  integer                 not null,
    quantity                 integer                 not null,
    CONSTRAINT               stock_pk PRIMARY KEY(item_id)
);


create table orderline
(
    orderinfo_id             integer                 not null,
    item_id                  integer                 not null,
    quantity                 integer                 not null,
    CONSTRAINT               orderline_pk PRIMARY KEY(orderinfo_id,
item_id)
);


create table barcode
(
    barcode_ean              char(13)                not null,
    item_id                  integer                 not null,
    CONSTRAINT               barcode_pk PRIMARY KEY(barcode_ean)
);
```

## Removing the Tables

If at some later date you wish to delete all the tables (also known as dropping the tables), and start again, you can. The command set is in `drop_tables.sql`, and looks like this:

```
drop table barcode;

drop table orderline;

drop table stock;

drop table orderinfo;

drop table item;

drop table customer;

drop sequence customer_customer_id_seq;

drop sequence item_item_id_seq;

drop sequence orderinfo_orderinfo_id_seq;
```

> **Be warned, if you drop the tables, you also lose any data in them!**

If you run this script after creating the tables, then run the `create_tables.sql` again before attempting to populate the tables with data.

## Populating the Tables

Last, but not least, we need to add some data to the tables or populate the tables.

These samples are all in the code bundle, as `pop_tablename.sql`. You can of course, use your own data, except your results will be different from the ones presented in the book. So until you are confident, it's probably best to stick with our sample data.

The line wraps are simply a necessity of the printing, you can type each command on a single line. You do need to note the terminating semi-colon however, this tells `psql` where each SQL command ends.

### Customer Table

```
insert into customer(title, fname, lname, addressline, town, zipcode, phone)
values('Miss','Jenny','Stones','27 Rowan Avenue','Hightown','NT2 1AQ','023 9876');
insert into customer(title, fname, lname, addressline, town, zipcode, phone)
values('Mr','Andrew','Stones','52 The Willows','Lowtown','LT5 7RA','876 3527');
insert into customer(title, fname, lname, addressline, town, zipcode, phone)
values('Miss','Alex','Matthew','4 The Street','Nicetown','NT2 2TX','010 4567');
insert into customer(title, fname, lname, addressline, town, zipcode, phone)
values('Mr','Adrian','Matthew','The Barn','Yuleville','YV67 2WR','487 3871');
insert into customer(title, fname, lname, addressline, town, zipcode, phone)
values('Mr','Simon','Cozens','7 Shady Lane','Oahenham','OA3 6QW','514 5926');
```

```
insert into customer(title, fname, lname, addressline, town, zipcode, phone)
values('Mr','Neil','Matthew','5 Pasture Lane','Nicetown','NT3 7RT','267 1232');
insert into customer(title, fname, lname, addressline, town, zipcode, phone)
values('Mr','Richard','Stones','34 Holly Way','Bingham','BG4 2WE','342 5982');
insert into customer(title, fname, lname, addressline, town, zipcode, phone)
values('Mrs','Ann','Stones','34 Holly Way','Bingham','BG4 2WE','342 5982');
insert into customer(title, fname, lname, addressline, town, zipcode, phone)
values('Mrs','Christine','Hickman','36 Queen Street','Histon','HT3 5EM','342
5432');
insert into customer(title, fname, lname, addressline, town, zipcode, phone)
values('Mr','Mike','Howard','86 Dysart Street','Tibsville','TB3 7FG','505 5482');
insert into customer(title, fname, lname, addressline, town, zipcode, phone)
values('Mr','Dave','Jones','54 Vale Rise','Bingham','BG3 8GD','342 8264');
insert into customer(title, fname, lname, addressline, town, zipcode, phone)
values('Mr','Richard','Neill','42 Thached way','Winersby','WB3 6GQ','505 6482');
insert into customer(title, fname, lname, addressline, town, zipcode, phone)
values('Mrs','Laura','Hendy','73 Margeritta Way','Oxbridge','OX2 3HX','821 2335');
insert into customer(title, fname, lname, addressline, town, zipcode, phone)
values('Mr','Bill','O\'Neill','2 Beamer Street','Welltown','WT3 8GM','435 1234');
insert into customer(title, fname, lname, addressline, town, zipcode, phone)
values('Mr','David','Hudson','4 The Square','Milltown','MT2 6RT','961 4526');
```

### Item Table

```
insert into item(description, cost_price, sell_price) values('Wood Puzzle', 15.23,
21.95);
insert into item(description, cost_price, sell_price) values('Rubic Cube', 7.45,
11.49);
insert into item(description, cost_price, sell_price) values('Linux CD', 1.99,
2.49);
insert into item(description, cost_price, sell_price) values('Tissues', 2.11,
3.99);
insert into item(description, cost_price, sell_price) values('Picture Frame',
7.54, 9.95);
insert into item(description, cost_price, sell_price) values('Fan Small', 9.23,
15.75);
insert into item(description, cost_price, sell_price) values('Fan Large', 13.36,
19.95);
insert into item(description, cost_price, sell_price) values('Toothbrush', 0.75,
1.45);
insert into item(description, cost_price, sell_price) values('Roman Coin', 2.34,
2.45);
insert into item(description, cost_price, sell_price) values('Carrier Bag', 0.01,
0.0);
insert into item(description, cost_price, sell_price) values('Speakers', 19.73,
25.32);
```

### Barcode Table

```
insert into barcode(barcode_ean, item_id) values('6241527836173', 1);
insert into barcode(barcode_ean, item_id) values('6241574635234', 2);
insert into barcode(barcode_ean, item_id) values('6264537836173', 3);
insert into barcode(barcode_ean, item_id) values('6241527746363', 3);
insert into barcode(barcode_ean, item_id) values('7465743843764', 4);
insert into barcode(barcode_ean, item_id) values('3453458677628', 5);
```

```
insert into barcode(barcode_ean, item_id) values('6434564564544', 6);
insert into barcode(barcode_ean, item_id) values('8476736836876', 7);
insert into barcode(barcode_ean, item_id) values('6241234586487', 8);
insert into barcode(barcode_ean, item_id) values('9473625532534', 8);
insert into barcode(barcode_ean, item_id) values('9473627464543', 8);
insert into barcode(barcode_ean, item_id) values('4587263646878', 9);
insert into barcode(barcode_ean, item_id) values('9879879837489', 11);
insert into barcode(barcode_ean, item_id) values('2239872376872', 11);
```

### Orderinfo Table

```
insert into orderinfo(customer_id, date_placed, date_shipped, shipping)
values(3,'03-13-2000','03-17-2000', 2.99);
insert into orderinfo(customer_id, date_placed, date_shipped, shipping)
values(8,'06-23-2000','06-24-2000', 0.00);
insert into orderinfo(customer_id, date_placed, date_shipped, shipping)
values(15,'09-02-2000','09-12-2000', 3.99);
insert into orderinfo(customer_id, date_placed, date_shipped, shipping)
values(13,'09-03-2000','09-10-2000', 2.99);
insert into orderinfo(customer_id, date_placed, date_shipped, shipping)
values(8,'07-21-2000','07-24-2000', 0.00);
```

### Orderline Table

```
insert into orderline(orderinfo_id, item_id, quantity) values(1, 4, 1);
insert into orderline(orderinfo_id, item_id, quantity) values(1, 7, 1);
insert into orderline(orderinfo_id, item_id, quantity) values(1, 9, 1);
insert into orderline(orderinfo_id, item_id, quantity) values(2, 1, 1);
insert into orderline(orderinfo_id, item_id, quantity) values(2, 10, 1);
insert into orderline(orderinfo_id, item_id, quantity) values(2, 7, 2);
insert into orderline(orderinfo_id, item_id, quantity) values(2, 4, 2);
insert into orderline(orderinfo_id, item_id, quantity) values(3, 2, 1);
insert into orderline(orderinfo_id, item_id, quantity) values(3, 1, 1);
insert into orderline(orderinfo_id, item_id, quantity) values(4, 5, 2);
insert into orderline(orderinfo_id, item_id, quantity) values(5, 1, 1);
insert into orderline(orderinfo_id, item_id, quantity) values(5, 3, 1);
```

### Stock Table

```
insert into stock(item_id, quantity) values(1,12);
insert into stock(item_id, quantity) values(2,2);
insert into stock(item_id, quantity) values(4,8);
insert into stock(item_id, quantity) values(5,3);
insert into stock(item_id, quantity) values(7,8);
insert into stock(item_id, quantity) values(8,18);
insert into stock(item_id, quantity) values(10,1);
```

With the PostgreSQL system running, the database created, the tables made and populated, we are ready to continue our exploration of PostgreSQL features.

## Stopping PostgreSQL

It is important that the PostgreSQL server process is shut down in an orderly fashion. This will allow it to write any outstanding data to the database, and free up shared memory resources it is using.

To cleanly shut down the database use the `pg_ctl` utility as `postgres` or `root` like this:

```
# /usr/local/pgsql/bin/pg_ctl -D /usr/local/pgsql/data stop
```

If startup scripts are in place you can of course use those:

```
# /etc/rc.d/init.d/MyPostgreSQL stop
```

The scripts also make sure that the database is shut down properly when the machine is halted or rebooted.

### Resources

You can get more information on the utilities `psql`, `initdb`, `createuser`, and `createdb` by referring to the manual pages, and other documentation provided with PostgreSQL. To make life a little easier when dealing with PostgreSQL it might be of some use to add the PostgreSQL applications directory to your execution path, and similarly the manual pages. To do this for the standard UNIX shell, place the following commands in your shell startup file (`.profile` or `.bashrc`):

```
PATH=$PATH:/usr/local/pgsql/bin
MANPATH=$MANPATH:/usr/local/pgsql/man
export PATH MANPATH
```

As mentioned above, the source code for the current and latest test releases of PostgreSQL can be found at http://www.postgresql.org. More resources about PostgreSQL are provided in the Chapter 18.

# Installing PostgreSQL on Windows

Let's begin this section with some good news for Windows users. Although PostgreSQL was developed for UNIX-like platforms, it has been written to be portable. It has been possible for some time now to write PostgreSQL client applications for Windows, and from version 7.1 onwards, PostgreSQL can be compiled, installed, and run as a PostgreSQL server on Microsoft Windows NT4 and Windows 2000. To achieve this, we'll need to install some additional software to support some UNIX features on Windows.

Many of the steps are the same as those we used to install on Linux and UNIX from source code. The key differences are that we need a UNIX-like development environment for Windows and we need to jump through a couple of small hoops to get the `postmaster` process started automatically. Nevertheless, it can be done, should you need to. In fact, having the PostgreSQL utilities like `psql` on the same machine as some client applications can be useful in testing out new database installations and troubleshooting connection problems even if you don't need to run the server on Windows.

## Cygwin – A UNIX Environment for Windows

To help those who would like to extend the capabilities of Microsoft Windows, Cygnus Solutions (now part of Red Hat) have developed a set of libraries that emulate some of the UNIX APIs on Windows NT and 2000. These DLLs allow programs written for UNIX or Linux to run on Windows. There are some restrictions, notably in the areas of file permissions and user privileges, due to the differences in approach between the two underlying operating systems, but nevertheless it is a very useful addition to free software.

The package is called Cygwin and can be freely downloaded from http://www.cygwin.com. In this section, we will show how to install Cygwin on Windows platform and use it to compile PostgreSQL from the source code:

Firstly, visit http://www.cygwin.com and click on the Install Cygwin now icon.

This is a link to a setup program you can either download and run, or run in place. We recommend downloading it to a suitable area and executing it once it is safely resident on the hard disk of a Windows machine.

**A complete Cygwin installation will require a download of 40Mb or more.**

Run setup.exe to begin the installation:

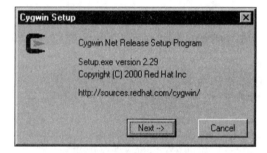

The program will take you through a number of simple steps, prompting for the information it needs to download and install the many packages that make up the total Cygwin suite of tools.

The next task is to decide on an installation strategy. You can download and install packages at once, or you can download the files and install later. We recommend that you download the files and install at your leisure. That way you will have the downloaded files to hand in case you want to re-install or install on another machine:

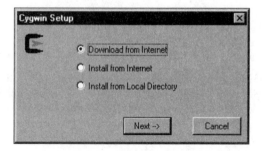

After we have downloaded the packages from the Internet we will re-run `setup.exe` and select Install from Local Directory specifying the location of the download. We are prompted for a local directory to place the download in, and then asked about the connection method we want to use for the download. If you are using Internet Explorer 5 or later, you can tell `setup.exe` to use the same settings as the browser:

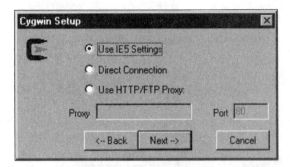

Then we are prompted to select a site to download from. There are a number of sites around the world that keep copies of Cygwin so that the main site does not get overloaded. You ought to choose a download site that is geographically close to you:

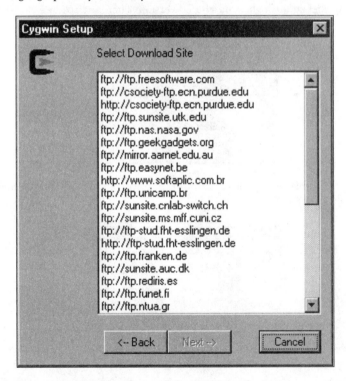

The next step is to decide which of the many packages which make up Cygwin we would like to download and install. The default is to download a set of binary packages with no source code for them, although source code is available. For compiling PostgreSQL, the default setting works fine:

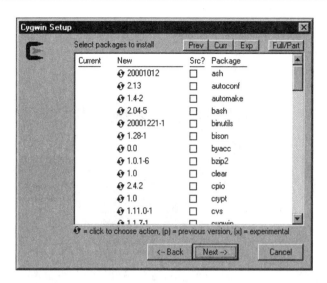

If you are sure that you do not want a particular package, you can click on the selection and set it to skip. If there is more than one version of a package available for download you can choose the one you want. It is probably best to stick to the highest numbered version. Then setup.exe starts downloading:

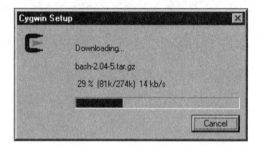

Once downloading is finished, we can re-run setup.exe and install from the local directory where we placed the download:

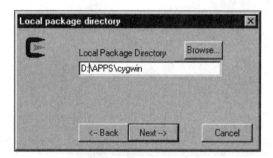

Next, we have to decide on a base location for Cygwin. Once installed, Cygwin will provide a directory tree very much like a traditional UNIX or Linux file system. It will have a root directory with subdirectories called bin, lib, usr, and so on. All of these will live under a directory in the NT/2000 file system in a place we can choose:

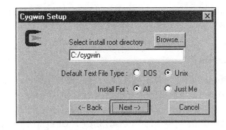

We recommend that you select the default text file type to be UNIX, as this will make sure that files created with Cygwin tools will always be compatible with other Cygwin tools.

If you need to edit Cygwin files with Windows applications, it is probably a good idea to use an editor that is aware of the different types of text file and handles them appropriately. A good one is PFE, The Programmer's File Editor available from many free software sites. The home page of PFE is http://www.lancs.ac.uk/people/cpaap/pfe/. Cygwin versions of UNIX favorites vi and emacs are also available.

If you select Install For All, a program group will be created for all Windows users, otherwise Cygwin will only be available for you. We recommend selecting All, which will then enable you to run Cygwin programs as the postgres user.

Finally, you can select the packages you want to install, the default is to install all of the packages you downloaded.

Once installation is finished, you will have an icon on your desktop and a Cygnus program group that will start a UNIX shell on your Windows PC:

With the Cygwin tools installed you have a version of the GNU C compiler, Bash command shell, and almost all the tools needed to compile PostgreSQL from source.

## IPC Services for Windows

One additional piece of software that you need for PostgreSQL to work on Windows is an IPC manager to handle UNIX-style shared memory and semaphores that PostgreSQL requires. A suitable package, not distributed by default with Cygwin is CygIPC available from http://www.neuro.gatech.edu/users/cwilson/cygutils/V1.1/cygipc/.

Installation of CygIPC is very easy. Simply download a Cygwin-compatible package and unpack it in the Cygwin root directory:

```
$ cd /
$ tar zxvf cygipc-1.09-2.tar.gz
```

## PostgreSQL for Cygwin

As at Cygwin version 2.29, there is a binary distribution of PostgreSQL included as a contributed package. This can be installed by the Cygwin setup program. The PostgreSQL programs are installed in `/usr/bin`, with the libraries in `/usr/lib` and shared files in `/usr/share`.

## Compiling PostgreSQL on Windows

The steps needed to compile PostgreSQL on Windows NT/2000 are pretty much the same as for UNIX and Linux so we will keep things brief here.

Copy a source 'tarball' (`postgresql-7.1.2.tar.gz`) to a local directory in the Cygwin root, say `/usr/src`.

> **The Cygwin root is visible from the normal Windows Explorer as the location you chose when installing Cygwin.**

Unpack the sources, run `configure`, and make as in the UNIX case:

```
$ tar zxvf postgresql-7.1.2.tar.gz
$ cd postgres-7.1.2
$ ./configure
$ make
$ make install
```

You will now have an installation of PostgreSQL installed in `/usr/local/pgsql`.

## Configuring PostgreSQL for Windows

As with UNIX and Linux, the PostgreSQL server process, `postmaster`, has to run as a distinguished user. The same is true on Windows, so the first task is to create a user called `postgres`.

Use the Control Panel 'Users and Passwords' application to create a user called `postgres` that is a member of the Administrators group. Set a password in the normal way. It is a good idea to set the password so that it never expires, as it will be used to start a Windows service.

Now you can log on as `postgres` and start a Cygwin `bash` session.

Before we can run the `postmaster` program, we need to start the IPC services daemon to handle the UNIX-style IPC. You can do this by executing:

```
$ /usr/local/bin/ipc-daemon.exe &
```

Now you can initialize the database just as in the UNIX and Linux environments:

```
pg$ /usr/local/pgsql/bin/initdb -D /usr/local/pgsql/data
```

To run the postmaster program with remote access allowed, you need to edit the `pg_hba.conf` file to add the following at the end of the file:

```
host all   192.168.0.0 255.255.0.0     trust
```

This means that all computers with an IP address that begins 192.168 can access all databases.

Start the server process in just the same way as before:

```
pg$ /usr/local/pgsql/bin/postmaster -i -D /usr/local/pgsql/data >logfile 2>&1 &
```

As before, we can create users and databases:

```
$ /usr/local/pgsql/bin/createuser neil
$ /usr/local/pgsql/bin/createdb test
```

We can check that our database is active by using `psql` either locally or remotely. Here's a couple of screenshots showing PostgreSQL running on Windows 2000 and being accessed from a Linux machine:

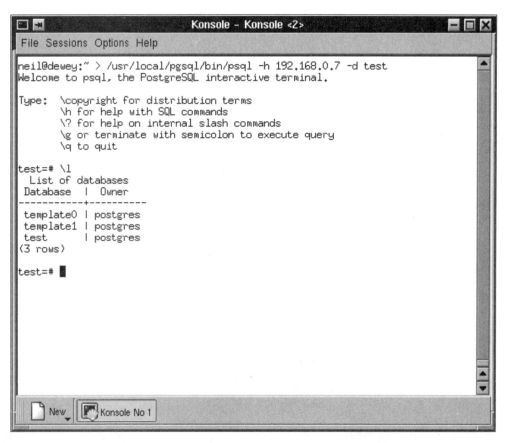

This could simultaneously be verified on Windows by starting another Cygwin bash session and executing:

```
$ /usr/local/pgsql/bin/psql -d test
```

## Starting PostgreSQL Automatically

As things stand, at the moment we are relying on starting the PostgreSQL server by hand. Now, if you have an NT or Windows 2000 computer that can be dedicated to running PostgreSQL, and you are prepared to log on as the postgres user and start the two processes needed (ipc-daemon and postmaster), each time the server restarts you can leave things as they are.

If you try to log out and login as a normal user you will find that the processes will get terminated.

We can do better than this however, and arrange for our two processes to get started automatically by Windows. We need to run the daemon processes as Windows Services. Ideally, the programs themselves would have been constructed to run as services, but even though they are not currently, we can persuade Windows to treat them as such.

It is possible that a future version of PostgreSQL will include an installable binary that will run as a service, once installed. It's probably worth keeping an eye on the web site for the latest developments.

What we need to do is employ the help of two handy little programs called INSTSRV and SRVANY. These are part of the Windows NT4 Resource Kit and together they allow any normal program to be run as if it was a service. They also work on Windows 2000. An updated version of the SRVANY utility obtained from ftp://ftp.microsoft.com/bussys/winnt/winnt-public/reskit/nt40/.

The instructions below require the use of a registry editor. Editing the Windows Registry can be dangerous as mistakes can be costly. If you are unsure, backup all of your data before proceeding.

Install the instsrv.exe and srvany.exe utilities into any local directory. srvany.exe will need to be present whenever the PostgreSQL services are started. Here we will assume that they have been installed in C:\NTRESKIT.

The plan is to create two new services in Windows, both of which will execute the srvany.exe utility. This utility will in turn start the application we actually need to run as a service.

We will start with the easier of the two, the IPC Daemon.

> **At the time of writing, work was underway to modify the IPC daemon to support its use as a service, without the need to use INSTSRV or SRVANY. If you use a version of cygipc later than 1.09 check out the README file for details.**

First, install a new service by running the instsrv.exe utility:

```
C:\NTRESKIT> instsrv "IPC Daemon"
c:\ntreskit\srvany.exe
The service was successfully added!

Make sure that you go into the Control Panel and use
the Services applet to change the Account Name and
Password that this newly installed service will use
for its Security Context.

C:\NTRESKIT>
```

Before editing the registry to create the parameters for this new service we need to set it to run as the postgres user. To do this, open the Control Panel Services applet again and change the Account Name and Password (in the Logon dialog for Windows 2000) to be postgres and whatever password you chose when you created the user. The name will show as .\postgres as it is a user on the local machine rather than an NT Domain, as shown in the screenshot on the following page:

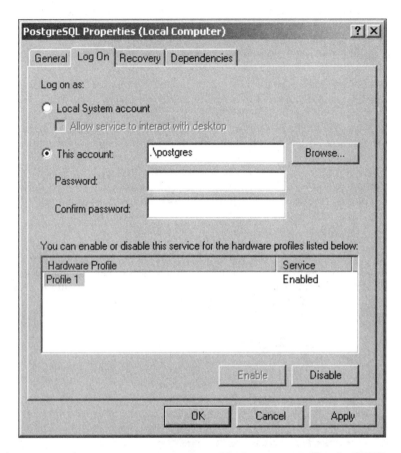

Now we use the registry editor, regedit.exe, to modify the new entry for the IPC Daemon process that we have created. We need to set parameters for srvany.exe so that it executes the ipc-daemon.exe program on our behalf.

Start regedit.exe and navigate to the entry:

```
HKEY_LOCAL_MACHINE\SYSTEM\CurrentControlSet\Services
```

You should see a new entry IPC Daemon. Make a new key within IPC Daemon called Parameters. Within Parameters make two new string values, Application and AppDirectory. Set these to the full path to the ipc-daemon.exe file and the Cygwin /bin directory.

For example, they might be F:\cygwin\usr\local\bin\ipc-daemon.exe and F:\cygwin\bin respectively.

The result should look something like this:

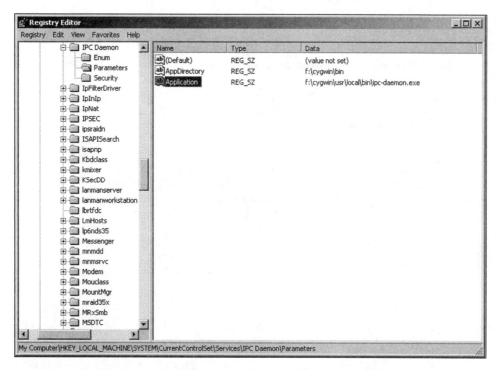

Now you can use the **Services** applet in the **Administrative Tools** group on Windows 2000, which is in the **Control Panel**, to try and start the service.

The `ipc-daemon.exe` program should start and will show up in **Windows Task Manager**:

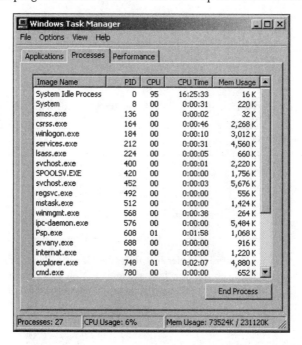

Now we can move on to the slightly trickier `postmaster` process. We start in the same way by creating a `SRVANY` service:

```
C:\NTRESKIT> instsrv "PostgreSQL" c:\ntreskit\srvany.exe
```

Before editing the registry to create the parameters for this second service we need to set it to run as the `postgres` user as we did for the IPC Daemon. To do this open the Control Panel Services applet again and change the Account Name and Password to be `.\postgres` as before.

So that we can start the `postmaster` process in a Cygwin UNIX-like environment we are going to have to invoke a couple of command processes. We are going to get `srvany.exe` to start a Windows command shell, `cmd.exe`. This we will give parameters telling it to run a particular program. The program will be the Cygwin command processor running a shell script we will provide. The script will start the `postmaster` process. It's not so bad if we do it step by step.

Create a bash script file in Cygwin `/usr/local/bin` and call it `startpg`. It must be a UNIX-style text file and contain the following lines:

```bash
#!/bin/bash

# Start PostgreSQL

PGDATA=/usr/local/pgsql/data
PATH=/bin:/usr/bin:/usr/local/bin:/usr/local/pgsql/bin
export PGDATA PATH

postmaster -i >/usr/local/pgsql/postmaster.log 2>&1 </dev/null
```

This script will actually start PostgreSQL for us.

Now we can use `regedit.exe` to setup the starting of the script. Like before, we need to navigate the registry to `HKEY_LOCAL_MACHINE\SYSTEM\CurrentControlSet\Services`. We should see an entry for `PostgreSQL`.

Create a new key here called `Parameters` and three string values within `Parameters` as follows:

| String | Parameter |
| --- | --- |
| Application | `cmd.exe` |
| AppDirectory | `f:\cygwin\bin` |
| AppParameters | `/c "f:\cygwin\bin\bash.exe /usr/local/bin/startpg"` |

Now we are ready to start the PostgreSQL service. Use the Control Panel Services applet to do this and check in the Task Manager that both our services are active. You will notice that the `postmaster` entry reads `postgres.exe` as that is the actual binary that the `postmaster` script invokes.

As a final test, if you reboot your Windows machine you should see that both services are started in Task Manager and the PostgreSQL database is accessible without having to log on as the `postgres` user.

That's all there is to it.

# Summary

In this chapter, we have taken a look at some of the options for installing PostgreSQL. The easiest way is from pre-compiled binary packages. Also, PostgreSQL is an Open Source product, we have the source code to use if we choose. Therefore, we can compile it on a wide range of UNIX and UNIX-like systems.

We have seen step-by-step instructions for compiling, installing and confirming a working installation on Linux from packages, UNIX from source and even Windows NT/2000 using Cygwin.

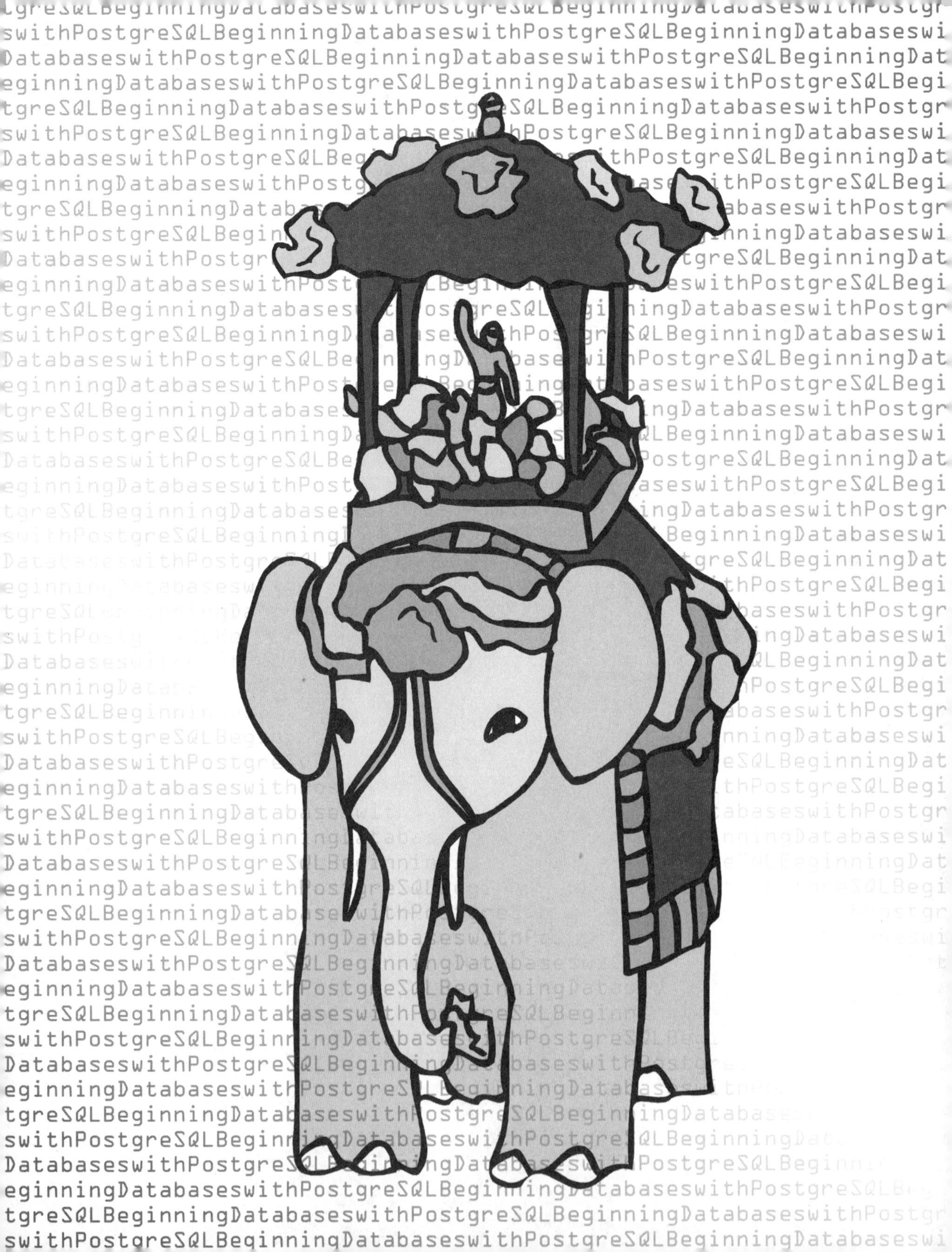

# Accessing Your Data

So far in this book, our encounters with SQL have been rather informal. We have seen some statements that retrieve data in various ways, and we also saw in the previous chapter some SQL for creating and populating tables. By now you should have PostgreSQL up and running. We will see in the next chapter, some of the GUI clients you can use, but for now we will be using a simple command line tool, psql, to access the database.

In this chapter, we are going to have a slightly more formal look at SQL, starting with the SELECT statement. In fact, this whole chapter is devoted to learning the SELECT statement. Your first impression might be that a whole chapter on one part of SQL is perhaps a bit excessive, but the SELECT statement is right at the heart of the SQL language. Once you understand SELECT, you really have done the hard part of learning SQL.

We will also see, in later chapters, how we can update and delete data, and further extend our understanding of SELECT to other statements for manipulating data. We will show SQL keywords in uppercase, to make them stand out clearly. SQL is not case sensitive, though a few implementations do make table names case sensitive. Data stored in SQL databases, is of course case sensitive, so the character string 'Newtown' is different from the character string 'newtown'.

We will also be using the command line tool, psql, but you should be able to try all of the examples in this chapter from any GUI tool that allows you to type SQL directly to PostgreSQL.

In this chapter we'll look at:

- ❑   Using psql
- ❑   Some simple SELECT statements
- ❑   Overriding column names
- ❑   Controlling the order of rows
- ❑   Suppressing duplicates
- ❑   Performing calculations

- ❏ More complex conditions
- ❏ Aliasing table names
- ❏ Pattern matching
- ❏ Comparisons using other types
- ❏ Multiple tables
- ❏ Relating three models

Throughout this chapter, we will be using the sample database we designed in Chapter 2, and created and populated in Chapter 3.

# Using psql

Assuming you have followed the instructions in Chapter 3, by now you should have a database called bpsimple, accessible by your normal login prompt.

> **You should never use the `postgres` user for accessing the PostgreSQL server, except in the special case of database administration. Just like when using Linux, you should avoid being the `root` user, unless you absolutely have to be that user to perform a command.**

To start psql accessing the bpsimple database, enter:

```
$ psql -d bpsimple
```

You should see:

```
Welcome to psql, the PostgreSQL interactive terminal.

Type:  \copyright for distribution terms
       \h for help with SQL commands
       \? for help on internal slash commands
       \g or terminate with semicolon to execute query
       \q to quit

bpsimple=#
```

We are now ready to enter commands. If psql complains about pg_shadow, then you have not yet created yourself as a database user. Use the su command to become the postgres user, rerun the createuser <login name> command and reply 'y'. Then exit that login. Now log in as yourself once more, run the createdb command to create the database bpsimple. Then restart psql and you should get the bpsimple=# prompt. You will then need to rerun the steps described at the end of the previous chapter, in order to create the sample tables and data we will use in this chapter.

To check if you have the tables created, enter \dt then press return, and you should see output similar to this:

```
bpsimple=# \dt
                List of relations
          Name          |   Type   |  Owner
------------------------+----------+----------
 barcode                |  table   |  rick
 customer               |  table   |  rick
 item                   |  table   |  rick
 orderinfo              |  table   |  rick
 orderline              |  table   |  rick
 stock                  |  table   |  rick

bpsimple=#
```

rick in the owner column above will be replaced by your login name.

There are only a few basic psql commands you need in this chapter (we will meet the full set in Chapter 5). For now, the commands you need to know, each of which must be followed by a return, are:

| Command | Description |
|---------|-------------|
| \? | Get a help message |
| \do | List operators |
| \dt | List tables |
| \Dt | List types |
| \h <cmd> | Get help on the SQL command |
| \i <filename> | Execute commands read from the filename <*filename*> |
| \r | Reset the buffer (discard any typing) |
| \q | Quit psql |
| \? | Get a help message |

On most Linux systems you should also be able to use the arrow keys to recall previous lines, and move about editing them as you require. This feature of psql depends on the presence of the GNU readline facility, which is usually, but not always, installed.

Now we are ready to start accessing PostgreSQL using SQL. In the next chapter, we will meet some of the GUI tools that you can use with PostgreSQL, but for this chapter we will stick to using the psql tool. If you prefer to use the GUI tools, you may want to look ahead to Chapter 5, first, then come back here using a GUI tool rather than psql.

# Simple SELECT Statements

We get data from PostgreSQL using the SELECT statement as in all relational databases. It's probably the most complex statement in SQL, but it really is at the heart of using relational databases effectively.

Let's start our investigation of SELECT by simply asking for all the data in a particular table. We do this by using a very basic form of the SELECT statement, specifying a FROM clause and a table name:

```
SELECT <comma separated list of columns> FROM <table name>
```

If we can't remember what the exact column names are called, or want to see all the columns, we can just use a '*' in place of the column list.

## Try it Out – Selecting All Columns from a Table

We will start by fetching all the data from the item table:

```
SELECT * FROM item;
```

Remember that the ';' is for the benefit of psql, to tell it you have finished typing. Strictly speaking, it is not part of SQL. If you prefer, you can terminate SQL statements typed into psql with \g, which has exactly the same effect as the semicolon. If you are using a different tool to send SQL to PostgreSQL, you may need neither of these terminators.

Once you have pressed return, PostgreSQL responds:

```
bpsimple=# SELECT * FROM item;
 item_id |  description  | cost_price | sell_price
---------+---------------+------------+------------
       1 | Wood Puzzle   |      15.23 |      21.95
       2 | Rubic Cube    |       7.45 |      11.49
       3 | Linux CD      |       1.99 |       2.49
       4 | Tissues       |       2.11 |       3.99
       5 | Picture Frame |       7.54 |       9.95
       6 | Fan Small     |       9.23 |      15.75
       7 | Fan Large     |      13.36 |      19.95
       8 | Toothbrush    |       0.75 |       1.45
       9 | Roman Coin    |       2.34 |       2.45
      10 | Carrier Bag   |       0.01 |       0.00
      11 | Speakers      |      19.73 |      25.32
(11 rows)

bpsimple=#
```

## How it Works

We simply asked PostgreSQL for all the data from all the columns in the item table, using a '*' for the column names, and PostgreSQL gave us just that, but neatly arranged with column headings and a pipe '|' symbol to separate each column. It even told us how many rows we retrieved.

That worked, but suppose we didn't want all the columns? In general, you should only ask PostgreSQL, or indeed any database, to retrieve the data you actually want. Each column of each row that is retrieved adds a little extra work. Remember, we would like to keep things neat and efficient.

You will also find that, once you start having SQL embedded in other languages (see Chapter 14), specifying exact columns also protects you against changes to the database schema. For example, if you use '*' and an additional column is added, you may find that you are processing data from a different column to the one you intended. If a column that you are using is deleted, then your SQL will fail, since the column can no longer be retrieved – but that is a much easier bug to track and correct than some application code simply running out of columns while processing data.

Of course, if you name the column you do have the possibility of searching all your code to see if the column name appears, and preventing that bug ever occurring.

Let's start by restricting the columns we retrieve. As we saw in the syntax earlier, we do this by specifying each column we want, separated by a comma. If we don't want the columns in the order we specified when we created the database table, that's fine; we can specify the columns in any order we like and they will be returned in that order.

## Try it Out – Selecting Named Columns in the Order We Choose

To retrieve the name of the town and last name of all our customers, we must specify the name of the columns for town and last name, and of course the table to retrieve them from. Here is the statement we need and PostgreSQL's response:

```
bpsimple=# SELECT town, lname FROM customer;
    town    |  lname
------------+---------
 Hightown   | Stones
 Lowtown    | Stones
 Nicetown   | Matthew
 Yuleville  | Matthew
 Oahenham   | Cozens
 Nicetown   | Matthew
 Bingham    | Stones
 Bingham    | Stones
 Histon     | Hickman
 Tibsville  | Howard
 Bingham    | Jones
 Winersby   | Neill
 Oxbridge   | Hendy
 Welltown   | O'Neill
 Milltown   | Hudson
(15 rows)

bpsimple=#
```

### How it Works

PostgreSQL returns all the data rows from the table we asked for, but only from the columns we specified. It also returns the column data in the order in which we specified the columns in the SELECT statement.

# Overriding Column Names

You will notice that the output uses the database column name as the heading for the output. Sometimes this is not very easy to read, particularly, as we shall see in Chapter 7, when the column in the output isn't an actual database column so it has no name. There is a very simple syntax for specifying the display name to use with each column, which is to add AS "<display name>" after each column in the SELECT statement. You can specify the name of all columns you select, or just a few. Where you don't specify the name, PostgreSQL just uses the column name.

For example, to change the above output to make lname be displayed as Last Name we would write:

```
SELECT town, lname AS "Last Name" FROM customer;
```

We will see an example of this in use in the next section.

# Controlling the Order of Rows

So far, we have retrieved the data from the columns we wanted, but the data is not always in the most suitable order for viewing. The data we are seeing may look as though it is in the order we inserted it into the database, but in fact, relational databases are under no obligation to return the data to you in any particular order, unless you specifically ask for it ordered in some way.

You may remember we mentioned in Chapter 2 that unlike a spreadsheet, the order of rows in a database is unspecified. The database server is free to store rows in the most effective way, which is not usually the most natural way for viewing the data. The output you see is not sorted in any meaningful order, and next time you ask for the same data, it could be displayed in a different order.

Generally, the data will be returned in the order it is stored in the database internally. Initially, this may look to be the same order as you inserted data into the database, but as you delete rows, and insert new rows, this order may begin to look more and more random. No SQL database, PostgreSQL included, is obliged to return the data in a particular order, unless you specifically request it to be ordered.

We can control the order in which data is displayed from a SELECT statement, by adding an additional clause to the SELECT statement, ORDER BY, that specifies the order we would like the data to be returned. The syntax is:

```
SELECT <comma separated list of columns> FROM < table name> ORDER BY <column name>
[ASC | DESC]
```

The slightly strange looking syntax at the end means that after the column name, we can write either ASC (short for ascending), or DESC (short for descending). By default, ascending is used. The data is then returned to us ordered by the column we specified, sorted in the direction we requested.

## Try it Out – Ordering the Data

In this example, we will sort the data by town, and we will also override the default column name for the lname column, as we saw in the last section, to make the output slightly easier to read.

Notice that since we want the data in ascending order, we can omit the ASC, as that is the default. Here is the command we require and PostgreSQL's response:

```
bpsimple=# SELECT town, lname AS "Last Name" FROM customer ORDER BY town;
    town    | Last Name
------------+-----------
 Bingham    | Stones
 Bingham    | Stones
 Bingham    | Jones
 Hightown   | Stones
 Histon     | Hickman
 Lowtown    | Stones
 Milltown   | Hudson
 Nicetown   | Matthew
 Nicetown   | Matthew
 Oahenham   | Cozens
 Oxbridge   | Hendy
 Tibsville  | Howard
 Welltown   | O'Neill
 Winersby   | Neill
 Yuleville  | Matthew
(15 rows)

bpsimple=#
```

As you can see, the data is now sorted in ascending order by town.

### How it Works

This time we made two changes to our previous statement. We added an AS clause to change the name of the second column to Last Name, which makes it easier to read, and we also added an ORDER BY clause to specify the order in which PostgreSQL should return the data to us.

Sometimes we need to go a little further, and order by more than a single column. For example, in the output above although the data is ordered by town, there is not much order in the Last Name. We can see, for example that Jones is listed after Stones under all the customers found in the town Bingham.

We can specify more precisely the order we would like the output to appear in, by specifying more than one column in the ORDER BY clause. If we want to, we can even specify that the order is ascending for one column, and descending for another column.

## Try it Out – Ordering the Data Using ASC and DESC

Let's try our SELECT again, but this time we will sort the town names into descending order, and the last names into ascending order where rows share the same town name. This time, we will not override the default column names.

The statement we need and PostgreSQL's response:

```
bpsimple=# SELECT town, lname FROM customer ORDER BY town DESC, lname ASC;
town      | lname
----------+----------
Yuleville | Matthew
Winersby  | Neill
Welltown  | O'Neill
Tibsville | Howard
Oxbridge  | Hendy
Oahenham  | Cozens
Nicetown  | Matthew
Nicetown  | Matthew
Milltown  | Hudson
Lowtown   | Stones
Histon    | Hickman
Hightown  | Stones
Bingham   | Jones
Bingham   | Stones
Bingham   | Stones
(15 rows)

bpsimple=#
```

### How it Works

As you can see, PostgreSQL first orders the data by town in descending order, which was the first column we specified in our ORDER BY clause. It then orders those entries in an ascending order that have multiple last names for the same town. This time, although Bingham is now last in the rows retrieved, the last names of our customers in that town are ordered in an ascending fashion.

Usually, the columns by which you can order the output are restricted, not unreasonably, to columns you have requested in the output. PostgreSQL, at least in the current version does not enforce this standard restriction, and will accept a column in the ORDER BY clause that is not in the selected column list. This is a non-standard SQL, and we strongly suggest that you avoid using it.

# Suppressing Duplicates

You may notice that there are several rows in the last output, for example the following appear twice:

```
Nicetown | Matthew
Bingham  | Stones
```

What's going on here? If we look back at our original data, back in Chapters 2 and 3, we will see that there are indeed two customers in Nicetown called Matthew, and two customers in Bingham called Stones. For reference, here are the rows showing the first names as well:

```
Nicetown | Matthew | Alex
Nicetown | Matthew | Neil
Bingham  | Stones  | Richard
Bingham  | Stones  | Ann
```

When PostgreSQL listed two rows for Nicetown and Matthew, and two rows for Bingham and Stones, it was quite correct. There are two customers in each of those towns with the same last names.

Even if they look the same because we have not asked for columns that distinguish them. The default behavior is to list all the rows, but is not always what we want.

Suppose we wanted just a list of towns where we had customers, perhaps in a much bigger scenario to determine where we should build distribution centers. Based on our knowledge so far, we might reasonably try:

```
bpsimple=# SELECT town FROM customer ORDER BY town;
    town
-----------
 Bingham
 Bingham
 Bingham
 Hightown
 Histon
 Lowtown
 Milltown
 Nicetown
 Nicetown
 Oahenham
 Oxbridge
 Tibsville
 Welltown
 Winersby
 Yuleville
(15 rows)

bpsimple=#
```

What we get back is correct, but not perhaps what we wanted.

PostgreSQL has listed all the towns, once for each time a town appeared in the customer table. Correct, but probably not quite the listing we would like. What we actually needed was a list where each town appeared just once, in other words a list of distinct towns.

In SQL you can suppress duplicate rows by adding the term DISTINCT to the SELECT statement. The syntax is:

```
SELECT DISTINCT <comma separated list of columns> FROM < table name>
```

As with pretty much all the clauses on SELECT, you can of course combine this with other clauses, such as renaming columns or specifying an order.

## Try it Out – Using DISTINCT

Let's get a list of all the towns that appear in our `customer` table, without duplicates. We can try the following code to get the response:

```
bpsimple=# SELECT DISTINCT town FROM customer;
   town
-----------
 Bingham
 Hightown
 Histon
 Lowtown
 Milltown
 Nicetown
 Oahenham
 Oxbridge
 Tibsville
 Welltown
 Winersby
 Yuleville
(12 rows)

bpsimple=#
```

### How it Works

The DISTINCT clause tells PostgreSQL to remove all duplicate rows. Notice that the output is now ordered by `town`. This is because of the way PostgreSQL has chosen to implement the search for your data. In general, you cannot assume the data will be sorted in this way. If you want the data sorted in a particular way, you must add an ORDER BY clause to specify the order.

Notice that the DISTINCT clause is not associated with a particular column. You can only suppress rows that are duplicated in all the columns you select, not suppress duplicates of a particular column. For example, if we asked:

```
SELECT DISTINCT town, fname FROM customer;
```

We would again get 15 rows, because there are 15 different town and first name combinations.

A word of warning is in order here. Although it might look like a good idea to always use the distinct version of SELECT, in practice this is a bad idea, for two reasons. First, by using DISTINCT you are asking PostgreSQL to do significantly more work in retrieving your data and checking for duplicates. Unless you know there will be duplicates that need to be removed, you shouldn't use the DISTINCT clause. The second reason is a bit more pragmatic. Occasionally, DISTINCT will mask errors in your data or SQL that would have been easy to spot if duplicate rows had been displayed. In short, use DISTINCT only where you actually need it.

# Performing Calculations

We can also perform simple calculations on data in the rows we retrieve, before we send them to the output.

Suppose we wanted to display the cost price of items in our item table. We could just execute SELECT as shown, which would give us output like this:

```
bpsimple=# SELECT description, cost_price FROM item;
  description   | cost_price
----------------+------------
 Wood Puzzle    |      15.23
 Rubic Cube     |       7.45
 Linux CD       |       1.99
 Tissues        |       2.11
 Picture Frame  |       7.54
 Fan Small      |       9.23
 Fan Large      |      13.36
 Toothbrush     |       0.75
 Roman Coin     |       2.34
 Carrier Bag    |       0.01
 Speakers       |      19.73
(11 rows)

bpsimple=#
```

Suppose however, we wanted to see the price in cents. We can do a simple calculation in SQL, like this, which would give us a response as shown:

```
bpsimple=# SELECT description, cost_price *100 FROM item;
  description   | cost_price
----------------+------------
 Wood Puzzle    |    1523.00
 Rubic Cube     |     745.00
 Linux CD       |     199.00
 Tissues        |     211.00
 Picture Frame  |     754.00
 Fan Small      |     923.00
 Fan Large      |    1336.00
 Toothbrush     |      75.00
 Roman Coin     |     234.00
 Carrier Bag    |       1.00
 Speakers       |    1973.00
(11 rows)

bpsimple=#
```

It seems a little weird, with the decimal points, so let's get rid of them using a trick we will see more of later.

We use the CAST to change the type of the column, which gives us the better looking:

```
bpsimple=# SELECT description, CAST(cost_price *100 AS INT) FROM item;
 description    | cost_price
----------------+--------------
 Wood Puzzle    |       1523
 Rubic Cube     |        745
 Linux CD       |        199
 Tissues        |        211
 Picture Frame  |        754
 Fan Small      |        923
 Fan Large      |       1336
 Toothbrush     |         75
 Roman Coin     |        234
 Carrier Bag    |          1
 Speakers       |       1973
 (11 rows)

bpsimple=#
```

It's not very often you will need to perform calculations on columns. They are used more when updating the database, as we will see in Chapter 7. It is handy to know however, that the ability to calculate in SQL statements exists.

# Choosing the Rows

So far, in this chapter, we have always worked with either all the rows of data, or at least all the distinct rows. It's time to look at how, just as with columns, we can choose the rows we want to see. You probably won't be surprised to learn that we do this with yet another clause on the SELECT statement.

The new clause we use for restricting the rows returned is WHERE.

The syntax, simplified, is:

```
SELECT <comma separated list of columns> FROM <table name> WHERE <conditions>
```

There are lots of possible conditions, which can also be combined by the operators AND, OR, and NOT.

The standard list of comparison operators is:

| Operator | Description |
|----------|-------------|
| < | Less than |
| <= | Less than or equal to |
| = | Equal to |
| >= | Greater or equal to |
| > | Greater than |
| <> | Not equal to |

These can be used on most types, both numeric and string, though there are some special conditions when working with dates which we will see later.

We will start with a simple condition, by just choosing to retrieve rows for people who live in the town Bingham. To get PostgreSQL's response as shown, the command we need is:

```
bpsimple=# SELECT town, lname, fname FROM customer WHERE town = 'Bingham';
town     | lname   | fname
---------+---------+---------
Bingham  | Stones  | Richard
Bingham  | Stones  | Ann
Bingham  | Jones   | Dave
(3 rows)

bpsimple=#
```

That was pretty straightforward, wasn't it? Notice the single quotes round the string Bingham, which are needed to make it clear that this is a string. Also notice that because Bingham is being matched against data in the database, it is case sensitive. If we had used ... town = 'bingham' no data would have been returned, because the string matching is case sensitive.

We can have multiple conditions, combined using AND, OR, and NOT, with parentheses to make the expression clear. We can also use conditions on columns that don't appear in the list of columns we have selected. You will remember that this generally isn't true for clauses such as ORDER BY.

## Try it Out – Using Operators

Let's try a more complicated set of conditions. Suppose we want to see the names of our customers who do not have a title of Mr, but do live in either Bingham or Nicetown.

The statement we need and PostgreSQL's response:

```
bpsimple=# SELECT title, fname, lname, town FROM customer WHERE title <> Mr'
bpsimple-# AND (town = 'Bingham' OR town = 'Nicetown');
title | fname | lname   | town
------+-------+---------+----------
 Miss | Alex  | Matthew | Nicetown
 Mrs  | Ann   | Stones  | Bingham
(2 rows)

bpsimple=#
```

### How it Works

Although it might look a little complex at first glance, this statement is actually quite simple. The first part is just our usual SELECT, listing the columns we want to see in the output. After the WHERE clause, we initially check that the title is not Mr, then we check that another condition is true, using AND. This second condition is that the town is either Bingham or Nicetown. Notice that we have to use parentheses to make it clear how the clauses are to be grouped.

You should be aware that PostgreSQL, or any other relational database, is not under any obligation to process the clauses in the order you write them in the SQL statement. All that is promised is that the result will be the correct answer to the SQL 'question'. Generally, relational databases have a complex optimizer, which looks at the request then calculates the 'best' way to satisfy it. Optimizers are not perfect, and you will occasionally come across statements that run better when rewritten in different ways. For reasonably simple statements like this one, we can safely assume the optimizer will do a good job.

> **If you want to know how PostgreSQL will process a SQL statement, you can get it to tell you by prefixing the SQL with 'explain' when, rather than execute the statement, PostgreSQL will tell you how the statement would be processed.**

# More Complex Conditions

One of the things that we frequently need to do when working with string, is to allow partial matching. For example, we may be looking for a person called Robert, but the name may have been shortened in the database to Rob, or even Bob. There are some special operations in SQL that make working with strings, either partial ones or lists of strings, easier.

The first new condition is IN, which allows us to check against a list of items, rather than using a string of OR conditions. Consider the following:

```
SELECT title, fname, lname, town FROM customer WHERE title <> 'Mr' AND (town =
'Bingham' OR town = 'Nicetown');
```

We can rewrite this as:

```
SELECT title, fname, lname, town FROM customer WHERE title <> 'Mr' AND town IN
('Bingham', 'Nicetown');
```

We will get the same result, although it's possible the output rows could be in a different order, since we did not use an ORDER BY clause. There is no particular advantage in using IN in this case, except for the simplification of the expression. Later, when we meet sub-selects, we will use IN again, as there it does offer more advantages.

The next new condition is BETWEEN, which allows us to check a range of values by specifying the end points. Suppose we wanted to select the rows with customer_id values between 5 and 9. Rather than write a sequence of OR conditions, or an IN with many values, we can simply write and get the response:

```
bpsimple=# SELECT customer_id, town, lname FROM customer WHERE customer_id
bpsimple-# BETWEEN 5 AND 9;
customer_id |   town   | lname
-------------+----------+---------
          5 | Oahenham | Cozens
          6 | Nicetown | Matthew
          7 | Bingham  | Stones
          8 | Bingham  | Stones
          9 | Histon   | Hickman
(5 rows)
bpsimple=#
```

It's also possible to use BETWEEN with strings, but care is needed, because the answer may not always be exactly what you were expecting, and you must know the case, since, as we have said before, string comparison is case sensitive.

## Try it Out – Complex Conditions

Let's try a BETWEEN statement, comparing strings. Suppose we wanted a distinct list of all the towns that started with letters between B and N. We know that all the towns in our table start with a capital letter, so we might well write the following, to get PostgreSQL's response:

```
bpsimple=# SELECT DISTINCT town FROM customer
bpsimple-# WHERE town BETWEEN 'B' AND 'N';
    town
 ----------
  Bingham
  Hightown
  Histon
  Lowtown
  Milltown
(5 rows)

bpsimple=#
```

Which if you look at closely, isn't what you were probably hoping for. Where is Newtown? It certainly starts with an N, but it hasn't been listed.

### Why it Didn't Work

The reason this statement didn't work, is that PostgreSQL, as per the SQL92 standard, pads the string you give it, with blanks till it is the same length as the string it is checking against. So when the comparison got to Newtown, PostgreSQL compared N (N followed by 6 spaces) with Newtown, and because whitespace appears in the ASCII table before all the other letters, it decided the Newtown came after N, so it shouldn't be included in the list.

### How to Make it Work

It's actually quite easy to make it work. Either we need to prevent the behavior of adding blanks to the search string by adding some z characters ourselves, or search using the next letter, O, in the BETWEEN clause. Of course, if there is a town called O we will then erroneously retrieve it, so this needs care. It's generally better to use z rather than Z, because z appears after Z in the ASCII table. Thus, our SQL should have read:

```
SELECT DISTINCT town FROM customer WHERE town BETWEEN 'B' AND 'Nz';
```

Notice that we didn't add a Z after the B, the B string being padded with blanks does work to find all towns that start with a B. Also if there was a town that started with the letters Nzz we would again fail to find it, because we would then compare Nz against Nzz and decide that Nzz came after Nz, because the third string location would have been padded to ' ' (space), which comes before the z in the third place of the string we are comparing against.

This type of matching has rather subtle behavior, and is so easy to go wrong that even experienced SQL users get caught out occasionally. For this reason, we recommend that you avoid using BETWEEN with strings.

# Pattern Matching

The string comparison operations we have seen till now are fine as far as they go, but they don't help very much with 'real world' string pattern matching. There is, of course, a SQL condition for doing this; it's the LIKE condition.

Unfortunately, LIKE uses a different set of string comparison rules from all other programming languages we know but, so long as you remember the rules, it's easy enough to use. When comparing strings with LIKE, you use % to mean any string of characters, and _ to match a single character.

For example, to match towns beginning with the letter B, we would write:

```
... WHERE town LIKE  'B%'
```

To match first names that end with e, we would write:

```
... WHERE fname LIKE '%e';
```

To match first names that are exactly 4 characters long, we would use 4 underscore characters, like this:

```
... WHERE fname LIKE '_ _ _ _';
```

We can also combine the two types in a single string if we need to.

## Try it Out – Pattern Matching

Let's find all the customers who have first names that have an a as the second character.

To get the following PostgreSQL response, we write:

```
bpsimple=# SELECT fname, lname FROM customer WHERE fname LIKE '_a%';
fname | lname
-------+--------
Dave  | Jones
Laura | Hendy
David | Hudson
(3 rows)

bpsimple=#
```

### How it Works

The first part of the pattern, _a matches strings that start with any single character, then have a lower case a. The second part of the pattern, %, matches any remaining characters. If we didn't use the trailing %, then only strings exactly two characters long would have been matched.

# Limiting the Result

In the examples we have been using so far, the number of result rows returned has always been quite small, because we only have a few sample rows in our 'experimental' database. In 'real' databases, we could easily have many thousands of rows that match the selection criteria, and if we are working on our SQL, refining our statements, we almost certainly do not want to see many thousands of rows scrolling past on our screen. A few sample rows to check our logic would be quite sufficient.

PostgreSQL has an extra clause on the SELECT statement, LIMIT, which is not part of the SQL standard, but is very useful when we want to restrict the number of rows returned.

You can use the LIMIT clause in two slightly different ways. If you append LIMIT and a number to your SELECT clause, only rows up to the number you specified will be returned, starting from the first row.

A slightly different way to use LIMIT, is to specify a pair of numbers with a 'comma' between them. If you use LIMIT M, N then only M rows will be returned, after N rows have been skipped.

It's easier to show it in action than to describe it. Here we only display the first 5 matching rows:

```
bpsimple=# SELECT customer_id, town FROM customer LIMIT 5;
customer_id |   town
-------------+-----------
          1 | Hightown
          2 | Lowtown
          3 | Nicetown
          4 | Yuleville
          5 | Oahenham
(5 rows)

bpsimple=#
```

The following skips the first two result rows, then returns the next 5 rows:

```
bpsimple=# SELECT customer_id, town FROM customer LIMIT 5,2;
 customer_id |   town
-------------+-----------
          3 | Nicetown
          4 | Yuleville
          5 | Oahenham
          6 | Nicetown
          7 | Bingham
(5 rows)

bpsimple=#
```

If you want to combine LIMIT with other SELECT clauses, then you should put the LIMIT clause at the end.

# Comparisons Using Other Types

There are two special cases of matching that we need to look at separately. You will remember from Chapter 2, the rather special column value NULL, which means either 'unknown' or 'not relevant'. We need to look at this separately, because if a column has the value NULL, then checking it needs special care to ensure that the results are as expected.

We also need to jump ahead slightly, and see how the PostgreSQL types for storing dates and times work in comparisons.

# Checking NULL Values

So far, we do not know a way of checking to see if a column contains a NULL value. We can check if it equals a value or string, or if it doesn't equal a value or string, but that's not sufficient. Suppose we have an integer column tryint in a table testtab that we know stores either 0, or 1, or NULL. We can check if it is 0 by writing:

```
SELECT * FROM testtab WHERE tryint = 0;
```

We can check if it is 1, by writing:

```
SELECT * FROM testtab WHERE tryint = 1;
```

We need another check however, to see if the value is NULL. PostgreSQL supports the standard SQL syntax for checking whether a value is NULL or not. We do this with the use of IS NULL, like this:

```
SELECT * FROM testtab WHERE tryint IS NULL;
```

Notice that we use the keyword IS rather than an = sign. We can also test to see if the value is something other than NULL, by adding a NOT, to invert the test:

```
SELECT * FROM testtab WHERE tryint IS NOT NULL;
```

Why do we suddenly need this extra bit of syntax? What is happening here is that instead of the logic you are probably more familiar with, a two-valued logic where everything is either TRUE or FALSE, we have stumbled into three-value logic, with TRUE, FALSE, and UNKNOWN.

Unfortunately, this property of NULL, being 'unknown', has some other effects outside the immediate concern of checking for NULL.

Suppose we ran our statement on a table where some values of tryint were NULL:

```
SELECT * FROM testtab WHERE tryint = 1;
```

What does our `tryint = 1` mean when `tryint` is actually NULL? We are asking the question, 'is Unknown = 1', which is interesting, because we can't claim it is FALSE, but neither can it be TRUE. So the answer must be unknown, hence the rows where NULL appears are not matched. If we reversed the test, and compared `tryint = 0`, they would also not be found, because that condition would not be true either. This can be confusing, because we have apparently used two tests, with opposite conditions, and still not retrieved all the rows from the table.

It's important to be aware of these issues with NULL, because it's all too easy to forget about NULL values. If you start getting slightly unexpected results when using conditions on a column that can have NULL values, check to see if rows where the column is NULL are the cause of your problems.

# Checking Dates and Time

Although, we haven't met all the PostgreSQL data types yet, we do need to be aware of some special functions we can use when checking dates and time.

PostgreSQL has two basic types for handling date and time information, TIMESTAMP, which holds both a date and a time, and DATE, which holds day, month, and year information. PostgreSQL has some built-in functions that help us manipulate dates and time, which are traditionally rather difficult units to manipulate. We won't go through all the functions available here (you can find them listed in the online documentation); we will concentrate on the main ones you will need.

Before we start, we need to tackle one of those apparently trivial problems that can so easily cause confusion. How do we specify a date?

When we write the date 1/2/1997, what do we mean? Europeans generally mean the first day of February 1997, but Americans usually mean the second day of January 1997. This is because Europeans generally read dates as DD/MM/YYYY, but Americans expect MM/DD/YYYY. We have always wondered why that is, but that's not a topic to discuss here.

This date confusion gives PostgreSQL a slight problem when you ask it to convert, such a string to a date. PostgreSQL lets you change the way dates are handled to suit your local needs, and before we get into checking dates and time, it's probably sensible to look at how you control this aspect of PostgreSQL's behavior.

## Setting the Time and Date Style

Unfortunately, PostgreSQL's method of setting the way date and time are handled is, at first sight at least, a little strange.

There are two things you can control:

❏   The order in which days and months are handled, US or European style

❏   The display format, or example, numbers only or more textual date output

The unfortunate part of the story, is that PostgreSQL uses the same variable to handle both settings, which frankly, can be a bit confusing.

The good news is that PostgreSQL defaults to using the unambiguous ISO-8601 style date and time output, which is always written in the form YYYY-MM-DD hh:mm:ss.sTZD. For example, a full date and time would look like 1997-02-01 05:23:43.23+5, which equates to February 1, 1997 at 23 minutes and 43.23 seconds past five o'clock in the morning. The TZD at the end of the format is a Time Zone Designator, which we'll leave for now.

For input in the form NN/NN/NNNN, PostgreSQL defaults to expecting month before day US style, in other words 2/1/97 is the first of February. Alternatively, you can use a format like 'February 1, 1997', or the ISO style '1997-02-01'. If that behavior is all you need, you are in luck, you don't need to know any more about controlling how PostgreSQL accepts and displays dates you could skip ahead to the next section on date and time functions.

If you want, or need, more control over how dates are handled, PostgreSQL does allow this, but it's a little tricky.

As we said above, there are two independent features to control, which act almost independently. The confusing thing is that you set them both using the same variable, DATESTYLE. Do remember however, that this is all to do with presentation. Internally, PostgreSQL stores dates in a way totally independent of any representation that users expect when data is input or retrieved. The syntax as a command to psql is:

```
SET DATESTYLE TO 'value';
```

Although, as with SQL statements in general, case is not important.

To set the order in which months and days are handled, you set the value to either 'US', for month first behavior, or 'European' for day first behavior:

| Value | Meaning | Example |
|---|---|---|
| US | Month before day | 02/01/1997 |
| European | Day before month | 01/02/1997 |

To change the display format, you also set DATESTYLE, but to one of four different values:

| Value | Meaning | Example |
|---|---|---|
| ISO | ISO-8601 standard, using '-' as the field separator | 1997-02-01 |
| SQL | Traditional style | 02/01/1997 |
| Postgres | Original style | Sat Feb 01 |
| German | German style | 01.02.1997 |

In the current release, the Postgres format defaults to displaying in SQL style for date types, but uses the longer format as shown in the example for TIMESTAMP types.

You set the DATESTYLE variable to the value pair by separating the values with a comma. So, for example, to specify that we want dates shown in SQL style, but using the European convention of day before month, we say:

```
SET DATESTYLE TO 'European, SQL';
```

Rather than set the date handling style locally in session, we can set it for an entire installation, or set the default for a session.

If you want to set the default style for date input for a complete installation, you must set the environment variable PGDATESTYLE before starting the postmaster master server process. Setting the same options using the environment variable in the UNIX, Linux, or Cygwin shell, we would use:

```
PGDATESTYLE="European, SQL"
export PGDATESTYLE
```

Alternatively, you can pass a backend option to the postmaster process, but we think that the environment variable is easier to manage.

If you want to set the date style for individual users, you use the same environment variable, but set for the local user, before psql is invoked. Local setting will override any global setting you have made.

Before we demonstrate how this all works, it's very handy to know about the special PostgreSQL function CAST, which allows you to convert one format into another. Although PostgreSQL makes a pretty good job of getting types correct, and you shouldn't need conversion functions often, they can be very useful occasionally. The conversion we need to use to investigate our date and time values is the following to get a date:

```
CAST('string' TO DATE)
```

Alternatively, to get a value that includes a time:

```
CAST('string' TO TIMESTAMP)
```

We are also going to use a little trick to demonstrate this. Perhaps ninety-nine out of a hundred times you use the SELECT statement, you will be fetching data out of a table. You can use SELECT in some limited circumstances however, to get data that isn't in a table at all. For example, we get this PostgreSQL response, if we write:

```
bpsimple=# SELECT 'Fred';
?column?
--------------
 Fred
(1 row)

bpsimple=#
```

PostgreSQL is warning us that we haven't selected any columns, but is quite happy to accept the SELECT syntax without a table name, and just returns the string we specified.

We can use the same feature, in conjunction with CAST, to see how PostgreSQL treats dates and time, without having to create a temporary table to experiment with.

## Try it Out – Date Formats

We start off with the environment variable PGDATESTYLE unset, so you can see the default behavior, and then set the date style, so you can see how things progress. We enter a date in ISO format, so this is always a safe option, and PostgreSQL outputs in the same format. No ambiguity in either of these:

```
bpsimple=# SELECT CAST('1997-02-1' AS DATE);
?column?
------------
1997-02-01
(1 row)

bpsimple=#
```

Changing the style to US and SQL format, we still enter the date in ISO style, which is unambiguous, it's still the first of February, but now the output shows the more conventional, but possibly ambiguous, US style MM/DD/YYYY output:

```
bpsimple=# SET DateStyle TO 'US, SQL';
SET VARIABLE
bpsimple=# SELECT CAST('1997-02-1' AS DATE);
?column?
------------
02/01/1997
(1 row)

bpsimple=#
```

Now is a good time to also ask psql what the variable datestyle is set to:

```
bpsimple=# SHOW datestyle;
NOTICE:  DateStyle is SQL with US (NonEuropean) conventions
SHOW VARIABLE

bpsimple=#
```

Now let's try some more formats. Same input date, but now the output is set to European, the display changes to DD/MM/YYYY:

```
bpsimple=# SET DateStyle TO 'European, SQL';
SET VARIABLE
bpsimple=# SELECT CAST('1997-02-1' AS DATE);
  ?column?
------------
 01/02/1997
(1 row)
bpsimple=#
```

Back to ISO input and output. The European has no effect, ISO is the same for all locales:

```
bpsimple=# SET DateStyle TO 'European, ISO';
SET VARIABLE
bpsimple=# SELECT CAST('1997-02-1' AS DATE);
  ?column?
------------
 1997-02-01
(1 row)

bpsimple=#
```

Now we use the TIMESTAMP type, which displays time. We didn't specify any hours or minutes, therefore they all default to zero:

```
bpsimple=# SELECT CAST('1997-02-1' AS TIMESTAMP);
        ?column?
------------------------
 1997-02-01 00:00:00+00
(1 row)

bpsimple=#
```

Now we see the unambiguous, and rather more reader-friendly, PostgreSQL style output:

```
bpsimple=# SET DateStyle TO 'European, Postgres';
SET VARIABLE
bpsimple=# SELECT CAST('1997-02-1' AS TIMESTAMP);
           ?column?
----------------------------
 Sat 01 Feb 00:00:00 1997 GMT
(1 row)

bpsimple=#
```

**101**

### How it Works

As you can see, we can vary the way both dates and times are displayed, as well as how ambiguous input strings, such as '01/02/1997' are interpreted.

Timezones are much simpler than date formats. Providing your local environment TZ is correctly set, PostgreSQL will manage timezones without further ado.

## Date and Time Functions

Now we have seen how dates work, we can look at a couple of useful functions you might need when comparing dates. These are:

```
date_part(units required, value to use);
now()
```

The first function, date_part(), allows you to extract a particular component of a date, such as the month.

Suppose we wanted to select the rows from our orderinfo table where the date the order was placed is in September. We know September is the ninth month, therefore we just ask:

```
bpsimple=# SELECT * FROM orderinfo WHERE date_part('month',date_placed)=9;
 orderinfo_id | customer_id | date_placed | date_shipped | shipping
--------------+-------------+-------------+--------------+----------
            3 |          15 | 2000-09-02  | 2000-09-12   |     3.99
            4 |          13 | 2000-09-03  | 2000-09-10   |     2.99
(2 rows)

bpsimple=#
```

PostgreSQL extracts the appropriate rows for us. Note the date is being displayed in ISO format. The parts we can extract from a DATE or TIMESTAMP are:

❑   year

❑   month

❑   day

❑   hour

❑   minute

❑   second

We can also compare dates, using the same operators $<>, <=, <, >, >=, =$, that we would use with numbers. For example:

```
bpsimple=# SELECT * FROM orderinfo WHERE date_placed >= CAST('2000-07-21' AS
bpsimple-# DATE);
 orderinfo_id | customer_id | date_placed | date_shipped | shipping
--------------+-------------+-------------+--------------+----------
            3 |          15 | 2000-09-02  | 2000-09-12   |     3.99
            4 |          13 | 2000-09-03  | 2000-09-10   |     2.99
            5 |           8 | 2000-07-21  | 2000-07-24   |     0.00
(3 rows)

bpsimple=#
```

Notice that we have to convert our string to a date, using the CAST operation, and that we stick to the unambiguous ISO style dates.

The second function, now(), simply gives us the current date and time, which would be handy if, for example, we were adding a new row for an order being placed whilst the customer was on the phone, or in 'real time' over the net. We could simply use now() as an easy way of getting at the current date:

```
bpsimple=# SELECT now();
          now
-----------------------
 2001-02-03 17:06:20+00
(1 row)

bpsimple=#
```

We can also do simple calculations using dates. For example, to discover the number of days between an order being placed and shipped, we could use a query like this:

```
bpsimple=# SELECT date_shipped - date_placed FROM orderinfo;
 ?column?
---------
        4
        1
       10
        7
        3
(5 rows)

bpsimple=#
```

This returns the number of days between the two dates stored in the database.

# Multiple Tables

By now you should have a good idea of how we can select data from a table, picking which columns we want, which rows we want, and how to control the order of the data. We have also seen how to handle the rather special date formats.

It's now time to move on to one of the most important features of SQL and indeed relational databases, relating data in one table to data in another table automatically. The good news is that it's all done with the SELECT statement, and all the good stuff you have learned so far about SELECT is just as true with many tables as it was with a single table.

## Relating Two Tables

Before we look at the SQL for using many tables at the same time, let's have a quick recap on the material we saw in Chapter 2 about relating tables.

You will remember that we have a `customer` table, which stores details of our customers, and an `orderinfo` table, which stores details of the orders they have placed. This allowed us to store details of each customer only once, no matter how many orders they placed. We linked the two tables together by having a common piece of data, the `customer_id`, stored in both tables.

If we think about this as a picture, we could imagine a row in the `customer` table, which has a `customer_id`, being related to none, one or many rows in the `orderinfo` table, where the same `customer_id` value appears:

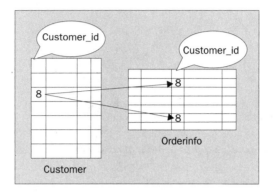

We could say that the value 8 for `customer_id` in the row in the `customer` table, relates to two rows in the `orderinfo` table, where the column `customer_id` also appears. Of course, we didn't have to have the two columns with the same name, but given that they both store the customer's ID, it would have been very confusing to give them different names.

Suppose we wanted to find all the orders that had been placed by our customer Ann Stones. Logically, what we do is look first, in our `customer` table to find this customer:

```
bpsimple=# SELECT customer_id FROM customer WHERE fname = 'Ann' AND lname =
bpsimple-# 'Stones';
customer_id
-------------
          8
(1 row)

bpsimple=#
```

Now that we know the `customer_id`, we can check for orders from this customer:

```
bpsimple=# SELECT * FROM orderinfo WHERE customer_id = 8;
 orderinfo_id | customer_id | date_placed | date_shipped | shipping
--------------+-------------+-------------+--------------+----------
            2 |           8 | 2000-06-23  | 2000-06-24   |     0.00
            5 |           8 | 2000-07-21  | 2000-07-24   |     0.00
(2 rows)

bpsimple=#
```

This has worked, but took us two steps, and we had to remember the `customer_id` between steps. If you think back to Chapter 2, we told you that SQL is a declarative language; that is you tell SQL what you want to achieve, rather than explicitly defining the steps of how to get to the solution. What we have just done is to use SQL in a procedural way. We have specified two discrete steps to get to our answer, the orders placed by a single customer. Wouldn't it be more elegant to do it all in a single step?

Indeed, in SQL we can do this all in a single step, by specifying that we want to know the orders placed by 'Ann Stones' and knowing that the information is in the `customer` table and `orderinfo` table, which are related by the column `customer_id` that appears in both tables.

The new bit of SQL syntax we need to do this, is an extension to the `WHERE` clause:

```
SELECT <column list> FROM <table list> WHERE <join condition> AND <row selection
conditions>
```

That looks a little complex, but actually it's quite easy. Just to make our first example a little easier, let's assume we know the customer ID is 8, and just fetch the order date(s) and customer first name(s).

We need to specify the columns we want, the customer first name and date the order was placed, that the two tables are related by `customer_id` column, and we only want rows where the `customer_id` is 8.

You will immediately realize we have a slight problem. How do we tell SQL which `customer_id` we want to use, the one in the `customer` table or the one in the `orderinfo` table? Although we are about to check that they are equal, in general this might not be the case, so how do we handle columns whose name appears in more than one table? We simply specify the column name using the extended syntax:

```
tablename.columnname
```

We can then unambiguously describe every column in our database. In general, PostgreSQL is quite forgiving, and if a column name only appears in one table in the `SELECT` statement, we don't have to explicitly use the table name as well. In this case, we will use `customer.fname`, even though `fname` would have been sufficient, because it's a little easier to read, especially when you are learning SQL. The first part of our statement, therefore, needs to be:

```
SELECT customer.fname, orderinfo.date_placed FROM customer, orderinfo;
```

That tells PostgreSQL the columns and tables we wish to use.

Now we need to specify our conditions. We have two different conditions, that the `customer_id` is 8, and that the two tables are related, or joined, using `customer_id`. Just like we saw earlier with multiple conditions, we do this by using the keyword `AND` to specify multiple conditions that must all be `TRUE`:

```
WHERE customer.customer_id = 8 AND customer.customer_id = orderinfo.customer_id;
```

Notice that we have to tell SQL a specific `customer_id` column, using `tablename.columnname` syntax, even though in practice, it would not matter which of the two tables' `customer_id` column was checked against 8, since we also specify that they must have the same value.

Putting it all together, the statement we need is:

```
bpsimple=# SELECT customer.fname, orderinfo.date_placed FROM customer, bpsimple-#
orderinfo WHERE customer.customer_id = 8 AND customer.customer_id  bpsimple-#
=orderinfo.customer_id;
 fname | date_placed
-------+-------------
 Ann   | 06/23/2000
 Ann   | 07/21/2000
(2 rows)

bpsimple=#
```

Much more elegant than multiple steps, isn't it? Perhaps more importantly, by specifying the entire problem in a single statement, we allow PostgreSQL to fully optimize the way the data is retrieved.

Now we know the principle, let's try our original question, to find all the orders placed by Ann Stones, assuming we don't know the `customer_id`.

## Try it Out – Relating Tables

We now only know a name, rather than a customer ID therefore, our SQL is slightly more complex. We have to specify the customer by name, and PostgreSQL responds:

```
bpsimple=# SELECT customer.fname, orderinfo.date_placed FROM customer, bpsimple-#
orderinfo WHERE customer.fname = 'Ann' AND customer.lname = bpsimple-# 'Stones'
AND customer.customer_id = orderinfo.customer_id;
 fname | date_placed
-------+-------------
 Ann   | 2000-06-23
 Ann   | 2000-07-21
(2 rows)

bpsimple=#
```

### How it Works

Just like we saw in our earlier example, we specify the columns we want, (`customer.fname`, `orderinfo.date_placed`), the tables involved (`customer, orderinfo`), the selection conditions (`customer.fname = 'Ann' AND customer.lname = 'Stones'`), and how the two tables are related (`customer.customer_id = orderinfo.customer_id`).

SQL solves the rest for us. You should also notice that it doesn't matter if the customer has placed no orders, one order or many orders as in the example, SQL is perfectly happy to execute the SQL query, provided it's valid, even if there are no rows that match the condition.

Let's now look at a different example. Suppose we want to list all the products we have, with their barcodes. You will remember that barcodes are held in the `barcode` table, and items in the `item` table. The two tables are related by having an `item_id` column in each table. You may also remember that the reason we split this out into two tables is that many products, or items, actually have multiple barcodes.

Using our newly found expertise in joining tables, we know that we need to specify the columns we want, the tables, and how they are related, or joined together. Being confident, we also decide to order the result by the cost price of the item.

We type in the statement and PostgreSQL responds as:

```
bpsimple=#  SELECT  description,  cost_price,  barcode_ean  FROM  item,  barcode
bpsimple-# WHERE barcode.item_id = item.item_id ORDER BY cost_price;
 description   | cost_price |  barcode_ean
---------------+------------+---------------
 Toothbrush    |       0.75 | 6241234586487
 Toothbrush    |       0.75 | 9473625532534
 Toothbrush    |       0.75 | 9473627464543
 Linux CD      |       1.99 | 6264537836173
 Linux CD      |       1.99 | 6241527746363
 Tissues       |       2.11 | 7465743843764
 Roman Coin    |       2.34 | 4587263646878
 Rubic Cube    |       7.45 | 6241574635234
 Picture Frame |       7.54 | 3453458677628
 Fan Small     |       9.23 | 6434564564544
 Fan Large     |      13.36 | 8476736836876
 Wood Puzzle   |      15.23 | 6241527836173
 Speakers      |      19.73 | 9879879837489
 Speakers      |      19.73 | 2239872376872
(14 rows)

bpsimple=#
```

This looks reasonable, except several items seem to appear more than once, and we don't remember stocking two different speakers. Also, we don't remember stocking that many items.

What's going on here?

Let's count the number of items we stock, using our newfound SQL skills:

```
bpsimple=# SELECT * FROM item;
```

PostgreSQL responds with the data, showing 11 rows.

We only stock 11 items, but our earlier query found 14 rows. Did we make a mistake?
No, all that's happened is that for some items, such as Toothbrush, there are many different barcodes against a single product. What happened was that PostgreSQL simply repeated the information from the item table against each barcode, so that it listed all the barcodes, and the item each one belonged to.

You can check this out by also selecting the item ID, by adding it to the SELECT statement, like this:

```
bpsimple=#  SELECT  item.item_id,  description,  cost_price,  barcode_ean  FROM
bpsimple-# item, barcode WHERE barcode.item_id = item.item_id ORDER BY bpsimple-#
cost_price;
 item_id |  description  | cost_price |  barcode_ean
---------+---------------+------------+---------------
   8 | Toothbrush    |    0.75 | 6241234586487
   8 | Toothbrush    |    0.75 | 9473625532534
   8 | Toothbrush    |    0.75 | 9473627464543
   3 | Linux CD      |    1.99 | 6264537836173
   3 | Linux CD      |    1.99 | 6241527746363
   4 | Tissues       |    2.11 | 7465743843764
   9 | Roman Coin    |    2.34 | 4587263646878
   2 | Rubic Cube    |    7.45 | 6241574635234
   5 | Picture Frame |    7.54 | 3453458677628
   6 | Fan Small     |    9.23 | 6434564564544
   7 | Fan Large     |   13.36 | 8476736836876
   1 | Wood Puzzle   |   15.23 | 6241527836173
  11 | Speakers      |   19.73 | 9879879837489
  11 | Speakers      |   19.73 | 2239872376872
(14 rows)

bpsimple=#
```

Notice that we have specified precisely which table, item_id comes from, since it appears in the item table as well as the barcode table.

It is now clear what exactly is going on. If the data you get returned from a SELECT statement looks a little odd, it's often a good idea to add all the 'id' type columns to the SELECT statement, just to see what was happening.

# Aliasing Table Names

You will remember, earlier in the chapter, we saw how we could change column names in the output using AS to give more descriptive names. It's also possible to alias table names, if you wish. This is handy in a few special cases, where you need two names for the same table, but more frequently it is used to save on typing. You will also see it used frequently in GUI tools, where it makes SQL generation a little easier.

To alias a table name, you simply put the alias name immediately after the table name in the FROM part of the SQL clause. Once you have done this, you can use the alias name, rather than the real table name in the rest of the SQL statement.

It's easier to show how this works than to describe it. Suppose we had a simple SQL statement:

```
SELECT lname FROM customer;
```

As we saw earlier, you can always explicitly name the column by preceding it with the table name, like this:

```
SELECT customer.lname FROM customer;
```

If we alias the `customer` table to `cu`, we could instead prefix the column `cu` like this:

```
SELECT cu.lname FROM customer cu;
```

Notice that we have added a `cu` after the table name, as well as prefixing the column with `cu`.

Now with a single table aliasing table names is not very interesting. With multiple tables, it can start to be a bit more useful.

If we look back at our earlier query:

```
SELECT customer.fname, orderinfo.date_placed FROM customer, orderinfo WHERE
customer.fname = 'Ann' AND customer.lname = 'Stones' AND customer.customer_id =
orderinfo.customer_id;
```

With aliases for table names, we could write this as:

```
SELECT c.fname, o.date_placed FROM customer c, orderinfo o WHERE c.fname = 'Ann'
AND c.lname = 'Stones' AND c.customer_id = o.customer_id;
```

# Relating Three Tables

Now that we know how to relate two tables together, can we extend the idea to three or even more tables? Of course, we can. SQL is a very logical language, so if we can do something with N items, we can almost always do it with N+1 items. Of course the more tables you include, the more work PostgreSQL has to do, so queries with many tables can be rather slow, if many of the tables are quite large.

Suppose we wanted to relate `customer` to actual item IDs ordered?

If you look back to our schema you will see we need to use three tables to get from customer to the actual ordered items. We need `customer`, `orderinfo`, and `orderline`:

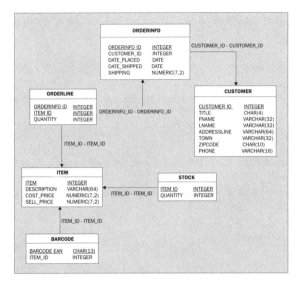

If we redraw our earlier diagram with three tables, it would look like this:

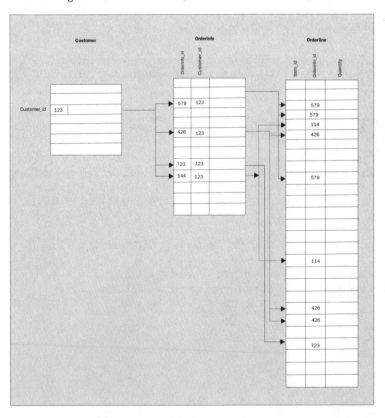

Here we can see that customer '123' matches several rows in the orderinfo table, those with orderinfo id's of '579', '426', '723', and '114', and each of these in turn relates to one or more rows in the orderline table.

Notice that there is no direct relationship between `customer` and `orderline`. We must use the `orderinfo` table, since that contains the information that binds the customer to their order.

## Try it Out – A Three Table Join

Let's build ourselves a three-table join to discover what `item_ids` the orders from Ann Stones actually comprised.

We start with the columns we need:

```
SELECT    customer.fname,    customer.lname,    orderinfo.date_placed,
orderline.item_id, orderline.quantity
```

Then we list the tables involved:

```
FROM customer, orderinfo, orderline
```

Then we specify how the `customer` and `orderinfo` tables are releated:

```
WHERE customer.customer_id = orderinfo.customer_id
```

We must also specify how the `orderinfo` and `orderline` tables are related:

```
orderinfo.orderinfo_id = orderline.orderinfo_id
```

Now our conditions:

```
customer.fname = 'Ann' AND customer.lname = 'Stones';
```

Putting them all together, we get:

```
bpsimple=# SELECT customer.fname, customer.lname,
orderinfo.date_placed, bpsimple-# orderline.item_id,orderline.quantity
bpsimple-# FROM customer, orderinfo, orderline
bpsimple-# WHERE
bpsimple-# customer.customer_id = orderinfo.customer_id AND
bpsimple-# orderinfo.orderinfo_id = orderline.orderinfo_id AND
bpsimple-# customer.fname = 'Ann' AND
bpsimple-# customer.lname = 'Stones';
 fname | lname  | date_placed | item_id | quantity
-------+--------+-------------+---------+----------
 Ann   | Stones | 2000-06-23  |       1 |        1
 Ann   | Stones | 2000-06-23  |       4 |        2
 Ann   | Stones | 2000-06-23  |       7 |        2
 Ann   | Stones | 2000-06-23  |      10 |        1
 Ann   | Stones | 2000-07-21  |       1 |        1
 Ann   | Stones | 2000-07-21  |       3 |        1
(6 rows)

bpsimple =#
```

Notice that whitespace outside strings is not significant to SQL, so we add extra spaces and line breaks to make the SQL easier to read. The `psql` program just waits till it sees a `;`, before it tries to interpret what we have been typing.

## Try it Out – A Four Table Join

Having seen how easy it is to go from two tables to three tables, let's take our query a step further, and list all the items by description that our customer Ann Stones has ordered. To do this we need to use an extra table, the `item` table, to get at the item description. The rest of the query however, is pretty much as before:

```
bpsimple=# SELECT customer.fname, customer.lname, orderinfo.date_placed,
bpsimple-# item.description, quantity
bpsimple-# FROM customer, orderinfo, orderline, item
bpsimple-# WHERE
bpsimple-# customer.customer_id = orderinfo.customer_id AND
bpsimple-# orderinfo.orderinfo_id = orderline.orderinfo_id AND
bpsimple-# orderline.item_id = item.item_id AND
bpsimple-# customer.fname = 'Ann' AND
bpsimple-# customer.lname = 'Stones';
 fname | lname  | date_placed | description | quantity
-------+--------+-------------+-------------+----------
 Ann   | Stones | 2000-06-23  | Wood Puzzle |        1
 Ann   | Stones | 2000-07-21  | Wood Puzzle |        1
 Ann   | Stones | 2000-07-21  | Linux CD    |        1
 Ann   | Stones | 2000-06-23  | Tissues     |        2
 Ann   | Stones | 2000-06-23  | Fan Large   |        2
 Ann   | Stones | 2000-06-23  | Carrier Bag |        1
(6 rows)

bpsimple= #
```

### How It Works

Once you have seen how three table joins work, it's not difficult to extend the idea to more tables. We added the item description to the list of columns to be shown, added the `item` table to the list of tables to select from, and added the information about how to relate the `item` table to the tables we already had, `orderline.item_id = item.item_id`.

You will see that Wood Puzzle is listed twice, since it was purchased on two different occasions.

In this SELECT, we have actually displayed at least one column from each of the tables we used in our join. There is actually no need to do this; if we had just wanted the customer name and item description, we could have simply chosen not to retrieve the columns we didn't need.

A version retrieving fewer columns is just as valid, and may be marginally more efficient than our earlier attempt:

```
SELECT customer.fname, customer.lname, item.description
FROM customer, orderinfo, orderline, item
WHERE
    customer.customer_id = orderinfo.customer_id AND
    orderinfo.orderinfo_id = orderline.orderinfo_id AND
    orderline.item_id = item.item_id AND
    customer.fname = 'Ann' AND
    customer.lname = 'Stones';
```

For our final example of SQL in this chapter, let's go back to something we learnt early in the chapter: how to remove duplicate information using the DISTINCT keyword.

## Try it Out – Adding Extra Conditions

Suppose we had wanted to discover what type of items Ann Stones bought. All we want listed is the description of items purchased, ordered by the description. We don't even want to list the customer name, since we know that already (we are using it to select the data). We only need to select the item.description, and we also need to use the DISTINCT option, to ensure that Wood Puzzle is only listed the once, even though it was bought several times:

```
bpsimple=# SELECT DISTINCT  item.description
bpsimple-# FROM customer, orderinfo, orderline, item
bpsimple-# WHERE
bpsimple-# customer.customer_id = orderinfo.customer_id AND
bpsimple-# orderinfo.orderinfo_id = orderline.orderinfo_id AND
bpsimple-# orderline.item_id = item.item_id AND
bpsimple-# customer.fname = 'Ann' AND
bpsimple-# customer.lname = 'Stones'
bpsimple-# ORDER BY item.description;
description
-------------
Carrier Bag
Fan Large
Linux CD
Tissues
Wood Puzzle
(5 rows)

bpsimple=#
```

### How it Works

We simply take our earlier SQL, remove the columns we no longer need, add the DISTINCT keyword after SELECT to ensure each row only appears once, and add our ORDER BY condition after the WHERE clause.

That's one of the great things about SQL: once you have learnt a feature, you can apply it in a general way. The ORDER BY for example, works with many tables in just the same way it works with a single table.

# Summary

This has been a pretty long chapter, but we have learned quite a lot.

We have covered the SELECT statement in some detail, discovering how to choose columns and rows, how to order the output, and how to suppress duplicate information. We also learnt a bit about the data type, and how to configure PostgreSQL's behavior in interpreting and displaying dates, as well has how we could use dates in condition statements.

We then moved on to the heart of SQL, the ability to relate tables together. After our first bit of SQL that joined a pair of tables we saw how easy it was to extend this to three, and even four, tables. We finished off by reusing some of the knowledge we gained early in the chapter to refine our four-table selection to home in on displaying exactly the information we were searching for, and removing all the extra columns and duplicate rows.

The good news is that we have now seen all the everyday features of the SELECT statement, and once you understand the SELECT statement, much of the rest of SQL is reasonably straightforward. We will be coming back to the SELECT statement in Chapter 7 to look at some more advanced features that you will need from time to time, but you will find that much of SQL you need to use in the real world has been covered in this chapter.

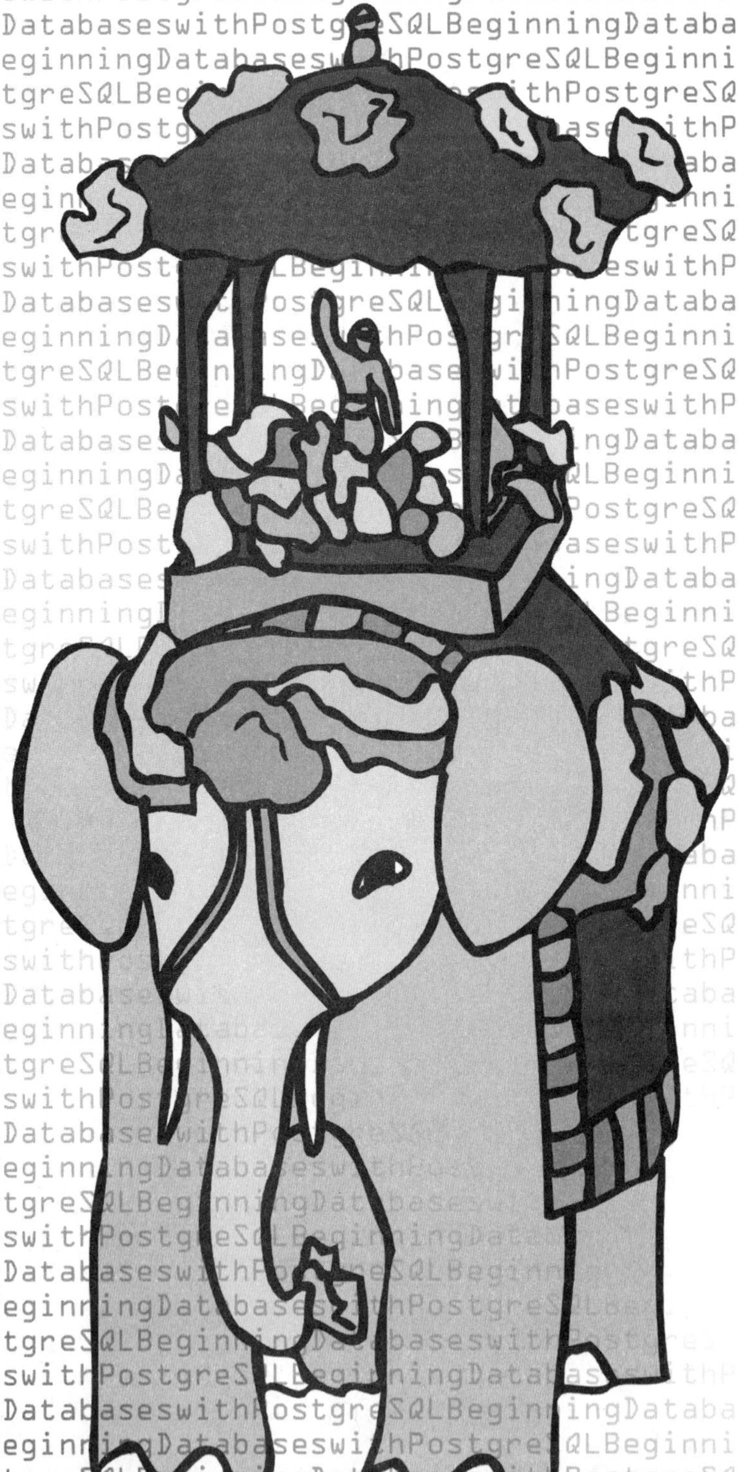

# PostgreSQL Graphical Tools

A PostgreSQL database is generally created and administered with the command line tool, psql, which we have used in earlier chapters to get started. Command line tools, similar to psql, are common with commercial databases. Oracle has one such tool called SQL*PLUS, for example. While command line tools are generally complete, in the sense that they contain ways to perform all the functions that you need, they can be a little unfriendly. On the other hand, they make no great demands in terms of graphics cards, memory and so on.

In this chapter, we will take a look at some of the alternatives to psql for accessing PostgreSQL databases. Some of the tools can also be used for administering databases. A special user with responsibility for managing the database performs administration tasks, such as creating new users, setting permissions, and optimizing the database. We will cover administration of PostgreSQL in Chapter 11. Here we will concentrate on functions that general users can perform.

We will start with a brief summary of the commands available in psql, and as the chapter progresses, we'll look at:

- psql
- ODBC
- pgAdmin
- Kpsql
- PgAccess
- Microsoft Access
- Microsoft Excel

## psql

The psql tool allows us to connect to a database, execute queries, and administer a database, including creating a database, adding new tables and entering or updating data, using SQL commands.

# Starting psql

The command syntax for psql is:

```
psql [options] [dbname [username]]
```

As we have already seen, we start psql by specifying the database we wish to connect to. We need to know the host name of the server, and the port number the database is listening on, plus a valid user name and password to use for the connection. The default database will be one on the local machine with the same name as the current user login name.

To connect to a named database on a server, we invoke psql with a database name like this:

```
$ psql -d bpsimple
```

Defaults for the database name, user name, server host name and listening port may be overridden by setting the environment variables PGDATABASE, PGUSER, PGHOST, and PGPORT respectively.

These defaults may also be overridden by using the -d, -U, -h, and -p command line options to psql.

> We can only run **psql** by connecting to a database. This gives a "chicken and egg" problem for creating our first database. We need a user account and a database to connect to. We created a default user, **postgres**, when we installed PostgreSQL in Chapter 3, so we can use that to connect to create new users and databases. To create a database we connect to a default database, included with all PostgreSQL installations, **template1**. Once connected to **template1** we can create a database, and then either quit and restart **psql** or use the \c internal **psql** command to reconnect to the new database.

The complete list of options to psql can be seen if we invoke psql with:

```
$ psql --help
```

# Commands in psql

When psql starts up, it will read a startup file, .psqlrc, if one exists and is readable in the current user's home directory. This file is similar to a shell script startup file and may contain psql commands to set the desired behavior, such as setting the format options for printing tables and so on. We can prevent the startup file being read by starting psql with the -X option.

Once running, psql will prompt for commands with a prompt that consists of the name of the database we are connected to, followed by =#. In some cases it is =>. Commands are of two different types, SQL and internal. We can issue any SQL statement that PostgreSQL supports to psql and it will execute it for us.

> You can ask for a list of all supported SQL commands by executing the internal command \h and help on a specific command with \h <sql command>. The internal command \? gives a list of all internal commands.

Commands to `psql` may be spread over multiple lines, and when this occurs, `psql` will change its prompt to `-#` or `->` to indicate that more input is expected:

```
$ psql -d bpsimple
...
bpsimple=#SELECT *
bpsimple-#FROM customer
bpsimple-#;
...
$
```

To tell `psql` that we have completed a long SQL command that might spread across multiple lines, we have to end the command with a semi-colon. Note that the semi-colon is not a required part of the SQL command, but is just there to help `psql` decide when we are finished. In the case above, we may have wanted to add a WHERE clause on the next line, for example.

We can tell `psql` that we will never split our commands over more than one line by starting `psql` with the `-S` option, in which case we do not need to add the semi-colon to the end of our commands. The `psql` prompt will change to `^>` to remind us that we are in single line mode.

Internal `psql` commands are used to perform operations not directly supported in SQL, such as listing the available tables and executing scripts. All internal commands begin with a backslash and cannot be split over multiple lines.

# Command History

Each command that you ask `psql` to execute is recorded in a history, and you can recall previous commands to run again or edit. Use the arrow keys to scroll through the command history and edit. This feature is available unless you have turned it off with the `-n` command line option (or it has not been compiled-in for your platform). The query history can be shown with the `\s` command or saved to a file with `\s <file>`.

The last query executed is kept in a query buffer. You can see what is in the query buffer with `\p` and you can clear it with `\r`. You can edit the query buffer contents with an external editor with `\e`. The editor will default to `vi` (on Linux and UNIX at least), but you can specify your own favorite editor by setting the EDITOR environment variable before starting `psql`.

# Scripting psql

We can collect a group of `psql` commands (both SQL and internal) in a file and use it as a simple script. The `\i` internal command will read a set of `psql` commands from a file.

This feature is especially useful for creating and populating tables. We used it earlier to create our sample database, `bpsimple`. Here is part of the `create_tables` script file that we used:

```
create table customer
(
    customer_id             serial                  ,
    title                   char(4)                 ,
    fname                   varchar(32)             ,
```

**119**

```
        lname               varchar(32)            not null,
        addressline         varchar(64)                   ,
        town                varchar(64)                   ,
        zipcode             char(10)               not null,
        phone               varchar(16)                   ,
        CONSTRAINT          customer_pk PRIMARY KEY(customer_id)
);

create table item
(
        item_id             serial                        ,
        description         varchar(64)            not null,
        cost_price          numeric(7,2)                  ,
        sell_price          numeric(7,2)                  ,
        CONSTRAINT          item_pk PRIMARY KEY(item_id)
);
```

We give script files a .sql extension by convention, and execute them with the \i internal command:

```
bpsimple=#\i create_tables.sql
CREATE TABLE
CREATE TABLE
...
bpsimple=#
```

Another use of script files is for simple reports. If we want to keep an eye on the growth of our database, we could put a few commands in a script file and arrange to run it every once in a while. To report the number of customers and orders taken, make a script file called report.sql that simply contains the following lines and execute it in a psql session:

```
select count(*) from customer;
select count(*) from orderinfo;
```

Alternatively, we can use the -f command line option to get psql to execute the file and then exit:

```
$ psql -f report.sql bpsimple
  count
--------
     15
(1 row)

  count
--------
      5
(1 row)
$
```

We can redirect query output to a file by using either the -o command line option, or to a file or filter program with the \o internal command from within a session.

# Examining the Database

We can explore the structure of our database using a number of internal `psql` commands.

The `\d` command will list all of the relations (that is, tables, sequences, and views, if any) in our database. `\dt` will restrict the listing to tables only.

We can get a detailed description of a particular table with `\d tablename`:

```
bpsimple=# \d customer
                    Table "customer"
   Attribute  |          Type          |         Modifier
-------------+------------------------+---------------------------------
 customer_id | integer                | not null default nextval(...)
 title       | character(4)           |
 fname       | character varying(32)  |
 lname       | character varying(32)  | not null
 addressline | character varying(64)  |
 town        | character varying(32)  |
 zipcode     | character(10)          | not null
 phone       | character varying(16)  |
 Index: customer_pk

bpsimple=#
```

Check out the reference tables below for more information on internal `psql` commands, or refer to the PostgreSQL online documentation.

# Command Line Quick Reference

The `psql` command line options and their meanings are reproduced in the table below:

| Option | Meaning |
|---|---|
| -a | Echo all input from script. |
| -A | Unaligned table output mode (same as -P format=unaligned). |
| -c <query> | Run only single query (or slash command) and exit. |
| -d <dbname> | Specify database name to connect to (default: $PGDATABASE or current login name). |
| -e | Echo queries sent to backend. |
| -E | Display queries that internal commands generate. |
| -f <filename> | Execute queries from file, then exit. |
| -F <string> | Set field separator (default: "\|") (same as -P fieldsep=<string>). |

*Table continued on following page*

| Option | Meaning |
|---|---|
| -h \<host\> | Specify database server host (default: $PGHOST or local machine). |
| -H | HTML table output mode (same as -P format=html). |
| -l | List available databases, then exit. |
| -n | Disable readline, prevents line editing. |
| -o \<filename\> | Send query output to filename. Use the form \|pipe to send output to a filter program. |
| -p \<port\> | Specify database server port (default: $PGPORT or compiled-in default – usually 5432). |
| -P var[=arg] | Set printing option var to arg (see \pset command). |
| -q | Run quietly (no messages, only query output). |
| -R \<string\> | Set record separator (default: newline) (same as -P recordsep=\<string\>). |
| -s | Single step mode (confirm each query). |
| -S | Single line mode (newline terminates query rather than semi-colon). |
| -t | Print rows only (same as -P tuples_only). |
| -T \<text\> | Set HTML table tag options (width, border) (same as -P tableattr=\<text\>). |
| -U \<username\> | Specify database username (default: $PGUSER or current login). |
| -v name=val | Set psql variable name to value. |
| -V | Show version information and exit. |
| -W | Prompt for password (should happen automatically, if a password is required). |
| -x | Turn on expanded table output (same as -P expanded). |
| -X | Do not read startup file (~/.psqlrc). |

# Internal Commands Quick Reference

The supported internal `psql` commands are reproduced in the table below:

| Command | Meaning |
|---------|---------|
| `\a` | Toggle between unaligned and aligned mode. |
| `\c[onnect] [dbname|-[user]]` | Connect to new database. Use – as the database name to connect to the default database if you need to give a user name. |
| `\C <title>` | Set table title for output (same as `\pset title`). |
| `\copy ...` | Perform SQL COPY with data stream to the client machine. |
| `\copyright` | Show PostgreSQL usage and distribution terms. |
| `\d <table>` | Describe table (or view, index, sequence). |
| `\d{t|i|s|v}` | List tables/indices/sequences/views. |
| `\d{p|S|l}` | List permissions/system tables/lobjects. |
| `\da` | List aggregates. |
| `\dd [object]` | List comment for table, type, function, or operator. |
| `\df` | List functions. |
| `\do` | List operators. |
| `\dT` | List data types. |
| `\e [file]` | Edit the current query buffer or `file` with external editor. |
| `\echo <text>` | Write text to stdout. |
| `\encoding <encoding>` | Set client encoding. |
| `\f <sep>` | Change field separator. |
| `\g [file]` | Send query to backend (and results in `file` or `|pipe`). |
| `\h [cmd]` | Help on syntax of SQL commands, * for detail on all commands. |
| `\H` | Toggle HTML mode. |
| `\i <file>` | Read and execute queries from file. |
| `\l` | List all databases. |
| `\lo_export, \lo_import, \lo_list, \lo_unlink` | Large object operations. |
| `\o [file]` | Send all query results to `file`, or `|pipe`. |

*Table continued on following page*

| Command | Meaning |
| --- | --- |
| \p | Show the content of the current query buffer. |
| \pset <opt> | Set table output opt, which can be one of: format, border, expanded, fieldsep, null, recordsep, tuples_only, title, tableattr, pager. |
| \q | Quit psql. |
| \qecho <text> | Write text to query output stream (see \o). |
| \r | Reset (clear) the query buffer. |
| \s [file] | Print history or save it in [file]. |
| \set <var> <value> | Set internal variable. |
| \t | Show only rows (toggles between modes). |
| \T <tags> | HTML table tags. |
| \unset <var> | Unset (delete) internal variable. |
| \w <file> | Write current query buffer to a <file>. |
| \x | Toggle expanded output. |
| \z | List table access permissions. |
| \! [cmd] | Shell escape or command. |

# ODBC

Several of the tools in this chapter use the ODBC standard interface to connect to PostgreSQL. ODBC defines a common interface for databases and is based on X/Open and ISO/IEC programming interfaces. In fact, ODBC stands for Open DataBase Connectivity and is not (as is often believed) limited to Microsoft Windows clients. To use ODBC on a particular client machine, we need both an application written for the ODBC interface and a driver for the particular database that we want to use.

PostgreSQL ships with an ODBC driver called psqlodbc as part of the sourcecode distribution, which you can compile and install for your clients if you wish. Normally our clients will be running on different machines, and possibly even a different architecture. So we will have to compile the ODBC driver on the client platform too. For example, we might have the database server on UNIX or Linux and our client applications running on Windows.

Happily, if we are using Microsoft Windows as our client, we can find a pre-compiled ODBC driver at the Great Bridge site.

The files we need are:

❑ psqlodbc-registry.zip

❑ psqlodbc-07_01_0003.zip

Both of these files, or later versions, can be found at http://www.greatbridge.org/project/pgadmin

On Microsoft Windows, ODBC drivers are made available through the Control Panel applet:

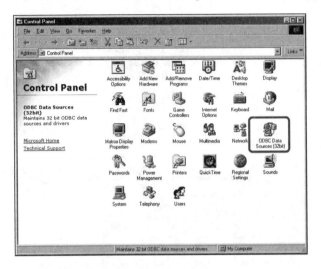

Selecting this applet shows us the installed ODBC drivers:

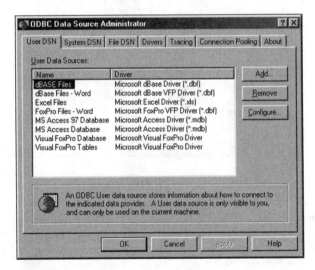

To install the PostgreSQL ODBC driver, we have to perform two steps. Firstly, we must copy the driver executable (in the form of a Windows DLL file) into the correct place. Secondly, we must register the ODBC driver, so that the ODBC applet knows that it is available to use.

The driver DLL file is called psqlodbc.dll and is contained in the `psqlodbc-07_01_0003.zip` file. It must be copied into the `SYSTEM` directory of the client machine's Windows installation, normally `C:\WINDOWS\SYSTEM` for Windows 9x/ME or `C:\WINNT\SYSTEM32` on Windows NT/2000.

We can register the driver DLL by creating appropriate registry settings ourselves, or we can execute the file `psqlodbc.reg` contained in `psqlodbc-registry.zip`. This will create the registry entries for us.

> **An earlier version of the ODBC driver for PostgreSQL was made available as part of a self-installing executable, `postdrv.exe`. This program performed both the installation and registration steps, but the version of the driver was not able to support versions of PostgreSQL later than 6.4. Check out the Great Bridge site for a more recent update if you would rather use a single executable.**

After we have performed these two steps, we can confirm that we have successfully installed the driver by selecting the Drivers tab in the ODBC applet and noting that PostgreSQL now appears in the list:

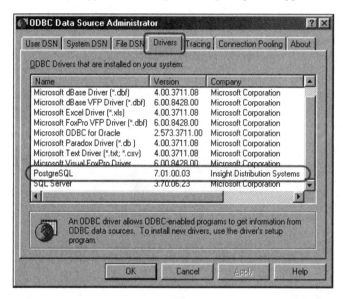

Now we will be able to use ODBC-aware applications to connect to our PostgreSQL databases. To make a specific database available, we have to create a data source. To do this select User DSN in the ODBC applet to create a data source that will be available to the current user. If you select System DSN you can create data sources that all users can see. Click on Add to begin the creation process this and will display a dialog box for selecting which driver the data source will use:

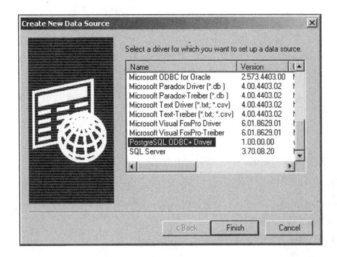

Click on Finish.

We now have a PostgreSQL driver entry that we need to configure. A Driver Setup box will appear for us to enter the details of this data source:

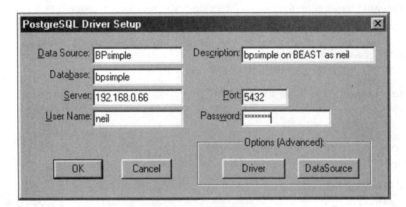

We give the Data Source a name, a Description and set the network configuration. Here we are using the IP address of a Linux server. If you are running a fully configured naming service such as DNS or WINS you can use a machine name for the server. We also specify the User Name and Password to be used at the server to access the database we have chosen.

Additional options are available under Driver and DataSource options. If you need to be able to update data in the PostgreSQL database using an ODBC application, be sure to uncheck the Read Only boxes in these options.

We are now ready to access our PostgreSQL database from ODBC applications. In this chapter we will look briefly at two such applications. Later we will see how we can use Microsoft Access to create PostgreSQL frontend applications, but first let's take a look at pgAdmin.

# pgAdmin

pgAdmin is a fully-featured graphical interface for PostgreSQL databases. It is free software maintained by Great Bridge and is released under the GNU General Public License (GPL).

According to the Great Bridge web site, "pgAdmin is a general purpose tool for designing, maintaining, and administering PostgreSQL databases. It runs under Windows 95/98/ME and NT/2000."

Features include:

❏ Arbitrary SQL entry with SQL Wizard

❏ Plug-in 'Exporter' modules allow exporting of the results of SQL queries

❏ Info Browsers and 'Creators' for databases, tables, indexes, sequences, views, triggers, functions, and languages

❏ User, Group and Privilege configuration dialog

❏ Revision tracking with upgrade script generation

❏ Data Import Wizard

❏ Database Migration Wizard

❏ Predefined reports on databases, tables, indexes, sequences, languages, and views

❏ User reports can be added (requires Seagate Crystal Reports)

We do not have the space in this chapter to cover all of the features of pgAdmin; we will instead concentrate on getting up and running with this versatile tool.

You will need to have installed the PostgreSQL ODBC driver psqlodbc on the client machine where you intend to install pgAdmin. See the *ODBC* section earlier in this chapter for details on how to do this.

Another pre-requisite for pgAdmin is the Microsoft Data Access Components 2.6 Runtime. We require version 2.6 or later of these components. These can be found as file mdac_type.exe from http://www.microsoft.com/data/download.htm.

A pre-compiled binary for pgAdmin can be downloaded from Great Bridge at http://www.greatbridge.org/project/pgadmin/. The file we need is pgadmin-7_1_0.zip or similar, depending on the currently released version.

If you are installing on Windows 9x or NT as opposed to Windows Me or 2000, you will also need the Microsoft Windows Installer (instmsia.exe for Windows 9x or instmsiw.exe for Windows NT) from http://msdn.Microsoft.com/downloads/ (search for "Windows Installer Re-distributable").

The installation steps for pgAdmin are therefore:

❏ Install the PostgreSQL OBDC driver psqlodbc

❏ Install MDAC 2.6 or later runtime, mdac_typ.exe

❏ Install Windows Installer if on Windows 9x or NT (instmsia.exe or instmsiw.exe)

❏ Unpack the pgAdmin zip file to extract pgAdmin.msi to a temporary directory

❏ Double-click on pgAdmin.msi to begin the installation

After installation, we should have a new program group (pgAdmin) on the Start Menu. Before we can use pgAdmin in earnest, we need to make sure that we can create objects in the database we want to maintain. This is because pgAdmin augments the database with objects of its own that are stored on the server.

First of all, we must ensure that we have enabled write access within the ODBC driver or the specific data sources we want to use. To do this, we must pay another visit to the ODBC Data Sources applet within the Control Panel.

Select the PostgreSQL Data Source and change the Driver options so that the default choice of ReadOnly access check box is cleared:

We could just change the Advanced Options for the data source:

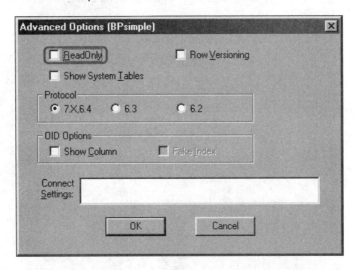

If you want to see the PostgreSQL internal tables, you can also check the Show System Tables check box.

Now we are ready to start pgAdmin and maintain our database. We are greeted with a **pgAdmin Logon** dialog box asking for the ODBC data source together with a user name and password:

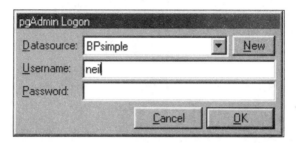

To perform all of the maintenance functions with pgAdmin, we need to logon as a user that has complete privileges for the database, a superuser in other words. If we choose a user without superuser status we will get an error:

We will be looking at users and permissions in Chapter 11. If your PostgreSQL installation was performed with the default setting, you should have a user postgres that is used to control the database and you can try to logon as that user.

Here is a screenshot of pgAdmin exploring the tables of the bpsimple database and examining the last name attribute of the customer table:

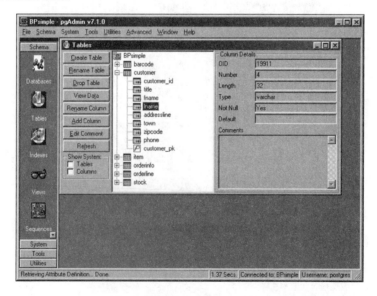

One feature of `pgAdmin` that will potentially be very useful is its data import functionality. If we have some data that we would like to import into a PostgreSQL table, `pgAdmin` can help.

One way of importing data is to arrange to make it available as a comma separated variable (CSV) file. Applications such as Microsoft Excel are able to export data in this format.

Here is a simple example. From an Excel spreadsheet we have saved some additional rows for the `numbers` table in the `test` database. The format we have saved them in is CSV with no headings. This means that there are no column names present in the first row, we only have the data. The file contains:

```
111,Nelson
0,Duck
22,Two Ducks
```

We start the **Table Import Wizard** by selecting **Tools | Import** from the `pgAdmin` menu:

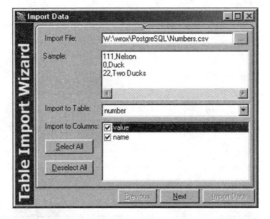

We select the **Import file** we want to import data from and which of the tables and columns to import into. We then have to set some options for the import, specifically whether the data is quoted and how columns are separated:

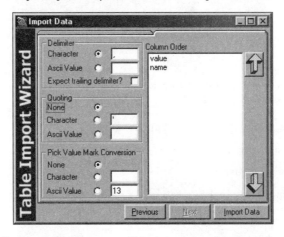

We can then click on **Import Data** and the new rows will be incorporated into our database table.

# Kpsql

A graphical alternative to psql on Linux is Kpsql from Mutiny Bay Software. Although no longer in active development, Kpsql is still quite useful. It is designed to run under the K Desktop Environment (KDE) and the current version (1.0) can be downloaded from http://www.mutinybaysoftware.com.

Kpsql is essentially an editor for SQL queries. You can create, save, and edit queries with a syntax highlighting editor that shows SQL keywords in different colors to help with creating valid queries. You can execute queries that you have created and see the results in a scrollable window.

It is a simple, but effective, tool if all you need to do is run a few simple reports. Here is a screenshot showing the result of a simple query:

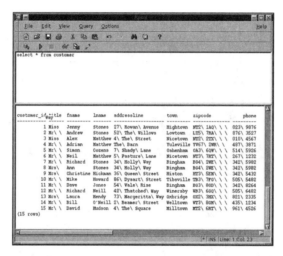

Kpsql ships with online help that describes the use of the query editor, and includes a reference for PostgreSQL SQL commands.

# PgAccess

The official distribution of PostgreSQL includes a graphical tool called PgAccess, an extremely useful tool for using with PostgreSQL databases. It can be used to:

❑   Browse tables, adding, deleting, and updating rows

❑   Create tables and alter the structure of existing tables

❑   Create and execute queries

❑   Use a visual query designer to create queries and save them as views

❑   Design, create, and execute data entry forms

❑   Create and modify user accounts

**132**

PgAccess is a Tcl/Tk program and requires `Tcl/Tk 8.0` or later to be installed on your client machine. It should run on any machine that meets this requirement, including both Linux and Microsoft Windows. In this chapter, we will look at a Linux installation, but Windows usage will be very similar.

PgAccess may not be installed by default. If you do not have it in your PostgreSQL installation, you can find it in the `src/bin` sub-directory of the sourcecode distribution. Alternatively, you can download the latest version from http://www.flex.ro/pgaccess.

Normally the only installation that is required is to copy the PgAccess files to a directory and edit the startup script, PgAccess, to set the variable `PATH_TO_WISH` to the location of the Tcl/Tk interpreter, `wish`, and `PGACCESS_HOME` to the directory where the PgAccess files can be found.

PgAccess is started with an optional database name as its only argument:

```
pgaccess [dbname]
```

With no database argument, PgAccess will attempt to open the last database it was connected to. This database name, the user identity used, and other configuration details are stored in the file `.pgaccessrc` in your home directory.

When connected to our sample database, the PgAccess main window will appear something like this:

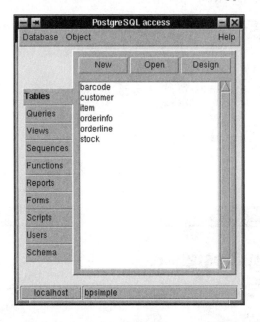

If you have used **pgAdmin** you will see additional tables in the database that are used by **pgAdmin** to store its server-side objects. Similarly if you use **PgAccess** to create forms you will see further tables.

The user interface for PgAccess is very straightforward with the functions made available as tabs along the left hand side of the main window and operations along the top. To browse the data in a table, we just highlight the table we want to look at and select **Open**:

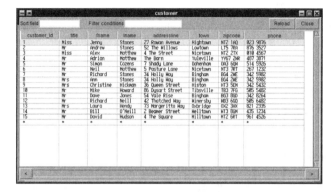

We can use this data window to make changes to the data, add new rows, and delete rows. To sort the data by a particular column, we simply enter the column name in the **Sort Field** box, and we can restrict the rows that are shown by entering a condition in the **Filter conditions** box. Here is the item table, sorted by description, but showing only those items that have a cost_price greater than $2:

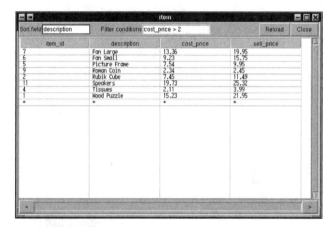

# Forms and Query Designers

Perhaps the two most interesting features of PgAccess are its abilities to create and store forms, and the visual query designer.

PgAccess forms can be created using a forms designer and stored in the database itself as Tcl/Tk code. They can then be executed from within PgAccess. Here is an example form taken from formdemo.sql, the forms demonstration code distributed with PgAccess. It shows many of the user interface components available:

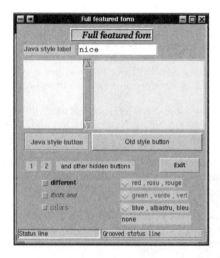

To make the most of PgAccess forms, you need to add Tcl code to perform actions when user interface widgets, the buttons and entry boxes, are activated.

The PgAccess visual query designer allows you to create a SQL query graphically. Although it does not support all query types it can be useful in getting started with a complex query. We can drag and drop attributes from one table to another to indicate relationships between tables that need to be satisfied in the query and we can add other criteria on columns. We can also view the equivalent SQL and execute it all, from the designer window.

In the next screenshot, we can see a query being developed that identifies customers from a certain town that have placed orders:

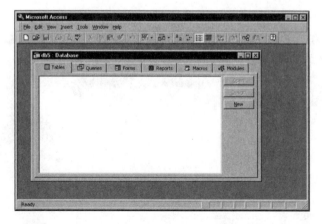

# Microsoft Access

Although it may seem an odd idea at first sight, we can use Microsoft Access with PostgreSQL. If Access is already a database system, why would we want to use PostgreSQL to store data? And, as PostgreSQL has PgAccess, why do we need to use Microsoft Access?

Firstly, when developing a database system, we need to consider the requirement for things such as data volumes, possibility of multiple concurrent users, security, robustness, and reliability. You may decide on PostgreSQL because it fits better with your security model, your server platforms, and your data growth predictions.

Secondly, although PostgreSQL running on a UNIX or Linux server may be the ideal environment for your data, it might not be the best, or most familiar, environment for your users and their applications.

There is a case for allowing users to use tools such as Access or other third-party applications to create reports or data entry forms for PostgreSQL databases. Since, PostgreSQL has an ODBC interface, this is not only possible but remarkably easy.

Here we will look at creating an Access database that uses data stored on a remote PostgreSQL server, and writing a simple report based on that data. We will be assuming that you are reasonably familiar with creating Access databases and applications.

Once you have established the link from Access to PostgreSQL you can use all of the features of Access to create easy-to-use PostgreSQL applications.

# Linked Tables

Access allows you to import a table into a database in a number of different ways? one of which is by means of a linked table. This is a table that is represented in Access as a query. The data is retrieved from another source as and when it is needed, rather than being copied into the database. This means that when the data changes in the external database the change is also reflected in Access.

Let's create a simple Access database to update and report on the products that we are selling on our example database system. In the `bpsimple` database we have a table called `item` that records a unique identifier for each product we sell, a description of that product together with a cost price and a selling price.

In Access, we create a new blank database:

In the Tables section of the tabbed dialog box, select New to create a new table, and choose the Link Table option:

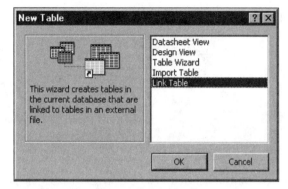

In the Link dialog box that appears, choose files of type ODBC Databases:

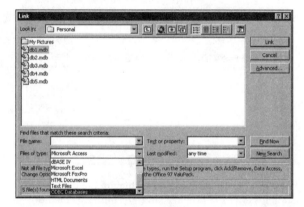

You should then see the ODBC data source selection dialog. Select Machine DSN and the appropriate PostgreSQL database connection:

Next, we have to provide the connection parameters, including a valid User Name and Password, for connecting to the database:

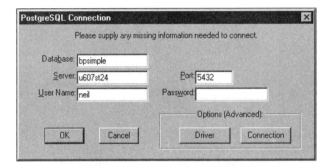

When the connection is made, we are presented with a list of available tables in the remote database. Click on item to link the item table into our Access database:

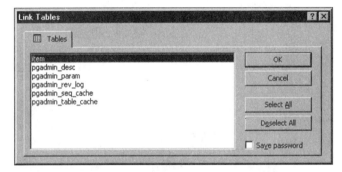

Before Access can finally link the table, it needs to know which of the fields it can use to uniquely identify each record. In other words, what fields form the primary key? For this table the item_id column is the primary key so we select that. For composite keys we can select more than one column:

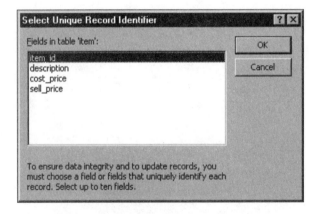

Now we will see that the Access database has a new table, also called item that we can browse just as if the data was held in Access:

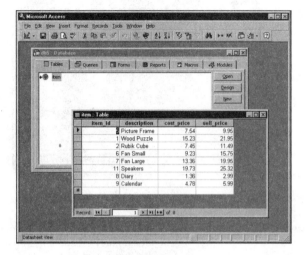

That's just about all there is to it.

> You might see slightly different screens to those shown here, depending on your version of Windows and Access. If you see an additional column in your table called oid, this is the internal PostgreSQL object identifier and can be ignored. To prevent the object_id column being shown, be sure to uncheck the OID column options in the ODBC data source configuration

# Data Entry

We can use the table browser in Access to examine data in the PostgreSQL table and to add more rows.

> Access may have some trouble mapping PostgreSQL data types such as NUMERIC(7,2) to its own floating point format, float8. This will affect our ability to modify and delete rows. If you plan to use Access with your PostgreSQL applications, you will need to consider using only simple types for your table columns.

Here's a screenshot of an Access data entry form being used to add further items to the item table. You can use the programming features of Access to create more sophisticated data entry applications that perform validation on entries, or prevent the modification of existing data:

# Reports

Reports are just as easy. Use the Access report designer to generate reports based on the data stored in PostgreSQL tables just as you would any other Access table. We can include derived columns in the report to answer questions about the data in the table. For example here is an Access report that shows the markup (that is, the difference between the sell_price and the cost_ price) that we are applying to the products in the item table:

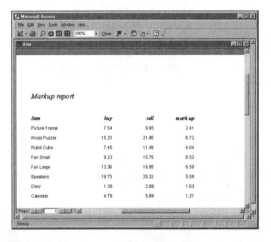

Combining Microsoft Access and PostgreSQL increases the number of options you have for creating database applications. The scalability and reliability of PostgreSQL with the familiarity and ease of use of Microsoft Access may be just what you need.

# Microsoft Excel

As with Microsoft Access, we can employ Microsoft Excel to add functionality to our PostgreSQL installation. The idea is much the same as with Access, we include data in our spreadsheets that is taken from (or rather, linked to) a remote data source. When the data changes, we can refresh the spreadsheet and have the spreadsheet reflect the new data.

Once we have made a spreadsheet based on PostgreSQL data, we can use Excel's features, such as charting, to create graphical representations of our data.

Let's extend our `product` table example from Access to make a chart showing the *markup* we have applied to our products in the `item` table.

In a similar way to Access, we have to tell Excel that some portion of a spreadsheet needs to be linked to an external database table. Starting from a blank spreadsheet, we choose the menu option to get external data with a new database query:

We are presented with a now familiar ODBC data source selection dialog:

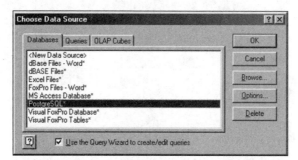

When the connection to the database is made, we can choose which table we want to use, and which columns we want to appear in the spreadsheet. Here we will select item identifier, the description, and both prices from the `item` table:

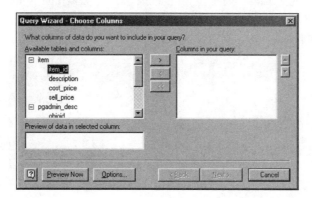

If we want to restrict the number of rows that appear in our spreadsheet we can do this by specifying selection criteria at the next dialog box. Here we select those products with a selling price greater than $2:

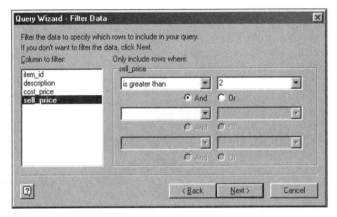

Finally, we can choose to have the data sorted by a particular column, or group of columns, in either sort direction:

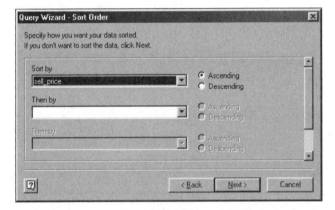

Before the data is returned to Excel, we get the chance to specify where in our spreadsheet we want the data to appear. It is probably a good idea to have data from a PostgreSQL table appear on a worksheet by itself. This is because we need to make sure that we cater for the number of rows increasing as the database grows. We will refresh the spreadsheet data and will need space for the data to expand into.

In this example, we simply allow the data to occupy the top left area of the sheet:

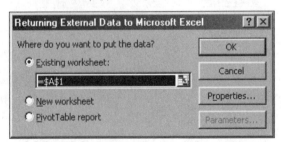

Now we can see the data present in our worksheet:

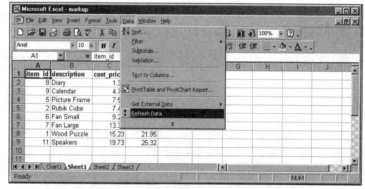

We can use this spreadsheet to perform calculations on the data if we want to. We could for example calculate the sales margin being earned from each product by setting up an additional column with an appropriate formula.

When the data changes in the database, Excel will not automatically update its version of the rows. To make sure that the data you are viewing in Excel is accurate, you must refresh the data. This is simply done by selecting Data | Refresh Data:

Now that we have data in our spreadsheet we can employ some of Excel's features to add value to our PostgreSQL application. In this example, we have added a chart showing the markup on each product. It is simply built by using the Excel Chart Wizard and selecting the PostgreSQL data area of the sheet as the source data for the chart:

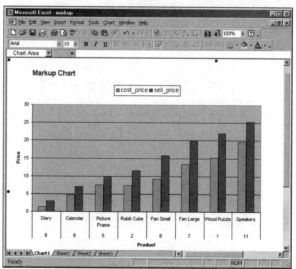

When the data in the PostgreSQL database changes and we refresh the spreadsheet the chart will automatically update.

> **Some versions of Excel may have display problems using Microsoft Query to connect to PostgreSQL databases. The examples in this chapter were created using Excel 2000 which performed satisfactorily.**

# Resources

A good place to start to look for tools to use with PostgreSQL is the Great Bridge site at http://www.greatbridge.org.

The Zeos database explorer program, available from http://www.zeos.dn.ua/eng/ is a more general-purpose database tool that has support for PostgreSQL.

A session monitor for PostgreSQL, called `pgmonitor`, is in development and can be found at http://www.greatbridge.org/project/pgmonitor/projdisplay.php. This is another Tcl/Tk program that allows you to monitor activity on your database. It needs to run on the database server, but can display on a client machine if you are running the X Window System on Unix or a Unix-like operating system.

# Summary

In this chapter, we have taken a look at some of the tools we have at our disposal for getting the most out of PostgreSQL. The standard distribution comes with the command line tool, `psql`, that is capable of carrying out most of the operations we need for creating and maintaining databases.

If we have Tcl/Tk installed, we also have the option of using a graphical tool, `PgAccess`, to perform updates to our data.

Database administration can be carried out on a Microsoft Windows machine using the very capable `pgAdmin` tool.

We can use Microsoft Office products, including Microsoft Excel and Accessm, to manipulate and report on data held in a PostgreSQL database. This allows us to combine the scalability and reliability of the PostgreSQL system running on a UNIX or Linux platform with the easy use of familiar tools.

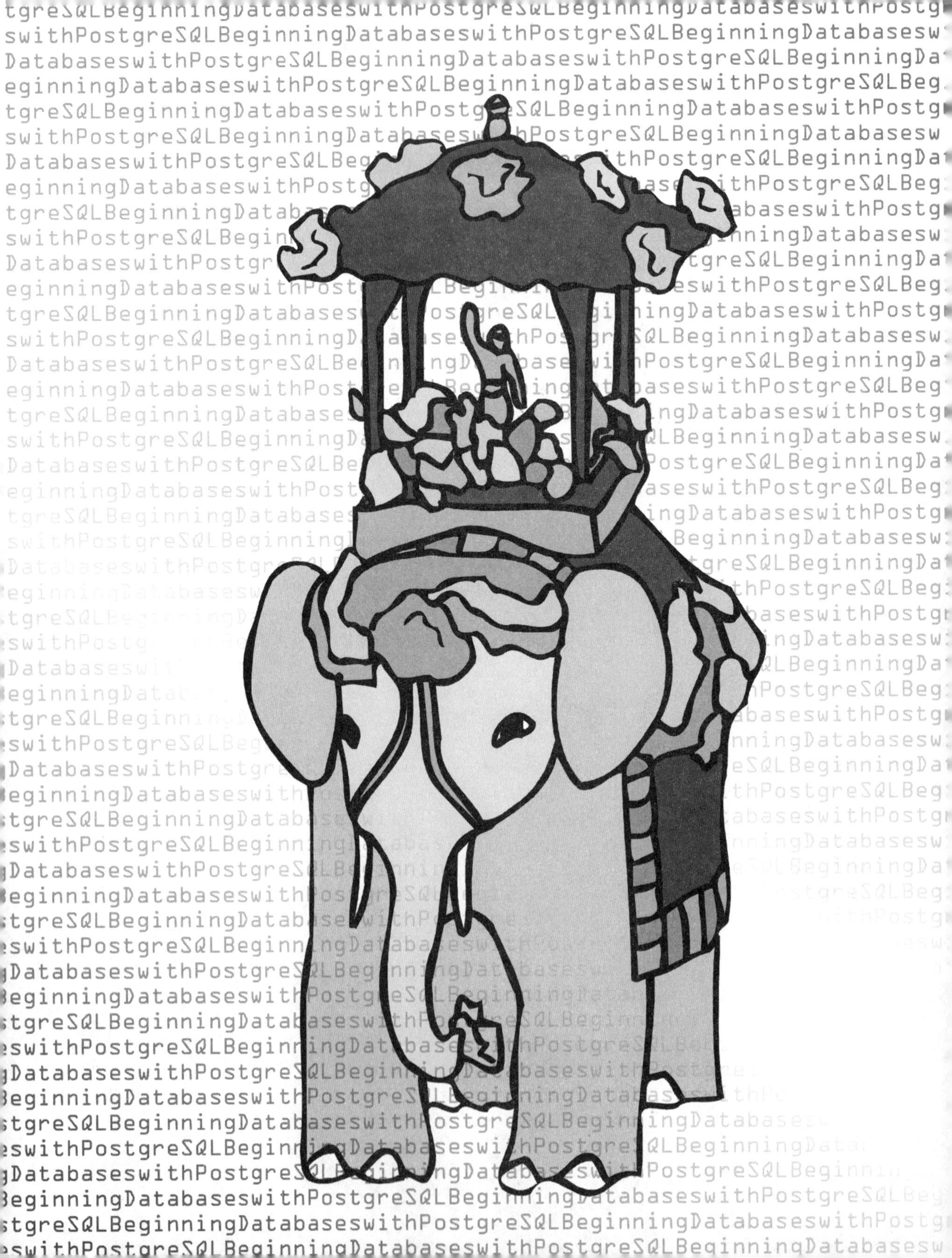
BeginningDatabaseswithPostgreSQL

# Data Interfacing

So far we have looked at why a relational database, and PostgreSQL in particular, is a powerful tool for organizing and retrieving data. In the previous chapter, we looked at some of the graphical tools such as `psql`, `pgAdmin`, `Kpsql`, and `PgAccess`, which can also be used for administering PostgreSQL. We even looked at how to use Microsoft Access with PostgreSQL and add more functionality to it by using Microsoft Excel. Of course, that's not much use to us until we have some data in the database to work with. So in this chapter, we are going to look at how to `INSERT` data into a PostgreSQL database, `UPDATE` data already in the database, and finally how to `DELETE` data from a database.

As we wade through the chapter, we will look at:

❑   Adding data to the database

❑   Basic `INSERT`s

❑   Inserting data into `SERIAL` columns

❑   Inserting `NULL` values

❑   The `\copy` command

❑   Loading data directly from another application

❑   Updating data in the database

❑   Deleting data from the database

## Adding Data to the Database

Surprisingly perhaps, after the complexities of the `SELECT` statement that we saw in Chapter 4, adding data into a PostgreSQL database is quite straightforward. We add data to PostgreSQL using the `INSERT` statement. We can only add data to a single table at any one time, and generally, we do that one row at a time.

# Basic INSERTs

The basic SQL INSERT statement has a very simple syntax:

```
INSERT INTO tablename VALUES (list of column values);
```

We specify a list of comma-separated column values, which must be in the same order as the columns in the table.

> **Although this syntax is very appealing because of its simplicity, it is also rather dangerous. We urge you to avoid this syntax, and instead use the 'safer insert syntax' shown later, where the column names are specified as well as the data values. We present it here, because you will see it in common use, but we do recommend you avoid using it.**

## Try It Out – \d customer

Let's add some new rows to our customer table. The first thing we must do, is to discover the correct column order. If we have the SQL statement used to create the table to hand, then the order of column values will simply be the same – the order in which they were listed in the CREATE TABLE command. If we don't have the SQL to hand, which is unfortunately all too common, then we can use the psql command line tool to describe the table to us, using the \d command. Suppose we wanted to have a look at the definition of the customer table in our database, as presented in Chapter 3. We would use the \d command to ask for its description to be shown. Let's do that now:

```
bpsimple=# \d customer
                                   Table "customer"
   Attribute   |         Type          |                     Modifier
-------------+-----------------------+-------------------------------------------
-----------------
 customer_id  | integer               | not null default
nextval('"customer_customer_id_seq"'::text)
 title        | character(4)          |
 fname        | character varying(32) |
 lname        | character varying(32) | not null
 addressline  | character varying(64) |
 town         | character varying(32) |
 zipcode      | character(10)         | not null
 phone        | character varying(16) |
Index: customer_pk
bpsimple=#
```

The display is slightly confused by the wrapping introduced to get it on the page, but it does show us the column order for our customer table. You will notice that the customer_id column isn't described exactly as we specified in the CREATE TABLE statement. This is because of the way PostgreSQL implements our SERIAL definition of customer_id. For now, you just need to remember that it is an integer field. We will be explaining how PostgreSQL implements SERIAL columns later in Chapter 8, *Data Definition Language*.

To insert character data we must enclose it in single quotes (`'`). If we need a single quote to appear in our character string, then precede it with a backslash (`\`). Numbers can be written as they are (unless they are taken as a single entity). For Nulls, we just write NULL, or, as we shall see later, in a more complex form of the INSERT statement, simply provide no data for that column.

Now that we know the column order, we can write our INSERT statement, like this:

```
INSERT INTO customer VALUES(16, 'Mr', 'Gavin', 'Smyth', '23 Harlestone',
'Milltown', 'MT7 7HI', '746 3725');
```

This is what we see:

```
bpsimple=# INSERT INTO customer VALUES(16, 'Mr', 'Gavin', 'Smyth', '23 bpsimple-#
Harlestone', 'Milltown', 'MT7 7HI', '746 3725');
INSERT 18944 1

bpsimple=#
```

The exact number you see after the INSERT will almost certainly be different in your case. The important thing is that PostgreSQL has inserted the new data. The first number is actually an internal PostgreSQL identification number, called an **OID**, which is normally hidden.

> The OID (Object IDentification number), is a unique, normally invisible number assigned to every row in PostgreSQL. When you initialize the database, a counter is created which is used to uniquely number every row. Here, the INSERT command has been executed and **18944** is the Object IDentification number assigned to the new row and **1** is the number of rows inserted. This OID number is not part of standard SQL, and will not normally be sequential within a table, so we urge you to be aware of its existence but never to use it in applications.

We can easily check that the data has been inserted correctly by using a SELECT statement to retrieve it, like this:

```
bpsimple=# SELECT * FROM customer WHERE customer_id > 15;
 customer_id | title | fname | lname |  addressline  |   town   | zipcode |
phone
-------------+-------+-------+-------+---------------+----------+---------+----
------
          16 | Mr    | Gavin | Smyth | 23 Harlestone | Milltown | MT7 7HI | 746
3725
(1 row)

bpsimple=#
```

The display is wrapped, because of the restrictions of the page width, but you can see that the data was correctly inserted.

Suppose we wanted to insert another row, where the last name was O'Rourke. What do we do with the single quote that is already in the data?

We escape it using a single backslash(\), like this:

```
INSERT INTO customer VALUES(17, 'Mr', 'Shaun', 'O\'Rourke', '32 Sheepy Lane',
'Milltown', 'MT9 8NQ', '746 3956');
```

Check that the data has been inserted:

```
bpsimple=# SELECT * FROM customer WHERE customer_id > 15;
 customer_id | title | fname |  lname  |   addressline   |   town   |  zipcode
 |  phone
-------------+-------+-------+---------+-----------------+----------+-----------
-+----------
          16 | Mr    | Gavin | Smyth   | 23 Harlestone   | Milltown | MT7 7HI
 | 746 3725
          17 | Mr    | Shaun | O'Rourke | 32 Sheepy Lane | Milltown | MT9 8NQ
 | 746 3956
(2 rows)

bpsimple=#
```

### How It Works

We used the INSERT statement to add additional data to the customer table, specifying column values in the same order as they were created in the table. To add a number to a column just write the number and to add a string, enclose it in single quotes. To insert a single quote into the string, we must precede the single quote with a backslash character(\). If we ever need to insert a backslash character, then we would write a pair, like this \\.

## Try It Out – The INSERT Statement

Suppose we wanted to insert another row, where the address was something strange, such as Midtown Street A\33. What do we do with the single backslash that is already in the data? We would escape the single backslash by using two backslashes, like this:

```
INSERT INTO customer VALUES(18, 'Mr', 'Jeff', 'Baggott', 'Midtown Street A\\33',
'Milltown', 'MT9 8NQ', '746 3956');
```

This is how it looks:

```
bpsimple=# SELECT * FROM customer WHERE addressline='Midtown Street A\\33';
 customer_id | title | fname |  lname  |     addressline      |   town   | zipco
de | phone
-------------+-------+-------+---------+----------------------+----------+-------
-----+----------
          18 | Mr    | Jeff  | Baggott | Midtown Street A\33  | Milltown | MT9 8N
Q  | 746 3956
(1 row)

bpsimple=#
```

## Safer INSERT Statements

While INSERT statements like the above work, it is not always convenient to specify every single column, or having to get the data order exactly the same as the table column order. This adds an element of risk, in that we may accidentally write an INSERT statement with the column data in the wrong order. This would result in us adding incorrect data to our database. In the previous example, suppose we had erroneously exchanged the position of the fname and lname columns. The data would have been inserted successfully, because both columns are text columns, and PostgreSQL would have been unable to detect our mistake. If we had later asked for a list of the last names of our customers, however Gavin would have appeared as a valid customer last name, rather than Smyth as we intended. Poor quality, or in this case just plain incorrect data, is a major problem in databases and we generally take as many precautions as we can to ensure that only correct data gets in. Simple mistakes might be easy to spot in our example database with just tens of rows, but in a database with tens of thousands of customers, spotting mistakes, particularly with in data with unusual names, would be very difficult indeed.

Fortunately, there is a slight variation of the INSERT statement, that is both easier to use, and much safer as well:

```
INSERT INTO tablename(list of column names) VALUES (list of column values
corresponding to the column names);
```

In this variant of the INSERT statement, we must list the column names and data values in the same order, which can be different from the order we used when we created the table. Using this variant, we no longer need to know the order in which the columns were defined in the database. We also have a nice, clear, almost 'side-by-side' list of column names and the data we are about to insert into them.

### Try It Out – Inserting Values Corresponding to Column Names

Let's add another row to our database, this time explicitly naming the columns, like this:

```
INSERT INTO customer(customer_id, title, fname, lname, addressline, town, zipcode,
phone) VALUES(19, 'Mrs', 'Sarah', 'Harvey', '84 Willow Way', 'Lincoln', 'LC3 7RD',
'527 3739');
```

We can also enter this over several lines, making it easier to read, and check that we have the column names and data values in the same order.

Let's execute this SQL, typing it in over several lines so it is easier to read:

```
bpsimple=# INSERT INTO
bpsimple-# customer(customer_id, title, lname, fname, addressline, town, bpsimple-
# zipcode, phone)
bpsimple-# VALUES(19, 'Mrs', 'Harvey', 'Sarah',   '84 Willow Way', 'Lincoln',
bpsimple-# 'LC3 7RD', '527 3739');
INSERT 22592 1

bpsimple=#
```

Notice how much easier it is to compare the names of the fields with the values being inserted into them. We deliberately swapped over the fname and lname columns, just to show it could be done. You can use any column order you like; all that matters is that the values match the order in which you list the columns.

You will also notice the psql prompt changes on subsequent lines, and remains until we terminate the command with a semicolon.

> We strongly recommend that you always use the named column form of the INSERT statement, because the explicit naming of columns makes it much safer to use.

# Inserting Data Into SERIAL Columns

At this point, it is time to confess to a minor sin we have been committing with the customer_id column. Up to this point in the chapter, we have not known how to insert data into some columns of a table, while leaving others alone. With the second form of the INSERT statement, using named columns, we can do this and see how it is particularly important when we are inserting data into tables with SERIAL type columns.

You will remember from Chapter 2, that we met the rather special data type SERIAL, which is effectively an integer, but automatically increments to give us an easy way of creating unique_id numbers for each row. So far in this chapter, we have been inserting data into rows, providing a value for the customer_id column, a SERIAL type data field.

Let's have a look at the data in our customer table so far:

```
bpsimple=# SELECT customer_id, fname, lname, addressline FROM customer;
 customer_id |   fname   |  lname   |      addressline
-------------+-----------+----------+---------------------
           1 | Jenny     | Stones   | 27 Rowan Avenue
           2 | Andrew    | Stones   | 52 The Willows
           3 | Alex      | Matthew  | 4 The Street
           4 | Adrian    | Matthew  | The Barn
           5 | Simon     | Cozens   | 7 Shady Lane
           6 | Neil      | Matthew  | 5 Pasture Lane
           7 | Richard   | Stones   | 34 Holly Way
           8 | Ann       | Stones   | 34 Holly Way
           9 | Christine | Hickman  | 36 Queen Street
          10 | Mike      | Howard   | 86 Dysart Street
          11 | Dave      | Jones    | 54 Vale Rise
          12 | Richard   | Neill    | 42 Thatched way
          13 | Laura     | Hendy    | 73 Margeritta Way
          14 | Bill      | O'Neill  | 2 Beamer Street
          15 | David     | Hudson   | 4  The Square
          16 | Gavin     | Smyth    | 23 Harlestone
          17 | Shaun     | O'Rourke | 32 Sheepy Lane
          18 | Jeff      | Baggott  | Midtown Street A\33
          19 | Sarah     | Harvey   | 84 Willow Way
(19 rows)

bpsimple=#
```

Certainly, all looks well, but in fact, there is a slight problem, because by forcing values into the customer_id column, we have inadvertently 'confused' PostgreSQL's internal SERIAL counter.

Suppose we try inserting another row, this time allowing the SERIAL type to provide our automatically incrementing customer_id value:

```
bpsimple=# INSERT INTO customer(title, fname, lname, addressline, town, bpsimple-#
zipcode, phone)
bpsimple-# VALUES('Mr', 'Steve', 'Clarke',  '14 Satview way', 'Lincoln', bpsimple-
# 'LC4 3ED', '527 7254');
ERROR:  Cannot insert a duplicate key into unique index customer_pk

bpsimple=#
```

Clearly, something has gone wrong, since we did not provide any duplicate values. What has happened is that earlier in the chapter, when we were providing values for customer_id, we have overridden PostgreSQL's automatic allocation of IDs in the SERIAL column, and caused the automatic allocation system to get out of step with the actual data in the table.

> **Avoid providing values for SERIAL data columns when inserting data.**

Having gotten ourselves into a bit of a mess, how do we recover? The answer is that we need to give PostgreSQL a helping hand, and put its internal sequence number back in step with the actual data.

## Accessing Sequence Numbers

When we created the customer table, we defined the customer_id column as having type SERIAL. You may have noticed that PostgreSQL then gave us some informational messages, saying that it was creating a customer_customer_id_seq sequence. Also, when we ask PostgreSQL to describe the table, using \d, we see the column is rather specially defined:

```
customer_id integer not null default nextval('customer_customer_id_seq'::text)
```

What has happened is that PostgreSQL has created a special counter for the column, a **sequence**, which it can use to generate unique IDs. Notice that the sequence is always named <tablename>_<column name>_seq. The default behavior for the column has been automatically specified by PostgreSQL to be the result of the function nextval('customer_customer_id_seq'). When we failed to provide data for the column in our INSERT statement, this is the function that was being automatically executed by PostgreSQL for us. By inserting or providing data to this column, we have upset this automatic mechanism, since the function will not get called if data is provided. Fortunately, we are not reduced to deleting all the data from the table and starting again, because PostgreSQL allows us to directly manipulate the sequence number.

You can always find the value of a sequence number using the currval function:

```
currval('sequence name');
```

PostgreSQL will tell you the current value of the sequence number.

For example:

```
bpsimple=# SELECT currval('customer_customer_id_seq');
 currval
---------
      17
(1 row)

bpsimple=#
```

As you can see, PostgreSQL thinks that the current number for the last row in the table is 17, but in fact the last row is 19. When we try and insert data into the customer table, leaving the customer_id column to PostgreSQL, it attempts to provide a value for the column by calling the nextval() function:

```
nextval('sequence number');
```

This function first increments the provided sequence number, then returns the result. We can try this directly:

```
bpsimple=# SELECT nextval('customer_customer_id_seq');
 nextval
---------
      18
(1 row)
bpsimple=#
```

Of course, we could get to the correct value for the sequence by repeatedly calling nextval(), but that would not be much use if the value were too large, or too small. Instead we can use the setval() function:

```
setval('sequence number', new value);
```

First, we need to discover what the sequence value should be. We do this by selecting the maximum value of the column that is already in the database. To do this, we will use the MAX(column name) function, which we will meet properly in the next chapter, but its use is quite intuitive, as it simply tells you the maximum numeric value stored in a column:

```
bpsimple=# SELECT MAX(customer_id) FROM customer;
 max
-----
  19

bpsimple=#
```

PostgreSQL will respond with the largest number that it found in the customer_id column in the customer table. Now we set the sequence, using the function setval(sequence, value), which allows us to set a sequence to any value we choose. The current largest value in the table is 19, and the sequence number is always incremented before its value is used,therefore the sequence should normally have the same number as the current biggest value in the table:

```
bpsimple=# SELECT setval('customer_customer_id_seq', 19);
 setval
--------
     19
(1 row)

bpsimple=#
```

Now that the sequence number is correct, we can insert our data allowing PostgreSQL to provide the value for the SERIAL column customer_id:

```
bpsimple=# INSERT INTO customer(title, fname, lname, addressline, town, bpsimple-#
zipcode, phone) VALUES('Mr', 'Steve', 'Clarke',  '14 Satview bpsimple-# way',
'Lincoln', 'LC4 3ED', '527 7254');
INSERT 21459 1

bpsimple=#
```

Success! PostgreSQL is now back in step, and will continue to create SERIAL values correctly.

This out of step problem is reasonably rare, but most commonly occurs because:

❑   You have dropped and re-created the table, but did not drop and re-create the sequence

❑   You mixed styles between adding data allowing PostgreSQL to pick values for SERIAL columns, and explicitly specifying a value for the SERIAL column yourself

# Inserting NULL values

We briefly mentioned in Chapter 2 that we could insert NULL values into columns using the INSERT statement. Let's look at this in a little more detail.

If you are using the first form of the INSERT statement, where you insert data into the columns in the order they were defined when the table was created, you simply write NULL in the column value. Note that you must not use quotes, as this is not a string. You should also remember that NULL is a special undefined value in SQL, not the same as an empty string.

Suppose from our previous example:

```
INSERT INTO customer VALUES(16, 'Mr', 'Gavin', 'Smyth', '23 Harlestone',
'Milltown', 'MT7 7HI', '746 3725');
```

That we did not know the first name. The table definition allows NULL in the fname column, so adding data without knowing the first name is perfectly valid. If we had written:

```
INSERT INTO customer VALUES(16, 'Mr', '', 'Smyth', '23 Harlestone', 'Milltown',
'MT7 7HI', '746 3725');
```

This would not be what we intended, because we would have added an empty string as the first name, perhaps implying that Mr. Smyth had no first name, when what we intended was to use a NULL, because we do not know the first name.

The correct INSERT statement would have been:

```
INSERT INTO customer VALUES(16, 'Mr', NULL, 'Smyth', '23 Harlestone', 'Milltown',
'MT7 7HI', '746 3725');
```

Notice the lack of quotes around NULL. If quotes had been used, fname would have been set to the string NULL, rather than the *value* NULL.

Using the second (safer) form of the INSERT statement, where columns are explicitly named, it is much easier to insert NULL values, where we neither list the column, nor provide a value for it, like this:

```
INSERT INTO customer(title, lname, addressline, town, zipcode, phone) VALUES('Mr',
'Smyth', '23 Harlestone', 'Milltown', 'MT7 7HI', '746 3725');
```

Notice that the fname column is neither listed nor is a value defined for it. Alternatively, we could have listed the column and then written NULL in the value list.

This will not work if we try and add a NULL value in a column that is defined as not allowing NULL values. Suppose we try to add a customer with no last name (lname) column:

```
bpsimple=# INSERT INTO customer(title, fname, addressline, town, zipcode,
bpsimple-# phone) VALUES('Ms', 'Gill', '27 Chase Avenue', 'Lowtown', 'LT5
bpsimple-# 8TQ', '876 1962');
ERROR:  ExecAppend: Fail to add null value in not null attribute lname

bpsimple=#
```

Notice that we did not provide a value for lname, so the INSERT was rejected, because the customer table is defined to not allow NULL in that column.

Check it out:

```
bpsimple=# \d customer
                            Table "customer"
   Attribute   |    Type     |                     Modifier

-------------+-------------+-----------------------------------------------------
------
 customer_id | integer     | not null default
nextval('customer_customer_id_seq'::text)
 title       | char(4)     |
 fname       | varchar(32) |
 lname       | varchar(32) | not null
 addressline | varchar(64) |
 town        | varchar(32) |
 zipcode     | char(10)    | not null
 phone       | varchar(16) |
Index: customer_pk

bpsimple=#
```

We will see in Chapter 8 *Data Definition Language*, how we can more generally define explicit default values to be used in columns when data is inserted with no value, by specifying a default value against a column.

# The \copy Command

Although INSERT is the standard SQL way of adding data to a database, it is not always the most convenient.

Suppose we had a large number of rows to add to the database, but already had the actual data available, perhaps in a spreadsheet. The only way we knew of getting data into the database was to use the Export command, so we would probably export the spreadsheet as a CSV (comma-separated variable) file. We can then use a text editor like EMACS, or at least one with a macro facility, to convert all our data into INSERT statements.

If we had started with data such as:

```
Miss,Jenny,Stones,27 Rowan Avenue,Hightown,NT2 1AQ,023 9876
Mr,Andrew,Stones,52 The Willows,Lowtown,LT5 7RA,876 3527
Miss,Alex,Matthew,4 The Street,Nicetown,NT2 2TX,010 4567
```

We might transform it into a series of INSERT statements, so it looked like this:

```
INSERT INTO customer(title, fname, lname, addressline, town, zipcode, phone)
VALUES('Miss','Jenny','Stones','27 Rowan Avenue','Hightown','NT2 1AQ','023
9876');
INSERT INTO customer(title, fname, lname, addressline, town, zipcode, phone)
VALUES('Mr','Andrew','Stones','52 The Willows','Lowtown','LT5 7RA','876 3527');
INSERT INTO customer(title, fname, lname, addressline, town, zipcode, phone)
VALUES('Miss','Alex','Matthew','4 The Street','Nicetown','NT2 2TX','010 4567');
```

Then save it in a text file with a .sql extension.

We could then use the \i command in psql to execute the statements in the file. This is how the pop_customer.sql file works (we used this in Chapter 3 to initially populate our database). Notice here that we allowed PostgreSQL to generate the unique customer_id value.

This isn't very convenient, however. It would clearly be much nicer if we could move data between flat files and the database in a more general way. There are a couple of ways of doing this in PostgreSQL. Rather confusingly, both are called the copy command. There is a PostgreSQL SQL command called COPY, which can save and restore data to flat files, but its use is limited to the database administrator, and files are read and written on the server. More useful is the general-purpose \copy command, which implements almost all the functionality of COPY, but can be used by everyone, and data is read and written on the client machine. The SQL-based COPY command is, therefore, almost totally redundant, so we won't cover it any further than beyond the next paragraph.

The COPY command does have one advantage. It is significantly quicker, because it executes directly in the server process, while the \copy command executes in the client process, potentially having to pass all the data across a network. It can also be slightly more reliable when errors occur. Unless you have very large amounts of data however the difference will not be that noticeable.

The `\copy` command has this basic syntax for importing data:

```
\copy tablename FROM 'filename' [USING DELIMITERS 'a single character to use as a
delimiter'] [WITH NULL AS 'a string that means NULL']
```

It looks a little imposing, but is quite simple to use. The sections in square braces, `[]`, are optional, so you only need to use them if required. do notice however that the filename needs to be enclosed in single quotes.

The option `USING DELIMITERS 'a single character...'` allows you to specify how each column is separated in the input file. By default, a tab character is assumed to separate columns in the input data. In our case, we will assume that we have started with a CSV file that we have exported from a spreadsheet. In practice, the CSV format is often not a good choice, since the comma character can appear in the data, and address data is particularly prone to containing comma characters. Unfortunately, spreadsheets are often not particularly good at offering sensible alternatives to CSV file exports, so you may have to work with what you've got. Given the choice, a pipe character, `|`, is often useful, as it very rarely appears in user data.

The option `WITH NULL AS 'a string...'` allows you to specify a string that should be interpreted as Null. By default `\N` is assumed. Notice that in the `\copy` command you must include single quotes around the string, because that tells PostgreSQL that it is a string, although quotes will not be expected in the actual data. So, if you want the string `NOTHING` to be loaded as a Null value in the database, you would specify the option `WITH NULL AS 'NOTHING'` and the data, if we did not know Mr. Hudson's first name for example, should look like:

```
15,Mr,NOTHING,Hudson,4 The Square, Milltown,MT2 6RT,961 4526
```

One thing that it is very important to watch out for when inserting data directly, is that the data is 'clean'. You do need to ensure that no columns are missing, all quote characters have been correctly escaped with a backslash, there are no binary characters present, and so on. PostgreSQL will catch most of these mistakes for you, and only load valid data, but untangling several thousand rows of data that have almost been completely loaded is a slow, unreliable, and unrewarding job. It is well worth going to the effort to clean the data as much as possible *before* attempting to 'bulk load' it with the `\copy` command.

## Try It Out – Loading Data Using \copy

Suppose we had some additional customer data in a file `cust.txt` that looked like this:

```
21,Miss,Emma,Neill,21 Sheepy Lane,Hightown,NT2 1YQ,023 4245
22,Mr,Gavin,Neill,21 Sheepy Lane,Hightown,NT2 1YQ,023 4245
23,Mr,Duncan,Neill,21 Sheepy Lane,Hightown,NT2 1YQ,023 4245
```

Conveniently, there are no Nulls to worry about, so we just need to specify comma as the column separator. To load this data, we simply execute the command:

```
\copy customer from 'cust.txt' using delimiters ','
```

Notice there is no `;` on the command, since it is a `\` command directly to psql, not SQL. psql responds with the rather brief `\.`, which tells us that all is well.

If we then run:

```
SELECT * FROM customer;
```

Then we will see that the additional rows have been added.

There is however a slight problem lurking. Remember the sequence number that can get out of step? Unfortunately, using \copy to load data is one way this can happen. Let's check what has happened to our sequence number:

```
bpsimple=# SELECT MAX(customer_id) FROM customer;
 max
-----
  23
(1 row)

bpsimple=# SELECT currval('customer_customer_id_seq');
 currval
---------
      20
(1 row)

bpsimple=#
```

Oops! The maximum value stored in customer_id is currently 22, so the next ID allocated should be 23, but the sequence is going to try and allocate 21 as the next value. Never mind – it's easy to correct:

```
bpsimple=# SELECT setval('customer_customer_id_seq', 23);
 setval
--------
     23
(1 row)

bpsimple=#
```

### How It Works

We used the \copy command to directly load data that had been exported from a spreadsheet in CSV format into our customer table. We subsequently had to correct the sequence number that generates customer_id numbers for the SERIAL column customer_id in the table, which takes significantly less effort than that we would have had to expend to convert our CSV format data into a series of INSERT statements.

# Loading Data Directly from Another Application

If we have data already in a desktop database, such as Microsoft Access, there is an even easier way to load the data into PostgreSQL. We can simply attach the PostgreSQL table to our Access database, via ODBC, and insert data into a PostgreSQL table.

Often, when you are doing this, you will find that your existing data is not quite what you need, or that it needs some reworking before being inserted into its final destination table. Even if the data is in the correct format, it is often a good idea not to attempt to insert it directly into the database, but rather to first move it to a loading table, and then transfer it from this load table to the real table. Using an intermediate load table is a common method in real applications for inserting data into a database, particularly when the quality of the original data is uncertain. The data is first loaded into the database in a holding table, checked, corrected if necessary, and then moved on into the final table.

Usually, you will write a custom application, or stored procedure (Chapter 10 *Stored Procedures and Triggers*) to check and correct the data. Once it is ready to load into the final table though, there is a useful variant of the INSERT command that allows us to move data between tables, moving multiple rows in one command. It is the only time an INSERT statement affects multiple rows with a single statement. This is the INSERT INTO statement.

The syntax for inserting data from one table into another is:

```
INSERT INTO tablename(list of column names) SELECT normal select statement
```

Suppose we have a holding table, tcust, that has some additional customer data to be loaded into our master customer table.

We will make our holding table definition look like this:

```
create table tcust
(
    title               char(4)             ,
    fname               varchar(32)         ,
    lname               varchar(32)         ,
    addressline         varchar(64)         ,
    town                varchar(32)         ,
    zipcode             char(10)            ,
    phone               varchar(16)
);
```

Notice that there are no primary keys or constraints of any kind. It is normal when cross-loading data into a load table to make it as easy as possible to get the data into the load table. Removing the constraints makes this easier. Also notice that all the required columns are there, except the customer_id sequence number, which PostgreSQL can create for us as we load the data.

Suppose we have loaded some data into tcust, either via ODBC, \copy, or some other method, validated and corrected it, then a SELECT output looks like this:

```
bpsimple=# SELECT * FROM tcust;
 title | fname |  lname  |   addressline   |  town   | zipcode  |  phone
-------+-------+---------+-----------------+---------+----------+----------
 Mr    | Peter | Bradley | 72 Milton Rise  | Keynes  | MK41 2HQ |
 Mr    | Kevin | Carney  | 43 Glen Way     | Lincoln | LI2 7RD  | 786 3454
 Mr    | Brian | Waters  | 21 Troon Rise   | Lincoln | LI7 6GT  | 786 7243
(3 rows)

bpsimple=#
```

## Try It Out – Loading Data Between Tables

The first thing to notice is that we have not yet managed to find a phone number for Mr. Bradley. This may or may not be a problem. Let's decide that for now we don't wish to load this row, but we do wish to load all the other customers. In a real-world scenario of course, we may be trying to load hundreds of new customers, and it is quite probable that we will want to load groups of them as the data for each group is validated or cleaned.

The first part of the INSERT is quite easy to write. We will use the full syntax of INSERT, specifying precisely the columns we wish to load. This is normally the sensible choice:

```
INSERT INTO customer(title, fname, lname, addressline, town, zipcode, phone);
```

Notice that we do not specify that we are loading the customer_id. You will remember that by leaving this blank, we allow PostgreSQL to automatically create values for us, which is always the safer way to allow SERIAL values to be created.

We now need to write the SELECT part of the statement, which will feed this INSERT statement. Remember, that we do not wish to insert Mr. Bradley yet, because his phone number is set to Null, as we are still trying to find it. We could, if we wanted to, load Mr. Bradley, since the phone column *will* accept Null values. What we are doing here, is applying a slightly more stringent business rule to the data than is required by the low-level database rules. We write a SELECT statement like this:

```
SELECT title, fname, lname, addressline, town, zipcode, phone FROM tcust WHERE
phone IS NOT NULL;
```

Of course, this is a perfectly valid statement on its own. Let's test it:

```
bpsimple=# SELECT title, fname, lname, addressline, town, zipcode, phone bpsimple-
# FROM tcust WHERE phone IS NOT NULL;
 title | fname | lname  |  addressline   |  town   | zipcode  |  phone
-------+-------+--------+----------------+---------+----------+----------
 Mr    | Kevin | Carney | 43 Glen Way    | Lincoln | LI2 7RD  | 786 3454
 Mr    | Brian | Waters | 21 Troon Rise  | Lincoln | LI7 6GT  | 786 7243
(2 rows)

bpsimple=#
```

That looks correct – it finds the rows we need, and the columns are in the same order as the INSERT statement. So we can now put the two statements together, and execute them, like this:

```
bpsimple=# INSERT INTO customer(title, fname, lname, addressline, town, bpsimple-#
zipcode, phone) SELECT title, fname, lname, addressline, town, bpsimple-# zipcode,
phone FROM tcust WHERE phone IS NOT NULL;
INSERT 0 2

bpsimple=#
```

Notice psql tells us that two rows have been inserted. Now, being extra cautious, let's fetch those rows from the customer table, just to be absolutely sure they were loaded correctly:

```
bpsimple=# SELECT customer_id, fname, lname, addressline FROM customer WHERE
bpsimple-# town = 'Lincoln';
 customer_id | fname | lname  |  addressline
-------------+-------+--------+---------------
          18 | Sarah | Harvey | 84 Willow Way
          24 | Kevin | Carney | 43 Glen Way
          25 | Brian | Waters | 21 Troon Rise
(3 rows)

bpsimple=#
```

Notice that we actually get three rows, because we already had a customer from Lincoln. We can see however, that our data has been inserted correctly, and customer_ids created for us. Now that some of the data from tcust has been loaded into the live customer table, we would normally delete those rows from tcust. For the purposes of the example, we are going to leave it alone for now, and delete it in a later example.

## How It Works

We specified the columns we wanted to load in the customer table, and then selected the same set of data, in the same order from the tcust table. To allow PostgreSQL to create unique customer_ids for us, we did not specify that we would load the customer_id column. So, PostgreSQL used its sequence to generate unique IDs for us.

An alternative method, which you may find easier, particularly if there is a lot of data to load, is to add an additional column to the temporary table, perhaps a column isvalid of type Boolean. You then load all the data into the temporary table, and set all the isvalid values to FALSE, using the UPDATE statement that we will meet more formally a little later:

```
UPDATE tcust SET isvalid = 'FALSE';
```

We have not specified a WHERE clause therefore, all rows have the isvalid column set to FALSE. We can then work on the data, and for each 'good' row update, set the isvalid column to TRUE, then load corrected data, selecting only the rows where isvalid is TRUE:

```
bpsimple=# INSERT INTO customer(title, fname, lname, addressline, town, bpsimple-#
zipcode, phone)
bpsimple=# SELECT title, fname, lname, addressline, town, zipcode, phone bpsimple-
#  FROM tcust WHERE isvalid = TRUE;
```

Once these rows are loaded, we can remove them (we will meet the DELETE statement in more detail near the end of this chapter) from the tcust table, like this:

```
DELETE FROM tcust WHERE isvalid = TRUE;
```

Then continue to work on the remaining data in the tcust table.

# Updating Data in the Database

Now we know how to get data into the database by using INSERT, and how to retrieve it again, using SELECT. Unfortunately, data does not tend to stay static for very long. People move house, change phone numbers and so on. We need a way of updating the data in the database.

In PostgreSQL, as in all SQL-based databases, this is done with the UPDATE statement.

The UPDATE statement is remarkably simple. Its syntax is:

```
UPDATE tablename SET columnname = value  WHERE condition
```

If we want to set several columns at the same time, we simply specify them as a comma-separated list, like this:

```
UPDATE customer SET town = 'Leicester', zipcode = 'LE4 2WQ' WHERE some condition
```

We can update as many columns simultaneously as we like, providing each column only appears once. You will notice that you can only use a single table name. This is due to the syntax of SQL. In the rare event that you need to update two separate, but related, tables, you must write two separate UPDATE statements. You can put them both into a **transaction** however (Chapter 9 *Transactions and Locking*), to ensure that either both updates are performed or no updates are performed.

## Try It Out – The UPDATE Statement

Suppose we have now tracked down the phone number of the Mr. Bradley in our tcust table, and want to update the data into our live customer table. The first part of the UPDATE statement is easy:

```
UPDATE tcust SET phone = '352 3442'
```

Now we need to specify the row to update, which is simply:

```
WHERE fname = 'Peter' and lname = 'Bradley';
```

With UPDATE statements, it is always a good idea to check the WHERE clause. Let's do that now:

```
bpsimple=# SELECT fname, lname, phone FROM tcust WHERE fname = 'Peter' AND
bpsimple-# lname = 'Bradley';
 fname | lname   | phone
-------+---------+-------
 Peter | Bradley |
(1 row)

bpsimple=#
```

We can see that the single row we want to update is being selected, so we can go ahead and put the two halves of the statement together and execute it:

```
bpsimple=# UPDATE tcust SET phone = '352 3442' WHERE fname = 'Peter' AND bpsimple-
# lname = 'Bradley';
UPDATE 1

bpsimple=#
```

PostgreSQL tells us that one row has been updated, and we could, if we wanted, re-execute our SELECT statement to check that all is well.

### How It Works

We built our UPDATE statement in two stages. First, we wrote the UPDATE command part that would actually change the column value, then we wrote the WHERE clause to specify which rows to update. After testing the WHERE clause, we executed the UPDATE, which changed the row as required.

## A Word of Warning

Why were we so careful to test the WHERE clause and warn about not executing the first part of the UPDATE statement? The answer is because it is perfectly valid to have an UPDATE statement with no WHERE clause. By default, UPDATE will then update all rows in the table, which is almost never what was intended. It can also be quite hard to correct.

tcust is just temporary experimental data, therefore let's just test out an UPDATE with no WHERE clause:

```
bpsimple=# UPDATE tcust SET phone = '999 9999';
UPDATE 3
bpsimple=#
```

Notice that psql has told us that 3 rows have been updated.

Now look at what we have:

```
bpsimple=# SELECT fname, lname, phone FROM tcust;
 fname  |  lname   |  phone
--------+----------+----------
 Kevin  | Carney   | 999 9999
 Brian  | Waters   | 999 9999
 Peter  | Bradley  | 999 9999
(3 rows)

bpsimple=#
```

Almost certainly not what we wanted!

> **Always test the WHERE clause of UPDATE statements before executing them.**

If you do intend to update many rows, then rather than retrieve all the data, you can simply check how many rows you are matching using the COUNT(*) syntax, which we will meet in more detail in the next chapter, *Advanced Data Selection*. For now, all you need to know is that replacing the column names in a SELECT statement with COUNT(*) will tell you how many rows were matched, rather than returning the data in the rows. In fact, that's about all there is to the COUNT(*) statement, but it does turn out to be quite useful in practice.

By way of a sample, here is our SELECT statement, just checking how many rows are matched by the WHERE clause:

```
bpsimple=# SELECT count(*) from tcust WHERE fname = 'Peter' AND lname = bpsimple-#
'Bradley';
 count
-------
     1
(1 row)

bpsimple=#
```

Which tells us that the WHERE clause is sufficiently restrictive to specify a single row. Of course, with different data, even specifying both fname and lname may not be sufficient to uniquely identify a row.

PostgreSQL has an extension that allows updates from another table, using the syntax:

```
UPDATE tablename FROM tablename WHERE condition
```

This is an extension to the SQL standard.

## Try It out – UPDATE with FROM

For the purpose of checking out this option, let's create a table custphone that contains the customer names and their phone numbers. The table would look like this:

```
create table custphone
(
    customer_id                 serial,
    fname                       varchar(32),
    lname                       varchar(32) not null,
    phone_num                   varchar(16)

);
```

Let's also insert some data into the newly created custphone table that holds the customers and their phone numbers:

```
bpsimple=#  INSERT  INTO  custphone(fname,  lname,  phone_num)  VALUES('Peter',
bpsimple-# 'Bradley', '352 3442');
INSERT 22593 1

bpsimple=#
```

Now we need to specify the row in the `tcust` table to be updated:

```
bpsimple=# UPDATE tcust SET phone = custphone.phone_num FROM custphone WHERE
bpsimple=# fname = 'Peter' AND lname = 'Bradley';
UPDATE 1

bpsimple=#
```

### How It Works

We created a new table that contains the phone numbers of the customers. Then, we inserted data into the new table. Finally, we executed the UPDATE, which changed the row as required.

While UPDATE uses sub-queries to control the rows that are updated, the FROM clause allows the inclusion of columns from other tables in the SET clause. In fact, the FROM clause isn't even required. This is because PostgreSQL creates a reference to any table used in a query by default.

# Deleting Data from the Database

The last thing we need to learn about in this chapter, is deleting data from tables. Prospective customers may never actually place an order, orders get cancelled, and so on, so we often need to delete data from the database.

The normal way of deleting data is to use the DELETE statement. This has syntax similar to the UPDATE statement:

```
DELETE FROM tablename WHERE condition
```

Notice that there are no columns listed, since DELETE works on rows. If you want to remove data from a column you must use the UPDATE statement to set the value of the column to NULL, or some other appropriate value.

Now that we have copied our data for our two new customers from `tcust` to our live `customer` table, we can go ahead and delete those rows from our `tcust` table.

### Try It Out – DELETE

Now we know just how dangerous omitting the WHERE clause in statements that change data can be, we can appreciate that accidentally deleting data is even more serious, so we will start by writing, and checking our WHERE clause using a SELECT statement:

```
bpsimple=# SELECT fname, lname FROM tcust WHERE town = 'Lincoln';
 fname | lname
-------+--------
 Kevin | Carney
 Brian | Waters
(2 rows)

bpsimple=#
```

That's good – it retrieves the two rows we were expecting.

Now we can prepend the DELETE statement on the front and, after a last visual check that it looks correct, execute it:

```
bpsimple=# DELETE FROM tcust WHERE town = 'Lincoln';
DELETE 2

bpsimple=#
```

> **Deleting from the database is that easy, so be very careful!**

### How It Works

We wrote, and tested, a WHERE clause to choose the rows that we wanted to delete from the database. We then executed a DELETE statement that deleted them.

Just like UPDATE, DELETE can only work on a single table at any one time. If we ever need to delete related rows from more than one table we will use a transaction, which we will meet in Chapter 9 *Transactions and Locking*.

There is one other way of deleting data from a table. It *always* deletes *all* data from a table, however, and even containing it in a transaction will give you no way of recovering the data. This is a command to be used only with caution. The command is TRUNCATE, and its syntax is:

```
TRUNCATE TABLE name of table
```

This is a command only to be used when you are very sure that you want to permanently delete all the data in a table. In some ways, it is similar to dropping and recreating the table, except it is much easier to use and doesn't reset the sequence number.

## Try It Out – The TRUNCATE Statement

Suppose we have now finished with our tcust table, and want to delete all the data in it. What we could do is drop the table, but then if we needed it again we would have to re-create it. Instead, we can TRUNCATE it, to drop all the rows in the table:

```
bpsimple=# TRUNCATE TABLE tcust;
TRUNCATE

bpsimple=# SELECT COUNT(*) FROM tcust;
 count
-------
     0
(1 row)

bpsimple=#
```

All the rows are now deleted.

### How It Works

TRUNCATE simply deletes all the rows from the specified table.

> **There are two ways to delete all the rows from a table – DELETE with a WHERE clause, and TRUNCATE. TRUNCATE, although not in SQL-92, is a very common SQL statement for efficiently deleting all rows from a table.**

If you have a large table, perhaps with many thousands of rows, and want to delete all the rows from it, by default PostgreSQL will temporarily hold a copy of the data. This is to restore the data in case the transaction is rolled back. Even though on the command line we might not have explicitly asked for a transaction, all commands automatically get executed inside a transaction. The action of taking a copy of many thousands of rows of a table, slows down execution and uses some temporary disk space. The TRUNCATE statement deletes the contents of the table very efficiently, with no backup copy of the data held. So, on very large tables it executes much more efficiently than DELETE. This also means that, used inside a transaction, however, a ROLLBACK statement that normally 'undoes' all changes, will be unable to reverse the effects of a TRUNCATE statement. You should stick to using DELETE almost all of the time, as it is a much safer way of deleting data. In a special case of wanting to efficiently, and irrevocably delete all rows from a table, However TRUNCATE is the answer.

# Summary

In this chapter, we have looked at the three other parts of data manipulation, along with SELECT. The ability to add data with the INSERT command, modify data with the UPDATE command, and finally, remove data with the DELETE command.

We learnt about the two forms of the INSERT command, with data explicitly included in the INSERT statement, or INSERT from data SELECTed from another table. We saw how it is safer to use the longer form of the INSERT statement, where all columns are listed, so there is less chance of mistakes. We also met INSERT's cousin command, the rather useful PostgreSQL extension \copy, which allows data to be inserted into a table directly from a local file.

We looked at how you need to be careful with the sequence counters for SERIAL fields, how to check the value of a sequence, and if necessary, change it. We saw that in general, it is better to allow PostgreSQL to generate sequence numbers for you, by not providing data for SERIAL type columns.

With the UPDATE and DELETE statements, we saw how these very simple statements work, and how you use them with WHERE clauses, just like the SELECT statement. We also mentioned that you should always test UPDATE and DELETE statements with WHERE clauses using a SELECT statement, as mistakes here can cause problems that are difficult to rectify.

Finally, we looked at the TRUNCATE statement, a very efficient way of deleting all rows from a table but since it is an irrevocable deletion and not managed by transactions, it should only be used with caution.

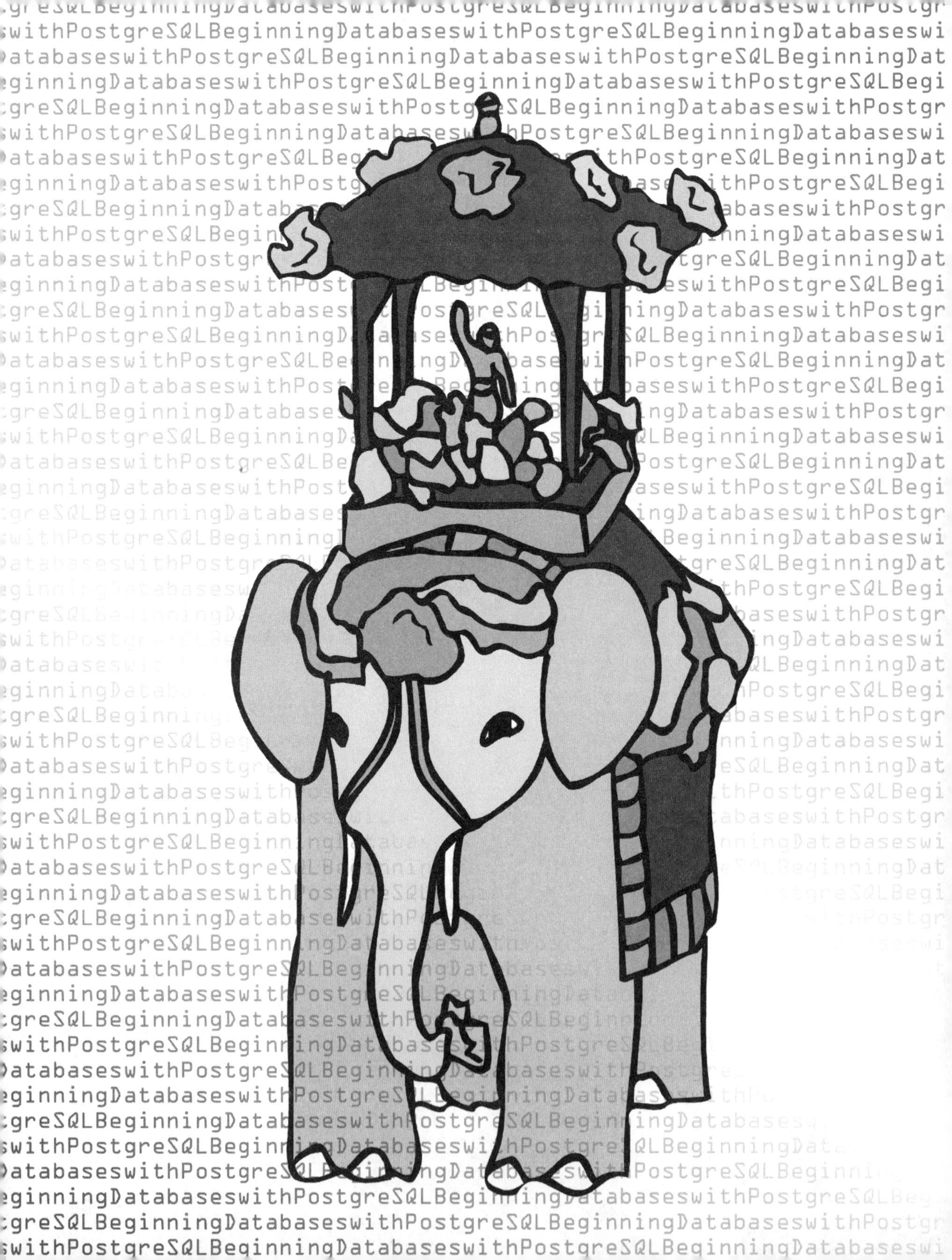
BeginningDatabaseswithPostgreSQL

# Advanced Data Selection

In Chapter 4, we looked in some detail at the SELECT statement and how we can use it to retrieve data for us. This included selecting columns, selecting rows, and joining tables together. In the previous chapter, we looked at ways of adding, updating, and removing data. In this chapter, we return to the SELECT statement, and look at its more advanced features. You will rarely need to use some of these features, but it's useful to know them, so that you have a good understanding of what is possible in SQL.

Readers who are working through the chapters, trying the examples, will notice that in this chapter, and others, we always start with clean base data in the example database, so readers can dip into chapters as they choose. This does mean that some of the output will be slightly different if you continue to use sample data from a previous chapter. The download bundle provides scripts to make it easy to drop the tables, re-create them, and re-populate them with clean data if you wish to do so.

Here, we will meet some special functions called aggregates, which allow us to get results based on a group of rows. We will then meet some more advanced joins that let us control results, where the join between tables is not as simple as those we have used previously. We will also meet a whole new group of queries called subqueries, where we use multiple SELECT statements in a single query. Finally, we will meet the very important outer join, which allows us to join tables together in a more flexible way than we have seen so far.

Along the chapter, we'll be looking at:

- ❑ Aggregate functions
- ❑ The UNION joins
- ❑ Subqueries
- ❑ Self joins
- ❑ Outer joins

## Aggregate Functions

In previous chapters, we have used a couple of special functions: the MAX(column name) function, to tell us the largest value in a column, and the COUNT(*) function, to tell us the number of rows in a table. These functions belong to a small group of SQL functions called aggregates.

The functions in this group are:

- ❏  COUNT(*)
- ❏  COUNT(column name)
- ❏  MIN(column name)
- ❏  MAX(column name)
- ❏  SUM(column name)
- ❏  AVG(column name)

They are often quite useful, and generally easy to use.

> **psql's \da command lists all of the aggregates used by PostgreSQL.**

# COUNT

We will start by looking at COUNT, which, as you will see from the list above, has two forms. The COUNT(*) function provides a row count for a table. It acts as a special column name in a SELECT statement. SELECT statements using any of these aggregate functions can use two optional clauses, GROUP BY and HAVING. The syntax is:

```
SELECT COUNT(*) column list FROM table name WHERE condition [GROUP BY column name
[HAVING aggregate condition]]
```

The new optional GROUP BY clause is an additional condition that can be applied to SELECT statements. It is normally useful only when an aggregate function is being used. It can also be used to provide a function similar to ORDER BY, but by working on the aggregate column. The optional HAVING clause allows us to pick out particular rows where the COUNT(*) meets some condition, and we have already used a GROUP BY clause.

This all sounds a bit complicated, but it's actually quite easy in practice. Let's try out a very simple COUNT(*) just to get the basic idea. We will see GROUP BY in use shortly.

## Try it Out – Basic Use of COUNT(*)

Suppose we wanted to know how many customers we have in our customer table who live in the town, Bingham. We could of course simply write a SQL query like this:

```
SELECT * FROM customer WHERE town = 'Bingham';
```

Or rather more efficiently, since it returns less data, write a SQL query like this:

```
SELECT customer_id FROM customer WHERE town = 'Bingham';
```

This works, but in a rather round about way. It involves retrieving a lot of data we don't actually need. Suppose we had a `customer` table with many thousands of customers, with perhaps over a thousand of them living in Bingham; we would be retrieving a great deal of data that we don't need. The `COUNT(*)` function solves this for us, by allowing us to retrieve just a single row with the count of the number of selected rows in it. We write our `SELECT` statement as we normally do, but instead of selecting real columns, we use `COUNT(*)`, like this:

```
bpsimple=# SELECT COUNT(*) FROM customer WHERE town = 'Bingham';
 count
-------
     3
(1 row)

bpsimple=#
```

If we want to count all the customers, we can just omit the `WHERE` clause:

```
bpsimple=# SELECT COUNT(*) FROM customer;
 count
-------
    15
(1 row)

bpsimple=#
```

You can see we just get a single row, with the count in it. If you want to check the answer, just replace `COUNT(*)` with `customer_id` to show the real data.

### How it Works

The function `COUNT(*)` allows us to retrieve a count of objects, rather than the objects themselves. It is vastly more efficient than retrieving the data for two reasons:

❑   All of the data that we don't need to see does not have to be retrieved from the database, or worse still, sent across a network

❑   `COUNT(*)` allows the database to use its internal knowledge of the table to retrieve the answer, quite probably without actually inspecting any real data rows at all

> **You should never retrieve data when all you need is a count of the number of rows.**

## GROUP BY and COUNT(*)

Frequently, the answer we got in the previous section is almost what we want, but not quite. Suppose we wanted to know how many customers live in each town. We could do it by selecting all the distinct towns, then counting how many customers we had in each town. This is However a rather procedural and tedious way of solving the problem. Wouldn't it be better to have a declarative way of simply expressing the question directly in SQL? You might be tempted to try something like this:

```
SELECT COUNT(*), town FROM customer;
```

It's a reasonable guess based on what we know so far, but PostgreSQL will produce an error message, as it is not valid SQL syntax. The additional bit of syntax you need to know to solve this problem is the `GROUP BY` clause.

**173**

The GROUP BY clause tells PostgreSQL that we want an aggregate function to spit out a result and reset each time a specified column, or columns, change value. It's very easy to use. You simply add a GROUP BY column name to the SELECT with a COUNT(*) function. PostgreSQL will tell you how many of each value of your column exist in the table.

## Try it Out – GROUP BY

Let's try and answer the question, how many customers live in each town?

Stage one is to write the SELECT statement to retrieve the count and column name, just like you may have guessed at before:

```
SELECT COUNT(*), town FROM customer;
```

We then add the GROUP BY clause, to tell PostgreSQL to produce a result and reset the count each time the town changes by issuing a SQL query like this:

```
SELECT COUNT(*), town FROM customer GROUP BY town;
```

Here it is in action:

```
bpsimple=# SELECT COUNT(*), town FROM customer GROUP BY town;
 count |   town
-------+-----------
     3 | Bingham
     1 | Hightown
     1 | Histon
     1 | Lowtown
     1 | Milltown
     2 | Nicetown
     1 | Oahenham
     1 | Oxbridge
     1 | Tibsville
     1 | Welltown
     1 | Winersby
     1 | Yuleville
(12 rows)

bpsimple=#
```

As you can see, we get a nice listing of towns and the number of customers in each town.

### How it Works

PostgreSQL orders the result by the column listed in the GROUP BY clause. It then keeps a running total of rows, and each time the town name changes, it writes a result row, and resets its counter to zero. You will agree that this is much easier than writing procedural code to loop through each town.

We can extend this idea to more than one column if we want to, provided all the columns we select are also listed in the GROUP BY. Suppose we wanted to know two pieces of information. Firstly, how many customers are in each town, and secondly, how many different last names they have. We would simply add lname to both the SELECT and GROUP BY parts of the statement:

```
bpsimple=# SELECT count(*), lname, town FROM customer GROUP BY town, lname;
 count |  lname   |    town
-------+----------+-----------
     1 | Jones    | Bingham
     2 | Stones   | Bingham
     1 | Stones   | Hightown
     1 | Hickman  | Histon
     1 | Stones   | Lowtown
     1 | Hudson   | Milltown
     2 | Matthew  | Nicetown
     1 | Cozens   | Oahenham
     1 | Hendy    | Oxbridge
     1 | Howard   | Tibsville
     1 | O'Neill  | Welltown
     1 | Neill    | Winersby
     1 | Matthew  | Yuleville
(13 rows)

bpsimple=#
```

Notice that the output is sorted first by `town`, then `lname`, since that is the order they are listed in the ORDER BY clause, and that Bingham is now listed twice, because there are customers with two different last names, Jones and Stones who live in Bingham.

## HAVING and COUNT(*)

The last optional part of the statement is the HAVING clause. This clause often causes some confusion with people new to SQL, but it's not difficult to use. You just have to remember that HAVING is a kind of WHERE clause for aggregate functions. We use HAVING to restrict the results returned to rows where a particular aggregate condition is true, such as COUNT(*) is >1. We use it in just the same way as WHERE to restrict the rows based on the value of a column.

> **Aggregates cannot be used in a WHERE clause; they are valid only inside the HAVING clause.**

Let's look at an example, which should make it nice and clear. Suppose we want to know all the towns where we have more than a single customer, we could do it using COUNT(*), and then visually look for the relevant towns. That's not a sensible solution in a situation however where there may be thousands of towns. Instead, we use a HAVING clause to restrict the answers to rows where COUNT(*) was greater than one, like this:

```
bpsimple=# SELECT COUNT(*), town FROM customer
bpsimple-# GROUP BY town HAVING COUNT(*) > 1;
 count |  town
-------+----------
     3 | Bingham
     2 | Nicetown
(2 rows)

bpsimple=#
```

Notice that we must still have our GROUP BY clause, and it appears before the HAVING clause. Now that we have all the basics of COUNT(*), GROUP BY and HAVING, let's put them together in a bigger example.

## Try it Out – HAVING

Suppose we are thinking of setting up a delivery schedule, and we want to know the last names and towns of all our customers, except, we want to exclude Lincoln (maybe it's our local town), and we are only interested in names and towns where there is more than one customer.

This is not as difficult as it might sound; we just need to build up our solution bit by bit. This is often a good approach with SQL. If it looks too difficult, then start by solving a simpler but similar, problem, and then extend the initial solution until you solve the more complex problem. Effectively, take a problem, break it down into smaller parts, and then solve each of the smaller parts.

Let's start with simply returning the data, rather than counting it. We sort by town to make it a little easier to see what is going on:

```
bpsimple=# SELECT lname, town FROM customer WHERE town <> 'Lincoln';
  lname  |   town
---------+-----------
 Stones  | Hightown
 Stones  | Lowtown
 Matthew | Nicetown
 Matthew | Yuleville
 Cozens  | Oahenham
 Matthew | Nicetown
 Stones  | Bingham
 Stones  | Bingham
 Hickman | Histon
 Howard  | Tibsville
 Jones   | Bingham
 Neill   | Winersby
 Hendy   | Oxbridge
 O'Neill | Welltown
 Hudson  | Milltown
 Smyth   | Milltown
 Garrett | Lowtown
(17 rows)

bpsimple=#
```

Looks good so far, doesn't it?

Now if we use COUNT(*) to do the counting for us, we also need to GROUP BY the lname and town:

```
bpsimple=# SELECT COUNT(*), lname, town FROM customer WHERE town <> bpsimple-#
'Lincoln' GROUP BY lname, town;
 count |  lname  |   town
-------+---------+-----------
     1 | Cozens  | Oahenham
     1 | Garrett | Lowtown
     1 | Hendy   | Oxbridge
     1 | Hickman | Histon
     1 | Howard  | Tibsville
     1 | Hudson  | Milltown
     1 | Jones   | Bingham
     2 | Matthew | Nicetown
     1 | Matthew | Yuleville
```

```
    1 | Neill    | Winersby
    1 | O'Neill  | Welltown
    1 | Smyth    | Milltown
    2 | Stones   | Bingham
    1 | Stones   | Hightown
    1 | Stones   | Lowtown
(15 rows)

bpsimple=#
```

We can actually see the answer now by visual inspection, but we are almost at the final answer, which is simply to add a HAVING clause to pick out those rows with a COUNT(*) greater than one:

```
bpsimple=# SELECT COUNT(*), lname, town FROM customer WHERE town <>
bpsimple-# 'Lincoln' GROUP BY lname, town HAVING COUNT(*) > 1;
 count | lname   | town
-------+---------+----------
     2 | Matthew | Nicetown
     2 | Stones  | Bingham
(2 rows)

bpsimple=#
```

Quite straightforward when you break the problem down into parts.

### How It Works

We solved our problem in three stages.

❑ We wrote a simple SELECT statement to retrieve all the rows we were interested in

❑ Next we added a COUNT(*) and a GROUP BY, to count the unique lname and town combination

❑ Finally, we added a HAVING clause to extract only those rows where the COUNT(*) was greater than one

There is However, one slight problem with this approach. If we were working with a customer database containing thousands of rows, we could have had customer lists scrolling past for a very long time while we developed our query. For our sample database it was not a problem, but on a big database this iterative development approach has some drawbacks. Fortunately, there is often an easy way to develop your queries on a sample of the data, but by using the primary key. If we add the condition WHERE customer_id < 50 to all our queries, we could work on a sample of the first 50 customer_ids in the database.

Once we were happy with our SQL, we could have simply removed the WHERE clause to execute our solution on the whole table. Of course we need to be careful that the sample data we used to test our SQL is representative of the full data set, and be wary that smaller samples may not have fully exercised our SQL.

## COUNT(column name)

A slight variant of the COUNT(*) is to replace the '*' with a column name. The difference is that COUNT(column name) counts occurrences in the table where the provided column name is not NULL.

**177**

Suppose we add some more data to our `customer` table, with some new customers having NULL telephone numbers:

```
INSERT INTO customer(title, fname, lname, addressline, town, zipcode)
VALUES('Mr','Gavin','Smyth','23 Harlestone','Milltown','MT7 7HI');
INSERT INTO customer(title, fname, lname, addressline, town, zipcode, phone)
VALUES('Mrs','Sarah','Harvey','84 Willow Way','Lincoln','LC3 7RD','527 3739');
INSERT INTO customer(title, fname, lname, addressline, town, zipcode)
VALUES('Mr','Steve','Harvey','84 Willow Way','Lincoln','LC3 7RD');
INSERT INTO customer(title, fname, lname, addressline, town, zipcode)
VALUES('Mr','Paul','Garrett','27 Chase Avenue','Lowtown','LT5 8TQ');
```

Let's check how many customers we have, whose phone numbers we don't know:

```
bpsimple=# SELECT customer_id FROM customer WHERE phone IS NULL;
 customer_id
-------------
          16
          18
          19
(3 rows)

bpsimple=#
```

We see that there are three customers for whom we don't have a phone number. Let's see how many customers are there in total:

```
bpsimple=# SELECT COUNT(*) FROM customer;
 count
-------
    19
(1 row)

bpsimple=#
```

There are 19 customers in total. Now if we count the number of customers where the phone column is not NULL, there hopefully will be 16 of them:

```
bpsimple=# SELECT COUNT(phone) FROM customer;
 count
-------
    16
(1 row)

bpsimple=#
```

That's the only difference between COUNT(*) and COUNT(column name). The form with an explicit column name counts only rows where the named column is not NULL, the '*' form counts all rows. In all other respects, such as using GROUP BY and HAVING, it works in just the same way as COUNT(*).

# The MIN() Function

Now that we understand COUNT(*) and have learnt the principles of aggregate functions, we can apply the same logic to all the other aggregate functions.

As you might expect, MIN() takes a column name parameter, and returns the minimum value found in that column. For numeric type columns the result would be as expected. For temporal types, such as dates, it returns the largest date, which might be either in the past or future. For variable length strings, the result is slightly unexpected; it compares the strings after they have been right padded with blanks. Be wary of using MIN() or MAX() on VARCHAR type columns, the results may not be what you expect.

Here are a couple of examples.

Find the smallest shipping charge we levied on an order:

```
bpsimple=# SELECT MIN(shipping) FROM orderinfo;
 min
------
 0.00
(1 row)

bpsimple=#
```

It was in fact zero. Notice what happens when we try the same function on our phone column, where we know there are NULL values:

```
bpsimple=# SELECT MIN(phone) FROM customer;
   min
----------
 010 4567
(1 row)

bpsimple=#
```

Now you might have expected the answer to be NULL, or an empty string. Given that NULL generally means unknown, However the MIN() function ignores NULL values. Ignoring NULL values is a feature of all the aggregate functions, except COUNT(*). Whether there is any value in knowing the smallest phone number is of course a different question.

# The MAX() Function

It's not going to be a surprise that the MAX() function is similar to MIN(), but in reverse.

As you might expect, MAX() takes a column name parameter, and returns the maximum value found in that column.

Here are a couple of examples.

Find the largest shipping charge we levied on an order:

```
bpsimple=# SELECT MAX(shipping) FROM orderinfo;
 max
------
 3.99
(1 row)

bpsimple=#
```

Just like MIN(), NULL values are ignored:

```
bpsimple=# SELECT MAX(phone) FROM customer;
    max
----------
 961 4526
(1 row)

bpsimple=#
```

That is pretty much all you need to know about MAX(), except that you can also use GROUP BY and HAVING clauses, just like COUNT(*).

# The SUM() Function

The SUM() function takes the name of a numeric column and provides the total. Just like MIN() and MAX(), NULL values are ignored:

```
bpsimple=# SELECT SUM(shipping) FROM orderinfo;
 sum
------
 9.97
(1 row)

bpsimple=#
```

SUM() does However, have one interesting variant. You can ask it to add up only the unique values, so that multiple rows with the same value only get counted once:

```
bpsimple=# SELECT SUM(DISTINCT shipping) FROM orderinfo;
 sum
------
 6.98
(1 row)

bpsimple=#
```

Note that real world uses for this variant are thin on the ground.

# The AVG() Function

The last aggregate function is AVG(), which also takes a column name and returns the average of the entries. Like SUM(), it also ignores NULL values and it can also take a DISTINCT keyword to work only on distinct values:

```
bpsimple=# SELECT AVG(shipping) FROM orderinfo;
      avg
--------------
 1.9940000000
(1 row)

bpsimple=#
```

The DISTINCT variant:

```
bpsimple=# SELECT AVG(DISTINCT shipping) FROM orderinfo;
      avg
--------------
 2.3266666667
(1 row)

bpsimple=#
```

Note that in standard SQL, and in PostgreSQL's implementation, there are no MODE or MEDIAN functions, though a few commercial vendors do support them as extensions.

# The UNION Join

We are now going to look at the way multiple SELECT statements can be combined to give us more advanced selection capabilities.

Remember the tcust table from the previous chapter that we used as a loading table, while adding data into our main customer table? Suppose that in the time period between loading our tcust table with new customer data, and being able to clean it and load it into our main customer table, we had been asked for a list of all the towns where we had customers including the new data. We might reasonably have pointed out that since we hadn't cleaned and loaded the customer data into the main table yet, we could not be sure of the accuracy of the new data, so any list of towns combining the two lists would not be accurate either. It may well be However that it wasn't important. Perhaps all that was needed was a general indication of the geographic spread of customers, not exact data.

We could solve this problem by selecting the town from the customer table, saving it, and then selecting the town from the tcust table, saving it again, and then combining the two lists. This does seem rather inelegant as we have two tables, However both with a list of towns.

Isn't there some way we could combine the list? As you might gather from the title of this section, there is a way, and it's called a UNION join. These joins are not very common, but in a few circumstances they are exactly what is needed to solve a problem, and they are also very easy to use.

Let's put some data back in our tcust table, so it looks like this:

```
bpsimple=# SELECT * FROM tcust;
title| fname  | lname   | addressline    |  town    | zipcode  |  phone
--+----+-----+-------+-----+-----+---
 Mr  | Peter  | Bradley | 72 Milton Rise | Keynes   | MK41 2HQ |
 Mr  | Kevin  | Carney  | 43 Glen Way    | Lincoln  | LI2 7RD  | 786 3454
 Mr  | Brian  | Waters  | 21 Troon Rise  | Lincoln  | LI7 6GT  | 786 7245
 Mr  | Malcolm | Whalley | 3 Craddock Way | Welltown | WT3 4GQ  | 435 6543
(4 rows)

bpsimple=#
```

Compare getting our list of towns from this table and our customer table.

We already know how to select the `town` from each table; it's a very simple pair of SELECT statements, like this:

```
SELECT town FROM tcust;
SELECT town FROM customer;
```

Each of which gives us a list of towns. In order to combine them, we use the UNION operator to stitch the two SELECT statements together:

```
SELECT town FROM tcust UNION SELECT town FROM customer;
```

## Try it Out – UNION Join

We enter our SQL statement, split across multiple lines to make it easier to read. Notice the `psql` prompt changes from =# to – # to show it's a continuation line, and that there is only a single semi-colon, right at the end, because this is all a single SQL statement:

```
bpsimple=# SELECT town FROM tcust
bpsimple-# UNION
bpsimple-# SELECT town FROM customer;
    town
-----------
 Bingham
 Hightown
 Histon
 Keynes
 Lincoln
 Lowtown
 Milltown
 Nicetown
 Oahenham
 Oxbridge
 Tibsville
 Welltown
 Winersby
 Yuleville
(14 rows)

bpsimple=#
```

### How it Works

PostgreSQL has taken the list of towns from both tables and combined them into a single list. Notice, however, that it has removed all duplicates. If we wanted a list of all the towns, including duplicates, we could have written UNION ALL, rather than just UNION.

This ability to combine SELECT statements is not limited to a single column; we could have combined both the towns and zip codes:

```
SELECT town, zipcode FROM tcust UNION SELECT town, zipcode FROM customer;
```

This would have produced a list with both columns present. It would have been a longer list, because `zipcode` is included, and hence there are more unique rows to be retrieved.

The UNION join is not magic though, the two lists of columns you ask to be combined from the two tables must each have the same number of columns, and the chosen corresponding columns must also have compatible types. Let's see:

```
bpsimple=# SELECT title FROM customer
bpsimple-# UNION
bpsimple-# SELECT town FROM tcust;
  title
----------
 Keynes
 Lincoln
 Miss
 Mr
 Mrs
 Welltown
(6 rows)

bpsimple=#
```

The query, although rather nonsensical, is valid, because PostgreSQL can combine the columns, even though title is a fixed length column and town a variable length column, because they are at least both strings of characters. If we tried to combine customer_id and town for example, then PostgreSQL would tell us that it could not be done, because the column types are different.

Generally, that is all you need to know about UNION joins, occasionally a very handy way to combine data from two (or more) tables.

# Subqueries

Now that we have met SQL statements which have more than a single SELECT in them, we can look at a whole class of data retrieval statements that combine SELECT statements in much more complex ways. These are rather more difficult to understand than single SELECT statement queries or UNION joins, but they are very useful, and open up a whole new area of data selection criteria.

A subquery is where we make one (or more) of the WHERE conditions of a SELECT to be another SELECT statement.

Suppose we want to find all items in the item table with a cost price greater than 10. The SELECT is slightly complicated by the need to cast the number we are testing against into a NUMERIC(7,2), to be compatible with the column type of cost_price in the item table, but is basically straightforward:

```
bpsimple=# SELECT * FROM item WHERE cost_price > CAST(10.0 AS NUMERIC(7,2));
 item_id | description | cost_price | sell_price
---------+-------------+------------+-----------
       1 | Wood Puzzle |      15.23 |      21.95
       7 | Fan Large   |      13.36 |      19.95
      11 | Speakers    |      19.73 |      25.32
(3 rows)

bpsimple=#
```

Suppose, we want to find the items that have a cost price that is higher than the average cost price. We can easily do it in two queries:

```
bpsimple=# SELECT AVG(cost_price) FROM item;
      avg
-------------
 7.2490909091
(1 row)

bpsimple=# SELECT * FROM item WHERE cost_price > CAST(7.249 AS
bpsimple-# NUMERIC(7,2));
 item_id |  description  | cost_price | sell_price
---------+---------------+------------+-----------
       1 | Wood Puzzle   |      15.23 |      21.95
       2 | Rubic Cube    |       7.45 |      11.49
       5 | Picture Frame |       7.54 |       9.95
       6 | Fan Small     |       9.23 |      15.75
       7 | Fan Large     |      13.36 |      19.95
      11 | Speakers      |      19.73 |      25.32
(6 rows)

bpsimple=#
```

This does seem However rather inelegant. What we really want to do is pass the result of the first query straight into the second query, without having to remember it and then type it back in for a second query.

This is just one of the things that subqueries allow us to do. What we do is put the first query in brackets, and use it as part of a WHERE clause to the second query, like this:

```
bpsimple=# SELECT * from ITEM WHERE cost_price > (SELECT AVG(cost_price)
bpsimple-# FROM item);
 item_id |  description  | cost_price | sell_price
---------+---------------+------------+-----------
       1 | Wood Puzzle   |      15.23 |      21.95
       2 | Rubic Cube    |       7.45 |      11.49
       5 | Picture Frame |       7.54 |       9.95
       6 | Fan Small     |       9.23 |      15.75
       7 | Fan Large     |      13.36 |      19.95
      11 | Speakers      |      19.73 |      25.32
(6 rows)

bpsimple=#
```

As you can see, we get the same result, but without needing the intermediate step or the cast, since the result is already of the right type.

PostgreSQL runs the query in brackets first. After getting the answer, it then runs the outer query substituting the answer from the inner query. We can have many subqueries using various WHERE clauses if we want. We are not restricted to just one, though needing multiple nested SELECT statements is rare.

Let's try a more complex example. Suppose we want to know all the items where the cost price is above the average cost price, but the selling price is below the average selling price. Something that probably suggests our margin is not very good, so hopefully there are not too many items that fit those criteria.

We already know how to find the average cost price, SELECT AVG(cost_price) FROM item. Finding the average selling price is similar, SELECT AVG(sell_price) FROM item.

The main query is going to be of the form:

```
SELECT * FROM item WHERE cost_price > average cost price AND sell_price < average
selling price
```

If we put these three queries together, what we get is:

```
bpsimple=# SELECT * FROM item WHERE cost_price > (SELECT AVG(cost_price)
bpsimple-# FROM item) AND sell_price < (SELECT AVG(sell_price) FROM item);
 item_id |  description  | cost_price | sell_price
---------+---------------+------------+-----------
       5 | Picture Frame |       7.54 |       9.95
(1 row)

bpsimple=#
```

Perhaps someone needs to look at the price of picture frames and see if it is correct!

### How It Works

PostgreSQL first scans the query and finds that there are two queries in brackets, the subqueries. It evaluates each of those subqueries independently, and then puts the answers back into the appropriate part of the main query of WHERE clause before executing it.

We could also have applied additional WHERE clauses, or ORDER BY clauses. It is perfectly valid to mix WHERE conditions that comes from subqueries, with more conventional conditions.

# Types of Subquery

So far we have only used subqueries that return a single result, because we used an aggregate function in the subquery. In general, subqueries can have three types of result:

❑ A single value (like those we have already seen)

❑ Zero or more rows

❑ A test for existence of something

Let's look at the second type of subquery, where several rows could be returned. Suppose we want to know what items we have in stock where the cost price is greater than 10.0. Now we could do this with a single SELECT statement, like this:

```
bpsimple=# SELECT s.item_id, s.quantity FROM stock s, item i WHERE
bpsimple-# i.cost_price > CAST(10.0 AS NUMERIC(7,2)) AND s.item_id =
bpsimple-# i.item_id;
 item_id | quantity
---------+----------
       1 |       12
       7 |        8
(2 rows)

bpsimple=#
```

Notice that we give the tables alias names (stock becomes s, item becomes i), to keep the query shorter. All we are doing is joining the two tables (s.item_id = i.item_id), while also adding a condition about the cost price in the item table (i.cost_price > CAST(10.0 AS NUMERIC(7,2))).

We can also write this as a subquery, using the keyword IN to test against a list of values. What we need to do is write a query that gives us a list of item_ids where the item has a cost price less than 10.0:

```
SELECT item_id FROM item WHERE cost_price > CAST(10.0 AS NUMERIC(7,2));
```

We also need a query to select items from the stock table:

```
SELECT * FROM stock WHERE item_id IN list of values
```

We can then put the two queries together, like this:

```
bpsimple=# SELECT * FROM stock WHERE item_id IN (SELECT item_id FROM item
bpsimple-# WHERE cost_price > CAST(10.0 AS NUMERIC(7,2)));
 item_id | quantity
---------+----------
       1 |       12
       7 |        8
(2 rows)

bpsimple=#
```

This gives us the same result. It is quite common to be able to rewrite subqueries as joins, however not all subqueries can be rewritten in this way, so it is important to understand them. Just like more conventional queries, we could negate the condition by writing NOT IN, and we could also add additional WHERE clauses and ORDER BY conditions.

If you have a subquery that can be rewritten as a join, which one should you use? There are two things to consider – readability and performance. If it is a query that you use occasionally on small tables that executes quickly, then use whichever form you find most easily readable. If it is a heavily used query on large tables, then it may be worth writing it in different ways and experimenting to discover which performs best. You may find that the query optimizer is able to optimize both styles, so the performance is identical between the two, in which case readability automatically wins.

> **Be careful in testing the performance of SQL statements. There are a lot of variables beyond your control, such as the caching of data by the operating system.**

You may also find that performance is critically dependent on the exact data in your database, or that it varies dramatically as the number of rows in different tables change.

We haven't yet met the last type of subquery, one that tests for existence, because it is rather complex. Don't worry, However we will be coming back to them before the end of the chapter.

# Correlated Subqueries

The types of subquery we have seen so far are those where we executed a query to get an answer, which we then 'plug in' to a second query. The two queries however are otherwise unrelated and are called uncorrelated subqueries. This is because there are no linked tables between the inner and outer queries. We may be using the same column from the same table in both parts of the SELECT, but they are related only by the result of the subquery being fed back into the main query's WHERE clause.

There is another group of subqueries, called correlated subqueries where the relationship between the two parts of the query is rather more complex. In a correlated subquery, a table in the inner SELECT will be joined to a table in the outer SELECT hence these two queries are correlated. This is a powerful group of subqueries, which quite often cannot be rewritten as simple SELECT statements with joins.

A correlated query has the general form:

```
SELECT columnA from table1 T1 WHERE T1.columnB = (SELECT T2.columnB FROM table2 T2
WHERE T2.columnC = T1.columnC)
```

We have written this as some pseudo SQL to make it a little easier to explain. The important thing to notice is that the table in the outer SELECT, T1, also appears in the inner SELECT. The inner and outer queries are, therefore, deemed to be correlated. You will notice we have aliased the table names. This is important, as the rules for table names in correlated subqueries are rather complex, and a slight mistake can give strange results.

> **We strongly suggest you always alias all tables in a correlated subquery, as this is the safest option.**

When this is executed, something quite complex happens. First, a row from table T1 is retrieved for the outer SELECT, then the column T1.columnB is passed to the inner query, which then executes selecting from table T2, but using the information that is passed in. The result of this is then passed back to the outer query, which completes evaluation of the WHERE clause, before moving on to the next row.

This is shown in the diagram below:

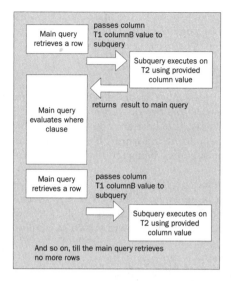

If this sounds a little long winded, then it is. Correlated subqueries often execute quite inefficiently. However they do occasionally solve some particularly complex problems. Hence, it's well worth knowing they exist, even though you may use them only infrequently.

## Try it Out – A Correlated Subquery

On a simple database, such as the one we are using, there is little need for correlated subqueries. They can generally be rewritten in other ways, however we can still use our sample database to demonstrate their use.

Let us suppose we want to know the date when orders were placed for customers in Bingham. Although we could write this more conventionally, we will use a correlated subquery, like this:

```
bpsimple=# SELECT oi.date_placed FROM orderinfo oi WHERE oi.customer_id =
bpsimple=# (SELECT c.customer_id from customer c WHERE c.customer_id =
bpsimple=# oi.customer_id and town = 'Bingham');
 date_placed
-------------
 2000-06-23
 2000-07-21
(2 rows)

bpsimple=#
```

### How it Works

The query starts by selecting a row from the orderinfo table. It then executes the subquery on the customer table, using the customer_id it found. The subquery executes, looking for rows where the customer_id from the outer query gives a row in the customer table that also has the town Bingham. If it finds one, it then passes the customer_id back to the original query, which completes the WHERE clause, and, if it is true, prints the date_placed column. The outer query then proceeds to the next row, and the sequence repeats.

Let's look at a different example. This time we will use the third type of subquery, the type we have not met yet, where the subquery tests for existence.

Suppose we want to list all the customers who have placed orders. In our sample database, these are not many. The first part of the query is easy, we write:

```
SELECT fname, lname FROM customer c;
```

Notice that we have aliased the table name `customer` to `c`, ready for the subquery. The next part of the query needs to discover if the `customer_id` also exists in the `orderinfo` table:

```
SELECT 1 FROM orderinfo oi WHERE oi.customer_id = c.customer_id;
```

There are two very important aspects to notice here. Firstly, we have used a common 'trick'. Where we need to execute a query but don't need the results, we simply place '1' where a column name would be. This means that if any data is found, a 1 will be returned, which is an easy and efficient way of saying 'true'. This is a weird idea, so let's just try it:

```
bpsimple=# SELECT 1 FROM customer WHERE town = 'Bingham';
 ?column?
----------
        1
        1
        1
(3 rows)

bpsimple=#
```

So it may look a little odd, but it does work. It is important not to use COUNT(*) here, because we need a result from each row where the town is Bingham, not just to know how many customers are from Bingham.

The second important thing to notice, is that we use the column `customer` in this sub-select, which was actually in the original select. This is what makes it correlated. As before we alias all the table names. Now we need to put the two halves together.

It's time to meet the last form of subquery, which we skipped over earlier. This subquery tests for existence using the EXISTS keyword in the WHERE clause, without needing to know what data is present.

For our query, using EXISTS is a good way of combining the two SELECT statements together, because we only want to know if the sub-select return a row. An EXISTS clause will normally execute more efficiently than other types of join or IN conditions. Hence, it's often worth using it in preference to other types of join, where you have a choice of how to write the subquery.

```
bpsimple=# SELECT fname, lname FROM customer c WHERE EXISTS ( SELECT 1 FROM
bpsimple-# orderinfo oi WHERE oi.customer_id = c.customer_id);
 fname  | lname
--------+---------
 Alex   | Matthew
 Ann    | Stones
 Laura  | Hendy
 David  | Hudson
(4 rows)

bpsimple=#
```

You can see here how correlated subqueries are written, and when you come across a problem that you can't seem to be able to solve in SQL with more common queries, you may find that the correlated subquery is the answer to your difficulties.

# Self Joins

One very special type of join is called a self join, and is used where we want to use a join between columns that are in the same table. It's quite rare to need to do this, but occasionally very useful, so we will mention it briefly.

Suppose we sell items that can be sold as a set, or individually. For the sake of example, let us suppose we sell a set of chairs and table item, and also the table and chairs separately. What we would like to do is store not only the individual items, but also the relationship between them when they are sold as a single item. This is frequently called 'parts explosion' and we will meet it again in Chapter 12.

Let's start by creating a table that can hold not only an item id and its description, but also a second item id, like this:

```
CREATE TABLE part (part_id INT, description VARCHAR(32), parent_part_id INT);
```

We will use the parent_part_id to store the component id of which this is a component. For example, suppose we had a table and chairs set, say item_id 1, which was composed of chairs, say item_id 2, and a table, say item_id 3. The INSERT statements, when executed, would look like this:

```
bpsimple=# INSERT INTO part(part_id, description, parent_part_id) VALUES(1,
bpsimple-# 'table and chairs', NULL);
INSERT 21579 1

bpsimple=# INSERT INTO part(part_id, description, parent_part_id) VALUES(2,
bpsimple-# 'chair', 1);
INSERT 21580 1

bpsimple=# INSERT INTO part(part_id, description, parent_part_id) VALUES(3,
bpsimple-# 'table', 1);
INSERT 21581 1

bpsimple=#
```

Now we have stored the data, but how do we retrieve the information about what individual parts make up a particular component? We need to join the part table to itself.

This turns out to be quite easy. What we need to do is alias the table names, then we can write a WHERE clause referring to the same table, but using different names:

```
bpsimple=# SELECT p1.description, p2.description FROM part p1, part p2 WHERE
bpsimple-# p1.part_id = p2.parent_part_id;
    description      | description
--------------------+-------------
 table and chairs   | chair
 table and chairs   | table
(2 rows)

bpsimple=#
```

This works, but is a little confusing, because we have two output columns with the same name. We can easily rectify this by naming them using AS:

```
bpsimple=# SELECT p1.description AS "Combined", p2.description AS "Parts"
bpsimple-# FROM part p1, part p2 WHERE p1.part_id = p2.parent_part_id;
    Combined      |  Parts
------------------+-------
 table and chairs | chair
 table and chairs | table
(2 rows)

bpsimple=#
```

We will see self joins again in Chapter 12, when we look at how a manager/subordinate relationship can be stored in a single table.

# Outer Joins

Our last major topic in this chapter is a class of joins known as outer joins. They are similar to more conventional joins, but use a slightly different syntax, which is why we had postponed meeting them till the end of this chapter.

Let's look at our item and stock tables:

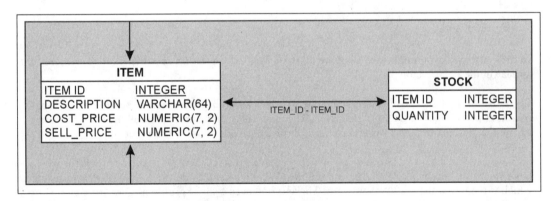

As you will remember, all the items that we might sell are held in the item table, but only items we actually stock are held in the stock table.

Suppose we want to have a list of all items we sell, indicating the quantity we have in stock. This apparently simple request, turns out to be surprisingly difficult in the SQL we know so far, though it can be done. It is quite instructive to work through a solution, so let's do it using only the SQL we know so far.

Let's try a simple SELECT, joining the two tables:

```
bpsimple=# SELECT i.item_id, s.quantity FROM item i, stock s WHERE i.item_id
bpsimple-# = s.item_id;
 item_id | quantity
---------+----------
       1 |       12
       2 |        2
```

```
          4 |         8
          5 |         3
          7 |         8
          8 |        18
         10 |         1
(7 rows)

bpsimple=#
```

It's easy to see (since we happen to know that our item_ids in the item table are sequential, with no gaps), that some item_ids are missing. The rows that are missing are those relating to items that we do not stock, since the join between the item and stock tables fails for these rows, as the stock table has no entry for that item_id.

We can find the missing rows, using a sub-select and an IN clause:

```
bpsimple=# SELECT i.item_id FROM item i WHERE i.item_id NOT IN (SELECT
bpsimple-# i.item_id FROM item i, stock s WHERE i.item_id = s.item_id);
 item_id
---------
       3
       6
       9
      11
(4 rows)

bpsimple=#
```

In ordinary speak, we might say "Tell me all the item_ids in the item table, excluding those that also appear in the stock table".

The inner SELECT statement is simply the one we used earlier, but this time we use the list of item_ids it returns as part of another SELECT statement. The main SELECT statement lists all the known item_ids, except that the WHERE NOT IN clause removes those item_ids found in the subquery.

So now we have a list of item_ids for which we have no stock, and a list of item_ids for which we do have stock, but retrieved using different queries. What we need to do now is join the two lists together, which is the job of the UNION statement. There is however a slight problem. Our first statement returns two columns, item_id and quantity, but our second SELECT returns only item_ids, as there is no stock for these items. We need to add a dummy column to the second SELECT, so it has the same number and types of columns as the first SELECT. We are going to use NULL, although we might equally well have used 0 (zero). You will see why we chose NULL a little later.

Here is our complete query:

```
SELECT i.item_id, s.quantity FROM item i, stock s WHERE i.item_id = s.item_id
UNION
SELECT i.item_id, NULL FROM item i WHERE i.item_id NOT IN
       (SELECT i.item_id FROM item i, stock s WHERE i.item_id = s.item_id);
```

Looks a bit complicated, but let's give it a try:

```
bpsimple=# SELECT i.item_id, s.quantity FROM item i, stock s WHERE i.item_id
bpsimple-# = s.item_id
bpsimple-# UNION
bpsimple-# SELECT i.item_id, NULL FROM item i WHERE i.item_id NOT IN (select
bpsimple-# i.item_id FROM item i, stock s WHERE i.item_id = s.item_id);
 item_id | quantity
---------+----------
       1 |       12
       2 |        2
       3 |
       4 |        8
       5 |        3
       6 |
       7 |        8
       8 |       18
       9 |
      10 |        1
      11 |
(11 rows)

bpsimple=#
```

In the early days of SQL, this was pretty much the only way of solving this type of problem, except that SQL89 did not allow the NULL we used in the second SELECT statement as a column. Fortunately, most vendors allowed the NULL, or life would have been even more difficult. If we had not been allowed to use NULL, we would have had to use 0, as the next best alternative. NULL is better, because 0 is potentially misleading, NULL will always be blank.

To get around this rather complex solution for what is a reasonably common problem, vendors invented what was called the outer joins. Unfortunately, because it did not appear in the standard, all the vendors invented their own solutions, with similar ideas, but different syntax.

Oracle and DB2 used a syntax where a '+' sign is used in the WHERE clause to indicate that all values of a table must appear (the preserved table), even if the join fails. Sybase used a *= in the WHERE clause to indicate the preserved table. Both of these syntaxes are reasonably straightforward, but unfortunately different, which is not good for the portability of your SQL.

When the SQL92 standard appeared, it specified a very general-purpose way of implementing outer joins, which has another syntax again. Vendors have been slow to implement the new standard. Sybase 11 did not support it, nor did Oracle 8. Both are products that came out after the standard. PostgreSQL implemented the standard method from version 7.1 onwards. So if you are running an older version, you will need to upgrade to try the last section of this chapter. It's probably worth upgrading if you are running a version older than 7.1 anyway, as version 7.1 has significant improvements over older versions.

The SQL92 syntax replaces the WHERE clause we are familiar with, an ON clause for joining tables, and adds the LEFT OUTER JOIN key words.

The syntax looks like this:

```
SELECT columns FROM table1 LEFT OUTER JOIN table2 ON table1.column = table2.column
```

The table name to the left of LEFT OUTER JOIN is always the preserved table, the one from which all rows are shown.

So now we can rewrite our query, using this new syntax:

```
SELECT i.item_id, s.quantity FROM item i LEFT OUTER JOIN stock s ON i.item_id =
s.item_id;
```

Looks almost too simple to be true? Let's give it a go:

```
bpsimple=# SELECT i.item_id, s.quantity FROM item i LEFT OUTER JOIN stock s
bpsimple-# ON i.item_id = s.item_id;
 item_id | quantity
---------+----------
       1 |       12
       2 |        2
       3 |
       4 |        8
       5 |        3
       6 |
       7 |        8
       8 |       18
       9 |
      10 |        1
      11 |
(11 rows)

bpsimple=#
```

Excellent, an identical answer. You can see why most vendors felt they needed to implement an outer join, even though it wasn't in the original SQL89 standard.

There is also the equivalent RIGHT OUTER JOIN, but the left join is almost always the one that is used, probably because logically, at least for Westerners, it makes more sense to list the known items down the left side of the output, rather than the right.

## Try it Out – A More Complex Condition

The simple left outer join we have used till now is great as far as it goes, but how do we add more complex conditions?

Suppose we want only rows from the stock table where we have more than 2 items in stock, and overall we are only interested in rows where the cost price is greater than 5.0. This is quite a complex problem, because we want to apply one rule to the item table (that cost price is $> 5.0$) and a different rule to the stock table (quantity $> 2$), but we still want to list all rows from the item table where the condition on the item table is true, even if there is no stock at all.

What we do is combine ON conditions that work on left outer joined tables only, with WHERE conditions, that limit all the rows returned after the table join has been performed.

The condition on the stock table is part of the outer join, we don't want to restrict rows where there is no quantity, so we write this as part of the ON condition:

```
ON i.item_id = s.item_id AND s.quantity > 2
```

For the `item` condition, which applies to all rows, we use a WHERE clause:

```
WHERE i.cost_price > CAST(5.0 AS NUMERIC(7,2));
```

Putting them both together, we get:

```
bpsimple=# SELECT i.item_id, i.cost_price, s.quantity FROM item i LEFT OUTER
bpsimple-# JOIN stock s ON i.item_id = s.item_id AND s.quantity > 2 WHERE
bpsimple-# i.cost_price > CAST(5.0 AS NUMERIC(7,2));
 item_id | cost_price | quantity
---------+------------+----------
       1 |      15.23 |       12
       2 |       7.45 |
       5 |       7.54 |        3
       6 |       9.23 |
       7 |      13.36 |        8
      11 |      19.73 |
(6 rows)

bpsimple=#
```

### How it Works

We use a LEFT OUTER JOIN to get all the values from the `item` table, optionally joining to the `stock` table where both a row exists and the quantity is greater than 2. This gives us a set of rows where all the rows from the `item` table appear, but the `quantity` column (from the `stock` table) will contain NULL unless it both has an entry for that item AND the quantity value is greater than 2. The WHERE clause is then applied, which only allows through rows where the cost price (from the `item` table) is greater than 5.0.

# Summary

We started the chapter looking at aggregate functions that we can use in SQL to select single values from a number of rows. In particular, we met the COUNT(*) function, which you will find widely used to determine the number of rows in a table.

We then met the GROUP BY clause, which allows us to select groups of rows to apply the aggregate function too, followed by the HAVING clause, which allows us to restrict the output of rows containing particular aggregate values. We then looked briefly at the UNION join, which allows us to combine the output of two queries in a single result set. Although this is not widely used, it can occasionally be very useful.

We then took a look at subqueries, where we use the results from one query in another query. We also saw some simple examples, and touched on a much more difficult kind of query, the correlated subquery, where the same column appears in both parts of a subquery.

Finally we met outer joins, a very important feature that allows us to perform joins between two tables, retrieving rows from the first table even when the join to the second table fails.

In this chapter, we have covered some difficult aspects of SQL. Don't worry if some parts seem a little unclear still, one of the best ways of truly understanding SQL is to use it, and use it extensively. Get PostgreSQL installed, install the test database and some sample data, and experiment.

We have now covered the SELECT statement in as much detail as we will need for this book. Although it is a Beginning book we have covered a wide range of SQL syntax, so should you meet some advanced SQL in existing systems, you will at least have a reasonable understanding of what is being done.

In the next chapter, we will be looking in more detail at types, creating tables, and more that you need to know to build your own database.

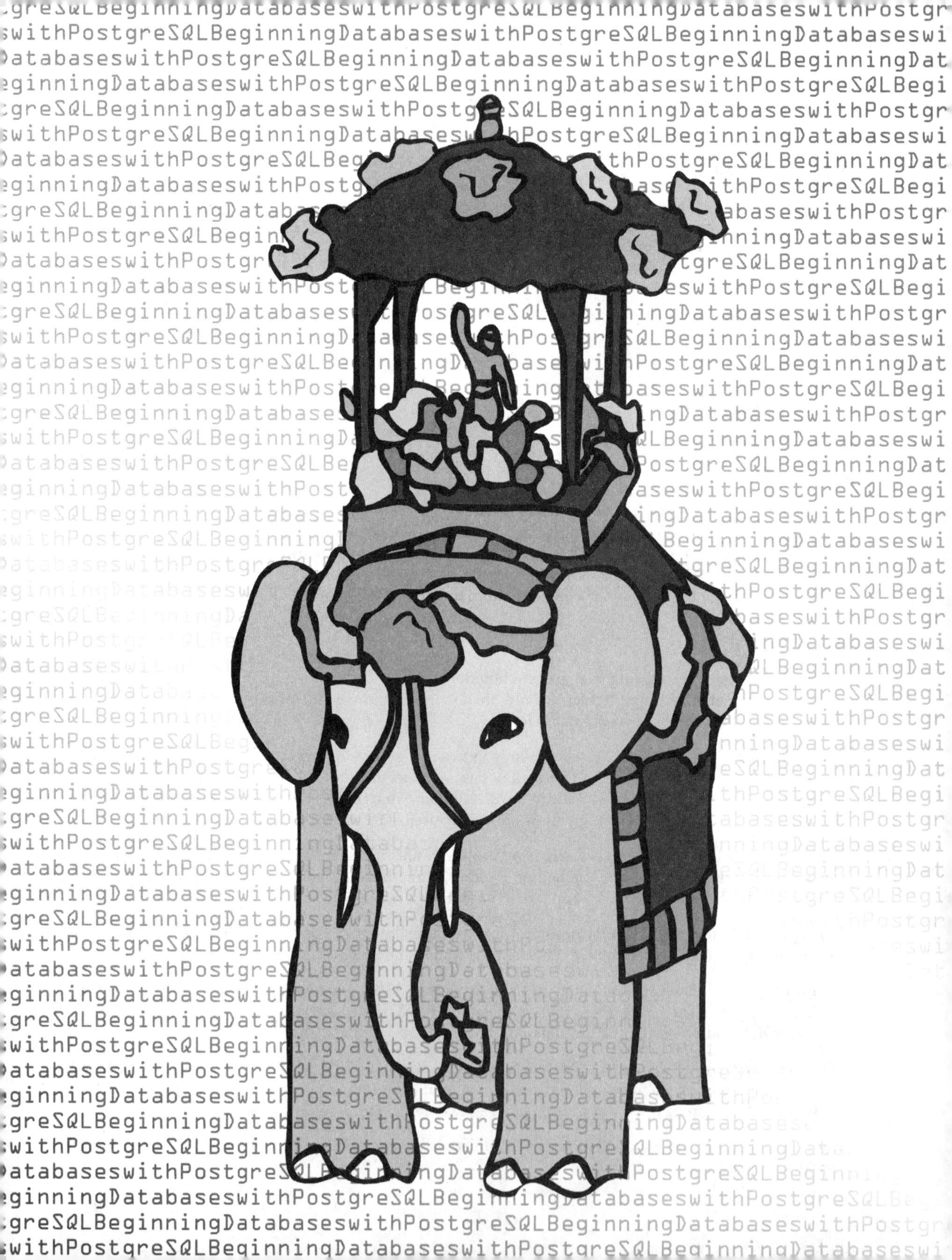
BeginningDatabaseswithPostgreSQL

# Data Definition and Manipulation

Up until now, we have concentrated on the PostgreSQL tools and data manipulation. Although we created a database for ourselves early in the book, we only looked superficially at table creation and the data types available in PostgreSQL. We kept our table definitions quite simple by just using primary keys and defining a few columns that do not accept Null values.

In a database, the quality of the data should always be one of our primary concerns, and in this chapter, we are going to look in more detail at the data types available in PostgreSQL, and how to manipulate them, including **casting** between data types.

We shall look more formally at how tables are managed, and most importantly how you can use more advanced features, such as **constraints**, to significantly tighten the rules we apply when data is added to, or removed from, the tables in the database.

Having very strict rules about the data enforced at the lowest level by the database, is one of the most effective measures you can use to maintain the data in a consistent state. This is also one of the features that distinguish true databases from simple indexed files, spreadsheets, and the like.

Throughout the chapter, we will be looking at:

- ❑ Data types
- ❑ PostgreSQL special types
- ❑ Manipulating tables
- ❑ Views
- ❑ Foreign key constraints

## Data Types

PostgreSQL supports a standard set of SQL data types, and in addition, a few more esoteric types that we will mention, but not cover in great depth, as their usefulness is rather limited.

At the most basic level, PostgreSQL supports these types of data:

- **Boolean**
- **Character**
- **Number**
- **Temporal (time-based)**
- **PostgreSQL extension types**
- **Binary Large Object (BLOB)**

Let's look at each of these in turn, except the Binary Large Objects (BLOB), which is beyond the scope of a *Beginning*-level book.

# Boolean

The Boolean type is probably the simplest possible type. It can only store two possible values, True and False, and our old friend Null, for unknown.

The type declaration for a Boolean column is simply `bool`.

When data is inserted into a Boolean column in a table, PostgreSQL is quite flexible about what it will interpret as True and False. Like SQL keywords, these are also case-insensitive:

| Interpreted as True | Interpreted as False |
| --- | --- |
| TRUE | FALSE |
| '1' | '0' |
| 'yes' | 'no' |
| 'y' | 'n' |
| 'true' | 'false' |
| 't' | 'f' |

Anything else will be rejected, apart from Null.

When PostgreSQL displays the contents of a Boolean column, it will only display t, f, and NULL for a True, False, and Null respectively. It doesn't matter how you set the column value, PostgreSQL only stores one of the three possible states, True, False, or Null, so the exact phrase (`true`, `y`, `t`, and so on) you used to set the column value is never stored, only the resulting value. This should never be a problem, since if you declared a column to be of type Boolean, why do you care how its value was initially set?

## Try It Out – Boolean Values

Let's create a simple table with a `bool` column, and experiment with some values. As we have seen before, to create a column with a name and a type, we simply give the name, some whitespace, and then the type what we want to associate with the name.

We will create a table, testtype, with a variable length string and a Boolean column, insert some data, and see what PostgreSQL stores. Rather than experiment in our bpsimple database with our real data, we create a test database to use as a 'play' area. If you worked with the examples in Chapter 3, you may already have created this database. If not, creating it is easy:

```
bpsimple=# CREATE DATABASE test;
CREATE DATABASE

bpsimple=# \c test
You are now connected to database test.

test=#
```

Here is our session:

```
test=# CREATE TABLE testtype (
test-# valused VARCHAR(10),
test-# boolres BOOL
test-# );
CREATE
test=# INSERT INTO testtype VALUES('TRUE', TRUE);
INSERT 19132 1
test=# INSERT INTO testtype VALUES('1', '1');
INSERT 19133 1
test=# INSERT INTO testtype VALUES('t', 't');
INSERT 19134 1
test=# INSERT INTO testtype VALUES('no', 'no');
INSERT 19135 1
test=# INSERT INTO testtype VALUES('f', 'f');
INSERT 19136 1
test=# INSERT INTO testtype VALUES('Null', NULL);
INSERT 19137 1
test=# INSERT INTO testtype VALUES('FALSE', FALSE);
INSERT 19138 1
test=#
```

Let's check that the data has been inserted:

```
test=# SELECT * FROM testtype;
 valused | boolres
---------+---------
 TRUE    | t
 1       | t
 t       | t
 no      | f
 f       | f
 Null    |
 FALSE   | f
(7 rows)

test=#
```

### How It Works

We create a table `testtype` with two columns, the first holds a string, and the second holds a Boolean. We then insert data into the table, each time making the first value a string to remind us what we inserted, the second the same value, but to be stored as a Boolean value. We also inserted a Null, to show that PostgreSQL (unlike at least one commercial database), does allow Null to be stored in a Boolean type. We then extracted the data again, which showed us how PostgreSQL had interpreted the value we passed to it as one of True, False, or Null.

# Character

The character data types are probably the most widely used in any database, and are divided into three sub-types:

❑   A single character

❑   Fixed length character strings

❑   Variable length character strings

These are standard SQL character types, but PostgreSQL also supports a TEXT type, which is similar to the variable length type, except that you do not have to declare any upper limit to the length. This is not a standard SQL type, However and so, should be used with caution. The standard types are defined using CHAR, CHAR(N) and VARCHAR(N):

| Definition | Meaning |
|---|---|
| CHAR | A single character. |
| CHAR(N) | A set of characters exactly N characters in length, padded with spaces. If you attempt to store a string that is too long, then the additional characters will be silently ignored. |
| VARCHAR(N) | A set of characters up to N characters in length, no padding. |
| TEXT | Effectively unlimited length character string, like VARCHAR but without the need to define a maximum. |

To all intents and purposes, the maximum length of the string you can store is unlimited in version 7.1 and above. The actual limit was raised to 1 GB (one Gigabyte) for any single field of a table from version 7.1 of PostgreSQL, but in practice you should never need a character string like anything this long.

Given a choice of three standard types to use for character strings, which should you pick? As always, there is no definitive answer.

If you know that your database is only ever going to be run on PostgreSQL, then TEXT is a good choice, since it is easy to use, and doesn't force you into maximum length decisions. Its length is limited only by the maximum row size that PostgreSQL can support. If you are using a version of PostgreSQL earlier than 7.1, the row limit is around 8 KB, unless you recompiled from sources and changed it. From 7.1 onwards, that limit is gone. Another good reason for upgrading! The downside is that TEXT is not a standard type, so if there is a chance that you will one day need to port your database to something other than PostgreSQL, it is best avoided. Generally, we have avoided the TEXT type in this book, preferring the more standard SQL type definitions.

The advantage of the VARCHAR(N) type, is that it only stores as many characters as required, plus a length. With CHAR(N) type, the length is fixed, so may be slightly more efficient in some circumstances. In general, if your string is short and a known length, it is probably best to use the CHAR(N) type. Where the length varies significantly between different rows of data, choose the VARCHAR(N) type. If in doubt, use VARCHAR(N).

Just like the Boolean type, all character types can also contain NULL, for unknown values.

## Try It Out – Character Types

First, we need to drop our testtype table, and then we can re-create it with some different column types:

```
test=# DROP TABLE testtype;
DROP
test=# CREATE TABLE testtype (
test-#         singlechar       CHAR,
test-#         fixedchar        CHAR(13),
test-#         variablechar     VARCHAR(128)
test-# );
CREATE
test=# INSERT INTO testtype VALUES('F', '0-349-10177-9', 'The Wasp
test-# Factory');
INSERT 19164 1
test=# INSERT INTO testtype VALUES('S', '1-85723-457-X', 'Excession');
INSERT 19165 1
test=# INSERT INTO testtype VALUES('F', '0-349-10768-8', 'Whit');
INSERT 19166 1
test=# INSERT INTO testtype VALUES(NULL, '', 'T.B.D.');
INSERT 19167 1
test=# SELECT * FROM testtype;

 singlechar |    fixedchar    |   variablechar
------------+-----------------+------------------
 F          | 0-349-10177-9   | The Wasp Factory
 S          | 1-85723-457-X   | Excession
 F          | 0-349-10768-8   | Whit
            |                 | T.B.D.
(4 rows)
test=#
```

### How It Works

We create a table with three columns, one for each of the different standard SQL types. The column singlechar holds a single character, fixedchar holds exactly 13 characters, and variablechar holds up to 128 characters. We then store different data in the columns, and retrieve them again to show, that PostgreSQL has stored the data correctly, although in the psql output, you can't actually see the padding.

# Number

The number types in PostgreSQL are slightly more complex than those we have met so far, but they are not particularly difficult to understand. There are two distinct types of numbers that we can store in the database, **integers** and **floating-point** numbers. These sub-divide again, with a special sub-type of integer, the SERIAL type, which we have already used to create unique values in a table, and different sizes of integers. Floating-point numbers also subdivide, into those offering general-purpose floating-point values, and fixed precision numbers, including the PostgreSQL specific MONEY type.

If we show all the number types in a table, it is easier to see what the choices are:

| Type | Sub-type | Standard Name | Description |
| --- | --- | --- | --- |
| Integer numbers | small integer | SMALLINT | A two byte signed integer, capable of storing numbers from -32768 to 32767. |
| | integer | INT | A four byte integer, capable of storing numbers from -2147483648 to +2147483647. |
| | serial | SERIAL | Same as INT, except that it is normally automatically entered by PostgreSQL, as we saw in Chapter 6. |
| Floating-point numbers | float | FLOAT(N) | A floating-point number with at least the precision N, up to a maximum of 8 bytes of storage. |
| | float8 | REAL | A double precision (8 byte) floating-point number. |
| | numeric | NUMERIC(P,S) | A real number with P digits, S of them after the decimal point. Unlike FLOAT, this is always an exact number, but less efficient to work with than ordinary floating point numbers. |
| | money | NUMERIC(9,2) | A PostgreSQL-specific type, though common in other databases. In PostgreSQL MONEY is an alternative name for NUMERIC(9,2). |

The split of the two types into integer and floating-point numbers is easy enough to understand, but what might be less obvious, is the purpose of the NUMERIC type.

Floating-point numbers are stored in scientific notation, with a **mantissa** and **exponent**. With the NUMERIC type, you get to specify both the precision and the exact number of digits stored when performing calculations., You can also specify the number of digits held after the decimal point. The actual decimal point location comes free!

> A common mistake is to think that **NUMERIC(5,2)** can store a number, such as 12345.12. This is not correct. The total number of digits stored is only five, so a declaration **NUMERIC(5,2)** can only store up to 999.99 before overflowing.

PostgreSQL will generally catch attempts to insert values into fields that cannot store them, so attempting to insert overly large numbers into any number column will fail.

## Try It Out – Number Types

First, we need to drop our `testtype` table, and then re-create it with some different column types:

```
test=# DROP TABLE testtype;
DROP
test=# CREATE TABLE testtype (
test-#        asmallint      SMALLINT,
test-#        anint          INT,
test-#        afloat         FLOAT(2),
test-#        areal          REAL,
test-#        anumeric       NUMERIC(5,2)
test-# );
CREATE
test=# INSERT INTO testtype VALUES(2, 2, 2.0, 2.0, 2.0);
INSERT 19244 1
test=# INSERT INTO testtype VALUES(-100, -100, 123.456789, 123.456789,
test-# 123.456789);
INSERT 19245 1
test=# INSERT INTO testtype VALUES(-32768, -123456789, 1.23456789,
test-# 1.23456789, 1.23456789);
INSERT 19246 1
test=# INSERT INTO testtype VALUES(-32768, -123456789, 123456789.123456789, test-#
123456789.123456789, 123456789.123456789);
ERROR:  overflow on numeric ABS(value) >= 10^8 for field with precision 5 scale 2
test=# INSERT INTO testtype VALUES(-32768, -123456789, 123456789.123456789, test-#
123456789.123456789, 123.123456789);
INSERT 19247 1
test=# SELECT * FROM testtype;

 asmallint |    anint    |   afloat    |    areal    | anumeric
-----------+-------------+-------------+-------------+----------
         2 |           2 |           2 |           2 |     2.00
      -100 |        -100 |     123.457 |     123.457 |   123.46
    -32768 |  -123456789 |     1.23457 |     1.23457 |     1.23
    -32768 |  -123456789 | 1.23457e+08 | 1.23457e+08 |   123.12
(4 rows)

test=#
```

## How It Works

We create a table with a small integer column, a normal integer column, a floating-point number, a real number, and a numeric with a precision of 5 and a scale of 2.

You can see that FLOAT and REAL behave in a similar fashion, but the numeric column behaves slightly differently, rather than storing approximate numbers, it rounds the number to store a fixed number of digits after the decimal place. The INSERT fails if we try and store a number in it that is too large. Also notice, that both FLOAT and REAL have rounded numbers, for example, 123.456789 has been rounded to 123.457.

# Temporal

We looked at temporal (types that store time related information) earlier when we saw how to control data formats.

PostgreSQL has a range of types relating to date and time, but we will confine ourselves to the standard SQL-92 types:

| Definition | Meaning |
|---|---|
| DATE | Stores date information |
| TIME | Stores time information |
| TIMESTAMP | Stores a date and time |
| INTERVAL | Stores information about a difference in timestamps |

We have already considered date and time in some detail in Chapter 4, we will not look at them further in this chapter.

# PostgreSQL Special Types

From its origins as a research database system, PostgreSQL has acquired some unusual data types. We will list them here for interest, but will not consider them in detail. For further information, consult the PostgreSQL user guide in the online documentation:

| Definition | Meaning |
|---|---|
| Box | A rectangular box |
| cidr or inet | A Ipv4 internet address such as 196.192.12.45 |
| Line | A set of points |
| Point | A geometric pair of numbers |
| Lseg | A line segment |
| polygon | A closed geometric line |

# Creating Your Own Types

PostgreSQL also allows you to create your own types for use in the database, using the SQL CREATE TYPE command. This is not commonly needed, and is performed in a manner unique to PostgreSQL. Further details can be found in the user documentation. Be aware that creating your own types is likely to result in a database schema that is specific to PostgreSQL, as user-created types tend not to be very portable.

## Array Types

PostgreSQL has another unusual feature; the ability to store arrays in tables. This is not a standard SQL feature. Normally, an array would be implemented using an additional table, but since they can occasionally be useful, and are easy to use, we will briefly cover PostgreSQL arrays here.

To declare a column in a table as an array, you simply add [ ] after the type, there is no need to declare the number of elements. Suppose we decided to have a table of employees, with an indicator to show which days of the week they worked. Normally, this would require a column for each day, or a separate table to hold the workdays. In PostgreSQL, we can simplify this and hold an array of working days directly:

```
test=# CREATE TABLE empworkday (
test-# refcode CHAR(5),
test-# workdays INT[]
test-# );
CREATE

test=#
```

This creates a table empworkday with two columns, a character reference code, and an array of integers called workdays. To insert values into the array column, we have to enclose a comma-separated list of values in a pair of { } delimiters, such as this:

```
test=# INSERT INTO empworkday VALUES('val01', '{0,1,0,1,1,1,1}');
INSERT 19290 1
test=# INSERT INTO empworkday VALUES('val02', '{0,1,1,1,1,0,1}');
INSERT 19291 1

test=#
```

We can now either select all the values of the array elements in one go:

```
test=# SELECT * FROM empworkday;
 refcode  |     workdays
----------+------------------
 val01    | {0,1,0,1,1,1,1}
 val02    | {0,1,1,1,1,0,1}
(2 rows)

test=#
```

Or, select individual elements by giving an array index:

```
test=# SELECT workdays[2] FROM empworkday WHERE refcode = 'val02';
 workdays
----------
        1
(1 row)

test=#
```

Unusually for computers, the first array element is 1. If you try and select a non-existent array element, a Null will be returned.

More about PostgreSQL's unique array handling can be found in the user manual on the web site.

# Converting Between Types

From time to time, we need to convert between types in a database. Generally, you should be concerned at seeing type conversions, since many type conversions may indicate a design flaw. Occasionally, however, it is necessary as we saw earlier in Chapter 4, to perform conversions, particularly with dates.

There is quite a degree of variation in how relational databases do this. PostgreSQL uses a CAST notation, with an alternative double colon syntax. The syntax is:

```
CAST(column-name AS type-definition-to-convert-to)
```

Or

```
column-name::type-definition-to-convert-to
```

Used in place of a simple column name in a SELECT statement.

Suppose we wanted to grab the date from the orderinfo table as a char(10). We would revert back to the bpsimple database and simply write:

```
SELECT CAST(date_placed AS CHAR(10)) FROM orderinfo;
```

When we execute this in our bpsimple database, we see:

```
bpsimple=# SELECT CAST(date_placed AS CHAR(10)) FROM orderinfo;
  ?column?
------------
 2000-03-13
 2000-06-23
 2000-09-02
 2000-09-03
 2000-07-21
(5 rows)

bpsimple=#
```

Notice that the column is now unnamed.

We can use CAST (or : : ) on values as well as columns, and we can name the result, to provide a column heading.

## Try It Out – Casting Types

Suppose we want to produce a list of items, showing the price to the nearest $, over $5. If we try the simplistic:

```
bpsimple=# SELECT sell_price::int FROM item WHERE sell_price > 5.0;
```

PostgreSQL is not happy:

```
ERROR:  Unable to identify an operator '>' for types 'numeric' and 'float8'
        You will have to retype this query using an explicit cast
```

What we need to do is not only cast the sell_price to an integer, but also the value we are supplying to test it with to a numeric, since that is the type of the sell_price column we are testing. We also forgot to name the resulting column. Let's try again:

```
bpsimple=# SELECT item_id, sell_price::int AS "Guide Price" FROM item WHERE
bpsimple-# sell_price > 5.0::NUMERIC(7,2);
 item_id | Guide Price
---------+-------------
       1 |          22
       2 |          11
       5 |          10
       6 |          16
       7 |          20
      11 |          25
(6 rows)

bpsimple=#
```

Success!

### How It Works

We cast the sell_price column to an integer (sell_price::int) and also name it (AS "Guide Price"). This gives us a named output column in integer format. To make the types compatible in the WHERE part of the statement, we also have to use a CAST to convert our 5.0 to a NUMERIC(7,2), the type of the sell_price column.

We could just as well have written this using the CAST(::) notation; the two are interchangeable. Note that it is not possible to universally convert between types. For example, you cannot cast a date as an integer.

# Other Data Manipulations

PostgreSQL also provides some general-purpose functions that you can use for manipulating columns. We will not list them all here – see instead the online documentation for more details.

Here, we present a few of the more generally useful ones:

| Function | Description |
|---|---|
| length(column-name) | Returns the length of a string. |
| trim(column-name) | Removes leading and trailing spaces. |
| strpos(column-name, string) | Returns the position of string in the column. |
| substr(column-name, position, length) | Returns the length characters from the string, starting the search from the given character position. The first character is counted as position 1. |
| round(column-name, length) | Rounds a number to a given number of decimal places. |
| Abs(number) | Gets the absolute value of a number. |

These are used just like the CAST function:

```
bpsimple=# SELECT substr(description, 3, 5), round(sell_price, 1) FROM item;
 substr | round
--------+-------
 od Pu  |  22.0
 bik C  |  11.5
 nux C  |   2.5
 ssues  |   4.0
 cture  |  10.0
 n Sma  |  15.8
 n Lar  |  20.0
 othbr  |   1.5
 man C  |   2.5
 rrier  |   0.0
 eaker  |  25.3
(11 rows)

bpsimple=#
```

# Magic Variables

Occasionally, we want to store some information in the database that relates to the current user or time in some way, perhaps to implement an audit trail.

PostgreSQL provides four magic variables for doing this:

- ❏ CURRENT_DATE
- ❏ CURRENT_TIME
- ❏ CURRENT_TIMESTAMP
- ❏ CURRENT_USER

You can use these just like column names, or you can SELECT them without a table name at all:

```
bpsimple=# SELECT item_id, quantity, CURRENT_TIMESTAMP FROM stock;
 item_id | quantity |        timestamp
---------+----------+------------------------
       1 |       12 | 2001-03-25 09:22:11+01
       2 |        2 | 2001-03-25 09:22:11+01
       4 |        8 | 2001-03-25 09:22:11+01
       5 |        3 | 2001-03-25 09:22:11+01
       7 |        8 | 2001-03-25 09:22:11+01
       8 |       18 | 2001-03-25 09:22:11+01
      10 |        1 | 2001-03-25 09:22:11+01
(7 rows)

bpsimple=# SELECT CURRENT_USER, CURRENT_TIME;
 current_user |    time
--------------+----------
 rick         | 09:22:20
(1 row)

bpsimple=#
```

These magic variables can also be used in INSERT and UPDATE statements such as this:

```
INSERT INTO orderinfo(orderinfo_id, customer_id, date_placed, date_shipped,
shipping) VALUES (5, 8, CURRENT_DATE, NULL, 0.0);
```

# The OID Column

You will have noticed that each time we insert data, PostgreSQL responds with an almost arbitrary looking number, as well as the number of rows inserted. This number is an internal reference number that PostgreSQL stores against each row, a normally hidden column called oid.

Most relational databases either do not have such a column, or it is never accessible to the users. With PostgreSQL, we can see this number by explicitly naming it when we SELECT from a table, such as this:

```
bpsimple=# SELECT oid, fname, lname FROM customer;
  oid  |   fname   |  lname
-------+-----------+---------
 19888 | Jenny     | Stones
 19889 | Andrew    | Stones
 19890 | Alex      | Matthew
 19891 | Adrian    | Matthew
 19892 | Simon     | Cozens
 19893 | Neil      | Matthew
 19894 | Richard   | Stones
 19895 | Ann       | Stones
 19896 | Christine | Hickman
 19897 | Mike      | Howard
 19898 | Dave      | Jones
 19899 | Richard   | Neill
 19900 | Laura     | Hendy
 19901 | Bill      | O'Neill
 19902 | David     | Hudson
(15 rows)

bpsimple=#
```

Your database will almost certainly have different values for the `oid` column. You will also see OID appear in ODBC driver configuration. You can choose to display it or hide it.

In a properly designed database, with well-constructed primary keys you should never need to use the OID. We mention it here for completeness, but urge you to resist the temptation to ever use it.

# Manipulating Tables

Now that we know about PostgreSQL data types, we can use them to create tables. We have already seen the CREATE TABLE SQL command, which we used to create tables in our example database, but we will cover it more formally here. We will also learn about additional features, such as temporary tables, altering tables after creation, and of course deleting tables, when they are no longer required.

## Creating Tables

The basic syntax for creating tables is:

```
CREATE [TEMPORARY] TABLE table-name (
    { column-name type [ column-constraint ] [,…] }
    [ CONSTRAINT table-constraint ]
) [ INHERITS (existing-table-name) ]
```

Although short, this looks a little complex, but is actually quite straightforward. The first line simply says that you create tables by using CREATE TABLE, followed by the name of the table and an opening parenthesis. We will come back to TEMPORARY shortly. After that, you list the column name, its type, and an optional column constraint. You can essentially have an unlimited number of columns in your table, each one separated by a comma. The optional column constraint allows us to specify additional rules for the column, and we have already seen the most common example, NOT NULL.

After the list of columns, comes an optional table-level constraint, which allows us to write additional table level rules that must be obeyed by the data in the table.

Last comes a PostgreSQL extension, INHERITS, which allows a new table to be created. This table inherits the columns from existing tables. The new table contains all the columns that are in the tables listed after the INHERITS keyword, in addition to those specified directly. More about INHERITS can be found in the online documentation.

We strongly advise you to always store the commands you use for creating your database in a script, and always use that script for creating your database. If you need to change the database design, it is so much easier, and more reliable, to modify the script, then re-create the database, rather than to try and recall the commands you used initially to create the database all those months (or was it just days...) ago. You will find that the effort of initially creating a script, and keeping it up to date, pays you back many, many times over.

## Column Constraints

We have already seen plenty of basic table creation commands in this chapter, therefore let's skip straight on to looking at the common column constraints you might need to use. It is common to have columns in your table where certain rules apply. We have seen some simple ones already, such as ensuring that a customer's last name is NOT NULL. Sometimes, we want to impose rules that govern the data when it is known, such as ensuring that a pay rate column will only accept values above a minimum value, or ensuring that columns are unique. Applying constraints to columns allows us to perform these checks at the lowest level of our complete application – in the database. For hard and fast basic rules, enforcing them at the database level is a good technique, since it is independent of the application, so any application bugs that might allow illegal values to slip through, will be caught by the database. It is also often easier to apply the rule by writing a definition when a table is created, rather than write application logic code to support the rule.

These are the principal constraints that you will find useful, although there are more advanced constraints, which you can find in the online documentation:

| Definition | Meaning |
| --- | --- |
| NOT NULL | The column cannot have a Null value stored in it. |
| UNIQUE | The value stored in the column must be different for each row in the database. See below for how Null is handled. |
| PRIMARY KEY | Effectively, a combination of NOT NULL and UNIQUE. Each table may only have a single column marked PRIMARY KEY (you can have multiple columns marked both NOT NULL and UNQIUE however). We will see a little later in the chapter, that if you need to create a composite primary key (a primary key that comprises more than one column), you have to use a table-level constraint, rather than the column-level constraints we are discussing here. |
| DEFAULT value | Allows you to provide a default value when inserting data. |
| CHECK (condition) | Allows you to check a condition when inserting or updating data. |
| REFERENCES | See the section *Foreign Key Constraints* near the end of this chapter. |

Apart from REFERENCES, which we will cover in more detail later in the chapter, these are all quite simple to understand. Apart from PRIMARY KEY, you can have as many columns with as many constraints as you need. It is possible, but not common, to name column-level constraints.

One particular point to note, is what happens when a Null value is added to a column with a UNIQUE constraint. PostgreSQL considers each Null to be unique, so it allows you to have as many rows as you like with Null in a column declared UNIQUE. According to the SQL standard, only a single Null should be allowed, so this is a slight deviation from the standard. Arguably, the SQL standard is more logical, since if Null is unknown, there is no way of knowing that two of them are different, but the PostgreSQL implementation, allowing multiple Nulls, is probably more intuitive.

## Try It Out – Column Constraints

The easiest way of understanding column constraints, is simply to see them in action. Let's create a table to experiment with, in the test database we created earlier, and use it to experiment with some constraints:

```
bpsimple=# \c test
You are now connected to database test
test=# CREATE TABLE testcolcons (
test-#        colnotnull INT NOT NULL,
test-#        colunique INT UNIQUE,
test-#        colprikey INT PRIMARY KEY,
test-#        coldefault INT DEFAULT 42,
test-#        colcheck INT CHECK( colcheck < 42)
test-# );
NOTICE:  CREATE TABLE/PRIMARY KEY will create implicit index 'testcolcons_pkey'
for table 'testcolcons'
NOTICE:  CREATE TABLE/UNIQUE will create implicit index
'testcolcons_colunique_key' for table 'testcolcons'
CREATE

test=#
```

You can see that PostgreSQL warns us that it has created indexes to enforce the PRIMARY KEY and UNIQUE constraints.

Now that we have created a table with a variety of constraints on the columns, we can try inserting some data, and see how the constraints work in practice:

```
test=# INSERT INTO testcolcons(colnotnull, colunique, colprikey, coldefault, test-
# colcheck) VALUES(1,1,1,1,1);
INSERT 19341 1
test=# INSERT INTO testcolcons(colnotnull, colunique, colprikey, coldefault, test-
# colcheck) VALUES(2,2,2,2,2);
INSERT 19342 1
test=# INSERT INTO testcolcons(colnotnull, colunique, colprikey, coldefault, test-
# colcheck) VALUES(2,2,2,2,2);
ERROR:  Cannot insert a duplicate key into unique index testcolcons_pkey

test=#
```

This INSERT has failed, because the index testcolcons_pkey found a duplicate value. We have to use a little bit of common sense here, and realize that an index called testcolcons_pkey is referring to a primary key index on the testcolcons table. Hardly a great leap of intuition! Each table can only have one primary key,therefore there is no ambiguity in the index being called tablename_pkey.

```
test=# INSERT INTO testcolcons(colnotnull, colunique, colprikey, coldefault, test-
# colcheck) VALUES(2,2,9,2,2);
ERROR:  Cannot insert a duplicate key into unique index testcolcons_colunique_key

test=#
```

This time, the INSERT fails, because the index testcolcons_colunique_key found a duplicate. You can have many columns all declared UNIQUE,therefore PostgreSQL names the index tablename_columnname_key so it is clear which column is causing the problem:

```
test=# INSERT INTO testcolcons(colnotnull, colunique, colprikey, coldefault, test-
# colcheck) VALUES(2,9,9,2,2);
INSERT 19345 1
test=# INSERT INTO testcolcons(colnotnull, colunique, colprikey, coldefault, test-
# colcheck) VALUES(3,3,3,3,100);
ERROR:  ExecAppend: rejected due to CHECK constraint testcolcons_colcheck

test=#
```

This time the INSERT fails, because the CHECK constraint failed. Notice the constraint is named tablename_columnname so the source of the problem is easy to locate:

```
test=# UPDATE testcolcons SET colunique = 1 WHERE colnotnull = 2;
ERROR:  Cannot insert a duplicate key into unique index testcolcons_colunique_key

test=#
```

We cannot update the value of colunique, because there is already a row in the table where the column has that value:

```
test=# INSERT INTO testcolcons(colnotnull, colunique, colprikey, colcheck)
VALUES(3,3,3,41);
INSERT 19346 1
test=# SELECT * FROM testcolcons ;
 colnotnull | colunique | colprikey | coldefault | colcheck
------------+-----------+-----------+------------+----------
          1 |         1 |         1 |          1 |        1
          2 |         2 |         2 |          2 |        2
          2 |         9 |         9 |          2 |        2
          3 |         3 |         3 |         42 |       41
(4 rows)`

test=#
```

Finally, we fail to provide a value for the coldefault column (notice it is not listed in the column list), and see that the default value is used.

If we ever want to check the constraints on a table, we can always ask psql to list them, using the \d tablename command, such as this:

```
test=# \d testcolcons
        Table "testcolcons"
 Attribute  |  Type   |  Modifier
------------+---------+------------
 colnotnull | integer | not null
 colunique  | integer |
 colprikey  | integer | not null
```

```
coldefault | integer | default 42
colcheck   | integer |
Indices: testcolcons_colunique_key,
         testcolcons_pkey
Constraint: (colcheck < 42)

test=#
```

### How It Works

PostgreSQL uses a variety of methods to implement constraints. It is not possible to control the order in which constraints are checked however; the exact error you get will depend on PostgreSQL internal implementations. What you can guarantee is that all constraints will be checked before the data is stored in the database. You can also use transactions, which we will be meeting in Chapter 9 *Transactions and Locking*, to ensure that all or none, of a set of changes are made to the database.

## Table Constraints

Table constraints are very similar to column constraints, but as the name suggests, apply to the table, rather than an individual column. Occasionally, we need to specify constraints, such as a primary key, at a table level rather than a column-level. For example, we saw in our `orderline` table we needed to use two columns, `orderinfo_id` and `item_id` together as a composite key to identify a row, since only the combination of columns has to be unique.

The four table-level constraints are:

| Name | Description |
| --- | --- |
| UNIQUE(column list) | The value stored in the columns must be different from that stored in all other rows of this column. |
| PRIMARY KEY(column list) | Effectively a combination of NOT NULL and UNIQUE. Each table may only have a single PRIMARY KEY constraint, either as a table constraint or as a column constraint. |
| CHECK (condition) | Allows you to check a condition when inserting or updating data. |
| REFERENCES | See the section *Foreign Key Constraints* near the end of this chapter. |

As you can see they bear more than a passing resemblance to the column-level constraints.

The differences are:

❑   Table-level constraints are listed after all the columns

❑   They take comma-separated lists of column names, so a table-level constraint can refer to more than one column

Let's dive straight in and give table level-constraints a go.

## Try It Out – Table Level Constraints

First, we create a table with some constraints:

```
test=# CREATE TABLE ttconst (
test-# mykey1 int,
test-# mykey2 int,
test-# mystring varchar(15),
test-# CONSTRAINT cs1 CHECK (mystring <> ''),
test-# CONSTRAINT cs2 PRIMARY KEY(mykey1, mykey2)
test-# );
NOTICE:  CREATE TABLE/PRIMARY KEY will create implicit index 'cs2' for table
'ttconst'
CREATE

test=#
```

Notice that like the column-level constraint, PostgreSQL has created an index to enforce the primary key constraint

```
test=# INSERT INTO ttconst VALUES(1,1,'Hello');
INSERT 19381 1
test=# INSERT INTO ttconst VALUES(1,2,'Bye');
INSERT 19382 1

test=#
```

Notice that although the value of mykey1 is 1 for both rows, since mykey2 has changed the constraint, that the pair are unique has not been violated

```
test=# INSERT INTO ttconst VALUES(1,2,'');
ERROR:  ExecAppend: rejected due to CHECK constraint cs1

test=#
```

The table level CHECK constraint works almost identically to the column-level one, rejecting the row, because the string was empty

```
test=# INSERT INTO ttconst VALUES(2,2,'Chow');
INSERT 19383 1
test=# INSERT INTO ttconst VALUES(2,2,'Hi');
ERROR:  Cannot insert a duplicate key into unique index cs2

test=#
```

When both mykey values are the same, the row is rejected, because the primary key constraint has now been violated.

As you can see, table-level constraints are very similar to their column-level equivalents. In general, it is better to use a column-level constraint if that is all that is required. Where you need a mix of column-level and table-level constraints, such as we needed when we created our bpsimple database, however many people prefer to use a table-level primary key constraint on all the tables, for the sake of consistency.

# Altering Table Structures

Unfortunately, life is complicated, and no matter how carefully you gather requirements and implement your database, the day will come when you need to alter the design of a table.

We saw one way we might solve this in Chapter 6, using INSERT INTO where the data is gathered by selecting data from an existing table. We could:

❑ Create a new working table with an identical structure to the existing table

❑ Use INSERT INTO to populate the working table with data identical to the original table

❑ Delete the existing table

❑ Re-create the table with the same name, but with the changes we need

❑ Use INSERT INTO again to populate the altered table from the working table

❑ Delete the working table

That is clearly a great deal of work, however especially if the table contains a lot of data, if all we wanted to do is add a column to a table. The SQL standard allows for columns to be added and deleted from a table 'in situ'. That is, while it contains data. At the time of writing, PostgreSQL only supports the ability to add new columns to a table, not to remove them.

You can also rename a column preserving its data, and rename the whole table too.

The syntax is simple:

```
ALTER TABLE table-name ADD COLUMN column-name column-type
ALTER TABLE table-name RENAME COLUMN old-column-name TO new-column-name
ALTER TABLE old-table-name RENAME TO new-table-name
```

Columns that are added to a table with existing data will have Null stored as their value for the existing rows.

Here they are in action:

```
test=# \d ttconst
            Table "ttconst"
 Attribute |         Type         | Modifier
-----------+----------------------+----------
 mykey1    | integer              | not null
 mykey2    | integer              | not null
 mystring  | character varying(15) |
Index: cs2
Constraint: (mystring <> ''::"varchar")

test=#
```

First, we add a new column:

```
test=# ALTER TABLE ttconst ADD COLUMN mydate DATE;
ALTER
test=# \d ttconst
                Table "ttconst"
  Attribute  |         Type          |  Modifier
-------------+-----------------------+-----------
 mykey1      | integer               | not null
 mykey2      | integer               | not null
 mystring    | character varying(15) |
 mydate      | date                  |
Index: cs2
Constraint: (mystring <> ''::"varchar")

test=#
```

Now, we rename the column we just added:

```
test=# ALTER TABLE ttconst RENAME COLUMN mydate TO birthdate;
ALTER
test=# \d ttconst
                Table "ttconst"
  Attribute  |         Type          |  Modifier
-------------+-----------------------+-----------
 mykey1      | integer               | not null
 mykey2      | integer               | not null
 mystring    | character varying(15) |
 birthdate   | date                  |
Index: cs2
Constraint: (mystring <> ''::"varchar")

test=#
```

Finally, we rename the whole table:

```
test=# ALTER TABLE ttconst RENAME TO ttconst2;
ALTER

test=#
```

As you can see, ALTER TABLE is very simple to use.

One thing you should be very wary of, is constantly changing a table structure by adding new columns. New columns are always added at the end of the table, and so may not logically reflect the logical purpose of the table very well.

Suppose we had forgotten a `title` column when we created our `customer` table, and then added it on later. The column would have been added at the end, which would have made the design of the `customer` table look a little strange, with a person's title coming after their phone number. For this reason, many people are very wary of adding columns to an existing table and hence prefer to:

❑ Create a new table with a temporary name, but the right columns in the most logical order

❑ Use INSERT INTO ... SELECT ... to populate it as a duplicate of the table being changed

❑ Delete the old table

❑ Rename the new table with the same name as the old table

You do need to be careful that sequences, and triggers, see Chapter 10 *Stored Procedures and Triggers*, may also need to be dropped and recreated when tables are dropped and renamed.

## Deleting Tables

Deleting a table is very simple:

```
DROP TABLE table-name
```

Presto! Your table has disappeared, along with any data that was in it. A command to be used with caution!

## Temporary Tables

All the SQL we have seen so far have managed to achieve our desired result in a single, albeit occasionally complex, SELECT statement. Usually, this is a good practice, because you will remember we said that SQL is a declarative language. If you define what you want to achieve, SQL finds the best way of getting the result for you. Sometimes it is just not possible, or convenient, to do everything in a single SELECT statement, and some temporary results need to be held.

Usually, the temporary storage you need is a table, so you can store many rows. Of course, you could always create a table, do your processing, and then delete the table again, but that entails a risk that the intermediate tables will occasionally fail to get deleted, either because your application has a bug, or due to simple forgetfulness from an interactive user. The net result is stray tables, usually with strange names, left around in your database. Unfortunately, it is not always clear which tables are intended to be just intermediate work tables and can be deleted, and which are currently in use.

SQL has a very simple solution to this problem, the idea of temporary tables. When you create the table, rather than use CREATE TABLE, you use CREATE TEMPORARY TABLE (you can also use CREATE TEMP TABLE, which is just a synonym). The table is created for you in the usual way, except that when your session ends and your connection to the database gets terminated, the temporary table is automatically deleted for you.

Be aware that the \dt command does not list temporary tables.

## Views

When you have a complex database, or sometimes when you have various users with different permissions, see Chapter 11 *PostgreSQL Administration*, you need to create the illusion of a table. Let's look at an example.

Suppose you want to allow people in the warehouse to look at the items and barcodes in our database. Currently, these are split across two tables, item and barcode. While correct from a design point of view, we might wish to present a simpler view to people accessing the data, perhaps in a very simplistic way using some of the GUI tools we saw in Chapter 5. Rather than change our design, what we need to do is create the illusion of one table, and we can do this with a **view**.

The syntax for creating a view is very simple:

```
CREATE VIEW name-of-view AS select-statement;
```

You can then use the view as though it is a table. At the time of writing, in PostgreSQL, views are read-only. In other databases, however views and hence the underlying data in the tables, can be updated, just like tables. You SELECT data from a view just as you would a table, including joining it to other tables and using WHERE clauses.

Each time you SELECT using the view, the data is rebuilt, so the data is always up-to-date. It is not a frozen copy stored at the time the view was created.

Suppose we want to create a view that provides a simplified view of the item table. We just want to see the item_id, description and the sell_price. The SELECT statement would be

```
SELECT item_id, description, sell_price FROM item;
```

So, to create this as a view called (for example) item_price we would write:

```
CREATE VIEW item_price AS SELECT item_id, description, sell_price FROM item;
```

You will remember from Chapter 5 that we had a minor difficulty with the price definition in the item table. Assuming that we consider our definition of price as NUMERIC(7,2) to be 'correct', we can still keep this definition, but present a different view of the type, using a view with a CAST in the SELECT statement.

## Try It Out – Creating a View

Let's create a view of the item table that alters what users see in two ways. Firstly, we want to hide the cost_price (we will see more about permissions in Chapter 11 *PostgreSQL Administration*, and how we could remove access to the original item table from ordinary users). Secondly, we want to present the sell_price as though it was a simple floating-point number, rather than a numeric field.

We can do this by creating a view, like this:

```
bpsimple=# CREATE VIEW item_price AS SELECT item_id, description,
bpsimple-# CAST(sell_price AS FLOAT) AS price FROM item;
CREATE

bpsimple=#
```

Now when we SELECT data from the view, it behaves like a subset of the columns in the original table:

```
bpsimple=# SELECT * FROM item_price;
 item_id |  description  | price
---------+---------------+-------
       1 | Wood Puzzle   | 21.95
       2 | Rubik Cube    | 11.49
       3 | Linux CD      |  2.49
       4 | Tissues       |  3.99
       5 | Picture Frame |  9.95
```

**219**

```
 6 | Fan Small     | 15.75
 7 | Fan Large     | 19.95
 8 | Toothbrush    |  1.45
 9 | Roman Coin    |  2.45
10 | Carrier Bag   |     0
11 | Speakers      | 25.32
(11 rows)

bpsimple=#
```

### How It Works

We create a view that has just the columns we want to allow people to see from the table. To convert the sell_price to a float we use the CAST operator. Notice that we also name the column (using AS price) to ensure that users see a named column.

We are not restricted to using only one table in a view – we can use as complex a piece of SQL, accessing as many tables as we like.

## Try It Out – Creating a View from Multiple Tables

Let's create a view, which will solve our problem of presenting a simplified view of the item and barcode tables, hiding the price information and the split of data into two tables. We call the VIEW all_items command:

```
bpsimple=# CREATE VIEW all_items AS SELECT i.item_id, i.description, bpsimple-#
b.barcode_ean FROM item i, barcode b WHERE i.item_id = b.item_id;
CREATE

bpsimple=#
```

This creates a new view, which we can now use just like a table:

```
bpsimple=# SELECT * FROM all_items;

 item_id | description   | barcode_ean
---------+---------------+---------------
       1 | Wood Puzzle   | 6241527836173
       2 | Rubik Cube    | 6241574635234
       3 | Linux CD      | 6264537836173
       3 | Linux CD      | 6241527746363
       4 | Tissues       | 7465743843764
       5 | Picture Frame | 3453458677628
       6 | Fan Small     | 6434564564544
       7 | Fan Large     | 8476736836876
       8 | Toothbrush    | 6241234586487
       8 | Toothbrush    | 9473625532534
       8 | Toothbrush    | 9473627464543
       9 | Roman Coin    | 4587263646878
      11 | Speakers      | 9879879837489
      11 | Speakers      | 2239872376872
(14 rows)

bpsimple=#
```

Notice that this is exactly the same as if we had typed:

```
SELECT i.item_id, i.description, b.barcode_ean FROM item i, barcode b WHERE
i.item_id = b.item_id;
```

As you can see however, it hides the complexity away from the end users.

If we want to list the views in our database, we can use the psql \dv command, and \d name-of-view
will describe the view, allowing us to see the SQL being used:

```
bpsimple=# \dv
     List of relations
    Name    | Type | Owner
------------+------+-------
 all_items  | view | rick
(1 row)

bpsimple=# \d all_items
                View "all_items"
  Attribute   |          Type          | Modifier
--------------+------------------------+----------
 item_id      | integer                |
 description  | character varying(64)  |
 barcode_ean  | character(13)          |
View definition: SELECT i.item_id, i.description, b.barcode_ean FROM item i,
barcode b WHERE (i.item_id = b.item_id);

bpsimple=#
```

### How It Works

We created a view called all_items, which behaves like a table, except that it builds its data from
some hidden SQL.

Some people are tempted to think that views are such a good idea, that all tables should be hidden
behind views. While some level of data hiding is often good, using a view is not as efficient as using the
actual tables, particularly if the SQL that defines the view is complex, and uses more than a single table.
Database designers who have hidden all the data behind views can suffer from poor performance, and
users are unable to optimize their SQL performance, perhaps because the column they need is in a
view, which does a big table join. Even though users want only one column, if you have forced them to
use the view they will be executing the complex SQL behind the view, lowering the performance. While
views can be good for you, too much of a good thing can be harmful!

Views are deleted just like tables:

```
DROP VIEW view-name
```

Unlike dropping a table, however, dropping a view does not affect the underlying data.

# Foreign Key Constraints

We now come to one of the most important kinds of constraints, called **foreign key constraints**.

When we drew our diagram of a sample `bpsimple` database, we had tables with data that joined, or were related, to other tables. Here is the relationship diagram from Chapter 2 again, as a reminder:

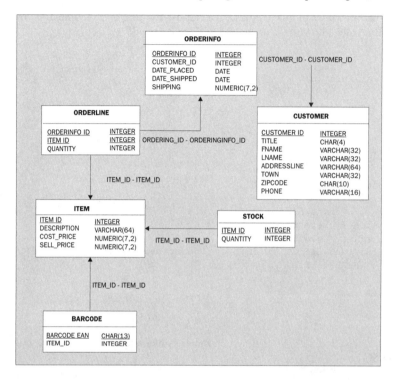

You will remember how columns in one table relate to columns in another. For example, the `customer_id` in the `orderinfo` table relates to the `customer_id` in the `customer` table. So, given an `orderinfo_id`, we can use the `customer_id` from the same row to discover the name and address of the customer to which the order relates. We learnt that the `customer_id` is a primary key in the `customer` table; that is it uniquely identifies a single row in the `customer` table. We can now learn another important piece of terminology – the `customer_id` in the `orderinfo` table is a **foreign key**. What we mean by foreign key is that although `customer_id` in the `orderinfo` table is not a primary key in that table; the column it joins to in the `customer` table is unique. Notice that there is no reverse relationship; no column in the `customer` table is a unique key of any other table. Hence, we say that the `customer` table has no foreign keys. When we create a foreign key constraint, PostgreSQL will check that the column in the particular table is declared such that it must be unique. It is very common for the column referenced by a foreign key to be the primary key in the other table.

Just as the `customer` table has no foreign key columns, it is possible for a table to have more than one foreign key. If we look at the `orderline` table, we see that `orderinfo_id` is a foreign key, since it joins with the `orderinfo_id`, which is a primary key in the `orderinfo` table, and `item_id` is also a foreign key, because it joins with `item_id` in the `item` table that is a primary key in the `item` table.

In the `item` table we discover that the `item_id` is both a primary key in the `item` table, since it uniquely identifies a row, and is also a foreign key in the `stock` table. It is perfectly acceptable for a single column to be both a primary and foreign key, and implies a (usually optional) one-to-one relationship between rows in the two tables.

Although we don't have any examples in our sample database, it is also possible for a pair of columns combined to be a foreign key, just as the `orderinfo_id` and `item_id` combined are a primary key in the `orderline` table.

These relationships are absolutely crucial to our database. If we have a row in our `orderinfo` table where the `customer_id` doesn't match a `customer_id` in the `customer` table, it is a major problem. We have an order and no idea of the customer who placed the order. Although we can use application logic to enforce our relationship rules, as we said with the column and table constraints we met earlier, it is much safer, and often easier, to declare them as database rules.

You will not be surprised to learn that it is possible to declare such foreign key relationships as constraints on columns and tables, much like the constraints we have already met. This is done when tables are created, as part of the CREATE TABLE command, using the REFERENCES type of constraint that we skipped over earlier in the chapter.

We are now going to move on from our `bpsimple` database, and create a `bpfinal` database, that implements foreign key constraints, to enforce data integrity.

# Foreign Key as a Column Constraint

The basic syntax for declaring a column to be a foreign key in another table, is:

```
[CONSTRAINT arbitrary-name] existing-column-name type REFERENCES foreign-table-
name(column-in-foreign-table)
```

The naming of the constraint is optional, but as we will see later, can help with the understanding of error messages. The full power of foreign key constraints is beyond the scope of this book. Generally, the basic syntax will cover your needs until you become very experienced. More details can be found in the online documentation.

To define a foreign key constraint on the `customer_id` column in the `orderinfo` table, relating it to the `customer` table, we use the REFERENCES keyword along with the name of the foreign table and column, such as this:

```
create table orderinfo
(
    orderinfo_id        serial ,
    customer_id         integer not null REFERENCES customer(customer_id),
    date_placed         date not null,
    date_shipped        date ,
    shipping            numeric(7,2) ,
    CONSTRAINT          orderinfo_pk PRIMARY KEY(orderinfo_id)
);
```

Notice that we have named the constraint as `orderinfo_pk`.

We will see the effect of `REFERENCES` constraint very shortly.

# Foreign Key as a Table Constraint

Although you can declare foreign key constraints at the column level, we prefer that you declare them at the table level, along with `PRIMARY KEY` constraints. You cannot use a column constraint when multiple columns in the current table are involved in the relationship, so in these cases, you have to write it as a table-level constraint.

> **We recommend that rather than mix column and table-level foreign key constraints, it is better to always use the table form.**

The table form is very similar to the column form, but comes after all columns have been listed:

```
[CONSTRAINT arbitrary-name] FOREIGN KEY (column-list) REFERENCES foreign-table-
name(column-list-in-foreign-table)
```

We can update our definition of the `orderinfo` table to declare a constraint that the column `customer_id` is a foreign key, because it relates to the primary key column `customer_id` in the `customer` table.

```
create table orderinfo
(
    orderinfo_id                serial ,
    customer_id                 integer not null,
    date_placed                 date not null,
    date_shipped                date ,
    shipping                    numeric(7,2) ,
    CONSTRAINT                  orderinfo_pk PRIMARY KEY(orderinfo_id),
    CONSTRAINT orderinfo_customer_id_fk FOREIGN KEY(customer_id) REFERENCES
            customer(customer_id)
);
```

If we drop and re-create the `orderinfo` table, (not forgetting the automatically created sequence), then populate it again, we can see the effect of our new constraint as follows:

```
bpfinal=# DROP SEQUENCE orderinfo_orderinfo_id_seq;
DROP

bpfinal=# DROP TABLE orderinfo;
DROP

bpfinal=# CREATE TABLE orderinfo
bpfinal-# (
bpfinal-#      orderinfo_id                serial,
bpfinal-#      customer_id                 integer not null,
bpfinal-#      date_placed                 date not null,
```

```
bpfinal-#        date_shipped                    date,
bpfinal-#        shipping                        numeric(7,2),
bpfinal-#        CONSTRAINT                      orderinfo_pk PRIMARY
bpfinal-#        KEY(orderinfo_id),
bpfinal-#        CONSTRAINT orderinfo_customer_id_fk FOREIGN KEY(customer_id)
bpfinal-#        REFERENCES customer(customer_id)
bpfinal-# );
NOTICE:  CREATE TABLE will create implicit sequence 'orderinfo_orderinfo_id_seq'
for SERIAL column 'orderinfo.orderinfo_id'
NOTICE:  CREATE TABLE/PRIMARY KEY will create implicit index 'orderinfo_pk' for
table 'orderinfo'
NOTICE:  CREATE TABLE will create implicit trigger(s) for FOREIGN KEY check(s)
CREATE

bpfinal=#
```

If you look carefully, you will see an additional NOTICE from the CREATE command we used early in the book:

```
CREATE TABLE will create implicit trigger(s) for FOREIGN KEY check(s)
```

Telling us that arrangements for additional checks are being made.

Now we can re-populate the orderinfo table from our SQL script:

```
bpfinal=# \i pop_orderinfo.sql
INSERT 20325 1
INSERT 20326 1
INSERT 20327 1
INSERT 20328 1
INSERT 20329 1

bpfinal=#
```

So now we are back to almost where we started, with one very important difference – the orderinfo table has a foreign key constraint, which says that rows in the orderinfo table have the customer_id column referring to the customer_id column in the customer table. This should mean that we cannot delete rows from the customer table if the row is being referenced by a column in the orderinfo table.

## Try It Out – Foreign Key Constraints

We will start by checking to see what customer_ids we have in the orderinfo table:

```
bpsimple=# select orderinfo_id, customer_id from orderinfo;
 orderinfo_id | customer_id
--------------+-------------
            1 |           3
            2 |           8
            3 |          15
            4 |          13
            5 |           8
            6 |           8
(6 rows)

bpsimple=#
```

We now know that there are five rows in orderinfo that have customer_ids that refer to customers in the customer table, and that the customers referred to have ids 3, 8, 13 and 15. There are only four customers referred to, because the row with orderinfo_ids 2 and 5, both refer to the same customer.

So let's try and delete the row from the customer table with customer_id 3:

```
bpfinal=# DELETE FROM customer WHERE customer_id = 3;
ERROR:  orderinfo_customer_id_fk referential integrity violation - key in customer
still referenced from orderinfo

bpfinal=#
```

PostgreSQL prevents us from deleting the row. Also, notice that naming the constraint orderinfo_customer_id_fk allows us to more easily identify the source of the complaint. If we had not named the constraint, PostgreSQL would simply have said <unnamed>. PostgreSQL will allow us to delete rows from the customer table where there is no related orderinfo entry:

```
bpfinal=# DELETE FROM customer WHERE customer_id = 4;
DELETE 1

bpfinal=#
```

### How It Works

Behind the scenes, PostgreSQL adds some additional checking ensuring that for each row we try and delete from the customer table, it checks that the row is not being referred to by a row in a different table, in this case the orderinfo table.

Any attempts to violate the rule-result in the command being rejected and the data left unchanged. Of course we can still delete a customer, but we have to ensure they have no orders first.

PostgreSQL also checks that we don't try and INSERT rows into the orderinfo table that refer to non-existent customers:

```
bpfinal=# INSERT INTO orderinfo(customer_id, date_placed, shipping) VALUEFS(250,
'07-25-2000', 0.00);
ERROR:  orderinfo_customer_id_fk referential integrity violation - key referenced
from orderinfo not found in customer

bpfinal=#
```

It is important to realize what a big step forward we have made here. We have taken very effective steps to ensure that the relationships between tables are enforced by the database. No longer is it possible to have rows in orderinfo referring to non-existent customers.

We can now update our create_tables.sql script to add foreign key constraints to all the tables that refer to other tables, that is orderinfo, orderline, stock, and barcode.

The only slightly complex one is `orderline`, where the `orderinfo_id` column refers to the `orderinfo` table, and the `item_id` column refers to the `item` table. This is not a problem; we simply specify two constraints, one for each column such as this:

```
create table orderline
(
    orderinfo_id                integer             not null,
    item_id                     integer             not null,
    quantity                    integer             not null,
    CONSTRAINT                  orderline_pk PRIMARY KEY(orderinfo_id,
item_id),
    CONSTRAINT orderline_orderinfo_id_fk FOREIGN KEY(orderinfo_id) REFERENCES
orderinfo(orderinfo_id),
    CONSTRAINT orderline_item_id_fk FOREIGN KEY(item_id) REFERENCES item(item_id)
);
```

The full set of constraints for all tables can be found in the code bundle that can be downloaded from the Wrox web site.

When you use this database, you will also find that you must populate the tables in an order that fulfills the foreign key constraints; you can no longer populate the `orderinfo` table before populating the `customer` table for the orders to reference.

The order that we suggest is:

❑   customer

❑   item

❑   orderinfo

❑   orderline

❑   stock

❑   barcode

# Foreign Key Constraint Options

We can take these referential integrity checks using foreign key constraints one step further, although since this is an advanced topic, we will only be touching on the details. More information can be found in the online documentation and advanced SQL books.

It might be that we get into a situation where we have entries in the `orderinfo` table referring to the `customer` table, but we need to update the `customer_id`. As it stands, we can't easily do this, because if we attempt to change the `customer_id` (actually a very bad idea, since it is a serial column!) the foreign key constraint in `orderinfo` will prevent it, since the rule says that the `customer_id` stored in each `orderinfo` row must always refer to a `customer_id` entry in the `customer` table.

We can't change the `customer_id` in the `orderinfo` table, because the entry in the `customer` table doesn't exist yet, and we can't change the entry in the `customer` table, because it is being referred to by the `orderinfo` table.

## *Deferrable*

The SQL standard allows two ways out of this. The first is to add the keyword DEFERRABLE at the end of the foreign key constraint such as this:

```
create table orderinfo
(
    orderinfo_id                serial ,
    customer_id                 integer not null,
    date_placed                 date not null,
    date_shipped                date ,
    shipping                    numeric(7,2) ,
    CONSTRAINT                  orderinfo_pk PRIMARY KEY(orderinfo_id),
    CONSTRAINT orderinfo_customer_id_fk FOREIGN KEY(customer_id) REFERENCES
customer(customer_id) DEFERRABLE
);
```

This changes the way foreign key constraints are enforced. Normally, PostgreSQL will check that foreign key constraints are met before any change is allowed to the database. If you use transactions, which we will meet in the next chapter, and the DEFERRABLE keyword, then PostgreSQL will allow foreign key constraints to be violated, but only inside a transaction. As we will see, a transaction is a group of SQL commands that must either be completely executed, or it must appear as though none of them were executed. Hence, we could start a transaction, update the customer_id in the customer table, update the related customer_ids in the orderinfo table, commit the transaction, and then PostgreSQL would permit this. All it will check is that the constraints are met when the transaction ends.

## *ON UPDATE and ON DELETE*

An alternative solution is to specify rules in the foreign key constraint about how to handle violation in two circumstances, UPDATEs and DELETEs. Two actions are possible. Firstly, we could CASCADE the change from the table with the primary key, and secondly, we could SET NULL to make the column Null, since it no longer references the primary table.

For example:

```
create table orderinfo
(
    orderinfo_id                serial ,
    customer_id                 integer not null,
    date_placed                 date not null,
    date_shipped                date ,
    shipping                    numeric(7,2) ,
    CONSTRAINT                  orderinfo_pk PRIMARY KEY(orderinfo_id),
    CONSTRAINT orderinfo_customer_id_fk FOREIGN KEY(customer_id) REFERENCES
customer(customer_id) ON DELETE CASCADE
);
```

Would tell PostgreSQL that if we delete a row in customer with a customer_id that is being used in the orderinfo table, it should automatically delete the related rows in orderinfo. This might be what we intended, but is normally a dangerous choice. It is usually much better to ensure applications delete rows in the correct order, so we make sure there are no orders for a customer before deleting the customer entry.

The SET NULL option is usually used with UPDATEs, and looks like this:

```
create table orderinfo
(
    orderinfo_id                    serial ,
    customer_id                     integer not null,
    date_placed                     date not null,
    date_shipped                    date ,
    shipping                        numeric(7,2) ,
    CONSTRAINT                      orderinfo_pk PRIMARY KEY(orderinfo_id),
    CONSTRAINT orderinfo_customer_id_fk FOREIGN KEY(customer_id) REFERENCES
customer(customer_id)ON UPDATE SET NULL
);
```

This says that should the row being referred to by customer_id be deleted from the customer table, set the column in the orderinfo table to NULL. The astute readers will have noticed that for our table, this isn't going to work. We declared customer_id as NOT NULL, so it cannot be updated to a null value. We did this because we did not want to allow the possibility of rows in the orderinfo table having Null customer_ids. After all, what does an order with an unknown customer mean? It's probably a mistake.

These options can be combined, so you can write:

```
ON UPDATE SET NULL ON DELETE CASCADE
```

We mention ON UPDATE and ON DELETE here for completeness. We do suggest however, you use them with considerable caution. It is much safer to force application programmers to code UPDATEs and DELETEs in the right order and use transactions, than it is to CASCADE DELETE rows and suddenly store Nulls in columns because a different table was changed.

In Chapter 10, *Stored Procedures and Triggers*, we will see how we can use triggers and stored procedures to give much the same effect, but in a way that gives us more control over the changes in other tables.

# Summary

We have covered a lot of material in this chapter. We started by looking more formally at the data types supported by PostgreSQL, especially the common SQL standard types, but also mentioning some of PostgreSQL's more unusual extension types, such as arrays.

We then looked at how you can manipulate column data, converting between types, using sub-strings of the data, and the small number of PostgreSQL 'magic' variables, that allow access to information, such as the current user.

We then moved on to look at a very important topic, that of constraints. We saw that there are effectively two ways of defining constraints, those against a single column, and those at a table level. We saw how even simple constraints can help us to enforce the integrity of data at the database level.

Our final topic was one of the most important types of constraints, foreign keys, which allow us to define formally in the database how different tables relate to each other. Most importantly, it allows us to enforce these rules, for example ensuring that we can never delete a customer that has order information relating to that customer in a different table.

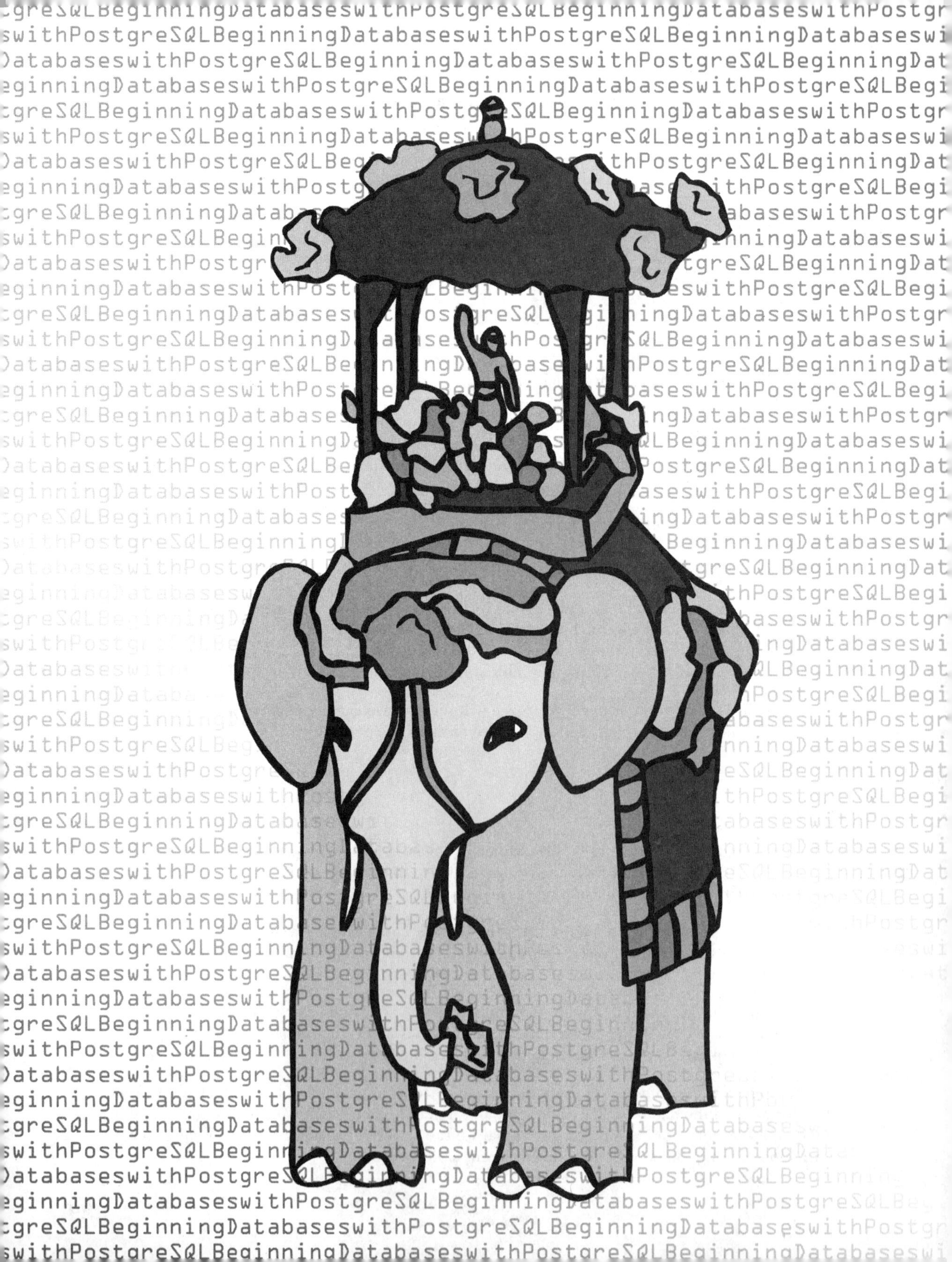

# Transactions and Locking

So far in this book, we have avoided any in-depth discussion of the multi-user aspects of PostgreSQL, simply stating the idealized view that like any good relational database, PostgreSQL hides the details of supporting multiple concurrent users. It simply provides a database server, which behaves as if all the simultaneous users have exclusive access, and that it remains efficient and each user appears to be independent of the others.

For many purposes, particularly with small and lightly loaded databases, this idealized view is almost achieved in practice. The reality is that PostgreSQL, although very capable, cannot perform magic However, and the isolation of each user from all the others requires work behind the scenes. Occasionally, the real world has to intrude on the idealized view that users can often consider that they have exclusive access to the database server.

In this chapter, we will be looking not so much at how PostgreSQL achieves its isolation of different users, but more at the practicalities of what this means for users of the database. We will also see how client programs can expect the database to behave, and how they can work with the database server to maximize its effectiveness. We will also look at how PostgreSQL allows you to collect a number of discrete changes to the database into a single work unit, a transaction. This is very important when you have a set of changes that must be made as a single unit of work.

We will be looking at:

- ❏ What are transactions?
- ❏ The ACID rules
- ❏ Transactions with a single user
- ❏ Transaction limitations
- ❏ Transaction with multiple users
- ❏ ANSI isolation levels
- ❏ Chained and unchained modes
- ❏ Locking
- ❏ Deadlocks and explicit locks

# What are Transactions?

The first topic we need to discuss is how updates are made to a database. We have said that wherever possible, you should write database changes as a single declarative statement, but in real world applications there soon comes a point at which you need to make several changes to a database that cannot be expressed in a single SQL statement. You still need all these changes to occur However, or none of them to occur if there is a problem with any part of the group of changes.

The classic example is that of transferring money between two accounts in a bank, perhaps represented in different tables in a database, and you need one account to be debited and the other credited. If you debit one account and fail to credit the second for some reason, you must return the money to the first account, or behave as though it was never debited in the first place. No bank could remain in business if it 'lost' money occasionally when transferring it between accounts.

In databases based on ANSI SQL, as PostgreSQL is, this is achieved with what are termed **transactions**.

> **A transaction is a logical unit of work that must not be subdivided.**

What do we mean by a logical unit of work? It is simply a set of logical changes to the database, which must either all occur, or must all fail. Just like the transference of money between accounts as mentioned above. In PostgreSQL, these changes are controlled by 3 key phrases:

- ❏ BEGIN WORK starts a transaction.

- ❏ COMMIT WORK says that all the elements of the transaction are complete and should now be made persistent and accessible to all concurrent and subsequent transactions.

- ❏ ROLLBACK WORK says that the transaction is to be abandoned, and all changes made to data by that SQL-transaction are cancelled. The database should appear to all users as though none of the changes have ever occurred since the previous BEGIN WORK.

The ANSI/ISO SQL standard does not define the BEGIN WORK SQL phrase, it defines transactions as starting automatically (hence the phrase would be redundant), but it is a very common extension present, and required, in many relational databases.

> **For both ROLLBACK WORK and COMMIT WORK, the WORK part may be omitted.**

A second aspect of transactions is that any transaction in the database is isolated from other transactions occurring in the database at the same time. In an ideal world, each transaction would behave as though it had exclusive access to the database. Unfortunately, as we will see later in this chapter, when we look at isolation levels, the practicalities of achieving good performance mean that some compromises often have to be made. Let's look at a different example of where a transaction is needed.

Suppose you are trying to book an airline ticket online. You check the flight you want and discover a ticket is available. Although unknown to you, it is the very last ticket on that flight. While you are typing in your credit card details another customer with an account at the airline makes the same check for tickets. You have not yet purchased your ticket, they see a free seat, and book it, while you are still typing in your credit card details. You now submit to buy 'your' ticket therefore, and because the system knew there was a seat available when you started the transaction, it incorrectly assumes a seat is still available, and debits your card.

You hang up, confident your seat has been booked, and perhaps even check that your credit card has been debited. The reality is, however that you purchased a non-existent ticket. At the instant your transaction was processed, there were no free seats.

The code executed by your booking may have looked a little like this:

```
Check if seats available.
If yes offer seat to customer.
If customer accepts offer ask for credit card number.
Authorize credit card transaction with bank.
Debit card.
Assign seat.
Reduce the number of free seats available by the number purchased.
```

Such a sequence of events is perfectly valid, if only a single customer ever uses the system at any one time. The trouble only occurred because we had two customers, and what actually happened was:

| Customer 1 | Customer 2 | Free seats on plane |
|---|---|---|
| Check if seats available | | 1 |
| | Check if seats available | 1 |
| If yes offer seat to customer | | 1 |
| | If yes offer seat to customer | 1 |
| If customer accepts offer ask for credit card or account number | | 1 |
| | If customer accepts offer ask for credit card or account number | 1 |
| Provides credit card number | Provides account number | 1 |
| Authorize credit card transaction with bank | | 1 |
| | Check account is valid | 1 |
| | Update account with new transaction | 1 |
| Debit card | Assign seat | 1 |
| Assign seat | Reduce the number of free seats available by the number purchased | 0 |
| Reduce the number of free seats available by the number purchased | | -1 |

We could improve things considerably by re-checking that a seat was available closer to the point at which we take the money, but however close we do the check, it's inevitable that the 'check a seat is available' step is separated from the 'take money' step, even if only by a tiny amount of time.

We could go to the opposite extreme to solve the problem, allowing only one person to access the ticket booking system at any one time, but the performance would be terrible and customers would go elsewhere. Alternatively, we could write our application using a semaphore, or similar technique, to manage access to critical sections of code. This would require every application that accessed the database to use the semaphore, which is a much more effective and logical place to tackle the problem. It's most unlikely that any airline would have such a simplistic system that basic ticket booking errors occur, but it does illustrate the principle.

In application terms what we have is a critical section of code, a small section of code that needs exclusive access to some data. As we have seen already, it is often easier to use a database to solve problems, rather than writing application logic. In database terms, what we have here is a transaction, the set of data manipulations from checking the seat availability through to debiting the account or card and assigning the seat, all of which must happen as a single unit of work.

# ACID Rules

ACID is a frequently used mnemonic to describe the properties a transaction must have:

❑ **Atomic**
A transaction, even though it is a group of actions, must happen as a single unit. A transaction must happen exactly once, with no subsets. In our banking example, the move must be atomic. The debit of one account and the credit of the other must both happen as though it were a single action, even if several consecutive SQL statements are required.

❑ **Consistent**
At the end of a transaction, the system must be left in a consistent state. We touched on this in Chapter 8, when we saw that we could declare a constraint as deferrable, in other words the constraint should only be checked at the end of a transaction. In our banking example, at the end of a transaction, all the accounts must add up to the correct amount.

❑ **Isolated**
This means that each transaction, no matter how many transactions are currently in progress in a database, must appear to be independent of all the other transactions. In our airline example, transactions processing two concurrent customers must behave as though they each have exclusive use of the database. In practice, we know this cannot be true if we are to have sensible performance on multi-user databases, and indeed this turns out to be one of the places where the practicalities of the 'real world' impinge most severely on our ideal database behavior. We will come back to the topic of isolating transactions a little later in the chapter.

❑ **Durable**

Once a transaction has completed, it must stay completed. Once money has been successfully transferred between accounts it must stay transferred, even if the power fails and the machine running the database has an uncontrolled power down. In PostgreSQL, like most relational databases, this is achieved using a transaction logfile. The way the transaction logfile works, is essentially simple. As a transaction executes, not only are the changes written to the database, but also to a `logfile`. Once a transaction completes, a marker is written to say the transaction has finished, and the `logfile` data is forced to permanent storage, so it is secure even if the database server crashes. Should the database server die for some reason in the middle of a transaction, then as the server restarts, it is able to automatically ensure that completed transactions are correctly reflected in the database (by 'rolling forward' transactions in the transaction log, but not in the database). No changes from transactions that were still in progress when the server went down appear in the database. Transaction durability happens without user intervention, so we do not need to consider it further.

# Transaction with Single Users

Before we look at the more complex aspects of transactions and how they behave with multiple concurrent users of the database, we need to have a look at how they behave with a single user.

Even in this rather simplistic way of working, there are real advantages to using transactions. The big benefit of transactions is that they allow you to execute several SQL statements, and then at a later stage, allow you to undo the work you have done, if you so decide. Using a transaction, the application does not need to worry about storing what changes have been made to the database and how to undo them. It can simply ask the database engine to undo a whole batch of changes in one go.

Logically, the sequence is:

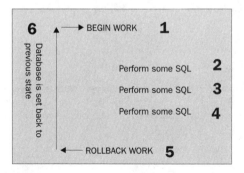

If you decide all your changes to the database are valid at step 5, however, and you wish to apply them to the database so they become permanent, then all you do is replace the ROLLBACK WORK statement with a COMMIT WORK statement:

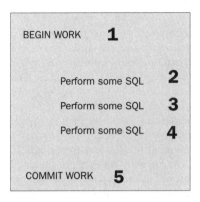

After step 5, the changes to the database are committed, and can be considered permanent, so they will not be lost by power failures, disk crashes, or application errors.

The transaction log that PostgreSQL maintains, not only records all the changes that are being made to the database, but also how to reverse them. Obviously, this file could get very large very quickly. Once a COMMIT WORK statement is issued for a transaction However, PostgreSQL then knows that it is no longer required to store the 'undo' information, since the database change is now irrevocable, at least by the database. The application could of course execute additional code to reverse changes.

## Try it Out – Transactions

Let's try a very simple transaction, where we change a single row in a table, to change a name from David to Dave, and then use the ROLLBACK SQL statement to cancel the change:

```
bpfinal=# BEGIN WORK;
BEGIN
bpfinal=# SELECT fname FROM customer WHERE customer_id = 15;
fname
-------
David
(1 row)

bpfinal=# UPDATE customer SET fname = 'Dave' WHERE customer_id = 15;
UPDATE 1
bpfinal=# SELECT fname FROM customer WHERE customer_id = 15;
fname
-------
Dave
(1 row)
bpfinal=# ROLLBACK WORK;
ROLLBACK
bpfinal=# SELECT fname FROM customer WHERE customer_id = 15;
fname
-------
David
(1 row)

bpfinal=#
```

### How it Works

We must start the transaction by using the BEGIN WORK command. We then make a change to the database, updating the fname column of the row where the customer_id is 15. When we do a SELECT on this row it shows the data has changed. We then call ROLLBACK WORK. PostgreSQL uses its internal transaction log to undo the changes since BEGIN WORK was executed, so next time we SELECT the row with customer_id 15, our change has been backed out.

In PostgreSQL the WORK part of BEGIN WORK, COMMIT WORK, and ROLLBACK WORK statements are just noise, and PostgreSQL will consider the keywords BEGIN, COMMIT, and ROLLBACK sufficient. We will use the full terms for clarity.

Transactions are not limited to a single table, or simple updates to data. Here is a more complex example, involving both an UPDATE and an INSERT, on different tables:

```
bpfinal=# BEGIN WORK;
BEGIN
bpfinal=# INSERT INTO customer(title, fname, lname, addressline, town, bpfinal-#
zipcode, phone)  VALUES('Mr', 'Steven', 'Harvey', '23 Millbank bpfinal-# Road',
'Nicetown', 'NT1 1EE', '267 4323');
INSERT 21099 1
bpfinal=# UPDATE item SET sell_price = 99.99 WHERE item_id = 2;
UPDATE 1
bpfinal=# ROLLBACK WORK;
ROLLBACK
bpfinal=# SELECT fname, lname FROM customer WHERE lname = 'Harvey';
 fname | lname
-------+-------
(0 rows)

bpfinal=# SELECT * FROM item WHERE item_id = 2;
 item_id | description | cost_price | sell_price
---------+-------------+------------+------------
       2 | Rubik Cube  |       7.45 |      11.49
(1 row)

bpfinal=#
```

The data added as a result of the INSERT statement has been removed, and the UPDATE to the item table reversed.

# Transaction Limitations

There are a few things you need to be careful of with transactions.

Firstly, you cannot nest transactions in PostgreSQL, or most other relational databases for that matter. In PostgreSQL, if you try and execute a BEGIN WORK statement while it's already in a transaction, PostgreSQL will give you a notice message, telling you a transaction is already in progress. A few databases have the concept of save points which are in the SQL standard, where you can set a marker part of the way through a transaction, and rollback as far as a save point, rather than the whole transaction.

Some databases silently accept several BEGIN WORK statements. A COMMIT WORK or ROLLBACK WORK command always works against the first BEGIN WORK statement, however so although it looked as though the transactions were nested, in reality subsequent BEGIN WORK commands were being ignored.

PostgreSQL doesn't currently support save points, but it does warn you if you attempt to perform nested transactions by using BEGIN WORK while a transaction is in progress. PostgreSQL doesn't support save points at this time,therefore we will not be considering them further here.

Secondly, it is advisable to keep transactions small. As we will see later in this chapter, PostgreSQL (and other relational databases) have to do a lot of work to ensure that transactions from different users are kept separate. A consequence of this is that the parts of a database involved in a transaction frequently need to become locked, to ensure that transactions are kept separate.

Although PostgreSQL locks the database automatically for you, a long running transaction usually prevents other users accessing data involved in the transaction, until the transaction is completed or cancelled. Consider an application which started a transaction when a person sat down to work at their terminal in the morning, and left the transaction running all day while s/he made various changes to the database. Supposing s/he committed the data only when s/he signed off at the end of the day, the performance of the database, and ability for other users to access the data would be severely impacted.

You should also avoid having a transaction in progress when any user dialogue is required. It is advisable to collect all the information required from the user first, then process the information in a transaction unhindered by unpredictable user responses.

A COMMIT WORK statement usually executes quite rapidly, since it generally has to do very little work to perform. Rolling back transactions however normally involve at least as much work for the database as performing them initially, and frequently more. Therefore, if you start a transaction, and it takes 5 minutes to execute all the SQL, then decide to do a ROLLBACK WORK to cancel it all, don't expect the rollback to be instantaneous. It could easily take longer than 5 minutes to undo all the changes.

# Transactions with Multiple Users

Before we look at how transactions need to work for multiple concurrent users and how they are isolated from each other, we need to return to our ACID rules and look more specifically at what we mean by the 'I' part of ACID, Isolated.

## ANSI Isolation Levels

As we said, one of the most difficult aspects of relational databases is isolation between different users for updates to the database. Of course achieving isolation is not difficult. Simply allowing a single connection to the database, with only a single transaction in progress at any one time, will ensure you have complete isolation between different transactions. The difficulty occurs in achieving more practical isolation without significantly damaging performance, preventing multi-user access to the database.

True isolation is extremely difficult to achieve without serious performance degradation therefore, the ANSI/ISO SQL standard defines different levels of isolation that databases can implement. Usually, a relational database will implement at least one of these levels by default, and normally allow users to specify at least one other isolation level they can choose to use.

Before we can understand the standard isolation levels, we need to tackle some more terminology. Although PostgreSQL's default behavior will suffice in most cases, there are circumstances where it is useful to understand it in more detail.

## Undesirable Phenomena

The ANSI/ISO SQL standard defines isolation levels in terms of undesirable phenomena that can happen in multi-users databases when transactions interact.

### Dirty Read

A dirty read occurs when some SQL in a transaction reads data that has been changed by another transaction, but the transaction changing the data has not yet committed its block of work.

As we discussed earlier, a transaction is a logical unit or block of work that must be atomic. Either all the elements of a transaction occur or none of them occur. Until a transaction has been committed, there is always the possibility that it will fail, or be abandoned with a ROLLBACK WORK command. Therefore, no other users of the database should see this changed data before a COMMIT.

We can illustrate this, by considering what a different transaction might see as the fname of the customer with customer_id 15. This is assuming dirty reads are permitted, which PostgreSQL never allows, so we can only show this as a theoretical example:

| Transaction 1 | Data seen by 1 | What a dirty read in other transactions would see | What other transactions would see if dirty reads did not occur |
|---|---|---|---|
| BEGIN WORK | | | |
| | David | David | David |
| UPDATE customer SET fname='Dave' | | | |
| WHERE customer_id = 15; | | | |
| | Dave | Dave | David |
| COMMIT WORK | | | |
| | Dave | Dave | Dave |
| BEGIN WORK | | | |
| UPDATE customer SET fname = 'David' WHERE customer_id = 15; | | | Dave |
| | David | David | Dave |
| ROLLBACK WORK | | | |
| | Dave | Dave | Dave |

Notice how a dirty read has permitted other transactions to 'see' data which is not yet committed to the database. This means they can see changes which are later discarded, because of the ROLLBACK WORK command.

> **PostgreSQL never permits dirty reads.**

### Unrepeatable Reads

This is very similar to the dirty read, but is more of a restrictive definition.

An unrepeatable read occurs where a transaction reads a set of data, then later re-reads the data, and discovers it has changed. This is much less serious than a dirty read, but not quite ideal. Let's look at what this might look like:

| Transaction 1 | Data seen by 1 | What an urepeatable read in other transactions would see | What other transactions would see if unrepeatable read did not occur |
|---|---|---|---|
| BEGIN WORK | | BEGIN WORK | BEGIN WORK |
| | David | David | David |
| UPDATE customer SET fname = 'Dave' WHERE customer_id = 15; | | | |
| | Dave | David | David |
| COMMIT WORK | | | |
| | Dave | Dave | David |
| | | COMMIT WORK | COMMIT WORK |
| | | BEGIN WORK | BEGIN WORK |
| SELECT fname FROM customer WHERE customer_id = 15; | | Dave | Dave |

Notice the unrepeatable read means that a transaction can 'see' changes committed by other transactions, even though the reading transaction has not itself committed. If unrepeatable reads are prevented, then other transactions do not see changes made to the database until they themselves have committed changes.

By default, PostgreSQL does permit unrepeatable reads, although as we will see later, we can change this default behavior.

### Phantom Reads

This is quite similar to the unrepeatable read problem, but occurs when a new row appears in a table, while a different transaction is updating the table, and the new row should have been updated, but wasn't.

Suppose we had two transactions updating the item table. The first is adding 1 dollar to the selling price of all items, the second adding a new item:

| Transaction 1 | Transaction 2 |
|---|---|
| BEGIN WORK | BEGIN WORK |
| UPDATE item SET sell_price = sell_price + 1; | |
| | INSERT INTO item(....) VALUES(...); |
| COMMIT WORK | |
| | COMMIT WORK |

What should the sell_price of the item added by Transaction 2 be? the INSERT started before the UPDATE was committed therefore, we might reasonably expect it to be greater by one, than the price we inserted. If a phantom read occurs, however the new record that appears after Transaction 1 determines which rows to UPDATE, and the price of the new item does not get incremented.

Phantom reads are extremely rare, and almost impossible to demonstrate, so generally you do not need to worry about them, although by default PostgreSQL will allow such phantoms reads.

### Lost Updates

Lost updates are slightly different from the previous three cases, which are generally an application level problem, not related to the way the relational database works. A lost update on the other hand occurs when two different changes are written to the database, and the second update causes the first to be lost.

Suppose two users are using a screen-based application, which updates the item table:

| User 1 | Data seen by 1 | User 2 | Data seen by 2 |
|---|---|---|---|
| Attempting to change the selling price from 21.95 to 22.55 | | Attempting to change the cost price from 15.23 to 16.00 | |
| BEGIN WORK | | BEGIN WORK | |
| SELECT cost_price , sell_price from item WHERE item_id = 1; | 15.23, 21.95 | SELECT cost_price, sell_price from item WHERE item_id = 1; | 15.23, 21.95 |

*Table continued on following page*

| User 1 | Data seen by 1 | User 2 | Data seen by 2 |
|---|---|---|---|
| UPDATE item SET cost_price = 15.23, sell_price = 22.55 WHERE item_id = 1; | | | |
| | 15.23, 22.55 | | |
| COMMIT WORK | | | |
| | | | 15.23, 22.55 |
| | | UPDATE item SET cost_price = 16.00, sell_price = 21.95 WHERE item_id = 1; | |
| | 15.23, 22.55 | | 16.00, 21.95 |
| | | COMMIT WORK | |
| | 16.00, 21.95 | | 16.00, 21.95 |

The sell_price change made by User 1 has been lost, not because there was a database error, but because User 2 read the sell_price, then 'kept it' for a while, and wrote it back to the database, destroying the change that User 1 had made. The database has quite correctly isolated the two sets of changes, but the application has still lost data.

There are several ways round this problem, and which is the most appropriate will depend on individual applications. As a first step, applications should take steps to keep transactions as short as possible, never holding them in progress for longer than is absolutely necessary. As a second step, applications should only ever write back data that they have changed. These two steps will prevent many occurrences of lost updates, including the mistake demonstrated above.

Of course, it is possible for both users to have been trying to update the sell_price, in which case a change would still have been lost. A more comprehensive way to prevent lost updates is to encode the value you are trying to change in the UPDATE statement:

| User 1 | Data seen by 1 | User 2 | Data seen by 2 |
|---|---|---|---|
| Attempting to change the selling price from 21.95 to 22.55 | | Attempting to change the selling price from 21.95 to 22.99 | |
| BEGIN WORK | | BEGIN WORK | |
| Read sell_price where item_id = 1 | 21.95 | Read sell_price where item_id = 1 | 21.95 |
| UPDATE item SET cost_price = 15.23, sell_price = 22.55 WHERE item_id = 1 and sell_price = 21.95; | | | |
| | 22.55 | | 21.95 |
| COMMIT WORK | | | |
| | | | 22.55 |
| | | UPDATE item SET cost_price = 16.00, sell_price = 21.95 WHERE item_id = 1 and sell_price = 21.95; | |
| | | Update fails with row not found, since the sell_price has been changed | |

Although this is not a perfect cure, since it only works if the first transaction COMMITs before the second UPDATE is run, it does reduce the risks of losing updates significantly.

# ANSI/ISO Isolation Levels

Using our newly found terminology, we are now in a position to understand the way ANSI/ISO defined the different isolation levels a database may use. Each ANSI/ISO level is a combination of the first three types of undesirable behavior that we listed above:

| ANSI/ISO isolation level definition | Dirty Read | Unrepeatable Read | Phantom |
| --- | --- | --- | --- |
| Read uncommitted | Possible | Possible | Possible |
| Read committed | Not Possible | Possible | Possible |
| Repeatable read | Not Possible | Not Possible | Possible |
| Serializable | Not Possible | Not Possible | Not Possible |

You can see that as the isolation level moves from 'Read uncommitted' through 'Read committed' and 'Repeatable read' to the ultimate 'Serializable', the types of undesirable behavior that might occur reduce in degree.

The isolation level is set using the SET TRANSACTION ISOLATION LEVEL command, using the following syntax:

```
SET TRANSACTION ISOLATION LEVEL { READ COMMITTED | SERIALIZABLE }
```

By default, the mode will be set to READ COMMITTED.

Notice that PostgreSQL, at the time of writing, cannot provide the intermediate level 'Repeatable read', nor the entry level 'Read uncommitted'. Generally, 'Read uncommitted' is such poor behavior that few databases offer it as an option, and it would be a rare application that was brave (or foolhardy!) enough to choose to use it.

Similarly, the intermediate level 'Repeatable read', only provides added protection against 'Phantom Reads', which as we said are extremely rare, so the lack of this level is of no real consequence. It is common for databases to offer less than the full set of possibilities, and providing 'Read committed' and 'Serializable' is a good compromise solution.

# Chained (Auto Commit) and Unchained Mode

Throughout this chapter, we have been explicitly using BEGIN WORK and COMMIT (or ROLLBACK) WORK to delimit our transactions. Earlier in the book, before we knew about transactions, however we were happily making changes to our database without a BEGIN WORK command to be seen.

By default PostgreSQL operates in an auto commit mode, sometimes referred to as **chained mode** or **implicit transaction mode**, where each SQL statement that can modify data acts as though it was a complete transaction in its own right. This is great for experimentation on the command line, and allowing new users to experiment without having to learn too much SQL, but not so good for real applications, where we want to have access to transactions with explicit COMMIT or ROLLBACK statements.

In other SQL servers that implement different modes, you normally have to issue an explicit command to change mode, for example SET CHAINED in Sybase, or SET IMPLICIT_TRANSACTIONS for Microsoft SQL Server.

In PostgreSQL, all you need to do is issue the command BEGIN WORK, and PostgreSQL automatically switches into a mode where following commands are in a transaction, until you issue a COMMIT or ROLLBACK statement.

The SQL standard considers all SQL statements to occur in a transaction, with the transaction starting automatically on the first SQL statement, and continuing until a COMMIT WORK or ROLLBACK WORK is encountered. Thus, standard SQL does not define a BEGIN WORK command. The PostgreSQL way of performing transactions, with an explicit BEGIN WORK, is however, very common.

# Locking

Most databases implement transactions, in particular isolating different user transactions from each other, using locks to restrict access to the data from other users. Simplistically, there are two types of locks:

❑ A **shared** lock, that allows other users to read, but not update the data

❑ An **exclusive** lock, which prevents other transactions even reading the data

For example, the server will lock rows that are being changed by a transaction, until such time as the transaction is complete, when the locks are automatically released. This is all done automatically, usually without users of the database even being aware that locking is happening.

The actual mechanics and strategies required for locking are highly complex, with many different types of locks being used depending on circumstances. The documentation for PostgreSQL describes seven different types of lock permutations. PostgreSQL also implements an unusual mechanism for isolating transactions using a multi-version model, which reduces conflicts between locks, and significantly improves its performance compared to other schemes.

Fortunately, users of the database generally only need to worry about locking in two circumstances, avoiding deadlocks (and recovering from them), and explicit locking by an application.

# Deadlocks

What happens when two different applications both try and change the same data at the same time? It's easy to see, just start up two psql sessions, and attempt to change the same row in both of them:

| Session 1 | Session 2 |
| --- | --- |
| UPDATE row 14 | |
| | UPDATE row 15 |
| UPDATE row 15 | |
| | UPDATE row 14 |

At this point, both sessions are blocked, since each is waiting for the other to release.

This behavior is a clue as to why PostgreSQL defaults to a 'Read committed' mode of transaction isolation. There is a trade-off between concurrency, performance, and minimizing the number of locks held on one side, and consistency and 'ideal' behavior on the other:

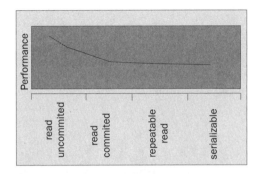

As the behavior of the database becomes more 'ideal', the number of locks required increases, the concurrency between different users decreases, and so overall performance falls. It's an unfortunate, but inevitable trade-off.

In our example above, although Session 2 was blocked while waiting for Session 1 to complete, there was no real impact, except for Session 2 taking longer. A much more serious occurrence is when two sessions block each other out.

## Try It Out – Deadlocks

Start two `psql` sessions, and try the following sequence of commands:

| Session 1 | Session 2 |
|---|---|
| BEGIN WORK | |
| | BEGIN WORK |
| UPDATE customer SET fname = 'D' WHERE customer_id = 15; | |
| | UPDATE customer SET fname = 'B' WHERE customer_id = 14; |
| UPDATE customer SET fname = 'Bill' WHERE customer_id = 14; | |
| | UPDATE customer SET fname = 'Dave' WHERE customer_id = 15; |

You will find that both sessions block, and then after a short pause the following will happen in one of the sessions:

```
ERROR:  Deadlock detected.
        See the lock(l) manual page for a possible cause.
```

The other session will continue. The session that had the deadlock message has been rolled back, and the changes lost. The other session can continue and execute a COMMIT WORK statement to make the database changes permanent.

PostgreSQL has detected a deadlock, both sessions are blocked, waiting for the other, and neither can progress.

### How it Works

Session 1 first locked row 15, then Session 2 came along and locked row 14. Session 1 then tries to lock 14, but can't proceed, because that row is locked by Session 2, and Session 2 tries to update row 15, but can't because that row is locked by Session 1. After a short interval, PostgreSQL's deadlock detection code detected that a deadlock was occurring, and automatically cancelled the transaction.

There is no way to be sure which session PostgreSQL will choose to kill in advance. It will try and pick the one that it considers to have 'done the least work', but this is far from a perfect science.

Applications can, and should, take steps to avoid deadlocks occurring. The simplest technique is the one we suggested earlier: keep your transactions as short as possible. The fewer the rows and the tables involved in a transaction, and shorter the time the locks have to be held, for there is lesser chance of conflict occurring.

The other technique is almost as simple: try and make application code always process tables and rows in the same order. In our example, if both sessions had tried to update the rows in the same order there would not have been a problem, since Session 1 would have been able to update both its rows and complete. While Session 2 briefly paused, before continuing when Session 1's transaction completed. It's also possible to write code that retries when a deadlock occurs, but it is always better to try and design your application to avoid the problem, than code a retry of a failure.

# Explicit Locking

Occasionally, you may find the automatic locking that PostgreSQL provides is not sufficient for your needs, and you will come across a situation where you need to explicitly lock either some rows or a whole table. You should avoid explicit locking if at all possible. The SQL standard does not even define a way of locking a complete table, it is a PostgreSQL extension.

It is only possible to lock rows or tables inside a transaction. Once the transaction completes, either with a COMMIT or ROLLBACK, all locks acquired during the transaction will be automatically released. There is also no way of explicitly releasing locks during a transaction, for the very simple reason that releasing the lock on a row that is changed during a transaction, might allow another application to change it, which would prevent a ROLLBACK undoing the initial change.

## Locking Rows

The most common need is to lock a number of rows in advance of performing changes to them. This can be a way of avoiding deadlocks as well. By locking in advance all the rows that you know you will need to change, you can ensure other applications will not conflict part of the way through your changes.

To lock a set of rows, we simply issue a SELECT statement, appending FOR UPDATE:

```
SELECT 1 FROM item WHERE sell_price > 5.0 FOR UPDATE;
```

Providing we are in a transaction, this will lock all the rows in item where the sell_price is greater than 5. In this case, we didn't want any rows returned, so we simply selected 1, as a convenient way of minimizing the data returned.

### Try it Out – Row Locking

Suppose we wanted to lock all the rows in the customer table where the customer lived in Nicetown, perhaps because we need to change the telephone code. We need to ensure we can access all the rows, but require some procedural code to then process each row in turn, calculating what the new telephone code should be, perhaps because the area code is being split into several new ones dependent on zip code:

```
bpfinal=# BEGIN WORK;
BEGIN
bpfinal=# SELECT customer_id FROM customer WHERE town = 'Nicetown' FOR bpfinal=#
UPDATE;
 customer_id
-------------
           3
           6
(2 rows)

bpfinal=#
```

At this point, the two rows with customer_ids 3 and 6 have been locked, and we can test this by trying to UPDATE them in a different psql session:

```
bpfinal=# BEGIN;
BEGIN
bpfinal=# UPDATE customer SET phone = '023 3376' WHERE customer_id = 2;
UPDATE 1
bpfinal=# UPDATE customer SET phone = '023 3267' WHERE customer_id = 3;
UPDATE 1

bpfinal=#
```

At this point, the second session blocks, until either we type *Ctrl+C* to interrupt it, or the first session COMMITs or does a ROLLBACK.

### How it Works

The first session, using `SELECT ... FOR UPDATE`, causes the rows with customer_ ids 3 and 6 to be locked. Other sessions are able to update different rows in the `customer` table, but not rows 3 and 6 until the transaction that locked them completes.

## Locking Tables

In PostgreSQL, it is possible to lock tables, though not recommended, since generally, performance suffers significantly.

The syntax is:

```
LOCK [ TABLE ] name
LOCK [ TABLE ] name IN [ ROW | ACCESS ] { SHARE | EXCLUSIVE } MODE
LOCK [ TABLE ] name IN SHARE ROW EXCLUSIVE MODE
```

The full details of the different types of locks are beyond the scope of this book, as it requires a comprehensive understanding of how locks work internally to the database. More details can be found in the online documentation.

Generally, applications that require a table to be locked, simply use:

```
LOCK TABLE table-name
```

This is the same as saying:

```
LOCK TABLE table-name ACCESS EXCLUSIVE MODE.
```

This prevents any application accessing the table in any way. Although rather draconian, this is probably the behavior required in the rare circumstances when a table level lock is required.

# Summary

In this chapter, we have been looking at transactions and locking. We have seen how transactions are useful even in single-user databases, by allowing us to group SQL commands together in a single atomic unit, which either happens or is abandoned.

We then moved on to look at how transactions work in a multi-user environment. We learnt about the ACID acronym rules for databases, and what Atomic, Consistent, Isolated, and Durable mean in database terms.

We then moved on to look at what the ANSI standard terms 'undesirable phenomena', and how different levels of transaction consistency are defined by eliminating different types of undesirable behavior. We also discussed briefly how eliminating undesirable features also caused performance degradation, and the need to strike a balance between 'ideal' behavior and improving performance.

We also saw how simple techniques can reduce the risk of deadlocks, where two or more applications can become stuck waiting for each other to complete.

Finally, we looked at explicit locking, and how we can lock specific rows in a table, or indeed a whole table, within a transaction.

Although transaction and locking are not always the most interesting of topics, a general understanding of how they work is very important to writing your applications in a solid fashion. So not only do they perform correctly, but also interact in the database in a way that minimizes the performance implications, to get the best out of the multi-user capabilities of PostgreSQL.

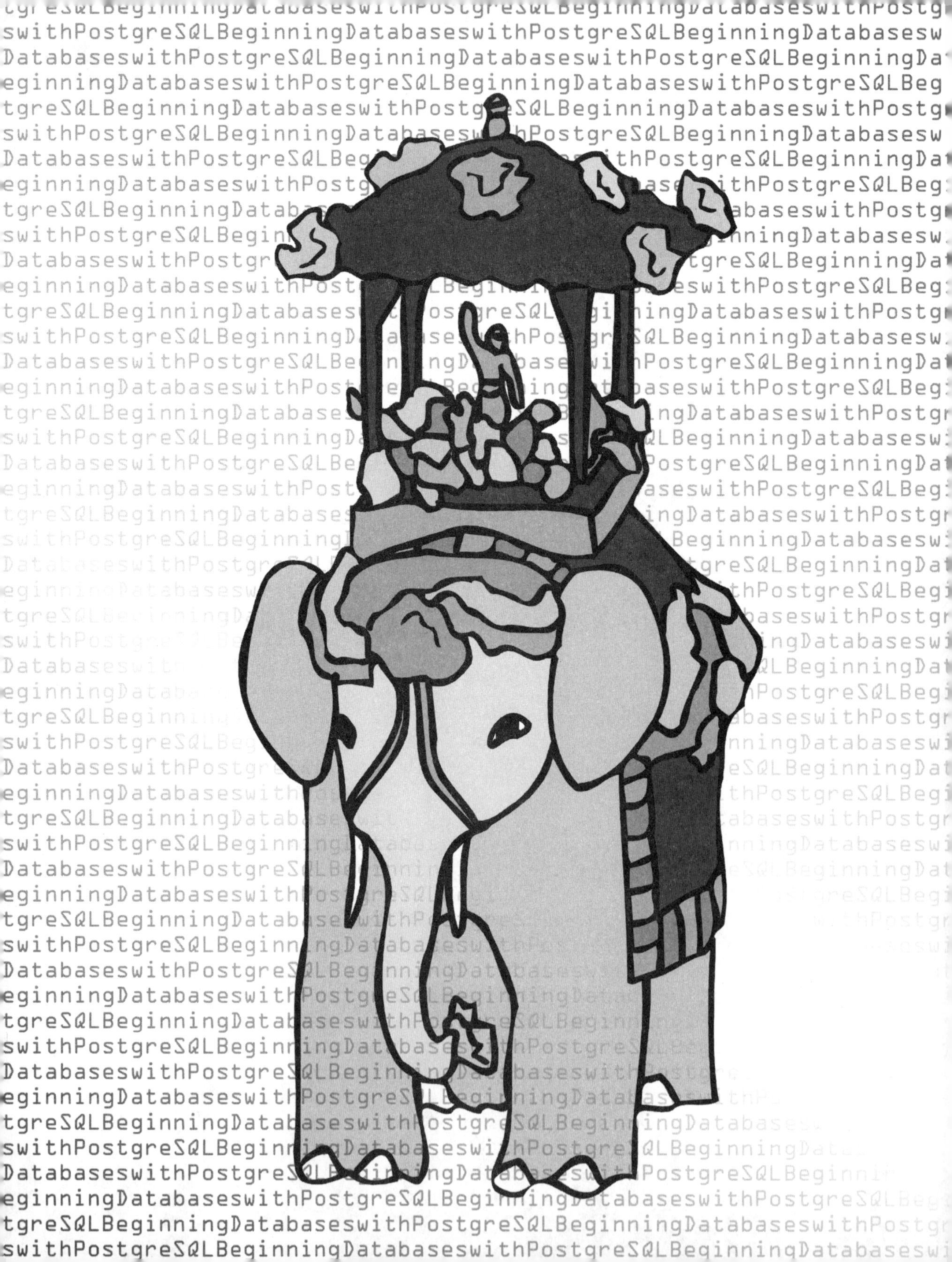

# Stored Procedures and Triggers

In this chapter, we are going to take a look at a few ways in which we can extend and enhance the features of PostgreSQL that we have seen so far. A lot of the material in this chapter is PostgreSQL specific, although most commercial RDBMS systems, such as Oracle, include similar features.

To begin with, we will take a look at more of the operators that PostgreSQL supports within SELECT statements, including advanced matching and mathematical operators that allow us to construct more sophisticated tests in WHERE clauses. Next, we will see how operators are implemented as functions in PostgreSQL and look at a few additional functions that add to the expressive power of our SELECTs.

PostgreSQL allows a developer to extend the database server functionality by writing functions in the C programming language and loading them into the server when the database starts up.

An extension can be as simple as a single extra function or as complex as a complete programming language in its own right. Several such extensions, known as loadable procedural languages, are included with the standard PostgreSQL distribution. These languages allow us to create our own functions quickly and more easily than writing in C.

We will take a brief look at one of the loadable languages, PL/pgSQL, in this chapter. Others, such as PL/Tcl and PL/Perl ,allow you to create PostgreSQL extensions in the Tcl and Perl programming languages respectively.

Functions, created as extensions, are executed by the server, rather than the client application, and are stored within the database itself. Therefore, they go by the name of stored procedures.

We will see some examples of stored procedures created with PL/pgSQL in this chapter. Again, PL/pgSQL is PostgreSQL-specific, but similar languages are available in other databases. For example, Oracle has PL/SQL and Sybase has Transact-SQL.

Stored procedures can also be executed automatically by the PostgreSQL server, when particular conditions arise within the database. For example, when a row deletion from a table is attempted, a stored procedure can be executed to enforce referential integrity by deleting related rows in other tables, or perhaps preventing the deletion from occurring. These autonomous actions are known as triggers, and we shall see them in action here as well.

In this chapter, we'll be looking at:

- ❑ Operators
- ❑ Functions
- ❑ Procedural languages
- ❑ PL/pgSQL
- ❑ Stored procedures
- ❑ SQL functions
- ❑ Triggers

# Operators

We have already seen and used some simple operators in SELECT statements from Chapter 8 onwards. For example, we can use a numerical comparison operator to limit a selection to rows that obey a condition, such as items that have a cost price greater than $4:

```
bpfinal=# SELECT * FROM item WHERE cost_price > 4;
 item_id |  description  | cost_price | sell_price
---------+---------------+------------+------------
       1 | Wood Puzzle   |      15.23 |      21.95
       2 | Rubik Cube    |       7.45 |      11.49
       5 | Picture Frame |       7.54 |       9.95
       6 | Fan Small     |       9.23 |      15.75
       7 | Fan Large     |      13.36 |      19.95
      11 | Speakers      |      19.73 |      25.32
(6 rows)

bpfinal=#
```

Here the operator > is applied between the cost_price attribute and a given number.

We can go further and include other attributes and operators to create more complex conditions:

```
bpfinal=# SELECT * FROM item WHERE (sell_price*100)%100 = 99;
 item_id | description | cost_price | sell_price
---------+-------------+------------+------------
       4 | Tissues     |       2.11 |       3.99
(1 row)

bpfinal=#
```

Here, we have used the multiplication operator in conjunction with a remainder to list the items that have a selling price that ends in 99¢.

Here's another operator. This operator performs a case insensitive regular expression match to discover which items have descriptions that start with a 'p' or an 'r' and end with an 'e':

```
bpfinal=# SELECT * FROM item WHERE description ~* '^[PR].*E$';
 item_id |   description   | cost_price | sell_price
---------+-----------------+------------+------------
       2 | Rubik Cube      |       7.45 |      11.49
       5 | Picture Frame   |       7.54 |       9.95
(2 rows)

bpfinal=#
```

As you can see, there are many operators supported by PostgreSQL. In fact, if you count the different variations of the same operator (that is, consider comparing integers as being distinct from comparing floating point numbers or comparing strings) there are almost 600 operators available.

# Operator Precedence and Associativity

Many of the PostgreSQL operators look and act very much like the normal arithmetic operators that you will find in many programming languages. The operators have a precedence hard-coded into the parser that determines the order in which operators, are executed in compound expressions. As usual, the precedence can be overridden using parentheses.

Note that PostgreSQL allows the use of operators, and, as we will see later, functions outside WHERE clauses of SELECTs:

```
bpfinal=# SELECT 1+2*3;
 ?column?
----------
        7
(1 row)
bpfinal=# SELECT (1+2)*3 AS answer;
 answer
--------
      9
(1 row)

bpfinal=#
```

Here we can see that the result of the expression 1+2*3 is reported as 7, displayed as an unknown column, given the name ?column? by default. In the second example, the operator precedence is overridden and the result is named as answer.

Although some of the operators behave exactly as you might expect if you have programmed in C or any other programming language, some of the operator precedences may just catch you out. As in C, the Boolean operators have a lower precedence than arithmetic operators, so parentheses are often required to get the desired operator execution order. If in doubt, make the order explicit with parentheses.

PostgreSQL operators also display associativity, either right or left, which determines the order in which operators of the same precedence are evaluated. Arithmetic operators, such as addition and subtraction are left associative so that 1+2-3 evaluates as if it had been written (1+2)-3. Others, such as the Boolean equality operator, are right associative so that x = y = z is evaluated as x = (y = z).

The table below lists the lexical precedence (in descending order) of the most common PostgreSQL operators:

| Operator | Associativity | Meaning |
| --- | --- | --- |
| UNION | Left | SQL SELECT statement clause |
| :: | | Typecast (synonym for CAST) |
| [] | Left | Array selection |
| . | Left | Attribute (column) selection |
| - | Right | Unary minus (integer negation) |
| ^ | Left | Exponentiation |
| * / % | Left | Multiplicative operators |
| + - | Left | Additive operators |
| IS | | Test (for TRUE, FALSE and NULL) |
| ISNULL | | Test (for NULL) |
| NOTNULL | | Test (for non-NULL) |
| OR | Left | Logical union |
| IN | | Test for membership of a set |
| BETWEEN | | Test for inclusion in a range |
| LIKE | | Test for a string match |
| <> | | Test for inequality |
| = | Right | Test for equality |
| NOT | Right | Logical negation |
| AND | Left | Logical intersection |
| All other operators | | User-defined and built-in operators not listed here, all have the same precedence |

> PostgreSQL supports operators for calculating natural logarithms and anti-logarithms (: and ;), but these are deprecated and may be removed from future releases of PostgreSQL. Use the functions `ln()` and `exp()` instead

# Arithmetic Operators

PostgreSQL provides a range of arithmetic operators. The most common are listed in the table below. All of these have the same precedence and are left associative:

| Operator | Example | Meaning |
|----------|---------|---------|
| + | `2+3 is 5` | Addition |
| – | `3-2 is 1` | Subtraction |
| * | `2*3 is 6` | Multiplication |
| / | `3/2 is 1` | Division |
|   | `3/2.0 is 1.5` | |
|   | `3/2::float8 is 1.5` | |
| % | `22 % 7 is 1` | Remainder (modulo) |
| ^ | `4^3 is 64` | Raise to power (exponentiation) |
| & | `14 & 23 is 6` | Binary AND |
| \| | `14 \| 23 is 31` | Binary OR |
| # | `14 # 23 is 25` | Binary XOR |
| >> | `128 >> 4 is 8` | Shift Right |
| << | `1 << 4 is 16` | Shift Left |

There are also a number of unary arithmetic operators, shown in the following table:

| Operator | Example | Meaning |
|----------|---------|---------|
| % | `%2.3 is 2` | Truncate |
| ! | `4! is 24` | Factorial |
| !! | `!!4 is 24` | Factorial as a left operator |
| @ | `@-2 is 2` | Absolute value |
| \|/ | `\|/64 is 8` | Square Root |
| \|\|/ | `\|\|/64 is 4` | Cube Root |
| ~ | `~15 is -16` | Binary NOT |

In general, the arithmetic operators "do the right thing". PostgreSQL will use the version of the operator that matches the argument used. So, when you divide one whole number by another, you will get a whole number result. When you divide a floating point number by another, you will get a floating point result. As shown in the table of examples, to force a floating point result, one of the arguments should be cast as a floating point number.

# Comparison and String Operators

PostgreSQL provides the usual array of comparison operators, such as less than and greater than. These operators work on many of the types that PostgreSQL supports, so for example, you can use the greater than operator to test for alphabetical ordering of strings, as well as relative sizes of numeric values.

The result of a comparison operator is either TRUE or FALSE, which psql will display as t or f:

| Operator | Example | Meaning |
|---|---|---|
| < | 2 < 3 | Less than |
|  | 'axy' < 'azz' |  |
| <= | 2 <= 3 | Less than or equal to |
| <> | 2 <> 3 | Not equal to |
| != | 2 != 3 |  |
| = | 3 = 1+2 | Equal to |
| > | 3 > 2 | Greater than |
| >= | 3 >= 2 | Greater than or equal to |
| IN | 3 in (1,2,3) | Included in a set |
| !!= | 4 !!= (2,3) | Not included (synonym for NOT IN) |

Strings have their own set of operators in PostgreSQL. There are operators for concatenating strings and for matching strings according to various rules. They are summarized in the next table:

| Operator | Example | Meaning |
|---|---|---|
| \|\| | 'abc' \|\| 'def' is 'abcdef' | String concatenation. |
| ~~ | 'xyzzy' ~~ '%zz%' | Synonym for LIKE. |
| !~~ | 'xyzzy' ~~ '%aa%' | Synonym for NOT LIKE. |
| ~ | 'xyzzy' ~ 'y.*y' | Regular expression substring match. Use leading ^ and trailing $ to anchor the match to the beginning or end or both. |
| ~* | 'xyzzy' ~* '^X.*Y$' | Regular expression match, case insensitive. |
| !~ | 'xyzzy' !~ 'aa' | Does not match (inverse of ~). |
| !~* | 'xyzzy' !~* 'AA' | Does not match, case insensitive (inverse of ~*). |

In a regular expression match, a string is compared to an expression similar to that used in the UNIX grep utility or the Perl match operators.

# Other Operators

PostgreSQL supports a whole host of additional operators for comparing and manipulating the PostgreSQL-specific data types such as points, circles, time intervals, and IP addresses. For more information, refer to the PostgreSQL User Guide.

> **The PostgreSQL documentation is provided as a set of HTML pages that can be viewed online with any web browser. Select file://usr/local/pgsql/doc/html**

The operators are all listed in the `pg_operator` table of the database and `psql` can list all of the operators and functions with the `\do` and `\df` internal commands.

# Functions

PostgreSQL boasts a very long list of built-in functions that we can use in `SELECT` expressions.

Here's the list:

- ❏ Functional equivalents to the operators we have already seen
- ❏ Additional mathematical functions
- ❏ More functions for handling strings of characters
- ❏ Functions for handling dates and times
- ❏ Text formatting functions
- ❏ Functions for the PostgreSQL geometric types such as point and circle
- ❏ IP address functions

The built-in functions (and in fact user-defined ones) are recorded in a system table of the PostgreSQL database, `pg_proc`. As at version PostgreSQL 7.1 and later, this table has over 1,100 entries.

In `psql`, you can list all functions and their arguments using `\df` command. Also, comments about any specific functions or group of functions can be displayed using the `\dd` command.

We cannot possibly hope to cover all of the available functions in this chapter, but we will take a peek at a few of the more useful ones. We have come across a few of the standard ones already in Chapters 7 and 8. For more information, seek out the PostgreSQL User Guide or browse the regression tests distributed with the PostgreSQL source code.

Many built-in functions provide an equivalent function for each mathematical and logical operator. Examples include `int4shl` and `float8mul` as the equivalent of the shift left operator (`<<`) for integers and the multiplication operator (`*`) for floating point values.

Additional mathematical functions are listed in the table below, all of which operate on floating point numbers and return a floating point number, unless otherwise stated:

| Function | Meaning |
|---|---|
| `abs(x)` | Absolute value |
| `degrees(r)` | Converts angular measures from radians to degrees |
| `radians(d)` | Converts angular measures from degrees to radians |

*Table continued on following page*

| Function | Meaning |
|----------|---------|
| exp(x) | Natural antilogarithm, raise *e* to a power |
| ln(x) | Natural logarithm |
| log(x) | Logarithm to base 10 |
| log(b,x) | Logarithm to a given base, b |
| mod(x,y) | Remainder after dividing x by y (also has an integer version) |
| pi() | Returns |
| pow(x,y) | Raises x to the power of y |
| random() | Returns a random number between 0.0 and 1.0 |
| Round(x) | Round to nearest whole number |
| Round(x,d) | Round to specified number of decimal places, d |
| Trunc(x) | Truncate to whole number (towards zero) |
| Trunc(x,d) | Truncate to specified number of decimal places, d |
| ceil(x) | Returns smallest integer not less than given argument |
| floor(x) | Returns largest integer not greater than given argument |
| sqrt(x) | Square root |
| cbrt(x) | Cube root |
| float8(i) | Takes an integer argument returns an equivalent float8 |
| float4(i) | Takes an integer argument, returns an equivalent float4 |
| int4(x) | Returns an integer, rounding if necessary |

Trigonometric functions are supported. All angular arguments and results are in radians:

| Function | Meaning |
|----------|---------|
| sin | Sine |
| cos | Cosine |
| tan | Tangent |
| Cot | Cotangent |
| asin | Inverse Sine |
| acos | Inverse Cosine |
| atan | Inverse Tangent |
| atan2 | Two argument arctangent, given a, b computes atan(b/a) |

PostgreSQL includes the standard SQL string functions, with their own syntax. For these functions, a string can be of type `char`, `varchar`, or `text`:

| Function | Meaning |
| --- | --- |
| `char_length(s)` `character_length(s)` | Length of a string. |
| `octet_length(s)` | Amount of storage consumed by a string. |
| `lower(s)` | Convert a string to lower case. |
| `upper(s)` | Convert a string to upper case. |
| `position(s1, s2)` | Position at which s1 appears in s2. |
| `substring(s from n for m)` | Extract a substring length m starting at position n. |
| `trim([leading \| trailing \| both] [s1] from s2)` | Remove characters s1 from string s2, either from the start, the end or both. Removes spaces by default if s1 not given. |

PostgreSQL extends string manipulation features with additional functions of its own. Refer to the User Guide for more information.

An important formatting function worth mentioning here, is the `to_char` function. It plays the same role in PostgreSQL that `printf` does in C, being responsible for all manner of formatting values for printing or display. It will format a date and time value according to a date template, and can format numeric values in many different ways (including roman numerals). Full details can be found in the User Guide.

# Procedural Languages

As was mentioned in the introduction to this chapter, it is possible to define your own functions for use within a PostgreSQL database. This is useful when we want to capture a particular calculation or query and reuse it in a number of places.

The SQL needed to create a new function is CREATE FUNCTION, which has the following basic syntax:

```
CREATE FUNCTION name ( [ ftype [, ...] ] )
    RETURNS rtype
    AS definition
    LANGUAGE 'langname'
```

> In fact, there is another form of **CREATE FUNCTION** that allows compiled object code to be incorporated into the PostgreSQL server, typically created from C source code. Extending the server by writing functions in C is beyond the scope of this chapter.

A very simple function, that simply increments its single argument might be written like this:

```
CREATE FUNCTION add_one(int4) RETURNS int4 AS '
    BEGIN
            RETURN $1 + 1;
    END;
' LANGUAGE 'plpgsql';
```

The definition of the function is given as a single string that may span several lines and may be written in any language supported by PostgreSQL as a loadable procedural language. In this case, PL/pgSQL is used, as indicated by the LANGUAGE clause specifying plpgsql.

To handle a procedural language, PostgreSQL must first be extended by including a handler function, typically written in C. For PL/pgSQL, a handler is included in the distribution as a shared library.

When a function is created, its definition is stored within the database. When the function is called for the first time, the definition is compiled by the handler into an executable form, and then executed. This means that we may not be advised of an error in our function until we try to use it.

Before we can write our own functions, in whatever loadable language we choose, we first have to arrange for PostgreSQL to support the language. This is what we will do next.

# Getting Started with PL/pgSQL

We will use PL/pgSQL as the loadable procedural language for our example stored procedures in this chapter. In a standard PostgreSQL installation, the handler function for PL/pgSQL is included in the shared library plpgsql.so in the directory /usr/local/pgsql/lib for UNIX and Linux, or plpgsql.dll in /usr/lib using Cygwin on Microsoft Windows.

Each PostgreSQL database is independent with regard to the languages that it supports, partly for security reasons. It is possible to create functions that will either accidentally or maliciously consume CPU resources by, for example, looping indefinitely. This could form the basis of a denial-of-service attack. Therefore, by default PostgreSQL databases do not support procedural languages. To use PL/pgSQL, we have to install the handler ourselves.

> **The database administrator can add languages to the template1 database, in which case all new databases will have those languages by default.**

To install PL/pgSQL for our bpfinal database, we could use the CREATE LANGUAGE command within psql and load the shared library, creating the handler function explicitly. This is complex enough to warrant a helper script, and one is provided in the PostgreSQL installation. The command we need is createlang:

```
createlang [options] [langname] dbname
```

The options are:

| Option | Meaning |
|---|---|
| -h, --host=HOSTNAME | Database server host |
| -p, --port=PORT | Database server port |
| -U, --username=USERNAME | Username to connect as |
| -W, --password | Prompt for password |
| -d, --dbname=DBNAME | Database to install language in |
| -L, --pglib=DIRECTORY | Find language interpreter file in DIRECTORY |
| -l, --list | Show a list of currently installed languages |

If a language name langname is not specified, you will be prompted for one. A database name dbname is mandatory. Normal users cannot add languages to databases, so you will usually connect as the postgres superuser:

```
$ createlang -U postgres plpgsql bpfinal
```

We can check that the language is present by listing languages with createlang, or by querying the system table pg_language with psql and pgAdmin:

```
$ createlang -l bpfinal
      Procedural languages
  Name    | Trusted? | Compiler
----------+----------+----------
 plpgsql  | t        | PL/pgSQL
(1 row)
```

```
$ psql -d bpfinal
```

```
bpfinal=# SELECT * FROM pg_language;
 lanname  | lanispl | lanpltrusted | lanplcallfoid | lancompiler
----------+---------+--------------+---------------+-------------
 internal | f       | f            |             0 | n/a
 C        | f       | f            |             0 | /bin/cc
 sql      | f       | f            |             0 | postgres
 plpgsql  | t       | t            |         21571 | PL/pgSQL
(4 rows)
```

```
bpfinal=#
```

Superusers can remove support for languages from databases by executing DROP LANGUAGE from within psql:

```
bpfinal=# DROP language 'plpgsql';
DROP
```

```
bpfinal=#
```

## Try it Out – A First Stored Procedure

We are now ready to begin working with PL/pgSQL stored procedures by writing our own functions. Let's start by checking that everything works by implementing the add_one function shown earlier:

```
bpfinal=# CREATE function add_one (int4) RETURNS int4 as '
bpfinal'# BEGIN return $1 + 1; end;' language 'plpgsql';
CREATE
bpfinal=# SELECT add_one(2) AS answer;
 answer
--------
      3
(1 row)

bpfinal=#
```

### How it Works

The CREATE FUNCTION stores the definition of the function add_one written in PL/pgSQL to the database. It is executed when the SELECT expression is evaluated. Note that the PL/pgSQL is not sensitive to either case of its keywords, such as BEGIN or layout. We could have easily defined the function like this:

```
bpfinal=# CREATE function
bpfinal-# add_one(int4) RETURNS int4
bpfinal-# AS '
bpfinal'# BEGIN
bpfinal'#   RETURN $1 + 1;
bpfinal'# END;
bpfinal'# '
bpfinal-# LANGUAGE 'plpgsql';
CREATE

bpfinal=#
```

# Function Overloading

PostgreSQL considers functions to be distinct if they have different names or if they have a different number of parameters, or if their parameters have different types. We can create further add_one functions that deal with different types if we wish. Consider what happens when we use our add_one function on a floating point value:

```
bpfinal=# SELECT add_one(3.1);
 add_one
---------
       4
(1 row)

bpfinal=#
```

Here we see that PostgreSQL has executed our add_one function, which takes an integer parameter, as specified by the parameter type int4. The value that we passed, 3.1, has been cast to an integer, effectively rounded to give 3, which is then incremented.

If we wish to create an increment function for floating point number, we just have to create another definition of add_one:

```
bpfinal=# CREATE function
bpfinal-# add_one(float8) RETURNS float8
bpfinal-# AS '
bpfinal'# BEGIN
bpfinal'#    RETURN $1 + 1;
bpfinal'# END;
bpfinal'# '
bpfinal-# LANGUAGE 'plpgsql';
CREATE
bpfinal=# SELECT add_one(3.1);
 add_one
---------
     4.1
(1 row)

bpfinal=#
```

This time we get the result we want because PostgreSQL executes the correct version of the add_one function. This behavior, known as **function overloading** can be quite useful, but also fairly confusing. To keep the functions distinct we must refer to them in a way that indicates their parameters. In this case, we have two functions that we can refer to as add_one(int4) and add_one(float8).

> A more convenient way to create functions is to edit script files containing function definitions and to use the **psql \i** command to read them.

# Listing Functions

If we need to see the source code for our functions once they have been loaded into the database, we can query the table used for storing procedures. This is the pg_proc table:

```
bpfinal=# SELECT prosrc FROM pg_proc WHERE proname = 'add_one';
           prosrc
-----------------------------

begin
        return $1 + 1;
end;


begin
        return $1 + 1;
end;

(2 rows)

bpfinal=#
```

# Deleting Functions

Functions can be dropped from a database with DROP FUNCTION. We must be sure to specify the correct version of a function for overloaded functions, and to drop all versions of a function if we want to remove the function completely:

```
bpfinal=# DROP function add_one(int4);
DROP
bpfinal=# DROP function add_one(float8);
DROP

bpfinal=#
```

# Quoting

One slight complication that arises when using PL/pgSQL for stored procedures concerns quoting. The entire function definition is given to the CREATE FUNCTION command as a single quoted string. This means that if we have single quotes within our function definition, they must be escaped. We do this by writing two quotes together to stand for a quote within a string. The examples in this chapter will show escaped quotes where necessary.

# Anatomy of a Stored Procedure

Now that we have created, executed, and dropped a sample stored procedure, it is time to move on to consider the construction of PL/pgSQL stored procedures in more detail.

PL/pgSQL is a block-structured language, such as Pascal or C, with variables having declarations and block scope. Each block has an optional label; it may have some variable declarations, and encloses statements that make up the block between BEGIN and END keywords. The syntax therefore for a block is:

```
[<<label>>]
[DECLARE declarations]
BEGIN
      statements
END;
```

> **PL/pgSQL is case insensitive. All keywords and variable names may be written in either case.**

A PL/pgSQL function is defined with a CREATE FUNCTION statement with a block as the definition part, enclosed in single quotes:

```
CREATE FUNCTION name ( [ ftype [, ...] ] )
    RETURNS rtype
    AS 'block definition'
    LANGUAGE 'plpgsql';
```

# Function Arguments

A PL/pgSQL function can take zero or more parameters, and the types of the parameters are given in parentheses after the function name. The types are built-in PostgreSQL types, such as int4, or float8. All stored procedures must return a value, and the return type is specified in the RETURNS clause of the function definition.

Within a function body, the parameters of the function are referred to as $1, $2, and so on, in the order that they are defined. We will see later that it is possible to give the parameters names using an ALIAS declaration.

Here is a simple stored procedure that provides a floating point geometric average of two integers:

```
-- geom_avg
-- get a geometric average of two integers
create function geom_avg(int4, int4) returns float8 as '
begin
    return sqrt($1 * $2::float8);
end;
' language 'plpgsql';
```

Notice that we have to cast one of the integer values to a floating point value so that we pass a floating point result of the multiplication to the sqrt function. If we do not do this, we will get an error saying that the function sqrt(int4) does not exist.

# Comments

As we can see from the examples so far, PL/pgSQL allows comments to be included in function definitions. In fact, there are two types of comments, single line comments and block comments.

A standard SQL single line comment is introduced by two dashes (--). Everything following the two dashes up to the end of the line is ignored:

```
-- This is a single line comment
create   -- comments can
function -- come anywhere, and extend to the end of the line
```

Block comments are used to introduce larger blocks of text as comments, or for temporarily removing sections of code not required. The syntax is the same as C and C++, with blocks of comments being surrounded by /* and */:

```
/*
    This is a block comment used to describe
    the use and behavior of the following function
*/
create function blah() returns integer as '
begin
    /* comment out call to func
    func();
    */
    return 1;
```

```
        end;
        ' language 'plpgsql';
```

Block comments cannot be nested, but you can use single line comments to prevent the block comment delimiters from being interpreted as a block comment if you need to.

# Declarations

PL/pgSQL functions can declare local variables for use within the function. Each variable has a type that can be one of the PostgreSQL built-in types, a user-defined type, or a type that corresponds to a row in a table.

Variable declarations for a function are written in the DECLARE section of a function definition, or a block within a function.

As is usual with block-structured languages such as C and C++, variables declared for a block are only visible within that block, or blocks within that block. Variables declared in an inner block with the same name as a variable outside that block hide the outer block's variable:

```
DECLARE
      n1 integer;
      n2 integer;
BEGIN
      -- can use n1 and n2 in here
      n2 := 1;
      DECLARE
            n2 integer; -- hides the earlier n2
            n3 integer;
      BEGIN
            -- can use n1, n2 and n3 in here
            n2 := 2;
      END;
      -- n3 no longer available here
      -- n2 still has value 1 here
END;
```

All variables used in a function must be declared before they can be used, except for loop control variables that we will meet later. A variable may not have the same name as a PL/pgSQL keyword, these are reserved, and include:

| | | |
|---|---|---|
| alias | begin | bpchar |
| Char | constant | debug |
| declare | Default | diagnostics |
| else | end | Exception |
| execute | exit | for |
| From | Get | if |
| in | Into | loop |

| not | notice | Null |
| --- | --- | --- |
| perform | processed | raise |
| Record | rename | result |
| return | Reverse | select |
| then | to | Type |
| varchar | when | while |

There are several ways to declare a variable, depending on its intended use.

## ALIAS

The simplest declaration is an ALIAS declaration, that gives a name to a positional parameter to a function. This helps us to write slightly more meaningful code, and code that is more robust against changes in parameter numbers and ordering. The ALIAS declaration has the syntax:

```
name ALIAS FOR $n;
```

A new variable called name is made available, which acts as another name for the specified positional parameter. For example, we might have written the geom_avg function as:

```
create function geom_avg(integer, integer) returns float8 as '
declare
      first alias for $1;
      second alias for $2;
begin
      return sqrt(first * second::float8);
end;
' language 'plpgsql';
```

## RENAME

It is also possible to rename variables with a RENAME declaration. This can be useful inside trigger functions as we will see later, but is generally not recommended, as it can make code difficult to read. The syntax of a RENAME declaration is:

```
RENAME original TO new;
```

## A Simple Variable Declaration

A simple variable is declared by giving it a name, a type, and optionally an initial value. The syntax is:

```
name [CONSTANT] type [NOT NULL] [:= value];
```

The CONSTANT modifier declares that the variable may not be changed. It must, therefore, include an initial value in its declaration.

The NOT NULL clause instructs PostgreSQL to raise a run-time error if the variable is ever given a NULL value.

**269**

The initial value need not be a constant and is evaluated and assigned each time the function is called, so for example giving an initial value of now for a timestamp variable would result in the variable taking the current time when it is executed, not when it was compiled.

The type may be a PostgreSQL built-in type, that is, you can declare variables with the same data type or structure of another database item. The advantage of specifying the variable's type in this indirect fashion is that, should changes be made in the database, the stored procedure code remains correct. The syntax is:

```
builtintype
variable%TYPE
table.column%TYPE
```

Here are some examples of variable declarations:

```
n integer := 1;
mypi constant float8 := pi();
pizza_pi mypi%TYPE;
mydesc item.description%type := ''extra large size pizza'';
```

Here the declaration of mydesc will result in a variable suitable for handling the description column in the item table of our sample database. If that is currently a char(64), say, and changes in the future to a char(80), the code using mydesc will still work and PostgreSQL will create the correct type of variable. Note that we have double-quoted the string we initialize with, as this declaration will be appearing inside a single-quoted string as part of a function definition.

## A Composite Variable Declaration

We can declare and use composite variables in our stored procedures. These correspond to complete rows in a particular table.

## ROWTYPE

To declare a composite variable, we use the ROWTYPE declaration syntax:

```
name table%ROWTYPE;
```

The result of this declaration will be a variable that itself has fields, one for each column in the table on which it is based. Consider the following:

```
contact customer%ROWTYPE;
```

This will create a variable called contact with fields corresponding to columns in the customer table. To use the fields, we use the syntax variable.field. Here is an example:

```
DECLARE
    contact customer%ROWTYPE;
    address text;
BEGIN
    contact.zipcode := ''XY1 6ZZ'';
    contact.fname := NULL;
    address := contact.addressline || contact.town;
END;
```

## RECORD

A second kind of composite type is the RECORD type. This is a type that acts much like a ROWTYPE, but is not based on a particular table when it is defined. The record will have fields that match whatever is assigned to the record at run-time. Records are useful in code that must work as triggers that are called from different tables. They can also be used to store the results of SELECT statements in a general way. A record declaration is very simple:

```
name RECORD;
```

We will see more of records when we cover assignment via selections and in triggers.

# Assignments

PL/pgSQL variables are assigned new values in assignment statements. The syntax for an assignment is:

```
reference := expression;
```

`reference` is a variable name or field in a composite type, such as a `rowtype` or `record`. The expression may be a constant, another variable or field reference of a complex expression constructed with operators, casts, and function calls. Examples of assignments are:

```
n1: = 23;
long_variable_names_are_OK := (n1 + 45)/2;
f2 := add_one(n1)::float8 * sqrt(2.0);

/*Composite types may be assigned one field at a time by referring to individual
fields: */

contact.zipcode := ''AB12 3CD'';
```

## SELECT INTO Statement

An alternative assignment mechanism is an extension to SELECT. With this we can assign a variable, a list of variables, an entire row type variable, or a record with a SELECT INTO statement. The syntax is an extension of the normal SQL SELECT:

```
SELECT expressions INTO target [FROM ...];
```

Some simple examples of using SELECT in place of an assignment operator are:

```
SELECT sqrt(2.0) INTO sqrt2;
SELECT add_one(n1) INTO n1;
SELECT 1,2,3,4 INTO n1, n2, n3, n4;
SELECT ''Mole'', ''Adrian'' INTO contact.lname, contact.fname;
```

We can assign an entire row type in one go, if we specify values for each column, in the right order:

```
DECLARE
    product item%ROWTYPE;
```

```
BEGIN
     select NULL, ''Widget'', ''1.45'', ''1.99'' into product;
END;
```

Where assigned values and variables are of different types, PostgreSQL will apply appropriate casts where it can. In the last example, the cost and sell prices are of type NUMERIC(7,2), but they are successfully assigned from text values.

Assignments are executed by the PostgreSQL server as SELECT statements even when the := operator form is used. We can use the power of SELECT to assign variables based on the content of the database by including a FROM clause, and optional WHERE conditions. For example:

```
SELECT * INTO product FROM item WHERE item_id = 9;
```

We must take care that our SELECT returns only one row, because additional rows will be silently discarded, only the first returned row is assigned to variables listed. We will see a little later that we can arrange for code to be executed for each row in a SELECT that returns multiple rows.

It is possible that a SELECT will return no rows, in which case, the assignment will not be performed. PostgreSQL provides a special Boolean variable, called FOUND, that is available immediately after an assignment using SELECT INTO, which we can use to determine if the assignment was successful:

```
SELECT * INTO product FROM item WHERE description ~~ ''%Cube%'';
IF NOT FOUND THEN
-- take some recovery action
END IF;
```

## PERFORM

In some cases, we may not wish to capture the result of a SELECT, possibly if it is used to call a function with side effects. In this case, we can evaluate the expression or query and discard the result with PERFORM:

```
PERFORM query;
```

The PERFORM statement essentially executes SELECT query over the SPI managers and ignores the result.

# Execution Control Structures

PL/pgSQL provides structures for controlling the flow of execution within a function. These are the branch, return, conditional, and loop statements.

# Returning from Functions

Returning a value from a function is accomplished by using a RETURN statement:

```
RETURN expression;
```

Processing for the function stops after the expression has been evaluated. The value of the expression is made available to the caller of the function as the function result. The value must be compatible with the return type declared for the function, and will be cast if necessary.

In PL/pgSQL, a function must return a value, and a run-time error will occur if the end of the outermost block of a function is reached without executing a RETURN.

## Exceptions and Messages

A function's execution can also be stopped should some condition arise that makes it impossible to continue. Rather than return a value, the function may raise an exception. An exception causes PostgreSQL to write an entry in the log, and can cause a stored procedure to terminate immediately:

```
RAISE level 'format' [, variable ...];
```

The RAISE statement logs the exception, which can be one of several levels of seriousness.

PostgreSQL defines three levels:

| Level | Behavior |
|---|---|
| DEBUG | Write a message in the log (usually suppressed) |
| NOTICE | Write a message in the log and send to application |
| EXCEPTION | Write a message in the log and terminate the stored procedure |

The DEBUG level is useful for capturing additional information during development. The NOTICE level provides warnings for non-fatal errors. The warnings are made available to client applications if required, by the NOTIFY mechanisms. The EXCEPTION level is used for fatal errors, where the stored procedure is unable to continue. For more information, refer to the PostgreSQL Programmer's Guide.

The format string is used to layout an error message. Within this string, each % character is replaced in turn by the values of the variables. Unlike printf in C, you may not use expressions in a RAISE statement, only identifiers.

Consider the following:

```
RAISE DEBUG '' The value of n is %'', n;
```

This results in a log entry in the PostgreSQL log file, /usr/local/pgsql/data/postmaster.log, that reads something like:

```
DEBUG: The value of n is 4
```

Here is an example procedure:

```
create function scope() returns integer AS '
BEGIN
DECLARE
```

```
  n integer := 4;
BEGIN
RAISE DEBUG ''n is %'', n;
return n;
END;
' language 'plpgsql';
```

If we execute this stored procedure within `psql`, we will see no message:

```
bpfinal=# SELECT scope();
 scope
-------
     4
(1 row)


bpfinal=#
```

Increasing the seriousness level in the RAISE statement to NOTICE however, we see a message from `psql` as well as in the log file:

```
bpfinal=# SELECT scope();
NOTICE:  n is 4
 scope
-------
     4
(1 row)


bpfinal=#
```

Finally, at level EXCEPTION, the stored procedure terminates prematurely with an error:

```
bpfinal=# SELECT scope();
ERROR:  n is 4

bpfinal=#
```

## Conditionals

PL/pgSQL supports several types of conditionals, constructs that execute one of two or more sets of statements, or return one of two or more results depending on a test. These are probably the most useful parts of PL/pgSQL. The most common is probably the IF statement, similar to many other programming languages.

### IF-THEN-ELSE

```
IF expression
THEN
statements
[ELSE
     statements]
END IF;
```

If the `expression` evaluates to `TRUE`, the statements in the `THEN` part of the `IF` are executed. Otherwise, if there is an (optional) `ELSE` part, the statements therein are executed.

As in other programming languages, `IF` statements can be nested by including another `IF` statement inside the `THEN` or `ELSE` parts.

### NULLIF and CASE

There are also two SQL conditional functions that return values depending on a test. These are `NULLIF` and `CASE` and they can be used in stored procedures and regular SQL in PostgreSQL.

The `NULLIF` function returns `NULL` if an input matches a specified value, and returns the input unchanged if not:

```
NULLIF(input, value)
```

This returns `NULL` if the test `input = value` is `TRUE`, and returns `input` otherwise.

The `CASE` function chooses one of a number of values, depending on an input value. The syntax is:

```
CASE
        WHEN expression
        THEN expression
        ...
ELSE expression
END;
```

There may be as many `WHEN`/`THEN` pairs as needed. The expression as a whole, returns the result of evaluating the expression in the `THEN` part corresponding to the first `WHEN` expression to yield `TRUE`. If no `WHEN` parts match, the `ELSE` expression is evaluated. For example, the following will set `res` to 5, 6, or 7 depending on whether n2 is 1, 2, or some other value:

```
res := CASE
            WHEN n2 = 1
            THEN 5
            WHEN n2 = 2
            THEN 6
            ELSE 7
END;
```

## Loops

PL/pgSQL has a particularly rich set of looping mechanisms alternatively known as iterative control structures or ways of executing statements a number of times.

The simplest loop is one that is uncontrolled, and unless terminated with an `EXIT` statement, will run indefinitely:

```
[<<label>>]
LOOP
        statements
END LOOP;
```

All of PL/pgSQL LOOP constructs may be labeled, as can BEGIN . . . END blocks. This label is used as a target for an EXIT statement that causes the specified loop to be terminated. For readers familiar with C this would be equivalent to a multi-level version break – something that C lacks:

```
The EXIT statement

EXIT [label] [WHEN expression];
```

This causes the LOOP labelled with label to be terminated, while execution continues at the next statement after the end of the loop. The label must refer to the current LOOP, or a containing LOOP. If no label is given, the current loop is terminated. If a WHEN clause is given, the EXIT is not performed unless expression evaluates to TRUE.

Here is an example of an infinite loop:

```
<<infinite>>
LOOP
    n := n + 1;
    EXIT infinite WHEN n >= 10;
END LOOP;
```

A more controlled loop is the WHILE loop, which executes a set of statements as long as a condition remains true.

### WHILE Loop

```
[<<label>>]

WHILE expression

LOOP
    statements
END LOOP;
```

We can arrange to execute a loop a fixed number of times with a FOR loop:

```
FOR name IN [REVERSE] from .. to
LOOP
    statements
END LOOP;
```

This type of loop executes its body once for each value in the range given by the integer expressions from and to. A new variable is created for the loop and is called name. It takes each of the values in the range in turn, incrementing by one each time the loop body is executed. If REVERSE is specified, the loop runs in the opposite direction with the variable name being decremented.

### FOR Loop

Here is a simple example of a FOR loop in action:

```
FOR cid IN 1 .. 15
LOOP
        SELECT * INTO row FROM customer
```

```
    WHERE customer_id = cid;
        -- process a customer
END LOOP;
```

This loop executes 15 times with the variable cid taking the values 1 through 15, selecting the customers one at a time into a row variable. The lower and upper bounds on the loop variable may be expressions, so we might try to scan the entire customer table, rather than just the first 15 by using:

```
SELECT COUNT(*) INTO ncustomers FROM customer;
FOR cid IN 1 .. ncustomers
...
```

A neater solution however, is an alternative form of the FOR loop that allows us to execute a loop once for each row in a table. In fact, once for each row returned by an arbitrary SELECT:

```
FOR row IN SELECT ...
LOOP
      statements
END LOOP;
```

For each of the rows returned by the SELECT, the row variable is assigned and the statements executed. The variable used to store the row must have been previously declared either as a record or a row type. The last row processed will still be available when the loop ends or is terminated with an EXIT.

The following procedure prints the family names of all our customers when run in psql:

```
DECLARE
      row record;
BEGIN
      FOR row IN SELECT * FROM customer
      LOOP
            RAISE NOTICE ''Family Name is %'', row.lname;
      END LOOP;
END:
```

Now that we have met all of the programming structures in PL/pgSQL, it is time to consider putting some of them to use.

## Try it Out – Stored Procedure

Suppose, in our example database we would like to think about using the database to help with ordering more products from our suppliers as we run low on stock. We already have a stock table that keeps track of the number of available items we have to sell. We would like to be able to use this information to automatically raise orders on our suppliers.

Below is a stored procedure that takes the first step towards the goal of automated re-ordering. The reorders function looks in the stock table for items that have a stock holding of less than a given value. For each of these items, it writes a record in a new table, reorders.

The next step (left as an exercise) would be to use the reorders table to generate orders:

```
-- Drop and create a temporary table for raising orders
drop table reorders;
create table reorders
(
  item_id  integer,
  message  text
);

-- reorders
-- scan the stock table to raise re-orders of item low on stock
create function reorders(int4) returns integer as '
declare
     min_stock alias for $1;
     reorder_item integer;
     reorder_count integer;
     stock_row stock%rowtype;
     msg text;
begin
     select count(*) into reorder_count from stock
             where quantity <= min_stock;
     for stock_row in select * from stock
                  where quantity <= min_stock
     loop
          declare
               item_row item%rowtype;
          begin
               select * into item_row from item
                       where item_id = stock_row.item_id;
               msg = ''order more '' ||
                      item_row.description || ''s at '' ||
                      to_char(item_row.cost_price,''99.99'');
               insert into reorders
                       values (stock_row.item_id, msg);
          end;
     end loop;
     return reorder_count;
end;
' language 'plpgsql';
```

Save the above code in `sproc.sql` or alternatively, download it from the Wrox website (http://www.wrox.com).

When we create the function and execute it specifying a minimum stock level of 3, we get a return result of 3, indicating that there are three items with a current stock level less than or equal to 3:

```
bpfinal=# \i sproc.sql
DROP
CREATE
CREATE
bpfinal=# SELECT reorders(3);
 reorders
----------
        3
(1 row)
```

```
bpfinal=#
```

The `reorders` table has been populated with the item identifiers of the three items we are running low on:

```
bpfinal=# SELECT * SELECT reorders ;
 item_id |               message
---------+------------------------------------
       2 | order more Rubik Cubes at    7.45
       5 | order more Picture Frames at    7.54
      10 | order more Carrier Bags at     .01
(3 rows)

bpfinal=#
```

We could have used CREATE TEMPORARY TABLE to create the `reorders` table. In that case, the table would automatically be dropped when we quit our database session. We have used a CREATE TABLE here so that the `reorders` table persists, which we might need if our re-ordering application is separate from the stock check.

We can verify the result by querying the `stock` table ourselves:

```
bpfinal=# SELECT * FROM stock;
 item_id | quantity
---------+----------
       1 |       12
       2 |        2
       4 |        8
       5 |        3
       7 |        8
       8 |       18
      10 |        1
(7 rows)

bpfinal=#
```

### How it Works

The `reorders` function uses a SELECT to retrieve all of the rows in the `stock` table that have a low quantity level. A LOOP is used to iterate over the results of the SELECT. The body of the loop, which uses an INSERT to add to the `reorders` table, is executed for each row in the results set. The return result from `reorders` is provided by another SELECT that counts the matching rows in the `stock` table.

To complete the automated ordering system, we would have to extract the items and place orders on the suppliers. We would also probably need to set minimum stock levels for each product and add that to the `item` table. Similarly, the number of products to order may need to be varied, perhaps on the basis of previous sales history, or seasonal factors.

# Dynamic Queries

Normally, database queries in a stored procedure are either fixed or simply parameterized. We usually query a table for rows that have a specific column that matches a given value, or UPDATE a row with new column values. This can be achieved using SELECT, UPDATE, and friends substituting the values of procedure variables where needed:

```
INSERT INTO reorders VALUES (stock_row.item_id, msg);
```

There are some rare instances where we might like to be able to use the value of a variable to specify a table or column name for an operation. PostgreSQL does not allow this as it needs to be able to optimize the query only once, rather than every time the query is executed.

PL/pgSQL however, supports a generic EXECUTE statement that allows us to execute an arbitrary SQL statement, specified as a string:

```
EXECUTE query-string
```

The string for the query can be dynamically created within a stored procedure, using the string manipulation operators that we met earlier.

Special care needs to be taken to ensure that quoting of names and literal values is correct within the string. To help with this two functions are available. All table and column names should be processed with quote_ident, which generates a string suitable for forming part of a query, and values should be processed with quote_value.

Here is an example that creates a general-purpose update using variables for names and values:

```
EXECUTE ''UPDATE ''
|| quote_ident(tablename)
|| '' SET ''
    || quote_ident(columnname)
    || '' = ''
    || quote_literal(columnvalue)
    || '' WHERE ''
...;
```

Note that this can be an inefficient way of accessing the database, as any queries that you make, have to be interpreted and planned each time they need to be run.

Dynamic queries may also be used in FOR loops in place of the SELECT statement for iterating across records. The syntax for this variant is:

```
FOR row IN EXECUTE query-string
LOOP
      statements
END LOOP;
```

# SQL Functions

Although in this chapter we have concentrated on PL/pgSQL as a method of creating stored procedures, it is also possible to use SQL to create functions. To do this, you specify the procedure language as 'sql' and use PostgreSQL SQL statements instead of PL/pgSQL.

SQL functions take parameters as with PL/pgSQL and can be referred to as $1, $2, and so on. In the function definition, $1 is automatically replaced by the first argument of the function call, and so on. There are no control structures, you are restricted to PostgreSQL SQL statements. That is, while PL/pgSQL includes features such as variables, conditional evaluation and looping, SQL functions allow only argument substitution. The value returned by an SQL function is the data returned by the last SQL statement executed, usually a SELECT.

The advantage of using SQL for stored procedures is that there is then no need to load the PL/pgSQL language handler into the database.

One trick that a SQL function allows us is to return more than one row of data from our function. If we declare the function return type as setof type and then use an appropriate SELECT, we can arrange to return multiple rows. Here's a function that returns all customers in a given town:

```
CREATE function sqlf(text) RETURNS setof customer AS '
    SELECT * FROM customer WHERE town = $1;
' language 'sql';
```

When we run the function in psql, we see three rows returned:

```
bpfinal=# SELECT sqlf('Bingham');
 ?column?
-----------
 136842856
 136842856
 136842856
(3 rows)


bpfinal=#
```

Unfortunately, we cannot handle entire rows at once in psql, so we need to select a column at a time. To do this, we use the syntax column(function()) to extract the required column. Here we list the last names of customers in Bingham and give the results column a name:

```
bpfinal=# SELECT lname(sqlf('Bingham')) AS customer;
 customer
----------
 Stones
 Stones
 Jones
(3 rows)

bpfinal=#
```

# Triggers

In our stored procedure example, we developed a function that would allow us to discover which products required restocking. We created a function that wrote reminder messages into a `reorders` table. For this to be useful, we would need to ensure that this procedure is executed on a regular basis, perhaps once a day, during an overnight batch process. It might be an advantage to find a way of making sure the `reorders` table is always up to date automatically, without having to program our client applications to keep updating the entries.

We have mentioned in Chapter 8, the concept of referential integrity, ensuring that the data in our database makes sense at all times. For example, if we delete a customer we need to ensure that all of the order history relating to that customer is deleted at the same time. We have seen constraints used to ensure that PostgreSQL enforces this kind of integrity.

For some applications, constraints are not quite enough – suppose we want to prevent the deletion of a customer when there are still outstanding orders for that customer, but allow the deletion if all orders have been shipped.

We saw in Chapter 8, how we could use column and table level constraints to enforce more complex rules of data integrity, but these rules were essentially static. We could specify that a related row must exist, or enforce a rule that you cannot delete while related rows exist, but had no way of specifying complex conditions. For example, that row must not exist unless some other condition is also true. Nor could we carry out more complex user-defined actions when rows were added or deleted.

One answer to these problems lies in triggers. With a trigger, we can arrange for PostgreSQL to execute a stored procedure when certain actions are taken, like an `INSERT`, `DELETE`, or `UPDATE` in a table.

The combination of stored procedures and triggers gives us the power to enforce quite sophisticated business rules directly in the database. As we have said before, the best place for enforcing business rules about the data is in the database.

To use a trigger, we need to first define a trigger procedure and then create the trigger itself, which defines when the trigger procedure will be executed.

## Creating Triggers

Triggers are created with the `CREATE TRIGGER` command, which has the syntax:

```
CREATE TRIGGER name { BEFORE | AFTER }
    { event [OR ...] }
    ON table FOR EACH { ROW | STATEMENT }
    EXECUTE PROCEDURE func ( arguments )
```

Here, `event` is one of `INSERT`, `DELETE`, or `UPDATE`.

The trigger effectively says "run this stored procedure every time this event occurs on this table".

The trigger is given a name that is used to delete the trigger when it is no longer required, by executing:

```
DROP TRIGGER name ON table;
```

The trigger fires when the specified event occurs – a DELETE, INSERT, or UPDATE. We can request that the trigger fires after the event occurs, in which case the called procedure will have access to both the original data (for updates and deletes) and the new data (for inserts and updates). We can also request that the trigger fire before the event occurs. In this case, we can prevent the update occurring, or change the data to be inserted or updated.

> **We can specify more than one event by listing them separated by OR.**

As we know, some SQL statements can affect multiple rows of data. Where a multiple-row-update causes a trigger to fire, we can choose whether the trigger fires for each row that is updated, or just once for the whole update. We specify ROW if we wish the trigger to fire multiple times, or STATEMENT otherwise.

The arguments passed to the function can be used to distinguish similar triggers, so that one function can be used for more than one trigger.

To automate the updates on our re-orders table, we might create a stored procedure called reorder_trigger and create a trigger to call it whenever the stock table changes:

```
CREATE TRIGGER trig_reorder
AFTER INSERT OR UPDATE ON stock
FOR EACH ROW EXECUTE PROCEDURE reorder_trigger(3);
```

Note that the trigger procedure (trig_reorder in this case) must have been defined before we create the trigger itself.

We use the trigger procedure argument to pass a minimum stock quantity, in this case 3.

## Trigger Procedures

A trigger fires when a condition is met, and executes a special type of stored procedure called a trigger procedure. A trigger procedure is very similar to a stored procedure, but is slightly more restricted due to the manner in which it gets called.

A trigger procedure is created as a function with no parameters and a special return type of OPAQUE. The OPAQUE return type is used for functions that return values which cannot be manipulated by PostgreSQL directly.

PostgreSQL will call a trigger procedure when changes are being made to a particular table. The procedure must either return NULL or a row that matches the structure of the table for which the trigger procedure has been called.

For AFTER triggers that are called following an UPDATE, it is generally recommended that a trigger procedure return NULL.

For BEFORE triggers, the return result is used to direct the update about to be performed. If the trigger procedure returns NULL, the UPDATE is not performed, and if a data row is returned, it is used as the source for the update, giving the trigger procedure the opportunity to change the data before it is committed to the database.

## Try it Out – Triggers

Here is a simple trigger procedure that updates our `reorders` table after stock has been adjusted:

```
Create function reorder_trigger() returns opaque AS '
declare
      mq integer;
      item_record record;
begin
      mq := tg_argv[0];
      raise notice ''in trigger, mq is %'', mq;
      if new.quantity <= mq
         then
            select * into item_record from item
            where item_id = new.item_id;
              insert into reorders
            values (new.item_id, item_record.description);
      end if;
      return NULL;
end;
' language 'plpgsql';
```

Now we have a trigger procedure and have defined a trigger that uses it, we can see it in action with `psql`.

Load the function and trigger definition from a script file:

```
bpfinal=# \i sproc.sql
...
CREATE
CREATE

bpfinal=#
```

Then try adjusting the stock of an item so that it drops to 3 or below:

```
bpfinal=# UPDATE stock SET quantity = 3 WHERE item_id = 1;
NOTICE:  in trigger, mq is 3
UPDATE 1

bpfinal=#
```

We can see that the trigger has fired and raised a notice to tell us. The update to the stock proceeds, but the trigger also updates the `reorders` table, adding a new row:

```
bpfinal=# SELECT * FROM reorders;
 item_id |   message
---------+-------------
       1 | Wood Puzzle
(1 row)

bpfinal=#
```

### How it Works

The trigger procedure is called whenever an INSERT or UPDATE takes place on the stock table. It checks the stock quantity as it appears after the update has taken place, and if it is less than the minimum quantity, adds a record to the reorders table.

You may have noticed that we have used a couple of new features in the trigger procedure. Firstly, the procedure arguments are not referred to as $1, $2, and so on, for trigger procedures. The arguments are made available via one of a number of special variables made available automatically to trigger procedures. The arguments are passed in an array named tg_argv, starting at tg_argv[0].

Secondly, inside the trigger procedures, two very special records are made available, OLD and NEW. These contain (for ROW triggers) the data from the row being affected by the update that fired the trigger. As you may guess OLD contains data from before the update and NEW contains data from after the update (or proposed update for a BEFORE trigger).

The special variables made available to trigger procedures are:

| Variable | Description |
| --- | --- |
| NEW | A record containing the new database row. |
| OLD | A record containing the old database row. |
| TG_NAME | A text variable containing the name of the trigger that fired and caused the trigger procedure to run. |
| TG_WHEN | A text variable containing the text 'BEFORE' or 'AFTER' depending on the type of the trigger. |
| TG_LEVEL | A text variable containing 'ROW' or 'STATEMENT' depending on the trigger definition. |
| TG_OP | A text variable containing 'INSERT', 'DELETE' or 'UPDATE' depending on the event that occurred resulting in this trigger being fired. |
| TG_RELID | An object identifier representing the table the trigger has been activated upon. |
| TG_RELNAME | The name of the table that the trigger has been fired upon. |
| TG_NARGS | An integer variable containing the number of arguments specified in the trigger definition. |
| TG_ARGV | An array of strings containing the procedure parameters, starting at zero. Invalid indexes return NULL values. |

As a final example, here is another trigger function that prevents customer being deleted if there are any orders outstanding for that customer. We check whether the date_shipped column in the orderinfo table is NULL for any orders placed by the customer about to be deleted and disallow the deletion. If there are no outstanding orders we, can allow the deletion to go ahead, but we need to tidy up by deleting orders placed by this customer in the past, and the information about the items in those orders.

## Try it Out – Another Trigger

```
create function customer_trigger() returns opaque AS
declare order_record record;
begin
    -- about to delete a customer
    -- disallow if orders pending
    select * into order_record from orderinfo
          where customer_id = old.customer_id
          and date_shipped = NULL;
    if not found
    then
          -- all OK, delete of customer can proceed
          raise notice ''deletion allowed - no outstanding orders'';

          -- for referential integrity we have to tidy up
          -- we will need to delete all completed orders
          -- but first delete the information about the orders
          for order_record in select * from orderinfo
             where customer_id = old.customer_id
          loop
                delete from orderline
                      where orderinfo_id = order_record.orderinfo_id;
          end loop;

          -- now delete the order records
          delete from orderinfo
                where customer_id = old.customer_id;

          -- return the old record to allow customer to be deleted
          return old;
    else
          -- orders present return NULL to prevent deletion
          raise notice ''deletion aborted - outstanding orders present'';
          return NULL;
    end if;
end;
' language 'plpgsql';

create trigger trig_customer before delete on customer
for each row execute procedure customer_trigger();
```

To verify the behavior of this trigger, let's check it out.

First, make one of the orders have a NULL shipped date to indicate that it is still pending:

```
bpfinal=# UPDATE orderinfo SET date_shipped = NULL WHERE orderinfo_id = 3;
UPDATE 1
bpfinal=# SELECT * FROM orderinfo;
 orderinfo_id | customer_id | date_placed | date_shipped | shipping
--------------+-------------+-------------+--------------+----------
            1 |           3 | 2000-03-13  | 2000-03-17   |    2.99
            2 |           8 | 2000-06-23  | 2000-06-24   |    0.00
```

```
              4 |          13 | 2000-09-03 | 2000-09-10 |       2.99
              5 |           8 | 2000-07-21 | 2000-07-24 |       0.00
              3 |          15 | 2000-09-02 |            |       3.99
(5 rows)

bpfinal=#
```

Now, if we try to delete customer number 15 whose order number 3 is outstanding, we get a notification that there are orders outstanding and the delete affected no rows, as it was not allowed to proceed:

```
bpfinal=# DELETE FROM customer WHERE customer_id = 15;
NOTICE:  deletion aborted - outstanding orders present
DELETE 0

bpfinal=#
```

Deleting customers with no outstanding orders presents no problem as long as we delete the entries in the orderinfo table first. This is because we are using a constraint on this table to prevent just this sort of maverick deletion. The trigger takes care of this and, therefore, provides us with another way to approach the referential integrity issue.

Customer number 3 has no outstanding orders, so we can delete him/her and let the trigger do all the work:

```
bpfinal=# DELETE FROM customer WHERE customer_id = 3;
NOTICE:  deletion allowed - no outstanding orders
DELETE 1

bpfinal=#
```

Checking the tables show no lingering sign of our deleted customer:

```
bpfinal=# SELECT * FROM orderinfo;
 orderinfo_id | customer_id | date_placed | date_shipped | shipping
--------------+-------------+-------------+--------------+----------
            2 |           8 | 2000-06-23 | 2000-06-24 |     0.00
            4 |          13 | 2000-09-03 | 2000-09-10 |     2.99
            5 |           8 | 2000-07-21 | 2000-07-24 |     0.00
            3 |          15 | 2000-09-02 |            |     3.99
(4 rows)

bpfinal=# SELECT * FROM orderline;
 orderinfo_id | item_id | quantity
--------------+---------+----------
            2 |       1 |        1
            2 |      10 |        1
            2 |       7 |        2
            2 |       4 |        2
            3 |       2 |        1
            3 |       1 |        1
            4 |       5 |        2
            5 |       1 |        1
            5 |       3 |        1
(9 rows)
```

```
bpfinal=#

bpfinal=# SELECT customer_id, fname, lname FROM customer;
 customer_id |   fname   |  lname
-------------+-----------+---------
           1 | Jenny     | Stones
           2 | Andrew    | Stones
           4 | Adrian    | Matthew
           5 | Simon     | Cozens
           6 | Neil      | Matthew
           7 | Richard   | Stones
           8 | Ann       | Stones
           9 | Christine | Hickman
          10 | Mike      | Howard
          11 | Dave      | Jones
          12 | Richard   | Neill
          13 | Laura     | Hendy
          14 | Bill      | O'Neill
          15 | David     | Hudson
(14 rows)
bpfinal=#
```

# Why Stored Procedures and Triggers?

There are almost as many reasons for using stored procedures and triggers as there are database applications. Some of them are:

❑ **Providing central validation**
You can enforce conditions on table updates in one place, independent of your client applications. If the conditions need to change, they change in one place only.

❑ **Tracking changes**
We can use a trigger to create an audit trial, writing to another table when rows in a table are updated, perhaps recording the user that made the change, the time and date, and perhaps even the data that changed.

❑ **Enhance security**
By using the PostgreSQL current_user variable, we can enforce our own security.

❑ **Deferred deletions**
We could use a trigger to mark rows for deletion at a later date, rather than deleting them when an application tries to.

❑ **Mapping for clients**
We can use triggers and stored procedures to create a simpler, single table version of some of our data that can be updated more easily by our users. For example, we could create a table and link it to Microsoft Excel. As rows in this table are updated, we can update rows in the 'real' tables that perhaps have a more complex structure.

# Summary

In this chapter, we have looked at ways in which we can extend the functionality of PostgreSQL queries. We have seen that PostgreSQL provides many operators and functions that we can use to refine queries and extract information.

The procedural languages supported by PostgreSQL allow us to develop quite sophisticated server-side processing by writing procedures in PL/pgSQL, SQL, and other languages. This provides the opportunity for the database server to implement complex application functionality, independently of the client.

Stored procedures are stored in the database itself, and may be called by the application or, in the form of triggers, called automatically when changes are made to database tables. This gives us another means of enforcing referential integrity.

For simple referential integrity, it's generally best to stick to constraints, as they are more straightforward, efficient and less error prone. The power of triggers and stored procedures comes when your declarative constraints become very complex, or you wish to implement a constraint that is too complex for the declarative form.

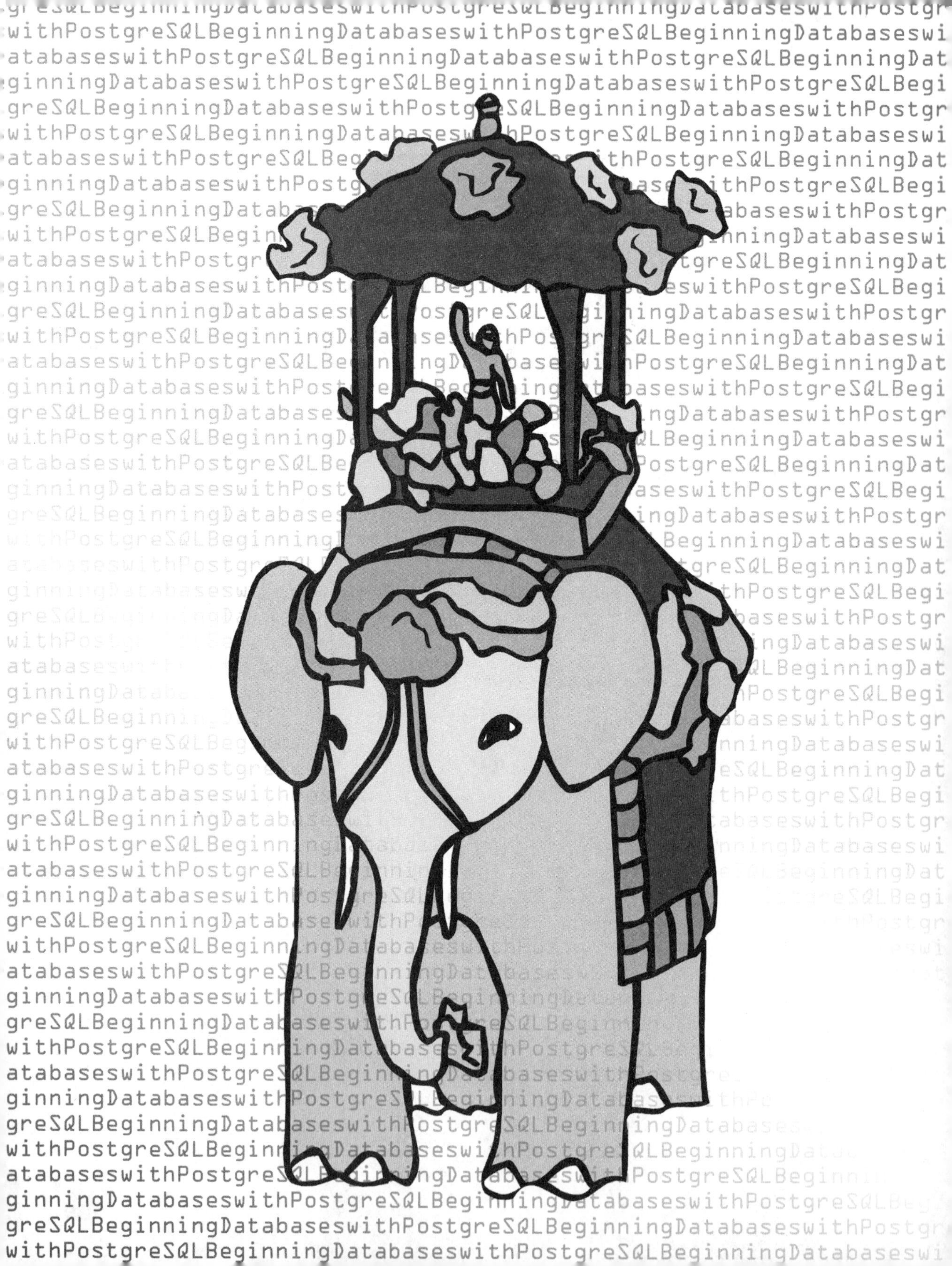

# PostgreSQL Administration

In this chapter, we will be looking at how to care for our PostgreSQL database. We will start by looking at the PostgreSQL default installation in a little more detail than we did in Chapters 3 and 4. Then we will move on to the housekeeping tasks that are needed to get the most from our database.

We recommend that you create a test database to experiment with. You may also find it helpful to install the pgAdmin application, which provides a graphical user interface to the administration functions from a Microsoft Windows client. See Chapter 5 for more details on pgAdmin.

There are a number of activities that we need to perform to effectively deploy and maintain a relational database system, all of which we will look at in this chapter:

- ❑ Server control
  - ❑ Starting, stopping, and monitoring the database server process
  - ❑ Remote (network) access
  - ❑ Use of log files
- ❑ User access
  - ❑ Creating and deleting user accounts
  - ❑ Managing privileges
- ❑ Data maintenance
  - ❑ Creating and deleting databases and schemas
  - ❑ Backups and restore of data
  - ❑ Upgrading PostgreSQL
- ❑ Security
- ❑ Configuration options
- ❑ Performance and Tuning
  - ❑ Creating indexes
  - ❑ Monitoring and Tuning

# Default Installation

If you compile PostgreSQL from source and install without overriding any of the default settings, you will create an installation that lives in /usr/local/pgsql as we have already seen.

If you install a pre-packaged version, you may find it installed in a different location, such as /var/lib/pgsql, but the directory structure beneath this install directory will generally be the same, although you may find the binary programs in a different location, such as /usr/bin.

There are seven subdirectories under the base install directory, used for storing the PostgreSQL programs, libraries, header files, and of course the database itself.

The directories are:

- ❑  bin
- ❑  include
- ❑  lib
- ❑  doc
- ❑  man
- ❑  share
- ❑  data

## bin

The bin directory contains programs that make up the PostgreSQL suite:

| Program | Description |
| --- | --- |
| postgres | Database backend server |
| postmaster | Database listener process (the same executable as postgres) |
| Psql | Command line tool for PostgreSQL |
| initdb | Utility to initialize the database system |
| pg_ctl | PostgreSQL control – start, stop, and restart the server |
| createuser | Utility to create a database user |
| dropuser | Utility to delete a database user |
| createdb | Utility to create a database |
| dropdb | Utility to delete a database |
| initlocation | Utility to create additional storage areas for a database |
| pg_dump | Utility to backup a database |

| Program | Description |
|---------|-------------|
| pg_dumpall | Utility to backup all databases in an installation |
| pg_restore | Utility to restore a database from backup data |
| pg_upgrade | Utility to help with PostgreSQL version upgrade |
| pg_passwd | Maintain host-specific password files for authentication |
| vacuumdb | Utility to help optimize the database (see *Performance* below) |
| ipcclean | Utility to delete shared memory segments after a crash |
| pg_config | Utility to report PostgreSQL configuration |
| createlang | Utility to add support for language extensions (see Chapter 10) |
| droplang | Utility to delete language support |
| ecpg | Embedded SQL compiler (see Chapter 14) |
| pg_id | Utility to report operating system user identity |

# include and lib

The include and lib directories contain all of the header files and libraries needed to create client applications for PostgreSQL. Here we can find the libraries needed to build libpq applications and C programs that contain embedded SQL. See Chapters 13 and 14 for more details on libpq and ecpg.

# doc

The doc directory contains PostgreSQL documentation. The most useful is probably doc/html/index.html, which is the start page for the online documentation that can be viewed with a web browser.

# man

The man directory contains UNIX-style manual pages. Adding this directory to your MANPATH environment variable, will allow you to use the standard man command to access these pages:

```
$ MANPATH=$MANPATH:/usr/local/pgsql/man
$ export MANPATH
$ man psql
...
```

# share

The share directory contains samples of PostgreSQL configuration files and backup files that are used by initdb to create an initial database.

# data

The data directory contains a PostgreSQL database installation. By running more than one listener process (postmaster) on different TCP/IP ports, it is possible to maintain more than one PostgreSQL database system on a single server. This directory contains the following files:

| File | Description |
|---|---|
| PG_VERSION | A text file containing the PostgreSQL version for this database (such as 7.1). |
| pg_hba.conf | A text file containing the configuration for PostgreSQL's host-based authentication. |
| pg_ident.conf | A text file containing the configuration for PostgreSQL's ident-based (user name) authentication. |
| postgresql.conf | PostgreSQL configuration file. |
| postmaster.log | PostgreSQL log file (if redirected from standard output). |
| postmaster.opts | A text file containing the command line options given to the postmaster process when it was started. |
| postmaster.pid | A text file containing the process id of the postmaster process for this database. Only present while the server is running, or has terminated abnormally. |

The database itself is stored in subdirectories global and base. Under normal circumstances, we would never need to examine files in these directories, as the entire configuration is performed via files in the data directory.

# The Initial Database

When PostgreSQL is first installed, we must arrange for a database to be created. We did this back in Chapter 3 by using initdb.

> **Some PostgreSQL installations arrange for initdb to be called automatically, if there is no database when the machine starts up.**

It is important to initialize the PostgreSQL database correctly, as database security is enforced by user permissions on the data directories. We need to stick to the following steps to ensure that our database will be secure. Often, an installation script for a PostgreSQL package will perform these steps for us automatically. If we need to change the defaults, or if we are manually installing, we need to perform these steps ourselves:

- ❏ Make a user to own the database. We recommend a user called postgres
- ❏ Create a directory (data) for the database files to live in
- ❏ Ensure that the postgres user owns that directory
- ❏ Run initdb, as postgres, not as root to initialize the database.

The initdb utility supports a few options. The most commonly used ones are listed in this table:

| Option | Description |
|---|---|
| -D dir<br>--pgdata=dir | Specify the location of the data directory for this database. |
| -i id<br>--sysid=id | Specify the (internal) user identity for the database superuser. May be omitted, defaults to the effective user identity of the user running initdb. |
| -W<br>--pwprompt | Causes initdb to prompt for a database superuser password. A password will be required to enable password authentication. |

The default database installation created by initdb contains information about the database superuser account (we have been using postgres), and among other things, a template database called template1.

To create additional databases in a PostgreSQL system, we must connect to the database system and request a new database be created. We can do this by hand or use the createdb utility, which we'll meet a little later. A connection requires a user and a database. In the initial installation we have only one user we can connect with, and only one database.

Before we can consider connecting to the database system, the server process must be running.

# Server Control

The PostgreSQL database server runs as a listener process on UNIX and Linux systems, and as a user program or system service on Windows systems. As we saw in Chapter 3, the server process is called postmaster and has to be running for client applications to be able to connect to and use the database.

If we wish to, we can start the postmaster process by hand. Without any command line arguments, the server will run in the foreground, log messages to the standard output, and use a database stored at the location given by the environment variable $PGDATA.

Normally though, we will want to start the process in the background and log messages to a file. When a connection attempt is made to the database, the postmaster process starts another process called postgres to handle the database access for the connecting client.

It is the backend server that reads the data and makes changes on behalf of one client application. There can be multiple postgres processes supporting many clients at once, but the total number of postgres processes is limited to a maximum, maintained by postmaster. The postmaster program has a number of parameters that allow us to control its behavior. The most commonly used options are listed below:

| Option: | Description: |
| --- | --- |
| -B nbufs | Set the number of shared memory buffers to nbufs. Each is 8K in size. The default is 64 buffers. Should be set to at least two times the number of server processes (see also -N). |
| -d level | Set the level of debug information written to the server log. Level set to 0 (the default) means no debugging, values up to 4 are supported. |
| -D dir | Set the database directory (/data) to dir. There is no default value. If no -D option is set, the value of the environment variable PGDATA is used. |
| -I | Allow remote TCP/IP connections to the database. Without this option, only clients on the server machine can connect to the database. See also Database Security, for other configuration required to allow network connections to succeed. |
| -l | Allow secure database connections using SSL, the Secure Sockets Layer protocol. This requires the -i option (network access) and support for SSL to have been compiled in to the server. |
| -N cons | Set the maximum number of simultaneous connections the server will accept. Default is 32. If increased, requires -B. |
| -o "opts" | Set options to be passed to the backend server process that handles individual clients (postgres). Refer to the PostgreSQL Administration Guide for server process options. |
| -p port | Set the TCP port number that the server should use to listen for database connections. Defaults to the value of $PGPORT or a compiled in default (normally 5432). |
| -c name=value | Set a run-time parameter. See the run-time server configuration section below. |

When it has successfully started, the postmaster process creates a file that contains its process id and the data directory for the database. By default, the file is:

```
/usr/local/pgsql/data/postmaster.pid
```

The server log file should be redirected using a normal shell redirect for the standard output and standard error:

```
postmaster >postmaster.log 2>&1
```

As mentioned earlier, the postmaster process needs to be run as a non-root user created to be the owner of the database. We created such a user (postgres) in Chapter 3.

# Starting and Stopping the Server

The standard PostgreSQL distribution contains a utility, pg_ctl, for controlling the postmaster process. It is able to start, stop, and restart the server, and can also report on the server's status:

```
pg_ctl start [ -w ] [ -D datadir ] [ -p path ]
[ -o options ]

pg_ctl stop [ -w ] [ -D datadir ]
[ -m [ s[mart] ] [ f[ast] ] [ i[mmediate] ] ]

pg_ctl restart [ -w ] [ -D datadir ]
[ -m [ s[mart] ] [ f[ast] ] [ i[mmediate] ] ]
[ -o options ]

pg_ctl status [ -D datadir ]
```

To use pg_ctl, you need to have permission to read the database directories, so you will need to be the superuser (root) or be using the postgres user identity.

The options to pg_ctl are:

| Option | Description |
| --- | --- |
| -D datadir | Specify the location of the database. Defaults to $PGDATA. |
| -w | Wait for the server to come up, instead of returning immediately. This waits for the server pid (process id) file to be created. Times out after 60 seconds. |
| -o "options" | Set options to be passed to the postmaster process when it is started. |
| -m mode | Set the shutdown mode (smart, fast or immediate). |

When stopping or restarting the server, we have a number of options for dealing with connected clients:

❑ Using pg_ctl stop (or restart) with smart (or s) is the default, and waits for all clients to disconnect before shutting down.

❑ fast (f) shuts down the database without waiting for clients to disconnect. In this case, transactions in progress are rolled back.

❑ immediate (i) shuts down immediately without giving the database server a chance to save data, requiring a recovery the next time the server is started. This mode should be used only when serious problems are occurring.

We can check that PostgreSQL is running using pg_ctl status. This will tell us the process id of the listener postmaster and the command line used to start it:

```
# pg_ctl status
pg_ctl: postmaster is running (pid: 486)
Command line was:
/usr/local/pgsql/bin/postmaster '-i' '-D' '/usr/local/pgsql/data'

#
```

# Users

Every request to a PostgreSQL database is associated with a user. In this section of the chapter we shall look at creating, altering, and dropping users. Further, we will also look at groups and the privileges that control access to the database.

Every user that is going to access the database must be made known to PostgreSQL and the user's details stored in an internal table, pg_user. We can list the users by selecting all of the rows of the pg_user table in psql:

```
bpfinal=# SELECT usename, usesysid, usecreatedb FROM pg_user;
 usename  | usesysid | usecreatedb
----------+----------+-------------
 postgres |       26 | t
 neil     |       28 | t
(2 rows)

bpfinal=#
```

Each user has an associated identifier (usesysid) and a number of abilities including the ability (or otherwise) to create databases, shown here as usecreatedb.

Note that PostgreSQL users are distinct from UNIX, Windows, or Linux login names. It is usual for PostgreSQL users to be created with the same names as login names, for the users that will connect to the database, but that need not be the case. Although when you connect to a database, a PostgreSQL client will by default present the login name to the database server, we can override that to provide a PostgreSQL-specific user name.

We can also arrange for a mapping between login names and PostgreSQL user names. If we have login names neil, rick, steve, and gavin, and PostgreSQL users author and reviewer, we could use this to create groups of users so that users neil and rick both access the database as PostgreSQL user author while gavin and steve access the database as PostgreSQL user reviewer. We will see how this is handled when we cover authentication a little later on.

## CREATE USER

PostgreSQL has a utility, createuser, to help with the creation of PostgreSQL users:

```
createuser [options...] username
```

Options to createuser allow us to specify the database server for which we want to create a user, and to set some of the user powers, such as database creation:

| Option | Description |
|---|---|
| -h host<br>--host host | Specify the database server host. Defaults to the local machine. |
| -p port<br>--port port | Specify the port. Defaults to the standard PostgreSQL listener port, 5432. |

| Option | Description |
|--------|-------------|
| -q <br> --quiet | Do not print a response. |
| -d <br> --createdb | Allow this user to create databases. |
| -a <br> --adduser | Allow this user to create new users. |
| -P <br> --pwprompt | Prompt for a password for this user. A user password is required for authentication. |
| -I <br> --sysid id | Specify the user's id, usesysid, for this new user. |
| -e <br> --echo | Print the command sent to the server to create the user. |

The createuser utility is simply a wrapper that uses psql to execute some PostgreSQL commands to create the user. You can see the command if you use the -e or --echo option to createuser:

```
$ createuser -e --pwprompt rick
Enter password for user "rick":
Enter it again:
Shall the new user be allowed to create databases? (y/n) n
Shall the new user be allowed to create more new users? (y/n) n
CREATE USER "rick" WITH  PASSWORD 'xxx' NOCREATEDB NOCREATEUSER
$
```

The underlying SQL (in fact DDL) command is CREATE USER, which has the full syntax like this:

```
CREATE USER username
[ WITH
[ SYSID uid ]
[ PASSWORD 'password' ] ]
[ CREATEDB | NOCREATEDB ]
[ CREATEUSER | NOCREATEUSER ]
[ IN GROUP groupname [, ...] ]
[ VALID UNTIL 'abstime' ]
```

We can use CREATE USER (from psql or other SQL client), to assign users to groups and to set a limit on the length of time this user is valid.

## *DROP USER*

If we need to remove a user from the PostgreSQL system, we can either use the SQL command DROP
USER name within psql or the shell utility dropuser:

```
dropuser [options...] username
```

The options to dropuser include the same server connection options as createuser, plus:

| Option | Description |
|---|---|
| -i<br><br>--interactive | Provide a prompt for confirmation before deleting the user |

## *ALTER USER*

We can change the attributes of an existing user with the ALTER USER command from psql:

```
ALTER USER username
[ WITH PASSWORD 'password' ]
[ CREATEDB | NOCREATEDB ] [ CREATEUSER | NOCREATEUSER ]
[ VALID UNTIL 'abstime' ]
```

## *GROUPS*

Groups of users are useful if we want to allow many users their own accounts, but treat them in the
same way, especially with regard to database privileges. The SQL command to create a user group is
CREATE GROUP:

```
CREATE GROUP name
[ WITH
[ SYSID gid ]
[ USER  username [, ...] ] ] ]
```

For example, to create the authors group with neil and rick, we would do this:

```
bpfinal=# CREATE GROUP authors WITH USER neil, rick;
CREATE GROUP

bpfinal=#
```

pgAdmin provides an easier way to manage users and groups if you can connect from a Microsoft
Windows client:

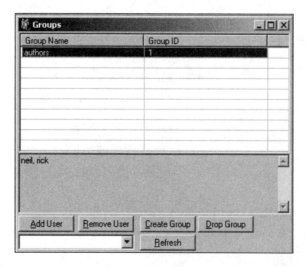

Details of user groups are stored in an internal system table, pg_group. The fields in the pg_group table are:

| Field | Description |
|-------|-------------|
| groname | The name of the group. Avoid non-alphanumeric characters such as punctuation. |
| grosysid | A numeric identifier for the group. |
| grolist | A list of user ids for members of the group. |

We can add or remove users from an existing group using ALTER GROUP:

```
ALTER GROUP name ADD USER username [, ... ]
ALTER GROUP name DROP USER username [, ... ]
```

To remove a user group, we need to use the DROP GROUP command:

```
DROP GROUP name
```

## PRIVILEGES

PostgreSQL controls access to the database by using a system of privileges that may be granted and revoked using the GRANT command. By default, users may not write data to tables that they did not create.

The GRANT command has the following syntax:

```
GRANT privilege [, ...] ON object [, ...]
TO { PUBLIC | GROUP group | username }
```

The supported privileges are:

| Privilege | Description |
| --- | --- |
| SELECT | Allows rows to be read |
| INSERT | Allows new rows to be created |
| DELETE | Allows rows to be deleted |
| UPDATE | Allows existing rows to be changed |
| RULE | Allows creation of rules for a table or view |
| ALL | Grants all privileges |

The `object` may be the name of a table, a view, or a sequence. The keyword PUBLIC is an abbreviation, meaning all users.

To allow the `authors` group to read the `customer` table and to add new customers, we could do this:

```
bpfinal=# GRANT SELECT,INSERT ON customer TO GROUP authors;
CHANGE

bpfinal=#
```

Privileges are revoked (taken away), by the REVOKE command, which is very similar to GRANT:

```
REVOKE privilege [, ...]
ON object [, ...]
FROM { PUBLIC | GROUP groupname | username }
```

We can deny the user `rick` any access to the `customer` table with:

```
bpfinal=# REVOKE ALL ON customer FROM rick;
CHANGE

bpfinal=#
```

A user group permission will still allow access. If, for example, the group `authors` has permission to access the `customer` table, and `rick` is a member of that group, he will still be allowed access. To complete the permission change, we have to delete `rick` from all groups that can access the table.

We can use `pgAdmin` to provide a more user-friendly interface to privileges:

# Views

The combination of user privileges and views allows us to restrict the information certain users can see in our database tables. Suppose we wish to store all information about employees in one table, but restrict access to sensitive information, such as salary details to senior managers. We can do this by revoking permissions for normal users, by creating a view (see Chapter 8) that selects only the non-sensitive columns, and granting permission on that view.

PostgreSQL uses a view to manage access to the `system` table for users, `pg_user`. The 'real' data about users, including their passwords, is held in a table called `pg_shadow`. Normal users do not have permission to read (`SELECT`) this table:

```
bpfinal=# SELECT * FROM pg_shadow;
ERROR:  pg_shadow: Permission denied.

bpfinal=#
```

We can partly read the table however, via the view, `pg_user`:

```
bpfinal=# SELECT usename,passwd FROM pg_user;
usename  |  passwd
---------+----------
postgres | ********
neil     | ********
rick     | ********
(3 rows)

bpfinal=#
```

The `passwd` column is returned as a string of asterisks, but other columns are available.

We can see the definition of the `pg_user` view using a `psql` internal command `\d`:

```
bpfinal=# \d pg_user
View "pg_user"
Attribute    | Type     | Modifier
-------------+----------+----------
usename      | name     |
usesysid     | integer  |
usecreatedb  | boolean  |
usetrace     | boolean  |
usesuper     | boolean  |
usecatupd    | boolean  |
passwd       | text     |
valuntil     | abstime  |
View definition: SELECT pg_shadow.usename, pg_shadow.usesysid,
pg_shadow.usecreatedb, pg_shadow.usetrace, pg_shadow.usesuper,
pg_shadow.usecatupd, '********'::text AS passwd, pg_shadow.valuntil FROM
pg_shadow;

bpfinal=#
```

In this case, the `pg_user` view selects all of the columns from the `pg_shadow` table, except that the password is set as a fixed text string.

# Data Maintenance

Data maintenance is a vital part of database administration, and we will look at the following aspects:

- ❑ Creating and deleting databases and schemas
- ❑ Backups and restore of data
- ❑ Upgrading PostgreSQL

## Creating and Deleting Databases

PostgreSQL databases are created within `psql` by the CREATE DATABASE command, which has the following syntax:

```
CREATE DATABASE name
[ WITH [ LOCATION = 'dbpath' ]
[ TEMPLATE = template ]
[ ENCODING = encoding ] ]
```

The database name must be unique within the PostgreSQL installation. It is possible to specify a location for the new database with the LOCATION option. See the PostgreSQL online documentation on `initlocation` for more details. The TEMPLATE and ENCODING options specify the database layout and the multi-byte encoding required. These are safely omitted in normal use. Refer to the PostgreSQL documentation for more details.

> To use **psql**, we must be connected to a database, so to create our first database we must connect to the default database, **template1**.

To delete a database we use DROP DATABASE:

```
DROP DATABASE name
```

We cannot drop a database that is currently selected in psql. We must switch to another database or template1 if we want to delete the database we are currently connected to.

PostgreSQL provides two wrapper utilities, createdb and dropdb to allow database creation and deletion respectively, from the normal UNIX or Linux command shell:

```
createdb [ options... ]  dbname [ description ]
dropdb [ options... ]  dbname
```

The options for these utilities are very similar to createuser and dropuser we saw earlier:

| Option | Description |
| --- | --- |
| -h host<br>--host host | Specify the database server host. Defaults to the local machine. |
| -p port<br>--port port | Specify the port. Defaults to the standard PostgreSQL listener port, 5432. |
| -q<br>--quiet | Do not print a response. |
| -e<br>--echo | Print the command sent to the server to create the user. |
| -U name<br>--username name | Specify the user name to use for the database connection. Defaults to the current user. |
| -W<br>--password | Prompt for a password. |
| -D dir<br>--location dir | Specify the database location (createdb only). Defaults to the installation location. |
| -E type<br>--encoding type | Specify the database multi-byte encoding type (createdb only). Refer to the PostgreSQL Reference Guide for database encoding options. |
| -I<br>--interactive | Prompt for confirmation before deleting the database (dropdb only). |

The optional description option to createdb, allows us to associate a comment with the new database.

# Backing Up and Restoring Data

All PostgreSQL databases should be backed up on a regular basis. Keeping a copy of your data elsewhere will protect you, should a problem arise.

Backup and recovery is an area all too often overlooked, with disastrous consequences. A database system depends on its data, and data can be lost in a number of ways – from a bolt of lightning frying the hard drive, to finger trouble deleting the wrong files, to bad programming corrupting the contents of the database. A well-thought out backup and recovery plan is one that has been tested and shown to work, preferably with an automated backup process. It will help reduce the impact of any data loss to a minor inconvenience, rather than an enterprise-terminating experience.

Even though PostgreSQL uses ordinary files in the file system to store its data, it is not advisable to rely on normal backup procedures for PostgreSQL databases. If the database is active when copies of the PostgreSQL files are taken, we cannot be sure that the internal state of the database will be consistent when it is restored. In theory, we could shut down the database server before copying the files, but there is a better way. PostgreSQL provides its own backup and restore mechanisms, `pg_dump`, `pg_dumpall`, and `pg_restore`.

The easiest way to backup a database is to run `pg_dump` and redirect its output to a file (we will discuss the options `pg_dump` offers shortly):

```
$ pg_dump bpfinal > bpfinal.backup
```

In essence, the backup scheme is to produce a large SQL (and PostgreSQL internal commands) script that, if executed, will re-create the database in its entirety. By default, the `pg_dump` output is a text script, and if we examine it, we can see in it statements for creating users and privileges, creating tables, and adding data.

Here is a small sample:

```
CREATE SEQUENCE "customer_customer_id_seq" start 1 increment 1 maxvalue 2147483647
minvalue 1  cache 1 ;

--
-- TOC Entry ID 18 (OID 24462)
--
-- Name: customer Type: TABLE Owner: neil
--

CREATE TABLE "customer" (
"customer_id" integer DEFAULT nextval('"customer_customer_id_seq"'::text) NOT
NULL,
"title" character(4),
"fname" character varying(32),
"lname" character varying(32) NOT NULL,
"addressline" character varying(64),
"town" character varying(32),
"zipcode" character(10) NOT NULL,
"phone" character varying(16),
Constraint "customer_pk" Primary Key ("customer_id")
```

```
);


--
-- TOC Entry ID 19 (OID 24462)
--
-- Name: customer Type: ACL Owner:
--

REVOKE ALL on "customer" from PUBLIC;
GRANT ALL on "customer" to "neil";
GRANT INSERT,SELECT on "customer" to GROUP "authors";


--
-- Data for TOC Entry ID 44 (OID 24502) TABLE DATA item
--
-- Disable triggers

UPDATE "pg_class" SET "reltriggers" = 0 WHERE "relname" ~* 'item';
COPY "item"  FROM stdin;
1       Wood Puzzle     15.23   21.95
2       Rubik Cube      7.45    11.49
3       Linux CD        1.99    2.49
4       Tissues 2.11    3.99
5       Picture Frame   7.54    9.95
6       Fan Small       9.23    15.75
7       Fan Large       13.36   19.95
8       Toothbrush      0.75    1.45
9       Roman Coin      2.34    2.45
10      Carrier Bag     0.01    0.00
11      Speakers        19.73   25.32
\.
```

To restore the database from a backup, we need to execute the script. The script will contain commands for creating and populating tables, but does not contain the database creation. We must first create a database to restore into, and then run the script. As a side-effect, this gives us a way of copying a database within an installation, or renaming it. Assuming we have an empty database created, say newbpfinal, we can restore the data from the original by using psql to execute the backup script:

```
$ createdb newbpfinal
$ psql -f bpfinal.backup newbpfinal
```

Here, the -f option to psql causes it to read commands from a file instead of from the user.

> If you use **pgAdmin** to maintain a PostgreSQL database, you will find that it creates tables for its own use. This may lead to errors being reported during a restore, unless these tables are deleted before the backup is taken, or are recreated by **pgAdmin** on the new database before restoring the data.

We can backup all of the databases in our installation (including internal system tables used by PostgreSQL), in one go by using pg_dumpall as the database superuser (postgres):

```
$ su - postgres
$ pg_dumpall >all.backup
```

This has the advantage of also backing up items that are common across all of the databases, such as user information. We lose the opportunity however, to rename databases.

To restore a backup that contains an entire installation, we need only connect to the default database, template1. A full backup created by pg_dumpall contains SQL statements to create each database in the backup. You will need to run the backup and restore as the database superuser to have sufficient permissions to read and write all of the data:

```
$ psql -f all.backup template1
```

Since backup scripts are text files that contain all of the data plus SQL statements therefore, the backup file will potentially be very large. You can arrange to compress the backup, as it is produced, using a compression program like gzip:

```
$ pg_dump bpfinal | gzip >bpfinal.backup.gz
$ gunzip -c bpfinal.backup.gz | psql newbpfinal
```

There are many arguments/options to pg_dump that allow us to select a single table to be dumped, whether to include table definitions and to specify the format of the dump output. The most useful options are listed in the table below:

```
pg_dump [dbname] [options...]
```

The options include:

| Option | Description |
| --- | --- |
| -h host | Server to connect to. Defaults to the local machine. |
| -p port | TCP/IP port to connect to. Defaults to the PostgreSQL standard listener port 5432. |
| -t table | Specifies a single table to dump, rather than the whole database. |
| -u | Use password authentication. Will prompt for a user and password. |
| -v | Verbose mode. |
| -S user | Specify a database superuser name for overriding triggers. |
| -c | Clean. Adds commands to the script to drop tables and other objects before creating new ones. |
| -C | Create. Add SQL to the script to create the database itself. For plain text output only. |

| Option | Description |
|---|---|
| -a | Dump only the data, not the object definitions. |
| -s | Dump only the object definitions (schema), not the data. |
| -x | Suppress dumping of access control (GRANT and REVOKE commands). |
| -b | Dump large object (BLOB) data. |
| -O | Do not set ownership of objects to match the original database. |
| -f file | Write the dump script to the specified file. Default is the standard output. |
| -F format | Specify the dump output format. The choices are: |
| | ❑      p for plain text SQL script (default). |
| | ❑      t for a tar archive. |
| | ❑      c for a custom format archive. |
| -Z 0..9 | For a custom archive, set the level of compression from 0 (least) to 9 (most). |

The archive formats for dump output (-F t and -F c) allow us some more flexibility when restoring the database. To restore using an archive, we need to use the pg_restore utility:

```
pg_restore [archive] [options...]
```

The most common options to pg_restore are listed in the following table:

| Option | Description |
|---|---|
| -h host | Server to connect to. Defaults to the local machine. |
| -p port | TCP/IP port to connect to. Defaults to the I standard listener port 5432. |
| -d dbname | Connect directly to the database dbname rather than using psql. Large objects (BLOBs) can only be restored in this way. |
| -t table | Specifies a single table to restore, rather than the whole database. Can only be given once. |
| -P proc | Specifies a single function (stored procedure) to restore. |
| -T trig | Specifies a single trigger to restore. |
| -I index | Specifies a single index definition to be restored. |
| -u | Use password authentication. Will prompt for a user and password. |
| -v | Verbose mode. |
| -l | List the contents of the archive. Useful with -U. |

| Option | Description |
|--------|-------------|
| -U file | Restore only those database elements listed in file. Useful for a selective restore. Elements may be commented out by prefixing with . |
| -S user | Specify a database superuser name for setting ownerships and overriding triggers. |
| -c | Drop tables and other objects before creating new ones. |
| -a | Restore only the data, not the object definitions. |
| -s | Restore only the object definitions (schema), not the data. |
| -x | Suppress restoration of access control (GRANT and REVOKE commands). |
| -O | Do not set ownership of objects to match the original database. |
| -f file | Read the dump archive from the specified file. Default is the standard input if not specified as the first argument. |

To backup a database and restore it under a new name, we can use the following sequence of commands:

```
$ pg_dump -F c bpsimple >bpsimple.bak
$ createdb bpsimple2
CREATE DATABASE
$ pg_restore -d bpsimple2 bpsimple.bak
NOTICE:  CREATE TABLE/PRIMARY KEY will create implicit index 'customer_pk' for
table 'customer'
NOTICE:  CREATE TABLE/PRIMARY KEY will create implicit index 'item_pk' for table
'item'
NOTICE:  CREATE TABLE/PRIMARY KEY will create implicit index 'orderinfo_pk' for
table 'orderinfo'
NOTICE:  CREATE TABLE/PRIMARY KEY will create implicit index 'stock_pk' for table
'stock'
NOTICE:  CREATE TABLE/PRIMARY KEY will create implicit index 'orderline_pk' for
table 'orderline'
NOTICE:  CREATE TABLE/PRIMARY KEY will create implicit index 'barcode_pk' for
table 'barcode'
$
```

Here we have backed up the bpsimple database to a custom format archive, bpsimple.bak. Then we created a new database to receive the archived data and restored it with pg_restore.

# Database Upgrades

From time to time, new versions of PostgreSQL are released, containing new features or enhancements that you will want to take advantage of. Before attempting to upgrade to a new version of PostgreSQL, backup your data. Unless you are sure that your data can be recreated, or it is not important, it is best to be safe.

Sometimes a database backup and restore is required when upgrading to a new version of PostgreSQL. In some circumstances however, it is possible to retain the existing data files when moving to a new version. This may be an advantage when dealing with large databases, and for some environments PostgreSQL provides a utility, `pg_upgrade`, to help with the creation of an upgraded database. Refer to the manual page for `pg_upgrade` for more details.

# Database Security

Most database applications have at least some requirements for security. We really do not want our data accessible to just anyone, whether people or applications. Ideally, we want to be able to control who and what have access. We have seen that PostgreSQL allows us to grant and revoke privileges to database users with GRANT and REVOKE respectively. This may not however, be enough in itself. We would like to be sure that the database files are secure against tampering. We might need to know that the connecting user is really who they claims to be.

PostgreSQL protects its database in several ways. First of all, the files that PostgreSQL uses to store the data are set to be accessible only by the PostgreSQL user, `postgres`.In reality, the operating system `superuser` can also read the data files.

When the database server starts up, it does not allow remote connections, serving only requests made from clients on the local machine. To allow network access, we have to explicitly configure PostgreSQL by invoking `postmaster` with the `-i` option. Before we do this we can, if we wish, restrict the network addresses that we allow connections from. This means we could allow access from our local network, but disallow connections from the Internet, for example. Someone trying to impersonate a PostgreSQL user would then not get very far and the database server would refuse the connection even before knowing who is trying to connect.

Once a connection is established to the server, we can configure PostgreSQL to use a number of methods of user authentication. Support is available for these authentication methods, which can be configured for particular network addresses:

| Authentication Method | Description |
| --- | --- |
| trust | Connection is always allowed |
| password | A password is requested and compared with a `pg_shadow` table entry |
| Crypt | Same as password authentication, but the password is encrypted instead of being passed as clear text |
| Ident | The client's ident (RFC 1413) server is used for authentication |
| Krb4 | Authentication is performed using Kerberos version 4 |
| Krb5 | Authentication is performed using Kerberos version 5 |
| reject | Connection always refused |

The configuration of PostgreSQL security, known as host-based security, is made using the file `pg_hba.conf` in the PostgreSQL data directory. The default configuration file contains extensive comments on the structure of entries for authentication configuration. Here, we will only consider basic authentication.

The `pg_hba.conf` file consists of single line records. Blank lines are ignored as are lines beginning with a #, which are used as comments. Each record specifies an authentication type for a particular connection method. At a minimum, we need to allow connections either from the local machine, or from at least one network address.

A local connection record has the form:

```
local database method [argument]
```

Local connections (those made via UNIX domain sockets, rather than network sockets) to the named database, will be authenticated using the specified method. The optional argument varies with authentication method. For local connections, only the `trust`, `password`, `crypt`, and `reject` methods are available.

Here is an example of some local authentication records:

```
# Allow everyone access the test database
local test trust

# Require encrypted authentication for the production database
local bpfinal crypt

# Disallow everything else
local all reject
```

When PostgreSQL performs its authentication, it scans the authentication records in order. The first record that matches the database being requested is used, so later records that apply are not used. The keyword `all` is an abbreviation meaning 'all databases'.

The `password` and `crypt` authentication methods support the use of per-host password files. The argument is the name of a file in the PostgreSQL data directory that is used to store the passwords to check against, rather than the internal system table `pg_shadow`. This can be useful if you want to maintain different passwords for the same user name connecting from different locations.

Network connections are allowed only from client machines that match a host authentication record (and the `postmaster` process has been started with `-i`). A network authentication record has the form:

```
host database address netmask method [argument]
```

The additional parameters are an IP address and a network mask. Any connecting machine whose network address matches will be authenticated by the specified method. Here are some examples:

```
# Allow connections from the loopback network
host 127.0.0.1 255.255.255.255 trust

# Allow connections by password on our local network
host 192.168.0.0 255.255.255.0 password

# Disallow one particular machine on another network
host 192.168.1.66 255.255.255.255 reject
```

```
# Allow others using a different password set
host 192.168.1.0 255.255.255.0 password mypasswords

# Everyone else gets rejected
```

Users connecting from the 192.168.1.0 network use a different set of passwords in this configuration. If we needed to, we could create as many password files as we have hosts that are allowed to connect.

The password files are maintained by the pg_passwd utility:

```
pg_passwd password_file
```

If the password file does not exist, pg_passwd can create a new one. To set up the mypasswords file used in one of the configuration examples, and create a host-specific password for the user neil, we would do this:

```
$ pg_passwd /usr/local/pgsql/data/mypasswords
File "/usr/local/pgsql/data/mypasswords" does not exist. Create? (y/n): y
Username: neil
New password:
Re-enter new password:
$
```

For further details on other authentication methods, such as ident and Kerberos, refer to the PostgreSQL Administrator's Guide or online documentation.

# Configuration Options

The PostgreSQL installation can be configured in two distinct ways. Firstly, when compiling PostgreSQL from source code we have the ability to compile in certain features and set some default values.

Secondly, once PostgreSQL is installed, we can set environment variables and command line options to override defaults or enable features. For example, we can change the TCP port that the backend server, postmaster, listens for connections on by compiling in a new default value at build time by using the --with-pgport=number option to the configure script. The default port can then be overridden when the server process is started by using the -p number argument to postmaster.

## Build Time Server Configuration

When building PostgreSQL from source code, the configure script that we used in Chapter 3 has a number of options. You can see a complete list by running configure with the --help flag:

```
$ ./configure --help
Usage: configure [options] [host]
Options: [defaults in brackets after descriptions]
Configuration:
--cache-file=FILE       cache test results in FILE
```

```
--help                  print this message
--no-create             do not create output files
--quiet, --silent       do not print `checking...' messages
--version               print the version of autoconf that created configure
Directory and file names:
--prefix=PREFIX         install architecture-independent files in PREFIX
[/usr/local/pgsql]
--exec-prefix=EPREFIX   install architecture-dependent files in EPREFIX
[same as prefix]
--bindir=DIR            user executables in DIR [EPREFIX/bin]
...
$
```

We will not cover the options in detail here, but be content ourselves with listing the most common build-time options that generally select the install directory, and the features to be included in the build:

| Option | Description |
| --- | --- |
| --prefix | Set the root of the installation, normally /usr/local/pgsql |
| --with-pgport=port | Set the default TCP port number for serving network connections |
| --with-maxbackends=n | Set the maximum number of simultaneous connections |
| --with-tcl | Build support for Tcl |
| --with-perl | Build support for Perl |
| --with-odbc | Build support for ODBC connections |

Once built and installed, we can query the configuration of a PostgreSQL system with pg_config:

```
pg_config
--bindir | --includedir | --libdir |
--configure | --version
```

pg_config will report the directory where the PostgreSQL programs are installed (--bindir), the location of C include files (--includedir) and object code libraries (--libdir), and the version of PostgreSQL (--version):

```
# pg_config --version
PostgreSQL 7.1
#
```

The build time configuration can be reported by using pg_config --configure. This will report the command line options passed to the configure script when the PostgreSQL server was configured for compilation.

# Run-time Server Configuration

The PostgreSQL backend server uses a number of parameters that alter its behavior, and can be altered at run-time. If we need to change any of these parameters, or configuration options, we can do so in one of the following three ways.

When started, the PostgreSQL server process reads a configuration file, `postgresql.conf` from its `data` directory. The default file is self-documenting, in that it contains an entry for each option and shows the default value for it. We can make changes to this configuration file, and then every time the server is started it will behave accordingly. Alternatively, we can use the `-c` command line option to set a configuration option when we invoke the `postmaster` process.

Finally, for some options, we can connect to a live database and execute a SQL SET command to make a configuration change while the system is active.

For example, one of the configuration options is the level of debug output written to the log file. The default is none (0), but if we wish, we can set the variable `debug_level` to 1 by editing `postgresql.conf` to contain the line:

```
debug_level=1
```

Now start `postmaster`:

```
postmaster -c debug_level=1
```

Run `psql` and use the `set` command to set the debug level for the entire system (not just the current `psql` session) such as this:

```
set debug_level=1;
```

Configuration options include:

| Option | Description |
|---|---|
| `tcpip_socket` | Allow network connections. |
| `Max_connections` | Maximum number of allowed simultaneous connections. Default is 32. |
| `Port` | TCP port to listen to for connections. |
| `Sort_mem` | Amount of memory to use for sorting workspace. |
| `shared_buffers` | Number of shared memory buffers to allocate (must be at least 2 * `Max_connections`). |
| `debug_level` | Level of debug output written to the log file. |

Refer to the online documentation for further information about PostgreSQL configuration.

# Performance

The last stop on our tour of PostgreSQL administration functions is potentially also one of the most important after backups: performance.

In this book, we have been working with a small database with relatively few tables, each containing a handful of rows. We have not been concerned with the speed at which PostgreSQL responds to queries, or the physical size of the database. For real world databases, these issues can become quite serious.

Optimizing databases is an advanced skill, requiring advanced database design and detailed knowledge of the internal workings of a database system. PostgreSQL includes a sophisticated optimizer that attempts to execute database queries as efficiently as possible, but in some cases it requires a helping hand.

We will not try to cover all the options available in PostgreSQL, but there are two relatively simple things we can do to help maintain our PostgreSQL databases in good condition. These are:

❑   Using the VACUUM command

❑   Creating indexes

## VACUUM

The PostgreSQL SQL command VACUUM has two uses:

❑   Reclaiming database storage

❑   Updating optimizer statistics

The command syntax is like this:

```
vacuum [verbose] analyse [table [ (column [, ... ] ) ] ]
```

Over a period of time, a PostgreSQL data table will accumulate defunct rows, rows that occupy space in the database, but that can no longer be accessed. This typically occurs as a result of a transaction rollback.

Recall from Chapter 9 that, during a transaction that is updating rows in a table, users must still be able to query the table and get consistent results. PostgreSQL creates new rows for the data in the transaction and makes them available once the transaction is committed. Meanwhile queries see the old rows. When the transaction is completed we have a table that contains both the old and new rows, but one set is no longer accessible. It is the space consumed by these inaccessible rows that VACUUM reclaims.

Here is an example of VACUUM output. We add the verbose option to see some statistics, and select the customer table for vacuuming. By default, VACUUM will reclaim storage in all tables in the active database:

```
bpfinal=# vacuum verbose customer;
NOTICE:  --Relation customer--
NOTICE:  Pages 1: Changed 1, reaped 1, Empty 0, New 0; Tup 14: Vac 1, Keep/VTL
```

```
0/0, Crash 0, UnUsed 0, MinLen 120, MaxLen 132; Re-using: Free/Avail. Space
6348/0; EndEmpty/Avail. Pages 0/0. CPU 0.00s/0.00u sec.
NOTICE:  Index customer_pk: Pages 2; Tuples 14: Deleted 1. CPU 0.00s/0.00u sec.
VACUUM

bpfinal=#
```

The ANALYZE option to VACUUM recomputes various statistics that PostgreSQL uses to plan its database queries.

We have seen in earlier chapters, that SQL is a declarative language. We tell PostgreSQL the result we want (find all the customers who ordered Linux CDs between two specific dates and live in Newtown), and it is up to the database to work out the best way of doing that. It will normally have a number of choices, for example, scanning the customer table and for each customer looking for their order information, or scanning the item table and for the item 'Linux CD', pick each order seeing which customer placed it and when.

Depending on the structure of the database, the primary keys, and the number of rows in the tables, one way may be much faster than another. PostgreSQL tries to work out which way to perform the query will be the fastest. This is what the query optimizer does. It creates a query plan for a query before executing it. This is normally based on both the structure of the database and the size of the tables involved in the query, and as we shall see, the availability of indexes on queried columns.

We can view the query plan for any particular query by using the EXPLAIN SQL statement:

```
explain [verbose] query
```

Here it is in action:

```
bpfinal=# EXPLAIN SELECT customer_id customer WHERE zipcode='BG3 8GD';
NOTICE:  QUERY PLAN:

Seq Scan on customer  (cost=0.00..1.18 rows=1 width=4)

EXPLAIN

bpfinal=#
```

In our example database, most queries will be performed using sequential scans of the tables. PostgreSQL estimates a cost associated with each part of the query that it is planning, and tries to minimize the total.

As we can see above, PostgreSQL is estimating a cost of between 0 and 1.18 for a scan of the customer table. PostgreSQL has no choice in this case, but to look at each customer record in turn comparing the zipcode.

The cost estimates that are used by PostgreSQL are based on the tables' vital statistics, such as the number of rows that are present. These statistics are not kept precisely up to date as the server runs, but have to be re-computed from time to time.

This is the second task for VACUUM, VACUUM ANALYZE:

```
bpfinal=# vacuum analyze;
VACUUM

bpfinal=#
```

PostgreSQL provides a utility, vacuumdb, for performing the database vacuum from the command line. Its syntax is:

```
vacuumdb [options] database
```

The options to vacuumdb are listed in the following table:

| Option | Description |
| --- | --- |
| -h host<br>--host host | Specify the database server host. Defaults to the local machine. |
| -p port<br>--port port | Specify the port. Defaults to the standard PostgreSQL listener port, 5432. |
| -q<br>--quiet | Do not print a response. |
| -U name<br>--username name | Specify the user name to use for the database connection. |
| -W<br>--password | Prompt for a password. |
| -d name<br>--dbname name | Specify the database to vacuum. |
| -a<br>-all | Vacuum all databases. |
| -z<br>--analyze | Re-compute optimizer statistics. |
| -v<br>--verbose | Report additional details on the vacuuming process, including statistics. |
| -t object<br>--table object | Specify table or column to be vacuumed. Note: The object specifier needs to be quoted if it contains parentheses denoting columns. |

> We strongly recommend that for a PostgreSQL database of any size, that VACUUM or vacuumdb be run daily, perhaps as part of an overnight routine. This will ensure that the space occupied by the data remains at a minimum, and the statistics used by the query optimizer remain up to date, keeping performance at its best.

# Indexes

We saw earlier that PostgreSQL creates a query plan for a query based on costs of selecting and scanning data. A sequential scan of all the rows in a table will become very expensive as the number of rows in the table increases. Databases use indexes to speed up searches for rows that contain specific data, as the cost of an index scan is typically much less than a sequential scan.

In fact, PostgreSQL will automatically create an index for a column defined as a primary key for a table. This means that, for example, locating a customer given their customer_id will be very quick, but locating a customer by zipcode will still require a sequential scan.

We can create additional indexes for a table, using the SQL CREATE INDEX command:

```
CREATE [unique] INDEX indexname ON table(column)
```

The unique option specifies that the column we are indexing, does not contain duplicate entries; each row has a unique value for this column. Once a unique index has been created, any attempt to add or alter data so that this condition is broken, will result in an error. Use this option, only if you are sure that your data will never have duplicate data for the index column.

Our example database has too little data to really benefit from indexes, therefore let's create a new table to demonstrate the effect of an index.

We can create a large table by reading in the UNIX dictionary into a table. This results in a table with over 40,000 rows. We can use the \copy command in psql to read data directly from a file, like this:

```
bpfinal=# CREATE TABLE words ( word text );
CREATE

bpfinal=# \copy words FROM  '/usr/dict/words'
\.

bpfinal=# SELECT count(*) FROM words;
count
-------
45407
(1 row)

bpfinal=#
```

Now that we have a large table, we can ask PostgreSQL how it would go about finding the word Zulu:

```
bpfinal=# EXPLAIN SELECT * FROM words WHERE word='Zulu';
NOTICE:   QUERY PLAN:

Seq Scan on words  (cost=0.00..22.50 rows=10 width=12)

EXPLAIN

bpfinal=#
```

Despite the fact that there are 45,000 rows, PostgreSQL estimates a maximum cost of 22.5 for a scan of the table. This is in fact just a guess, and is wildly inaccurate. To help PostgreSQL make a better estimate, we need to use VACUUM ANALYZE to update the table statistics after our insertion:

```
bpfinal=# VACUUM ANALYZE words;
VACUUM

bpfinal=# EXPLAIN SELECT * FROM words WHERE word='Zulu';
NOTICE:   QUERY PLAN:


Seq Scan on words  (cost=0.00..843.59 rows=1 width=12)


EXPLAIN

bpfinal=#
```

Now PostgreSQL is estimating a cost of up to 843 for a scan on this table. This is an illustration of why it is important to run VACUUM regularly to keep the statistics up to date, especially after significant data updates, insertions, or deletions.

When we perform the query to retrieve Zulu we see a slight pause, (of course, on fast computers, this query will be complete in the blink of an eye):

```
bpfinal=# SELECT * FROM words WHERE word='Zulu';
word
------
Zulu
(1 row)

bpfinal=#
```

We can speed up access to the words table by creating an index like this:

```
bpfinal=# CREATE INDEX words_idx ON words(word);
CREATE

bpfinal=#
```

We can see the predicted benefit by looking at the query plan again. The estimate cost has dropped dramatically, to a maximum of 2 (from 843), and the query runs effectively instantly:

```
bpfinal=# EXPLAIN SELECT * FROM  words WHERE  word='Zulu';
NOTICE:   QUERY PLAN:

Index Scan using words_idx on words  (cost=0.00..2.09 rows=1 width=12)

EXPLAIN

bpfinal=# SELECT * FROM words WHERE word='Zulu';
word
------
Zulu
(1 row)

bpfinal=#
```

We might expect an index to help with search for exact matches, but PostgreSQL is a little cleverer than that. It can use the index to help with prefix matches too. If we want to find all of the words that start with Zu, PostgreSQL uses the index to find partial matches. It will still need to check against our precise match string, but the cost compared with a sequential scan is very small.

We can see the estimated cost with EXPLAIN again:

```
bpfinal=# EXPLAIN SELECT * FROM words WHERE word LIKE 'Zu%';
NOTICE:   QUERY PLAN:

Index Scan using words_idx on words  (cost=0.00..16.25 rows=14 width=12)

bpfinal=#
```

While indexes can dramatically speed up a database, and are the key to maximizing performance, they do not come at no cost. An index will speed up access where selections are being made on matches with the indexed column. But they will make data insertions and updates slower, because the index has to be updated. Indexes also consume space within the database.

We need to take care in selecting which database tables and columns to index, balancing the improved selection performance against increased database size and decreased update speed. So which tables and columns should we index? There are no hard and fast rules, and sometimes experimentation is needed. Think about what each table is used for and what kind of queries are likely to be made.

Consider creating an index for:

❑ Tables that have many rows and are updated infrequently

❑ Columns that are not primary or foreign keys, but may be used in complex joins

❑ Columns that will be searched for an exact or prefix match

# Summary

In this chapter, we covered:

❑ Some routine database maintenance tasks that are needed to maintain a PostgreSQL system

❑ Ways to control and access the PostgreSQL backend server

❑ Managing user accounts, and, controlling access by users

❑ Data backup and recovery using the pg_dump and pg_restore tools, which can also help when upgrading PostgreSQL as new versions are released

❑ Creating Indexes and improving performance thereby

The documentation included with PostgreSQL contains an Administrator's Guide that covers advanced topics that are not covered here.

Although we have used the command line a lot in this chapter, you can also use pgAdmin as a GUI for more intuitive management of many database features, including user and table permissions.

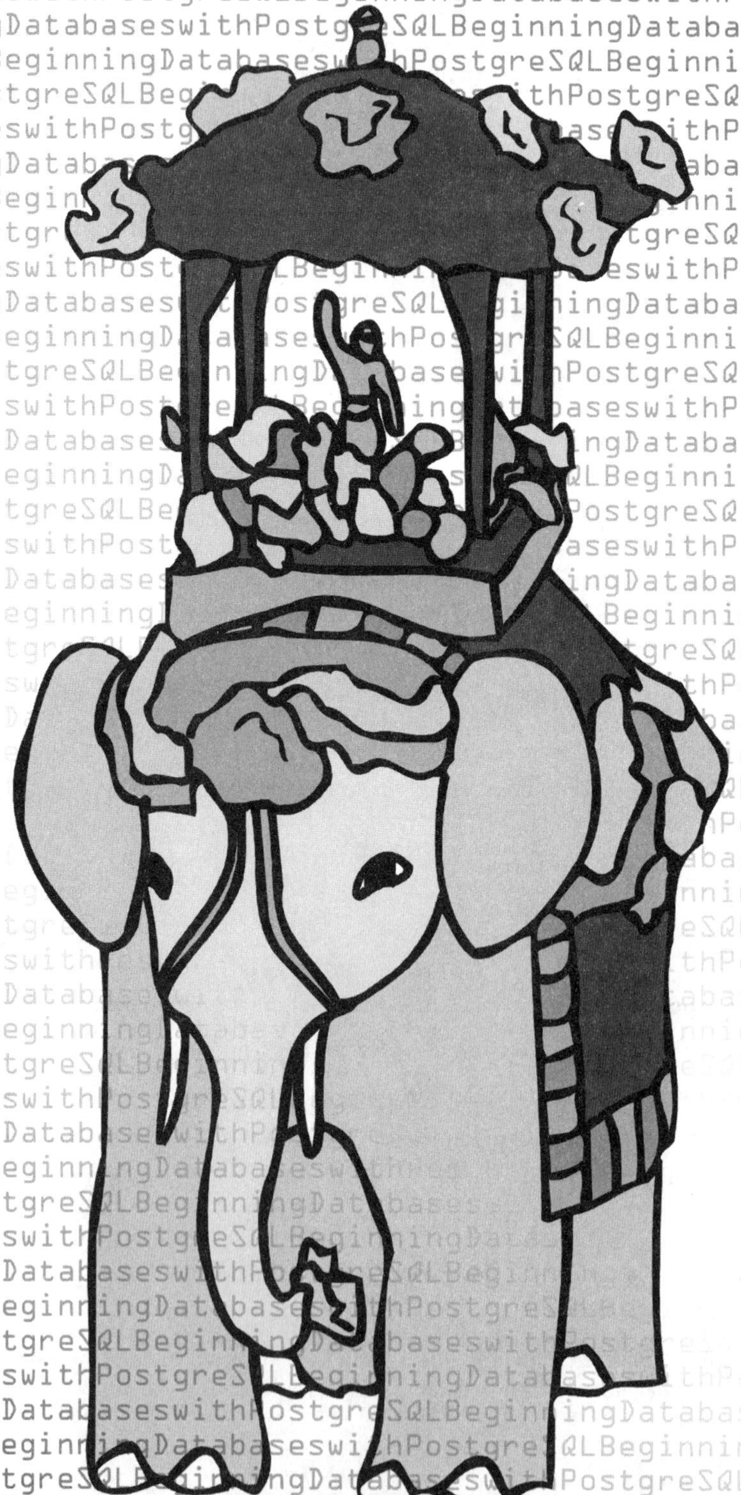

# Database Design

So far in this book, we have been working with our database schema for our simple customer/orders/products data, but we have taken the design of the tables and columns for granted. Now that we understand more about the capabilities of relational databases, we are in a position to backtrack a little, and look at the very important aspect of databases that is designing the database structure, more formally known as a database schema.

When researching this chapter, we asked a friend with excellent database design skills, honed over several years, what they thought was the most important aspect of database design. Their simple answer was 'practice'. Unfortunately, we can't provide a substitute for practice, but we will explain the basics in this chapter. Also, we'll work through how the design in our example database was arrived at, and provide some pointers to other books, so you can go and gain the experience from a solid base of understanding.

In this chapter, we'll be looking at the following aspects of a database design:

- ❑ Understanding the problem
- ❑ What is a good database design?
- ❑ Stages in database design
- ❑ Logical design
- ❑ Converting to a physical model
- ❑ Normal forms
- ❑ Common design patterns

## Understanding the Problem

The very first step in designing a database is to understand the problem. Just like designing applications, it is important to understand the problem area well, before getting immersed in any detailed design.

Is your planned system going to replace an existing system? If so, you have a head start, because whatever its failings or shortcomings, an existing system will have captured many important features required of the replacement system. Even so, the most important thing that you should do is to talk to the potential users of the system. If it's a database for your personal use, you still need to ask questions, but ask them of yourself.

If you are interviewing a group, there are some steps you can take to make the interview as productive as possible:

❑ Don't try and interview too many people at the same time. Two or three are enough.

❑ Warn people in advance what you are trying to discover and if possible send them your headline questions in advance.

❑ See if you can get a helper to jot down notes for you, so you can concentrate on understanding what the users are saying to you.

❑ Keep the interview session short, and ensure you cover a reasonable amount of breadth, even if you have to leave some minor details undecided during the actual meeting. If some items are left unresolved, ensure you action someone to come back to you with an answer by a specified date, say in a week.

❑ Always circulate detailed minutes after the meeting, no later than the next working day, with an explicit request to return comments within a week if any points are disputed.

Actual questions will depend very much on your particular application. At initial interviews, however, asking users to describe the purpose of the system and its principal functions are good opening topics. Always try and avoid the 'how', and focus on the 'what'. People will often try and tell you how things are done in the current system, what you need to know is 'why' they are done, so you can understand the purpose better.

Potential users hold the key to a good design, even if they don't know it. Even if you are creating a system for your personal use, it is worthwhile to take the time to consider precisely what you need to do, and to try and anticipate how this may change over the time.

# What is a Good Database Design?

It's important to understand what we are trying to achieve with a database design. Different features will be important in different systems. For example, you may be building a database to collect some survey data, where, once the results have been extracted, there will be no further use for the database. In this case, it's probable that designing in flexibility for future expansion is not the most effective use of time.

Let's look at the aspects of design that may need to be taken into account when designing a database.

### Ability to Hold the Required Data

This is a fairly crucial requirement of all databases, since storing data is the very reason for having a database. Even this apparently universal requirement however, can have degrees of necessity. If we are designing a reasonably complex database that we expect to evolve over time, we should seriously consider what are the 'must have' requirements, and implement those first, putting to one side 'nice to have' requests.

Database design can evolve through a number of design iterations, just like the spiral model of application design, where the design iterates through a number of design-code-implement loops as the system evolves. There is quite an important difference, however, in that with database design, getting the fundamentals correct the first time tends to be even more important than with application design. Once the first iteration of the database is in use and storing real data, significant design changes to the core structure will generally prove difficult, time consuming, and may require design changes in applications accessing the database.

Most database designs, even very complex ones, will probably have at most 25% of the tables in the final design as what might be termed 'key tables': tables fundamental to the design. Identifying and designing these core tables must be our first goal. The remaining tables are important, but usually peripheral the design.

### Ability to Support the Required Relationships

The design of the database should support the relationships between the data entities. It is all too easy to become so focused on the details of the data to be stored that relationships between the data items are overlooked, yet this is the key breakthrough of relational databases. A database design that captures all the data, but neglects the relationships between data items will tend to suffer in the longer run from data integrity problems and excessive application complexity, as other parts of the system attempt to make up for its design failings.

### Ability to Solve the Problem

The best-designed databases are worthless if they don't solve the problem that they were created to tackle. Throughout the design process, you must stay in touch with the problem area. If possible, communicate with, and explain to your intended users the design, at the major design points.

Simply mailing your users your database schema will almost certainly not do. You need to sit with them and talk through the design, explaining in business terms what the design achieves. When you do this, remember the previous two points, and explain not only the data stores, but also how each major data entity can relate to other entities. If your design only allows a local IT support person to support a single department, you must mention such details.

It's also important, where practical, to carefully select the users you talk to. The most valuable people to talk to are usually those with the broadest experience of the problem. Unfortunately, these also tend to be most senior, and therefore often the busiest.

### Ability to Impose Data Integrity

This aspect is closely related to the earlier point about relationships. The whole purpose of a database is to store data, and the quality of that data must be very important to us. A lot of real world data inevitably has deficiencies: uncertainties, hand written forms that have illegible entries, or missing data. These are never excuses for allowing any further deterioration in data quality in our database.

We should choose our data types with care, impose column constraints, and if necessary write trigger functions to maintain the data in the database with as much rigor as is reasonably possible. Of course, we must apply some common sense and be practical, but never invent data if something is missing. If we are entering a survey into the database, and some users are unable to answer some questions, then it is better to store the fact that the answer was unknown than to enter a best guess.

### Ability to Impose Data Efficiency

This is a difficult aspect of database design, because, as Donald Knuth is widely quoted as saying, "Premature optimization is the root of all evil". Although he was referring to application design, this is just as true, perhaps even more so, with database design.

Unfortunately, in a large heavily-used database, it is sometimes necessary to do things that spoil the purity of the design in order to achieve more practical performance goals. You should always, always get the design right first, however, before you even consider any optimizations. Often there are quite simple things, such as adding an index, or rewriting a query, than can give dramatic performance improvements, without compromising the core design.

What you should avoid is the temptation to arbitrarily make many small changes, such as changing a VARCHAR type to a CHAR type. Generally, these are a waste of time, and just result in a poor and inconsistent database schema. You need to invest time in profiling the application first, to determine where any bottlenecks lie, and only then consider what may need changing. Even then, changing the database design itself (as opposed to less-structural changes such as adding an index or rewriting a query) should be very much a last resort.

### Ability to Accommodate Future Change

People in the software business are often surprised at just how long software remains in use, usually well beyond its design lifetime. With databases, this is even more noticeable than with applications, because migrating data from an old design to a new one is often a significant problem in its own right. There will always be pressure to enhance the existing database design, rather than start from scratch and then migrate the data at a later date.

Often you will find that any changes you have made to your design in the supposed interests of efficiency make your design harder to evolve. As Alan Perlis said in one of his programming epigrams "Optimization hinders evolution" (http://www.cs.yale.edu/homes/perlis-alan/quotes.html).

# Stages in Database Design

So now we have some idea what we are trying to achieve with our database design, we can look at the steps we should take in order to achieve it. As we hinted earlier, when discussing the need to understand the problem, database design is rarely a purely technical problem. A significant aspect is to understand the needs and expectations of users, before converting those requirements into a technical design.

# Gather Information

The first stage in designing a database is to gather information about what it is for. Why are we designing a database in the first place? You should be able to define in a small number of sentences, perhaps just a single sentence, your aim with the database. If you can't come up with a simple way of describing your objective, then perhaps the objective is not yet well understood or defined.

It is important to have a clear objective before you attempt to collect more detailed requirements. Bear this initial simple definition in mind and if, further down the track, it all seems to be getting over-complicated and suffering from 'feature bloat', then go back to basics. Once you have a clear idea of what you are trying to achieve, you can start to expand on this initial requirement.

If your new database will be replacing an existing database, then your first task should be to understand the structure of the original database, be it relational, flat file, or perhaps just a spreadsheet. Even if the existing system is badly flawed, you can still learn from it, both good things and bad. It's likely that many of the items it currently stores will also be required in the new system, and having a look at existing sample data can often give you a good feel for what real world data looks like. Ask what the existing system does well, and what it does badly, or not at all. This will all give you clues as to how the existing design needs amending.

You should write down what the system needs to do, because writing things down focuses the mind. If reports will be generated, try mocking one up for users to comment on. If it will take data that comes from existing paper-based forms, get hold of a copy, if possible with some sample data already filled in.

At this stage, you should also be thinking about relationships and business rules, and noting any specific features and requirements that are mentioned. You need to be careful to determine which rules are simply rather arbitrary 'this is the way we do things'-type rules and prone to change, however, and which are factual rules about the nature of things, much less likely to change. The former, we will probably choose to enforce only with triggers or else enforce them at application level, so they are easy to modify; the latter, we should probably build into the design of our database, enforcing data integrity at a low level since they are fundamental and very unlikely to change.

# Logical Design

## Determining Entities

Once we have gathered information, we should be in a position to identify the **principal entities** (the key objects that will need to appear in our database). At this point, you generally shouldn't worry too much about minor entities. You need to pick out the key objects that define the problem area. In our sample database, we would be identifying customers, orders, and products as the key objects that we need to work with.

Additional details, such as the need to track stock and worry about barcodes, are not important at this stage, nor should you worry just yet about how the different entities relate to each other.

Once you believe you have identified the major components of your database, you need to identify the attributes of those components, in a non-formal way. For example, we would probably draw up a list of our main components, with the attributes written in plain language, like this:

| **Customers and Potential customers** |
| --- |
| Name |
| Address |
| Phone number |

| **Orders** |
| --- |
| Products ordered |
| Date placed |
| Date delivered |
| Shipping information |

| **Product Information** |
| --- |
| Description |
| Buy price |
| Sell price |
| Barcodes |
| Stock on hand |

Name is currently a non-reserved keyword in the standard, so may become a reserved word in the future. Currently PostgreSQL will accept this as a column identifier, but at some point in the future it may become illegal, so it is best avoided. At this stage, we are just working with plain language so for initial design purposes we will continue to use Name.

Notice that we have not yet worried about how we might store an address, nor about difficulties, such as the possibility that each product might have several different barcodes. We have also kept the attributes names quite general, for example Address and Shipping information. This helps to keep the list of attributes reasonably short and general, so we avoid focusing on the finer details too early, and losing sight of the bigger picture.

At this stage, some people find it helpful to write a brief description of each entity. In our small database, this is a little superfluous, as the components are so simple, but in larger databases, particularly those dealing with more abstract ideas, this can be helpful.

If we were writing descriptions for the Product Information, we might have:

| Product Information | Description |
|---|---|
| Description | Up to 75 characters that describe the product, including any size or volume information |
| Buy price | The price that we paid the supplier per item of product, excluding any delivery costs or tax |
| Sell price | The price to be paid for the item, excluding sales tax and shipping costs |
| Barcodes | The EAN13 barcode |
| Stock on hand | The quantity in stock, including any corrections applied during a stock take |

Once you have finished this stage, pause to check back to the information you gathered initially, and make sure nothing important has been missed.

## Convert Entities to Tables

Now we are ready to take a more technical step, and start converting our components and attribute lists into something that will start to look like a database. Firstly, we need to pick some sensible names for our tables.

If possible, always name tables in the singular, and try to stick a single word, even if that is slightly artificial. In our sample database, it's easy to convert our names to more succinct versions such as `customer` or `order`. So rather than Product Information, we will use `item`.

Now we can convert our attributes into more meaningful names, and also break down some of our more general descriptions into the columns we would like to see in a database. When breaking down descriptions into column names, it's very important to ensure that each column holds just a single attribute. As we will see later in the chapter, this is essential to ensuring our database is in First Normal Form, a key design requirement for relational databases.

Let's start with our `customer` table:

| Customer |
| --- |
| Name |
| Address |
| Phone number |

Name is reasonably easy to break down. People normally have a title of some form, such as Mr, Miss, or Dr, so we need to have a column for this. Names are quite complex. People are often tempted to use a single column for name assuming that they can always break down the name later, should the last name only be required. The clue is in the word 'assume'. Never assume.

Suppose you have a customer with a double-barrelled last name, such as 'Rose Martin', or a German last name such as 'von Neumann'. Some people might choose to enter two first names as well as a last name, such as 'Jennifer Ann Stones'. When you have a table of data like this:

| Title | Name |
| --- | --- |
| Miss | Jennifer Ann Stones |
| Dr | John von Neumann |
| Mr | Andrew Stones |
| Mr | Adrian Alan Matthew |
| Mr | Robert Rose Martin |

It's going to be impossible to reliably extract the first and last names at a later date. Much better to capture the separation of names at the point of entry, and store them separated in the database like this:

| Title | Fname | Lname |
| --- | --- | --- |
| Miss | Jennifer | Stones |
| Dr | John | von Neumann |
| Mr | Andrew | Stones |
| Mr | Adrian | Matthew |
| Mr | Robert | Rose Martin |

Notice that we have also decided that we are not interested in middle names, and will decide as a point of principle only to ever store a single first name.

Now it's possible at some point in the future to handle the components of the name separately, so we can write to Dr J von Neumann, and start the letter Dear John...., rather than write to Dr Neumann, and start the letter Dear John von. That sort of carelessness does not impress customers.

Our next item is Address. Addresses are always hard to handle in a database, because the form of address varies widely even in a single country, never mind between different countries.

For example in the United Kingdom addresses are written in the form:

20 James Road,
Great Barr,
Birmingham
M11 2BA

Another address however, might have no house number at all:

Arden House,
Warwick Road,
Acocks Green,
Birmingham
B27 6BH

American addresses are similar:

29 S. La Salle St,
Suite 520
Chicago
Illinois
60603

In Germany and Austria however addresses are written very differently:

Getreidegasse 9
A-5020 Salzburg

Getreidegasse in Salzburg. Mozart was born at number 9.

Designing a standard address structure is not easy and there is no right answer. Usually, a minimum design would be to separate out a postal town, and Zip code or equivalent, which is what we have done in our sample database. In real use, it is probably better to have at least three lines for an address, plus a town, Zip code, state (if in the US), and if relevant a country.

If you live outside the US, a common fault you see on web forms is assuming that everyone has a State part of the address and providing a handy drop down box to select the state, or making it a mandatory field, but forgetting to allow the 'not relevant' option for the rest of the world. It is very annoying for people outside the US trying to enter an address and discovering that State is mandatory, when in fact it is not relevant.

It is usually best to avoid trying to insist on a house number, as you will cause problems for people in office buildings with a name, or people who live in apartments in condominiums and have an apartment number as well as a street address number.

Another possibility, is to accept an undefined number of address lines, by splitting the address lines out into a separate table. If we do this, we must remember to impose an order on the lines, so we get the address details in the correct order. Generally, designers decide that this is overkill, and splitting the address into a fixed number is sufficient. Occasionally, too much subdivision is a bad thing.

Assuming a simplified design for our address columns, we get:

| **Customer** |
| --- |
| Title |
| Fname |
| Lname |
| Addressline |
| Town |
| Zip code |
| Phone |

Our Item (Product Information) table is already very close to having columns described:

| **Item** |
| --- |
| Description |
| Buy price |
| Sell price |
| Barcodes (may be several) |
| Stock Quantity |

Notice that we have postponed the problem of multiple barcodes per item for now. We will pick this up later.

Our `orders` table is similar. We have again postponed some issues, such as multiple products being put on the same order, and the possibility of more than one of each product being ordered at the same time. It's clear we will need to break this table down further before we can implement it in a real database:

| Orders |
| --- |
| Items ordered |
| Quantity of each item |
| Date placed |
| Date delivered |
| Shipping information |

# Determine Relationships and Cardinality

At this point, we have a list of our main entities, and although possibly not a complete list, we do at least have a reasonable first pass at the main attributes for each entity. Now comes an important phase in designing our database: breaking out those attributes that can occur several times for each entity, and deciding how our different entities relate to each other. This is often referred to as **cardinality**.

Some people like to consider the relationships even before generating an attribute list. We find that listing the main attributes helps in understanding the entities, so we perform that step first. There is no definitive right and wrong way: use whichever works best for you.

## Drawing Relationship Diagrams

With databases, a graphical representation of the structure of the data can be extremely helpful in understanding the design. There are many different diagramming techniques and styles in use in database circles. We will use a common notation; you will find other notations in use.

At this stage, we are working on what is termed a **conceptual model**. We are not yet concerned about the finer implementation detail, but more about the logical structure of our data. In a conceptual data model, tables are shown as boxes, with relationships between the tables shown using lines, with symbols at the end of the line indicating the type of relationship. The symbols we will be using are:

| Relationship | Symbol |
| --- | --- |
| Zero or one | Table |
| Exactly one | Table |
| Zero or many | Table |
| One or many | Table |

Relationships between tables are always in two directions, therefore there will always be a symbol at each end, and you 'read' the diagram towards the table you are interested in.

Suppose we had a relationship between two tables, A and B, drawn like this:

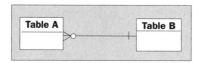

What this means is that:

❑   For each row in A there must be exactly one row in B

❑   For each row in B there can be zero, one or many rows in A

For example, if table A was `orders`, and table B `customer`, this would say, 'For each order there must be exactly one customer. For each customer there can be zero, one or many orders'.

## The Example Database

Now that we have the basics of drawing table relationships, we can look at our example with customers, orders, and products. Our `customer` table has no multiple attributes, so we can leave it alone for now. Let's tackle our `item` table next, as this is reasonably straightforward.

Our only difficulty with the `item` table, is that each item could have more than one barcode. As we discussed earlier in the book, having an unknown number of repeating columns in a database table is not possible (although PostgreSQL does have an array data type, that is quite unusual and should be used with caution). Suppose most items have two barcodes, but some we know have three, so we decide that an easy solution was to add three columns to the `item` table, `barcode1`, `barcode2`, `barcode3`?

This seems like a nice easy solution to the problem, but it doesn't stand up to closer scrutiny. What happens when a product comes along that has four barcodes? Do we re-design our database structure to add a fourth barcode column? How many columns is 'enough'? As we saw in Chapter 2, having repeated columns is very inflexible, and is almost always the wrong solution.

Another solution we might think of is to have a variable length string, and 'hide' barcodes in that string, perhaps separated by a character we know doesn't appear in barcodes. Again, this is a very bad solution, because we have stored many pieces of information in the same location. As with a good spreadsheet, it's very important to ensure that each entity is stored separately, so they can be processed independently.

We need to separate out the repeating information, the barcodes, into a new table. That way, we can arrange to store an arbitrary number of barcodes for each item. While we are breaking out the `barcode`, we also need to consider the relationship between an `item` and a `barcode`.

Thinking from the item side first, we know that each item could have no barcodes, one barcode, or many bar codes. Thinking from the barcode end, we know that each barcode must be associated with exactly one item. A barcode on a product is always the lowest level of identifier, identifying different versions of products, such as promotional packs or overfill packs, while the core product remains the same.

We can draw this relationship like this:

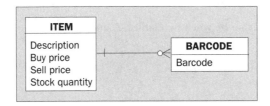

This shows that each item can have zero, one or many barcodes, but a barcode belongs to exactly one item. You will notice that we have not identified any columns to join the two tables. This will come later. The important thing at this point is to determine relationships, not how we will express them in SQL.

Now we can move on to the `orders` table, which is slightly harder to analyze. The first problem is how to represent the products that have been ordered. Often orders will consist of more than one product, so we know that we have a repeating set of information relating to orders. As before, this means that we must split out the products into a separate table. We will call our main order table `orderinfo`, and the table we split out to hold the products ordered, `orderline`, since we can imagine each row of this table corresponding to a line on a paper order.

Now we need to think about the relationship between the two. It makes no sense to have an order for nothing, or to prevent an order having multiple items on the same order, so we know that `orderinfo` to `orderline` must be a one-to-many relationship. Thinking about an `orderline`, we realize that each `orderline` must relate to exactly one actual order, so the relationship between the two is that for each `orderline` entry, there must be exactly one `orderinfo` entry.

Thus, we can draw the relationship like this:

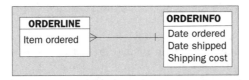

If we think about this a little longer, we can see a possible snag. When people go into a shop, they do not generally order things one at a time:

```
I'd like a coffee please

I'd like a coffee please

I'd like a donut please

I'd like a coffee please

I'd like a donut please
```

They tend to order:

```
I'd like three coffees and two donuts please
```

Currently, our design copes perfectly with the first situation, but can only cope with the second situation by converting it to the many single lines situation.

Now we might decide this is OK, but if we are going to print out an order for a large round of coffees, milk shakes, and donuts, it's going to look a bit silly to the customer if each item has a separate line. We are also making life difficult for ourselves if we do a discount on multiple items order at the same time.

For these reasons, we decided it would be better to store a quantity against each line, like this:

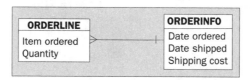

This way, we can store each type of product in an order only once, and store the quantity of the product required in a separate column.

Now we have a basic conceptual design for all our entities, it's time to relate them to each other. At the moment we have this:

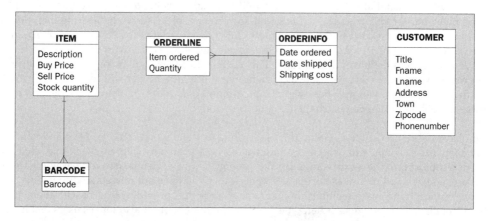

Now we can look at how the three groups relate to each other. In this simple database, it's immediately obvious that customer rows must relate to orderinfo rows. Looking at the relationship between items and orders, we can see that the relationship is not between the orderinfo and the item, it is between the orderline and the item.

How exactly do customers relate to orders? Clearly each order must relate to a single customer, and each customer could have had many orders, but could we have a customer with no orders? Although not very likely, it is possible in some situations, perhaps while a customer account is being setup; so we will allow the possibility of a customer with no orders.

Similarly, we must define the exact relationship between item and orderline. Each orderline is for an item, so this relationship is exactly one. In the opposite direction, item to orderline, any individual item could have never been ordered, or could appear on many different orderliness, so the relationship is zero or many. Adding these relationships gives us a diagram like this:

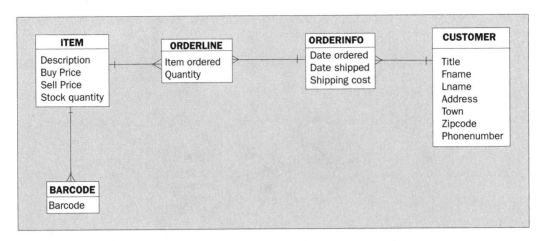

At this stage, we have what we believe to be a complete map of all the major entities and their most important attributes, broken down where we think we need to store them in individual columns, and a diagram showing the relationship between them all. We have our first conceptual database design.

At this point, it's vital that you stop and validate this initial conceptual design. A mistake at this stage will be much harder to correct later. It is a well-known tenet of software engineering that, the earlier you find an error, the less it costs to fix. Some studies have suggested that the cost of correcting an error increases by a factor of 10 for each stage in the development process. Invest in getting the requirements capture correct, and the initial design right. This doesn't mean you can't take an iterative approach if you prefer – you just need to get each stage right, but it is a little harder with database design, because after the first iteration, you may have significant volumes of live data in your database, and migrating this data to a later design can be challenging in its own right.

If you have future users of the system, this is the point at which you should go back and talk to them. Show them the diagram, and explain to them what it means, step by step, to check that what you have designed conforms to their expectations of the system. If your design is partially based on an existing database, go back and re-visit the original, to check that you have not missed anything vital. Most users will understand basic entity relationship diagrams such as this, providing you sit with them and talk them through it. Not only does it help you validate the design, but it also makes users feel involved and consulted in the development.

# Convert to a Physical Model

Now that we have a logical model of our data, which has been checked for logical correctness, we can start to move towards a physical representation of this design.

## Establish Primary Keys

Our first step is usually to decide what the primary keys of each table will be. We will work through our tables one at a time, considering them individually, and decide which piece of data in each row will make that row unique.

What we will be doing is generating **candidate keys**, possible data items that make each row uniquely identifiable, then picking one of the candidate keys to be the **primary key**. If we can't find any candidate keys, or think them poor candidates, we may resort to a logical primary key, which we create specially to act as a primary key. If you do find yourself having to create a special key to act as a primary key, this may be an indication that your attribute list is not complete. It's always worth revisiting your attribute list if you find there is no obvious primary key.

We will first check for a single column that will be unique, and then look for combinations that will be unique. We must also check that none of the columns in our candidate key could ever be null. It would make no sense to have a primary key whose value, or part of whose value, could be unknown. Indeed, SQL databases, including PostgreSQL, will automatically enforce the restriction that you may not store a NULL value in a column being used as a primary key.

When looking for columns to use as a primary key, we need to be aware that the shorter the field length, the more efficient searching for particular values will be, and the smaller the overhead in the database will be. When we make a column a primary key, an index is constructed for that column, both to enforce the requirement that its values are unique, and also to enable the database to find values in the column efficiently. Generally, tables are searched using their primary key columns far more often than any other column, so it is important that this can be done efficiently. You can imagine that searching a column for a description that is 200 characters long is going to be much slower than searching for a particular integer value.

Having a primary key column that has many characters, also makes the index tree that has to be built very large, adding to the overheads. For these reasons, it is important that we try and choose columns with small fields as primary keys; integer values are ideal, short strings, particularly fixed length strings tolerable. Using other data types as primary key columns is best avoided.

### Barcode Table

Let's look at the barcode table first, because it is nice and straightforward. We have only one column, there is only one candidate key, therefore barcode. Barcodes are unique, and generally short, therefore this candidate key makes a good primary key.

### Customer Table

It's reasonably easy to see that no single column is going to give us a unique key for each row, so we move on to look at combinations of columns we might use. Let's consider some possibilities:

- ❑ First names and last name combined. This might be unique, but we can't be certain we will never have two customers with the same name.

- ❑ Last name and Zip code. This is better, but still not guaranteed to be unique, since it could just be a husband and wife, both being customers.

- ❑ First name, last name, and Zip code. This is probably unique, but again not a certainty. It's also rather messy to have to use three columns to get to a unique key. One is much preferable, though we will accept two.

There is no clear candidate key, so we will have to generate a logical key that is unique for each customer. To be consistent, we will always name logical keys <table name>_id, which in this case gives us customer_id.

### Orderinfo Table

This table has exactly the same problem as the customer table. There is no clear way of uniquely identifying each row, so again we will create a key, this time orderinfo_id.

### Item Table

We could use description here, but descriptions could be quite a large text string, and long text strings do not make good keys, since they are slow to search. Again we will create a key, item_id.

### Orderline Table

The orderline table sits between the orderinfo table and the item table. If we decide that any particular item will only appear on an order once, because we handle multiple items on the same order using a quantity column, we could consider the item to be a candidate key. In practice, this won't work, because if two different customers order the same item it will appear in two different orderline rows.

We know that will we have to find some way of relating each orderline row to its parent order in orderinfo, and since there is no column present yet that can do this, we know we will have to add one. We can postpone briefly the problem of candidate keys in the orderline table, and come back to it in a moment.

## Establish Foreign Keys

Now that we have established our primary keys for most of the tables, we can work on the mechanism we are going to use to relate our tables together. Our conceptual model has told us the way the tables relate to each other, and we have also established what uniquely identifies each row in a table. When we establish foreign keys, often all we need to do is ensure that the column we have in one table identified as a primary key, also appears in all the other tables that are directly related to that table.

After adjusting some column names to make them a little more meaningful, and changing the relationship lines to a physical model version, where we simply draw an arrow that points at the 'must exist' table, we have a diagram that looks like this:

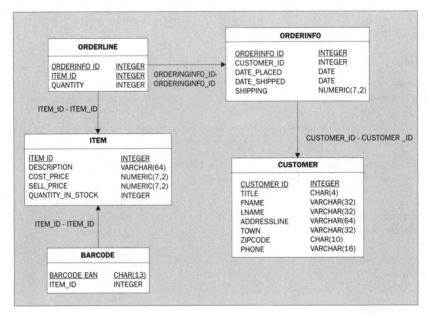

Notice how the diagram has changed from the conceptual model as we move to the physical model. Now we are showing information about how tables could join, not about the cardinality of those relationships. Notice that we have shown the primary key columns underlined.

Don't worry about the data types or sizes for columns yet; that will be a later step. We have deliberately left all the column types as CHAR(10). We will re-visit the type and sizes of all the columns shortly.

For now, we need to work out how to relate tables. Usually, this simply entails checking that the primary key in the 'must exist' table also exists in the table that is related to it. In this case, we needed to add customer_id to orderinfo, orderinfo_id to orderline, and item_id to barcode.

Now look at our orderline table:

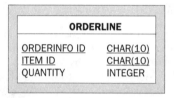

We can see that the combination of item_id and orderinfo_id will always be unique. Adding in the extra column we need has solved our missing primary key problem.

We have one last optimization to make to our schema. We know for our particular business we have a very large number of items, but only wish to keep a few of them in stock. This means that for our item table, quantity_in_stock will almost always be zero. Now for just a single column this is unimportant, but consider the problem if we had a large amount of information for a stocked item, that was always empty for un-stocked items. For example, we might store the date it arrived at the warehouse, a warehouse location, expiry dates, and batch numbers. For the purposes of demonstration, we are going to separate out the stock information from the item information, and hold it in a separate table.

Our physical design, with relationships added and primary keys underlined, now looks like this:

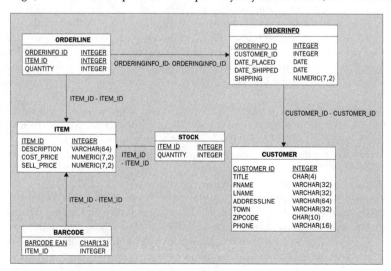

Notice we have been careful to ensure that all related columns have the same name. We didn't have to do this. We could have had a `customer_ident` in the `orderinfo` table that matched `customer_id` in the `customer` table. You will find that database designs that emphasis consistency are much easier to work with so, unless there are very good reasons indeed, we strongly urge you to try and keep column names identical for columns that are related to each other.

It's also a good idea to be consistent in your naming. If you need an `ident` column as a primary key for a table, then stick to a naming rule, preferably one that is `<table name>_<something>`. It doesn't matter if you want to use `id`, `ident`, `key`, or `pk` as the suffix, what is important is that the naming is consistent across the database.

## Establish Data Types

Now we have our tables, columns, and relationships, we can work through each table in turn adding data types to each column. At this stage, we also need to identify any columns that will need to accept NULL values, and declare the remaining columns as NOT NULL. Notice that we start from the assumption that columns should be declared NOT NULL, and look for exceptions. This is a better approach than assuming NULL is allowed, because, as we saw earlier, NULL values in columns are often hard to handle, so we should minimize their occurrence where we can.

Generally, columns to be used as primary keys or foreign keys should be set to a native data type that can be efficiently stored and processed, such as integer. PostgreSQL will automatically enforce a constraint to prevent them from storing NULL values.

Currency is often a difficult choice. Some people prefer a MONEY type, if the database supports it. PostgreSQL does have a MONEY type, but the user guide urges people to use numeric instead, which is what we have chosen to do. You should generally avoid using a type with undefined rounding characteristics, such as a floating point type like `float(P)`. Fixed precision types, such as `numeric(P,S)`, are much safer for working with financial information because the rounding is defined.

For text strings, we have a wide choice of options. When we know the length of a field exactly, and it is a fixed length, such as barcode, we will choose a `CHAR(N)` where N is the length we require (assuming we are sticking to EAN13 codes, which are far from the only barcodes in use, but this is a simplification we can make for the purposes of example). For other short text strings we also prefer to use fixed length strings, such as `CHAR(4)` for title. This is largely a matter of preference however, and it would be just as valid to use a variable length type for this.

For variable length text columns, PostgreSQL has the `text` type, which supports variable length character strings. Unfortunately, this is not standard and, although similar extensions do appear in other commercial databases, the ISO/ANSI definition defines only a `VARCHAR(N)` text type, where N specifies a maximum length of the string. We value portability quite highly, therefore we will stick with the standard `VARCHAR(N)` type.

Again consistency is very important. Make sure all your Money type fields have exactly the same precision. Check that commonly-used columns such as description and name, which might well appear in several tables in your database, aren't defined differently (and thus used in different ways) in each. The fewer unique types that you need to use, the easier your database will be to work with. Let's work through the `customer` table, seeing how we assign types.

The first thing to do is give a type to `customer_id`. It's a primary key and a column we added specially to be a primary key, so we can make it nice and efficient by using an `INTEGER` type. Title will be things like, Mr, Mrs, or Dr. This is always a short string of characters, therefore we make it a `CHAR(4)` type, though some designers prefer to always use `VARCHAR` to reduce the number of types being used. There is very little to choose between the two. `VARCHAR` would be a perfectly valid choice. It's perfectly possible not to know the title, so we will allow this field to store `NULL` values.

We then come to `fname` and `lname`, the first and second names. It's unlikely these ever need to exceed 32 characters, but we know the length will be quite variable, so we make them both `VARCHAR(32)`. We also decide that we could accept `fname` being a `NULL`, but not `lname`. Not knowing a customer's last name seems unreasonable.

In this database, we have chosen to keep all the address together, in a single long character array. As was discussed earlier, this is probably a little over-simplified for the real world, but addresses are always a design challenge: there is no 'right' answer.

We continue assigning types to the columns in this way, the only inserting point to note is perhaps 'phone' which we store as a character string. It is almost always a mistake to store phone numbers as numbers in a database, because it does not allow international dialing codes to be stored, for example +44 (0)116 ... would be a common way of giving a UK dialing code, where the country code is 44, but if you are already in the UK you need to add a 0 before the area code. Also, storing a number with leading zeros will not work in a numeric field, and in telephone numbers leading zeros are very important.

The final type allocation for our database is shown in this table:

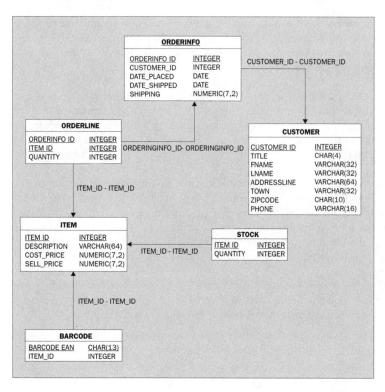

# Complete Table Definitions

We now need to go back and double check that all the information we wish to store in the database is present. All the entities should be represented, and all the attributes listed with appropriate types.

At this point, we may also decide to add some **lookup**, or **static data** tables; for example we might have a lookup table of towns. Generally, these lookup tables are unrelated to any other tables, and are simply used by the application as a convenient way of soft coding values to offer the user. Of course we could hard code these options into our application, but generally storing them in a database, from which they can be loaded into an application at run-time, makes it much easier to add additional options. The application doesn't need to be changed, we just need to insert additional rows in our database lookup table.

# Implement Business Rules

At this point, we would write, or generate from a tool, the SQL to create our database schema. If all is well, we can use the knowledge, from Chapters 8 and 10, to implement any additional business rules. For each rule we must consider if it is best implemented as a constraint, as we saw in Chapter 8, or if we must use a trigger, as shown in Chapter 10. In general, you use constraints, as these are much easier to work with. Some example constraints that we might wish to use in our simple database were shown in Chapter 10.

# Check the Design

By now, you should have a database implemented, complete with constraints and possibly triggers to enforce business rules. Before handing over your completed work, and celebrating a job well done, it's time to test your database again. Just because a database isn't 'code' in the conventional sense, that doesn't mean you can't test it.

Get some sample data, if possible part of the live data that will go into the database. Insert some of these sample rows. Check that attempting to insert NULL values into columns you don't think should ever be NULL results in an error. Attempt to delete data that is referenced by other data. Try and manipulate data to break the business rules you have implemented as triggers or constraints. Write some SQL to join tables together to generate the kind of data you would expect to find on reports.

Once your database has gone into production, it is difficult, although not impossible, to update your design. Anything other than the most minor change probably means stopping the system, unloading live data into text files, updating the database design, and reloading the data. This is not something you want to undertake any more than absolutely necessary. Similarly, once faulty data has been loaded into a table, you will often find it is referenced by other data, and difficult to correct or remove from the database. Time spent testing the design before it goes live is time well spent.

If possible, go back to your intended users and show them the sample data being extracted from the database, and how you can manipulate it. Even at this belated stage, there is much to be gained by picking up an error, even a minor one, before the system goes live.

# Normal Forms

No chapter on database design would be complete without a mention of **normal forms**, and database normalization. We have left these to the end of the chapter, since they are rather dry when presented on their own, but after the design stages we have just walked through, you should see how the final design has conformed to these rules.

What is commonly considered the origins of database normalization, is a paper written by E.F.Codd in 1969, and published in *Communications of the ACM*, Vol. 13, No. 6, June 1970. In later work, various normal forms were defined. Each normal form builds on previous rules and applies more stringent requirements on the design.

In total there are six normal forms: First, Second, and Third normal form, then Boyce Codd Normal Form, and finally Fourth and Fifth normal forms. You will be pleased to learn that only the first three forms are commonly used, and those are all that we will be looking at in this book.

The advantage of structuring your data so that it conforms to at least the first three normal forms, is that you will find it much easier to manage. Databases that are not well normalized are generally much harder to maintain, and more prone to storing invalid data.

# First Normal Form

First normal form requires that each attribute in a table cannot be further sub-divided, and that there are no repeating groups. For example, in our database design we separate the customer name into a title, first name, and last name. We know we may wish to use them separately, we must consider them therefore as separate attributes, and store them separately.

The second part, no repeating groups, we saw in Chapter 2 when we looked at what happened when we tried to use a simple spreadsheet to store customers and their orders. Once a customer had more than one order, we had repeating information for that customer, and our spreadsheet no longer had the same number of rows in all columns.

If we had decided earlier to hold both first names in the `fname` column of our `customer` table, this would have violated first normal form, because the column `fname` would actually be holding 'first names' which are clearly divisible entities. Sometimes you have to take a pragmatic approach and argue that, providing you are confident you will never need to consider different first names separately, they are for the purposes of the design a single entity. Alternatively, we could decide only to ever store a single first name, which is an equally valid approach and the one taken here.

Another example of violating first normal form that is seen worryingly frequently, is to store in a single column a character string where different character positions have different meanings. For example, characters 1-3 tell you the warehouse, 4-11 the bay, and 12 the shelf. These are a clear violation of first normal form, since we do need to consider sub-divisions of the column separately. In practice, they also turn out to be very hard to manage, and should always be considered a design fault, not a judicious stretching of the first normal form rule.

# Second Normal Form

Second normal form says that no information in a row must depend on only part of the primary key. Suppose in our `orderline` table we had stored the date that the order was placed in this table:

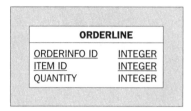

You will remember that our primary key for `orderline` is a composite of `orderinfo_id` and `item_id`. The date the order was placed depends only on the `orderinfo` information, not on the item ordered, so this would have violated second normal form. Sometimes you may find you are storing data that looks as though it may violate second normal form, but in practice it does not.

Suppose we changed our prices frequently. Customers would rightly expect to pay the price shown on the day they ordered, not on the day it was shipped. In order to do this, we would have to store the sell price in the `orderline` table to store the price in operation on the day the order was placed. This would not violate second normal form, because the price stored in the `orderline` table would depend on both the item and the actual order.

# Third Normal Form

Third normal form is very similar to second normal form, but more general. It says that no information in a column that is not the primary key can depend on anything except the primary key. This is often stated as "Non key values must depend upon 'The key, the whole key and nothing but the key'". Suppose in our `customer` table we had stored a customer's age and date of birth:

This would violate third normal form, because the customer's age depends on their date of birth, a non key column, as well as the actual customer, which is given by `customer_id`, the primary key.

Although putting your database into third normal form (that is to say making its structure conform to all the first three normalization rules) is almost always the preferred solution, there are occasions when it's necessary to break the rules. This is called de-normalizing the database, and is occasionally necessary to improve performance. You should always design a fully normalized database first, however, and only de-normalize if you know that you have a serious problem with performance.

# Common Patterns

In database design, there are a number of common patterns that occur over and over again, and it's useful to recognize these, because generally they can be solved in the same way. Before we conclude this chapter, we will look briefly at three standard problems that have standard solutions.

## Many-to-Many

You have two entities, which seem to have a many-to-many relationship between them. It is never correct to implement a many-to-many table relationship in the physical database, so you need to break the relationship.

The solution is almost always to insert an additional table, a link table, between the two tables that apparently have a many-to-many relationship. Suppose we had two tables, `author` and `book`. Each author could have written many books, and each book, like this one, could have had contributions from more than one author. How do we represent this in a physical database?

The solution is to insert a table in between the other two tables, which normally contains the primary key of each of the other tables. In this case, we create a new table, `bookauthor`, which has a composite primary key, where each component is the primary key of one of the other tables:

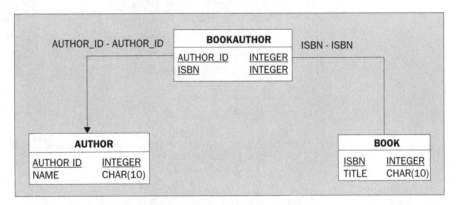

Now each author can appear in the `author` table exactly once, but have many entries in the `bookauthor` table, one for each book they have written. Each book appears exactly once in the `book` table, but can appear in the `bookauthor` table more than once, if there was more than one author. Each individual entry in the `bookauthor` table is however unique, the combination of book and author only ever occurs once.

## Hierarchy

Another frequent pattern is a hierarchy. This can appear in many different guises. Suppose we have many shops, and each shop is in a geographic area, and in turn areas are grouped into larger areas known as groups. It might be tempting to store it like this, where each shop stores the area and region in which it resides:

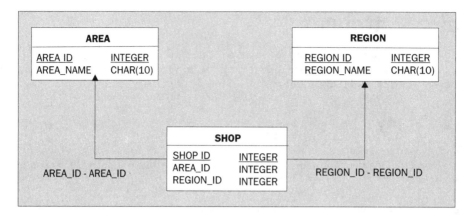

Although this might work, it's not ideal because once we know the area, we also know the region, so storing both the area and region in the shop table is violating third normal form – the region stored in the shop table depends on the area, which is not the primary key for the shop table:

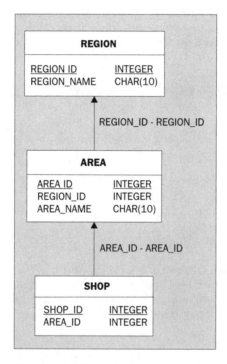

The design correctly shows the hierarchy of shop in area in region.

It may still be that you need to de-normalize this ideal design for performance reasons, and need to store the region_id in the shop. In this case, you should write a trigger to ensure that the region_id stored in the shop table is always correctly aligned with that found by looking for the region via the area table. What we would have done is added cost to the design, and increased the complexity of updates, in order to reduce the database query costs.

# Recursive Relationships

Our last pattern is not quite as common as the other two, but occurs frequently in a couple of situations, representing the hierarchy of staff in a company, and 'parts explosion', where parts in an `item` table are themselves composed of other parts from the same table.

Let us consider the staff example. All staff, from the most junior to senior managers, have many attributes in common, such as name, employee number, salary, grades, and addresses, therefore it seems logical to have a single table that is common to all members of staff to store those details. How do we then store the hierarchy of management, particularly as different areas of the company may have a different number of levels of management to be represented?

The answer is a recursive relationship, where each entry for a member of staff in the `person` table stores a `manager_id`, to record the person who is their manager. The clever bit is that the managers' information is stored in the same `person` table, generating a recursive relationship. So to find a person's manager, we pick up their `manager_id`, and look back in the same table for that to appear as an `emp_id`. We have stored a complex relationship, with an arbitrary number of levels in a simple one-table structure:

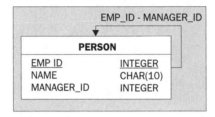

Suppose we wanted to represent a hierarchy like this:

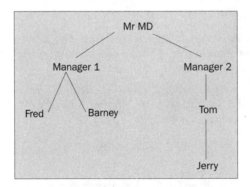

We would insert rows like this:

```
test=# INSERT INTO person(emp_id, name, manager_id) VALUES(1, 'Mr MD', NULL);
test=# INSERT INTO person(emp_id, name, manager_id) VALUES(2, 'Manager1', 1);
test=# INSERT INTO person(emp_id, name, manager_id) VALUES(3, 'Manager2', 1);
test=# INSERT INTO person(emp_id, name, manager_id) VALUES(4, 'Fred', 2);
test=# INSERT INTO person(emp_id, name, manager_id) VALUES(5, 'Barney', 2);
test=# INSERT INTO person(emp_id, name, manager_id) VALUES(6, 'Tom', 3);
test=# INSERT INTO person(emp_id, name, manager_id) VALUES(7, 'Jerry', 6);
```

**347**

Notice that the first number, emp_id is unique, but the second number is the emp_id of the manager next up the hierarchy. For example, Tom has an emp_id of 6, but a manager_id of 3, the emp_id of Manager2, since this is his manager.

This is fine until we need to extract data from this hierarchy. That is, when we need to join the person table to itself, a **self join**. To do this we need to alias the table names, as we saw earlier, and we can write the SQL like this:

```
test=# SELECT n1.name AS "Manager", n2.name AS "Subordinate" FROM person n1,
test-# person n2 WHERE n1.emp_id = n2.manager_id;
```

We are creating two alternative names for the person table, n1 and n2, and then we can join the emp_id column to the manager_id column. We also name our columns, using AS, to make the output more meaningful.

Which gives us a complete list of the hierarchy in our person table:

```
   Manager   | Subordinate
-------------+-------------
 Mr MD       | Manager1
 Mr MD       | Manager2
 Manager1    | Fred
 Manager1    | Barney
 Manager2    | Tom
 Tom         | Jerry
(6 rows)
```

# Resources

A couple of good books that deal with design issues are :

❑ *Database Design for Mere Mortals*, Michael J. Hernandez. Addison-Wesley (ISBN 0-201-69471-9). Covers the topic of obtaining design information, documenting it, and database design in far more detail than we have space to cover here, and

❑ *The Practical SQL handbook*, Judith S. Bowman, Sandra L. Emerson and Marcy Darnovsky. Addison-Wesley (ISBN 0-201-44787-8). This book has a short, but well written, section on database design and normalization.

# Summary

In this chapter, we have taken an all too brief look at database design, from capturing requirements, through generating a conceptual design and finally converting the conceptual design into a physical database design or schema. Along the way, we covered selecting candidate keys, primary keys, and foreign keys.

We also looked at choosing data types for our columns, and talked about the importance of consistency in database design.

We briefly mentioned normal forms, an important foundation of good design with relational databases. Finally, we looked at three common problem patterns that appear in database design, and how they are conventionally solved.

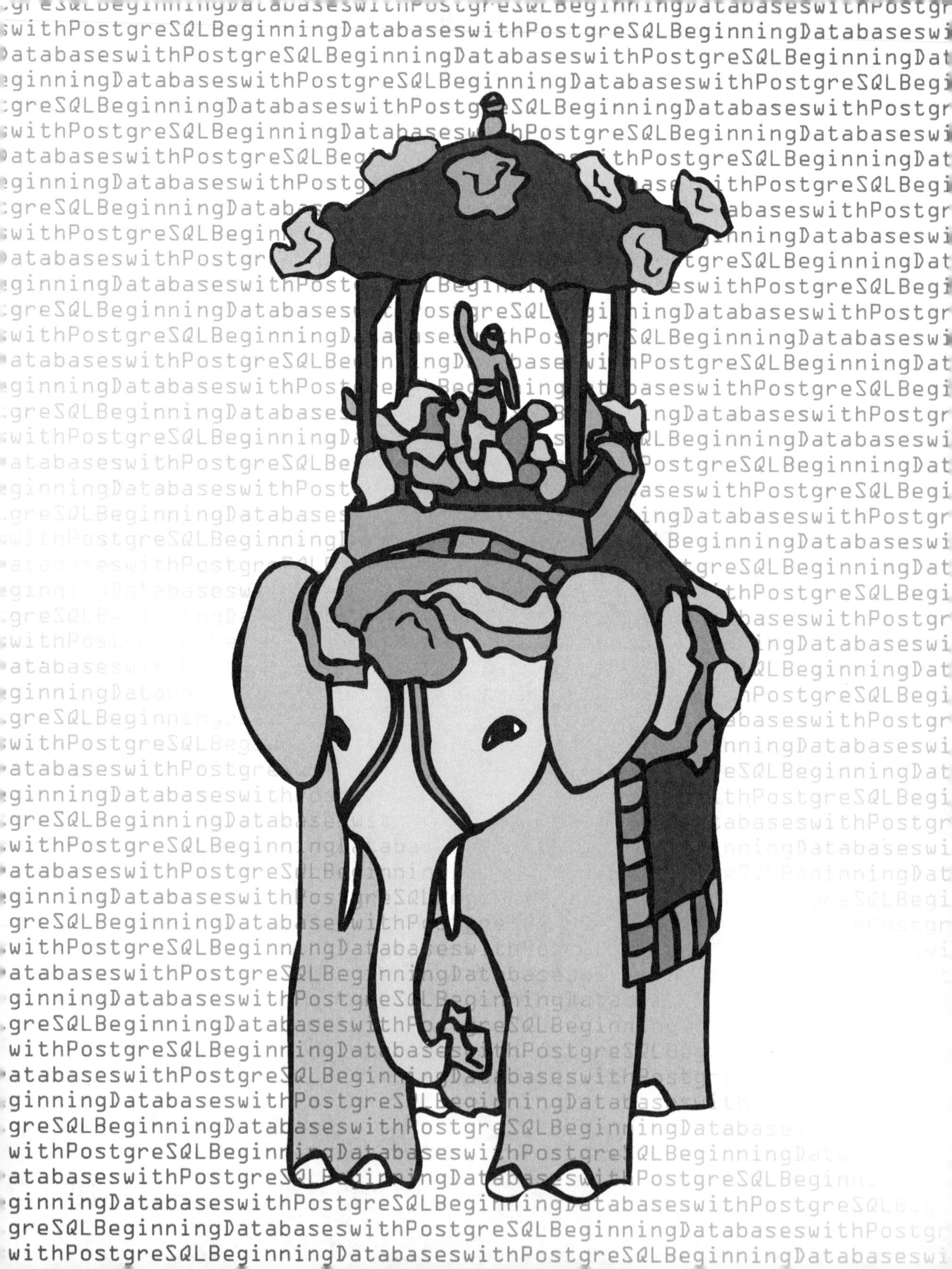
BeginningDatabaseswithPostgreSQL

# Accessing PostgreSQL From C Using libpq

In this chapter, we are going to start looking at ways to create our own client applications for PostgreSQL. Up until now, we have mostly used either command line applications such as psql that are part of the PostgreSQL distribution, or graphical tools such as pgAdmin that have been developed specifically for PostgreSQL. General-purpose tools such as Microsoft Access and Sun StarOffice, can also be used to view and update data via ODBC links, and to create applications. If we want complete control over our client applications, then we can consider making our own. That's where libpq comes in.

Recall that a PostgreSQL system is built around a client-server model. Client programs, such as psql and pgAdmin could run on one machine, maybe a desktop PC running Windows, and the PostgreSQL server itself could run on a UNIX or Linux server. The client programs send requests across a network to the server. These messages are effectively just the same as the SELECT or other SQL statements that we have used in psql. The server sends back resultsets that the client then displays.

Messages that are conveyed between PostgreSQL clients and the server are formatted and transported according to a particular protocol. The client-server protocol (which has no official name, but is sometimes referred to as the Frontend/Backend protocol) makes sure that appropriate action is taken, should messages get lost, and it ensures that results are always delivered complete. It can also cope, to a degree, with client and server version mismatches. Clients developed to work with PostgreSQL 6.4 or later should inter-work with later versions without too many problems.

Routines for sending and receiving these messages are included in the libpq library. To write a client application, all we have to do is use these routines and link our application with the library. We are going to assume some knowledge of the C programming language.

The functions provided by the libpq library fall into three distinct categories:

❑ Connecting to a database and managing the connection

❑ Executing SQL statements

❑ Reading the resultsets obtained from queries

As with many products that have grown and evolved over many releases, there is often more than one way of doing the same thing in libpq. Here we will concentrate on the most common methods and provide hints concerning alternatives and where they might be useful.

# Using the libpq Library

All PostgreSQL client applications that use the libpq library must include the appropriate header file, which defines the functions libpq provides, and link with the correct library, which contains the code for those functions.

Client applications are known as **frontend** (fe) programs to PostgreSQL and must include the header file libpq-fe.h. This header file provides definitions of the libpq functions and hides the internal workings of PostgreSQL that may well change between releases. The header file libpq-int.h that is also provided with the PostgreSQL distribution includes definitions of the internal structures that libpq uses, but it is not recommended that it be used in normal client applications.

Sticking with libpq-fe.h will ensure that your programs will compile with future releases of libpq. The header files are installed in the include subdirectory of your PostgreSQL installation (the default is /usr/local/pgsql/include). We need to direct the C compiler to this directory so that it can find the header files using the -I option.

The libpq library will be installed in the lib directory of your PostgreSQL installation (the default is /usr/local/pgsql/lib). To incorporate the libpq functions in your application, you need to link against that library. The simplest way is to tell the compiler to link with -lpq and specify the PostgreSQL library directory as a place to look for libraries by using the -L option.

A typical libpq program has this structure:

```
#include <libpq-fe.h>

main()
{
    /* Connect to a PostgreSQL database */

    LOOP:
    /* Execute SQL statement */
        /* Read query results */

    /* Disconnect from database */
}
```

The program would be compiled and linked into an executable program by using a command line similar to this:

```
$ gcc -o program program.c -I/usr/local/pgsql/include -L/usr/local/pgsql/lib -lpq
```

On a Red Hat Linux distribution, the libpq library is installed in a location that the compiler searches by default, so you need only specify the include directory option like this:

```
$ gcc -o program program.c -I/usr/local/pgsql/include -lpq
```

Other Linux distributions may place the include files and libraries in different places. On Microsoft Windows, using the Cygwin tools include files that are in /usr/include/postgresql and libraries are in /usr/lib.

We'll see later that, using a Makefile can make building PostgreSQL applications a little easier.

# Database Connections

In general, a PostgreSQL client application may connect to one or more databases as it runs. In fact, we can connect to many databases managed by many different servers all at the same time if we need to. The libpq library provides functions to create and maintain these connections.

When we connect to a PostgreSQL database on a server, libpq returns a handle to that database connection. This is represented by an internal structure defined in the header file as PGconn and we can think of it as an analog to a file handle. Many of the libpq functions require a PGconn pointer argument to identify the particular database connection we want to operate on, in much the same way that the standard I/O library in C uses a FILE pointer.

We create a new database connection using PQconnectdb:

```
PGconn *PQconnectdb(const char *conninfo);
```

The PQconnnectdb function returns a pointer to the new connection descriptor. The return result will be NULL if, for some reason, a new descriptor could not be allocated, perhaps if there is a lack of memory to allocate the new descriptor. A non-NULL pointer returned from PQconnectdb does not mean that the connection succeeded however, as we shall see in a moment.

The single argument to PQconnectdb is a string that specifies to which database to connect. It has embedded in it various options we can use to modify the way the connection is made. The conninfo string argument consists of space-separated options of the form option=value. The most commonly used options and their meaning are given in the table below:

| Option | Meaning | Default |
|---|---|---|
| dbname | Database to connect to | $PGDATABASE |
| user | User name to use when connecting | $PGUSER |
| password | Password for the specified user | $PGPASSWORD or none |
| host | Name of the server to connect to | $PGHOST or localhost |
| hostaddr | IP address of the server to connect to | $PGHOSTADDR |
| port | TCP/IP port to connect to on the server | $PGPORT or 5432 |

To connect to the bpsimple database on the local machine, we would use a conninfo string like this:

```
"dbname=bpsimple"
```

To include spaces in our option values, or to enter an empty value, the value must be quoted with single quotes, like this:

```
"host=monster password='' user=rick"
```

The host option names the server we want to connect to. The PQconnectdb call will result in a name lookup to determine the IP address of the server, so that the connection can be made. Usually, this is done by using DNS, the Domain Naming Service, and can take a short while to complete. If you already know the IP address of the server, you can use the hostaddr option to specify the address and, thus, avoid any delay while a name lookup takes place. The format of the hostaddr value is a **dotted quad**, the normal way of writing an IP address as four byte values separated by dots:

```
"hostaddr=192.168.0.22 dbname=neil"
```

If no `host` or `hostaddr` option is specified then `PQconnectdb` will try to connect to the local machine.

By default, a PostgreSQL server will listen for client connections on TCP port 5432. If you need to connect to a server listening on a non-default port number you can specify this with the `port` option.

The options can also be specified by using environment variables as listed in the table above. If for example, there is no `host` option set in the `conninfo` argument, then `PQconnectdb` will interrogate the environment to see if the variable `PGHOST` is set. If it is, the value `$PGHOST` will be used as the host name to connect to. We could then code a client program to call `PQconnectdb` with an empty string and provide all the options by environment variable:

```c
#include <libpq-fe.h>

int main()
{
    PGconn *conn = PQconnectdb("");
    ...
}
```

```
$ PGHOST=monster PGUSER=neil ./program
```

As mentioned earlier, the fact that `PQconnectdb` returns a non-NULL connection handle does not mean that the connection was made without error.

We need to use another function to check the state of our connection. This is `PQstatus`:

```c
ConnStatusType PQstatus(const PGconn *conn);
```

The `ConnStatusType` is an enumerated type that includes the following constants:

```
CONNECTION_OK
CONNECTION_BAD
```

For connection descriptors returned by `PQconnectdb` the status will be one of these two values, depending on whether connection succeeded or not. There are other status values in `ConnStatusType` that are used for other connection methods.

When we have finished with a database connection we must close it, as we would with open file descriptors. We do this by passing the connection descriptor pointer to `PQfinish`:

```c
void PQfinish(PGconn *conn);
```

A call to `PQfinish` allows the `libpq` library to release resources being consumed by the connection.

We can now write possibly the shortest useful PostgreSQL program (`connect.c`), which can be used to check whether a connection can be made to a particular database. We will use environment variables to pass options in to `PQconnectdb`, but we could consider using command line arguments or even hard-coding if it was appropriate for our application:

```
#include <stdlib.h>
#include <libpq-fe.h>

int main()
{
  PGconn *myconnection = PQconnectdb("");
  if(PQstatus(myconnection) == CONNECTION_OK)
    printf("connection made\n");
  else
    printf("connection failed\n");
  PQfinish(myconnection);
  return EXIT_SUCCESS;
}
```

```
$ gcc -o connect connect.c -lpq
$ ./connect
connection failed
$ PGDATABASE=bpsimple PGUSER=neil ./connect
connection made
$
```

# Makefile

In the earlier program, we omitted the -L and -I options to the compiler to aid readability. Always remember, that these are required to compile programs using libpq. If you use a Makefile to control the compilation, you can add them to the CFLAGS and LDLIBS variables respectively.

Here is an extremely simple Makefile that can be used to compile all of the sample programs in this chapter. You can download it and the source code to the examples from the Wrox web site (http://www.wrox.com):

```
# Makefile for sample programs
# in Beginning PostgreSQL

# Edit the base directories for your
# PostgreSQL installation

INC=/usr/local/pgsql/include
LIB=/usr/local/pgsql/lib

CFLAGS=-I$(INC)
LDLIBS=-L$(LIB) -lpq

ALL: async1 connect create cursor cursor2 print select1 select2          all:
$(ALL)

        clean  :
               @rm -f  *.o *~  $(ALL)
```

Now we can create a program with:

```
$ make program
```

# More Information

Note that both PQstatus and PQfinish can cope with a NULL pointer for the connection descriptor, so in this case, we do not check the return result from PQconnectdb is valid.

You can get a readable string that describes the state of the connection or an error that has occurred by calling PQerrorMessage:

```
char *PQerrorMessage(const PGconn *conn);
```

This function returns a pointer to a descriptive string. This string will be overwritten by other libpq functions, so it should be used, or copied, immediately after the call to PqerrorMessage, and before any call to other libpq functions. For example, we could have made our connection failure message rather more helpful, like this:

```
printf("connection failed: %s", PQerrorMessage(myconnection));
```

If you need more information about a connection after it has been made, you can consider using the members of the PGconn structure directly (defined in libpq-fe.h), but this would be a bad idea. Our code would probably break in some future release of libpq if the internal structure of PGconn changed.

We may have a genuine need to know more about the connection, so libpq provides a number of access functions that return the values of attributes of the connection:

```
char *PQdb(const PGconn *conn);
char *PQuser(const PGconn *conn);
char *PQpass(const PGconn *conn);
char *PQhost(const PGconn *conn);
char *PQport(const PGconn *conn);
char *PQoptions(const PGconn *conn);
```

These functions return respectively the database name, user name, user password, server name, server port number, and the options associated with a connection. All of these values will not change during the lifetime of a connection.

Should problems arise with a connection, it may be useful to attempt to reset it. The function PQreset is provided for this purpose. It will close the connection to the backend server and try to make a new connection with the same parameters that were used in the original connection setup:

```
void PQreset(PGconn *conn);
```

# Executing SQL with libpq

Now that we can connect to a PostgreSQL database from within a C program, the next step is to execute SQL statements. This is quite straightforward in fact, and our interface starts with the function PQexec:

```
PGresult *PQexec(PGconn *conn, const char *sql_string);
```

Essentially we pass a SQL statement to PQexec and the server we are connected to via the non-NULL connection conn executes it. The result is communicated via a result structure, a PGresult. On rare occasions, PQexec may return a NULL pointer if there is not enough memory to allocate a new result structure. Even when there is no data to return, PQexec will return a valid non-NULL pointer to a result structure that contains no data records.

We can determine the status of the SQL statement execution by probing the result with the function PQresultStatus that returns one of a number of values that make up the enumerated type ExecStatusType:

```
ExecStatusType PQresultStatus(const PGresult *result);
```

The status types include:

| Status Type | Description |
| --- | --- |
| PGRES_EMPTY_QUERY | Database access not required. Usually the result of an empty query string. |
| PGRES_COMMAND_OK | Success. Command does not return data. |
| PGRES_TUPLES_OK | Success. Query returned zero or more rows. |
| PGRES_BAD_RESPONSE | Failure, server response not understood. |
| PGRES_NONFATAL_ERROR | Failure, non-fatal, can be retried. |
| PGRES_FATAL_ERROR | Failure, fatal, cannot be retried. |

Other status types indicate some unexpected problem with the server, such as it being backed up or taken offline.

The status PGRES_EMPTY_QUERY often points to a problem with the client program, sending a query that requires the server to do no work at all.

The status PGRES_COMMAND_OK means that the SQL executed correctly, and the statement was of the type that does not return data, such as CREATE TABLE.

The status PGRES_TUPLES_OK means that the SQL executed OK, and is of a type that may return data, such as SELECT. It does not mean that there is, in this instance, data to return. We will have to make further enquiries to determine how much data is actually available.

The remaining status types PGRES_BAD_RESPONSE, PGRES_NONFATAL_ERROR, and PGRES_FATAL_ERROR indicate that the SQL failed to execute.

Here's an example code fragment that uses `PQresultStatus` to determine the precise results of a call to `PQexec`:

```
PGresult *result;
result  = PQexec(myconnection,
"SELECT customer_id FROM customer");
switch(PQresultStatus(result)) {
    case PGRES_TUPLES_OK:
            /* may have some data to process, find out */
            if(PQntuples(result)) {
                    /* process data */
                    break;
            }
            /* no data, drop through to no data case */
    case PGRES_COMMAND_OK:
            /* all OK, no data to process */
            break;
    case PGRES_EMPTY_QUERY:
            /* server had nothing to do, a bug maybe? */
            break;
    case PGRES_NONFATAL_ERROR:
            /* can continue, possibly retry the command */
            break;
    case PGRES_BAD_RESPONSE:
case PGRES_FATAL_ERROR:
default:
            /* fatal or unknown error, cannot continue */
}
```

We will cover `PQntuples` in more detail when we come back to the `PGRES_TUPLES_OK` case for `SELECT` later in the chapter.

One useful function that can aid with troubleshooting is `PQresStatus`. This function converts a result status code into a readable string:

```
const char *PQresStatus(ExecStatusType status);
```

When an error has occurred, you can retrieve a more detailed textual error message by calling `PQresultErrorMessage` in much the same way as we did for connections:

```
const char *PQresultErrorMessage(const PGresult *result);
```

As with connection structures, result objects must also be freed when you are finished with them. We can do this with `PQclear`, which will also handle `NULL` pointers. Note that results are not cleared automatically, even when the connection is closed, so they can be kept indefinitely if required:

```
void PQclear(PGresult *result);
```

Let's look at some simple examples of executing SQL statements. We will use a very small table in our `test` database as way of trying things out. Later, we will perform some operations on our sample `customer` table to return larger amounts of data.

We are going to create a database table called number. In it we will store numbers and an English description of them. The table will look like this:

```
value |     name
-------+-------------
   42 | The Answer
   29 | My Age
   66 | Clickety-Click
```

To create the table and insert values into it, we just need to call PQexec with an appropriate string containing the SQL query we need to execute. Our program will contain calls like this:

```
PGconn *myconnection;
...
PQexec(myconnection,"CREATE TABLE number ( value INTEGER, name
VARCHAR)");
PQexec(myconnection,"INSERT INTO number VALUES (42, 'The Answer')");
```

We will need to take care of errors that arise, for example if the table already exists we will get an error when we try to create it. In the case of creating the number table when it already exists, PQresultErrorMessage will return a string that says:

```
ERROR:  Relation 'number' already exists
```

To make things a little easier, we will develop a function of our own to execute SQL statements, check the results, and print errors. We will add more functionality to it as we go along. Here's a first version:

Now we can execute SQL queries almost as easily as we can enter commands to psql. Save this code in a file called create.c:

```c
#include<stdlib.h>
#include<libpq-fe.h>

void doSQL(PGconn *conn, char *command)
{
  PGresult *result;

  printf("%s\n", command);

  result = PQexec(conn, command);
  printf("status is %s\n", PQresStatus(PQresultStatus(result)));
  printf("result message: %s\n", PQresultErrorMessage(result));
  PQclear(result);
}

int main()
{
  PGresult *result;
  PGconn *conn;

  conn = PQconnectdb("");

  if(PQstatus(conn) == CONNECTION_OK) {
    printf("connection made\n");
```

```
        /* doSQL(conn, "DROP TABLE number"); */
        doSQL(conn, "CREATE TABLE number (
                        value INTEGER,
                        name  VARCHAR
                    )");
        doSQL(conn, "INSERT INTO number values(42, 'The Answer')");
        doSQL(conn, "INSERT INTO number values(29, 'My Age')");
        doSQL(conn, "INSERT INTO number values(29, 'Anniversary')");
        doSQL(conn, "INSERT INTO number values(66, 'Clickety-Click')");
    }
    else
        printf("connection failed %s\n", PQerrorMessage(conn));

    PQfinish(conn);
    return EXIT_SUCCESS;
}
```

Here we create the number table and add some entries to it. If we rerun the program, we will see a fatal error reported, as we cannot create the table a second time. Uncomment the DROP TABLE command to change the program into one that destroys and re-creates the table each time it is run.

Of course, in production code we would not be quite so cavalier in our approach to errors. Here we have omitted to return a result from doSQL to keep things brief and we push on regardless of failures.

When we compile and run this program, we should see the command being executed and some status information:

```
$ make create
$ PGDATABASE=bpsimple ./create
connection made
...
INSERT INTO number VALUES(66, 'Clickety-Click')
status is PGRES_COMMAND_OK
result message:
$
```

To include user-specified data into the SQL, we have to create a string to pass to PQexec that contains the values we want. To add all single digit integers we might write:

```
for(n = 0; n < 10; n++) {
     sprintf(buffer,
"INSERT INTO number VALUES(%d, 'single digit')", n);
     PQexec(buffer);
}
```

If we want to update or delete rows in a table, we can use the UPDATE and DELETE commands respectively:

```
UPDATE number SET name = 'Zaphod' WHERE value = 42
DELETE FROM number WHERE value = 29
```

If we add suitable calls to PQexec (or doSQL) to our program we will first change the descriptive text of the number 42 to Zaphod, and then delete both of the entries for 29. We can check the result of our changes using psql:

```
$ psql -d bpsimple
bpsimple=# SELECT * FROM number;
 value |       name
-------+----------------
    66 | Clickety-Click
    42 | Zaphod

bpsimple=#
```

DELETE and UPDATE may affect more than one row in the table (or **tuples** as PostgreSQL likes to call them), therefore it is often useful to know how many rows have been changed. We can get this information by calling PQcmdTuples:

```
const char *PQcmdTuples(const PGresult *result);
```

Strangely perhaps, PQcmdTuples returns not an integer as you might expect but a string containing the digits. We can modify doSQL function to report the rows affected very simply:

```
printf("#rows affected %s\n", PQcmdTuples(result));
```

We will now see that PQcmdTuples returns an empty string for commands that do not have any effect on rows at all – like CREATE TABLE, and the strings "1" and "2" for those that do (the INSERT and DELETE commands).

We have to be careful to distinguish commands that affect no rows, and those that fail and therefore affect no rows. We must always check the result status to determine errors, rather than the rows affected.

# Transactions

Sometimes we will want to ensure that a group of SQL commands are executed as a group, so that the changes to the database are made either all together or none at all if an error occurs at some point.

As in standard SQL, we can manage this with libpq by using the transaction support. We simply arrange to call PQexec with SQL statements that contain BEGIN, COMMIT, and ROLLBACK:

```
PQexec(conn, "BEGIN WORK");

/* make changes */

if(we changed our minds) {
      PQexec(conn, "ROLLBACK WORK");
}
else {
      PQexec(conn, "COMMIT WORK");
}
```

We have already discussed transactions and locking in detail in Chapter 9. We can use all of the facilities described there in our libpq programs by passing the appropriate SQL query string to PQexec.

# Extracting Data from Queries

Up until now, we have only been concerned with SQL statements that have not returned any data. Now it is time to consider how to deal with data returned by calls to PQexec, that is the results of SELECT statements.

When we perform a SELECT with Pqexec, the resultset will contain information about the data the query has returned.

Query results can seem a little tiresome to handle, as we do not always know exactly what to expect. If we execute a SELECT, we do not know in advance whether we will be returned zero, one, or several millions of rows. If we use a wildcard (*) in the SELECT, we do not even know what columns will be returned, and what their names are.

In general, we will want to program our application so that it selects specified columns only. That way, if the database design changes, perhaps when new columns are added, then a function that does not rely on the new column will still work as expected.

Sometimes (for example, if you are writing a general-purpose SQL program that is taking statements from the user and displaying results) it would be better if we could program in a general way, and with libpq, we can. There are just a few more functions to get to know.

When PQexec executes a SELECT without an error, we expect to see a result status of PGRES_TUPLES_OK. The next step is to determine how many rows are present in the resultset. We do this by calling PQntuples:

```
int PQntuples(const PGresult *result);
```

This will give us the total number of rows in our result, which may of course be zero.
We can retrieve the number of fields (attributes or columns) in our tuples by calling PQnfields:

```
int PQnfields(const PGresult *result);
```

The fields in the result are numbered starting from zero, and we can retrieve their names calling PQfname:

```
char *PQfname(const PGresult *result, int index);
```

The size of the field is given by PQfsize:

```
int PQfsize(const PGresult *result, int index);
```

For fixed sized fields, PQfsize returns the number of bytes that a value in that particular column would occupy. For variable length fields PQfsize returns −1.

Should we ever need to, we can retrieve the index number for a column with a given name by calling PQfnumber:

```
int PQfnumber(const PGresult *result, const char *field);
```

Let's modify our doSQL function to print out some information about the data returned from a SELECT query. Here's our next version:

```
void doSQL(PGconn *conn, char *command);
{
  PGresult *result;

  printf("%s\n", command);

  result = PQexec(conn, command);
  printf("status is %s\n", PQresStatus(PQresultStatus(result)));
  printf("#rows affected %s\n", PQcmdTuples(result));
  printf("result message: %s\n", PQresultErrorMessage(result));

  switch(PQresultStatus(result)) {
  case PGRES_TUPLES_OK:
    {
      int n = 0;
      int nrows = PQntuples(result);
      int nfields = PQnfields(result);
      printf("number of rows returned = %d\n", nrows);
      printf("number of fields returned = %d\n", nfields);
      /* Print the field names */
      for(n = 0; n < nfields; n++) {
          printf(" %s:%d",
                  PQfname(result, n), PQfsize(result, n));
      }
      printf("\n");
    }
  }
  PQclear(result);
}
```

Now when we execute a SELECT, we can see the characteristics of the data being returned:

```
doSQL(conn, "SELECT * FROM number WHERE value = 29");
```

The call above results in the following output:

```
status is PGRES_TUPLES_OK
#rows affected
result message:
number of rows returned = 2
number of fields returned = 2
 value:4 name:-1
```

Notice that an empty string is returned by PQcmdTuples for queries that cannot affect rows, and PQresultErrorMessage returns an empty string where there is no error. Now we are ready to extract the data from the fields returned in the rows of our resultset. The rows are numbered, starting from zero.

Normally all data is transferred from the server as strings. We can get at a character representation of the data by calling the function PQgetvalue:

```
char *PQgetvalue(const PGresult *result, int tuple, int field);
```

If we need to know in advance how long the string returned by `PQgetvalue` is going to be, we can call `PQgetlength`:

```
int PQgetlength(const PGresult *result, int tuple, int field);
```

As mentioned earlier, both the tuple (row) number and field (column) number start at zero.

Let's add some data display to our `doSQL` function:

```
void doSQL(PGconn *conn, char *command)
{
  PGresult *result;

  printf("%s\n", command);

  result = PQexec(conn, command);
  printf("status is %s\n", PQresStatus(PQresultStatus(result)));
  printf("#rows affected %s\n", PQcmdTuples(result));
  printf("result message: %s\n", PQresultErrorMessage(result));

  switch(PQresultStatus(result)) {
  case PGRES_TUPLES_OK:
    {
      int r, n;
      int nrows = PQntuples(result);
      int nfields = PQnfields(result);
      printf("number of rows returned = %d\n", nrows);
      printf("number of fields returned = %d\n", nfields);
      for(r = 0; r < nrows; r++) {
        for(n = 0; n < nfields; n++)
          printf(" %s = %s(%d),",
              PQfname(result, n),
              PQgetvalue(result, r, n),
              PQgetlength(result, r, n));
        printf("\n");
      }
    }
  }
  PQclear(result);
}
```

The complete result of the `SELECT` query is printed, including the lengths of the strings containing the data:

```
SELECT * FROM number WHERE value = 29
Status is PGRES_TUPLES_OK
#rows affected
result message:
number of rows returned = 2
number of fields returned = 2
 value = 29(2), name = My Age(6),
 value = 29(2), name = Anniversary(11),
```

Note that the length of the data string does not include a trailing null, which is present in the string returned by PQgetvalue.

> **String data, such as that used in columns defined as CHAR(n), is padded with spaces. This can give unexpected results if you are checking for a particular string value or comparing values for a sort. If you insert the value 'Zaphod' into a column defined as CHAR(8) you will get back "Zaphod<space><space>" which will not compare equal to "Zaphod" if you use the C library function strcmp. This little problem has been known to catch out some very experienced developers.**

There is one small complication that we must deal with before we go any further. The fact that our query results are being returned to us encoded within character strings, means that we cannot readily tell the difference between an empty string and an SQL NULL value.

Fortunately, the libpq library provides us with a function that we can call to determine whether a particular value of a field in a resultset tuple is a NULL:

```
int PQgetisnull(const PGresult *result, int tuple, int field);
```

We should call PQgetisnull when retrieving any field that may possibly be NULL. It returns 1 if the field contains a NULL value, 0 otherwise. The inner loop of the last example program would then become:

```
for(n = 0; n < nfields; n++) {
    if(PQgetisnull(result, r, n))
        printf(" %s is NULL,", PQfname(result, n));
    else
      printf(" %s = %s(%d),",
        PQfname(result, n),
        PQgetvalue(result, r, n),
        PQgetlength(result, r, n));
}
```

# Printing Query Results

The functions we have covered so far are sufficient to query and extract data from a PostgreSQL database. If all we want to do is print the results, we can consider taking advantage of a printing function supplied by libpq that outputs resultsets in a fairly basic form.

The PQprint function formats a resultset in a tabular form, similar to that used by psql and sends it to a specified output stream. The function is:

```
void PQprint(FILE *output, const PGresult *result, const PQprintOpt *options);
```

PQprint is no longer actively supported by the PostgreSQL maintainers however and care needs to be taken not to rely on it for production code. If you'd like to try it out, the arguments are an open file handle (output) to print to, a resultset (result) and a pointer to a structure that contains options that control the printing format (options). The structure is:

```
struct {
    pqbool header;           /* print out names of columns in a header */F
    pqbool align;            /* pad out the values to make them line up */
    pqbool html3;            /* format as an HTML table */
    pqbool expanded;  /* expand tables */
    pqbool pager;            /* use pager for output if needed */
    char *fieldSep;   /* field separator */
    char *tableOpt;   /* options for HTML table - place in <TABLE …> */
    char *caption;    /* HTML <caption> */
    char **fieldName;        /* Replacement set of field names */
} PQprintOpt;
```

The members of the PQprintOpt structure are fairly straightforward. The header member, if set non-zero, causes the first row of the output table to consist of the field names, which can be overridden by setting the fieldName list of strings.

Each row in the output table consists of field values separated by the string fieldSep and padded out to align with the other rows if align is non-zero.

Example output might look like this:

```
+-------------+-------+-----------+--
| customer_id | title | fname     | town       | zipcode | phone    |
+-------------+-------+-----------+--
|           1 | Miss  | Jenny     | Hightown   | NT2 1AQ | 023 9876 |
+-------------+-------+-----------+--
|           3 | Miss  | Alex      | Nicetown   | NT2 2TX | 010 4567 |
+-------------+-------+-----------+--
```

If the output is likely to be very long you can set pager to a non-zero value to ask for the output to be paged, that is passed through a filter that pauses the output every page or so. If expanded is set non-zero, the output format is changed to list each field in each row on a line by itself.

We can produce HTML output suitable for inclusion in web page if we set html3 non-zero. We can specify table options and a caption by setting the tableOpt and caption strings.

Here's an example program (print.c) using PQprint to generate the HTML output:

```c
#include <stdlib.h>
#include <libpq-fe.h>

int main()
{
  PGresult *result;
  PGconn *conn;

  conn = PQconnectdb("");
  if(PQstatus(conn) == CONNECTION_OK) {
    printf("connection made\n");

    result = PQexec(conn, "SELECT * FROM customer
                          WHERE town = 'Bingham'");

    {
      PQprintOpt pqp;
      pqp.header = 1;
```

```
            pqp.align = 1;
            pqp.html3 = 1;
            pqp.expanded = 0;
            pqp.pager = 0;
            pqp.fieldSep = "";
            pqp.tableOpt = "align=center";
            pqp.caption = "Bingham Customer List";
            pqp.fieldName = NULL;
            printf("<HTML><HEAD><TITLE>Customers</TITLE></HEAD><BODY>\n");
            PQprint(stdout, result, &pqp);
            printf("</BODY></HTML>\n");
        }

    }

    PQfinish(conn);
    return EXIT_SUCCESS;
}
```

The output of the above program is HTML code, which is displayed onto the screen (`stdout`). The output is as follows:

```
$ PGDATABASE=bpsimple  ./print
```

```
<HTML><HEAD></HEAD><BODY>
<table align=center><caption align=high>Bingham Customer List</caption>
<tr><th align=right>customer_id</th><th align=left>title</th><th align=left>fnam
e</th><th align=left>lname</th><th align=left>addressline</th><th align=left>tow
n</th><th align=left>zipcode</th><th align=right>phone</th></tr>
<tr><td align=right>7</td><td align=left>Mr  </td><td align=left>Richard</td><td
 align=left>Stones</td><td align=left>34 Holly Way</td><td align=left>Bingham</t
d><td align=left>BG4 2WE   </td><td align=right>342 5982</td></tr>
<tr><td align=right>8</td><td align=left>Mrs </td><td align=left>Ann</td><td ali
gn=left>Stones</td><td align=left>34 Holly Way</td><td align=left>Bingham</td><t
d align=left>BG4 2WE   </td><td align=right>342 5982</td></tr>
<tr><td align=right>11</td><td align=left>Mr  </td><td align=left>Dave</td><td a
lign=left>Jones</td><td align=left>54 Vale Rise</td><td align=left>Bingham</td><
td align=left>BG3 8GD   </td><td align=right>342 8264</td></tr>
</table>
</BODY></HTML>
```

To view this on a browser, all we have to do is to redirect the output of the program to a file (say `list.html`) and then view it. The following command illustrates this:

```
$ PGDATABASE=bpsimple ./print > list.html
```

Here is what the HTML page looks like when viewed in a browser:

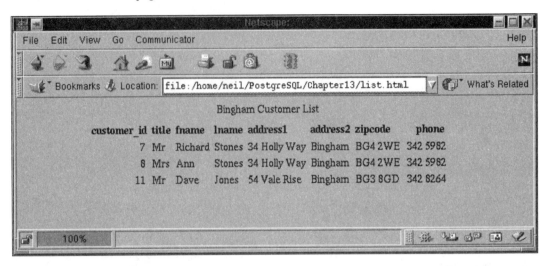

# Cursors

In the real world, when we are writing complete applications, we may find that we need to deal with large quantities of data. A PostgreSQL database is capable of storing tables with very large numbers of rows in them.

When it comes to processing the results of queries that produce a large amount of data however, we are rather at the mercy of the client application and its operating environment. A desktop PC may well have trouble dealing with a million tuples returned all at once in a resultset from a single SELECT. A large resultset can consume a great deal of memory, and, if we are running across a network, may consume a lot of bandwidth and take a substantial time to be transferred.

What we really need to do, is perform the query and deal with the results bit-by-bit. For example, if in our application we want to show our complete customer list, we could retrieve all them in one go. It is smarter to fetch them, say, a page of 25 at a time and display them in our application page by page.

We can do this with libpq by employing cursors. Cursors are an excellent general-purpose way of catering for an unknown number of rows being returned. If you search for a Zip code, particularly one provided by a user, you have no idea in advance if zero, one, or many rows will be returned.

In general, you should avoid writing code that assumes either a single row or no rows are returned from a SELECT statement, unless that statement is a simple aggregate, such as SELECT COUNT(*) FROM type query, or a SELECT on a primary key where you can be guaranteed the result will always be exactly one row. If in doubt, use a cursor.

To deal with multiple rows being returned from a query, we will retrieve them one (or more) at a time using a FETCH, with the column values being received into a resultset in the same way that we have seen for all-at-once SELECTs.

We will declare a cursor to be used to scroll through a collection of returned rows. The cursor will act as our bookmark and we will fetch the rows until no more data is available.

To use a cursor, we must declare it and specify the query that it relates to. We may only use a cursor declaration within a PostgreSQL transaction, so we must begin a transaction too:

```
PQexec(conn, "BEGIN work");
PQexec(conn, "DECLARE mycursor CURSOR FOR SELECT ..."
```

Now we can start to retrieve the result rows. We do this by executing a FETCH to extract the data rows as many at a time as we wish (including all that remain):

```
result = PQexec(conn, "FETCH 1 IN mycursor");
result = PQexec(conn, "FETCH 4 IN mycursor");
result = PQexec(conn, "FETCH ALL IN mycursor");
```

The resultset will indicate that it contains no rows when all of the rows from the query have been retrieved.

When we have finished with the cursor, we close it and end the transaction:

```
PQexec(conn, "COMMIT work");
PQexec(conn, "CLOSE mycursor");
```

Here is an example program that queries and processes the customer list from the bpsimple database page by page using a cursor.

The general approach is to structure our programs like this:

```
#include <libpq-fe.h>

main()
{
    /* Connect to a PostgreSQL database */

    /* Create cursor for SQL SELECT statement */
    DO
            /* Fetch batch of query results */
            /* Process query results */

        UNTIL no more results
        /* close cursor */

    /* Disconnect from database */
}
```

For each of the batches of query results we fetch, we will have access to a PGresult pointer that we can use in exactly the same way as before. Let's see a cursor in use (in cursor.c), first of all fetching all the results at once to make sure we've got the SQL correct:

```
#include <stdlib.h>
#include <libpq-fe.h>

void doSQL(PGconn *conn, char *command)
{
  PGresult *result;
```

```
  printf("%s\n", command);

  result = PQexec(conn, command);
  printf("status is %s\n", PQresStatus(PQresultStatus(result)));
  printf("#rows affected %s\n", PQcmdTuples(result));
  printf("result message: %s\n", PQresultErrorMessage(result));

  switch(PQresultStatus(result)) {
  case PGRES_TUPLES_OK:
    {
      int r, n;
      int nrows = PQntuples(result);
      int nfields = PQnfields(result);
      printf("number of rows returned = %d\n", nrows);
      printf("number of fields returned = %d\n", nfields);
      for(r = 0; r < nrows; r++) {
      for(n = 0; n < nfields; n++)
        printf(" %s = %s(%d),",
               PQfname(result, n),
               PQgetvalue(result, r, n),
               PQgetlength(result, r, n));
      printf("\n");
       }
    }
  }
  PQclear(result);
}

int main()
{
  PGresult *result;
  PGconn *conn;

  conn = PQconnectdb("");

  if(PQstatus(conn) == CONNECTION_OK) {
    printf("connection made\n");

    doSQL(conn, "BEGIN work");
    doSQL(conn, "DECLARE mycursor CURSOR FOR "
                      "SELECT fname, lname FROM customer");
    doSQL(conn, "FETCH ALL IN mycursor");
    doSQL(conn, "COMMIT work");
    doSQL(conn, "CLOSE mycursor");

  }
  else
    printf("connection failed\n");

  PQfinish(conn);
  return EXIT_SUCCESS;
}
```

When we execute this program, we see the customers listed all at once:

```
connection made
DECLARE mycursor CURSOR FOR SELECT fname, lname FROM customer
status is PGRES_COMMAND_OK
#rows affected
result message:
BEGIN work
status is PGRES_COMMAND_OK
#rows affected
result message:
FETCH ALL IN mycursor
status is PGRES_TUPLES_OK
#rows affected
result message:
number of rows returned = 15
number of fields returned = 2
 fname = Jenny(5), lname = Stones(6),
 fname = Andrew(6), lname = Stones(6),
 fname = Adrian(6), lname = Matthew(7),
 fname = Simon(5), lname = Cozens(6),
 fname = Neil(4), lname = Matthew(7),
 fname = Richard(7), lname = Stones(6),
 fname = Ann(3), lname = Stones(6),
 fname = Christine(9), lname = Hickman(7),
 fname = Mike(4), lname = Howard(6),
 fname = Dave(4), lname = Jones(5),
 fname = Richard(7), lname = Neill(5),
 fname = Laura(5), lname = Hendy(5),
 fname = Bill(4), lname = O'Neill(7),
 fname = David(5), lname = Hudson(6),
 fname = Alex(4), lname = Matthew(7),
COMMIT work
status is PGRES_COMMAND_OK
#rows affected
result message:
CLOSE mycursor
status is PGRES_COMMAND_OK
#rows affected
result message:
```

To modify the program to deal with the results, say four at a time, we need to be able to tell when we have retrieved all of the results. This was easy when we were handling all of them at once, since PQntuples will tell us how many results there are in our set. If we fetch results four at a time, then PQntuples will return four, for each batch of results except the last which will be less than four, possibly zero. This is the test we shall use (in cursor2.c). As our doSQL function does not return a result, we will handle the batches directly with PQexec:

```c
#include <stdlib.h>
#include <libpq-fe.h>
void printTuples(PGresult *result)
{
        int r, n;
        int nrows = PQntuples(result);
        int nfields = PQnfields(result);
        printf("number of rows returned = %d\n", nrows);
```

```
        printf("number of fields returned = %d\n", nfields);
        for(r = 0; r < nrows; r++) {
      for(n = 0; n < nfields; n++)
        printf(" %s = %s(%d),",
               PQfname(result, n),
               PQgetvalue(result, r, n),
               PQgetlength(result, r, n));
      printf("\n");
        }
}

void doSQL(PGconn *conn, char *command)
{
  PGresult *result;

  printf("%s\n", command);

  result = PQexec(conn, command);
  printf("status is %s\n", PQresStatus(PQresultStatus(result)));
  printf("#rows affected %s\n", PQcmdTuples(result));
  printf("result message: %s\n", PQresultErrorMessage(result));

  switch(PQresultStatus(result)) {
  case PGRES_TUPLES_OK:
    printTuples(result);
    break;
  }
  PQclear(result);
}

int main()
{
  PGresult *result;
  PGconn *conn;
  int ntuples = 0;

  conn = PQconnectdb("");

  if(PQstatus(conn) == CONNECTION_OK) {
    printf("connection made\n");

    doSQL(conn, "BEGIN work");
    doSQL(conn, "DECLARE mycursor CURSOR FOR "
                         "SELECT fname, lname FROM customer");
    do {
      result = PQexec(conn, "FETCH 4 IN mycursor");
      if(PQresultStatus(result) == PGRES_TUPLES_OK) {
          ntuples = PQntuples(result);
          printTuples(result);
          PQclear(result);
      }
      else ntuples = 0;
    } while(ntuples);

    doSQL(conn, "CLOSE mycursor");
    doSQL(conn, "COMMIT work");
```

```
  }
  else
    printf("connection failed\n");

  PQfinish(conn);
  return EXIT_SUCCESS;
}
```

With this version of the program, we can see several batches of four results processed at a time, followed by a short batch:

```
connection made
...
DECLARE mycursor CURSOR FOR SELECT fname, lname FROM customer
status is PGRES_COMMAND_OK
#rows affected
result message:
number of rows returned = 4
number of fields returned = 2
 fname = Jenny(5), lname = Stones(6),
 fname = Andrew(6), lname = Stones(6),
 fname = Adrian(6), lname = Matthew(7),
 fname = Simon(5), lname = Cozens(6),
number of rows returned = 4
number of fields returned = 2
 fname = Neil(4), lname = Matthew(7),
 fname = Richard(7), lname = Stones(6),
 fname = Ann(3), lname = Stones(6),
 fname = Christine(9), lname = Hickman(7),
number of rows returned = 4
number of fields returned = 2
 fname = Mike(4), lname = Howard(6),
 fname = Dave(4), lname = Jones(5),
 fname = Richard(7), lname = Neill(5),
 fname = Laura(5), lname = Hendy(5),
number of rows returned = 3
number of fields returned = 2
 fname = Bill(4), lname = O'Neill(7),
 fname = David(5), lname = Hudson(6),
 fname = Alex(4), lname = Matthew(7),
number of rows returned = 0
number of fields returned = 2
COMMIT work
status is PGRES_COMMAND_OK
#rows affected
result message:
...
$
```

We can use all of the options of FETCH that we saw earlier to fetch results one at a time (with the NEXT option), a batch at a time (by specifying a number), or all at once (with ALL).

# Binary Values

All of the data that we have dealt with in this chapter has been transferred in strings. We have created INSERT statements with values in strings and dealt with the results of a SELECT again in strings.

You might think that all this to-ing and fro-ing between formats is wasteful, wouldn't it be better to have a binary interface? If we want to insert or select a floating point value, such as average fuel consumption isn't it better to have it transferred directly from and to a C double?

The answer is "yes, and no". PostgreSQL does have in libpq some ability to deal with binary values, but the benefits are probably fairly slim. Currently, you can only retrieve binary values if you use a cursor and include the BINARY option in its declaration:

```
DECLARE mycursor BINARY CURSOR FOR...
```

Then the function PQbinaryTuples will confirm that a resultset returned from a FETCH of that cursor contains binary data:

```
int PQbinaryTuples(const PGresult *result);
```

Now, in the case where binary tuples are being used, PQgetvalue will return not a string pointer, but a pointer to a binary representation of the field, in the binary format native to the server. Dealing with issues, such as variable length data and the byte-ordering of multi-byte values (like currency data), can soon become decidedly messy. It is recommended that you stick with string representations when using libpq. We will see that when we discuss ecpg in the next chapter, we can handle binary values a little easier with embedded SQL.

# Asynchronous Functionality

All of the examples we have looked at so far are using the libpq functions in a blocking mode. This simply means that our programs call a libpq function and wait for it to return values. As we saw earlier, we might generate a large amount of data that may take some time to be received. In a single-threaded (normal) application, if we're using Pqexec, there is nothing we can do until PQexec returns. Our user must wait. It's also tricky to cancel a query if we no longer need the results. For most programs this will be sufficient, and short waits will not be a problem.

Fetching results a few at a time with a cursor is probably all you will need. In this section, we will cover a more advanced technique that can give you precise control over the behavior of your application if you need it.

An alternative approach to blocking, typically used for applications with a graphical user interface, is to run in a non-blocking mode. In this type of program, we are sent messages when something has happened and our application must respond to those messages. So, in a point-and-click application, we might be told when the user has pressed a mouse button, or entered data in a field, or moved a window, and so on.

The structure of a non-blocking program generally revolves around an event loop:

```
main()
{
    LOOP:
            /* wait for an event to occur */
            /* find out what has event has occurred */
            switch(event type) {
                    /* process event */
        }
}
```

We essentially do nothing until some event occurs. We receive a notification that something has happened, we find out exactly what has occurred and perform an appropriate action.

Sometimes the programming language we are writing in hides the event loop from us, and we just arrange for particular functions we have written to be called when a particular event occurs. These functions are often called callbacks, and the main loop that forms the heart of the application, calls you back when it has something to say. This is the case for Visual Basic, for example.

In libpq, PostgreSQL has some support for this non-blocking way of programming. It is referred to as working asynchronously, because database actions performed on the server are not synchronized with the client application which can be performing other tasks instead of waiting. Instead, we have to ask PostgreSQL if anything has happened, and when it has, we then resume processing.

Let's take a look at how we can execute a query in asynchronous mode. We are going to use a pair of functions that PQexec uses to do its work, PQsendQuery and PQgetResult. The idea is that we call PQsendQuery to send our SQL to the server. Once it is on its way, we can get on with other things. If the server responds immediately, the resultset will be kept waiting for us until we are ready to retrieve it. When we are ready, we will call PQgetResult one or more times to retrieve the query results as they come in:

```
int PQsendQuery(PGconn *conn, const char *query);
```

PQsendQuery returns zero if the query is not dispatched, and sets an error condition we can retrieve with PqerrorMessage. Otherwise it returns 1 to indicate successful sending of the query:

```
PGresult *PQgetResult(PGconn *conn);
```

PQgetResult will return a resultset each time we call it, until all the results from the active query have been returned. The resultset may contain no tuples if no further data was immediately available, but this does not mean that all the data has been received. At that point, PQgetResult returns a NULL pointer. Each of the results sets returned by PQgetResult must be cleared when are finished with them by calling PQclear.

The main thing we have to contend with is making sure that neither PQsendQuery nor PQgetResult will block, and have our application waiting for them. To help with PqsendQuery, we can set the connection itself to a non-blocking state by calling Pqsetnonblocking:

```
int PQsetnonblocking(PGconn *conn, int arg);
```

To prevent PqsendQuery from blocking, we make a call to PQsetnonblocking with a non-zero argument. Then PQsendQuery will return an error if it would have otherwise blocked, and the application may try again at a later point.

PQsetnonblocking returns zero if successful, and −1 if there is a problem in changing the mode of the connection. We can check the blocking mode of a connection by calling PQisnonblocking:

```
int PQisnonblocking(const PGconn *conn);
```

We get a non-zero value if the connection is in a non-blocking mode.

The programming we need to run this non-blocking operation is something like this (async1.c):

```c
#include <stdlib.h>
#include <libpq-fe.h>

void printTuples(PGresult *result)
{
    int r, n;
    int nrows = PQntuples(result);
    int nfields = PQnfields(result);
    printf("number of rows returned = %d\n", nrows);
    printf("number of fields returned = %d\n", nfields);
    for(r = 0; r < nrows; r++) {
    for(n = 0; n < nfields; n++)
      printf(" %s = %s(%d),",
            PQfname(result, n),
            PQgetvalue(result, r, n),
            PQgetlength(result, r, n));
    printf("\n");
    }
}

int main()
{
  PGresult *result;
  PGconn *conn;

  conn = PQconnectdb("");

  if(PQstatus(conn) == CONNECTION_OK &&
     PQsetnonblocking(conn,1) == 0) {
    printf("connection made\n");

    PQsendQuery(conn, "SELECT * FROM customer");
    while(result = PQgetResult(conn)) {
      printTuples(result);
      PQclear(result);
    }
  }
  else
    printf("connection failed\n");

  PQfinish(conn);
  return EXIT_SUCCESS;
}
```

This program sends off a query and then collects the results without blocking. As with the cursor, we saw earlier we now have no easy way of telling how many rows will be returned altogether, but this is rarely a problem in practice.

There are still some rare circumstances under which PQgetResult can block, one of them being while the backend server is busy. There are ways around this, using some lower-level libpq functions. If you need to have very precise control over your connection, and you are executing very complex queries that will cause the server to be busy for significantly long periods, check out the functions PQisBusy, PqconsumeInput, and PQflush in the PostgreSQL Programmer's Guide that is included in the source code distribution:

```
int PQisBusy(PGconn *conn);
```

PQisBusy returns 1 if the current query is busy, and PQgetResult would block if it were called:

```
int PQflush(PGconn *conn);
```

PQflush tries to send any outstanding data that is waiting to go to the server. It returns zero if it successfully empties the queue, or it was already empty:

```
int PQconsumeInput(PGconn *conn);
```

PQconsumeInput is the libpq function that transfers data waiting to be read on the database connection into the internal libpq data structures. It is normally called by functions like PQexec, but we can make explicit calls to it when we need control over blocking behavior of our applications.

If your application is using the SELECT system call to react to read and write events on file descriptors or network sockets, then you can include the PostgreSQL connection in the SELECT too.

To do this, you must obtain the socket that is being used by the database connection. This can be obtained from PQsocket:

```
int PQsocket(const PGconn *conn);
```

The socket will signal activity when there is backend data to be processed, but there are a couple of conditions that must be met for this to work. Firstly, there must be no data outstanding to be sent to the server. You can ensure this by calling PQflush until it returns zero. Secondly, data must be read from the connection by PQconsumeInput before calling PQgetResult.

If we need to cancel a query before we have read all of the results we can do this by calling PQcancelRequest, which will send an indication to the server to stop processing the query:

```
int PQcancelRequest(PGconn *conn);
```

PQcancelRequest will return 1 if it was able to send the cancellation, or 0 if it was unable to, possibly because the query had already completed. A cancelled query will manifest itself as a resultset bearing an error. Regardless of the result of PqcancelRequest, we may still be too late to stop the results from appearing and may not see any error in a results set.

Although `PQcancelRequest` is useful when working in a non-blocking mode it is also possible to call it from a signal handler to terminate a long-running query on a blocking connection. It is also possible to establish the initial connection to the database in a non-blocking way by using `PQconnectStart` and `PqconnectPoll`:

```
PGconn *PQconnectStart(const char *conninfo);
PostgresPollingStatusType *PQconnectPoll(PGconn *conn);
```

`PQconnectStart` is similar to `PQconnectdb`, except that it returns immediately, before the connection requested in the `conninfo` string has been established. As long as the host name parameter does not result in a DNS lookup, `PQconnectStart` will not block.

Before we can use the new connection, we must be sure that it is ready for use. First, we must call `PQstatus` to make sure that the call to `PQconnectStart` did not fail and leave a connection with a status of `CONNECTION_BAD`. We can then check on the connection's condition with `PQconnectPoll`, which will not block. The return results from `PQconnectPoll` include:

```
PGRES_POLLING_FAILED    /*the connection has failed*/
PGRES_POLLING_OK        /*the connection has been made*/
```

By polling while the result is not `PGRES_POLLING_FAILED`, and until it becomes `PGRES_POLLING_OK`, we can detect the end of the connection establishment process in a non-blocking fashion.

Here is a sample program (`async2.c` ) that makes an asynchronous database connection:

```c
#include <stdlib.h>
#include <libpq-fe.h>

int main()
{
  PGresult *result;
  PGconn *conn;

  /* Start an asynchronous connection */
  conn = PQconnectStart("");

  if(PQstatus(conn) == CONNECTION_BAD) {
    printf(" cannot start connect: %s\n", PQerrorMessage(conn));
  }
  else {
    /* do some work, calling PQconnectPoll from time to time */
    PostgresPollingStatusType status;
    do {
      printf("polling\n");
      status = PQconnectPoll(conn);
    }
    while(status != PGRES_POLLING_FAILED &&
        status != PGRES_POLLING_OK);

    if(status == PGRES_POLLING_OK)
      printf("connection made!\n");
    else
      printf("connection failed: %s\n", PQerrorMessage(conn));
  }
  PQfinish(conn);
  return EXIT_SUCCESS;
}
```

When we run this program, we see many polling messages before the connection is reported as made or failed:

```
$ PGDATABASE=bpsimple ./async2
polling
polling
...
connection made!
$
```

# Summary

In this chapter, we have looked at creating PostgreSQL applications in C. We will see in later chapters how other languages have interfaces to PostgreSQL.

We have seen how the libpq library provides access to the low-level functions of PostgreSQL, allowing us to connect to a database on a local machine or on a server across the network. We have used our example programs to make and close connections, and execute SQL statements to query, insert, or update rows in our database tables.

We have considered problems of handling large volumes of data and used cursors to marshal query results into manageable units. We have looked at the problem of blocking and considered ways of creating applications that continue to service the user while accessing a database server.

We can also access PostgreSQL from C using embedded SQL, which is the subject of discussion of the next chapter.

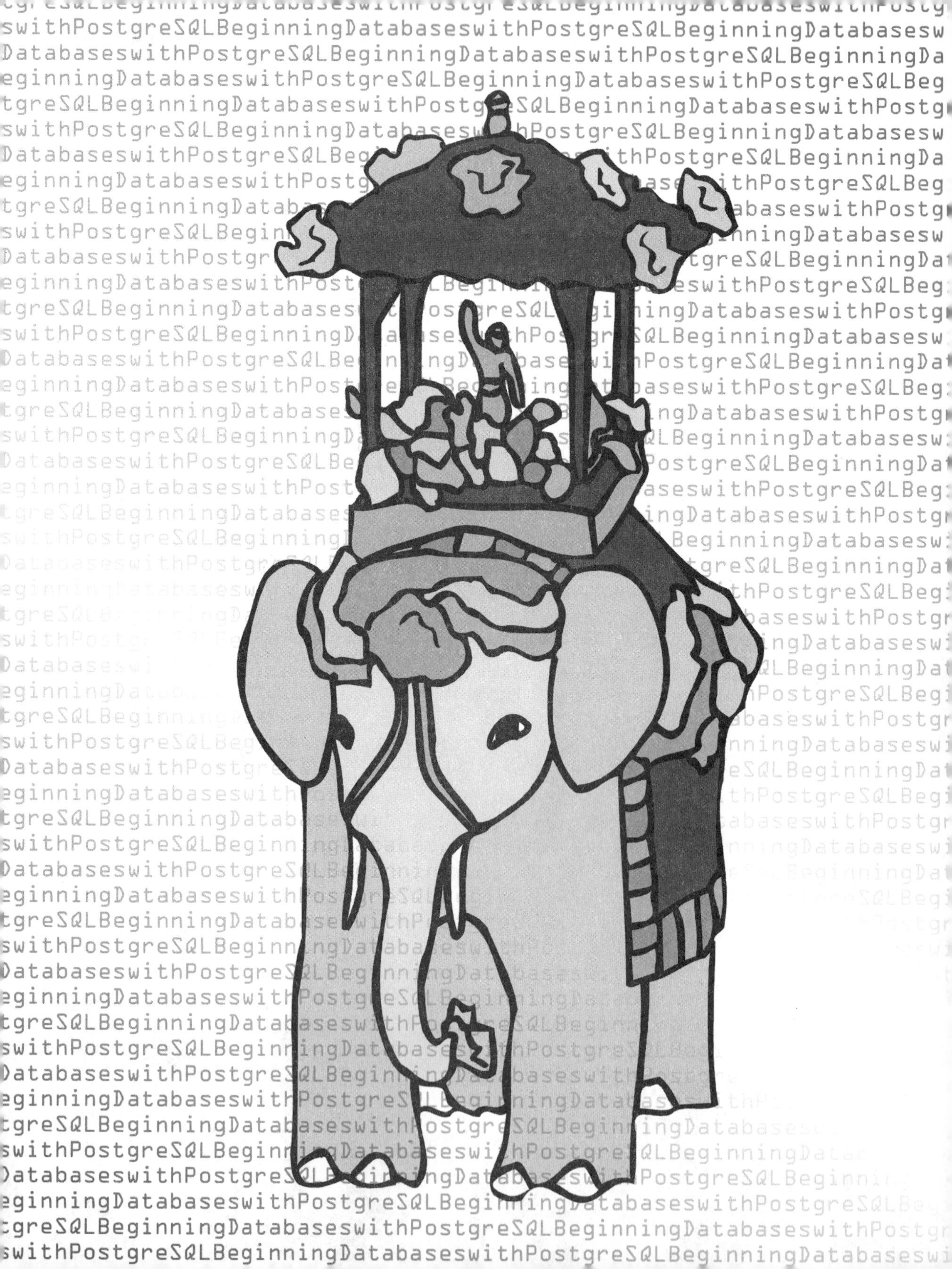

# Accessing PostgreSQL From C Using Embedded SQL

In the last chapter, we looked at a common way to create client applications for PostgreSQL, writing a C program that communicated with a PostgreSQL database. We used the libpq library, a collection of functions specific to PostgreSQL that allowed our program to connect to a database, and select data from tables. We saw that we could effectively execute standard SQL queries, and perform updates, inserts, and deletes, on rows in the database tables.

Although libpq does unleash the power of the PostgreSQL database system for our applications, it is in some ways unfortunate that the interface itself is in a sense, proprietary; that is, it is unique to PostgreSQL. It is also not that easy to see the SQL, as the supporting code tends to hide the all-important SQL statements.

Help is at hand however. Many database systems, particularly commercial ones, support the concept of embedded SQL. The SQL92 standard specified interfaces for embedding SQL in other languages, not only in C, but also in FORTRAN, ADA, and others. In December 1998, ANSI also ratified a standard for embedding SQL in Java, SQLJ.

PostgreSQL also provides a translator that expands the SQL you write embedded in C code into libpq calls. Simply put, this is a method of writing SQL statements in your C program, rather than using libpq function calls directly. Oracle and Informix have such translators in PRO*C and ESQL/C respectively, as do many other commercial relational database systems. The PostgreSQL equivalent, ecpg, closely follows the ANSI standard.

The translator, strictly speaking a preprocessor, works in much the same way as the C preprocessor. It reads your program file, which for PostgreSQL we conventionally use the extension pgc, and produces a C program file that the compiler can understand. The embedded SQL is replaced with calls to ecpg library routines, which in turn, call the libpq library routines.

Using embedded SQL and following the SQL standards for embedding SQL in C code, enables us to create applications that are more portable to other databases. It also enables us to transfer knowledge between different databases more easily. If you have used embedded SQL in another database system, you will be right at home in this chapter.

# A First Embedded SQL Program

The PostgreSQL embedded SQL preprocessor, ecpg, closely follows the ANSI standard. Before we start, let's use psql to create a database test, with a table number to experiment with, much like we did in the previous chapter. If you have deleted the test database from the previous chapter already, you can skip the DROP DATABASE step:

```
bpsimple=# DROP database test;
DROP DATABASE
bpsimple=# CREATE database test;
CREATE DATABASE
bpsimple=# \c test
You are now connected to database test.
test=# create table number (
test(# intval integer,
test(# name varchar
test(# );
CREATE
test=# INSERT INTO number(intval, name) VALUES(42, 'six times seven');
INSERT 19107 1
test=# INSERT INTO number(intval, name) VALUES(1, 'Numero Uno');
INSERT 19231 1
test=# INSERT INTO number(intval, name) VALUES(111, 'Nelson ');
INSERT 19253 1
test=#
```

## Try it Out – First Embedded SQL Program

Now let's look at a very simple example of esqlc program, update.pgc:

```c
int main()
{
  EXEC SQL connect to test;
  EXEC SQL UPDATE number
          SET name = 'The Answer to the Ultimate Question'
          WHERE intval = 42;
  EXEC SQL commit work;
  EXEC SQL disconnect all;
  return 0;
}
```

### How it Works

This program simply connects to the database (assumed to be on the local machine), and updates one of the rows in the number table.

> **The database name is not quoted. In versions of ecpg prior to 2.1.0, the database name had to be inside single quotes, so you may see this in some older programs. If you use a more recent version of ecpg with an application coded with a quoted database name the program will fail, and PostgreSQL will log an error claiming that database 'test' does not exist.**

You can see that we have simply written some SQL inside the main program. The embedded SQL syntax is fairly simple, prefixing each SQL statement that has to be translated with the string exec sql and terminating it with a semicolon:

```
EXEC SQL <some SQL statement>;
```

The keywords in embedded SQL are case insensitive, including EXEC SQL, so we may write them in either upper case or lower case. Some developers like to use upper case so that the SQL stands out from the surrounding C code; others regard that as ugly and use lower case. You should pick one case style and stick to it. We will stick to our convention of putting all SQL keywords in upper case, which we feel helps them to stand out from the surrounding C code. Variable names that we use in embedded SQL are case sensitive and must match the corresponding declarations.

The next step is to use the translator to create a C file that we can compile. We can translate our example program by running ecpg, giving our program as argument:

```
$ ecpg -t update.pgc
$
```

If you need to tell ecpg where to find additional include files, you can do so by adding a command line argument -I<include file directory>.

Now we also have a C program file, update.c, that includes the translated source code for our program. If we are curious, we can take a peek and see what is going on. Here is a slightly tidied up translation of update.pgc:

```
#include <ecpgtype.h>
#include <ecpglib.h>
#include <ecpgerrno.h>

main()
{
   { ECPGconnect(__LINE__, "test" , NULL,NULL , NULL, 1); }
   { ECPGdo(__LINE__, NULL, "UPDATE  number SET name  = 'The Answer to the Ultimate
Question'  WHERE intval  = 42", ECPGt_EOIT, ECPGt_EORT);}
   { ECPGtrans(__LINE__, NULL, "commit");}
   { ECPGdisconnect(__LINE__, "ALL");}
}
```

We can see that the SQL has been replaced by calls to functions. These ecpg functions all have names beginning ecpg, and are similar to the libpq ones we saw in the previous chapter. The ecpg functions are made available as a library and use the libpq library for their implementation.

To create an executable program, we have to compile update.c and link it with both the ecpg and libpq libraries. The exact location you need to specify with -L may be different on your system, depending on how PostgreSQL was installed:

```
$ cc -o update update.c -L/usr/local/pgsql/lib -lecpg -lpq
$
```

You may also need to add a `-Idirectory` command line argument to specify the location of the ECPG include files.

Now when we run the program, it connects to the database, updates the row, and disconnects:

```
$ ./update
$
```

There is nothing to see, because this program does not produce any output. We can check with `psql` to see whether the update has happened correctly.

If when you try to run the program you get an error that the shared library file `libecpg.so.<some-numbers>` does not exist, you may also need to set `LD_LIBRARY_PATH` to include the directory containing this file. For example:

```
$ LD_LIBRARY_PATH=$LD_LIBRARY_PATH:/usr/local/pgsql/lib
$ export LD_LIBRARY_PATH
$

$ psql -d test
test=# SELECT * FROM number;
  intval |                 name
---------+-------------------------------------
       1 | Numero Uno
     111 | Nelson
      42 | The Answer to the Ultimate Question
(3 rows)
test=# \q
$
```

By default, `ecpg` arranges for our statements to be executed within an open transaction, but it does not automatically end the transaction. At the end of our program, we have to explicitly end the transaction by executing a `COMMIT`, if we are happy with all of our database changes. We will see a little later how to take complete control over the way transactions are handled.

To make the process of invoking the translator and building embedded SQL applications easier, we will use a Makefile very similar to the one in the previous chapter. Here is a suitable Makefile for `ecpg` programs:

```
# Makefile for sample programs
# In Beginning PostgreSQL

# Edit the base directories for your
# PostgreSQL installation

INC=/usr/local/pgsql/include
LIB=/usr/local/pgsql/lib

CFLAGS=-I$(INC)
LDLIBS=-L$(LIB) -lecpg -lpq
ECPGFLAGS=-t -I$(INC)

.SUFFIXES: .pgc
.pgc.c:
        ecpg $(ECPGFLAGS) $<

ALL= cursor insert insert2 select select2 select3 update update2
```

This Makefile says that to create a .c file from a .pgc file you need to run ecpg on the .pgc file. We set a variable ECPGFLAGS to pass any command line arguments we need to the translator. We have specified -t here to take manual control of transactions. The default rules take care of compiling and linking, so all we need to add is the ecpg library to the LDLIBS variable.

More details on Makefile can be found in *Beginning Linux Programming* by Neil Matthew and Richard Stones (Wrox Press, ISBN 1-861-00297-1), as well as in the GNU Make Manual available from the http://www.gnu.org web site.

Using the Makefile, we can see the steps taken in creating our program:

```
$ rm -f update.c update
$ make update
ecpg -t -I/usr/local/pgsql/include update.pgc
cc -I/usr/local/pgsql/include -c -o update.o update.c
cc update.o -L/usr/local/pgsql/lib -lecpg -lpq-o update
rm update.o update.c
$
```

Here we have removed the intermediate file update.c and the executable update to force make to carry out all of the required steps in building our program. Notice too that (for the GNU version at least) make deletes the intermediate file and object to keep things nice and tidy. We end up with just update.pgc, the source code of our embedded SQL program, and an executable binary, update.

# Arguments to ecpg

We can use some command line arguments to control the behavior of ecpg. The full command is:

```
ecpg [-v] [-t] [-I include-dir] [-o output-file] file1 [file2 …]
```

The arguments have the following use:

| Argument | Result |
|----------|--------|
| -v | Print version information to the standard error output (stderr). |
| -t | Turn off auto-transaction mode, where each individual statement is automatically executed inside a transaction. A COMMIT is needed to close the transaction. |
| -o | Specify the name of the output file for the processed program code. Defaults to the same name as the input file name, substituting .c for .pgc as the extension. |
| -I | Add the named directory to the list of directories searched to find header files included in the source file. |

The -t argument controls the way that ecpg uses transactions. By default (without -t), ecpg will arrange for all transactions to be executed inside a transaction, as if you had written BEGIN WORK immediately before it. As PostgreSQL does not nest transactions, these results in all statements are executed in a single transaction. If you need to commit changes, you have to explicitly use a COMMIT statement. You can do this as many times as you need. The next SQL statement will automatically start another transaction.

If you want to take control of transactions within your program, which is normally a good idea, we recommend that you specify the −t argument to ecpg and use explicit BEGIN WORK and COMMIT WORK SQL statements.

> **The remaining examples in the chapter will only work correctly if they are processed by ecpg with the −t argument, or the Makefile above is used**

In the sample Makefile, we have specified an explicit search path for include files (exactly as we did in the previous chapter for compiling libpq applications) and the option to control transactions ourselves.

# Logging SQL Execution

Many of the ecpg library functions call a logging function internally for debugging purposes. We can use this feature to generate a log of the SQL statements that our embedded SQL program executes. To do this, we enable the debug output with a call to ECPGdebug:

```
void ECPGdebug(int logging, FILE *logstream);
```

We pass any non-zero value as the parameter logging to enable the debug output, and a zero value to turn it off again. The information will be printed to the output stream given as the logstream parameter.

Add the following line to the start of main in update.pgc and rebuild:

```
ECPGdebug(1,stderr);
```

We will now be able to see the progress of our program as it runs:

```
$ make update
$ ./update
[1597]: ECPGdebug: set to 1
[1597]: ECPGconnect: opening database test
[1597]: ECPGexecute line 15: QUERY: update number set name  = 'The Answer to the
Ultimate Question' where intval  = 42 on connection test
[1597]: ECPGexecute line 15 Ok: UPDATE 1
[1597]: ECPGtrans line 16 action = commit connection = test
[1597]: ecpg_finish: finishing test.
```

The number given in brackets at the start of each debug line is the process identifier for the program, and will be different for each run. This is useful for separating the output from several programs running at the same time.

As ECPGdebug (and the other ECPG functions if you call them explicitly) is PostgreSQL specific, if you use it in your applications they will not be portable to other database implementations that support embedded SQL. It is probably best confined to the test and debug phases of your application development and either removed or included only conditionally using the C preprocessor.

# Database Connections

The example program update.pgc contains a very simple variant of the SQL statement to connect to the database, where almost all of the options we might have used in the equivalent libpq functions have been set to default values.

The following statement will attempt to connect to the database called test on the local machine, using the current user as the login account and offering no password:

```
EXEC SQL connect to test;
```

We can specify in more detail which server to connect to, which port the database server is listening on, and the user identity and password to use, by employing the full version of the connect statement:

```
EXEC SQL CONNECT database_url
     AS connection_name
     USER login_name
     USING password;
```

The database_url specifies the location of the database and the method to be used to connect to it in much the same way as a URL on the Internet locates a file or a web page. Its form can be one of:

| Form | Description |
|---|---|
| database_name | Database on the local machine |
| database_name@server | Database on a remote server |
| database_name@server:port | Remote database on a non-standard port |
| tcp:postgresql://server | Default database on remote server connected via TCP socket |
| tcp:postgresql://server:port | Remote database on a non-standard port |
| tcp:postgresql://server/database_name | Named remote database |
| Unix:postgresql://server | Database connected by UNIX domain socket |
| Default | Default database, specified by PGDATABASE environment variable |
| :host_variable | Connection details taken from a C string variable |

The connection_name is an identifier that can be used to identify the connection in subsequent SQL statements.

The login_name is the user identity to use. The password may be added to the user name, separated by a slash.

The password is the user's password. The keyword identified by may be used as a synonym for using in a connect statement when using passwords. The user details may be taken from a variable if required. See the *Host Variables* section later in this chapter for details on using variables in SQL statements.

If you are writing a program that uses multiple connections, then assigning them names allow you to identify them as targets for SQL statements. To specify a particular database connection we use an extended form of the exec sql syntax:

```
EXEC SQL AT connection_name <sql statement> ;
```

We can also change the connection that is used for SQL statements (the current connection), by using a SET statement:

```
EXEC SQL SET CONNECTION TO connection_name ;
```

A database connection is closed with the disconnect statement:

```
EXEC SQL DISCONNECT connection;
```

Where the optional connection argument may be one of:

| Option | Description |
|---|---|
| Default | The default connection |
| Current | The current connection |
| All | All connections |
| *connection_name* | A named connection |

One function that is included in the ecpg library that can sometimes come in handy is ECPGstatus, which returns a non-zero Boolean value (true) if a database connection is valid (that is, it is connected to a database) and false otherwise:

```
bool ECPGstatus(int lineno, char *connection_name);
```

The parameters to ECPGstatus follow the standard for ECPG functions, having a first parameter that is a line number (usually the C preprocessor macro __LINE__ is used). The second parameter is a string used to identify the connection we are interested in. You can use the same connection specifier or name, as used in the embedded SQL connect statement that established the connection.

To check that our sample program connected successfully, we could add this test to the code:

```
if(!ECPGstatus(__LINE__,"test")) {
      /* failed to connect */
}
```

Again, using ECPGstatus will make our program PostgreSQL specific, and as we shall see there is a more standard way of detecting whether the connection failed, but only immediately after the attempt to connect is made.

# Error Handling

Our example program currently is rather cavalier in its approach. It carries on regardless, oblivious to any errors that might occur in executing any of the embedded SQL. As such, it is possible that the program will hang if it fails to connect to a database and then attempts the update. As responsible developers, we will want to catch and recover from errors that may occur.

The embedded SQL standard defines a mechanism for reporting errors in embedded SQL, and PostgreSQL supports this. A standard structure, the SQL control area, is defined and named `sqlca`. It has the following layout, expressed as a C structure:

```
struct
{
    char        sqlcaid[8];
    long        sqlabc;
    long        sqlcode;
    struct
    {
        int         sqlerrml;
        char        sqlerrmc[70];
    } sqlerrm;
    char        sqlerrp[8];
    long        sqlerrd[6];
    char        sqlwarn[8];
    char        sqlext[8];
} sqlca;
```

The `sqlca` structure is used for communicating error messages and status values from embedded SQL statement execution. It is rather arcane, and the different codes can appear a little odd. Furthermore, PostgreSQL does not implement all of the possible information that can be communicated through `sqlca` fields. Commercial databases, such as Oracle, provide additional information, but the PostgreSQL implementation is perfectly usable. Only the fields implemented by PostgreSQL are described here.

The `sqlca` structure is reset after every embedded SQL statement, so you must retrieve any information you need from one statement before executing the next. The fields that are set in the structure will depend on precisely what has happened, and the key to that is the `sqlcode` field.

The `sqlca.sqlcode` will be set to a result code, which will be zero if all went well. For serious errors, a negative value will be returned. For example, if a database connection attempt fails, `sqlca.sqlcode` will be set to -402. Non-fatal errors return positive values. A very important positive result is the code 100, which is returned in the case where a SELECT returned no data, not in itself an error.

If an error occurs, the string `sqlca.sqlerrm.sqlerrmc` will contain a message that describes the error. The length of the error message string (which is null terminated) is given in `sqlca.sqlerrm.sqlerrml`. With PostgreSQL, the error message might seem unhelpful as it may contain text like "error #-203" rather than anything truly meaningful. Error codes and their meaning include:

| Code | Description |
|------|-------------|
| -12 | Out of memory. |
| -201 | Too many arguments. Probably caused by PostgreSQL returning more data values than the program allows for as a result of a SELECT. |
| -202 | Too few arguments. Probably caused by PostgreSQL returning fewer data values than expected by the program. |
| -203 | Too many matches. A query has returned multiple rows but the variables receiving that data are only sufficient for a single row. |
| -208 | Empty query. This is equivalent to PGRES_EMPTY_QUERY being returned from libpq and probably indicates a program bug as the server was asked to do no work. |
| -220 | No such connection. The program has named a connection that does not exist. |
| -221 | Not connected. The program has attempted to access data without a valid connection being established. |
| -400 | PostgreSQL error. The message will contain details of the error from the server. |
| -401 | Transaction error. An error has occurred during a begin, commit or rollback of a transaction. |
| -402 | Open failed. A connection to the database could not be established. |
| 100 | Not found. No data was returned by a query. |

After an INSERT, UPDATE, or DELETE has successfully been executed, the number of rows that were affected is made available in sqlca.sqlerrd[2]. This field is also used when returning data with SELECT and using cursors.

In some circumstances, a condition arises, that while not a fatal error, needs to be brought to the programs attention. These are warnings that are raised for non-fatal errors and in some other cases. When data is returned as a result of an SQL statement, such as a SELECT, we can arrange for C variables in our program to received the data, as we shall see a little later in this chapter. If the data is too long for the variable, it is truncated and a warning is raised.

The sqlca.sqlwarn array is used to convey information about warnings. sqlca.sqlwarn[0] will be set to W if a warning has been issued. sqlca.sqlwarn[1] will be set to W if data has been truncated when been received into a C variable. sqlca.sqlwarn[2] will be set to W when a non-fatal error has occurred.

To use the sqlca structure in our program we need to instruct ecpg to include its definition for us. We do this by using an include directive such as this:

```
EXEC SQL INCLUDE sqlca;
```

## Try it Out – Updates

Let's create a second example update program to check the number of rows affected by our update. This version (update2.pgc) alters the cost and sell price for an item in our main sample database, bpsimple:

```
#include <stdio.h>

EXEC SQL include sqlca;

main()
{
  ECPGdebug(1,stderr);

  EXEC SQL connect to bpsimple;

  EXEC SQL UPDATE item
          SET cost_price = 1.75, sell_price = 2.99
          WHERE description = 'Linux CD';

  if(sqlca.sqlcode == 0)
    printf("rows affected: %d\n", sqlca.sqlerrd[2]);

  EXEC SQL disconnect all;
}
```

### How it Works

The program extracts the number of rows affected by the UPDATE, if it completes successfully. A zero code in sqlca.sqlcode indicates a successful UPDATE, and sqlca.sqlerrd[2] contains the number of rows affected.

# Trapping Errors

We can arrange for our ecpg program to execute some code automatically whenever an error or warning occurs. We can also arrange for code to run whenever we encounter the no data pseudo-error code 100.

The construct we use is the whenever statement:

```
EXEC SQL whenever condition action;
```

Where condition can be one of the following:

| Option | Description |
| --- | --- |
| Sqlerror | A fatal error has occurred |
| Sqlwarning | A non-fatal error has occurred |
| Not found | No data was returned |

`Action` can then be one of the following:

| Option | Description |
|--------|-------------|
| Sqlprint | Print the error message to the standard error |
| do *c_code* | Execute a C function |

If it is acceptable just to print out messages for non-fatal errors, and to exit the program for fatal errors we can include code such as this in our application to trap and handle errors:

```
EXEC SQL whenever sqlwarning sqlprint;
EXEC SQL whenever sqlerror do GiveUp();

void GiveUp()
{
    fprintf(stderr, "Fatal error\n");
    sqlprint();
    exit(1);
}
```

PostgreSQL implements the `whenever` statement in `ecpg` by generating code to check `sqlca.sqlcode` and `sqlca.sqlwarn[0]` after each embedded SQL statement and executing the specified action if the check fails. The keyword `sqlprint` is a shorthand for `do sqlprint()` which calls a library function to print out the associated error message.

These `whenever` functions are PostgreSQL specific, and not available in standard embedded SQL. For this reason, you shouldn't rely on them in your final program code if there is any possibility of needing to port your code to another database at a later date.

# Host Variables

So far we have simply executed fixed SQL statements in our sample program, and you may be wondering how we can introduce some variable data. After all, using `libpq` we could construct an SQL statement in a string using `sprintf` perhaps, and thereby arrange for it to contain data taken from variables.

Embedded SQL can also use variables in its statements, in a manner that is rather easier to use than the string manipulation we have to go through with `libpq`. We can refer to variables in our embedded SQL by using their names prefixed by a colon. So if we want to insert a new row in our `item` table, we can do it like this:

```
EXEC SQL INSERT INTO item VALUES(:description, :cost_price, :sell_price);
```

Notice that we can omit a value for `item_id` as it is generated automatically when a row is added to the `item` table. The variables here (`description`, `cost_price` and `sell_price`) are referred to as host variables, as they are variables contained in the client application, not within the server database.

Before we can use host variables in our program, we must let ecpg know about them. We do this by declaring the variables we want to use in SQL statements in special declaration sections:

```
EXEC SQL BEGIN declare section;
declare host variables here
    . . . .
EXEC SQL END declare section;
```

Declaration sections must appear where it is legal to declare a C variable, in other words at the start of a block or outside of functions. This is because they will be processed into normal C variable declarations, as well as being recorded by ecpg as host variables.

For simple values like integers and fixed length strings we can declare the host variables as we would in C.

## Try it Out – Host Variables

Let's start by writing a program (insert.pgc) that will allow us to add new barcodes for items in our database. We will take the item identifier and barcode as command line parameters:

```
#include <stdio.h>

#include <string.h>

EXEC SQL include sqlca;
EXEC SQL whenever sqlwarning sqlprint;
EXEC SQL whenever sqlerror do GiveUp();

void GiveUp()
{
    fprintf(stderr, "Fatal Error\n");
    sqlprint();
}

main(int argc, char *argv[])
{
  EXEC SQL begin declare section;
  int item_id;
  char barcode[13];
  EXEC SQL end declare section;

  if(argc != 3) {
    printf("usage: INSERT item barcode\n");
    exit(1);
  }

  item_id = atoi(argv[1]);
  strncpy(barcode, argv[2], sizeof(barcode));

  EXEC SQL connect to bpsimple;

  EXEC SQL insert into barcode values(:barcode, :item_id);

  EXEC SQL disconnect all;

}
```

### How it Works

Here we declare two host variables, item_id and barcode, that correspond to the data types (integer and fixed length character field) for columns in the item table. We can use them in our C code, because they are normal C variables. We can use them in embedded SQL, because we have declared them to ecpg within a declare section. We simply prefix their names with a colon when we use them in SQL.

When we compile and run the program, we can use it to add new barcodes to the database. If we try to add a duplicate barcode, we see a fatal error occurs which is handled by a sql whenever construction:

```
$ make insert
$ ./insert 2 1234567890123
$ ./insert 2 1234567890123
Fatal Error
sql error 'ERROR:  Cannot insert a duplicate key into unique index barcode_pk'
$
```

If we want to deal with other data types for our attributes, we declare them accordingly. For floating point numbers to handle prices that are stored in the database as NUMERIC(7,2) we use the C double type. For dates, we can use a character type long enough to store the date as a string.

We encounter a slight problem when we come to the VARCHAR database type. This type contains a variable number of characters, not necessarily null terminated as type contains a variable number of characters, and also not necessarily null terminated as with normal C character strings. We have no simple way of representing a VARCHAR type in C, so we will have to resort to a structure with two members, a character array of maximum length and an integer count that records the number of valid characters in the array.

Fortunately, ecpg can take care of the declaration for us. We just have to use the pseudo-type VARCHAR instead of char when declaring the variable. ecpg declares a structure with two members called arr and len, containing the characters and the length respectively.

## Try it Out – Variable Length Data

In the next example, insert2.pgc, we will look at a program for adding new products to the item table in our database. We take a product description (which is a VARCHAR(64)) and two floating point numbers representing cost and sell prices, and insert a new row in the table:

```c
#include <stdio.h>
#include <string.h>
#include <stdlib.h>

EXEC SQL include sqlca;
EXEC SQL whenever sqlwarning sqlprint;
EXEC SQL whenever sqlerror do GiveUp();

void GiveUp()
{
    fprintf(stderr, "Fatal Error\n");
    sqlprint();
```

```
    }

    main(int argc, char *argv[])
    {
      EXEC SQL begin declare section;
      char dbname[] = "bpsimple";
      double cost_price, sell_price;
      VARCHAR description[64];
      EXEC SQL end declare section;

      if(argc != 4) {
        printf("usage: insert description cost_price sell_price\n");
        exit(1);
      }

      strncpy(description.arr, argv[1], sizeof(description.arr));
      description.len = strlen(description.arr);
      cost_price = atof(argv[2]);
      sell_price = atof(argv[3]);

      EXEC SQL connect to :dbname as bpsimple;
      EXEC SQL at bpsimple insert into
        item(description, cost_price, sell_price)
        values(:description, :cost_price, :sell_price);

      EXEC SQL disconnect bpsimple;
    }
```

We can insert a new item with a simple invocation:

```
$ ./insert2 "Widget" 1.87 2.93
$
```

Now check that the item table is updated with psql:

```
bpsimple=# SELECT * FROM item;
 item_id |  description  | cost_price | sell_price
---------+---------------+------------+------------
...
      12 | Widget        |       1.87 |       2.93

bpsimple=#
```

### How It Works

We declare our host variables in the declare section, and use both members of the description structure to create a host variable suitable to be used in the SQL statement for inserting a new row.

As the item table uses a serial item_id, we can (and should) omit an item_id when adding a new row to the table. We can do this by explicitly naming the columns we are going to supply data for in the INSERT.

> If we need to insert a **NULL** into a column of a table row, we can use the keyword null
> in the values part of the **INSERT** statement.

In this program, by way of variation, we are also using a host variable to specify the database to connect
to and demonstrate the use of a named connection.

# Retrieving Data with ecpg

Now that we have introduced host variables, we are in ready to consider extracting data from the
database as host variables provide the storage for tuples (rows) returned by SELECT. Here is a very
simple example to get started with. Let's count the number of customers we have:

```
EXEC SQL begin declare section;
int count;
EXEC SQL end declare section;

EXEC SQL SELECT count(*) INTO :count FROM customer;
```

We extend our SELECT with an INTO clause that specifies the host variables we want to use to retrieve
information. In this example, we would declare an integer called count, which after successful
execution of this SQL statement will contain the number of customers in our database.

Similarly, we can extract a row of data into variables by giving a list of host variables in the INTO clause
that matches the data we are selecting. To extract the details of a particular customer by customer_id
we could write:

```
EXEC SQL SELECT addressline, zipcode INTO :addr, :zip
        FROM customer
        WHERE customer_id = 15;
```

The selected columns should always be explicitly listed in SELECT statements, rather than using '*'. If
there is a change to the database schema, your code will be much more resilient, and if it does fail,
because a column you refer to has been removed, will at least give a helpful error message.

We can use host variables in the other clauses of SELECT statements too. To take the customer_id
from a host variable we would write:

```
WHERE customer_id = :id;
```

In our sample database, the customer table has a serial customer_id, so the last customer added
always has the id that is the largest in the table.

## Try it Out – Retrieving Data

Here's a program that finds the maximum `customer_id` and uses it to retrieve the Zip code and first line of the address for that customer:

```
#include <stdio.h>
#include <string.h>
#include <stdlib.h>

EXEC SQL include sqlca;
EXEC SQL whenever sqlwarning sqlprint;
EXEC SQL whenever sqlerror do GiveUp();

void GiveUp()
{
    fprintf(stderr, "Fatal Error\n");
    sqlprint();
}

main(int argc, char *argv[])
{
    EXEC SQL begin declare section;
    int id;
    char zip[10];
    VARCHAR address[64];
    int address_ind;
    EXEC SQL end declare section;
    EXEC SQL connect to bpsimple;
    EXEC SQL SELECT max(customer_id) INTO :id FROM customer;
    printf("We have %d customers\n", id);

    EXEC SQL SELECT addressline, zipcode
             INTO :address:address_ind, :zip
             FROM customer
             WHERE customer_id = :id;

    printf("The address is%sNULL\n", address_ind ? " " : " not ");
    printf("customer id: %d\n", id);
    printf("%.*s <%.*s>\n", sizeof(zip), zip, address.len, address.arr);

    EXEC SQL disconnect all;
}
```

`select.pgc`

When we compile and run this program, we get the output shown below:

```
$ ./select
We have 15 customers
The address is not NULL
customer id: 15
MT2 6RT  <4 The Square>
```

### How it Works

The program extracts data returned by a SELECT into a number of host variables, and in doing so exposes a handful of pitfalls along the way. These pitfalls are the result of some subtleties in this program that we need to consider quite carefully.

The first, is that we are handling character data from the database retrieved into C strings. Ordinarily C strings are terminated with a null character, and many library functions assume that one is present. So, for example, if you simply print a string, the printf function outputs characters until it reaches a null in the string. Potentially worse, is the case of copying character data, as strcpy will blindly copy until a null is encountered.

Character data in the database is not necessarily null terminated and column data returned from a SELECT may, therefore, cause us a problem. When we print it with printf we may see garbage as printf outputs characters from memory locations beyond the limit of our data until it hits a null. Copying with strcpy will continue until a null is found, which may be at a location well beyond the end of the character data and, therefore, cause corruption as the target string is overwritten.

One way to deal with this is to be very careful when copying character data for use in your programs and make sure that you allow additional space for a null character and place one at the end of your string.

Our example program here uses a feature of printf to limit the amount of character data that it will output. The precision field for the %s format allows us to state that we want a maximum of a certain amount of output for the character data.

The following line will print the 10 characters of the fixed length Zip code without requiring a trailing null and up to 64 characters of the first address line:

```
printf("%.10s %.64s\n", zip, address.arr);
```

In fact, for variable length data, we will generally see a null terminator, except when the data is of maximum length.

We can be a little more general with the printing of character data by supplying the field precision in arguments to printf, so that if the database design changes we can be a little more robust. Here's a version of the printf call that avoids explicit data lengths:

```
printf("%.*s %.*s\n", sizeof(zip), zip, address.len, address.arr);
```

The second subtlety that we need to address is our old friend null database values. It is possible that our customer has not given us an address and the column contains NULL.

We cannot readily distinguish between an empty string and a NULL value, or a zero integer value and NULL, when we retrieve data into host variables. The situation is similar to that we met in the previous chapter. In libpq, we have the function PQgetisnull to tell us whether a result we have retrieved represents a NULL. In embedded SQL, we need to use **indicator variables** if we need to be able to tell whether a returned value is NULL.

An indicator variable is an integer host variable that is used to show whether a retrieved column value is NULL. The indicator is specified with its associated host variable by appending the indicator to the variable, using a colon as a separator:

```
SELECT addressline
       INTO :address:address_ind FROM customer
       WHERE ...
```

Here we have used an indicator variable called address_ind, which will be set to a non-zero value if the value retrieved into host variable address represents a NULL. We should not rely on any particular value (empty string, zero, and so on) being transferred into a host variable that has a NULL value.

It is a good idea to name your indicator variables in a way that makes it clear which host variable it relates to. We would suggest a naming convention, such as the one used here, adding a suffix _ind to mean indicator variable.

# Transactions

Transactions are extremely simple to implement with ecpg. As you might expect, you can use standard SQL as you would with libpq. The relevant statements are:

```
EXEC SQL BEGIN WORK;
EXEC SQL COMMIT WORK;
EXEC SQL ROLLBACK;
```

As mentioned earlier, by default (when we do not specify -t) ecpg will arrange for each of our embedded SQL statements to be run within a transaction, what is termed autocommit or unchained mode. Each new statement starts or continues a transaction, and we have to use COMMIT to make our changes stick.

If we want to take complete control of transactions we have to pass the -t option to ecpg when we process the pgc files that make up our application.

# Handling Data

So far in our sample programs in this chapter, we have been careful to make sure that when we retrieve data we obtain exactly one row. The column values are then extracted into host variables for our program to use.

If we make a small change to our select program to lookup customers by Zip code we can demonstrate handling cases where no rows are returned.

## Try it Out – Handling the "no data" Case

The next example program (`select2.pgc`) detects the case where no data is returned from a SELECT:

```c
#include <stdio.h>
#include <string.h>
#include <stdlib.h>

EXEC SQL include sqlca;
EXEC SQL whenever sqlwarning sqlprint;
EXEC SQL whenever sqlerror do GiveUp();

void GiveUp()
{
    fprintf(stderr, "Fatal Error\n");
    sqlprint();
    exit(1);
}

main(int argc, char *argv[])
{
  EXEC SQL begin declare section;
  int id;
  char title[4];
  int title_ind;
  char zip[10];
  VARCHAR lname[32];
  VARCHAR town[64];
  int town_ind;
  EXEC SQL end declare section;

  if(argc != 2) {
     printf("Usage: select2 zipcode\n");
     exit(1);
  }

  strncpy(zip, argv[1], sizeof(zip));

  EXEC SQL connect to bpsimple;

  EXEC SQL SELECT customer_id, title, lname, town
          INTO :id, :title:title_ind, :lname, :town:town_ind
          FROM customer
          WHERE zipcode = :zip;

  if(sqlca.sqlerrd[2] == 0) {
    printf("no customer found\n");
  }
  else {
    printf("title is%sNULL\n", title_ind ? " " : " not ");
    printf("town is%sNULL\n", town_ind ? " " : " not ");
    printf("customer id: %d\n", id);
    printf("%.*s %.*s <%.*s>\n",
        sizeof(title), title,
        lname.len, lname.arr,
        town.len, town.arr);
  }
  EXEC SQL disconnect all;
}
```

### How it Works

In this program, we use the fact the SQL control area will contain information about the number of rows returned in `sqlca.sqlerrd[2]`. If this is zero, then we found no rows. Let's use the program to query some data. The sample database contains these records for customers:

```
customer_id | title |  lname   |   town    |  zipcode
------------+-------+----------+-----------+-----------
          1 | Miss  | Stones   | Hightown  | NT2 1AQ
          2 | Mr    | Stones   | Lowtown   | LT5 7RA
          4 | Mr    | Matthew  | Yuleville | YV67 2WR
          5 | Mr    | Cozens   | Oahenham  | OA3 6QW
          6 | Mr    | Matthew  | Nicetown  | NT3 7RT
          7 | Mr    | Stones   | Bingham   | BG4 2WE
          8 | Mrs   | Stones   | Bingham   | BG4 2WE
          9 | Mrs   | Hickman  | Histon    | HT3 5EM
         10 | Mr    | Howard   | Tibsville | TB3 7FG
         11 | Mr    | Jones    | Bingham   | BG3 8GD
         12 | Mr    | Neill    | Winersby  | WB3 6GQ
         13 | Mrs   | Hendy    | Oxbridge  | OX2 3HX
         14 | Mr    | O'Neill  | Welltown  | WT3 8GM
         15 | Mr    | Hudson   | Milltown  | MT2 6RT
          3 | Miss  | Matthew  | Nicetown  | NT2 2TX
```

```
$ make select2
$ ./select2 "NT2 2TX"
title is not NULL
town is not NULL
customer id: 3
Miss Matthew <Nicetown>
$ ./select2 "BG4 2XE"
no customer found
$ ./select2 "BG4 2WE"
Fatal Error
sql error SQL error #-203 in line 39.
$
```

When we specify a `zipcode` search, where there are no corresponding records, we get no records returned. The query then detects this and prints a suitable message. Where we find a customer with a `zipcode` that matches, we print out the details.

The third run caused a fatal error, because we have chosen a `zipcode` that is shared between multiple customers. In this case' two customers have the same `zipcode`. As we cannot store both customers' details in our host variables we get an error. To solve the problem of multiple rows being returned, we need to use a cursor, as we did in the previous chapter. We will return to this shortly.

We can use the `exec sql whenever` construction to help us with the case where we have no rows returned by arranging to execute code when the situation arises. Take a look at this code snippet:

```
EXEC SQL whenever not found do break;

do {
  EXEC SQL SELECT customer_id, title, lname, town
    INTO :id, :title:title_ind, :lname, :town:town_ind
    FROM customer
    WHERE zipcode = :zip;

  printf("title is%sNULL\n", title_ind ? " " : " not ");
  printf("town is%sNULL\n", town_ind ? " " : " not ");
  printf("customer id: %d\n", id);
```

```
        printf("%.*s %.*s <%.*s>\n",
            sizeof(title), title,
            lname.len, lname.arr,
            town.len, town.arr);
    } while(0);
```

Here we have arranged for a C break statement to be executed when no rows are returned from a query. Now a break is only valid within a loop, so we create a run-once loop using a common trick in C, a do{} while(0); which will execute the code inside the do block, and then not loop back to the beginning as the continuation test fails. Now when we run a program using this method, we will only print out the customer details when we find one.

If you find this a little bit tricky, try imagining what the ecpg translator is doing in the presence of this sql whenever. It translates:

```
exec sql whenever not found <some code>;
exec sql <some query>;
```

Into something like:

```
ECPGdo(… <some query> …);
if(sqlca.sqlcode == ECPG_NOT_FOUND) <some code>;
```

The code we specify in our sql whenever statement must be valid in the context that the translator uses it. That's why we need to construct a dummy loop for the break to jump out of avoiding the printing of customer details when none were returned. If we wish to, we can even put a function call that uses local variables in the sql whenever action as long as wherever the translator uses the code, the variable is accessible.

Unfettered use of sql whenever can make your code impossible to follow, with some developers claiming that it's just as bad as using gotos. Having said that, it may be worth experimenting with sql whenever in small doses and with simple action code, as it can make for applications that are easier to understand.

In general though, the best way to solve the problem of not knowing for certain that you will get exactly one row, is to use a cursor, so that's what we'll tackle next.

# Cursors

The final subject that we will cover in this chapter, is the implementation of cursors in embedded SQL. As we saw in the previous chapter, cursors are an excellent general-purpose way of catering for an unknown number of rows being returned.

In case you skipped the previous chapter, it is worth reiterating the advice given there. In general, you should avoid writing code that assumes a single row or no rows are returned from a SELECT statement; unless that statement is a simple aggregate, such as SELECT COUNT(*) FROM type query, or a SELECT on a primary key where you can guarantee the result will always be exactly one row. If in doubt, use a **cursor**.

To deal with multiple rows being returned from a query, we will retrieve them one at a time using a FETCH, with the column values being received into host variables in the same way has we have seen for single row SELECTs. As with the libpq library, we will declare a cursor to be used to scroll through a collection of returned rows. The cursor will act as our bookmark and we will fetch the rows until no more data is available.

To use a cursor we must declare it and specify the query that it relates to. We may only use a cursor declaration within a PostgreSQL transaction, so if we are not using ecpg auto-transaction mode we must begin a transaction too:

```
EXEC SQL begin work
EXEC SQL declare mycursor cursor for SELECT ... ;
```

The SELECT statement that we use to define the cursor may contain host variables for conditions in WHERE clauses and so on, but it does not contain an INTO clause as we are not at this stage extracting data into host variables.

The next step is to open the cursor, to make it ready for fetching the results:

```
EXEC SQL open mycursor;
```

Now we can start to retrieve the result rows. We do this by executing a FETCH with an INTO clause to extract the data values:

```
EXEC SQL fetch next from mycursor into :var1, :var2, ... ;
```

When there are no more result rows left to fetch, we will get a row count in sqlca.sqlerrd[2] of zero, a sqlca.sqlcode of 100 and activation of any sql whenever not found code we may have specified.

When we have finished with the cursor, we close it and end the transaction:

```
EXEC SQL close mycursor;
EXEC SQL commit work;
```

## Try it Out – Cursors

Here is an example program (cursor.pgc) that uses a cursor to retrieve the results similar to a query we saw in Chapter 7, extracting the dates on which the orders were placed by customers living in a specified town:

```
#include <stdio.h>
#include <string.h>
#include <stdlib.h>

EXEC SQL include sqlca;
EXEC SQL whenever sqlwarning sqlprint;
EXEC SQL whenever sqlerror do GiveUp();
```

```
void GiveUp()
{
    fprintf(stderr, "Fatal Error\n");
    sqlprint();
    exit(1);
}

main(int argc, char *argv[])
{
  EXEC SQL begin declare section;
  char town[32];
  double shipping;
  char date[15];
  EXEC SQL end declare section;

  if(argc != 2) {
      printf("Usage: cursor town\n");
      exit(1);
  }

  strncpy(town, argv[1], sizeof(town));

  EXEC SQL connect to bpsimple;
  EXEC SQL begin work;
  EXEC SQL declare mycursor cursor for
    SELECT oi.date_placed, oi.shipping
           FROM orderinfo oi, customer c
           WHERE oi.customer_id = c.customer_id
           AND town = :town;

  EXEC SQL open mycursor;

  EXEC SQL fetch next from mycursor into :date, :shipping;

  while(sqlca.sqlcode == 0) {
    printf("%.*s <%.2f>\n", sizeof(date), date, shipping);
    EXEC SQL fetch next from mycursor into :date, :shipping;
  }

  EXEC SQL close mycursor;
  EXEC SQL commit work;
  EXEC SQL disconnect all;

  return EXIT_SUCCESS;
}
```

### How it Works

This program now neatly takes care of the three cases we might have, namely finding no orders, exactly one order, and many orders:

```
$ make cursor
$ ./cursor Erewhon
$ ./cursor Milltown
2000-09-02 <3.99>
$ ./cursor Bingham
2000-06-23 <0.00>
2000-07-21 <5.55>
```

# Debugging ecpg Code

Although ecpg does a good job of generating C code from pgc files, occasionally you will have a problem compiling the code. This is usually because of a mistake in your C code rather than anything ecpg has done, or you will want to look at the generated code from ecpg, using the real line numbers in the generated C code.

To do this, you need to employ a little trick, to remove the #line preprocessor directives ecpg inserts, which generally force compiler errors to refer to the original .pgc file, not the .c file that is actually being compiled.

The first steps are:

- ❑ Manually run ecpg to generate a .c file from the .pgc file

- ❑ Use grep to remove the #line directives

- ❑ Move the temporary file back to its rightful place

- ❑ Allow compilation to continue, or invoke the C compiler manually

Here is an example of how we might do this with cursor.pgc:

```
$ ecpg -t -I/usr/local/pgsql/include cursor.pgc
$ grep -v '^#line' cursor.c > _1.c
$ mv _1.c cursor.c
$ make
cc -I/usr/local/pgsql/include  -L/usr/local/pgsql/lib -lecpg -lpq  cursor.c   -o
cursor
```

# Summary

We have seen in this chapter, how we can use SQL in our C programs by embedding SQL statements directly in the source code. The translator ecpg then generates C code that the compiler can understand to produce an executable.

We have covered how to connect to a database and deal with errors that may occur. We have seen how to use host variables to provide values for INSERTs and UPDATEs.

Next we saw how to implement simple SELECTs and extract row data into host variables and using host variables to specify part of the WHERE clause. We also saw how to use indicator variable to detect null values in the data being retrieved. Finally, we used a cursor to retrieve multiple rows returned as a result of a more complex query.

In this chapter, we have built on what we learned in the previous chapter and used a more portable way of interfacing PostgreSQL to C. In some ways, the libpq method allows slightly more control over resultsets and status information. It also allows an asynchronous mode of operation. On the other hand, embedding SQL makes it easier to deal with binary values as ecpg takes care of all of the conversions needed, is more portable, and generally much easier to read the underlying SQL in the program. You will need to make a decision based on the requirements of your application on a case by case basis.

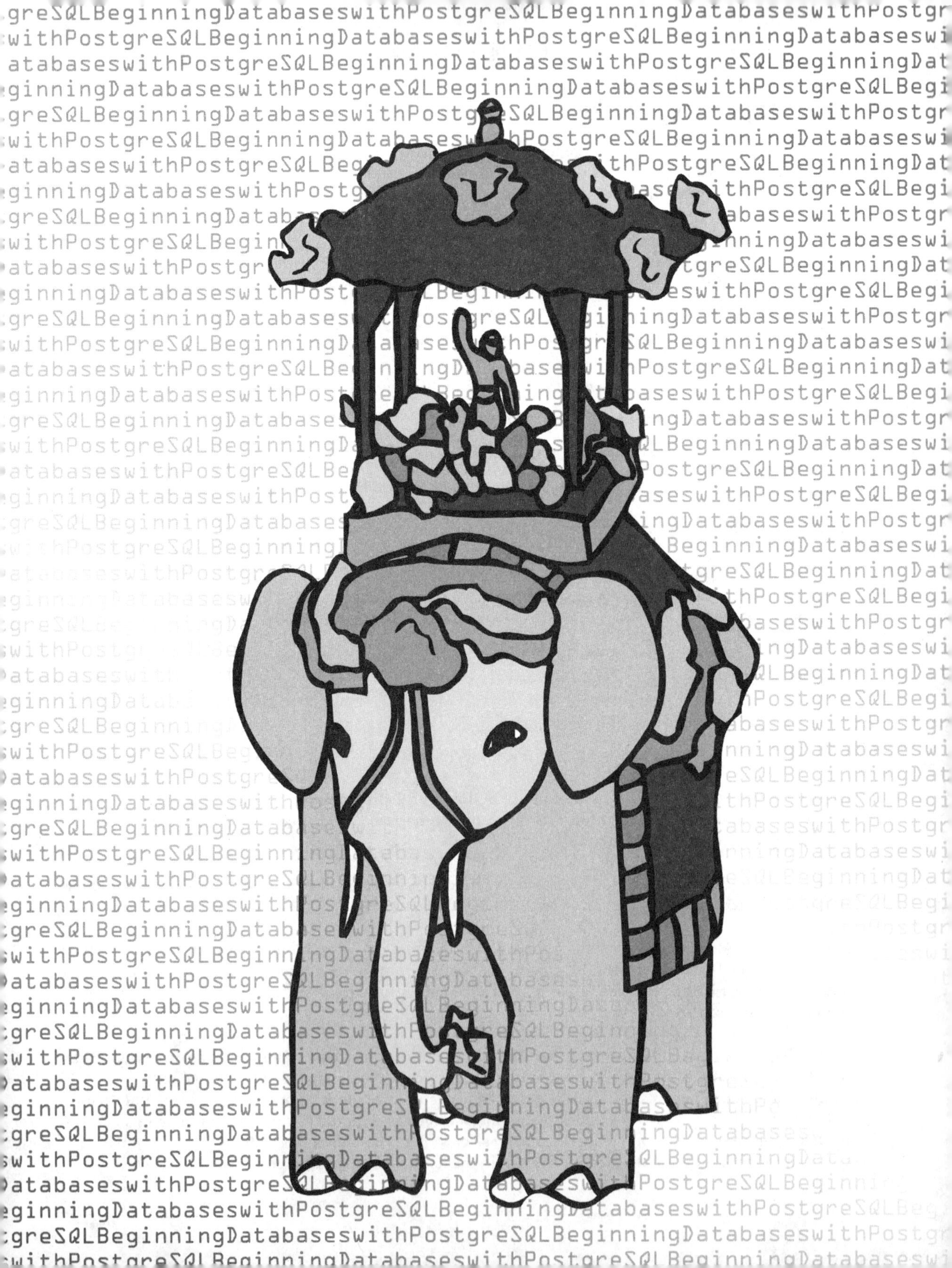

# Accessing PostgreSQL from PHP

Recently, there has been a strong trend towards providing web-based interfaces to online databases. There are a number of reasons supporting this movement, including:

❑ Web browsers are common and familiar interfaces for browsing data

❑ Web-based applications can easily be integrated into an existing web site

❑ Web (HTML) interfaces are easily created and modified

In this chapter, we will explore various methods for accessing PostgreSQL from PHP. PHP is a server-side, cross-platform scripting language for writing web-based applications. It allows you to embed program logic in HTML pages, which enables you to serve dynamic web pages. PHP allows us to create web-based user interfaces that interact with PostgreSQL.

In this chapter, we will assume at least a basic understanding of the PHP language. If you are completely unfamiliar with PHP, you might want to explore some of the following resources first:

❑ The home site of PHP http://www.php.net

❑ *Beginning PHP 4*, Wankyu Choi, Allan Kent, Ganesh Prasad, and Chris Ullman, with Jon Blank and Sean Cazzell, Wrox Press (ISBN 1-861003-73-0)

There are many different schools of thought concerning PHP development methodologies. It is not within the scope of this book to discuss them. Instead, we will focus on designing PHP scripts that make effective use of PHP's PostgreSQL interface.

Note that we will be focusing on PHP version 4. While most of the following code examples and descriptions will apply to earlier versions of PHP, there may be a few differences in functionality. In addition, it is assumed that all code snippets fall within the context of valid PHP scope (generally meaning with the `<?php ?>` tags), unless otherwise specified.

# Adding PostgreSQL Support to PHP

Before you can begin developing PHP scripts that interface with a PostgreSQL database, you will need to include PostgreSQL support in your PHP installation.

If you're not sure whether your existing PHP installation already has PostgreSQL support, create a simple script named `phpinfo.php` (which should be placed in your web server's document root), containing the following line:

```
<?php
phpinfo();
?>
```

Examine the output of this script in your web browser. If PostgreSQL support has already been included, the output will contain a section similar to the following:

**pgsql**

| PostgreSQL | Enabled |
|---|---|
| Active Persistent Links | 0 |
| Active Links | 0 |

| Directive | Local Valu | Master Value |
|---|---|---|
| pgsql.allow_persiste | On | On |
| pgsql.max_links | Unlimited | Unlimited |
| pgsql.max_persisten | Unlimited | Unlimited |

If your PHP installation already has PostgreSQL support, you can continue on to the next section.

If you have the PHP source code, it is fairly easy to add PostgreSQL support. Simply pass the `--with-pgsql` option to the `configure` script:

       **$ ./configure** --with-pgsql

You can optionally specify the directory of your PostgreSQL installation if the `configure` script is unable to locate it by itself:

       **$ ./configure** --with-pgsql=/var/lib/pgsql

Remember that you might need to pass additional options to the `configure` script depending on your build requirements. For example, to build PHP with support for PostgreSQL, LDAP, and XML, you would use the following command line:

       **$ ./configure** --with-pgsql --with-imap --enable-xml

Refer to the PHP documentation (specifically the `INSTALL` document included with the PHP distribution) for additional compilation options and installation instructions. You can also find them at http://www.php.net/manual/en/html/installation.html.

# Using the PHP API for PostgreSQL

All of the interaction with the PostgreSQL database is performed through the PostgreSQL extension, which is a comprehensive set of PHP functions. For a complete list of functions and further information about the same, refer to http://www.php.net/manual/ref.pgsql.php.

A simple PHP script that opens a connection to a PostgreSQL database, selects some rows, prints the number of rows in the resultset, and closes the connection would look something like this:

```php
<?php
$db_handle = pg_connect("dbname=bpsimple");
$query = "SELECT * FROM item";
$result = pg_exec($db_handle, $query);
echo "Number of rows: " . pg_numrows($result);
pg_freeresult($result);
pg_close($db_handle);
?>
```

As you can see, interacting with the database from within PHP is fairly straightforward. We will now cover the various aspects of the PHP PostgreSQL extension in more depth.

# Database Connections

Before you can interact with the database, you must first open a connection to it. Each connection is represented by a single variable (we'll refer to this variable as the **connection handle**). PHP allows you to have multiple connections open at once, each with its own connection handle.

### pg_connect()

Database connections are opened using the pg_connect() function. This function takes a connect string as its only argument and returns a database connection handle. Here's an example:

```php
$db_handle = pg_connect("dbname=bpsimple user=jon");
```

You can create your own user name and use it to connect to the database as user=<username>.

If you want to use PHP variables, remember to surround the connection string in double quotes instead of single quotes:

```php
$db_handle = pg_connect("dbname=$dbname user=$dbuser");
```

All of the standard PostgreSQL connection parameters are available in the connection string. The most commonly used options and their meanings are given in the table below:

| Option | Meaning | Default |
|--------|---------|---------|
| Dbname | Database to connect to | $PGDATABASE |
| User | User name to use when connecting | $PGUSER |
| password | Password for the specified user | $PGPASSWORD or none |
| Host | Name of the server to connect to | $PGHOST or localhost |
| hostaddr | IP address of the server to connect to | $PGHOSTADDR |
| Port | TCP/IP port to connect to on the server | $PGPORT or 5432 |

If the connection attempt fails, the `pg_connect()` function will return false. Failed connection attempts can, thus, be detected by testing the return value:

```php
<?php
$db_handle = pg_connect("dbname=bpsimple");
if ($db_handle) {
    echo 'Connection attempt succeeded.';
} else {
    echo 'Connection attempt failed.';
}
pg_close($db_handle);
?>
```

As mentioned above, PHP supports multiple concurrent database connections:

```php
$db_handle1 = pg_connect("dbname=database1");
$db_handle2 = pg_connect("dbname=database2");
```

## Persistent Connections

PHP also supports **persistent** database connections. Persistent connections are held open beyond the lifetime of the page request, whereas normal connections are closed at the end of the page request. PHP maintains a list of currently open connections and, if a request is made for a new persistence database connection with the same connection parameters as one of the open connections in this list, a handle to the already opened connection is returned instead. This has the advantage of saving the script the additional overhead of creating a new database connection when a suitable one already exists in the connection pool.

### pg_pconnect()

To open a persistent connection to PostgreSQL, use the `pg_pconnect()` function. This function behaves exactly like the `pg_connect()` function described above, except that it requests a persistent connection, if one is available.

It is suggested however that you use persistent connections with care. Overusing persistent connections could lead to a large number of idle database connections to your database. The ideal use of a persistent connection is in those instances where multiple pages will also request the same kind of database connection (meaning one containing same connection parameters). In such cases, persistent connections offer a substantial performance boost.

## Closing Connections

### pg_close()

Database connections can be explicitly closed using the `pg_close()` function:

```php
pg_close($db_handle);
```

There are a few things however that need to be pointed out here. Firstly, in the case of persistent connections, this function will not actually close the connection. Instead, the connection will just be returned to the database connection pool. Secondly, PHP will automatically close any open non-persistent database connections at the end of the script's execution. Both of these points make calling pg_close() largely unnecessary, but the function is included for completeness and for those instances where there is truly a need to close the connection immediately.

If the provided connection handle is invalid, pg_close() will return false. Otherwise, pg_close() will return true upon success.

### Connection Information

PHP provides a number of simple functions for retrieving information on the current database connection based on the connection handle provided. Such functions include:

| Function | Description |
| --- | --- |
| pg_dbname() | Returns the name of the current database |
| pg_host() | Returns the hostname associated with the current connection |
| pg_options() | Returns the options associated with the current connection |
| pg_port() | Returns the port number of the current connection |
| pg_tty() | Returns the TTY name associated with the current connection |

All of these functions require a connection handle as their sole argument and will return either a string or a number upon success. Otherwise, they will return false:

```php
<?php
$db_handle = pg_connect("dbname=bpsimple");
echo "<h1>Connection Information</h1>";
echo "Database name: ' . pg_dbname($db_handle) . "<br>\n";
echo "Hostname: " . pg_host($db_handle) . "<br>\n";
echo "Options: " . pg_options($db_handle) . "<br>\n";
echo "Port: " . pg_port($db_handle) . "<br>\n";
echo "TTY name: " . pg_tty($db_handle) . "<br>\n";
pg_close($db_handle);
?>
```

# Building Queries

We have already seen a simple example of executing a query from PHP. In this section, we will cover the topic of query building and execution in more depth.

SQL queries are merely strings, so they can be built using any of PHP's string functions. The following are three examples of query string construction in PHP:

```php
$lastname = strtolower($lastname);
$query = "SELECT * FROM customer WHERE lname = '$lastname'";
```

This example performs the lower case conversion of $lastname first. Then, it builds the query string using PHP's standard string syntax.

Note that the value of $lastname will remain lower case after these lines:

```
$query = "SELECT * FROM customer WHERE lname = '" .strtolower($lastname) . "'";
```

This example uses an inline call to strtolower(). Functions can't be called from inside string literals (in other words between quotation marks), so we need to break our query string into two pieces and concatenate them (using the "dot" operator) with the function call in between.

Unlike the previous example, the result of the strtolower() function will not affect the value of $lastname after this line is executed by PHP:

```
$query = sprintf("SELECT * FROM customer WHERE lname = '%s'",
strtolower($lastname));
```

This final example uses the sprintf() function to generate the query string. The sprintf() function uses special character combinations (the %s in the above line, for example) to format strings. More information on the sprintf() function is available at http://www.php.net/manual/en/function.sprintf.php.

Each of these approaches will produce exactly the same query string. The best method to use, like most things, will depend on the situation. For simple queries, a direct string assignment will probably work best, but when the situation calls for the interpolation or transformation of a large number of variables, you might want to explore different approaches. In some cases, you might encounter a trade-off between execution speed and code readability. This is true of most programming tasks, so you will have to apply your best judgment.

Here's an example of a complex query written as a long assignment string:

```
$query = "UPDATE table $tablename SET " . strtolower($column) . " = '" .
strtoupper($value) . "'";
```

This could be rewritten using the PHP sprintf() function as:

```
$query = sprintf("UPDATE table %s SET %s = '%s'", $tablename, strtolower($column),
strtoupper($value));
```

The second expression is clearly more readable than the first, although benchmarking will show that this readability comes at a slight performance cost as programmer time is much more expensive than machine time. In this case, the tradeoff of readability over execution speed is probably worth it, unless you are doing hundreds of these types of string constructions per page request.

## Complex Queries

In an ideal world, all of our queries would be as simple as those used in the previous examples, but we all know that is seldom true. In those cases where more complex queries need to be built, we find that PHP offers a number of convenient functions to aid us in our task.

For example, consider the case where a large number of table deletions need to be performed. In raw SQL, the query might look something like this:

```
DELETE FROM items WHERE item_id = 4 OR item_id = 6
```

Now, that query alone doesn't appear all that complicated, but what if this query needed to delete a dozen rows, specifying the item_id of each row in the WHERE clause? The query string gets pretty long at that point, and because the number of expressions in the where clause probably needs to be varying we need to account for these details in our code.

We will probably be receiving our list of item IDs to be deleted from the user via some method of HTML form input, so we can assume they will be stored in some kind of array format (at least, that's the most convenient means of storing the list). We'll assume this array of item IDs is named $item_ids. Based on that assumption, the above query could be constructed as follows:

```php
<?php
$db_handle = pg_connect("dbname=bpsimple");
$query = "DELETE FROM items WHERE ";
$query .= "item_id = " . $item_ids[0];
if (count($item_ids) > 1) {
array_shift($item_ids);
$query .= " or item_id = " .
implode(" or item_id =", $item_ids);
pg_close($db_handle);
?>
```

This will produce an SQL query with an arbitrary number of item IDs. Based on this code, we can write a generic function to perform our deletions:

```php
<?php
$db_handle = pg_connect("dbname=bpsimple");

function sqlDelete($tablename, $column, $ids)
{
    $query = '';
    if (is_array($ids)) {
        $query = "DELETE FROM $tablename WHERE ";
        $query .= "$column = " . $ids[0];
        if (count($ids) > 1) {
            array_shift($ids);
            $query .= " or $column = " .
                implode(" or $column =", $ids);
        }
    }
    return $query;
}
pg_close($db_handle);
?>
```

### *Executing Queries*

Once the query string has been constructed, the next step is to execute it. Queries are executed using the pg_exec() function.

#### *pg_exec()*

The pg_exec() function is responsible for sending the query string to the PostgreSQL server and returning the resultset.

Here's a simple example to illustrate the use of pg_exec():

```php
<?php
$db_handle = pg_connect("dbname=bpsimple");
$query = 'SELECT * FROM customer';
$result = pg_exec($db_handle, $query);
pg_close($db_handle);
?>
```

As you can see, pg_exec() requires two parameters: an active connection handle and a query string. You should already be familiar with each of these from the previous sections. pg_exec() will return a resultset upon successful execution of the query. We will work with resultsets in the next section.

If the query should fail, or if the connection handle is invalid, pg_exec() will return false. It is, therefore, prudent to test the return value of pg_exec() so that you can detect such failures.

The following example includes some result checking:

```php
<?php
$db_handle = pg_connect("dbname=bpsimple");
$query = "SELECT * FROM customer";
$result = pg_exec($db_handle, $query);
if ($result) {
    echo "The query executed successfully.<br>\n";
} else {
    echo "The query failed with the following error:<br>\n";
    echo pg_errormessage($db_handle);
}
pg_close($db_handle);
?>
```

In this example, we test the return value of pg_exec(). If it is not false (in other words it has a value), $result represents a resultset. Otherwise, if $result is false, we know that an error has occurred. We can then use the pg_errormessage() function to print a descriptive message for that error. We will cover error messages in more detail later in this chapter.

# Working with Resultsets

Upon successful execution of a query, pg_exec() will return a resultset identifier, through which we can access the resultset. The resultset stores the result of the query as returned by the database. For example, if a selection query were executed, the resultset would contain the resulting rows.

PHP offers a number of useful functions for working with resultsets. All of them take a resultset identifier as an argument, so they can only be used after a query has been successfully executed. We learned how to test for successful execution in the previous section.

### pg_numrows() and pg_numfields()

Now we'll start with the two simplest result functions: `pg_numrows()` and `pg_numfields()`. These two functions return the number of rows and the number of fields in the resultset, respectively. For example:

```php
<?php
$db_handle = pg_connect("dbname=bpsimple");
$query = "SELECT * FROM customer";
$result = pg_exec($db_handle, $query);
if ($result) {
    echo "The query executed successfully.<br>\n";
    echo "Number of rows in result: " . pg_numrows($result) . "<br>\n";
    echo "Number of fields in result: " . pg_numfields($result);
} else {
    echo "The query failed with the following error:<br>\n";
    echo pg_errormessage($db_handle);
}
pg_close($db_handle);
?>
```

These functions will return −1 if there is an error.

### pg_cmdtuples()

There's also the `pg_cmdtuples()` function, which will return the number of rows **affected** by the query. For example, if we were performing insertions or deletions with our query, we wouldn't actually be retrieving any rows from the database, so the number of rows or fields in the resultset would not be indicative of the query's result. Instead, the changes take place inside of the database. `pg_cmdtuples()` will return the number of rows that were affected by these types of queries (in other words the number of rows inserted, deleted, or updated):

```php
<?php
$db_handle = pg_connect("dbname=bpsimple");
$query = "DELETE FROM item WHERE cost_price > 10.00";
$result = pg_exec($db_handle, $query);
if ($result) {
    echo "The query executed successfully.<br>\n";
    echo "Number of rows deleted: " . pg_cmdtuples($result);
} else {
    echo "The query failed with the following error:<br>\n";
    echo pg_errormessage($db_handle);
}
pg_close($db_handle);
?>
```

The `pg_cmdtuples()` function will return 0 if no rows in the database were affected by the query, as in the case of a selection query.

## *Extracting Values from Resultsets*

There are a number of ways to extract values from resultsets. We will start with the pg_result() function.

### pg_result()

The pg_result() function is used when you want to retrieve a single value from a resultset. In addition to a resultset identifier, you must also specify the row and field that you want to retrieve from the result. The row is specified numerically, while the field may be specified either by name or by numeric index. Numbering always starts at zero.

Here's an example using pg_result():

```php
<?php
$db_handle = pg_connect("dbname=bpsimple");
$query = "SELECT title, fname, lname FROM customer";
$result = pg_exec($db_handle, $query);
if ($result) {
    echo "The query executed successfully.<br>\n";
    for ($row = 0; $row < pg_numrows($result); $row++) {
        $fullname = pg_result($result, $row, 'title') . " ";
        $fullname .= pg_result($result, $row, 'fname') . " ";
        $fullname .= pg_result($result, $row, 'lname');
        echo "Customer: $fullname<br>\n";
    }
} else {
    echo "The query failed with the following error:<br>\n";
    echo pg_errormessage($db_handle);
}
pg_close($db_handle);
?>
```

Using numeric indices, this same block of code could also be written like this:

```php
<?php
$db_handle = pg_connect("dbname=bpsimple");
$query = "SELECT title, fname, lname FROM customer";
$result = pg_exec($db_handle, $query);
if ($result) {
    echo "The query executed successfully.<br>\n";
    for ($row = 0; $row < pg_numrows($result); $row++) {
        for ($col = 0; $col < pg_numfields($result); $col++) {
        $fullname = pg_result($result, $row, $col) . " ";
            $fullname .= pg_result($result, $row, $col) . " ";
            $fullname .= pg_result($result, $row, $col);
            echo "Customer: $fullname<br>\n";
        }
    }
} else {
    echo "The query failed with the following error:<br>\n";
    echo pg_errormessage($db_handle);
}
pg_close($db_handle);
?>
```

The first example is a bit more readable, however, and doesn't depend on the order of the fields in the resultset. PHP also offers more advanced ways of retrieving values from resultsets, because iterating through rows of results isn't especially efficient,

### pg_fetch_row()

PHP provides two functions, `pg_fetch_row()` and `pg_fetch_array()`, that can return multiple result values at once. Each of these functions returns an array.

`pg_fetch_row()` returns an array that corresponds to a single row in the resultset. The array is indexed numerically, starting from zero. Here is the previous example rewritten to use `pg_fetch_row()`:

```php
<?php
$db_handle = pg_connect("dbname=bpsimple");
$query = "SELECT title, fname, lname FROM customer";
$result = pg_exec($db_handle, $query);
if ($result) {
    echo "The query executed successfully.<br>\n";
    for ($row = 0; $row < pg_numrows($result); $row++) {
        $values = pg_fetch_row($result, $row);
        for ($col = 0; $col < count($values); $col++) {
        $fullname = $values[$col] . " ";
            $fullname .= $values[$col] . " ";
            $fullname .= $values[$col];
        echo "Customer: $fullname<br>\n";
            }
        }
} else {
    echo "The query failed with the following error:<br>\n";
    echo pg_errormessage($db_handle);
}
pg_close($db_handle);
?>
```

As you can see, using `pg_fetch_row()` eliminates the multiple calls to `pg_result()`. It also places the result values in an array, which can be easily manipulated using PHP's native array functions.

In this example, However, we are still accessing the fields by their numeric indices. Ideally, we should also be able to access each field by its associated name. To accomplish that, we can use the `pg_fetch_array()` function.

### pg_fetch_array()

The `pg_fetch_array()` function also returns an array, but it allows us to specify whether we want that array indexed numerically or associatively (using the field names as keys). This preference is specified by passing one of the following as the third argument to `pg_fetch_array()`:

| Option | Description |
| --- | --- |
| PGSQL_ASSOC | Index the resulting array by field name |
| PGSQL_NUM | Index the resulting array numerically |
| PGSQL_BOTH | Index the resulting array both numerically and by field name |

If you don't specify one of the above indexing methods, PGSQL_BOTH will be used by default. Note that this will double the size of your resultset, so you're probably better off explicitly specifying one of the above. Also note, that the field names will always be returned in lower case letters, regardless of how they're represented in the database itself.

Here's the example rewritten once more, now using pg_fetch_array():

```php
<?php
$db_handle = pg_connect("dbname=bpsimple");
$query = "SELECT title, fname, lname FROM customer";
$result = pg_exec($db_handle, $query);
if ($result) {
    echo "The query executed successfully.<br>\n";
for ($row = 0; $row < pg_numrows($result); $row++) {
        $values = pg_fetch_array($result, $row, PGSQL_ASSOC);
$fullname = $values['title'] . " ";
        $fullname .= $values['fname'] . " ";
        $fullname .= $values['lname'];
echo "Customer: $fullname<br>\n";
    }
} else {
    echo "The query failed with the following error:<br>\n";
    echo pg_errormessage($db_handle);
}
pg_close($db_handle);
?>
```

### pg_fetch_object()

PHP also allows you to fetch the result values with the pg_fetch_object() function. Each field name will be represented as a property of this object. Thus, fields can not be accessed numerically. Written using pg_fetch_object(), our examples looks like this:

```php
<?php
$db_handle = pg_connect("dbname=bpsimple");
$query = "SELECT title, fname, lname FROM customer";
$result = pg_exec($db_handle, $query);
if ($result) {
    echo "The query executed successfully.<br>\n";
for ($row = 0; $row < pg_numrows($result); $row++) {
        $values = pg_fetch_object($result, $row, PGSQL_ASSOC);
$fullname = $values->title . " ";
        $fullname .= $values->fname . " ";
        $fullname .= $values->lname;
echo "Customer: $fullname<br>\n";
    }
} else {
    echo "The query failed with the following error:<br>\n";
    echo pg_errormessage($db_handle);
}
pg_close($db_handle);
?>
```

## Field Information

PHP allows you to gather some information on the field values in your resultset. These functions may be useful in certain circumstances, so we will cover them briefly here.

### pg_fieldisnull()

PostgreSQL supports a notion of NULL field values. PHP doesn't necessarily define NULL the same way PostgreSQL does, however. To account for this, PHP provides the `pg_fieldisnull()` function so that you may determine whether a field value is NULL based on the PostgreSQL definition of NULL:

```php
<?php
$db_handle = pg_connect("dbname=bpsimple");
$query = "SELECT title, fname, lname FROM customer";
$result = pg_exec($db_handle, $query);
if (pg_fieldisnull($result, $row, $field)) {
    echo "$field is NULL.";
} else {
    echo "$field is " . pg_result($result, $row, $field);
}
pg_close($db_handle);
?>
```

### pg_fieldname() and pg_fieldnum()

These functions return the name or number of a given field. The fields are indexed numerically, starting with zero:

```php
<?php
$db_handle = pg_connect("dbname=bpsimple");
$query = "SELECT title, fname, lname FROM customer";
$result = pg_exec($db_handle, $query);
if (pg_fieldisnull($result, $row, $field)) {
    echo "$field is NULL.";
    echo "Field 1 is named: " . pg_fieldname($result, 1);
    echo "Field item_id is number: " . pg_fieldnum($result, "item_id");
} else {
    echo "$field is " . pg_result($result, $row, $field);
}
pg_close($db_handle);
?>
```

Note that `pg_fieldname()` will return the field name as specified in the SELECT statement.

### pg_fieldsize(), pg_fieldprtlen(), and pg_fieldtype()

The size, printed (character) length, and type of fields can be determined:

```php
<?php
$db_handle = pg_connect("dbname=bpsimple");
$query = "SELECT title, fname, lname FROM customer";
$result = pg_exec($db_handle, $query);
if (pg_fieldisnull($result, $row, $field)) {
    echo "$field is NULL.";
    echo "Field 1 is named: " . pg_fieldname($result, 1);
    echo "Field 1 is named: " . pg_fieldname($result, 1);
    echo "Field item_id is number: " . pg_fieldnum($result, "item_id");
```

```
        echo  "Size of field 2:" . pg_fieldsize($result, 2);
        echo "Length of field 2: " . pg_fieldprtlen($result, $row, 2);
        echo "Type of field 2: " . pg_fieldtype($result, 2);
    } else {
        echo "$field is " . pg_result($result, $row, $field);
    }
    pg_close($db_handle);
    ?>
```

As usual, the numeric field indices start at zero. Field indices may also be specified as a string representing the field name.

Also, if the size of the field is variable, pg_fieldsize() will return a –1, or false on an error pg_fieldprtlen() will return –1 on an error.

## Freeing Resultsets

### pg_freeresult()

It is possible to free the memory used by a resultset by using the pg_freeresult() function:

```
pg_freeresult($result);
```

PHP will automatically free up all result memory at the end of the script's execution anyway, so this function only needs to be called if you're especially worried about memory consumption in your script, and you know you won't be using this resultset again later on in your script's execution.

### Type Conversion of Result Values

PHP does not offer the diverse data type support you might find in other languages, so values in resultsets are sometimes converted from their original data type to a PHP-native data type. For the most part, this conversion will have very little or no effect on your application, but it's important to be aware that some type conversion may occur:

❑   All integer, boolean, and OID types are converted to integers

❑   All forms of floating point numbers are converted to doubles

❑   All other types (arrays, etc.) are represented as strings

# Error Handling

We touched on error handling very briefly in an earlier section. We will now cover it in a bit more detail.

Nearly all PostgreSQL related functions return some sort of predictable value upon an error (generally false or –1). This makes it fairly easy to detect error situations so that your script can fail gracefully. For example:

```
$db_handle = pg_connect('dbname=bpsimple');
if (!$db_handle) {
    header("Location: http://www.example.com/error.php");
    exit;
}
```

In the above example, the user was to be redirected to an error page if the database connection attempt were to fail.

### pg_errormessage()

pg_errormessage() can be used to retrieve the text of the actual error message as returned by the database server. pg_errormessage() will always return the text of the last error message generated by the server. Be sure to take that into consideration when designing your error handling and display logic.

You will find that, depending on your level of error reporting, PHP can be fairly verbose when an error occurs, often outputting several lines of errors and warnings. In a production environment, it is often undesirable to display this type of message to the end user.

### The @ Symbol

The most direct solution is to lower the level of error reporting in PHP (controlled via the error_reporting configuration variable in the php.ini). The second option is to suppress these error messages directly from PHP code on a per-function-call basis. PHP uses the @ symbol to indicate error suppression. For example, no errors will be output from the following code:

```
$db_handle = pg_connect("host=nonexistent_host");
$result = @pg_exec($db_handle, "SELECT * FROM item");
```

Without the @ symbol, the second line above would generate an error complaining about the lack of a valid database connection (assuming your error reporting level was high enough to cause that error to be displayed, of course).

Note that the above error could still be detected by testing the value of $result, though, so suppressing the error message output doesn't preclude our dealing with error situations programmatically. Furthermore, we could display the error message at our convenience using the pg_errormessage() function.

> If (!result ....) outputs an error, it means that there is an error in the SQL query.    If (!pg_cmdTuples($result)) outputs an error, there is an error in at least one of the values in SQL query.

# Character Encoding

If character encoding support is enabled in PostgreSQL, PHP provides functions for getting and setting the current client encoding. By default, the encoding is set to SQL ASCII.

The supported character sets are: SQL_ASCII, EUC_JP, EUC_CN, EUC_KR, EUC_TW, UNICODE, MULE_INTERNAL, LATINX (X=1...9), KOI8, WIN, ALT, SJIS, BIG5, WIN1250.

### pg_client_encoding()

The pg_client_encoding() function will return the current client encoding:

```
$encoding = pg_client_encoding($db_handle);
```

### pg_set_client_encoding()

You can set the current client encoding using the `pg_set_client_encoding()` function:

```
pg_set_client_encoding($db_handle, 'UNICODE');
```

# PEAR

PEAR (The PHP Extension and Application Repository) is an attempt to replicate the functionality of Perl's CPAN in the PHP community. To quote the official PEAR goals:

❑ To provide a consistent means for library code authors to share their code with other developers

❑ To give the PHP community an infrastructure for sharing code

❑ To define standards that help developers write portable and reusable code

❑ To provide tools for code maintenance and distribution

PEAR is primarily a large collection of PHP classes, which make use of PHP's object-oriented programming capabilities. You will therefore, need to become familiar with PHP's syntax for working with classes. PHP's object-oriented extensions are documented here: http://www.php.net/manual/en/language.oop.php.

More information on PEAR is available at:

❑ http://pear.php.net

❑ http://php.weblogs.com/php_pear_tutorials/

## PEAR's Database Abstraction Interface

PEAR includes a database (DB) abstraction interface, which is included with the standard PHP distribution. The advantage to using a database abstraction interface instead of calling the database's native functions directly is code independence. Should you need to move your project to a different database, it would probably involve a major code rewrite. If you had used a database abstraction interface, however, the task would be trivial.

PEAR's DB interface also adds some value-added features, such as convenient access to multiple resultsets and integrated error handling. All of the database interaction is handled through the DB classes and objects. This is conceptually similar to Perl's DBI interface.

The main disadvantage to a database abstraction interface is the performance overhead it incurs on your applications execution. Once again, this is a situation where there is a trade-off between code flexibility and performance.

### Using the DB Interface

The following example illustrates the use of the DB interface: note that this example assumes that the PEAR DB interface has already been installed and that it can be found via the current `include_path` setting. Both of these are the default for newer PHP4 installations:

```php
<?php

/* Import the PEAR DB interface. */
require_once "DB.php";

/* Database connection parameters. */
$username = "jon";
$password = "secret";
$hostname = "localhost";
$dbname = "bpsimple";

/* Construct the DSN - Data Source Name. */
$dsn = "pgsql://$username:$password@$hostname/$dbname";

/* Attempt to connect to the database. */
$db = DB::connect($dsn);

/* Check for any connection errors. */
if (DB::isError($db)) {
    die ($db->getMessage());
}

/* Execute a selection query. */
$query = "SELECT title, fname, lname FROM customer";
$result = $db->query($query);

/* Check for any query execution errors. */
if (DB::isError($result)) {
    die ($result->getMessage());
}

/* Fetch and display the query results. */
while ($row = $result->fetchRow(DB_FETCHMODE_ASSOC)) {
$fullname = $row['title'] . " ";
    $fullname .= $row['fname'] . " ";
    $fullname .= $row['lname'];
echo "Customer: $fullname<br>\n";
}

/* Disconnect from the database. */
$db->disconnect();

?>
```

As you can see, this code, while not using any PostgreSQL functions directly, still follows the same programmatic logic of our previous examples. It is also easy to see how the above example could easily be adapted to use another type of database (Oracle or MySQL, for example) without much effort.

## PEAR's Error Handling

Using the PEAR DB interface offers you as a developer a number of additional advantages. For example, PEAR includes an integrated error handling system. Here is some code to demonstrate error handling:

```php
<?php

/* Import the PEAR DB interface. */
require_once 'DB.php';

/* Construct the DSN - Data Source Name. */
$dsn = "pgsql://jon:secret@localhost/bpsimple";
```

**423**

```
    /* Attempt to connect to the database. */
    $db = DB::connect($dsn);

    /* Check for any connection errors. */
    if (DB::isError($db)) {
        die ($db->getMessage());
    }
```

Above, we see the first instance of PEAR's error handling capabilities: `DB::isError()`. If the call to `DB::connect()` fails for some reason, it will return an `PEAR_Error` instance, instead of a database connection object. We can test for this case using the `DB::isError()` function, as shown above.

Knowing an error occurred is important, but finding out why that error occurred is even more important. We can retrieve the text of the error message (in this case, the connection error generated by PostgreSQL) using the `getMessage()` method of the `PEAR_Error` object. This is also demonstrated in the example above.

Our example continues with some queries:

```
    /* Make errors fatal. */
    $db->setErrorHandling(PEAR_ERROR_DIE);

    /* Build and execute the query. */
    $query = "SELECT title, fname, lname FROM customer";
    $result = $db->query($query);

    /* Check for any query execution errors. */
    if (DB::isError($result)) {
        die ($result->getMessage());
    }

    while ($row = $result->fetchRow(DB_FETCHMODE_ASSOC)) {
    $fullname = $row['title'] . " ";
        $fullname .= $row['fname'] . " ";
        $fullname .= $row['lname'];
    echo "Customer: $fullname<br>\n";
    }

    /* Disconnect from the database. */
    $db->disconnect();

    ?>
```

Note that we have changed PEAR's error handling behavior with the call to the `setErrorHandling()` method. Setting the error handling behavior to `PEAR_ERROR_DIE` will cause PHP to exit fatally if an error occurs.

Here's a list of the other error handling behaviors:

| Behavior | Description |
| --- | --- |
| PEAR_ERROR_RETURN | Simply return an error object (default) |
| PEAR_ERROR_PRINT | Print the error message and continue execution |
| PEAR_ERROR_TRIGGER | Use PHP's trigger_error() function to raise an internal error |
| PEAR_ERROR_DIE | Print the error message and abort execution |
| PEAR_ERROR_CALLBACK | Use a callback function to handle the error before aborting execution |

Additional information on the PEAR_Error class and PEAR error handling is available here: http://php.net/manual/en/class.pear-error.php.

## Query Preparation and Execution

PEAR also includes a handle method of preparing and executing queries. Here's an abbreviated example demonstrating the prepare() and execute() methods of the DB interface. This example assumes we already have a valid database connection (from a DB::connect()):

```
/* Set up the $items array. */
$items = array(
     '6241527836190' => 20,
     '7241427238373' => 21,
     '7093454306788' => 22
);

/* Prepare our template SQL statement. */
$statement = $db->prepare("INSERT INTO barcode VALUES(?,?)");

/* Execute the statement for each entry in the $items array. */
while (list($barcode, $item_id) = each($items)) {
     $db->execute($statement, array($barcode, $item_id));
}
```

This example probably requires some explanation for those of you who are unfamiliar with prepared SQL statements.

The call to the prepare() method creates a SQL template that can be executed repetitively. Note the two wildcard spots in the statement that are specified using question marks. These placeholders will be replaced with actual values later on when we call the execute() method.

Assuming we have an array of $items that contain barcodes and item IDs, we will want to perform one database insertion per item. To accomplish this, we construct a loop to iterate over each entry in the $items array, extract the barcode and item ID, and then execute the prepared SQL statement.

As mentioned above, the execute() method will replace the placeholder values in the prepared statement with those values passed to it in the second argument in array form. In the above example, this would be the array($barcode, $item_id) argument. The placeholder values are replaced in the order these new values are specified, so it's important to get them right.

Hopefully, you'll find this feature of the PEAR DB interface very useful in your own projects.

# Summary

In this chapter, we examined the various ways that a PostgreSQL database can be accessed from the PHP scripting language.

We covered the various aspects of database connections, query building and execution, resultset manipulation, and error handling. We also introduced the PEAR database abstraction interface.

From this foundation, you should now have enough of the basic tools to begin developing your own web-based database applications.

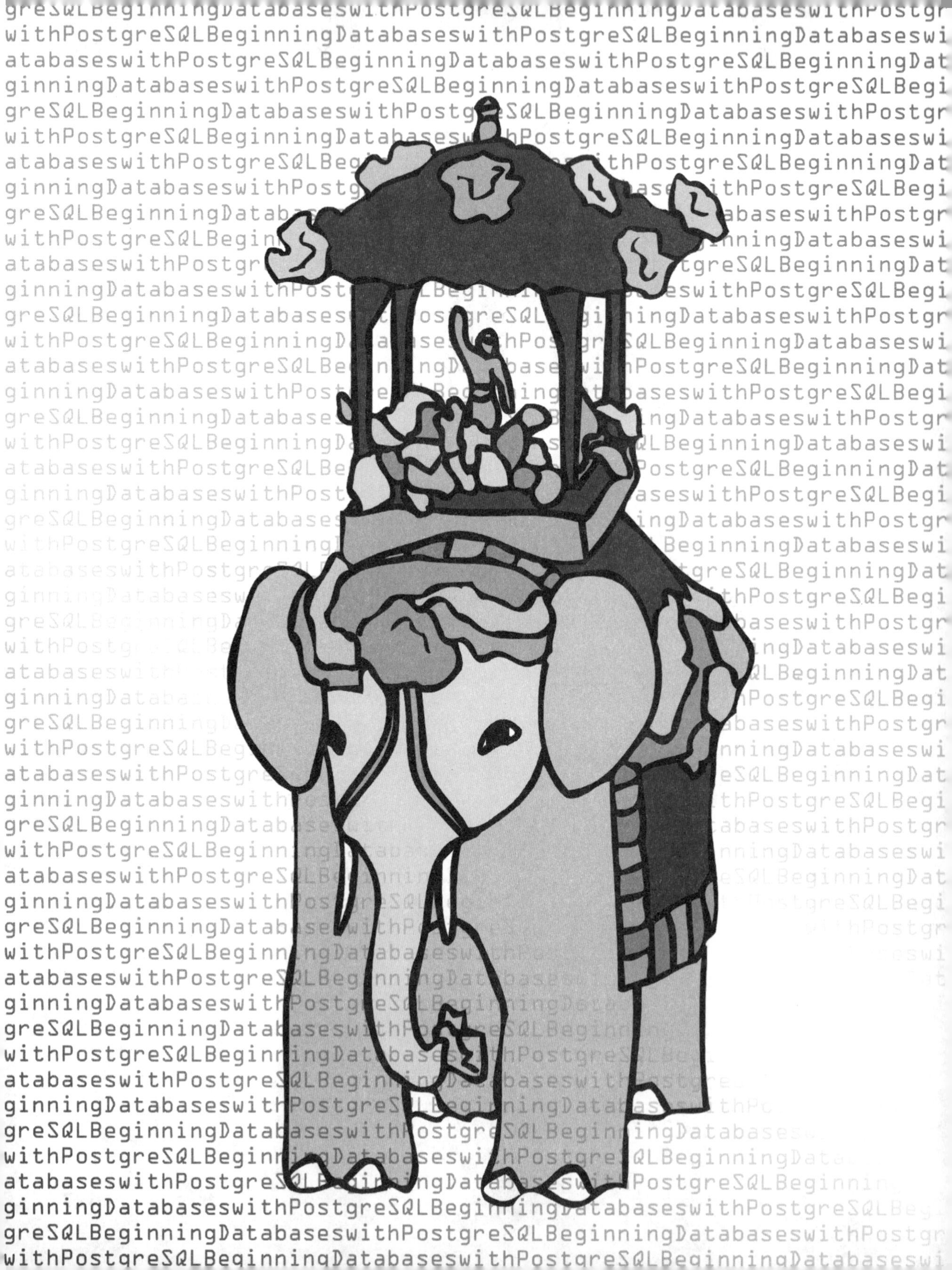

# Accessing PostgreSQL From Perl

As earlier chapters have shown, communicating with PostgreSQL generally involves a lot of string manipulation. One language that excels at string manipulation is Perl. In this chapter, we'll see how to use Perl with PostgreSQL.

In Chapter 13, we demonstrated that the libpq interface is powerful, but it is readily apparent that C's native string representation is quite primitive. We used NULL terminated sequence of characters, and for short programs, code dealing with strings can overshadow the database interaction. As Chapter 13 pointed out, although binary access is possible, its benefits are minimal. With Perl, strings are much more sophisticated, supporting functionality such as joining, splitting, pattern matching, and automatic conversion to and from other data types.

Perl has also historically been associated with web server processing, and having interfaces to databases definitely adds benefits. More modern mechanisms, however, such as PHP described in the previous chapter, are taking over these days.

We will not attempt to teach Perl here, but if you are completely unfamiliar with the language, some useful starting points are:

- ❑ http://www.perl.org and http://www.cpan.org
- ❑ *Beginning Perl*, Simon Cozens. Wrox Press (ISBN 1-861003-14-5)
- ❑ *Learning Perl*, Randal L. Schwartz and Tom Christiansen. O'Reilly (ISBN 1-56592-284-0)

The code in this chapter will not make use of many Perl idioms, so it should be readable by most C programmers. Things to remember are that:

- ❑ Scalar variables (numbers or strings – Perl, converts between these as required) begin with a $ symbol
- ❑ Lists (simple arrays) begin with a @ symbol
- ❑ And hashes (associative arrays) with a % character

One aspect that might confuse the newcomers to the language is that you only use @ or % when referring to the complete collection. For individual elements, you still use a $ symbol.

If you know even a little about Perl, you will be aware that one of the language's axioms is that there is always more than one way to tackle any given job – in fact, Perl enthusiasts would be disappointed if they had to limit their options to single figures. We do not propose to bombard you with numerous techniques for accessing PostgreSQL databases from Perl however: instead, we will present two best of breed mechanisms.

There are essentially three ways to access PostgreSQL from Perl:

❑   Low level – more or less a Perl mapping of the libpq C interface (pqsql_perl5)

❑   High level – a database independent layer

❑   Embedding the Perl interpreter (similar to the description in Chapter 14)

We will present an example of low-level access, because its use is very close to the C interface discussed in Chapter 13, and we will describe high-level access, because it is very flexible and powerful. We will not, however, touch on the final option here, PL/Perl does not offer as many benefits as, say, ecpg does for C since string manipulation is much easier in Perl than C. In addition, it is tricky to build PL/Perl because it requires a version of Perl to have been initially built as a shared library (libperl.so as opposed to the more usual libperl.a), which is beyond the scope of this book (see the instructions for building Perl to be found in Perl source distributions).

# The pgsql_perl5 or Pg Module

There are several Perl modules, which offer direct (or, as direct as Perl permits) access to libpq functionality, one of which is Edmund Mergl's pgsql_perl5, otherwise known as Pg. This particular PostgreSQL access module is the one you are most likely to come across first, if only because it is part of the PostgreSQL distribution.

## Installing pgsql_perl5

The PostgreSQL web site points to a number of downloads pre-built for different operating systems, which may offer the easiest way to install the module. For example, if you have a RedHat Linux distribution, simply select the following:

```
postgresql-perl- version - release . architecture .rpm
```

Install it with one of the GUI RPM tools or using a command, such as:

```
$ rpm -i$ rpm -i postgresql-perl-7.1.2-1.i386.rpm
```

On the other hand, you may be forced to (or simply want to) build from source. If you have the whole PostgreSQL source tree, you can either include the Perl interfaces as part of the complete build or deal with them separately. To do the former, append the --with-perl option to the configure command (the first step in building PostgreSQL, as described in Chapter 3), and then build the complete PostgreSQL distribution as normal.

If you want to build this Perl module by itself, maybe you have found a newer version (version 1.8.0 is included with PostgreSQL 7.1.2, but version 1.9.0, the latest at the time of writing, may be found at CPAN) then unpackage the tarball:

```
$ tar xfz pgsql_perl5-1.9.0.tar.gz
```

Before building, set POSTGRES_INCLUDE to the directory containing the libpq include files (such as /usr/local/pgsql/include on a standard Red Hat distribution) and POSTGRES_LIB to that containing the library files (for example, /usr/local/pgsql/lib). Note that this is the procedure for building version 1.9.0: version 1.8.0 uses the single environment variable POSTGRES_HOME instead, which should point to where you have installed PostgreSQL (such that the PostgreSQL include files may be found in $POSTGRES_HOME/include and the libraries in $POSTGRES_HOME/lib). After that, execute the following commands:

```
$ perl Makefile.PL
$ make
$ make test
```

Then the final step, which must be done as root:

```
# make install
```

### CPAN

CPAN is the Comprehensive Perl Archive Network, at http://www.cpan.org, a central repository for virtually every Perl module in existence. It is a familiar resource to just about any Perl programmer.

The command sequence shown above is the one used for all CPAN modules: a configuration step, producing a real Makefile, which can then be built. The third step, verifying that the build succeeded, is optional, but usually a good idea. The final step copies the built files to their correct places within the operating system file space.

The build and install sequence is so uniform that there is a convenient shortcut. If you grab and install the CPAN module (you **will** have to do this one manually), you can then download, build, and install any module from CPAN with, for example:

```
perl -MCPAN -e 'install DBI'
```

Users of ActiveState's (http://www.activestate.com) Perl have a similar shortcut in the ppm command. Do ppm -h for details.

Incidentally, CPAN modules adopt conventions beyond this build sequence, such as documentation, which can be viewed using the perldoc command after the module has been installed, for example:

```
perldoc DBI
```

# Using pgsql_perl5

The pgsql_perl5 interface looks very similar to the C interface, so the function names should be familiar. In fact, the Perl interface is so close to the C interface that the following is an almost line-by-line "port" of Chapter 13's select2.c program:

```
select_c.pl
#!/usr/bin/perl -w
```

```perl
use Pg;
use strict;

sub doSQL
{
    my ($conn, $command) = @_;

    print $command, "\n";

    my $result = $conn->exec($command);
    print "status is ", $result->resultStatus, "\n";
    print "#rows affected ", $result->cmdTuples, "\n";
    print "result message: ", $conn->errorMessage, "\n";

    if($result->resultStatus eq PGRES_TUPLES_OK) {
        print "number of rows returned = ", $result->ntuples, "\n";
        print "number of fields returned = ", $result->nfields, "\n";

        for(my $r = 0; $r < $result->ntuples; ++$r) {
            for(my $n = 0; $n < $result->nfields; ++$n) {
                print " ", $result->fname($n), " = ",
                        $result->getvalue($r, $n), "(",
                        $result->getlength($r, $n), "),";
            }
            print "\n";
        }
    }
}

my $conn = Pg::connectdb("");

if($conn->status eq PGRES_CONNECTION_OK) {
    print "connection made\n";

    doSQL($conn, "DROP TABLE number");
    doSQL($conn, "CREATE TABLE number ( value INTEGER, name  VARCHAR )");
    doSQL($conn, "INSERT INTO number values(42, 'The Answer')");
    doSQL($conn, "INSERT INTO number values(29, 'My Age')");
    doSQL($conn, "INSERT INTO number values(29, 'Anniversary')");
    doSQL($conn, "INSERT INTO number values(66, 'Clickety-Click')");
    doSQL($conn, "SELECT * FROM number WHERE value = 29");
    doSQL($conn, "UPDATE number SET name = 'Zaphod' WHERE value = 42");
    doSQL($conn, "DELETE FROM number WHERE value = 29");
} else {
    print "connection failed\n";
}
```

Actually, this is **new style** – there is an old style interface, which maps even more closely to libpq. For example, instead of $conn->exec($command), the old style interface uses PQexec($conn, $command). However, the new style is more Perl-ish. The old style is deprecated and will be dropped in a future version of the module.

You run the script with the command:

```
$ perl select_c.pl
```

Note that, as with the C version from which this has been ported, this uses the PG* environment variables, or connects to the default database.

Alternatively, if you mark the script as executable (with chmod 750 select_c.pl), you can simply type:

```
$ ./select_c.pl
```

The output, shown below, is practically identical to that produced by the corresponding C code:

```
connection made
DROP TABLE number
status is 1
#rows affected is
error message:
CREATE TABLE number ( value INTEGER, name  VARCHAR )
status is 1
#rows affected is
error message:
INSERT INTO number values(42, 'The Answer')
status is 1
#rows affected is 1
error message:
INSERT INTO number values(29, 'My Age')
status is 1
#rows affected is 1
error message:
INSERT INTO number values(29, 'Anniversary')
status is 1
#rows affected is 1
error message:
INSERT INTO number values(66, 'Clickety-Click')
status is 1
#rows affected is 1
error message:
SELECT * FROM number WHERE value = 29
status is 2
#rows affected is
error message:
number of rows returned = 2
number of fields returned = 2
 value = 29(2), name = My Age(6),
 value = 29(2), name = Anniversary(11),
UPDATE number SET name = 'Zaphod' WHERE value = 42
status is 1
#rows affected is 1
error message:
DELETE FROM number WHERE value = 29
status is 1
#rows affected is 2
error message:
```

Let's examine the PostgreSQL specific operations in this code. The first line of interest is the equivalent of a C #include <libpq-fe.h> and makes the module's functionality available to our code:

```
use Pg;
```

Hopping past doSQL to the main routine, the database connection is made with:

```
$conn = Pg::connectdb("");
```

As with PQconnectdb(), this takes a connection string, such as dbname=bpsimple user=rick and the same PG* environment variables are read for values not explicitly given, as listed below:

| Data | Environment Variable | Default |
|------|---------------------|---------|
| Database host | PGHOST | "localhost" |
| Port number | PGPORT | 5432 |
| Options | PGOPTIONS | Empty string |
| Dataset | PGDATABASE | Current user id |
| User | PGUSER | Current user id |
| Password | PGPASSWORD | Empty string |

$conn is a connection handle, corresponding to C's pointer to PGconn. Status values in Perl are not enumerations as in C, but plain strings and, because of this, they must be compared using eq rather than ==. The pgsql_perl5 module provides a set of suitable string constants: for example, PGRES_EMPTY_QUERY, PGRES_COMMAND_OK, and PGRES_TUPLES_OK.

After this, assuming a successful connection, doSQL is invoked a number of times to perform database operations.

The Perl garbage collector takes care of tidying up at the end, and there is no equivalent to PQfinish(), though you can indicate that you no longer want to access the database by setting $conn to some other value, such as undef. The risk still remains that the database connection remains open longer than if there were an explicit disconnect.

Within the doSQL function, a query or command is executed with:

```
$result = $conn->exec($command);
```

$result is a results handle, corresponding to C's PGresult*. The results handle offers access to such customary fields as resultStatus, cmdStatus, ntuples, and nfields. Note that pgsql_perl5 does not make the results error message available, so we're restricted to the connection message ($conn->errorMessage). This is the only significant difference in this program between the direct Perl and C interfaces to PostgreSQL.

Details about an individual field may be extracted via:

```
$fname   = $result->fname($fieldNum);
$fnumber = $result->fnumber($fieldName);
$ftype   = $result->ftype($fieldNum);
$fsize   = $result->fsize($fieldNum);
```

These are identical to their `libpq` counterparts: `$fieldNum` is the column number, starting at zero, and `$fieldName` is the column name. Similarly, the query results may be examined via:

```
$value  = $result->getvalue($tupleNum, $fieldNum);
$length = $result->getlength($tupleNum, $fieldNum);
$isNull = $result->getisnull($tupleNum, $fieldNum);
```

Again these are the same as the similarly named `libpq` operations, with `$tupleNum` being the row number in the query results, starting at zero.

There is no explicit clear operation – no equivalent to `PQclear()`. This is not an error: Perl's garbage collector takes care of cleaning up afterwards, as with database disconnection.

As was said earlier, this is a very close match to the C example in Chapter 13, and is more like writing C in Perl than genuine Perl code. For example, the nested `for` loop in the middle is a direct copy of the C example, but is not very Perl-ish. A better idiom is shown below, using `pgsql_perl5`'s convenient `fetchrow` function to return the next row in the query results as an array (and NULL at the end):

```
while(my @row = $result->fetchrow) {
    print " ", join(" ", @row), "\n";
}
```

The `join` function simply concatenates all the elements in an array regardless of its size, with the given separator string. If we do know how many columns there are, however, we can use another of Perl's tricks, an array of variables on the left side of an assignment:

```
($number, $value) = $result->fetchrow
```

Here `$number` and `$value` are a pair of variables to which the first and second column values will be assigned.

The following is the same program written in a more Perl-savvy manner. This particular script will form the basis for the other snippets of Perl code in this chapter, so that we can show the changes required for the different database access mechanisms more clearly:

```
select.pl
#!/usr/bin/perl -w

use Pg;
use strict;

# Function for non-query commands
sub doSQL
```

```
{
    my ($conn, $command) = @_;

    print $command, "\n";

    my $result = $conn->exec($command);
    print "status is ", $result->resultStatus, "\n";
    print "#rows affected ", $result->cmdTuples, "\n";
    print "result message: ", $conn->errorMessage, "\n";
}


# Function specifically for queries
sub doSQLquery
{
    my ($conn, $command) = @_;

    print $command, "\n";

    my $result = $conn->exec($command);
    print "status is ", $result->resultStatus, "\n";

    return if($result->resultStatus ne PGRES_TUPLES_OK);

    print "number of rows returned = ", $result->ntuples, "\n";
    print "number of fields returned = ", $result->nfields, "\n";

    print "fields: ";
    for(my $n = 0; $n < $result->nfields; ++$n) {
        print " ", $result->fname($n);
    }
    print "\n";

    while(my @row = $result->fetchrow) {
        print " ", join(" ", @row), "\n";
    }
}

my $conn = Pg::connectdb("") or die "connection failed";

doSQL($conn, "DROP TABLE number");
doSQL($conn, "CREATE TABLE number ( value INTEGER, name  VARCHAR )");
doSQL($conn, "INSERT INTO number values(42, 'The Answer')");
doSQL($conn, "INSERT INTO number values(29, 'My Age')");
doSQL($conn, "INSERT INTO number values(29, 'Anniversary')");
doSQL($conn, "INSERT INTO number values(66, 'Clickety-Click')");
doSQLquery($conn, "SELECT * FROM number WHERE value = 29");
doSQL($conn, "UPDATE number SET name = 'Zaphod' WHERE value = 42");
doSQL($conn, "DELETE FROM number WHERE value = 29");
```

This uses Perl's die function to abort the script on connection error, removing some clutter from the script, this is adequate for the sort of quick programming tasks for which Perl tends to be employed. The other significant change from the previous script is that we have split the SQL processing function into two, one for queries, and one for non-queries, the reason for this will become apparent as we progress.

Before leaving pgsql_perl5, we would like to mention that there are Perl variations of PQprint()
and the asynchronous processing described in Chapter 13 (as well as most other libpq functionality),
but since their use is so similar to their C counterparts, you are referred to that chapter and the
pgsql_perl5 documentation.

# The Perl DBI

If you have programmed databases in Windows, you will be familiar with ODBC, the Open Database
Connectivity API, or more recent APIs, such as ADO or OLE DB. Similarly, if you have used Java with
databases, you will have come across JDBC (see next chapter). These programming interfaces are an
attempt to abstract from the details of the actual database in use, and provide some higher level
database independent layer. The benefit to us is that we only have to learn one API, but can still use our
applications with numerous different databases.

DBI, the Database Interface, is Perl's implementation of this sort of scheme. As with other database
independent APIs, DBI is structured as the client API module and one or more driver, or DBD
(Database Driver), modules. You can have several different databases open at the same time, and access
them via essentially the same code in your Perl scripts, as illustrated below:

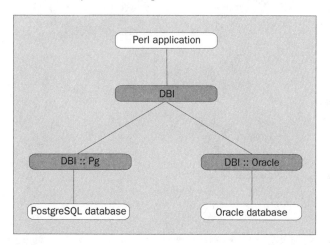

It is interesting to note that one of the available DBDs is for ODBC – a database independent interface.
On the subject of ODBC, a Win32::ODBC module exists which could also be used to connect to
PostgreSQL, but this will not be discussed further in this book.

You can find more information about DBI at its home page,
http://www.symbolstone.org/technology/perl/DBI/, or in *Programming the Perl DBI*, by Alligator
Descartes and Tim Bunce. O'Reilly (ISBN 1-56592-699-4).

# Installing DBI and the PostgreSQL DBD

The first port of call, as usual, is the installation of the required modules, DBI itself, and any DBDs you
may want. As always, download the tarball from CPAN and build and install (or use the shortcut shown
earlier). You are likely to see a lot of compiler warnings about unused variables. Though this is untidy,
it is harmless.

The DBI bundle itself contains a few DBDs (ADO, Multiplex, Proxy, and ExampleP, a very limited functionality stub mainly for the benefit of DBD writers), but not one for PostgreSQL, so you have to find that yourself. Edmund Mergl comes to the rescue again, with the DBD::Pg module. Download this from CPAN, set environment variables POSTGRES_INCLUDE to the directory containing the libpq include files and POSTGRES_LIB to that containing the library files, and then perform the customary build and install steps.

Diverting our attention from PostgreSQL for a moment, another useful driver is DBD::CSV. This emulates database accesses using comma-separated value (CSV) text files, and can be useful for quickly prototyping scripts without the need to set up a real database server.

# Using DBI

As you might expect, a database independent layer does not have the same API as the PostgreSQL specific API we have been using so far. In fact, precisely because it aims to be totally database independent, you will find that you simply cannot achieve the conciseness and efficiency of using a PostgreSQL specific interface, such as pgsql_perl5 directly.

DBI does bring some additional functionality which we will examine after a look at the earlier script recoded to use DBI, with the changed lines highlighted:

```perl
select_dbi.pl
#!/usr/bin/perl -w

use DBI;
use strict;

# Function for non-query commands
sub doSQL
{
    my ($conn, $command) = @_;

    print $command, "\n";

    my $sth = $conn->prepare($command);
    my $nrows = $sth->execute;
    print "status is ", $DBI::err, "\n" if $DBI::err;
    print "#rows affected is ", $nrows, "\n";
    print "error message: ", $DBI::errstr, "\n" if $DBI::err;
}

# Function specifically for queries
sub doSQLquery
{
    my ($conn, $command) = @_;

    print $command, "\n";

    my $sth = $conn->prepare($command);
    my $nrows = $sth->execute;
```

```
        print "status is ", $DBI::err, "\n" if $DBI::err;


        print "number of rows returned (unreliable) = ", $sth->rows, "\n";
        print "number of fields returned = ", $sth->{NUM_OF_FIELDS}, "\n";
        print "fields: ", join(" ", @{$sth->{NAME}}), "\n";

        while(my @row = $sth->fetchrow_array) {
            print " ", join(" ", @row), "\n";
        }
    }
```

```
    my $conn = DBI->connect("DBI:Pg:") or die $DBI::errstr;
```

```
    doSQL($conn, "DROP TABLE number");
    doSQL($conn, "CREATE TABLE number ( value INTEGER, name  VARCHAR )");
    doSQL($conn, "INSERT INTO number values(42, 'The Answer')");
    doSQL($conn, "INSERT INTO number values(29, 'My Age')");
    doSQL($conn, "INSERT INTO number values(29, 'Anniversary')");
    doSQL($conn, "INSERT INTO number values(66, 'Clickety-Click')");
    doSQLquery($conn, "SELECT * FROM number WHERE value = 29");
    doSQL($conn, "UPDATE number SET name = 'Zaphod' WHERE value = 42");
    doSQL($conn, "DELETE FROM number WHERE value = 29");
```

```
    $conn->disconnect;
```

The first thing to notice is that **only** the DBI module is referenced. You don't have to explicitly import the specific drivers for any particular databases you may be using:

```
    use DBI;
```

When the database connection is made (see later), DBI will locate and load the appropriate DBD if it is not already present, or fail with an error.

In the main routine, the database is opened with:

```
    $conn = DBI->connect("DBI:Pg:");
```

The first argument to connect is the data source, which must start with DBI and then the name of the driver, the remainder of this string is DBD specific, the whole data source string is of the form:

```
    DBI: driver name : driver parameters
```

Case is not important for the DBI, but the driver name is case sensitive, and the rest of the string depends on the driver's conventions. For PostgreSQL, the driver parameters correspond to the string passed to PQconnectdb(), such as dbname=bpsimple and it can be omitted, in which case the environment variables are used as explained in the earlier description of pgsql_perl5.

DBI adds another layer of environment variables; if the driver name part is empty (in other words nothing between the first and second colons, for example DBI::dbname=bpsimple), DBI takes the DBD name from the DBI_DRIVER environment variable. Finally, as a convenience, the data source string can be omitted or left empty, and DBI will use the DBI_DSN environment variable instead. The script has shown the short form of the connect function, which automatically looks up the user id and password from environment variables DBI_USER and DBI_PASS if they exist. The complete form is:

```
$dbh = DBI->connect($dsn, $uname, $pwd, \%attrs);
```

The second and third arguments are the user id and password with which to access the database, and the final, optional, argument is a hash containing attributes to pass to DBI.

One important attribute is AutoCommit – setting this to 1 causes DBI to treat each operation as a single transaction; setting it to 0 gives you explicit transaction processing.

An example of a complete connection statement is:

```
$dbh = DBI->connect("DBI:Pg:dbname=bpsimple",
                    "rick", "",
                    { AutoCommit => 0 });
```

In this instance, automatic committing is disabled, so you must insert calls to $dbh->commit (or $dbh->rollback) as necessary to end transactions.

As you can see from the above explanation, the username can be given, or can come from $DBI_USER or even $PGUSER. This clearly shows that there are a number of ways to specify the database connection parameters. You should pick one mechanism consistently to avoid confusion about which ones take precedence over the others.

The return value from connect is a handle to the database connection, or undef on error. If there has been an error, $DBI::err and $DBI::errstr are set appropriately. In the code above, processing is simply terminated on error with the error string being printed out via Perl's die function.

At the end of processing, the database connection is closed with:

```
$conn->disconnect;
```

Although the connection will be closed anyway when the application exits (with a warning message appearing), it is recommended that you explicitly disconnect to avoid problems with uncommitted transactions. If you have a number of connections open simultaneously, you can close all of them at once with DBI->disconnect_all.

Jumping back into the doSQL functions, DBI splits an operation into two steps (three for a query): preparation and execution (and fetching the results for a query). This is because you may want to execute the same operation several times and the database back end may let you optimise access by preparing once and executing multiple times:

```
my $sth = $conn->prepare($command);
my $nrows = $sth->execute;
```

The result of the preparation step is a statement handle, which we use to process the operation, and the result value of the execution is the number of rows affected, or undef if there was an error. In some cases, we do only want to execute the statement once, the two steps can be combined into a single function call, the line below replaces the two lines above:

```
my $nrows = $conn->do($command);
```

Notice the lack of a statement handle here; However, this means there is no way to extract the results of a query, so do is only useful for non-query operations.

The next thing to notice is that, while pgsql_perl5 lets us use the same processing regardless of whether the SQL statement was a query or a non-query, DBI does not do this because some databases use different mechanisms for these two operations. This was the reason for splitting the general doSQL function into query and non-query variants. Furthermore, because some databases cannot actually report the number of rows returned by a query, they just return rows until none are left. Strictly speaking, the return value of the execute function is deemed to be unreliable, but it does always appear to be correct for a PostgreSQL backend.

Processing query results is similar to our previous example, using the fetchrow_array function in the statement handle after the statement has been executed. There are other variants of this function:

❏ fetchrow_arrayref
Hands back a reference to an internal array (which is reused when the next fetch occurs) thus avoiding the copy that fetchrow_array does though the application must consume the data immediately.

❏ fetchrow_hashref
Returns a reference to a hash with the column names as keys and the data as the corresponding values.

❏ fetchall_arrayref
Returns all of the query results in a reference to a single array. Incidentally, this will give you a portable and reliable way to determine the number of rows, but may lead to excessive memory use if there are a lot of them.

The do function for non-query statements was mentioned above. There is a similar shortcut, or to be more precise, a set of them, for queries that you know you will not want to reuse: selectrow_array and selectall_arrayref perform the prepare and execute operations followed by the corresponding fetch function in one call. Consult the documentation for further details on these and other variants of the query operations that DBI makes available.

When you have finished with a statement handle, you should release it by setting the variable to undef, or simply leaving its scope. An alternative is to call:

```
$sth->finish;
```

You should also call this if you intend to reuse a query to flush the results buffer, otherwise you run the risk of getting rows back from a previous query. Placeholders are discussed later in the chapter.

We said earlier that DBI splits operations into a preparation stage and an execution step, so that you could execute the same query multiple times. Why would you want to do that? Wouldn't you get the same result each time, assuming that some other process is not changing the database? This is true except for one of the extra bits of functionality that DBI offers, the ability to bind parameters.

Instead of having a completely specified string as a SQL statement, you can insert question marks as placeholders with which actual values are associated later. This is similar to ecpg's host variable syntax described in Chapter 14. You prepare the statement once and execute it with different values with one argument for each placeholder. As an example, the following will return rows with value 14 and 15:

```
my $sth = $conn->prepare("SELECT * FROM number WHERE value = ?");
$sth->execute(14);
# Process rows...
$sth->execute(15);
# Process rows...
```

Each question mark placeholder in the SQL statement is replaced by corresponding argument in execute. $sth->execute(14) can be expressed as:

```
$sth->bind_param(1, 14);  # Note: parameters are numbered from 1
$sth->execute;
```

This hasn't bought us much, in fact it's more typing. It can be useful however when a statement has a large number of placeholders and you want to change only a few between executions. DBI also supports binding by reference, which, although intended for passing values in and out of shared procedures, can reduce the amount of typing a little:

```
my $num;
my $sth = $conn->prepare("SELECT * FROM number WHERE value = ?");
$sth->bind_param_inout(1,\$num, 10);
$num = 14;
$sth->execute;
# Process rows...
$num = 15;
$sth->execute;
# Process rows...
```

As this uses a reference, any changes in the value of the variable are immediately available to DBI without extra effort. Additionally, a third argument is necessary, to indicate the maximum size of a returned value, irrelevant in this particular instance, but required nonetheless.

Binding also works on the results of queries – the following is a replacement for doSQLquery's results processing:

```
sub doSQLquery
{
    my ($conn, $command) = @_;

    print $command, "\n";

    my $sth = $conn->prepare($command);
    my $nrows = $sth->execute;
    print "status is ", $DBI::err, "\n" if $DBI::err;

    print "number of rows returned (unreliable) = ", $sth->rows, "\n";

    my( $name, $value );
    $sth->bind_col(1, \$value); # 1st column mapped on to $value
    $sth->bind_col(2, \$name);  # 2nd column mapped on to $name

    while($sth->fetch) {
        print " name = ", $name, ", value = ", $value, "\n";
    }
}
```

Binding may offer some efficiency gains (this depends on the database in use), but it definitely can improve clarity of code.

# What Else Can We Do With DBI?

So far we've mainly looked at PostgreSQL specific use of DBI – now let's briefly investigate some of the additional database independent features.

You can enumerate the available drivers, and in some cases databases, quite easily, as shown in the following script:

```perl
dbi_sources.pl
#!/usr/bin/perl -w

use DBI;
use strict;

foreach my $driver (DBI->available_drivers())
{
    print "Driver ", $driver;

    eval { print "\n", join("\n ", DBI->data_sources($driver)), "\n\n" };
    print " - error ", $@, "\n\n" if ($@);
}
```

The `DBI->available_drivers` function returns a list of all the DBDs on the system, though it performs no tests that they are usable, or even loadable. For some DBDs, it is possible to determine what databases are available, via `DBI->data_sources` – this function does attempt to load the driver, which could fail for some reason, so we enclose it in an `eval` block. The return value of an `eval` is the expression inside the block, and any error status shows up in `$@`, hence the check for that being non-null. This script generates the following on one of our computers:

```
Driver ADO

Driver ExampleP
 dbi:ExampleP:dir=.

Driver Multiplex

Driver Pg
 dbi:Pg:dbname=bpsimple
 dbi:Pg:dbname=pgperltest
 dbi:Pg:dbname=template1

Driver Proxy
```

Executing this without the `eval` wrapper returned the following error with a premature script exit:

```
install_driver(Proxy) failed: Can't locate RPC/PlClient.pm in @INC (@INC contains:
/usr/lib/perl5/5.6.0/i386-linux /usr/lib/perl5/5.6.0
/usr/lib/perl5/site_perl/5.6.0/i386-linux /usr/lib/perl5/site_perl/5.6.0
```

```
/usr/lib/perl5/site_perl .) at
/usr/lib/perl5/site_perl/5.6.0/i386-linux/DBD/Proxy.pm line 28.
BEGIN failed--compilation aborted at
/usr/lib/perl5/site_perl/5.6.0/i386-linux/DBD/Proxy.pm line 28.
Compilation failed in require at (eval 5) line 3.
Perhaps a module that DBD::Proxy requires hasn't been fully installed
 at dbi_sources.pl line 10
```

This is telling us, in no uncertain terms, that loading the proxy DBD failed.

We mentioned the `AutoCommit` attribute above. Some additionally interesting attributes are:

❑ `PrintError`
As well as filling in $DBI::errstr, this causes the error message to be sent to `stderr`

❑ `RaiseError`
Errors will cause the program to `die` (unless you wrap the call in an `eval` block) instead of just returning an error status

❑ `Name`
The name of the database, usually the same as the string passed into connect

The first two can be useful for quick and dirty testing, but generally are not particularly friendly towards end users. There are a few other less common attributes – see the DBI and PostgreSQL DBD documentation for details.

You can access the attributes after connection and, in some cases, change them though it is recommended that you don't. This is because some DBDs do not support dynamic changing and, therefore, you would be limiting script portability. For example, the following reads and sets the transaction state:

```
$oldState = $conn->{ AutoCommit };
$conn->{ AutoCommit } = 0;
```

It is not only database handles that have associated attributes, statement handles have them as well. There was an example of this earlier:

```
print "number of fields returned = ", $sth->{NUM_OF_FIELDS}, "\n";
```

Statement attributes include:

| Attribute | Description |
| --- | --- |
| NUM_OF_FIELDS | Number of fields returned in a query |
| NUM_OF_PARAMS | Number of placeholders |
| NAME | Reference to an array containing the names of the columns |
| NAME_lc | As NAME, but always returns lowercase |

| Attribute | Description |
|-----------|-------------|
| NAME_uc | As NAME, but always returns uppercase |
| NULLABLE | Reference to an array containing flags indicating if each column can contain NULL values |
| Statement | The string used to create the statement |
| TYPE | Reference to an array indicating the type of each column |

Note that these are all read only and since, depending on the database, some may not be available until after execute has been called, it is best to examine them only after execution.

We have only scratched the surface of DBI, there is much more information in the online documentation. One extra thing worth mentioning is the DBI shell, dbish. This is similar to psql but, as with DBI itself, is database independent.

We will leave this section with a very brief comparison of the two mechanisms for accessing PostgreSQL databases from Perl, DBI and pgsql_perl5. DBI gives you database independence, and relatively sophisticated binding and parameter handling capabilities. pgsql_perl5, on the other hand is simpler and gives a more direct, thus more efficient route to the database. In addition, if you have used libpq, you should be familiar with pgsql_perl5.

Finally, both mechanisms include **BLOB handling** (see Appendix F). This is very comprehensive in case of pgsql_perl5, but DBI's database independence does not permit it to offer a complete level of support. If you expect the application to use many databases, the only answer is DBI; for quick one-off scripts, pgsql_perl5 is simpler.

# Using DBIx::Easy

If you have been browsing the database sections of CPAN, you will have noticed a number of DBIx modules. These are miscellaneous modules enhancing various aspects of DBI programming. One of these modules is particularly interesting – DBIx::Easy (home page http://www.linuxia.de/DBIx/Easy/, though you should be able to find everything via CPAN), a simplified interface to DBI. DBIx::Easy supports only a limited subset of DBDs, but fortunately PostgreSQL is one of them.

This module makes some database operations look, well, a little less database-y – we'll leave it to you to decide whether this is a good thing. As an example, you can have the results of a query returned as a hash (strictly, a reference to a hash). One other useful feature, is that you do not have to check the return value of every database operation. You can install a single error handler instead.

Here's our ubiquitous Perl script again, using DBIx::Easy, showing both these features:

```
select_easy.pl
#!/usr/bin/perl -w

use DBIx::Easy;
use strict;
```

```
sub myErrorHandler
{
    my( $statement, $err, $msg ) = @_;
    die"Oops, \"$statement\" failed ($err) - $msg";
}

# Note: we have to specify the DB type and the dbname explicitly
my $conn = new DBIx::Easy("Pg", "bpsimple");

$conn->install_handler(\&myErrorHandler);

$conn->process("DROP TABLE number");
$conn->process("CREATE TABLE number ( value INTEGER, name  VARCHAR )");
$conn->insert("number", name => "The Answer",     value => 42);
$conn->insert("number", name => "My Age",         value => 29);
$conn->insert("number", name => "Anniversary",    value => 29);
$conn->insert("number", name => "Clickety-Click", value => 66);

my $numbers = $conn->makemap("number", "name", "value", "value = 29");
foreach my $name (keys(%$numbers)) {
    print $name, " has value ", $$numbers{$name}, "\n";
}

$conn->update("number", "value = 42", name => "Zaphod");
$conn->process("DELETE FROM number WHERE value = 29");
$conn->disconnect;
```

Now, this looks quite a bit different to earlier scripts. This is because DBIx::Easy provides separate process, insert, update, and makemap (query) operations, so it would be inappropriate to combine them all into the previous pair of doSQL functions.

Before we get to those, notice how the error handler is installed, instead of testing each function for success or failure (which, admittedly, we have not been particularly rigorous about in earlier code samples), we can rely on the handler being called on any error. In this case, all it does is abort the script, but you may wish to provide something more sophisticated in your own programs.

The impact of process, insert, and update should be fairly obvious, but makemap deserves some explanation. This function takes the name of a table, two column names, and an optional where clause:

```
$conn->makemap($table, $keycol, $valuecol, $where)
```

This effectively executes the query:

```
SELECT $keycol, $valuecol FROM $table WHERE $where
```

The results are inserted into a hash as if by the following code fragment:

```
while(my ($key, $value) = $sth->fetchrow_array) {
    $map{$key} = $value;
}
```

As a hash can map each key on to only one value, multiple mappings in the source table will be lost: for example, if the table contained two rows (A, B) and (A, C), only one of those will appear in the resultant hash, since the earlier one returned from the database is overwritten by the later one.

Another limitation is that only two columns can be processed at a time, unlike a general query that can return any specified number of columns. Note that this is not the same as the hash returned by fetchrow_hashref function in DBI. This function returns a single row, with the key being the column name and the value of the column data.

# DBI and XML

Now that we've broached the subject of DBIx modules, it will be worth mentioning Matt Sergeant's DBIx::XML_RDB, for simplifying the creation of well-formed XML from the results of DBI queries.

Here is a version of the Perl script, this time producing XML as the query result (changes from the select_dbi.pl highlighted):

```perl
select_xml.pl
#!/usr/bin/perl -w

use DBI;
use DBIx::XML_RDB;
use strict;

# Function for non-query commands
sub doSQL
{
    my ($conn, $command) = @_;

    print $command, "\n";

    my $sth = $conn->prepare($command);
    my $nrows = $sth->execute;
    print "status is ", $DBI::err, "\n" if $DBI::err;
    print "#rows affected is ", $nrows, "\n";
    print "error message: ", $DBI::errstr, "\n" if $DBI::err;
}

# Function specifically for queries
sub doSQLquery
{
    my ($conn, $command) = @_;

    print $command, "\n";

    $conn->DoSql($command);

    print $conn->GetData;
}

my $connXml = DBIx::XML_RDB->new("", "Pg") or die $DBI::errstr;
my $conn = $connXml->{dbh};
```

```
doSQL($conn, "DROP TABLE number");
doSQL($conn, "CREATE TABLE number ( value INTEGER, name  VARCHAR )");
doSQL($conn, "INSERT INTO number values(42, 'The Answer')");
doSQL($conn, "INSERT INTO number values(29, 'My Age')");
doSQL($conn, "INSERT INTO number values(29, 'Anniversary')");
doSQL($conn, "INSERT INTO number values(66, 'Clickety-Click')");
doSQLquery($connXml, "SELECT * FROM number WHERE value = 29");
doSQL($conn, "UPDATE number SET name = 'Zaphod' WHERE value = 42");
doSQL($conn, "DELETE FROM number WHERE value = 29");
```

This time the database is opened with:

```
my $connXml = DBIx::XML_RDB->new("", "Pg") or die $DBI::errstr;
my $conn = $connXml->{dbh};
```

DBIx::XML_RDB->new returns an XML_RDB connection handle, which is not the same as a DBI handle. An examination of the module's source shows that it contains one, however, which can be used for any non-query operations (though, strictly, you should not rely on this, and it would be better not to mix XML_RDB operations with other database operations).

XML_RDB's query operation, DoSql, appends XML to an internal string, which can be extracted by GetData, as shown in the doSQLquery function. The results of our query are as follows:

```
<?xml version="1.0"?>
<DBI driver="dbname=book">
    <RESULTSET statement="SELECT * FROM number WHERE value = 29">
        <ROW>
                <value>29</value>
                <name>My Age</name>
        </ROW>
        <ROW>
                <value>29</value>
                <name>Anniversary</name>
        </ROW>
    </RESULTSET>
</DBI>
```

The DBIx::XML_RDB module itself is limited to producing XML from database queries, though the package includes a couple of scripts for converting a table to and from XML. sql2xml.pl uses the XML query facility to dump a complete table and xml2sql.pl reads it back in again.

The first one of the scripts has the following options:

| Option | Description |
| --- | --- |
| -sn servername | Data source name |
| -driver dbi_driver | Driver that DBI uses (default is ODBC) |
| -uid username | Username |
| -pwd password | Password (optional) |
| -table tablename | Table to extract |
| -output outputfile | File to place XML output in |

If you dump the usage, for example, by executing the command with no parameters, it identifies itself as sql2xls.pl and mentions Excel files, so it looks like the documentation has not quite kept up with the code.

You can run the script on the table created by the earlier Perl programs with the command (all one line):

```
$ /usr/lib/perl5/site_perl/5.6.0/DBIx/sql2xml.pl
          -sn dbname=bpsimple -driver Pg
          -table number -output xml.txt -uid rick
```

It is more than likely that your path does not include the directory containing these scripts, hence the full path specification above (you may need to alter this for your Perl installation's location). The output file, xml.txt, contains the following:

```
<?xml version="1.0"?>
<DBI driver="dbname=bpsimple">
    <RESULTSET statement="SELECT * FROM number ORDER BY 1">
        <ROW>
            <value>42</value>
            <name>Zaphod</name>
        </ROW>
        <ROW>
            <value>66</value>
            <name>Clickety-Click</name>
        </ROW>
    </RESULTSET>
</DBI>
```

As you can see, this looks almost identical in format to the query example above, showing that the script is a fairly thin wrapper on top of the DBIx::XML_RDB module's functionality.

The reverse script, xml2sql.pl, has similar options:

| Option | Description |
| --- | --- |
| -sn servername | Data source name |
| -driver dbi_driver | Driver that DBI uses (default is ODBC) |
| -uid username | Username |
| -pwd password | Password (optional) |
| -table tablename | Table to create |
| -input inputfile | File to read XML input from |
| -x | Delete contents of table before inserting |

Before you can use it, however you need to install XML::Parser, again to be found via CPAN.

There are other packages, such as Ron Bourret's XML-DBMS, which permit more complex interactions, but this is beyond the scope of this book. You are referred to http://www.rpbourret.com/xmldbms/ for more information.

**449**

# Summary

We have examined a number of ways of accessing PostgreSQL databases from Perl, letting us use its powerful string manipulation capabilities to avoid the task of writing C code to do the same. Although, there are numerous ways to use databases with Perl, we concentrated on what are probably the two most important of them all as far as PostgreSQL programming is concerned, a direct route which copies the C interface very closely and a database independent layer, DBI.

Within the scope of DBI, we have the option of easily using other database backends with the same client code. There is also a lot of existing DBI extension code, in the form of DBIx modules, to make our programming job simpler.

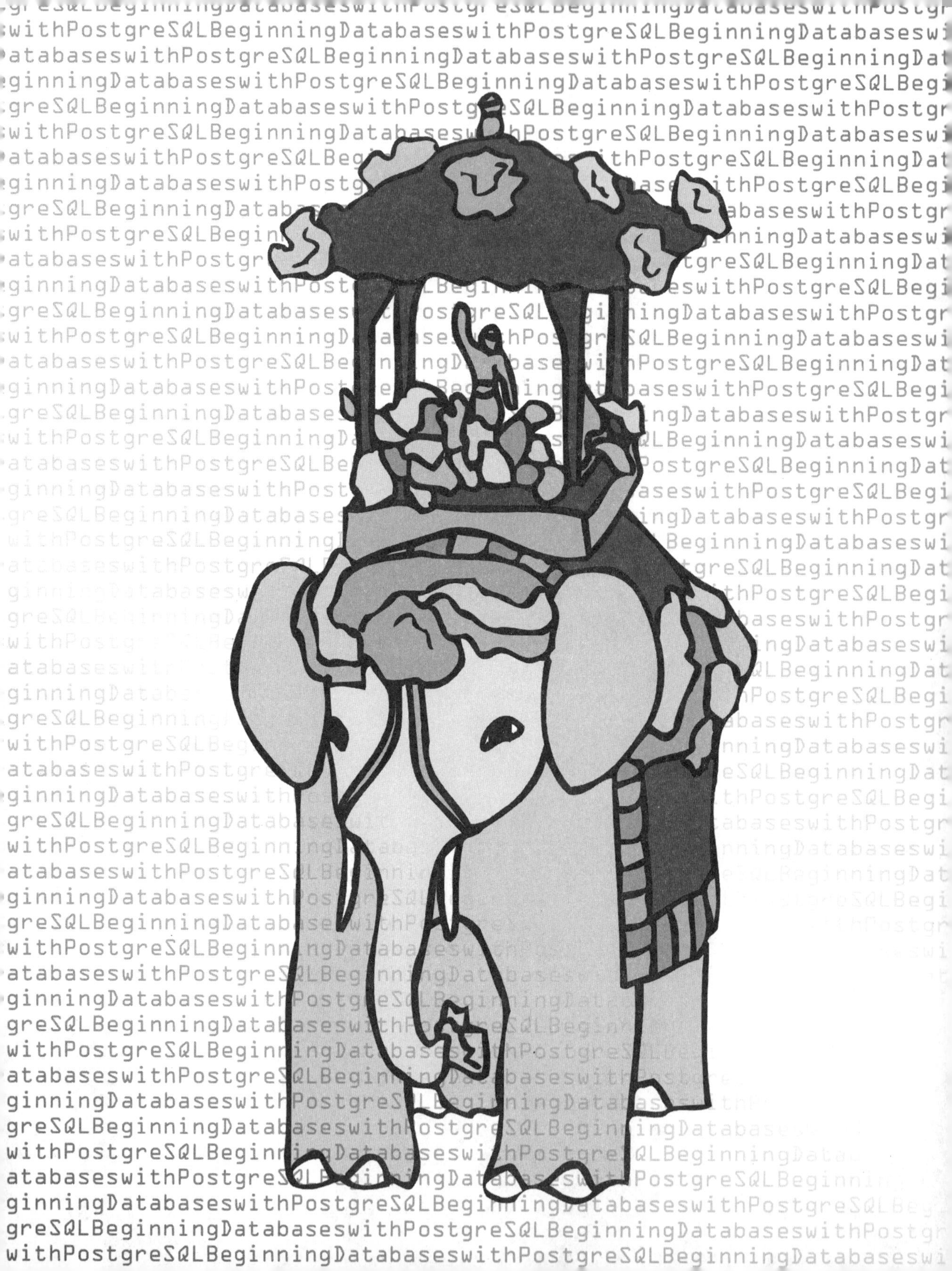
BeginningDatabaseswithPostgreSQL

# Accessing PostgreSQL from Java

JDBC has been the de-facto standard used by Java language programs for accessing relational databases. In this chapter, we will be covering the JDBC API in detail and looking into how Java language programs can use JDBC for accessing relational data residing in PostgreSQL databases.

In this chapter, we'll look at:

- ❑  An overview of JDBC
- ❑  JDBC drivers
- ❑  The PostgreSQL JDBC driver
- ❑  JDBC connections
- ❑  JDBC statements for issuing various DDL and DML statements
- ❑  Resultset retrieval from PostgreSQL databases
- ❑  JDBC prepared statements for issuing pre-compiled SQL statements
- ❑  JDBC callable statements for executing stored procedures
- ❑  Batch updates
- ❑  Database and resultset meta data queries
- ❑  A brief overview of the new features mentioned in the JDBC 3.0 API that is currently in the proposed final draft

We will conclude the chapter by building a GUI based Java application accessing a PostgreSQL database.

## JDBC Overview

JDBC is a standard API that can be used by programs written using the Java language for accessing external resource managers, mainly relational databases, in a resource manager-independent manner. This means a Java application written using standard JDBC classes and interfaces is portable across databases from different RDMS vendors, if it uses only standard ANSI compliant SQL. The JDBC API comprises the core JDBC API and the extension API.

The core API mainly defines the standard interfaces for:

- ❏ Creating a connection to the database
- ❏ Creating statements
- ❏ Accessing resultsets
- ❏ Querying database and resultset meta data

The core classes and interfaces are defined in the `java.sql` package and are available with the Java 2 Platform, Standard Edition.

The extension API defines more sophisticated interfaces for handling XA resources, distributed transactions, pooled connections, and connection factories. XA resources can be used to handle distributed transactions and two-phase commits, where a single transaction may need to span several multiple databases. These classes and interfaces belong to the `javax.sql` package and are available with the Java 2 Platform, Enterprise Edition.

In this chapter, we will be concentrating on the JDBC core API.

# JDBC Drivers

The JDBC API only defines interfaces for the objects used for performing various database-related tasks like opening and closing connections, executing SQL statements, and retrieving the results. It doesn't provide the implementation classes for these interfaces. Nevertheless, portable Java language programs need not be aware of the implementation classes and should only use the standard interfaces.

As good object oriented citizens, we all write our programs to interfaces and not implementations. Either the resource manager vendor or a third party provides the implementation classes for the standard JDBC interfaces. These software implementations are called **JDBC drivers**. JDBC drivers transform the standard JDBC calls to the external resource manager-specific API calls. The diagram below depicts how a database client written in Java accesses an external resource manager using the JDBC API and the JDBC driver:

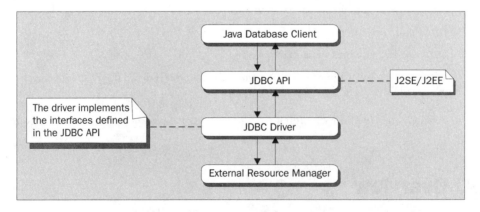

Depending on the mechanism of implementation, JDBC drivers are broadly classified into four types.

# Type 1

Type 1 JDBC drivers implement the JDBC API on top of a lower level API like ODBC. These drivers are not generally portable because of the dependency on native libraries. These drivers translate the JDBC calls to ODBC calls and ODBC sends the request to the external data source using native library calls. The JDBC-ODBC driver that comes with the software distribution for J2SE is an example of a type 1 driver.

# Type 2

Type 2 drivers are written in a mixture of Java and native code. Type 2 drivers use vendor specific native APIs for accessing the data source. These drivers transform the JDBC calls to vendor specific calls using the vendor's native library. These drivers are also not portable like type 1 drivers because of the dependency on native code.

# Type 3

Type 3 drivers use an intermediate middleware server for accessing the external data sources. The calls to the middleware server are database independent. However, the middleware server makes vendor specific native calls for accessing the data source. In this case, the driver is purely written in Java.

# Type 4

Type 4 drivers are written in pure Java and they implement the JDBC interfaces and translate the JDBC specific calls to vendor specific data access calls. They implement the data transfer and network protocol for the target resource manager. Most of the leading database vendors provide type 4 drivers for accessing their database servers.

# Building the PostgreSQL JDBC Driver

The PostgreSQL software bundle comes with a type 4 JDBC driver. This section explains how to build the PostgreSQL JDBC driver from the source files. The steps involved in building the PostgreSQL JDBC driver are listed below:

- ❑ Download and install the latest version of the Ant build tool from http://jakarta.apache.org/builds/jakarta-ant/release/v1.3/bin/ for the binary distribution, and http://jakarta.apache.org/builds/jakarta-ant/release/v1.3/src/ for the source files.

- ❑ Unpack the PostgreSQL source file bundle to the local file system.

- ❑ Under the source directory structure change to /src/interfaces/jdbc.

- ❑ Make sure there is a file called build.xml file in the directory.

- ❑ Run the Ant build script by typing ant from the directory mentioned in step 3.

- ❑ Make sure you have all the required class files for Ant in the classpath. These classes include the Ant classes available in the lib directory of the Ant installation and a JAXP compliant XML parser. Xerces from Apache is a JAXP compliant XML parser that can be downloaded from http://xml.apache.org. If you are using Xerces please make sure that xerces.jar is in your class path.

On successful completion, two files are created in the output directory specified in the `build.xml` file. One is `postgresql.jar` that contains the JDBC driver, and the other is `postgresql-examples.jar` that contains the examples. Since Ant is a Java based build tool, the steps explained above are applicable to both Linux and Cygwin environments.

Alternatively, the pre-compiled JDBC drivers for PostgreSQL may be downloaded from: http://jdbc.postgresql.org/download/.

# DriverManager and Driver

The `java.sql` package defines an interface called `java.sql.Driver` that needs to be implemented by all the JDBC drivers and a class called `java.sql.DriverManager` that acts as the interface to the database clients for performing tasks like connecting to external resource managers, and setting log streams. When a JDBC client requests the `DriverManager` to make a connection to an external resource manager, it delegates the task to an appropriate driver class implemented by the JDBC driver provided either by the resource manager vendor or a third party. In this section, we will discuss in detail the roles of `java.sql.DriverManager` and `java.sql.Driver` in JDBC API.

## java.sql.DriverManager

The primary task of the class `DriverManager` is to manage the various JDBC drivers registered. In the section on `java.sql.Driver`, we will see how JDBC drivers register themselves with the `DriverManager`. It also provides methods for:

❑ Getting connections to databases

❑ Managing JDBC logs

❑ Setting login timeout

### Managing Drivers

This section discusses the methods provided by the `DriverManager` class for managing drivers:

```
public static void registerDriver(Driver driver) throws SQLException
```

This method is normally used by the implementation classes of the interface `java.sql.Driver`, provided by the JDBC drivers, to register themselves with the `DriverManager`. This method throws an instance of `java.sql.SQLException` if a database error occurs. `DriverManager` uses registered drivers for delegating database connection requests:

```
public static void deregisterDriver(Driver driver) throws SQLException
```

This method is used for de-registering a driver that is already registered with the `DriverManager`:

```
public static Enumeration getDrivers()
```

This method returns an enumeration of all the drivers currently registered with the `DriverManager`:

```
public static Driver getDriver(String url) throws SQLException
```

This method is used for getting the driver registered with the `DriverManager` corresponding to the passed JDBC URL. It throws an instance of `SQLException` if a database access error occurs. JDBC URLs are used for uniquely identifying the resource manager type and resource manager location. This means that even though a JDBC driver can handle any number of connections identified by different JDBC URLs, the basic URL format including the protocol and sub-protocol is specific to the driver used.

JDBC clients specify the JDBC URL when they request a connection. The `DriverManager` can find a driver that matches the requested URL from the list of registered drivers and delegate the connection request to that driver if it finds a match. JDBC URLs normally take the following format:

**<protocol>:<sub-protocol>:<resource>**

The protocol is always `jdbc` and the sub-protocol and resource depend on the type of resource manager you use. The URL for PostgreSQL is in the format:

**jdbc:postgres://<host>:<port>/<database>**

Here `host` is the host address on which `postmaster` is running and `database` is the name of the database to which the client wishes to connect.

## Managing Connections

This section discusses the methods provided by the `DriverManager` class for managing connections to databases:

```
public static Connection getConnection(String url) throws SQLException
```

This method gets a connection to the database specified by the JDBC URL. The class `java.sql.Connection` is covered in detail in a later section. This method throws an instance of `SQLException` if a database access error occurs:

```
public static Connection getConnection(String url,String user,String password)
throws SQLException
```

This method gets a connection to the database specified by the JDBC URL using the specified user name and password. This method throws an instance of `SQLException` if a database access error occurs:

```
public static Connection getConnection(String url,Properties info) throws
SQLException
```

This method gets a connection to the database specified by the JDBC URL. The instance of the class `java.util.Properties` is used for specifying the security credentials. The property name user for specifying the user name is `user` and that for password is `password`. This method throws an instance of `SQLException` if a database access error occurs.

## Managing JDBC Logging

This section discusses the methods provided by the `DriverManager` class for managing JDBC logs:

```
public static PrintWriter getLogWriter()
```

This method gets a handle to an instance of the class `java.io.PrintWriter` to which the logging and tracing information are written. This method throws an instance of `SQLException` if a database access error occurs:

```
public static void setLogWriter(PrintWriter writer)
```

This method sets the `PrintWriter` to which all the log information is written by the `DriverManager` and all the registered drivers:

```
public static void println(String message) throws SQLException
```

This method writes the message to the current log stream.

## Managing Login Timeouts

This section discusses the methods provided by the `DriverManager` class for managing login:

```
public static int getLoginTimeout()
```

This method gets the maximum time in seconds the `DriverManager` would wait for getting a connection:

```
public static void setLogWriter(PrintWriter writer)
```

This method sets the maximum time, in seconds, the `DriverManager` would wait for getting a connection.

# java.sql.Driver

This interface defines the methods that need to be implemented by all JDBC drivers. The driver implementation classes are required to have static initialization code to register them with the current `DriverManager`. This is done so that the `DriverManager` has the driver in the list of registered drivers, and delegates a connection request to an appropriate driver class depending on the JDBC URL specified. Have a look at the sourcecode for the class `org.postgresql.Driver` that is the driver implementation for PostgreSQL used in this chapter (this class can be found in the `interfaces/jdbc/org/postgresql` directory under your PostgreSQL source structure). You will find the following code snippet:

```
static {
    try {
        java.sql.DriverManager.registerDriver(new Driver());
    } catch (SQLException e) {
        e.printStackTrace();
    }
}
```

So whenever the class loader loads the class `org.postgresql.Driver` it registers itself with the `DriverManager`. Hence JDBC clients need to load the class definition of the driver they wish to use so that the `DriverManager` can use it for obtaining database connections. One obvious way of doing this is using the static `forName()` method on the class `java.lang.Class` as shown below:

```
try {
    Class.forName("org.postgresql.Driver");
}catch(ClassNotFoundException e) {
    //Handle exception
}
```

This will throw a `ClassNotFoundException` if the class `org.postgresql.Driver` is not found in the classpath. Hence you need to make sure that the `postgres.jar` file which contains the required classes is available in the classpath.

The sequence diagram shown below depicts a typical JDBC client getting a connection to a PostgreSQL database called `bpsimple` running locally using the user name "meeraj" and the password "waheeda":

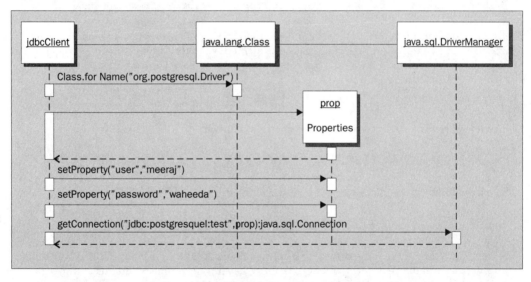

The code snippet below corresponds to the sequence of events depicted in the diagram shown above:

```
try {

    //Load the JDBC driver
    Class.forName("org.postgresql.Driver");

    //Create a properties object with user name and password
    Properties prop = new Properties();
    prop.setProperty("user","meeraj");
    prop.setProperty("password","waheeda");

    //Set the JDBC URL
    String url = "jdbc:postgresql:test";
```

```
        //Get the connection
        Connection con = DriverManager.getConnection(url,prop);

}catch(ClassNotFoundException e) {
        //Handle exception
}catch(SQLException e) {
        //Handle exception
}
```

Now we will have a look at the methods defined by the interface `java.sql.Driver`:

```
public boolean acceptsURL(String url) throws SQLException
```

This method returns True if the driver implementation class can open a connection to the specified URL. The implementation classes normally return True if they can recognize the sub-protocol specified in the JDBC URL. This throws an instance of SQLException if a database access error occurs:

```
public Connection connect(String url,Properties info) throws SQLException
```

This method returns a connection to the specified URL using the properties defined in the argument info. The DriverManager normally calls this method when it receives connection requests from JDBC clients. This method throws an instance of SQLException if a database access error occurs:

```
public int getMajorVersion()
```

This method returns the major revision number of the driver:

```
public int getMinorVersion()
```

This method returns the minor revision number of the driver:

```
public boolean jdbcCompliant()
```

This method returns True if the driver is JDBC compliant. A fully compliant JDBC driver should conform strictly to the JDBC API and SQL92 Entry Level. The various standards and specifications related to SQL may be found at http://www.opengroup.org. If it doesn't, this method should return False.

# Connections

The interface `java.sql.Connection` defines the methods required for a persistent connection to the database. The JDBC driver vendor implements this interface. A database 'vendor neutral' client never uses the implementation class and will always use only the interface. This interface defines methods for the following tasks:

❑   Statements, prepared statements, and callable statements are the different types of statements for issuing SQL statements to the database by the JDBC clients. Statements are discussed in later sections.

❑ For getting and setting auto-commit mode.

❑ Getting meta information about the database.

❑ Committing and rolling back transactions.

In this section we cover the various methods defined in the interface `java.sql.Connection` in detail.

# Creating Statements

The interface `java.sql.Connection` defines a set of methods for creating database statements. Database statements are used for sending SQL statements to the database:

```
public Statement createStatement() throws SQLException
```

This method is used for creating instances of the interface `java.sql.Statement`. This interface can be used for sending SQL statements to the database. The interface `java.sql.Statement` is normally used for sending SQL statements that don't take any arguments. This method throws an instance of `SQLException` if a database access error occurs:

```
public Statement createStatement(int resType, int resConcurrency) throws
SQLException
```

This is the same as the previous method, but it lets the JDBC clients specify the resultset type and resultset concurrency. Resultsets are used for retrieving the results back to the client from the database. Resultsets are discussed in more detail later in this chapter. The resultset type identifies the direction in which the resultset can be traversed, whereas concurrency defines how multiple threads can access the resultset simultaneously:

```
public PreparedStatement prepareStatement(String sql) throws SQLException
```

This method is used to create instances of the interface `java.sql.PreparedStatement`. The interface `java.sql.PreparedStatement` is normally used for sending SQL statements that take any arguments. Prepared statements can pre-compile and store SQL statements. This method throws an instance of `SQLException` if a database access error occurs. The SQL statements passed to prepared statements can use parameter placeholders using "?" for sending IN parameters:

```
public Statement prepareStatement (String sql,int resType, int resConcurrency)
throws SQLException
```

This is the same as the previous method, but it lets the JDBC clients specify the resultset type and resultset concurrency:

```
public CallableStatement prepareCall(String sql) throws SQLException
```

This method is used to create instances of the interface `java.sql.CallableStatement`. The interface `java.sql.CallableStatement` is normally used for sending calls to the database's stored procedures that take IN and OUT parameters. This method throws an instance of `SQLException` if a database access error occurs. The stored procedure calls, passed to prepared statements, can use parameter placeholders using "?" for specifying both IN and OUT parameters:

```
public Statement prepareCall (String sql,int resType, int resConcurrency) throws
SQLException
```

This is the same as the previous method, but it lets the JDBC clients specify the resultset type and resultset concurrency.

# Handling Transactions

The connection interface defines a set of methods for handling database transactions:

```
public void setAutoCommit(boolean autoCommit) throws SQLException
```

This method sets the auto-commit mode. If set to True, SQL statements are automatically committed, otherwise the clients need to issue an explicit commit. This method throws an instance of SQLException if a database access error occurs:

```
public boolean getAutoCommit() throws SQLException
```

This method gets the current auto-commit mode. This method throws an instance of SQLException if a database access error occurs:

```
public void commit() throws SQLException
```

This method commits the current transaction associated with the connection. This method throws an instance of SQLException if a database access error occurs:

```
public void rollback() throws SQLException
```

This method rolls back the current transaction associated with the connection. This method throws an instance of SQLException if a database access error occurs:

```
public int getTransactionIsolation() throws SQLException
```

This method gets the current transaction isolation level. Transaction isolation level, discussed in Chapter 9, dictates whether dirty reads, repeatable reads, or phantom reads can be performed or not. This method throws an instance of SQLException if a database access error occurs:

```
public void getTransactionIsolation(int level) throws SQLException
```

This method sets the transaction isolation level. This method throws an instance of SQLException if a database access error occurs.

# Database Meta Data

The connection interface provides a method to get the database meta data:

```
public DatabaseMetaData getMetaData() throws SQLException
```

This method returns an instance of a class that implements `java.sql.DatabaseMetaData` interface. This method throws an instance of `SQLException` if a database access error occurs. This interface provides 149 methods to obtain information about the database. Please refer to the JDBC API's Javadocs for a complete listing of these methods.

## Retrieving PostgreSQL Meta Data

In this section we will write an example to fetch a very small subset of the PostgreSQL meta data. The class will first load the PostgreSQL JDBC driver and get a connection to the database called `bpsimple` running on `localhost`. Then it obtains a handle to the database meta data from the connection and prints the following information:

❑ Database product name

❑ Database product version

❑ Driver major version

❑ Driver minor version

❑ Driver name

❑ Driver version

❑ JDBC URL

❑ Transaction support

❑ Information on whether PostgreSQL uses local files to store tables

The source for the class is listed below. Save this into `PostgreSQLMetaData.java`:

```
import java.sql.Connection;
import java.sql.DatabaseMetaData;
import java.sql.DriverManager;

public class PostgreSQLMetaData {

    public static void main(String args[]) throws Exception {

        Class.forName("org.postgresql.Driver");
        String url = "jdbc:postgresql:bpsimple";
        Connection con =
            DriverManager.getConnection(url,"meeraj","password");
        DatabaseMetaData dbmd = con.getMetaData();

        System.out.print("Database Product Name : ");
        System.out.println(dbmd.getDatabaseProductName());

        System.out.print("Database Product Version : ");
        System.out.println(dbmd.getDatabaseProductVersion());

        System.out.print("Driver Major Version : ");
        System.out.println(dbmd.getDriverMajorVersion());

        System.out.print("Driver Minor Version : ");
```

```
            System.out.println(dbmd.getDriverMinorVersion());

            System.out.print("Driver Name : ");
            System.out.println(dbmd.getDriverName());

            System.out.print("Driver Version : ");
            System.out.println(dbmd.getDriverVersion());

            System.out.print("JDBC URL : ");
            System.out.println(dbmd.getURL());

            System.out.print("Supports Transactions : ");
            System.out.println(dbmd.supportsTransactions());

            System.out.print("Uses Local Files : ");
            System.out.println(dbmd.usesLocalFiles());

            con.close();

        }

}
```

Compile the class with the following command:

$ **javac PostgreSQLMetaData.java**

Invoke the Java interpreter on the class with the `postgresql.jar` file in the classpath:

$ **java PostgreSQLMetaData**

This will produce the following output depending on the version of PostgreSQL you are running. Please make sure that you have the `postgresql.jar` file in your system classpath when you invoke the JVM:

```
Database Product Name : PostgreSQL
Database Product Version : 7.1
Driver Major Version : 7
Driver Minor Version : 1
Driver Name : PostgreSQL Native Driver
Driver Version : PostgreSQL 7.1 JDBC2
JDBC URL : jdbc:postgresql:test
Supports Transactions : true
Uses Local Files : false
```

The database meta data interface can be used to get a lot more information than this, like getting catalog and table names and SQL features supported. Please refer to the Javadoc for more details.

# JDBC Resultsets

A JDBC resultset represents a two dimensional array of data produced as a result of executing SQL SELECT statements against databases using JDBC statements. JDBC statements are covered in detail in the next section. JDBC resultsets are represented by the interface java.sql.ResultSet. The JDBC vendor provider provides the implementation class for this interface.

# Resultset Concurrency and Type

Executing appropriate methods against JDBC statement objects creates objects of type java.sql.ResultSet. As we have already seen in the section on connections, when we create statement objects, we can specify the type and scroll sensitivity of the resultsets that may be created by those statement objects. In this section we will have a look at resultset types and scroll sensitivity in detail.

## Type

Resultsets can be of one of the following types:

- ❏ TYPE_FORWARD_ONLY
  Forward only resultsets can be traversed only in the forward direction. This means once you move the current cursor pointer to the $n^{th}$ row you can't move back to $(n-1)^{th}$ row.

- ❏ TYPE_SCROLL_INSENSITIVE
  This type of ResultSet object is scrollable and not sensitive to changes made by other threads.

- ❏ TYPE_SCROLL_SENSITIVE
  This type of ResultSet object is scrollable and sensitive to changes made by other threads.

The interface defines a method to get the resultset type. The type can be set only when the statements are created using connection objects, as explained in the previous section:

```
public int getType() throws SQLException
```

## Concurrency

Resultsets can have one of the two following concurrency types:

- ❏ CONCUR_READ_ONLY
  Concurrent read only resultsets are not updateable.

- ❏ CONCUR _UPDATEABLE
  Concurrent updateable resultsets are updateable.

The ResultSet interface defines a method to get the resultset type. The type can be set only when the statements are created using connection objects as explained in the previous section:

```
public int getConcurrency() throws SQLException
```

# Traversing Resultsets

The `ResultSet` interface defines various methods for traversing the resultsets, manipulating the cursor position, and accessing fetch direction. In this section we will have a look at these methods in detail.

## Scrolling Resultsets

In this section, we will have a look at the methods available for scrolling resultsets:

```
public boolean next() throws SQLException
```

This method moves the current cursor pointer to the next row and returns True if there are more rows. Otherwise this method returns False. An instance of `SQLException` is thrown if a database access error occurs:

```
public boolean first() throws SQLException
```

This method moves the current cursor pointer to the first row and returns True if the cursor is on the first row. Otherwise this method returns False. This method cannot be executed against a forward only cursor. An instance of `SQLException` is thrown if a database access error occurs:

```
public boolean last() throws SQLException
```

This method moves the current cursor pointer to the last row and returns True if the cursor is on the last row. Otherwise this method returns False. This method cannot be executed against a forward only cursor. An instance of `SQLException` is thrown if a database access error occurs:

```
public boolean absolute(int rows) throws SQLException
```

This method moves the current cursor pointer forward or backward from the start or end of the resultset to the row specified by the argument. The cursor is moved forward from the start if the value of `rows` is positive and it is moved backward from the end if the value of `rows` is negative. An instance of `SQLException` is thrown if a database access error occurs:

```
public boolean relative(int row) throws SQLException
```

This method moves the current cursor pointer forward or backward from the current position to the row specified by the argument. The cursor is moved forward if the value of `rows` is positive and it is moved backward if the value of `rows` is negative. An instance of `SQLException` is thrown if a database access error occurs:

```
public boolean previous() throws SQLException
```

This method moves the current cursor pointer to the previous row. This method cannot be executed against a forward only cursor. An instance of `SQLException` is thrown if a database access error occurs.

## Querying the Cursor Position

In this section we will see the different methods available for querying the cursor position:

```
public boolean next() throws SQLException
```

This method moves the current cursor pointer to the next row and returns True if there are more rows. Otherwise this method returns False. An instance of SQLException is thrown if a database access error occurs:

```
public boolean isBeforeFirst() throws SQLException
```

Returns True if the cursor position is before the first row. An instance of SQLException is thrown if a database access error occurs:

```
public boolean isAfterLast() throws SQLException
```

Returns True if the cursor position is after the last row. An instance of SQLException is thrown if a database access error occurs:

```
public boolean isFirst() throws SQLException
```

Returns True if the cursor position is at the first row. An instance of SQLException is thrown if a database access error occurs:

```
public void isLast() throws SQLException
```

Returns True if the cursor position is at the last row. An instance of SQLException is thrown if a database access error occurs:

```
public void beforeFirst() throws SQLException
```

Moves the cursor to the start of the resultset, before the first row. An instance of SQLException is thrown if a database access error occurs:

```
public boolean afterLast() throws SQLException
```

Moves the cursor to the end of the resultset, after the last row. An instance of SQLException is thrown if a database access error occurs.

## Fetch Direction and Size

Now we will have a look at the methods for manipulating the fetch direction and size. These methods give a hint to the driver of the direction and the size in which the rows will be fetched, so that it can fetch records from the database accordingly:

```
public int getFetchDirection() throws SQLException
```

Returns the current fetch direction. An instance of SQLException is thrown if a database access error occurs. The JDBC API defines three fetch directions:

❑ FETCH_FORWARD

❑ FETCH_REVERSE

❑ FETCH_UNKNOWN

```
public void setFetchDirection(int direction) throws SQLException
```

This method sets the fetch direction. An instance of SQLException is thrown if a database access error or a fetch direction other than FETCH_FORWARD to a forward only resultset occurs:

```
public int getFetchSize() throws SQLException
```

Gets the current fetch size. An instance of SQLException is thrown if a database access error occurs.

```
public void setFetchDirection(int direction) throws SQLException
```

This method gives a hint to the driver on the fetch size. An instance of SQLException is thrown if a database access error occurs.

# Accessing Resultset Data

The interface defines methods for getting data from the current row in the resultset. The data can be retrieved as appropriate data types. These methods take the general format getXXX(int col). Where XXX can be one of the different types like int, short, string, and col is the column number in the current row from which data is to be fetched. Column numbers start from 1.

Alternatively, you can specify the column names as well. Regardless of the data type, all columns can be fetched as a string. All these methods throw an instance of SQLException if a database error occurs.

The table below shows some of the data access methods, and those that are missing can be extrapolated from the methods already described by referring to the Javadoc:

| Method Name | Purpose |
| --- | --- |
| public boolean getBoolean(int i)<br><br>public boolean getBoolean(String col) | Gets the data in the specified column as a boolean |
| public int getInt(int i)<br><br>public inr getInt(String col) | Gets the data in the specified column as an int |
| public String getString(int i)<br><br>public String getString(String col) | Gets the data in the specified column as a string |

# Mapping PostgreSQL Data Types

In this section, we will map the Java types to PostgreSQL data types and the JDBC.

The table below lists the mapping of Java types to PostgreSQL data types and JDBC data types. The different JDBC types are defined in the class `java.sql.Types`:

| Java Type | JDBC Type | PostgreSQL Type |
|---|---|---|
| `java.lang.Boolean` | `TINYINT` | `INT2` |
| `java.lang.Byte` | `TINYINT` | `INT2` |
| `java.lang.Short` | `SMALLINT` | `INT2` |
| `java.lang.Integer` | `INTEGER` | `INT4` |
| `java.lang.Long` | `BIGINT` | `INT8` |
| `java.lang.Float` | `FLOAT` | `FLOAT(7)` |
| `java.lang.Double` | `DOUBLE` | `FLOAT8` |
| `java.lang.Character` | `CHAR` | `CHAR(1)` |
| `java.lang.String` | `VARCHAR` | `TEXT` |
| `java.sql.Date` | `DATE` | `DATE` |
| `java.sql.Time` | `TIME` | `TIME` |
| `java.sql.Timestamp` | `TIMESTAMP` | `TIMESTAMP` |
| `java.lang.Object` | `JAVA_OBJECT` | `OID` |

# Updateable Resultsets

Updateable resultsets can be created from statements that were created by specifying the resultset concurrency as `CONCUR_UPDATEABLE`. The data in updateable resultsets can be modified and rows can be added and removed. In this section we will have a look at the methods available for modifying the state of resultsets.

## Deleting Data

The interface defines a method for deleting the current row from the resultset as well as the database:

```
public void deleteRow() throws SQLException
```

This method deletes the current row from the resultset and from the database. This method cannot be called when the cursor is on `INSERT` row. `INSERT` row is explained in the section on inserting data into the database. An instance of `SQLException` is thrown if a database access error occurs.

```
public boolean rowDeleted() throws SQLException
```

This method checks whether the current row has been deleted. An instance of `SQLException` is thrown if a database access error occurs.

## Updating Data

The resultset interface defines a set of `updateXXX()` methods for updating the data in the current row of the resultset. However, these methods don't update the underlying data in the database. The table below lists a few of these methods, and the rest can be extrapolated by referring to the Javasoc:

| Method Name | Purpose |
| --- | --- |
| `public void updateBoolean(int i, boolean x)` `public void updateBoolean(String col, boolean x)` | Sets the data in the specified column to the specified boolean value |
| `public void updateInt(int i, int x)` `public void updateInt(String col, int x)` | Sets the data in the specified column to the specified int value |
| `public void updateString(int i, String x)` `public void updateString(String col, String x)` | Sets the data in the specified column to the specified string value |

```
public void updateRow() throws SQLException
```

This method can be called to update the underlying database with the data changed using the `updateXXX()` methods. An instance of `SQLException` is thrown if a database access error occurs:

```
public void refreshRow() throws SQLException
```

This method refreshes the current row with the most recent data from the database. An instance of `SQLException` is thrown if a database access error occurs:

```
public void cancelRowUpdates() throws SQLException
```

This method cancels the updates made to the current row. An instance of `SQLException` is thrown if a database access error occurs:

```
public boolean rowUpdated() throws SQLException
```

This method checks whether the current row has been updated. An instance of `SQLException` is thrown if a database access error occurs.

## Inserting Data

Resultsets have a special row called `INSERT` row for adding data to the underlying database:

```
public boolean moveToInsertRow() throws SQLException
```

The cursor can be moved to the INSERT row by using this following method:

```
public boolean moveToCurrentRow() throws SQLException
```

The cursor can be moved from the INSERT row back to the previous row using this method. This method throws an instance of SQLException if a database access error occurs or if the resultset is not updateable:

```
public boolean insertRow() throws SQLException
```

Once the cursor is on the insert row appropriate updateXXX() methods can be called to set the data for the new row. This method can then be called to create the new record in the database. An instance of SQLException is thrown if a database access error occurs or if the cursor is not on INSERT row.

# Other Relevant Methods

This section explains the other relevant methods available with the interface java.sql.ResultSet:

```
public void close() throws SQLException
```

This method releases the database and JDBC resources. An instance of SQLException is thrown if a database access error occurs:

```
public ResultSetMetaData getMetaData() throws SQLException
```

This method gets the resultset meta data as an instance of a class that implements the interface java.sql.ResultSetMetaData. This interface defines a host of methods for accessing the resultset meta data including:

- ❏ Catalog name
- ❏ Column class name
- ❏ Column count
- ❏ Column display size
- ❏ Column label
- ❏ Column Type
- ❏ Column type name

Please refer to the Javadoc for a complete listing. An instance of SQLException is thrown if a database access error occurs.

# JDBC Statements

JDBC API defines three types of statements for sending SQL statements to the database:

❏ **Statements**
Statements are generally used for sending SQL statements that don't take any arguments. The methods required for statement objects are defined by the interface `java.sql.Statement`. The JDBC driver provider provides the implementation class for this interface.

❏ **Prepared Statements**
Prepared statements are generally used for sending pre-compiled SQL statements that take IN arguments. The methods required for prepared statement objects are defined in the interface `java.sql.PreparedStatement`. This interface extends the `java.sql.Statement` interface.

❏ **Callable Statements**
Callable statements are generally used for making calls to database stored procedures and can take both IN and OUT arguments. The methods required for prepared statement objects are defined in the interface `java.sql.CallableStatement`. This interface extends the `java.sql.PreparedStatement`.

> **Callable statements are not supported in this release of the PostgreSQL JDBC driver.**

# Statement

The interface `java.sql.Statement` is normally used for sending SQL statements that don't have IN or OUT parameters. The JDBC driver vendor provides the implementation class for this interface. The common methods required by the different JDBC statements are defined in this interface. The methods defined by `java.sql.Statement` can be broadly categorized as follows:

❏ Executing SQL statements

❏ Querying results and resultsets

❏ Handling SQL batches

❏ Other miscellaneous methods

The interface `java.sql.Statement` defines methods for executing different SQL statements like SELECT, UPDATE, INSERT, DELETE, and CREATE.

```
public ResultSet executeQuery(String sql) throws SQLException
```

This method can be used for sending a SELECT statement to the database and getting back the result. An instance of SQLException is thrown if a database error occurs. An example code snippet is shown below:

```
try {
    Connection con = DriverManager.getConnection(url,prop);
    Statement stmt = con.createStatement();
    ResultSet res = stmt.executeQuery("SELECT * FROM MyTable");
}catch(SQLException e) {
    //Handle exception
}
```

This code simply returns a resultset containing everything from the `MyTable` table:

```
public boolean execute(String sql) throws SQLException
```

This method can be used for sending an SQL statement that may fetch multiple resultsets like a stored procedure. This returns True if next result is a `ResultSet` object. An instance of `SQLException` is thrown if a database error occurs:

```
public int executeUpdate(String sql) throws SQLException
```

This method can be used for sending SQL statements that don't return resultsets, like `INSERT`, `UPDATE`, and `DELETE` statements as well as data definition language statements. This returns the number of rows affected by the SQL statement. An instance of `SQLException` is thrown if a database error occurs.

## Querying Results and Resultsets

The `Statement` interface defines various methods for getting information about the result of executing a SQL statement:

```
public ResultSet getResultSet() throws SQLException
```

Although executing a SQL statement can create several resultsets, a `Statement` object can have only one resultset open at a time. This method returns the current resultset associated with the `Statement` object. This method returns `NULL` if there is no more resultset available or the next result is an update count generated by executing an `UPDATE`, `INSERT`, or `DELETE` statement. An instance of `SQLException` is thrown if a database error occurs:

```
public int getUpdateCount() throws SQLException
```

This method returns the update count for the last executed `UPDATE`, `INSERT`, or `DELETE` statement. This method returns `-1` if there is no more update count available or the next result is a resultset generated by executing a `SELECT` statement. An instance of `SQLException` is thrown if a database error occurs:

```
public boolean getMoreResults() throws SQLException
```

This gets the statement object's next resultset. This method returns False if there is no more resultset available or the next result is an update count. An instance of `SQLException` is thrown if a database error occurs.

Methods are also provided for performing the get or set tasks:

- ❑ The resultset concurrency with which the statement was created
- ❑ The resultset fetch direction
- ❑ Fetch size

## Handling SQL Batches

The statement interface also provides methods for sending a batch of SQL statements to the database:

```
public void addBatch(String sql) throws SQLException
```

This method adds the specified sql to the current batch. Generally the SQL statements are INSERT, UPDATE, or DELETE. An instance of SQLException is thrown if a database error occurs:

```
public void clearBatch() throws SQLException
```

Clears the current batch. An instance of SQLException is thrown if a database error occurs:

```
public int[] executeBatch() throws SQLException
```

Executes the current batch. This method returns an array of updated counts. An instance of SQLException is thrown if a database error occurs.

## Miscellaneous Methods

Miscellaneous methods include methods for:

- ❑ Getting and setting query time out
- ❑ Closing the statement to release resources
- ❑ Getting and setting escape processing
- ❑ Getting and clearing SQL warnings
- ❑ Getting and setting cursor names

## An Example JDBC Client

In this section we will be using all the JDBC concepts we have learned. We will be writing a JDBC client that will perform the following tasks:

- ❑ Gets a connection to the database
- ❑ Creates a Statement object
- ❑ Inserts two records into the customer table
- ❑ Selects those records back from the database
- ❑ Deletes those records
- ❑ Closes the connection

Import the relevant classes:

```java
import java.sql.Connection;
import java.sql.Statement;
import java.sql.ResultSet;
import java.sql.DriverManager;

public class StatementClient {

    public static void main(String args[]) throws Exception {
```

Load the JDBC driver and get a connection. Create a statement from the connection:

```java
Class.forName("org.postgresql.Driver");
String url = "jdbc:postgresql:bpfinal";
Connection con =
    DriverManager.getConnection(url,"meeraj","password");

Statement stmt = con.createStatement();
```

Add two SQL statements for inserting records into the `customer` table into a batch:

```java
System.out.println("Inserting records");
stmt.addBatch("INSERT INTO customer(title,fname," +
    "lname,addressline,town,zipcode,phone) values " +
    "('Mr','Fred','Flintstone','31 Bramble Avenue'," +
    "'London','NT2 1AQ','023 9876')");
stmt.addBatch("INSERT INTO customer(title,fname," +
    "lname,addressline,town,zipcode,phone) values " +
    "('Mr','Barney','Rubble','22 Ramsons Avenue'," +
    "'London','PWD LS1','111 2313')");
```

Execute the batch:

```java
stmt.executeBatch();
System.out.println("Records Inserted");
System.out.println();
```

Select the records from the `customer` table and print the contents to the standard output:

```java
System.out.println("Selecting records");
String selectSQL = "SELECT * FROM customer";
ResultSet res = stmt.executeQuery(selectSQL);

while(res.next()) {
    for(int i = 1;i <= res.getMetaData().getColumnCount();i++) {
        System.out.print(res.getString(i) + "\t");
    }
    System.out.println();
}
System.out.println();
```

Delete the records from the `customer` table and print the number of records deleted:

```
System.out.println("Deleting records");
String deleteSQL = "DELETE FROM customer";
System.out.println("Records deleted: " +
    stmt.executeUpdate(deleteSQL));
```

Close the resultset, statement and connection to free up resources:

```
res.close();
stmt.close();
con.close();

    }

}
```

Name the class `StatementClient.java`, compile the class, and run the JVM on the compiled class with the `postgresql.jar` file in the classpath:

**# java -cp ./postgresql.jar StatementClient**

This will produce the following output depending on the records in the `customer` table. Please make sure that you have the `postgresql.jar` file in your system classpath when you invoke the JVM:

```
Inserting records
Records Inserted

Selecting records
81   Mr Fred Flinstone   31 Bramble Avenue   London   NT2 1AQ   023 9876
82   Mr Barney Rubble    22 Ramsons Avenue   London   PWD LS1   111 2313

Deleting records
Records deleted: 2
```

# Prepared Statements

Prepared statements are used for executing pre-compiled SQL statements, and are modelled in the JDBC API using the interface `java.sql.PreparedStatement`. This interface extends the interface `java.sql.Statement`. The JDBC driver vendor provides the implementation class for this interface. Prepared statements are created using the connection objects as we have already seen. They can also be used for executing SQL statements with parameter placeholders for IN statements defined using the symbol "?". Prepared statements are recommended for executing the same SQL statements more than once using different values for the IN parameters.

The methods defined in `java.sql.PreparedStatement` can be broadly classified into the following in addition to the ones already defined in the statement interface:

❑ Methods for executing SQL statements

❑ Methods for handling SQL batches

❑ Methods for setting the values of SQL IN parameters if the defined SQL have IN parameter placeholders

## Executing SQL Statements

The interface `java.sql.PreparedStatement` defines methods for executing different SQL statements like SELECT, UPDATE, INSERT, DELETE, and CREATE. Unlike the corresponding methods defined in the statement interface, these methods don't take the SQL statements as arguments. The SQL statements are defined when the prepared statements are created using the connection objects:

```
public ResultSet executeQuery() throws SQLException
```

This method can be used for executing the select statement associated with the prepared statement and getting back the result. An instance of `SQLException` is thrown if a database error occurs. An example code snippet is shown below:

```
try {
        String sql = "SELECT * FROM customer WHERE fname = ? ";
        Connection con = DriverManager.getConnection(url,prop);
        PreparedStatement stmt = con.prepareStatement(sql);
        stmt.setString(1, "Fred");
        ResultSet res = stmt.executeQuery();
}catch(SQLException e) {
        //Handle exception
}
```

```
public boolean execute() throws SQLException
```

This method can be used for executing the SQL statement associated with the prepared statement. This returns True if the next result is a `ResultSet` object. An instance of `SQLException` is thrown if a database error occurs:

```
public int executeUpdate() throws SQLException
```

This method can be used for executing the SQL statement associated with the prepared statements that don't return resultsets, like insert, update, etc. This returns the number of rows affected by the SQL statement. An instance of `SQLException` is thrown if a database error occurs.

## Updating Data

The prepared statement interface defines a set of `setXXX()` methods for setting the values of the IN parameters for the pre-compiled SQL statement defined using the symbol "?". The parameter indexes start from 1. The `setXXX()` method used should be compatible with the expected SQL type. The table below lists a few of these methods, and the rest can be extrapolated by referring to the Javadoc:

| Name | Purpose |
| --- | --- |
| `public void setBoolean(int index, boolean x)` | Sets the IN parameter specified by the argument index to the boolean value specified by x |
| `public void setInt(int index, int x)` | Sets the IN parameter specified by the argument index to the int value specified by x |

*Table continued on following page*

| Name | Purpose |
|------|---------|
| `public void setString(int index, string x)` | Sets the IN parameter specified by the argument `index` to the string value specified by `x` |

The interface also defines a method for clearing the current values of all parameters immediately:

```
public void clearParameters() throws SQLException
```

## An Example Using Prepared Statements

Now we will rewrite the previous example using prepared statements and see how the same INSERT statement can be executed multiple times using different values:

```java
import java.sql.Connection;
import java.sql.PreparedStatement;
import java.sql.ResultSet;
import java.sql.DriverManager;

public class PreparedStatementClient {

    public static void main(String args[]) throws Exception {

        Class.forName("org.postgresql.Driver");
        String url = "jdbc:postgresql:bpfinal";
        Connection con =
            DriverManager.getConnection(url,"meeraj","password");

        PreparedStatement stmt;

        String insertSQL = "INSERT INTO customer(title,fname," +
            "lname,addressline,town,zipcode,phone) VALUES " +
            "(?,?,?,?,?,?,?)";

        stmt = con.prepareStatement(insertSQL);

        System.out.println("Inserting records");

        stmt.setString(1,"Mr");
        stmt.setString(2,"Fred");
        stmt.setString(3,"Flinstone");
        stmt.setString(4,"31 Bramble Avenue");
        stmt.setString(5,"London");
        stmt.setString(6,"NT2 1AQ");
        stmt.setString(7,"023 9876");
        stmt.executeUpdate();

        stmt.clearParameters();

        stmt.setString(1,"Mr");
        stmt.setString(2,"Barney");
        stmt.setString(3,"Rubble");
```

```
        stmt.setString(4,"22 Ramsons Avenue");
        stmt.setString(5,"London");
        stmt.setString(6,"PWD LS1");
        stmt.setString(7,"111 2313");
        stmt.executeUpdate();

        System.out.println("Records Inserted");
        System.out.println();

        System.out.println("Selecting records");
        String selectSQL = "SELECT * FROM customer";
        stmt = con.prepareStatement(selectSQL);
        ResultSet res = stmt.executeQuery();
        while(res.next()) {
            for(int i = 1;i <= res.getMetaData().getColumnCount();i++) {
                System.out.print(res.getString(i) + "\t");
            }
            System.out.println();
        }
        System.out.println();

        System.out.println("Deleting records");
        String deleteSQL = "DELETE FROM customer";
        stmt = con.prepareStatement(deleteSQL);
        System.out.println("Records deleted: " +
            stmt.executeUpdate());

        res.close();

        stmt.close();
        con.close();

    }

}
```

# SQL Exceptions and Warnings

The core JDBC API provides four exceptions:

❑    `BatchUpdateException`
This exception is thrown when an error occurs during the execution of a SQL batch. This class gives a method to get the update counts of the SQLs that were executed successfully in the batch as an array of integers.

❑    `DataTruncation`
This exception is thrown when the data is unexpectedly truncated during data reads or writes. The class provides methods to access the following information:

     ❑    Number of bytes that should have been transferred.

     ❑    Number of bytes actually transferred.

❑ Whether the truncation occurred for a column or a parameter.

❑ Whether the truncation occurred on a read or a write.

❑ Index of the column or the parameter.

❑ SQLException
This is the superclass of all the other SQL exceptions. This class provides access methods for the database error code and SQL state for the error that caused this exception.

❑ SQLWarning
This subclass of SQLException is thrown to indicate warnings during database access.

# A JDBC GUI Application

In this section we will develop a small GUI based JDBC application to maintain the data in the customer table. The requirements for the application have been formulated and modelled into a use case diagram shown below:

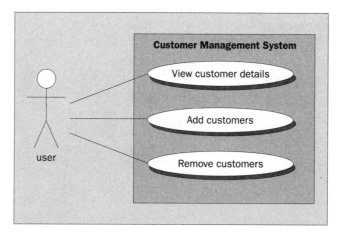

The identified use cases are:

❑ View the customer details in a list

❑ Add new customers

❑ Delete existing customers

We will implement the application as a standalone Java application using the Java swing classes. It has been further decided to list the details of existing customers using a read-only list probably implemented using JTable and to provide a form for entering the details of a new customer using a JPanel with the brequired fields for entering the information.

# Class Diagram

After detailed analysis and design, the following classes have been identified to model the system:

- ❑ The main class to start the application
- ❑ A class to model the customer entity
- ❑ A class that implements the `TableModel` interface to function as the data model for the list displaying the customer information
- ❑ A class to model the form for entering the details of a new customer

## Customer

This class models a customer entity in the database:

- ❑ Private instance variables that correspond to the columns in the `customer` table
- ❑ Accessors and mutators for all the attributes
- ❑ A constructor for initializing the values of the instance variables

## CustomerTableModel

This class acts as a model for the `JTable` instance that displays the customer information. This class implements the interface `javax.swing.table.TableModel` by extending the class `javax.swing.table.AbstractTableModel`:

- ❑ This class holds a collection of `Customer` class instances that represents the customers currently stored in the database
- ❑ It implements the required callback methods used by the controller for rendering the data. Note that `JTable` and `TableModel` fit into the classic MVC pattern
- ❑ It provides a method to set the current list of customers
- ❑ A method is also provided to remove the customer from the list for the specified index

## CustomerApp

This class models the form used for entering the details of a new customer:

- ❑ Input fields are provided for entering the customer details like title, first name, last name, address, and phone
- ❑ A method is provided to return a `Customer` object created from the values entered by the user
- ❑ The required fields are initialized and laid out in a grid in the constructor
- ❑ A method is also provided for blanking out the current values in the form

## *CustomerPanel*

This class contains the main method:

❑   This class has instance variables of type `CustomerPanel` and `CustomerTableModel`.

❑   This class extends `javax.swing.JFrame`.

❑   When the application starts, a connection is obtained from the database, the data is retrieved from the `customer` table and the instance of the class `CustomerTableModel` is populated.

❑   This object is used to initialize an instance of the `JTable` that displays the customer info and is added to the frame.

❑   An instance of the class `CustomerPanel` is also added to the frame.

❑   Two buttons, one for adding a new customer and one for deleting the selected customer from the list, are added to the frame.

❑   The class provides callback methods to handle the events when the buttons are clicked and the frame is closed. When the frame is closed, the connection to the database is released.

The figure below depicts the class diagram for the system:

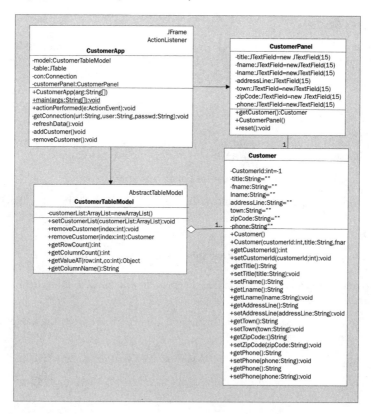

# System Interaction

In this section we will see the sequence of events instigated by the use cases associated with the system.

## View Customer Details

The sequence diagram below depicts the sequence of events involved in viewing the customer details:

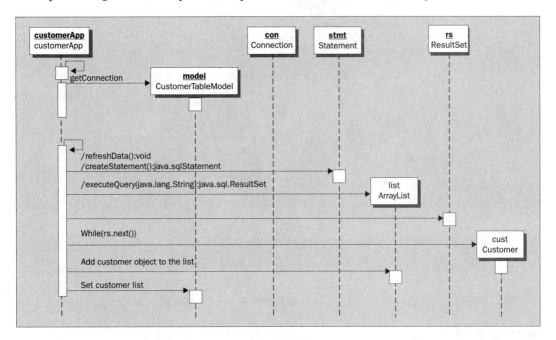

- ❑ The main class gets a connection to the database

- ❑ An instance of the class CustomerTableModel is instantiated

- ❑ Now the private method refreshData is called

- ❑ The connection is used to create a Statement object

- ❑ The Statement object issues the SQL statement to get all the records from the customer table

- ❑ The information in each record in the resultset is used to create a Customer object and this is added to a list

- ❑ Finally this list is used to populate the model that will use the instance of JTable to render the data

## Adding New Customer

The sequence diagram below depicts the sequence of events involved in adding a new customer to the database:

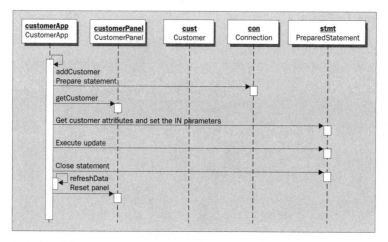

- ❑ The data entered by the user is retrieved from the CustomerPanel instance encapsulated in an instance of Customer class

- ❑ A prepared statement is created using the connection

- ❑ The IN parameters for the SQL statements are set using the data retrieved from the Customer object

- ❑ Finally the update is issued, the data in the table is refreshed and the form is reset

## Deleting a Customer

The sequence diagram below depicts the sequence of events involved in deleting a customer from the database:

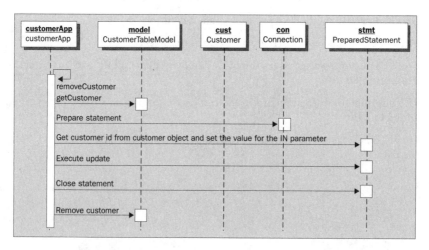

- ❏ The `Customer` object corresponding to the selected row in the table is retrieved from the model

- ❏ A prepared statement is created using the connection

- ❏ The `IN` parameter of the SQL statement for the customer Id is set using the data retrieved from the `Customer` object

- ❏ Finally the update is issued and the corresponding `Customer` object is removed from the model

# Source Files

In this section we will have a look at the source files in detail.

## The Customer Class

Declare the instance variables to model the database columns:

```java
public class Customer {

    private int customerId = -1;
    private String title = "";
    private String fname = "";
    private String lname = "";
    private String addressLine = "";
    private String town = "";
    private String zipCode = "";
    private String phone = "";

    public Customer() {
    }
```

Constructor to initialize the instance variables:

```java
    public Customer(int customerId,String title,
        String fname,String lname,
        String addressLine,String town,
        String zipCode,String phone) {

        this.customerId = customerId;
        this.title = title;
        this.fname = fname;
        this.lname = lname;
        this.addressLine = addressLine;
        this.town = town;
        this.zipCode = zipCode;
        this.phone = phone;


    }
```

Accessor and mutator for customer ID:

```
public int getCustomerId() {
    return customerId;
}
public void setCustomerId(int customerId) {
    this.customerId = customerId;
}
```

Accessor and mutator for title:

```
public String getTitle() {
    return title;
}

public void setTitle(String title) {
    this.title = title;
}
```

Accessor and mutator first name:

```
public String getFname() {
    return fname;
}

public void setFname(String fname) {
    this.fname = fname;
}
```

Accessor and mutator for last name:

```
public String getLname() {
    return lname;
}

public void setLname(String lname) {
    this.lname = lname;
}
```

Accessor and mutator for address:

```
public String getAddressLine() {
    return addressLine;
}

public void setAddressLine(String addressLine) {
    this.addressLine = addressLine;
}
```

Accessor and mutator for town:

```
public String getTown() {
    return town;
}

public void setTown(String town) {
    this.town = town;
}
```

Accessor and mutator for zip code:

```
public String getZipCode() {
    return zipCode;
}

public void setZipCode(String zipCode) {
    this.zipCode = zipCode;
}
```

Accessor and mutator for phone:

```
public String getPhone() {
    return phone;
}

public void setPhone(String phone) {
    this.phone = phone;
}

}
```

## The CustomerTableModel Class

Import the required classes:

```
import javax.swing.table.AbstractTableModel;
import java.util.ArrayList;

public class CustomerTableModel extends AbstractTableModel {
```

List to hold the current customer entities in the database:

```
private ArrayList customerList = new ArrayList();
```

Set the list of customers. When the list is changed all the listeners are notified. This is to notify the table to redraw itself:

```
public void setCustomerList(ArrayList customerList) {
    this.customerList = customerList;
    fireTableDataChanged();
}
```

Remove a specific customer. When the list is changed all the listeners are notified:

```
public void removeCustomer(int index) {
    customerList.remove(index);
    fireTableDataChanged();
}
```

Get a specific customer:

```
public Customer getCustomer(int index) {

    if(index >= customerList.size()) {
        return null;
    }
    return (Customer)customerList.get(index);
}
```

Callback method to get the number of rows to be rendered in the table:

```
public int getRowCount() {
    return customerList.size();
}
```

Callback method to get the number of columns to be rendered in the table:

```
public int getColumnCount() {
    return 7;
}
```

Callback method to get the value of the specified cell to be rendered in the table:

```
public Object getValueAt(int row, int col) {

    if(row >= customerList.size()) {
        throw new IllegalArgumentException("Invalid row");
    }

    Customer customer = (Customer)customerList.get(row);
    switch(col) {
        case 0:
            return customer.getTitle();
        case 1:
            return customer.getFname();
        case 2:
            return customer.getLname();
        case 3:
            return customer.getAddressLine();
        case 4:
            return customer.getTown();
        case 5:
            return customer.getZipCode();
```

```
            case 6:
                    return customer.getPhone();
            default:
                    throw new IllegalArgumentException("Invalid column");
        }

    }

}
```

## The CustomerPanel Class

Import the required classes:

```
import javax.swing.JTextField;
import javax.swing.JPanel;
import javax.swing.JLabel;

import javax.swing.border.TitledBorder;
import javax.swing.border.EtchedBorder;

import java.awt.GridLayout;
import java.awt.FlowLayout;

public class CustomerPanel extends JPanel {
```

Instantiate the input fields for entering the details for a new customer:

```
    private JTextField title = new JTextField(15);
    private JTextField fname = new JTextField(15);
    private JTextField lname = new JTextField(15);
    private JTextField addressLine = new JTextField(15);
    private JTextField town = new JTextField(15);
    private JTextField zipCode = new JTextField(15);
    private JTextField phone = new JTextField(15);
```

Instantiate and return a `Customer` object using the values entered into the form fields by the user:

```
    public Customer getCustomer() {

        return new Customer(-1,title.getText(),
                fname.getText(),lname.getText(),
                addressLine.getText(),town.getText(),
                zipCode.getText(),phone.getText());

    }
```

The constructor initializes the user interface for the form:

```
    public CustomerPanel() {
```

Set the layout to a 7 x 1 grid:

```
        setLayout(new GridLayout(7,1));
```

Add the field for entering the title:

```
        JPanel panel1 = new JPanel();
        panel1.setLayout(new FlowLayout(FlowLayout.RIGHT));
        panel1.add(new JLabel("Title:"));
        panel1.add(title);
        add(panel1);
```

Add the field for entering the first name:

```
        JPanel panel2 = new JPanel();
        panel2.setLayout(new FlowLayout(FlowLayout.RIGHT));
        panel2.add(new JLabel("First Name:"));
        panel2.add(fname);
        add(panel2);
```

Add the field for entering the last name:

```
        JPanel panel3 = new JPanel();
        panel3.setLayout(new FlowLayout(FlowLayout.RIGHT));
        panel3.add(new JLabel("Last Name:"));
        panel3.add(lname);
        add(panel3);
```

Add the field for entering the address:

```
        JPanel panel4 = new JPanel();
        panel4.setLayout(new FlowLayout(FlowLayout.RIGHT));
        panel4.add(new JLabel("Address:"));
        panel4.add(addressLine);
        add(panel4);
```

Add the field for entering the town:

```
        JPanel panel5 = new JPanel();
        panel5.setLayout(new FlowLayout(FlowLayout.RIGHT));
        panel5.add(new JLabel("Town:"));
        panel5.add(town);
        add(panel5);
```

Add the field for entering the Zip code:

```
        JPanel panel6 = new JPanel();
        panel6.setLayout(new FlowLayout(FlowLayout.RIGHT));
        panel6.add(new JLabel("Zip Code:"));
        panel6.add(zipCode);
        add(panel6);
```

Add the field for entering the phone number:

```
            JPanel panel7 = new JPanel();
            panel7.setLayout(new FlowLayout(FlowLayout.RIGHT));
            panel7.add(new JLabel("Phone:"));
            panel7.add(phone);
            add(panel7);

            setBorder(new TitledBorder(new EtchedBorder(),"Add Customer"));

    }
```

This method blanks out the form for entering customer information:

```
    public void reset() {

            title.setText("");
            fname.setText("");
            lname.setText("");
            addressLine.setText("");
            town.setText("");
            zipCode.setText("");
            phone.setText("");

    }

}
```

## The CustomerApp Class

Import the required classes:

```
import javax.swing.JTable;
import javax.swing.JFrame;
import javax.swing.JScrollPane;
import javax.swing.JPanel;
import javax.swing.JButton;

import java.awt.BorderLayout;

import java.awt.event.ActionEvent;
import java.awt.event.ActionListener;
import java.awt.event.WindowEvent;
import java.awt.event.WindowAdapter;

import java.util.ArrayList;

import java.sql.DriverManager;
import java.sql.Connection;
import java.sql.Statement;
import java.sql.PreparedStatement;
import java.sql.ResultSet;
import java.sql.SQLException;

public class CustomerApp extends JFrame implements ActionListener {
```

An instance of the model that feeds the table that lists the customer details:

```
private CustomerTableModel model;
```

Table in which the customer details are listed:

```
private JTable table;
```

Connection to the PostgreSQL database:

```
private Connection con;
```

Panel that contains the form for entering the customer data:

```
private CustomerPanel customerPanel;

public CustomerApp(String[] arg) throws Exception {

    super("Customer Management System");
```

Get a connection to the database:

```
getConnection(arg[0],arg[1],arg[2]);
```

Create an instance of the table model and populate it with the data:

```
model = new CustomerTableModel();
refreshData();
```

Create the table using the model and add the table to a scroll pane. The pane is then added to the parent frame:

```
table = new JTable(model);
table.setAutoCreateColumnsFromModel(true);
JScrollPane pane = new JScrollPane(table);

getContentPane().setLayout(new BorderLayout());

getContentPane().add(pane,BorderLayout.CENTER);
```

Add two buttons, one for adding new customers and one for deleting selected customers. The current class is registered as the action listener for the two buttons:

```
JPanel buttonPanel = new JPanel();
JButton newButton = new JButton("Add Customer");
newButton.addActionListener(this);
buttonPanel.add(newButton);
JButton deleteButton = new JButton("Remove Customer");
deleteButton.addActionListener(this);
buttonPanel.add(deleteButton);
getContentPane().add(buttonPanel,BorderLayout.SOUTH);
```

Create an instance of the customer panel and add it to the frame:

```
customerPanel = new CustomerPanel();
getContentPane().add(customerPanel,BorderLayout.WEST);
```

Display the frame:

```
pack();
show();
setLocation(50,50);
setSize(800,375);
setResizable(false);

validate();
```

Add an inner class that listens to the window closing events and closes the database connections:

```
addWindowListener(new WindowAdapter() {

    public void windowClosing(WindowEvent e) {
        try {
            con.close();
        }catch(SQLException ex) {
            ex.printStackTrace();
        }
        System.exit(0);
    }

});

}
```

The `main()` method expects the JDBC URL, user name and password for the database as commandline arguments:

```
public static void main(String args[]) throws Exception {

    if(args == null || args.length != 3) {
        System.out.print("Usage");
        System.out.println("java EmployeeApp
            <jdbcURL> <user> <passwd>");
        return;
    }
    CustomerApp app = new CustomerApp(args);

}
```

Callback method for listening to the button actions:

```
public void actionPerformed(ActionEvent e) {

    JButton button = (JButton)e.getSource();

    try {
```

If the button for adding customers is clicked, call the method to add customers:

```
        if("Add Customer".equals(button.getText())) {
            addCustomer();
```

If the button for removing customers is clicked, call the method to remove customers:

```
        }else if("Remove Customer".equals(button.getText())) {
            removeCustomer();
        }
    }catch(SQLException ex) {
        ex.printStackTrace();
    }

    validate();

}
```

This method gets a connection to the database:

```
private void getConnection(String url,String user,String passwd)
    throws Exception {

    Class.forName("org.postgresql.Driver");
    con = DriverManager.getConnection(url,user,passwd);

}
```

This method refreshes the table model data:

```
private void refreshData() throws SQLException {

    String sql = "select * from customer";
    Statement stmt = con.createStatement();
    ResultSet res = stmt.executeQuery(sql);

    ArrayList list = new ArrayList();
    while(res.next()) {
        Customer cust = new Customer(res.getInt(1),
            res.getString(2),res.getString(3),
            res.getString(4),res.getString(5),
            res.getString(6),res.getString(7),
            res.getString(8));
        list.add(cust);
    }

    model.setCustomerList(list);

    res.close();
    stmt.close();
}
```

This method inserts a record to the database:

```
private void addCustomer() throws SQLException {

    String sql = "insert into customer(" +
                    "title,fname,lname, " +
                    "addressline,town,zipcode,phone)" +
                    "values(" +
                    "?,?,?,?,?,?,?)";
```

Prepare the statement:

```
    PreparedStatement stmt = con.prepareStatement(sql);

    Customer cust = customerPanel.getCustomer();
```

Set the SQL IN parameters:

```
    stmt.setString(1,cust.getTitle());
    stmt.setString(2,cust.getFname());
    stmt.setString(3,cust.getLname());
    stmt.setString(4,cust.getAddressLine());
    stmt.setString(5,cust.getTown());
    stmt.setString(6,cust.getZipCode());
    stmt.setString(7,cust.getPhone());
```

Execute the SQL:

```
    stmt.executeUpdate();

    stmt.close();
```

Refresh the table:

```
    refreshData();
    customerPanel.reset();

}
```

This method deletes a record from the database:

```
private void removeCustomer() throws SQLException {

    String sql = "delete from customer where customer_id = ?";
    PreparedStatement stmt = con.prepareStatement(sql);
```

Get the selected customer:

```
int selectedRow = table.getSelectedRow();

Customer cust = model.getCustomer(selectedRow);
if(cust == null) {
      return;
}
```

Set the customer ID:

```
stmt.setInt(1,cust.getCustomerId());
```

Execute the delete SQL:

```
stmt.executeUpdate();
stmt.close();
```

Remove the customer from the model:

```
model.removeCustomer(selectedRow);

      }
   }
```

# Compile and Run the Application

Compile the classes using the following command:

```
$ javac Customer*.java
```

This will produce the following class files:

- ❑  Customer.class
- ❑  CustomerTableModel.class
- ❑  CustomerPanel.class
- ❑  CustomerApp.class

Run the application using the following command:

```
$ java CustomerApp <JDBC-URL> <User> <password>
```

The screenshot over the page shows the application running. Please make sure that you have the postgresql.jar file in your system classpath when you invoke the JVM:

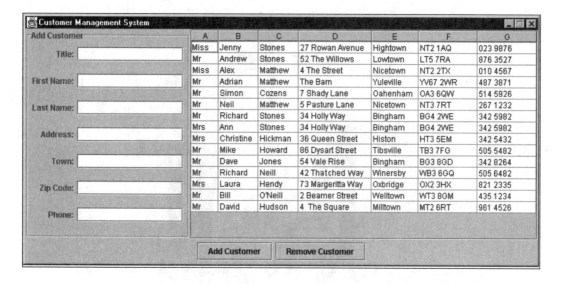

# Summary

In this chapter, we have seen how PostgreSQL databases can be accessed from Java language programs using JDBC. We have seen the following in this chapter:

❑ JDBC drivers

❑ Building PostgreSQL JDBC driver

❑ Database connections. JDBC statements

❑ Prepared statements for sending pre-compiled SQL

❑ JDBC resultsets

❑ Database and resultset meta data

The JDBC API continues to evolve, and some interesting new features will become available as vendors move to support version 3.0 of the JDBC API. New features in 3.0 include:

❑ Support for save points

❑ Integration of extension API with the core API and making them available with both J2EE and J2SE

❑ Parameter meta data

❑ Ability to have multiple resultsets open simultaneously against a statement

❑ Callable statement enhancements

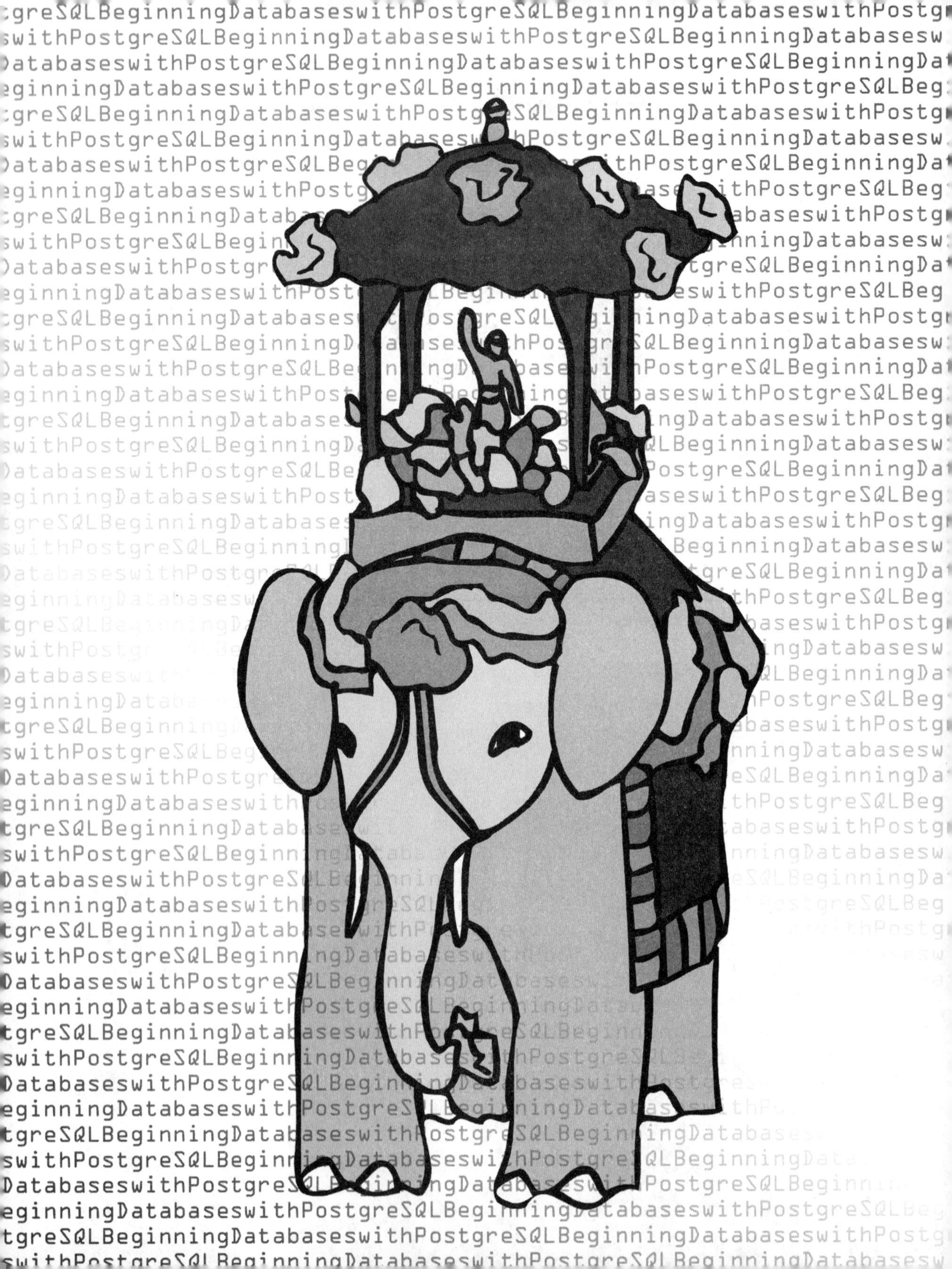
BeginningDatabaseswithPostgreSQL

# Further Information and Resources

As you have read through this book, hopefully you will have come to appreciate that PostgreSQL is a very advanced and capable relational database. From version 7.1 onwards, PostgreSQL almost attains compliance with the base standard of SQL92, and it seems probable that complete compliance is close at hand.

We have seen that PostgreSQL is accessible from many different programming languages, and also from remote clients across a network. The ODBC driver makes PostgreSQL a valid choice as a backend database server even where all the clients are Microsoft Windows-based PCs.

In this book, we have concentrated on getting PostgreSQL up and running, but have not had the scope to investigate some of PostgreSQL's more unusual features, particularly its ability to create tables derived from other tables, using inheritance. We have not attempted to delve into the source of PostgreSQL, all of which is of course available for inspection and can, if you wish to, be modified for your own use. Who knows, maybe one day you could contribute to the mainstream PostgreSQL source.

## Non-Relational Storage

The relational model has been around for over 30 years now, and has proved itself a very powerful and flexible concept. Its sound underpinnings in mathematics have not only stood the test of time, but also the harsh realities of real world problem solving.

There have been several challenges to the relational model through the years, most notably from object databases in the 1990s. Although there have been several successful pure object databases, much of the market has remained faithful to the relational model, particularly as the main relational vendors have added features to their relational databases to enable them to support objects more easily.

A more recent challenge is appearing in the wake of the establishment of XML as an interchange format, from vendors who allow XML to be stored and queried in what is effectively an XML-based database. Although these are very flexible, it seems to us that the relational model will adapt again, with XML interfaces added to the more traditional relational databases, to enable them to interface more easily to XML. Although XML is a very flexible format, the data it conveys is almost always highly structured and amenable to storage and retrieval from a relational database. It is expected that the relational model will adapt and rise to this latest challenge.

# OLTP, OLAP, and Other Database Terminology

The world of databases abounds with jargon terms; OLTP, OLAP, Data Warehouses, Data Marts, and many others. Although often used almost as magic incantations, they are basically just different strategies for storing data, so that it is better optimized for its intended purpose.

In this book, we have been using our relational database in a very interactive way. We have considered the relational database very much a source of live data, with ongoing updates as orders are added, goods shipped and so on, with many users simultaneously updating and accessing the data. These are **On Line Transaction Processing** (OLTP) type characteristics.

There is another class of data, not used for interactive processing, but for after the event' analysis. These are often termed **Decision Support Systems** (DSS), **Data Warehouses**, **Executive Information Systems** (EIS), and **Management Information System** (MIS). We will use the more technical term, **On Line Analytical Processing** (OLAP). These systems have quite different demands from the more common OLTP type databases.

Some essential differences between OLAP and OLTP type databases:

| OLTP | OLAP |
| --- | --- |
| Live data, usually continuously updated | Historic data, updated at fixed times, perhaps nightly or less frequently |
| Used for live processing during operations | Used for analysis over a longer time frame |
| Usually limited to tens of gigabytes in size | Can be many terabytes in size |
| Usually have a limited amount of historic data | May store many years of historic data |
| Optimized in a relational model for efficient data updates | Optimized for data retrieval, usually in a non-relational model such as star or snowflake schemas |

Our examples in this book have been based around a very simple store database bpsimple, with customers, customers placing orders, and items being sold. The database schema we have been using is very much an OLTP type database. It was optimized as a relational database, to allow dynamic processing of orders, and very efficient storage of data.

If we had a large business that was doing well, after a while the size of the data in the database would become quite significant, and performance would start to slow. Realistically, the best way of quickly improving the performance would be to simply throw away older data. We might well decide that we had no interest in customers who had not ordered from us for two years or what items we had shipped a year ago.

However, we might want to try and perform some analysis of our customers and their ordering habits, in order to improve our merchandising. We could perhaps organize a targeted marketing campaign, or promotions to allow us to sell more goods.

A classic, though perhaps 'urban legend', story is of the supermarket which discovered that sales of baby nappies and beer were linked, and that placing beer next to nappies improved sales. The reasoning was that some husbands sent shopping for nappies on the way home from work were tempted to pick up some beer at the same time, when the items were placed close together.

For this sort of analysis what we need is lots of data, probably collected over many years, and the ability to query it efficiently. We don't care if the last day's or last week's sales are not yet included, because what we are looking at is long term trends. This sort of work is done by OLAP databases. Although they can, and often are, built on conventional relational databases, the data stored in them is organized to allow it to be retrieved as efficiently as possible.

An OLAP database is often organized using a star schema, where there is a central **fact** table, and a number of **dimension** tables that are linked to it. If we were building an OLAP database for our store, we would perhaps have a central fact table that stored sales, with all the other data, such as who bought the item, when it was sold, and details of the item, relegated to dimension tables:

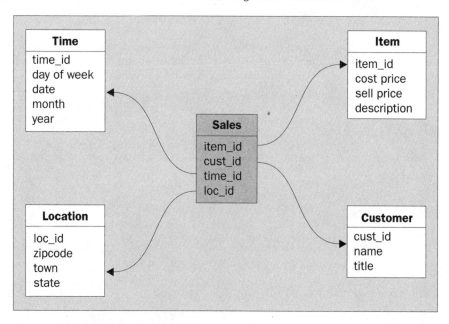

To get data into this OLAP database we would probably export the data from our normal database, and then use some custom data loading procedures to build the data in this new format.

If our business was very large, we might find that we needed to break down our OLAP database into smaller, more focused, segments of data. These are often referred to as data cubes or data marts. They are smaller collections of data about specific facts organized as an OLAP database:

Thus, a common flow of data in a large organization with heavy online processing needs and sophisticated data analysis requirements could be depicted like this:

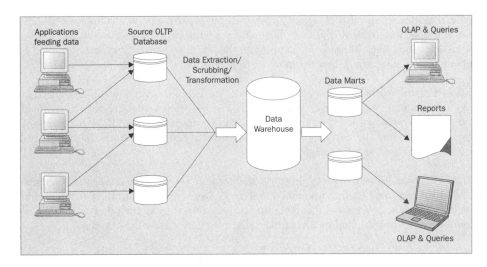

Although these OLAP databases use a very different schema design from the more normal relational schema, they are still normally implemented using relational databases. Major vendors, such as Oracle and Microsoft, have added features to their databases to make them easier to work with, as OLAP databases.

# Resources

The long-standing nature of the relational model means that there is a good range of reference material available.

# Web Resources

These of course change all the time, but some useful starting points are:

## *PostgreSQL*

- ❑  http://www.postgresql.org
- ❑  http://www.unixodbc.org
- ❑  http://www.greatbridge.org
- ❑  http://www.greatbridge.com
- ❑  http://pgdemo.acucore.com
- ❑  http://www.pgsql.com
- ❑  http://www.redhat.com and search for 'Red Hat Database'

## *PHP*

- ❑  http://www.php.net
- ❑  http://www.phpbuilder.com
- ❑  http://www.phpwizard.net

### Perl

- ❑ http://www.perl.com
- ❑ http://www.perl.org
- ❑ http://www.cpan.org
- ❑ http://activestate.com

### Java and JDBC

- ❑ http://www.java.sun.com

# General Tools

DeZign for databases is a database development tool using an entity relationship diagram. It visually supports the layout of the entities and relationships, and automatically generates SQL schemas for most leading databases. Supports ERDs, runs on Windows. Evaluation download available:

- ❑ http://www.datanamic.com/dezign/index.html

The Toolkit for Conceptual Modeling is a collection of software tools to present conceptual models of software systems in the form of diagrams, tables, and trees. Includes ERDs, but no code generation yet. Runs on UNIX and Linux:

- ❑ http://wwwhome.cs.utwente.nl/~tcm/

Database Design Studio (DDS) is a tool for the design of a database using an Entity Relationship Diagram. Runs on Windows using ODBC:

- ❑ http://www.chillisource.com/dds/

# Books

## SQL

- ❑ *PostgreSQL – Introduction and Concepts*, Bruce Momjian. Addison-Wesley (ISBN 0-201-70331-9). A book by one of the core PostgreSQL developers, also available in HTML format on the Web.

- ❑ *Database Design for Mere Mortals – A Hands-On guide to Relational Database Design*, Michael J. Hernandez. Addison-Wesley (ISBN 0-201-69471-9). A book that concentrates on the collection of information and basic design of databases, written in a very easy–to-read style.

- ❑ *The Practical SQL Handbook – Using Structured Query Language*, Judith S. Bowman, Sandra L. Emerson, Marcy Darnovsky. Addison-Wesley (ISBN 0-201-44787-8). Some clear explanations of the more practical aspects of using SQL.

- ❑ *Mastering SQL*, Martin Gruber. Sybex (ISBN 0-7821-2538-7). A well-written guide to standard SQL.

- ❑ *SQL for Smarties*, Joe Celko. Morgan Kaufmann Publishers (ISBN 1-55860-576-2). An excellent book on getting the most out of the more advanced features of SQL.

- ❑ *Instant SQL Programming*, Joe Celko. Wrox Press (ISBN 1-874416-50-8). A straightforward guide to the SQL syntax and usage.

## *PHP*

- ❏ *Professional PHP Programming,* Jesus Castagnetto, Chris Scollo, Sascha Schumann, Harish Rawat, Deepak Veliath. Wrox Press (ISBN 1-861002-96-3). This book is about multi-tier programming with PHP, with coverage of the core PHP language and database addressing.

- ❏ *Beginning PHP 4*, Wankyu Choi, Chris Lea, Ganesh Prasad, Chris Ullman with Jon Blank and Sean Cazzell. Wrox Press (ISBN 1861003730). A tutorial in the PHP language, including an introduction to relational databases.

## *Perl*

- ❏ *Beginning Perl,* Simon Cozens. Wrox Press (ISBN 1861003439). A tutorial in Perl on Windows and Unix, including working with databases.

- ❏ *Perl Cookbook* (Third Edition), Tom Christiansen and Nathan Torkington. O'Reilly and Associates (ISBN 0-596-00027-8). This edition of the well-known "Camel Book" has been expanded to cover Perl 5.6 and all other essentials.

- ❏ *Professional Perl Programming,* Peter Wainwright with Aldo Caplini, Simon Cozens, JJ Merelo-Guervos, Aalhad Saraf and Chris Nandor. Wrox Press (ISBN 1-861004-49-4). This book has an in-depth coverage of Perl 5.6, object-oriented programming, and more.

## *Java*

- ❏ *Beginning Java 2,* Ivor Horton. Wrox Press (ISBN 1-861003-66-8). A book for anyone who wants to program in Java. It teaches the Java language from scratch, as well as object-oriented programming, connecting to databases using JDBC and more.

- ❏ *Professional Java Data,* Danny Ayers, John Bell, Carl Calvert-Bettis, Thomas Bishop, Bjarki Holm, Glenn E. Mitchell, Kelly Lin Poon, Sean Rhody with Mike Bogovich, Matthew Ferris, Rick Grehan, Tony Loton, Nitin Nanda and Mark Wilcox . Wrox Press (ISBN 1-861004-10-9). Information about accessing data in relational and object-oriented databases using Java.

# Summary

PostgreSQL has progressed enormously from its early research days, and matured into a very capable and stable product suitable for use in many production systems. Its support for standard SQL, already strong, continues to improve with each release, as does its already strong scalability.

The Open Source license means that you can deploy PostgreSQL with no client or server license costs. Coupled with the knowledge you have hopefully gained from this book, you should now be in a position to deploy a true database server in situations where license costs may have otherwise driven a less elegant solution.

PostgreSQL already has a distinguished past, and as it matures rapidly into a very stable and capable database, we are sure it will be challenging the commercial vendors with their huge development budgets and dedicated development teams. We wish it well.

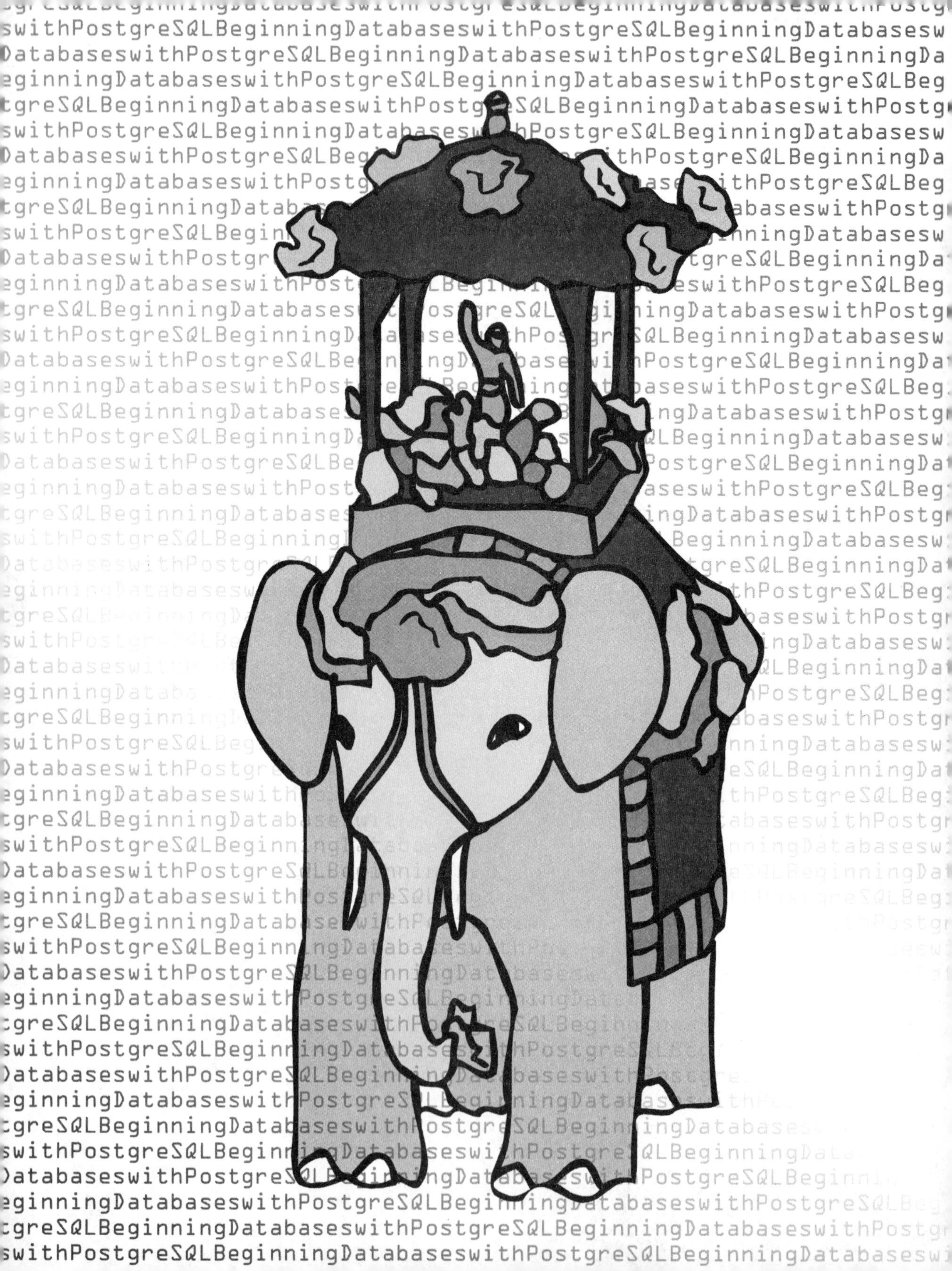
BeginningDatabaseswithPostgreSQL

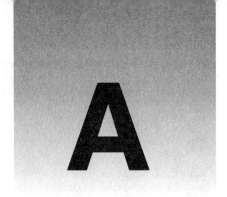

# PostgreSQL Database Limits

When we use a database to store information, creating tables and adding rows to them, we are tempted to ignore the fact that on no platform do we have the luxury of infinite storage.

All database systems will be limited in some way, and PostgreSQL is no exception. The amount of data that can be stored in a single column, the maximum number of columns allowed in a table and the total size of any table, all have limits, albeit quite large ones.

Recent releases of PostgreSQL have seen most database limits relaxed, and in many cases effectively removed. Here we will mention some of the restrictions that remain as of PostgreSQL 7.1.

For updates on limits for later versions, check out the site: http://www.postgresql.org

> **The information here is derived from the PostgreSQL FAQ and mailing list contributions made by PostgreSQL developers.**

Where a size is given as "no limit" this means that PostgreSQL by itself imposes no limit. The maximum size will be determined by other factors, such as the amount of available disk space or virtual memory.

As a limit is approached, the performance of the database will degrade. If we are, for example, manipulating very large fields consuming a large fraction of available (virtual) memory, it is likely that performance will begin to be unacceptable. Finally, PostgreSQL will be physically unable to perform an update.

Other limits, not discussed here, may be imposed by the operating system, or network transport. For example, there are typical limits on the size of a query that can be made via ODBC, depending on the driver. Memory limits may also be applied that would prevent very large columns, rows, or resultsets from being created, transferred across a network (which in itself will be slow), or received by the client.

## Database Size: No Limit

PostgreSQL does not impose a limit on the total size of a database. Databases over 60Gb are reported to exist. A 60Gb database is more than sufficient for all but the most demanding applications.

Due to the way that PostgreSQL arranges its data storage, you may see some performance degradation associated with databases containing many tables. PostgreSQL will use a large number of files for storing the table data, and, if the operating system does not cope well with many files in a single directory, performance may suffer.

# Table Size: 16Tb-64Tb

PostgreSQL normally stores its table data in chunks of 8k. The number of these blocks is limited to a 32-bit signed integer (just over two billion), giving a maximum table size of 16 terabytes. The basic block size can be increased when PostgreSQL is built, up to a maximum of 32k, thereby giving a theoretical table size limit of 64 terabytes.

Some operating systems impose a file size limit that prevent, files of this size being created, so PostgreSQL stores table data in multiple files, each 1Gb in size. For large tables, this will result in many files and potential operating system performance degradation, as noted earlier.

# Rows in a Table: No Limit

PostgreSQL does not impose a limit, on the number of rows in any table.

But, the aggregate function COUNT returns a 32-bit integer. So for tables with over two billion rows, the result from COUNT will be meaningless.

# Table Indexes: No Limit

There is no PostgreSQL-imposed limit on the number of indexes we can create on a table. Of course, performance may degrade if we choose to create more and more indexes on a table with more and more columns.

# Column Size: 1Gb

PostgreSQL has a limit of one gigabyte for the size of any one field in a table. In practice, the limit comes from the amount of memory available for the server to manipulate the data and transfer it to the client.

# Columns in a Table: 250+

The maximum number of columns that can be accommodated in a PostgreSQL table depends on the configured block size and the type of the column. For the default block size of 8k at least 250 columns can be stored. This can rise to 1600 if all of the columns are very simple fields, such as integer values. Increasing the block size increases these limits accordingly.

# Row Size: No Limit

There is no explicit maximum size of a row. But, of course, the size of columns and their number is limited as described above.

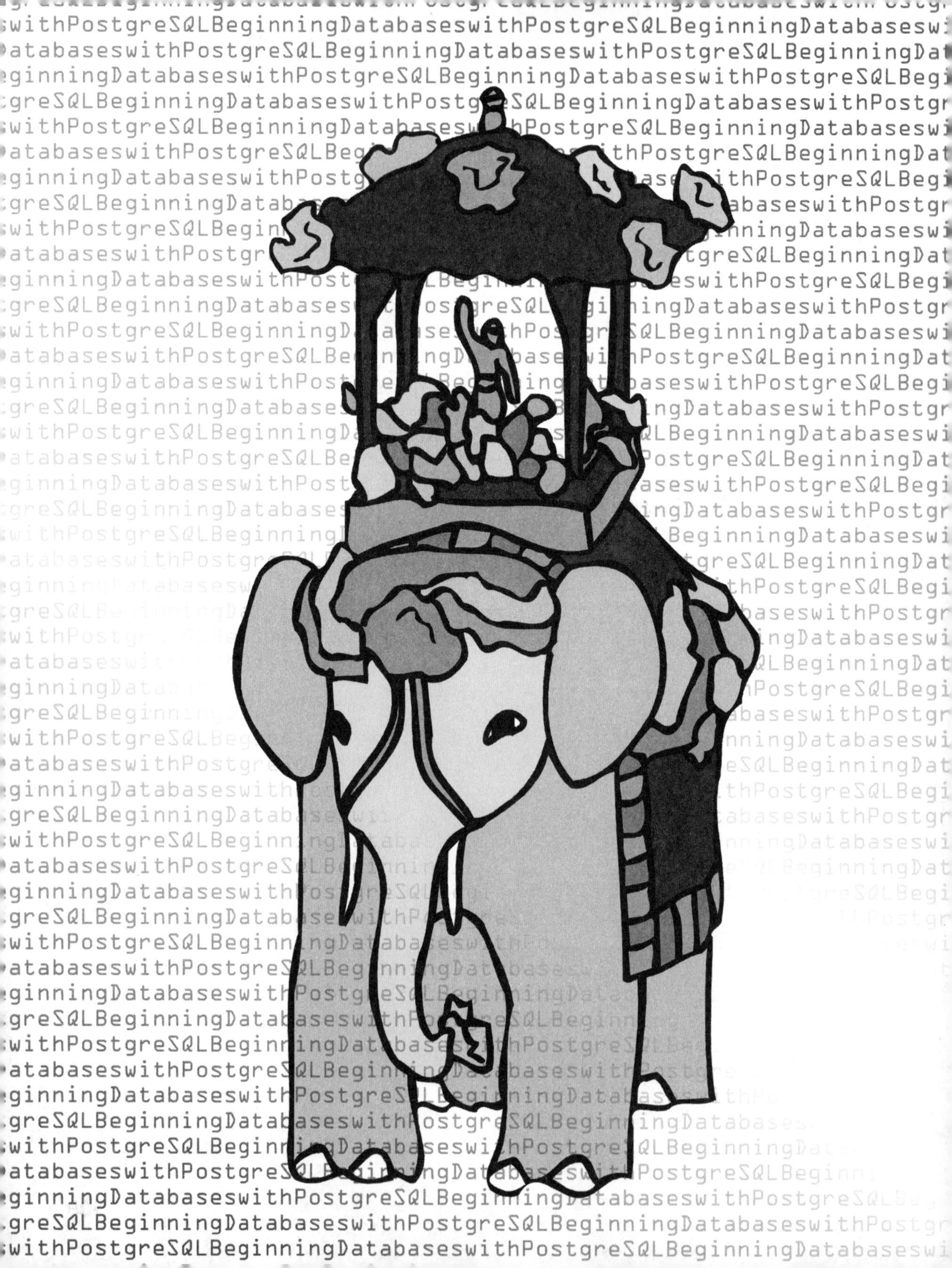

# B

# PostgreSQL data types

PostgreSQL has a particularly rich set of data types, which are described in the User Guide and from `psql` using the `\dT` command. Here we list the more useful types, ignoring some of the very specialist types and those types used only internally by PostgreSQL. Use `\dT` in `psql` for a definitive list.

In these tables, the standard SQL name appears first, which PostgreSQL generally accepts, and then, any PostgreSQL-specific alternative names.

Some types are specific to PostgreSQL. In such cases no SQL name is given. As long as it's practical, we suggest you stick to the standard SQL types and names.

## Logical Types

| SQL Name | PostgreSQL alternative name | Notes |
|---|---|---|
| Boolean | bool | Holds a truth value. Will accept values such as TRUE, 't', 'true', 'y', 'yes', '1' as true. |
| | | Uses 1 byte of storage, and can store NULL, unlike a few proprietary databases. |
| | | Boolean was not officially added to the SQL language until the SQL99 standard, although it was in common use long before that. |

# Exact Number Types

| SQL Name | PostgreSQL alternative name | Notes |
|---|---|---|
| smallint | int2 | A signed two-byte integer which can store -32768 to +32767. |
| integer, int | int4 | A signed 4-byte integer which can store -2147483648 to +2147483647. |
| | int8 | A signed 8-byte integer, giving approximately 18 digits of precision. |
| bit | | Stores a single bit, 0 or 1. |
| bit varying | Varbit | Stores a sequence of bits. To insert into a table use syntax such as INSERT INTO … VALUES(011101::varbit);. |

# Approximate Number Types

| SQL Name | PostgreSQL alternative name | Notes |
|---|---|---|
| numeric (precision, scale) | | Stores an exact number to the precision specified. The user guide states there is no limit to the precision. |
| decimal (precision, scale) | | By default precision will be 9, and scale 0. Range is approximately 8000 digits according to the user guide. In standard SQL, the difference between decimal and numeric is that with numeric the precision must be exactly as requested, with decimal the implementation may choose to store additional precision. We suggest you stick to numeric rather than use decimal. |
| float (precision) | float4, float8 | A floating point number with at least the given precision. If the precision requested is less than 7 digits float4 is used, otherwise float8 will be used with a maximum precision of 15 digits. Use float(15) to get an equivalent to the standard SQL type of double precision. |
| real | float4 | We recommend you stick to float(precision). |

| SQL Name | PostgreSQL alternative name | Notes |
|---|---|---|
| double precision | float8 | Same as float(15). |
| | money | This is the same as decimal(9,2). Its use is discouraged as it is deprecated and support may be dropped in later versions of PostgreSQL. |

## Temporal Types

| SQL Name | PostgreSQL alternative name | Notes |
|---|---|---|
| Timestamp | datetime | Stores times from 4713BC to 1465001AD, with a resolution of 1 microsecond. |
| timestamp with timezone | | Stores times from 1903AD to 2037AD, with a resolution of 1 microsecond. |
| Interval | interval, timespan | Can store an interval of approximately +/- 178000000 years, with a resolution of 1 microsecond. |
| Date | | Stores dates from 4713BC to 32767AD with a resolution of 1 day. |
| Time | | Stores a time of day, from 0 to 23:59:59.99 with a resolution of 1 microsecond. |
| time with timezone | | Same as time, except a time zone is also stored. |

## Character Types

| SQL Name | PostgreSQL alternative name | Notes |
|---|---|---|
| char | | Stores a single character. |
| char(n) | | Stores exactly n characters, which will be padded with blanks if less characters are actually stored. Recommended only for short strings of known length. |

*Table continued on following page*

| SQL Name | PostgreSQL alternative name | Notes |
| --- | --- | --- |
| char varying(n) | varchar(n) | Stores a variable number of characters, up to a maximum of n characters, which are not padded with blanks. This is the 'standard' choice for character strings. |
| | text | A PostgreSQL specific variant of varchar, which does not require you to specify an upper limit on the number of characters. |

# Geometric Types

| SQL Name | PostgreSQL name | Notes |
| --- | --- | --- |
| | point | An x,y value |
| | line | A line (pt1, pt2) |
| | lseg | A line segment (pt1, pt2) |
| | box | A box specified by a pair of points |
| | path | A sequence of points, which may be closed or open |
| | polygon | A sequence of points, effectively a closed path, but handled differently internal to PostgreSQL |
| | circle | A point and a length, which specify a circle |

# Miscellaneous Types

| SQL Name | PostgreSQL alternative name | Notes |
| --- | --- | --- |
| serial | | In standard, SQL a serial is a numeric column in a table that increases each time a row is added. |
| | | PostgreSQL does not implement the serial type as a separate type, although it accepts the standard SQL syntax. Internally PostgreSQL uses an integer to store the value, and a sequence to manage the automatic incrementing of the value. When a table is created with a serial type an implicit sequence is created to manage the serial data column. This implicit sequence will not be dropped automatically when the table is dropped. |
| | oid | An object id. Internally PostgreSQL adds a hidden oid to each row, and stores a 4 byte integer, giving a maximum value of approximately 4 billion. This type is also used as a reference when storing binary large objects. |

| SQL Name | PostgreSQL alternative name | Notes |
|---|---|---|
| | cidr | Stores a network address of the form x.x.x.x/y where y is the netmask.<br><br>CIDR is Classless Inter-Domain Routing. In "normal" IP you have three classes A, B, and C that have a network part of 8, 16, and 24-bits respectively, allowing 16.7 million, 65 thousand, and 254 hosts per network. CIDR allows network masks of any size, so you can better allocate IP addresses and route between them in a hierarchical fashion. |
| | inet | Similar to cidr except the host part can be 0. |
| | macaddr | A MAC address of the form XX:XX:XX:XX:XX:XX. |

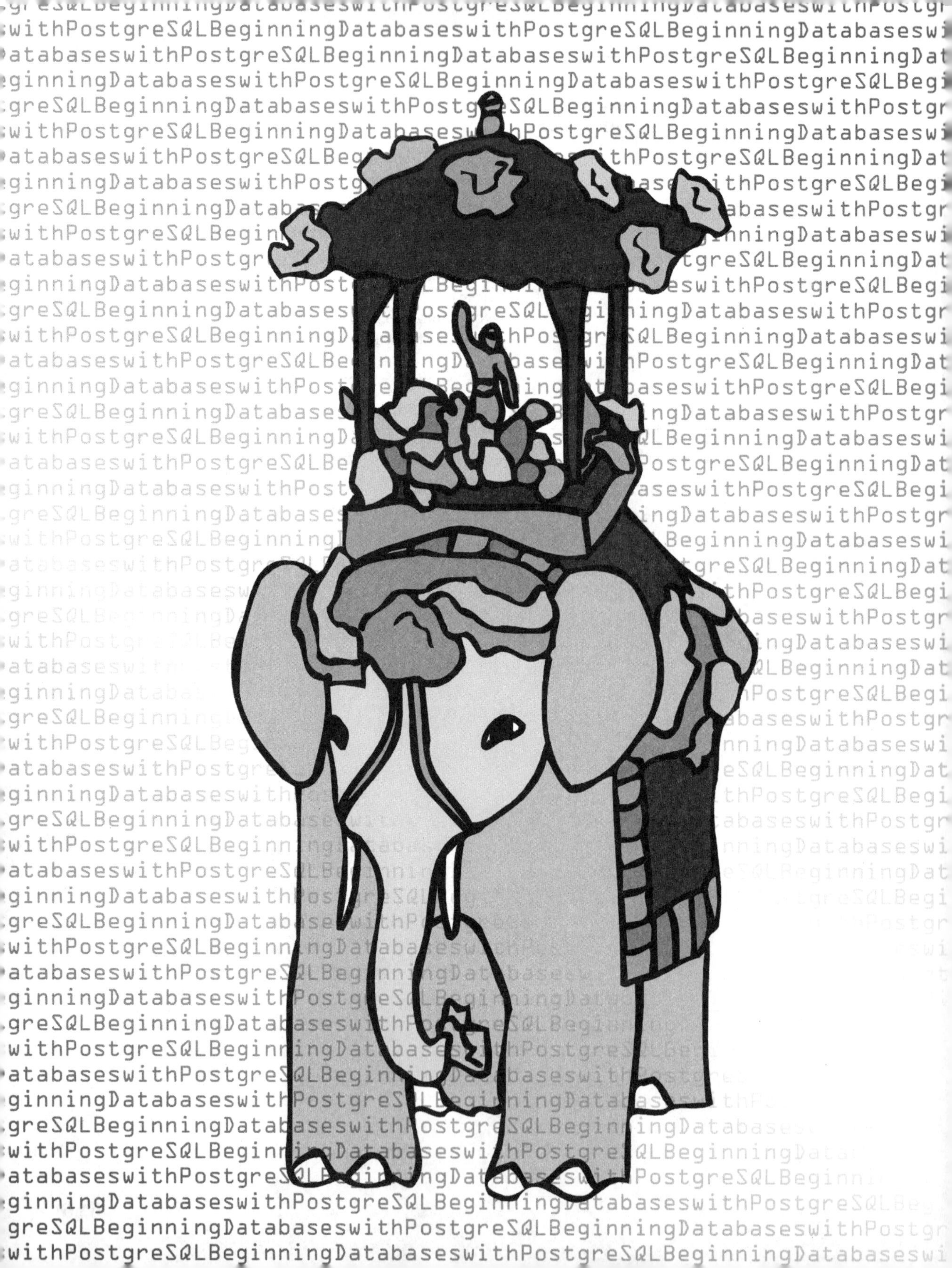
BeginningDatabaseswithPostgreSQL

# PostgreSQL SQL Syntax

## PostgreSQL SQL Commands

| | | |
|---|---|---|
| ABORT | CREATE TRIGGER | GRANT |
| ALTER GROUP | CREATE TYPE | INSERT |
| ALTER TABLE | CREATE USER | LISTEN |
| ALTER USER | CREATE VIEW | LOAD |
| BEGIN | DECLARE | LOCK |
| CHECKPOINT | DELETE | MOVE |
| CLOSE | DROP AGGREGATE | NOTIFY |
| CLUSTER | DROP DATABASE | REINDEX |
| COMMENT | DROP FUNCTION | RESET |
| COMMIT | DROP GROUP | REVOKE |
| COPY | DROP INDEX | ROLLBACK |
| CREATE AGGREGATE | DROP LANGUAGE | SELECT |
| CREATE CONSTRAINT TRIGGER | DROP OPERATOR | SELECT INTO |
| CREATE DATABASE | DROP RULE | SET |
| CREATE FUNCTION | DROP SEQUENCE | SET CONSTRAINTS |
| CREATE GROUP | DROP TABLE | SET TRANSACTION |
| CREATE INDEX | DROP TRIGGER | SHOW |
| CREATE LANGUAGE | DROP TYPE | TRUNCATE |
| CREATE OPERATOR | DROP USER | UNLISTEN |
| CREATE RULE | DROP VIEW | UPDATE |
| CREATE SEQUENCE | END | VACUUM |
| CREATE TABLE | EXPLAIN | |
| CREATE TABLE AS | FETCH | |

# PostgreSQL SQL Syntax

### ABORT

```
ABORT [ WORK | TRANSACTION ]
```

Description:   Aborts the current transaction

### ALTER GROUP

```
ALTER GROUP name ADD USER username [, ... ]
ALTER GROUP name DROP USER username [, ... ]
```

Description:   Adds users to a group, remove users from a group

### ALTER TABLE

```
ALTER TABLE [ ONLY ] table [ * ]
    ADD [ COLUMN ] column type
ALTER TABLE [ ONLY ] table [ * ]
    ALTER [ COLUMN ] column { SET DEFAULT value | DROP DEFAULT }
ALTER TABLE table [ * ]
    RENAME [ COLUMN ] column TO newcolumn
ALTER TABLE table
    RENAME TO newtable
ALTER TABLE table
    ADD table constraint definition
ALTER TABLE table
    OWNER TO new owner
```

Description:   Modifies table properties

### ALTER USER

```
ALTER USER username
    [ WITH PASSWORD 'password' ]
    [ CREATEDB | NOCREATEDB ] [ CREATEUSER | NOCREATEUSER ]
    [ VALID UNTIL 'abstime' ]
```

Description:   Modifies user account information

### BEGIN

```
BEGIN [ WORK | TRANSACTION ]
```

Description:   Begins a transaction in chained mode

### CHECKPOINT

```
CHECKPOINT
```

Description:   Forces transaction log checkpoint

### CLOSE

```
CLOSE cursor
```

Description:   Closes a cursor

### CLUSTER

```
CLUSTER indexname ON tablename
```

Description:   Gives storage clustering advice to the server

### COMMENT

```
COMMENT ON
[
  [ DATABASE | INDEX | RULE | SEQUENCE | TABLE | TYPE | VIEW ]
  object_name |
  COLUMN table_name.column_name|
  AGGREGATE agg_name agg_type|
  FUNCTION func_name (arg1, arg2, ...)|
  OPERATOR op (leftoperand_type rightoperand_type) |
  TRIGGER trigger_name ON table_name
] IS 'text'
```

Description:   Adds comment to an object

### COMMIT

```
COMMIT [ WORK | TRANSACTION ]
```

Description:   Commits the current transaction

### COPY

```
COPY [ BINARY ] table [ WITH OIDS ]
    FROM { 'filename' | stdin }
    [ [USING] DELIMITERS 'delimiter' ]
    [ WITH NULL AS 'null string' ]
COPY [ BINARY ] table [ WITH OIDS ]
    TO { 'filename' | stdout }
    [ [USING] DELIMITERS 'delimiter' ]
    [ WITH NULL AS 'null string' ]
```

Description:   Copies data between files and tables

### CREATE AGGREGATE

```
CREATE AGGREGATE name ( BASETYPE = input_data_type,
    SFUNC = sfunc, STYPE = state_type
    [ , FINALFUNC = ffunc ]
    [ , INITCOND = initial_condition ] )
```

Description:   Defines a new aggregate function

### CREATE CONSTRAINT TRIGGER

```
CREATE CONSTRAINT TRIGGER name
    AFTER events ON
    relation constraint attributes
    FOR EACH ROW EXECUTE PROCEDURE func '(' args ')'
```

Description:   Creates a trigger to support a constraint

### CREATE DATABASE

```
CREATE DATABASE name
    [ WITH [ LOCATION = 'dbpath' ]
           [ TEMPLATE = template ]
           [ ENCODING = encoding ] ]
```

Description:   Creates a new database

### CREATE FUNCTION

```
CREATE FUNCTION name ( [ ftype [, ...] ] )
    RETURNS rtype
    AS definition
    LANGUAGE 'langname'
    [ WITH ( attribute [, ...] ) ]
CREATE FUNCTION name ( [ ftype [, ...] ] )
    RETURNS rtype
    AS obj_file , link_symbol
    LANGUAGE 'langname'
    [ WITH ( attribute [, ...] ) ]
```

Description:   Defines a new function

### CREATE GROUP

```
CREATE GROUP name
    [ WITH
    [ SYSID gid ]
    [ USER  username [, ...] ] ]
```

Description:   Creates a new group

### CREATE INDEX

```
CREATE [ UNIQUE ] INDEX index_name ON table
    [ USING acc_name ] ( column [ ops_name ] [, ...] )
CREATE [ UNIQUE ] INDEX index_name ON table
    [ USING acc_name ] ( func_name( column [, ... ]) [ ops_name ] )
```

Description:   Constructs a secondary index

### CREATE LANGUAGE

```
CREATE [ TRUSTED ] [ PROCEDURAL ] LANGUAGE 'langname'
    HANDLER call_handler
    LANCOMPILER 'comment'
```

Description:   Defines a new language for functions

### CREATE OPERATOR

```
CREATE OPERATOR name ( PROCEDURE = func_name
    [, LEFTARG = type1 ] [, RIGHTARG = type2 ]
    [, COMMUTATOR = com_op ] [, NEGATOR = neg_op ]
    [, RESTRICT = res_proc ] [, JOIN = join_proc ]
    [, HASHES ] [, SORT1 = left_sort_op ] [, SORT2 =
            right_sort_op ] )
```

Description:   Defines a new user operator

### CREATE RULE

```
CREATE RULE name AS ON event
    TO object [ WHERE condition ]
    DO [ INSTEAD ] action
```

where action can be:

```
NOTHING
|
query
|
( query ; query ... )
|
[ query ; query ... ]
```

Description:   Defines a new rule

### CREATE SEQUENCE

```
CREATE SEQUENCE seqname [ INCREMENT increment ]
    [ MINVALUE minvalue ] [ MAXVALUE maxvalue ]
    [ START start ] [ CACHE cache ] [ CYCLE ]
```

Description:   Creates a new sequence number generator

### CREATE TABLE

```
CREATE [ TEMPORARY | TEMP ] TABLE table_name (
    { column_name type [ column_constraint [ ... ] ]
      | table_constraint } [, ... ]
    ) [ INHERITS ( inherited_table [, ... ] ) ]
```

where `column_constraint` can be:

```
[ CONSTRAINT constraint_name ]
{ NOT NULL | NULL | UNIQUE | PRIMARY KEY | DEFAULT value | CHECK (condition) |
  REFERENCES table [ ( column ) ] [ MATCH FULL | MATCH PARTIAL ]
   [ ON DELETE action ] [ ON UPDATE action ]
   [ DEFERRABLE | NOT DEFERRABLE ] [ INITIALLY DEFERRED | INITIALLY IMMEDIATE ]
}
```

`table_constraint` can be:

```
[ CONSTRAINT constraint_name ]
{ UNIQUE ( column_name [, ... ] ) |
  PRIMARY KEY ( column_name [, ... ] ) |
  CHECK ( condition ) |
  FOREIGN KEY ( column_name [, ... ] ) REFERENCES table [ ( column [, ... ] ) ]
   [ MATCH FULL | MATCH PARTIAL ] [ ON DELETE action ] [ ON UPDATE action ]
   [ DEFERRABLE | NOT DEFERRABLE ] [ INITIALLY DEFERRED | INITIALLY IMMEDIATE ]
}
```

Description:   Creates a new table

### CREATE TABLE AS

```
CREATE TABLE table [ (column [, ...] ) ]
     AS select_clause
```

Description:   Creates a new table

### CREATE TRIGGER

```
CREATE TRIGGER name { BEFORE | AFTER } { event [OR ...] }
     ON table FOR EACH { ROW | STATEMENT }
     EXECUTE PROCEDURE func ( arguments )
```

Description:   Creates a new trigger

### CREATE TYPE

```
CREATE TYPE typename ( INPUT = input_function, OUTPUT = output_function
     , INTERNALLENGTH = { internallength | VARIABLE }
     [ , EXTERNALLENGTH = { externallength | VARIABLE } ]
     [ , DEFAULT = "default" ]
     [ , ELEMENT = element ] [ , DELIMITER = delimiter ]
     [ , SEND = send_function ] [ , RECEIVE = receive_function ]
     [ , PASSEDBYVALUE ]
     [ , ALIGNMENT = alignment ]
     [ , STORAGE = storage ]
)
```

Description:   Defines a new base data type

### CREATE USER

```
CREATE USER username
    [ WITH
      [ SYSID uid ]
      [ PASSWORD 'password' ] ]
    [ CREATEDB   | NOCREATEDB ] [ CREATEUSER | NOCREATEUSER ]
    [ IN GROUP   groupname [, ...] ]
    [ VALID UNTIL  'abstime' ]
```

Description:   Creates a new database user

### CREATE VIEW

```
CREATE VIEW view AS SELECT query
```

Description:   Constructs a virtual table

### DECLARE

```
DECLARE cursorname [ BINARY ] [ INSENSITIVE ] [ SCROLL ]
    CURSOR FOR query
    [ FOR { READ ONLY | UPDATE [ OF column [, ...] ] ] ]
```

Description:   Defines a cursor for table access

### DELETE

```
DELETE FROM [ ONLY ] table [ WHERE condition ]
```

Description:   Removes rows from a table

### DROP AGGREGATE

```
DROP AGGREGATE name type
```

Description:   Removes the definition of an aggregate function

### DROP DATABASE

```
DROP DATABASE name
```

Description:   Removes an existing database

### DROP FUNCTION

```
DROP FUNCTION name ( [ type [, ...] ] )
```

Description:   Removes a user-defined C function

## DROP GROUP

```
DROP GROUP name
```

Description:   Removes a group

## DROP INDEX

```
DROP INDEX index_name [, ...]
```

Description:   Removes existing indexes from a database

## DROP LANGUAGE

```
DROP [ PROCEDURAL ] LANGUAGE 'name'
```

Description:   Removes a user-defined procedural language

## DROP OPERATOR

```
DROP OPERATOR id ( lefttype | NONE , righttype | NONE )
```

Description:   Removes an operator from the database

## DROP RULE

```
DROP RULE name [, ...]
```

Description:   Removes existing rules from the database

## DROP SEQUENCE

```
DROP SEQUENCE name [, ...]
```

Description:   Removes existing sequences from a database

## DROP TABLE

```
DROP TABLE name [, ...]
```

Description:   Removes existing tables from a database

## DROP TRIGGER

```
DROP TRIGGER name ON table
```

Description:   Removes the definition of a trigger

## DROP TYPE

```
DROP TYPE typename [, ...]
```

Description:   Removes user-defined types from the system catalogs

### DROP USER

```
DROP USER name
```

Description:   Removes a user

### DROP VIEW

```
DROP VIEW name [, ...]
```

Description:   Removes existing views from a database

### END

```
END [ WORK | TRANSACTION ]
```

Description:   Commits the current transaction

### EXPLAIN

```
EXPLAIN [ VERBOSE ] query
```

Description:   Shows statement execution plan

### FETCH

```
FETCH [ direction ] [ count ] { IN | FROM } cursor
FETCH [ FORWARD | BACKWARD | RELATIVE ] [ # | ALL | NEXT | PRIOR ] { IN | FROM }
cursor
```

Description:   Gets rows using a cursor

### GRANT

```
GRANT privilege [, ...] ON object [, ...]
    TO { PUBLIC | GROUP group | username }
```

Description:   Grants access privilege to a user, a group or all users

### INSERT

```
INSERT INTO table [ ( column [, ...] ) ]
    { DEFAULT VALUES | VALUES ( expression [, ...] ) | SELECT query }
```

Description:   Inserts new rows into a table

### LISTEN

```
LISTEN name
```

Description:   Listens for a response on a notify condition

## LOAD

```
LOAD 'filename'
```

Description:  Dynamically loads an object file

## LOCK

```
LOCK [ TABLE ] name
LOCK [ TABLE ] name IN [ ROW | ACCESS ] { SHARE | EXCLUSIVE } MODE
LOCK [ TABLE ] name IN SHARE ROW EXCLUSIVE MODE
```

Description:  Explicitly locks a table inside a transaction

## MOVE

```
MOVE [ direction ] [ count ]
    { IN | FROM } cursor
```

Description:  Moves cursor position

## NOTIF

```
NOTIFY name
```

Description:  Signals all frontends and backends listening on a notify condition

## REINDEX

```
REINDEX { TABLE | DATABASE | INDEX } name [ FORCE ]
```

Description:  Recovers corrupted system indexes under standalone PostgreSQL

## RESET

```
RESET variable
```

Description:  Restores run-time parameters to default values

## REVOKE

```
REVOKE privilege [, ...]
    ON object [, ...]
    FROM { PUBLIC | GROUP groupname | username }
```

Description:  Revokes access privilege from a user, a group or all users

## ROLLBACK

```
ROLLBACK [ WORK | TRANSACTION ]
```

Description:  Aborts the current transaction

## SELECT

```
SELECT [ ALL | DISTINCT [ ON ( expression [, ...] ) ] ]
    * | expression [ AS output_name ] [, ...]
    [ INTO [ TEMPORARY | TEMP ] [ TABLE ] new_table ]
    [ FROM from_item [, ...] ]
    [ WHERE condition ]
    [ GROUP BY expression [, ...] ]
    [ HAVING condition [, ...] ]
    [ { UNION | INTERSECT | EXCEPT [ ALL ] } select ]
    [ ORDER BY expression [ ASC | DESC | USING operator ] [, ...] ]
    [ FOR UPDATE [ OF tablename [, ...] ] ]
    [ LIMIT { count | ALL } [ { OFFSET | , } start ]]
```

where `from_item` can be:

```
[ ONLY ] table_name [ * ]
    [ [ AS ] alias [ ( column_alias_list ) ] ]
|
( select )
    [ AS ] alias [ ( column_alias_list ) ]
|
from_item [ NATURAL ] join_type from_item
    [ ON join_condition | USING ( join_column_list ) ]
```

Description:   Retrieves rows from a table or view

## SELECT INTO

```
SELECT [ ALL | DISTINCT [ ON ( expression [, ...] ) ] ]
    * | expression [ AS output_name ] [, ...]
    INTO [ TEMPORARY | TEMP ] [ TABLE ] new_table
    [ FROM from_item [, ...] ]
    [ WHERE condition ]
    [ GROUP BY expression [, ...] ]
    [ HAVING condition [, ...] ]
    [ { UNION | INTERSECT | EXCEPT [ ALL ] } select ]
    [ ORDER BY expression [ ASC | DESC | USING operator ] [, ...] ]
    [ FOR UPDATE [ OF tablename [, ...] ] ]
    [ LIMIT { count | ALL } [ { OFFSET | , } start ]]
```

where `from_item` can be:

```
[ ONLY ] table_name [ * ]
    [ [ AS ] alias [ ( column_alias_list ) ] ]
|
( select )
    [ AS ] alias [ ( column_alias_list ) ]
|
from_item [ NATURAL ] join_type from_item
    [ ON join_condition | USING ( join_column_list ) ]
```

Description:   Creates a new table from an existing table or view

## SET

```
SET variable { TO | = } { value | 'value' | DEFAULT }
SET TIME ZONE { 'timezone' | LOCAL | DEFAULT }
```

Description:  Sets run-time parameters

## SET CONSTRAINTS

```
SET CONSTRAINTS { ALL | constraint [, ...] } { DEFERRED | IMMEDIATE }
```

Description:  Sets the constraint mode of the current SQL-transaction

## SET TRANSACTION

```
SET TRANSACTION ISOLATION LEVEL { READ COMMITTED | SERIALIZABLE }
SET SESSION CHARACTERISTICS AS TRANSACTION ISOLATION LEVEL { READ COMMITTED |
SERIALIZABLE }
```

Description:  Sets the characteristics of the current SQL-transaction

## SHOW

```
SHOW name
```

Description:  Shows run-time parameters

## TRUNCATE

```
TRUNCATE [ TABLE ] name
```

Description:  Empties a table

## UNLISTEN

```
UNLISTEN { notifyname | * }
```

Description:  Stops listening for notification

## UPDATE

```
UPDATE [ ONLY ] table SET col = expression [, ...]
    [ FROM fromlist ]
    [ WHERE condition ]
```

Description:  Replaces values of columns in a table

## VACUUM

```
VACUUM [ VERBOSE ] [ ANALYZE ] [ table ]
VACUUM [ VERBOSE ] ANALYZE [ table [ (column [, ...] ) ] ]
```

Description:   Cleans and analyzes a PostgreSQL database

> **This set of commands is taken from the psql command line tool. At any point you can generate the first list using the command \h and the more specific syntax help using \h <command>.**

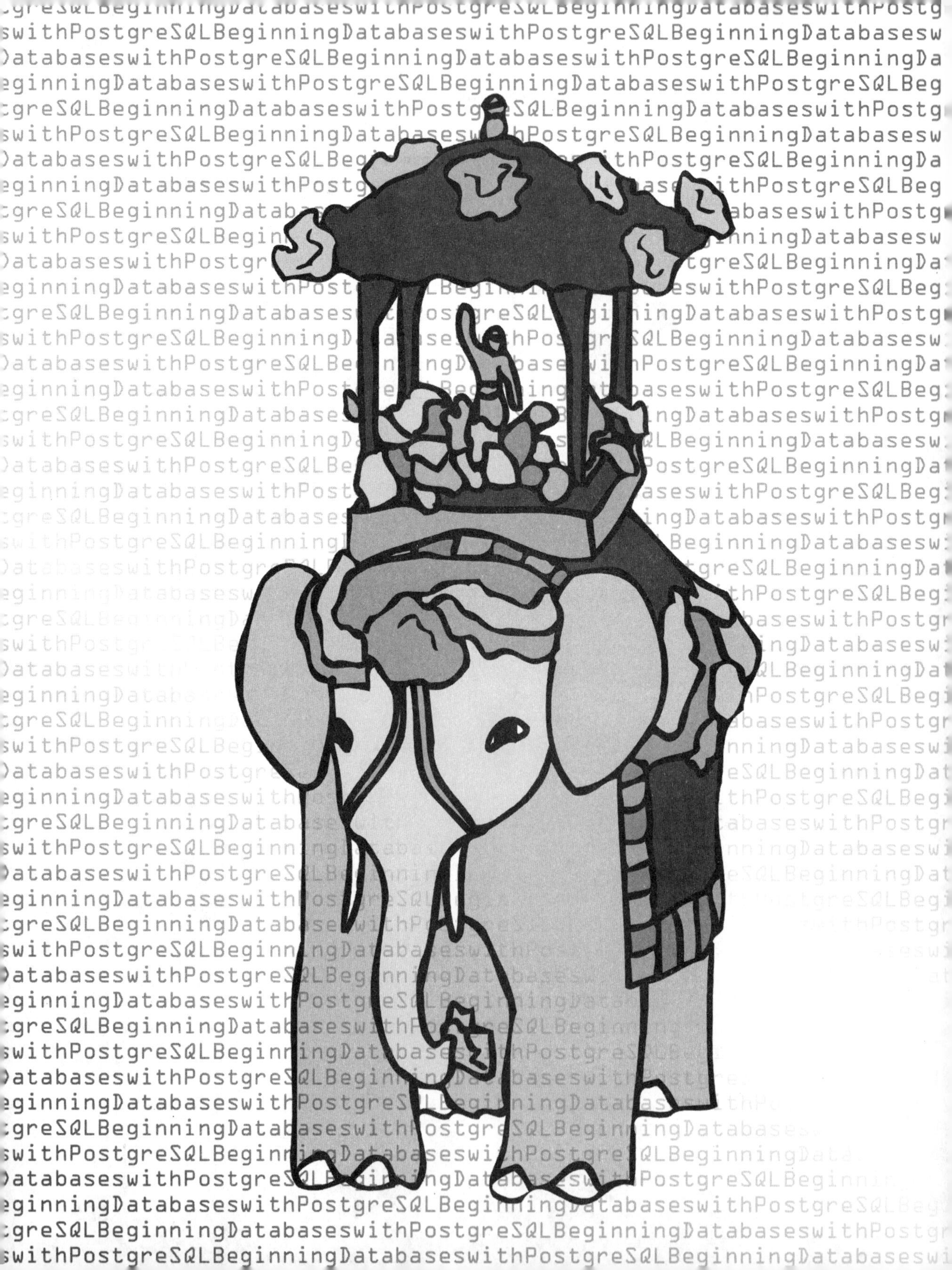
BeginningDatabaseswithPostgreSQL

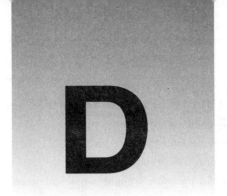

# psql Reference

## psql Command Line Options

### Usage:

```
psql [options] [dbname [username]]
```

### Options:

| | |
|---|---|
| `-a` | Echo all input from script |
| `-A` | Unaligned table output mode (`-P format=unaligned`) |
| `-c <query>` | Run only single query (or slash command) and exit |
| `-d <dbname>` | Specify database name to connect to |
| `-e` | Echo queries sent to backend |
| `-E` | Display queries that internal commands generate |
| `-f <filename>` | Execute queries from file, then exit |
| `-F <string>` | Set field separator (default: "`\|`") (`-P fieldsep=`) |
| `-h <host>` | Specify database server host |
| `-H` | HTML table output mode (`-P format=html`) |
| `-l` | List available databases, then exit |
| `-n` | Disable readline |
| `-o <filename>` | Send query output to `filename` (or `\|pipe`) |
| `-p <port>` | Specify database server port |
| | Set printing option `var` to `arg` (see `\pset` command) |
| `-q` | Run quietly (no messages, only query output) |
| `-R <string>` | Set record separator (`-P recordsep=`) |
| `-s` | Single step mode (confirm each query) |
| `-S` | Single line mode (newline terminates query) |

## Options cont...

| | |
|---|---|
| `-t` | Print rows only (`-P tuples_only`) |
| `-T text` | Set HTML table tag options (width, border) (`-P tableattr=`) |
| `-U <username>` | Specify database username |
| `-v name=val` | Set `psql` variable `name` to `value` |
| `-V` | Show version information and exit |
| `-W` | Prompt for password (should happen automatically) |
| `-x` | Turn on expanded table output (`-P expanded`) |
| `-X` | Do not read startup file (`~/.psqlrc`) |

## *psql Internal Commands*

| | |
|---|---|
| `-a` | Toggle between unaligned and aligned mode |
| `\c[onnect] [dbname|-` | Connect to new database |
| `\C <title>` | Table title |
| `\copy ...` | Perform SQL COPY with data stream to the client machine |
| `\copyright` | Show PostgreSQL usage and distribution terms |
| `\d <table>` | Describe table (or view, index, sequence) |
| `\d{t|i|s|v}` | List tables/indices/sequences/views |
| `\d{p|S|l}` | List permissions/system tables/lobjects |
| `\da` | List aggregates |
| `\dd [object]` | List comment for table, type, function, or operator |
| `\df` | List functions |
| `\do` | List operators |
| `\dT` | List data types |
| `\e [file]` | Edit the current query buffer or `[file]` with external editor |
| `\echo <text>` | Write `text` to stdout |
| `\encoding <encoding>` | Set client encoding |
| `\f <sep>` | Change field separator |
| `\h [cmd]` | Help on syntax of sql commands, * for all commands |
| `\i <file>` | Read and execute queries from `<file>` |
| `\l` | List all databases |
| `\lo_export,` | Large object operations |
| `\o [file]` | Send all query results to `[file]`, or `|pipe` |
| `\p` | Show the content of the current query buffer |
| `\pset <opt>` | Set table output `<opt>` = {format | border | expanded | fieldsep | null | recordsep | tuples_only | title | tableattr |pager} |
| `\q` | Quit `psql` |

## *psql Internal Commands*

| | |
|---|---|
| \qecho <text> | Write text to query output stream (see \o) |
| \r | Reset (clear) the query buffer |
| \s [file] | Print history or save it in [file] |
| \set <var> <value> | Set internal variable |
| \t | Show only rows |
| \T <tags> | HTML table tags |
| \unset <var> | Unset (delete) internal variable |
| \w <file> | Write current query buffer to a <file> |
| \x | Toggle expanded output |
| \z | List table access permissions |
| \! [cmd] | Shell escape or command |

This set of commands is taken from the psql command line tool's online help.

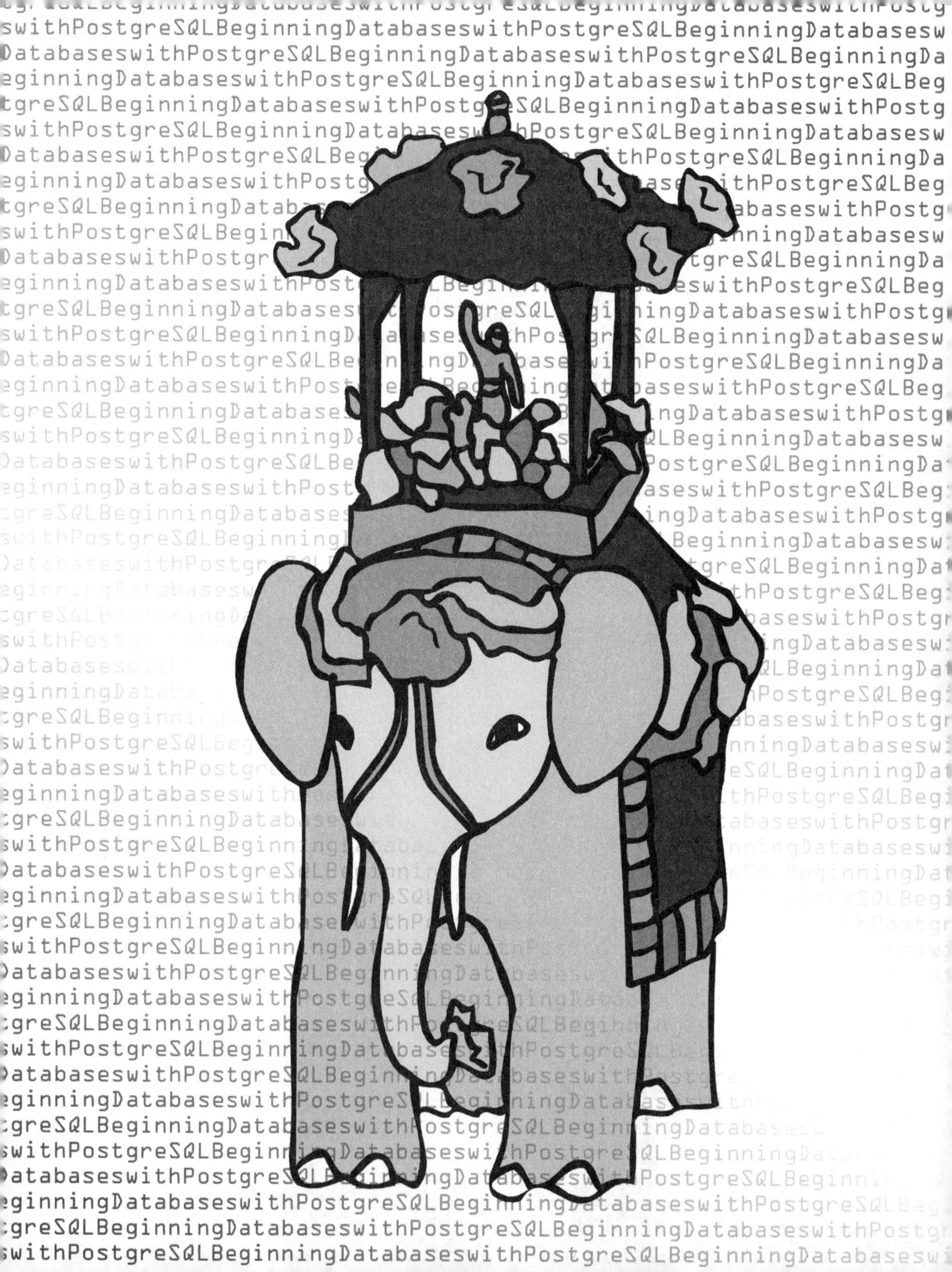
BeginningDatabaseswithPostgreSQL

# Database Schema and Tables

The database schema used in the examples in this book is a simplified customer/orders/items database as described below:

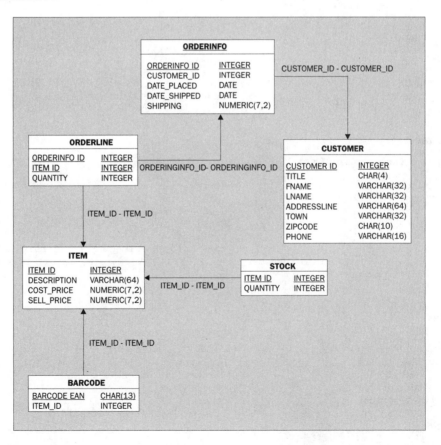

The tables need to be created in an appropriate order such that dependent tables are created first, because of the foreign key constraints. This is the same order to be followed as data is inserted into the tables. Such an order is:

- ❑ CUSTOMER
- ❑ ORDERINFO
- ❑ ITEM
- ❑ ORDERLINE
- ❑ STOCK
- ❑ BARCODE

The SQL to create the final version of this sample database, bpsimple, including the foreign key constraints, is:

### customer table

```
create table customer
(
        customer_id                     serial,
        title                           char(4),
        fname                           varchar(32),
        lname                           varchar(32) not null,
        addressline                     varchar(64),
        town                            varchar(32),
        zipcode                         char(10) not null,
        phone                           varchar(16),
        CONSTRAINT                      customer_pk PRIMARY KEY(customer_id)
);
```

### orderinfo table

```
create table orderinfo
(
        orderinfo_id                    serial,
        customer_id                     integer not null,
        date_placed                     date not null,
        date_shipped                    date,
        shipping                        numeric(7,2) ,
        CONSTRAINT                      orderinfo_pk PRIMARY KEY(orderinfo_id) ,
        CONSTRAINT orderinfo_customer_id_fk FOREIGN KEY(customer_id) REFERENCES
customer(customer_id)
);
```

### item table

```
create table item
(
        item_id                         serial,
        description                     varchar(64) not null,
        cost_price                      numeric(7,2),
        sell_price                      numeric(7,2),
        CONSTRAINT                      item_pk PRIMARY KEY(item_id)
);
```

### orderline table

```
create table orderline
(
    orderinfo_id                integer not null,
    item_id                     integer not null,
    quantity                    integer not null,
    CONSTRAINT                  orderline_pk PRIMARY KEY(orderinfo_id,
item_id),
    CONSTRAINT orderline_orderinfo_id_fk FOREIGN KEY(orderinfo_id) REFERENCES
orderinfo(orderinfo_id),
    CONSTRAINT orderline_item_id_fk FOREIGN KEY(item_id) REFERENCES item(item_id)
);
```

### stock table

```
create table stock
(
    item_id                     integer not null,
    quantity                    integer  not null,
    CONSTRAINT                  stock_pk PRIMARY KEY(item_id),
    CONSTRAINT stock_item_id_fk FOREIGN KEY(item_id) REFERENCES item(item_id)
);
```

### barcode table

```
create table barcode
(
    barcode_ean                 char(13) not null,
    item_id                     integer not null,
    CONSTRAINT                  barcode_pk PRIMARY KEY(barcode_ean),
    CONSTRAINT barcode_item_id_fk FOREIGN KEY(item_id) REFERENCES item(item_id)
);
```

The download code bundle has the table population commands for bpsimple in an appropriate order ready.

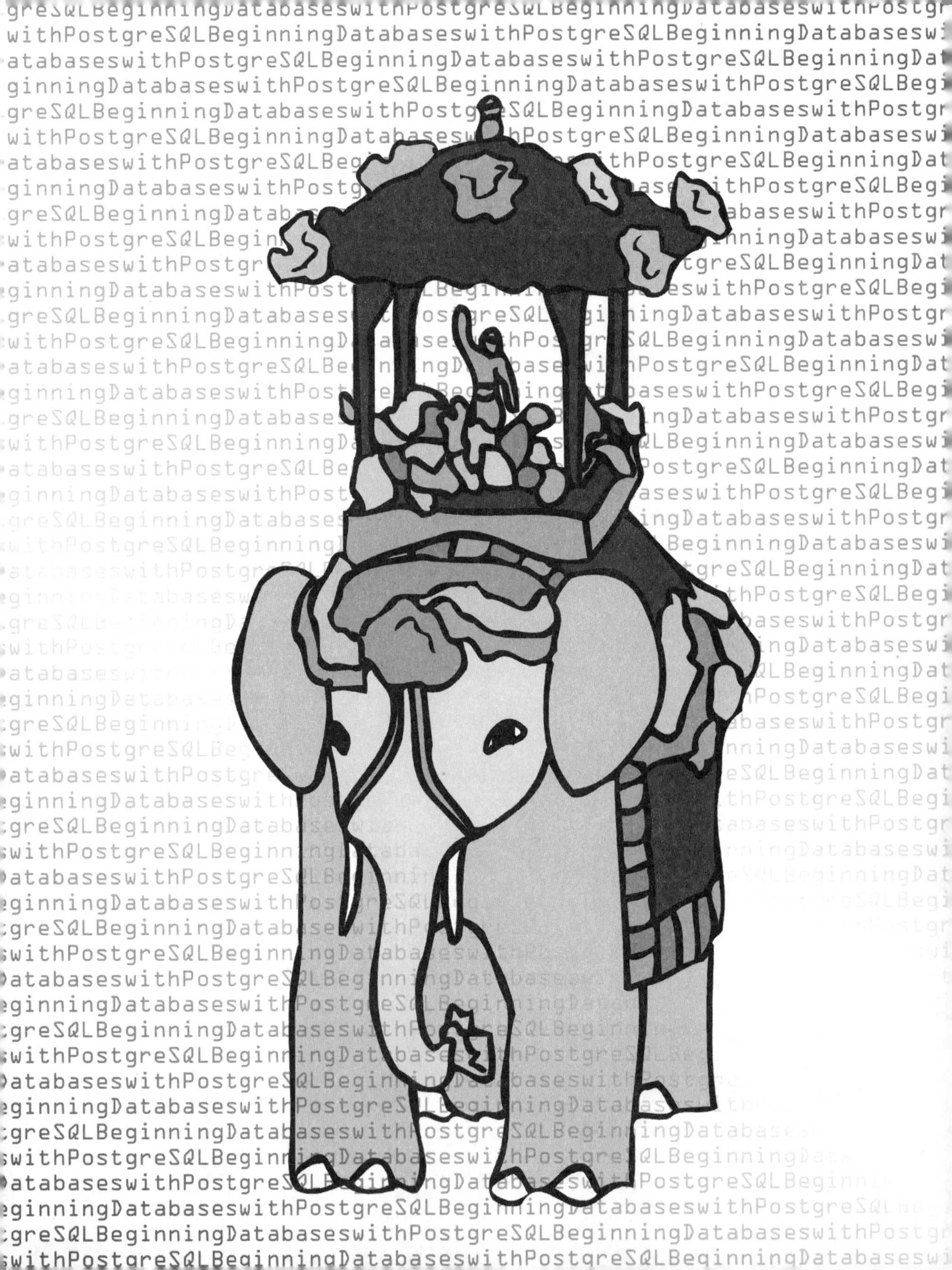
BeginningDatabaseswithPostgreSQL

# Large Objects Support in PostgreSQL

Traditionally, databases have been able to store data in a limited number of forms. Usually, as numeric values (integers, floating point, and fixed point) and text strings. Often, the size of the text data is limited. In the past, PostgreSQL has enforced a limit of a few thousand characters as the maximum length of a field.

In contrast, PostgreSQL provides support for a wide variety of data types for columns in a table, including geometric objects, network addresses, and arrays.

We can even define our own types if we wish. We will not cover these esoteric object types here, but more information can be found in the online PostgreSQL documentation.

It might be useful for us to be able to create a database application that can handle *arbitrary* unstructured data formats, for example, for images. We might want to add photographs of the products to our sample database so that our web-based interface can provide an on-line catalog.

PostgreSQL supports an arbitrary data type, the binary large object, or BLOB, suitable for storing large data items. We will concentrate on these here.

## Adding Images to the Database

Let's consider adding product photographs to our database. There are several ways we could do this:

❑ Use links into a file system or the Web

❑ Use encoded long text strings

❑ Use BLOBs

Our first option is to avoid storing images in the physical database at all. The idea is to place all of the images in the normal filing system of a server, which may be the database server, a file sharing server, or a web server. The database itself then need only contain a text link to the file. Any client application would follow the link to retrieve the image.

We need to create an additional table in the database to store the image links. It is very similar to the `stock` table in that we are providing additional information for each item we carry:

```
CREATE TABLE image
(
    item_id     INTEGER NOT NULL,
    picture     VARCHAR(512),
    CONSTRAINT  image_pk PRIMARY KEY(item_id),
    CONSTRAINT  image_item_id_fk FOREIGN KEY(item_id) REFERENCES
    item(item_id)
);
```

Here, we have added constraints to ensure that we can only add images for items that exist.

Now we can update the `image` table with links to product photographs:

```
INSERT INTO image VALUES (3, 'http://server/images/rubik.jpg');
INSERT INTO image VALUES (9, '//server/images/coin.bmp');
INSERT INTO image VALUES (5, '/mnt/server/images/frame.png');
```

This solution has both advantages and disadvantages.

Storing links rather than pictures means that the database size is kept to a minimum and applications will be portable to other database systems, as we have not used any esoteric features to handle images.

Retrieving the actual images will also be very fast, as reading a file from the file system will typically be many times quicker than querying a database.

Also we have a wide choice of locations for storing the images. In the example above we have used:

❑   a URL to provide a link into a web server

❑   a UNC file reference for a Windows file server

❑   a reference to an NFS mounted UNIX server

However, by using links we are unable to enforce referential integrity in the database.

If the images, which are stored elsewhere, are changed or deleted, the database is not automatically updated. To backup our system, we will have to attend to image files on the file system (and elsewhere) as well as the database itself. We must also ensure that the links we use are in a form that all possible clients can use. For example, the NFS form requires that all clients access the shared files in the same way.

In PostgreSQL 7.1 the limit on the size of a field has been lifted to 1Gb. For all practical purposes this is effectively unlimited. We could consider using the `text` type to store the images in the database directly. This is possible, if a little tricky.

Images are in general binary data, not well suited to a `character` type. So we need to encode the image in some way, perhaps by using hexadecimal or MIME encoding. Handling the very long strings that result may also cause a problem with limits imposed by client applications, network transport mechanisms or ODBC drivers. The storage space needed for encoded strings will also be up to double the size of the binary image file.

We can store our image data, in fact any large or binary data object in a PostgreSQL database, by using what PostgreSQL calls **large objects**, also known as Binary Large Objects, or BLOBs.

# BLOBs

PostgreSQL supports a column type of `oid`, which is an object identifier, a reference to arbitrary data. These are BLOBs and can be used to transfer the contents of any file into the database, and to extract an object from the database into a file. They can therefore be used to handle our product images, or any other data that we might wish to store.

We can modify the `image` table definition to use BLOBs by specifying `oid` as the image data type:

```
CREATE TABLE image
(
    item_id     INTEGER NOT NULL,
    picture     OID,
    CONSTRAINT  image_pk PRIMARY KEY(item_id),
    CONSTRAINT  image_item_id_fk FOREIGN KEY(item_id) REFERENCES item(item_id)
);
```

## Import and Export

PostgreSQL provides a number of functions that can be used in SQL queries for inserting into, retrieving from, and deleting BLOB data in a table.

To add an image to the table we can use the SQL function `lo_import` like this:

```
INSERT INTO image VALUES (3, lo_import('/tmp/image.jpg'));
```

The contents of the specified file are read into a BLOB object and stored in the database. The `image` table will now have a non-NULL `oid` that references the BLOB:

```
bpfinal=# SELECT * FROM image;
item_id | picture
---------+---------
3 |   163055
(1 row)

bpfinal=>
```

We can see all of the large objects stored in the database by using a `psql` internal command, `\lo_list`, or `\dl`, to list them:

```
bpfinal=# \dl
    Large objects
    ID   | Description
--------+-------------
 163055 |
(1 row)

bpfinal=>
```

Large objects are retrieved from the database using `lo_export`, which writes a file containing the contents of the BLOB:

```
bpfinal=# SELECT lo_export(picture, '/tmp/image2.jpg')
bpfinal-# FROM image WHERE item_id = 3;
 lo_export
-----------
         1
(1 row)

bpfinal=#
```

We can delete a large object from the database with `lo_unlink`:

```
bpfinal=# SELECT lo_unlink(picture) FROM image WHERE item_id = 3;
 lo_unlink
-----------
         1
(1 row)

bpfinal=# \dl
  Large objects
 ID | Description
----+-------------
(0 rows)

bpfinal=#
```

We must be careful when we delete large objects as any references to the BLOB will remain:

```
bpfinal=# SELECT * FROM image;
 item_id | picture
---------+---------
       3 |  163055
(1 row)

bpfinal=#
```

As operations on a large object and its object identifier are essentially decoupled, we must make sure to take care of both when manipulating BLOBs. So, when deleting a BLOB, we should set the object reference to NULL to prevent errors in our client applications:

```
bpfinal=# UPDATE image SET picture=null WHERE item_id = 3;
```

In the examples here we have used psql to manipulate binary objects. It is important to understand that the import and export functions lo_import and lo_export are executed by the backend database server and not by psql. Any client application using SQL statements can use these SQL functions to add and update BLOBs.

There are three caveats though.

The first is that, as the import is performed by the server, the files read and written by the `import` and `export` must be specified using a path and file name that is accessible to the server, rather than the client. If in `psql` we had simply said:

```
INSERT INTO image VALUES (3, lo_import('image.jpg'));
```

and expected PostgreSQL to insert the contents of a file in the current directory, we would have received an error message. This is because the import fails to find the file. We have to arrange for files for import so that they are (temporarily) placed in a location that the server can access. Similarly, we need to use full file names for exporting binary objects.

The second point, to watch out for is that exported files must be placed in a directory that the server user can write, that is the user `postgres` has permission to create files.

The third caveat is that all large object manipulation must take place within an SQL transaction, that is, between `BEGIN` and `COMMIT` or `END` statements. By default `psql` executes each SQL statement in its own transaction so this is not a problem, but client applications that perform imports and exports must be written with transactions.

## Remote Import and Export

Because the SQL functions `lo_import` and `lo_export` use the server file system, this can be inconvenient when creating BLOBs. However, `psql` contains internal commands that can be used to import and export binary objects from a remote client machine.

We can add a BLOB to the database using `\lo_import` and passing it a local file name. In this case files in the current directory will work just fine, and we can see the object listed with `\lo_list`:

```
bpfinal=# \lo_import image.jpg
lo_import 163059
bpfinal=# \lo_list
    Large objects
   ID  | Description
--------+-------------
 163059 |
(1 row)

bpfinal=#
```

Now, we need to associate the BLOB with the `image` table by updating the appropriate row:

```
bpfinal=# UPDATE image SET picture=163059 WHERE item_id = 3;
UPDATE 1
bpfinal=# SELECT * FROM image;
 item_id | picture
---------+---------
       3 |  163059
(1 row)

bpfinal=#
```

We can extract a BLOB with \lo_export, specifying the required object identifier and a file to write. Again, a local file name is fine:

```
bpfinal=# \lo_export 163059 image2.jpg
lo_export

bpfinal=#
```

Finally we can delete a large object with \lo_unlink:

```
bpfinal=# \lo_unlink 163059
lo_unlink 163059

bpfinal=#
```

# Programming BLOBs

As you might expect, it is possible to use BLOB import and export functions from the programming languages supported by PostgreSQL.

From C, using the libpq library we can use the functions lo_import, lo_export, and lo_unlink in much the same way as above:

```
Oid lo_import(PGconn *conn, const char *filename);
int lo_export(PGconn *conn, Oid lobjId, const char *filename);
int lo_unlink(PGconn *conn, Oid lobjId);
```

Here is an example program that imports an image file into the database. Note that the large object functions have to be called within a transaction:

```
#include <stdlib.h>
#include <libpq-fe.h>

int main()
{
  PGconn *myconnection = PQconnectdb("");
  PGresult *res;
  Oid blob;

  IF(PQstatus(myconnection) == CONNECTION_OK)
    printf("connection made\n");
  ELSE
    printf("connection failed\n");

  res = PQexec(myconnection, "begin");
  PQclear(res);

  blob = lo_import(myconnection, "image.jpg");
  printf("import returned oid %d\n", blob);

  res = PQexec(myconnection, "end");
  PQclear(res);

  PQfinish(myconnection);
  return EXIT_SUCCESS;
}
```

When we compile and run the program we can see the new binary object identifier reported. See Chapter 13 for more details on compiling and running libpq programs:

```
$ make import
cc -I/usr/local/pgsql/include  -L/usr/local/pgsql/lib -lpq  import.c   -o import
$ PGDATABASE=bpfinal ./import
connection made
import returned oid 163066
$
```

BLOBs can be imported and exported from other languages in similar ways. For example the Tcl interface to PostgreSQL contains functions pg_lo_import, pg_lo_export, and pg_lo_unlink.

For finer control over large object access PostgreSQL provides a suite of low-level functions akin to open, read, write, and friends for ordinary files:

```
int lo_open(PGconn *conn, Oid lobjId, int mode);
int lo_close(PGconn *conn, int fd);
int lo_read(PGconn *conn, int fd, char *buf, size_t len);
int lo_write(PGconn *conn, int fd, char *buf, size_t len);
int lo_lseek(PGconn *conn, int fd, int offset, int whence);
Oid lo_creat(PGconn *conn, int mode);
int lo_tell(PGconn *conn, int fd);
```

Refer to the on-line documentation for more details on these functions.

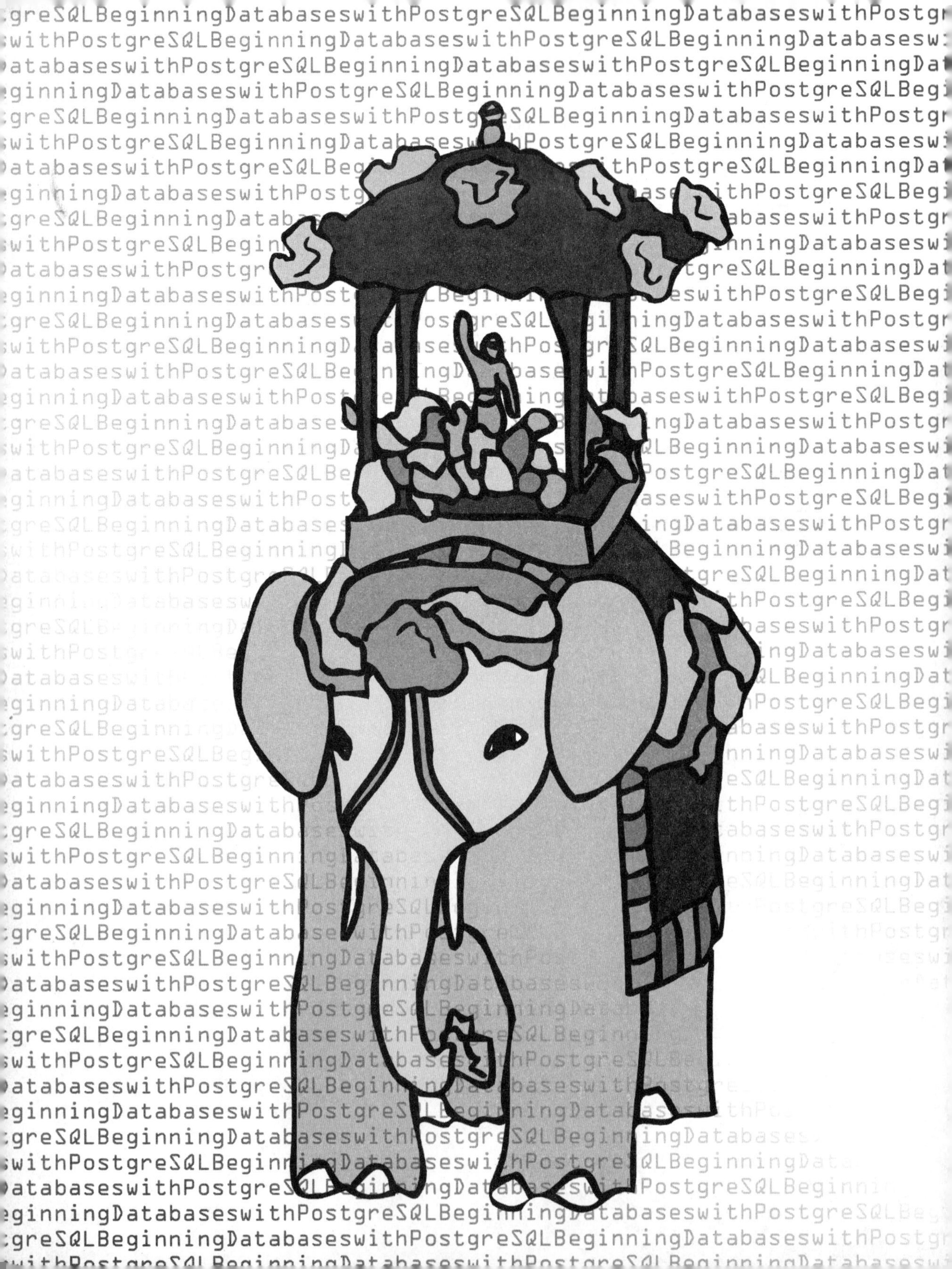
BeginningDatabaseswithPostgreSQL

# Index

## A Guide to the Index

The index is arranged hierarchically, in alphabetical order, with symbols preceding the letter A. Most second-level entries and many third-level entries also occur as first-level entries. This is to ensure that users will find the information they require however they choose to search for it.

# F

# G

# X

# Y

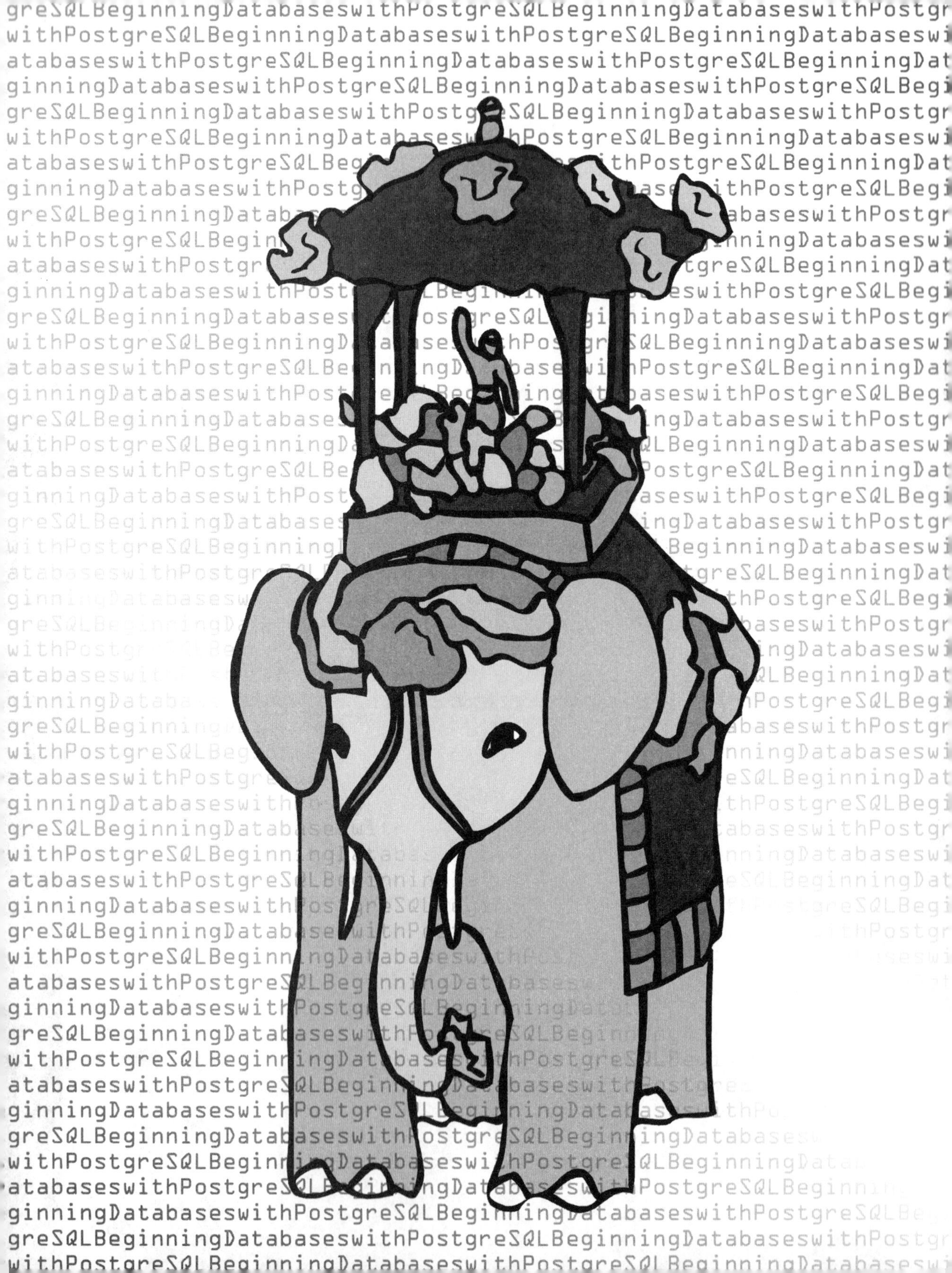
BeginningDatabaseswithPostgreSQL

# p2p.wrox.com
### The programmer's resource centre

## A unique free service from Wrox Press
### with the aim of helping programmers to help each other

Wrox Press aims to provide timely and practical information to today's programmer. P2P is a list server offering a host of targeted mailing lists where you can share knowledge with your fellow programmers and find solutions to your problems. Whatever the level of your programming knowledge, and whatever technology you use, P2P can provide you with the information you need.

**ASP**
Support for beginners and professionals, including a resource page with hundreds of links, and a popular ASP+ mailing list.

**DATABASES**
For database programmers, offering support on SQL Server, mySQL, and Oracle.

**MOBILE**
Software development for the mobile market is growing rapidly. We provide lists for the several current standards, including WAP, WindowsCE, and Symbian.

**JAVA**
A complete set of Java lists, covering beginners, professionals,and server-side programmers (including JSP, servlets and EJBs)

**.NET**
Microsoft's new OS platform, covering topics such as ASP+, C#, and general .Net discussion.

**VISUAL BASIC**
Covers all aspects of VB programming, from programming Office macros to creating components for the .Net platform.

**WEB DESIGN**
As web page requirements become more complex, programmer sare taking a more important role in creating web sites. For these programmers, we offer lists covering technologies such as Flash, Coldfusion, and JavaScript.

**XML**
Covering all aspects of XML, including XSLT and schemas.

**OPEN SOURCE**
Many Open Source topics covered including PHP, Apache, Perl, Linux, Python and more.

**FOREIGN LANGUAGE**
Several lists dedicated to Spanish and German speaking programmers, categories include .Net, Java, XML, PHP and XML.

## How To Subscribe

Simply visit the P2P site, at **http://p2p.wrox.com/**

Select the 'FAQ' option on the side menu bar for more information about the subscription process and our service.